IN HARM'S WAY

East German Latter-day Saints in World War II

IN HARM'S WAY

East German Latter-day Saints in World War II

ROGER P. MINERT

RSC

RELIGIOUS STUDIES CENTER
BRIGHAM YOUNG UNIVERSITY

To the many Latter-day Saint soldiers
of the East German Mission
whose whereabouts remain a mystery
and to their families who await
a glorious reunion

RSC

RELIGIOUS STUDIES CENTER
BRIGHAM YOUNG UNIVERSITY

Published by the Religious Studies Center, Brigham Young University, Provo, Utah
http://rsc.byu.edu/

Printed in the United States of America by Sheridan Books, Inc.

Cover design by Kristin Call

Library of Congress Cataloging-in-Publication Data

Minert, Roger P. (Roger Phillip), 1952–
    In harm's way : East German Latter-day Saints in World War II / Roger P. Minert.
        p.   cm.
    Includes index.
    ISBN 978-0-8425-2746-0 (hard cover : alk. paper)
    1. Mormons—Germany (East)—Biography.   2. Church of Jesus Christ of Latter-day Saints—Germany (East)—History—20th century.   3. Mormon Church—History—20th century.   4. World War, 1939–1945—Personal narratives, German.   5. Germany (East)—Church history—20th century.   I. Title.

    BX8693.M56 2009
    289.3'4309044—dc22   2009033908

Printed in the United States of America
Sheridan Books, Chelsea, MI
10   9   8   7   6   5   4   3   2   1

CONTENTS

ACKNOWLEDGMENTS

It should be evident that a work of this expanse could not emanate from the hand of one person in less than three years. This book is no exception, and I am quite pleased to admit it. First and foremost, I express my gratitude to the hundreds of eyewitnesses who agreed to share their stories. Conducting these interviews was a difficult task on occasion, but each eyewitness has had the opportunity to see his or her family members memorialized in this volume. None of the participants would call themselves heroes, but what they did was very often heroic. Less than 5 percent of the surviving eyewitnesses declined to participate in our study, and I did not debate their decisions.

I am grateful to the many members of The Church of Jesus Christ of Latter-day Saints (LDS Church) who provided names of friends whom they thought were qualified as eyewitnesses. Their vigilance led to interviews with persons who otherwise would not have been identified. Other friends directed our attention to published stories and other media that turned out to be of importance to this work.

The staff and missionaries of the Church History Library in Salt Lake City have been most cordial in assisting us in our search for pertinent literature and other items in their collection. I am especially grateful to Matthew Heiss, an archivist specializing in Germany, who opened many doors for us through his enthusiastic support of the research. One of his great-aunts perished in the firebombing of Dresden, and her name is included among the losses of the Dresden-Altstadt Branch.

The Religious Studies Center at Brigham Young University, under the direction of Professor Richard Neitzel Holzapfel, has proffered support in many ways since this project began in earnest in 2005. The center's principal support has come in the form of funds to pay the wages of student research assistants. The assistance of Devan Jensen, Brent R. Nordgren, Richard Peterson, and Joany O. Pinegar has also been invaluable. The Department of Church History and Doctrine and the Office of Research and Creative Activities (ORCA) at Brigham Young University also awarded grants to fund student research assistants' wages and to fund travel to Europe to conduct interviews, examine historical venues, and present programs on this topic to Church members and friends.

Members of the Church in Germany and Austria have also come to my aid by identifying eyewitnesses and helping to establish interview times and venues. Several were so kind as to take me into their homes for a night or two as I traversed the two countries.

Significant contributions from private individuals allowed me to retain the services of student research assistants (see below); in this regard, I offer my thanks to Cal Wing, Renate Sward, and Detlef Lehnardt.

Patty Smith in the Faculty Support Office of Religious Education has been most supportive of this project by allowing her student employees to transcribe more than one hundred eyewitness interviews conducted in English. My colleagues in the Religious Education department have offered excellent suggestions and critical readings of portions of the text.

Readers and reviewers have been solicited from the ranks of my friends and associates and from eyewitnesses. They have served with distinction in locating text in need of clarification or revision. I express my appreciation to my father, Roy T. Minert, my brother Brian Minert with his wife, Debbie, and my daughter, Stephanie Seegmiller, for their reviews of the initial text. I am also indebted to readers Marietta Glauser, Walter Kindt, Kate Adams, Robert Hasara, the late Bernie Roper, Todd Roach, Daniel Boden, Melissa Burton, Miriam Burton, and Jim Cavens. My wife, Jeanne, compiled the index.

One of the greatest pleasures of my academic career has been my association with student research assistants. I have engaged twenty-two such students in the process of writing this book. What a gratifying experience it has been to see them take ownership of significant aspects of the book and to carry out their stewardship with enthusiasm and dedication. The more they were involved with the research, the more they understood the importance of completing this work and presenting it to the Church and to the world as a monument to the people about whom it is written. I have expressed my gratitude to them collectively and personally, and list them here as well:

Archivists: Mary Wade, Sarah Gibby Peris, Rachel Gale Tolman, Kiarah Sue Cox

Interviews in German: Jennifer Heckmann, Judith Sartowski, Michael Corley

Interviews in English: Jennifer Heckmann, Michael Corley, Judith Sartowski, Rachel Gale Tolman

Interview translation (German to English): Judith Sartowski

Archival research: Kathryn Penfield Price, Colter Kennedy, Emily Cox, Nicole Gibb Taylor

Memorial Book compilation (English sources): Nicole Gibb Taylor

Memorial Book compilation (German sources): Julianna Baumann Edlinger, Emily Cox

Correspondence: Erin Collins, Zach Alleman, Samantha Boden, Jennifer Heckmann, Nicole Taylor, Mary Wade

Interview text editing: Mary Wade, Kelly Goff, Elizabeth Stubbs

Book text editing: Mary Wade, Kellyanne Ure

Eyewitness contacts: Erin Collins, Katie Althoff, Zach Alleman

Time line: Zach Alleman

Webmaster and computer support: Trevor Brown, Casidy A. Andersen

Maps and demographics: Samantha Boden, Amelia Hollingsworth

A longtime friend and family history research colleague, Marion Wolfert, conducted interviews, searched for documents in the Church History Library, and offered ideas regarding the research process. James Larsen, a son-in-law, served as my photographer on a lengthy research trip, and his creations are seen on several pages of this book.

I am very grateful to my personal mentor and professor, Douglas F. Tobler, who first employed me in 1975–76 to study the Church in Germany prior to 1945. It was under his tutelage that I first began to consider the fate of the Latter-day Saints whom I readily recognized to be in harm's way. When I finally found the opportunity to make the formal study a reality, he immediately expressed his enthusiastic support. Conversations with him on this topic have been most rewarding.

One of the great figures in postwar Church history in East Germany is Walter Kindt. He provided me with historical details from his vivid memory, as well as historical literature and photographs of the years 1930 to 1953. There is probably no living Latter-day Saint who knows more than this man does about the membership of the Church, the status of the branches, and the lives of the missionaries in East Germany in that era.

Finally, to my dear wife, Jeanne, I express the thanks of a dependent husband who must constantly use his wife as a sounding board for new ideas and impressions. She heard most of the stories before they were written and has examined the entire text with a careful eye at least twice. When I was rendered a temporary invalid due to a total knee replacement that went awry, it was Jeanne who suggested that I had been granted additional time at home where I could devote myself to writing this book. She then did everything she could to prevent interruptions during the writing. What a glorious institution is marriage!

Roger P. Minert
Provo, Utah

Members of the Schneidemühl Branch in about 1932, shortly before the Boy Scout program in Germany was forbidden by Hitler's government. The scout leader is Johannes Kindt (first row at left), who later became the district president. (W. Kindt)

INTRODUCTION

Historical Background

The Church of Jesus Christ of Latter-day Saints has a fascinating history that spans more than 170 years and includes peoples of every continent. The missionary effort that began in the German states in the 1840s resulted in the establishment of branches of the Church in nearly every corner of that land by 1900. Though many converts in Germany and Austria chose to immigrate to the United States, others remained in the fatherland to help the Church grow and prosper there. However, given the religious, cultural, and political traditions of this relatively young Germany (officially established in 1871), being a Latter-day Saint in the country was not easy.

Joining the Church in central Europe made German Latter-day Saints outsiders in their native country. They no longer worshipped with their Catholic or Protestant neighbors, business colleagues, school comrades, or best friends. Even in their new church, they may have felt like second-class citizens. Instead of wards and stakes, they were organized into branches and districts. Instead of listening regularly to prophets, apostles, seventies, and bishops, they received instruction mainly at the hands of mission presidents and young missionaries from small towns and farms in the American West. Instead of meeting in beautiful neighborhood churches with park-like surroundings, they gathered in taverns, apartment houses, or renovated factory rooms in the smoky industrial districts of large cities.

Nevertheless, they worshipped the same Heavenly Father, prayed in the name of the same Savior, studied the same scriptures, supported the same missionary program, and lived and preached the same gospel to their neighbors as their fellow Saints who lived in other nations.

Immigration to North America before and after World War I (1914–18) had weakened large branches in Germany and Austria and in some locations had made smaller branches defunct. As in other European countries, Latter-day Saint branches in Germany were constantly "starting over."[1] However, as the history of the Church in Germany approached its centennial mark in the late 1930s, emigration had essentially stopped, missionary work had increased, and the branches of the East German Mission (Berlin) and the West German Mission (Frankfurt am Main) were strong and growing slowly. Unfortunately, World War II would seriously weaken the Church in Germany and end for decades its presence in eastern German

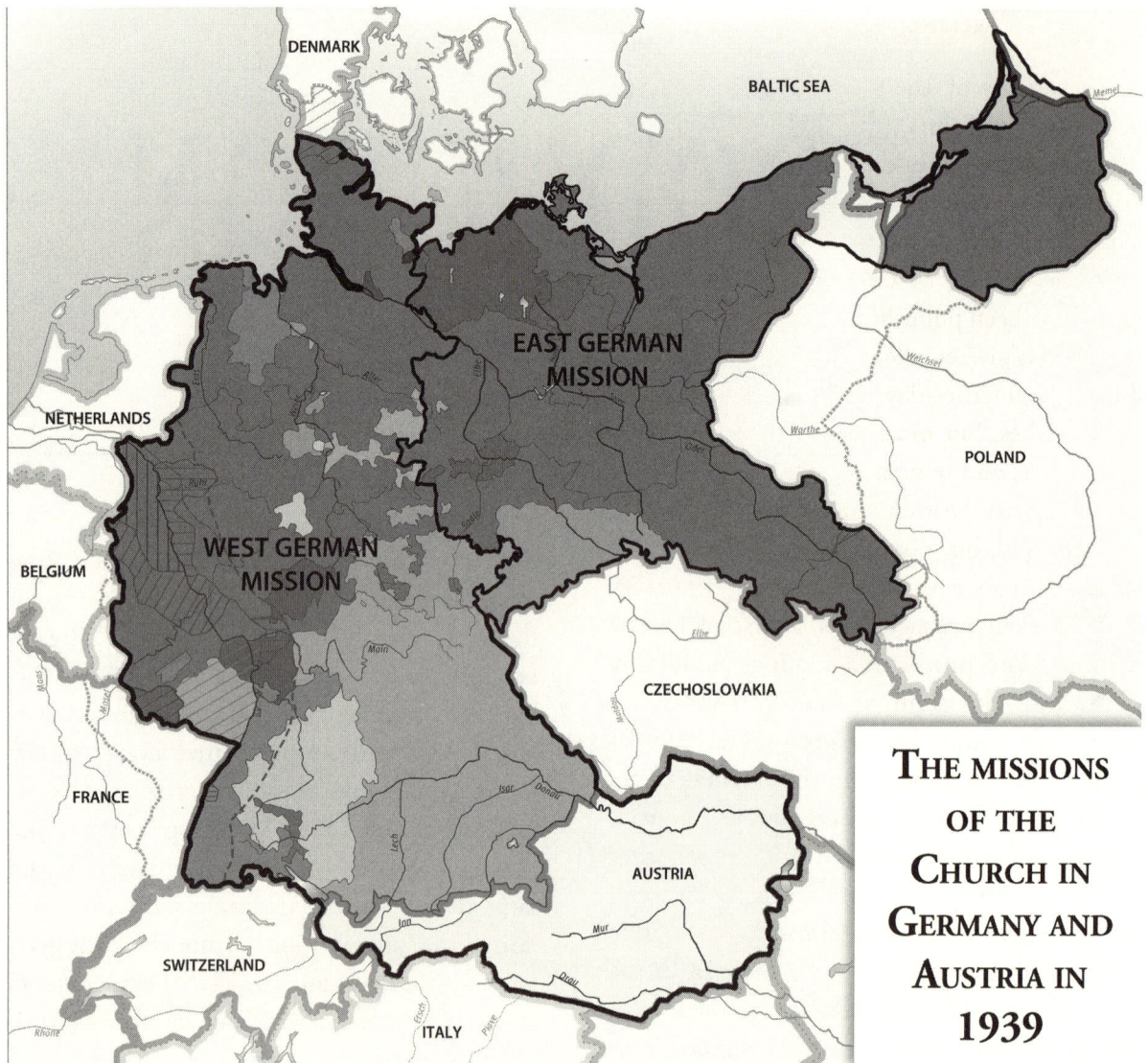

THE MISSIONS
OF THE
CHURCH IN
GERMANY AND
AUSTRIA IN
1939

territories that became part of post–World War II Poland and the Soviet Union.

Latter-day Saints in Germany during the Hitler era (1933–45) found themselves subjected to a unique set of challenges. For the first time, large numbers of Latter-day Saints were subjects of a totalitarian regime. Under a government that convinced or compelled more and more of its citizens to march to the same dark tune, members of a church that exalted the concepts of freedom of choice and moral agency were bound to feel at odds with the party line. When Hitler's armies achieved bloodless conquests of Austria (1938) and

parts of Czechoslovakia (1938 and 1939), some Latter-day Saint Germans saw a war coming. By the time the German army invaded Poland on September 1, 1939, Germans were no longer allowed to emigrate. Thirteen thousand Latter-day Saints were trapped and compelled to share the fate of their eighty million countrymen. What happened to them by the time Germany surrendered on May 8, 1945, is tragic, and for some of them, although the war had ended, their tribulations were far from over. But how these faithful Saints reacted to the events of the time is inspiring.

TELLING THE STORY

The history of The Church of Jesus Christ of Latter-day Saints (the LDS Church) in Germany during World War II has never been written in more than a few pages. Gilbert Scharffs devoted a chapter to the topic in his book *Mormonism in Germany.*[2] A few dozen books have been published by eyewitnesses, and those books give excellent detail about the lives of individual Latter-day Saints in specific towns and branches, but most were written for family members and remain essentially unknown.[3] Several diaries written during the war years have survived, but none have been published.[4] Many survivors have written short accounts of their experiences; few of these have ever found their way into print, though some have been submitted to the Family History Library and to the Church History Library in Salt Lake City.

In 1974, I began to focus my interest on the history of the Church in Germany. From a review of the wartime issues of the Church magazine *Der Stern,* it was clear to me that the Church suffered heavy losses during the Third Reich. I began asking questions to which nobody had ever researched the answers: How many members in Germany and Austria died from 1939 to 1945? How many priesthood holders were lost? How many branch meeting places were damaged or destroyed? How many Latter-day Saint families lost their homes? What happened to the branches in territories later ceded to Poland and the Soviet Union? What happened to Primary classes, Relief Society work meetings and bazaars, and Young Women and Young Men programs? How was the missionary effort sustained, if at all? Answers to these questions will be found in the pages of this book.

This story needed to be told—not in general, but in sufficient detail that the experiences of members of every branch of the Church in Germany and Austria could be described. Why

had this not been done in the six decades since the end of the war? This one question I can now answer, after thirty-two years of thinking and planning and three years of intense investigation. The effort required to write such a history is enormous and daunting. Such a story could be composed only after years of research and with the help of talented student assistants.

Interest in such a history is great. There could currently be as many as forty thousand members of the Church who have served missions in Germany and Austria. At least two hundred fifty thousand Latter-day Saints and others are related to the persons whose stories are featured in this history. The possibility that a German soldier in a photograph taken during the D-day invasion in 1944 could have been a priest from the Darmstadt Branch or that a Relief Society president might be among the dead in the aftermath of the Dresden firebombing of 1945 might motivate readers of World War II history books to think about the conflict from a different perspective.

In 2003, when Brigham Young University invited me to join the faculty of Religious Education as the instructor of Germanic family history, I realized that I now had the opportunity to write this history. I knew that nobody had attempted such a work, and I was more convinced than ever that it must be done. Finally, these faithful members of the Church—living or deceased—would have the chance to tell their stories.

My goal from the beginning has been to describe in great detail the lives of typical Latter-day Saints. Rather than an investigation of the relationship of the Church with the government of Hitler's Germany or the National Socialist (Nazi) Party, this is the story of everyday Saints. How did they maintain a testimony of the everlasting gospel under conditions few Church members have ever experienced? How did they conduct worship services without priesthood holders, locate each other after air raids, support each other after they lost their homes and loved ones? The remarkable stories they tell answer such questions.

When all foreign missionaries were evacuated from Germany and Austria in August 1939, the leadership of the Church was placed in the hands of local members. All contact with Church leadership in Salt Lake City was lost when the United States was drawn into the war in December 1941. How did the leaders of the East and West German Missions administer the affairs of the Church? How did they communicate with district and branch presidents? Did they continue to hold conferences, print and distribute literature for instruction, keep membership records, promote genealogical research, or do missionary work? These matters are described within the stories of eyewitnesses quoted here.

Compiling the Data

In order to present this history from the perspective of first-person experience, my assistants and I set out initially to interview all available surviving eyewitnesses, to locate biographies and autobiographies by and about eyewitnesses, and to study all available documents produced by Church units in the East and West German Missions. It was also decided early on that this history should be augmented with photographs, maps, and historical documents depicting the lives of the Latter-day Saints described in the pages of this book. To accomplish some of these goals, we needed the assistance of many individuals as well as the public media.

We immediately began assembling lists of survivors by conducting interviews with people we already knew and asking them to share with us the names of their living relatives and friends. Our list eventually grew to more than five hundred persons (of the thirteen thousand members of the Church in the two missions in 1939). Interviewees provided not only excellent first-person narratives regarding conditions and events in Germany during World War II, but also written stories of their own lives and the lives of deceased siblings, parents, and friends.

As we began our search for documents produced by Church units such as branches and mission offices, we were enthusiastically supported by the staff of the Church History Library in Salt Lake City. Church History Library call numbers appear in citations, such as CR 4 12, followed by the page number.

The *Church News* section of the *Deseret News* was kind enough to feature an introduction of our research on the cover of the February 11, 2006, issue, which coverage yielded more than three hundred responses from individuals wishing to share their stories or to recommend persons for us to contact. The same article was translated and featured in the German *Liahona* later that year and likewise attracted many responses from readers in Germany and Austria.

Organizing the data collected was, of course, a major challenge. The most efficient way proved to be the storage of data under the name of the branch to which each member belonged on September 1, 1939, when the war began. Hundreds of Saints, including displaced members and returning soldiers, had changed their branch affiliations by the time the war officially ended on May 8, 1945, and in the years that followed. The archival collection that emerged is monumental and will likely be transferred to the Harold B. Lee Library of Brigham Young University in Provo, Utah.

THE STATUS OF THE CHURCH IN
GERMANY AND AUSTRIA AT THE
ONSET OF WORLD WAR II

1939	East	West
Elders	402	390
Priests	194	179
Teachers	243	161
Deacons	445	345
Other Adult Males	1,245	939
Adult Females	4,336	3,172
Male Children	384	329
Female Children	358	280
Total	7,607	5,795

Mission	East (Berlin)	West (Frankfurt am Main)	Total
Districts	13	13	26
Branches	75	69	144

From reports compiled in the years before World War II, quite a lot is known about the membership of the Church in the two German missions.[5] The missions were similar in population and in geographical size (see map above).[6] No stakes of Zion had been established in Europe by 1939; members were organized instead into districts and branches. Each German mission had thirteen districts, and each district included from three to ten branches. The largest district in either mission was Berlin (East German Mission) with ten branches and 1,270 members. The smallest district was Hindenburg (East German Mission) with only four branches and sixty-five members.

The average size of a branch in Germany in 1939 was slightly more than one hundred members. Each branch had a presidency, clerks and secretaries, a Sunday School, a priesthood group, a Relief Society, a Primary organization, and youth groups. Each district had a presidency and clerks and leaders for each of the auxiliaries. Districts also had genealogical specialists, choir leaders, and in some cases recreational specialists.

The Largest LDS Branches in Germany in 1939		
	Branch	*Membership*
1	Chemnitz Center	469
2	Königsberg	465
3	Hamburg-St. Georg	400
4	Dresden	369
5	Stettin	359
6	Leipzig Center	328
7	Nuremberg	284
8	Annaberg-Buchholz	274
9	Berlin Center	268
10	Breslau West	265

In the two German missions, only one meetinghouse actually belonged to the Church—a modest but excellent structure erected in Selbongen, East Prussia (East German Mission), in 1929. The typical location for branch meetings was something far less prominent. Freestanding structures were very rare in the Church in Germany and Austria in those days. Most branches rented rooms in large buildings erected primarily for commercial use. Factories, warehouses, office buildings, and the like were sought out for space. Renovations were usually financed by the branch and resulted in chapels of appropriate size. In most cases there were also two or more classrooms. Most branch facilities featured restrooms and a cloakroom, but there was almost never an office for the branch presidency or the clerks. Some locations included a cultural hall, but most cultural activities took place on a stage or a rostrum in the main meeting room. Most chapels were used during the week for auxiliary meetings.

Decorations in branch chapels were sparse and modest. In most cases, one or two pictures were hung on the walls. The Savior was the most common subject of those pictures, but contemporary photographs also show small depictions of the Salt Lake Temple and the Prophet Joseph Smith or photographs of then Church President Heber J. Grant. The phrase "The Glory of God Is Intelligence" was often seen painted on the wall of the chapel, on the pulpit, or even on embroideries somewhere at the front of the room.

Church meetings for smaller groups were usually held in private homes, and attendees could number as high as thirty. This became progressively more common as branches lost their meeting rooms as the war drew to a close. In 1945, schools became popular meeting venues, and in such cases no signs of the presence of the Church were visible.

District presidencies had no specific physical locations or offices. Instead, district leaders conducted their business in the rooms of local branch buildings or in their own homes. Each mission rented office space in an affluent neighborhood, the East German Mission at Händelallee 6 in Berlin and the West German Mission at Schaumainkai 41 in Frankfurt am Main.

The standard meeting format in a branch was similar to that of branches and wards in other countries: Sunday School was held on Sunday morning; sacrament meeting took place in the late afternoon or evening; and meetings for the Relief Society, priesthood groups, and the Mutual Improvement Association (MIA) were held on evenings during the week. In most branches throughout the two missions, the Primary organization for children held meetings on Wednesday afternoons, mostly because public schools in Germany dismissed by 1:00 P.M. on Wednesdays. German Saints have traditionally sung the hymns of Zion with great enthusiasm, and choirs were integral parts of German branches and districts. Choir practice was usually held weekly on a convenient evening.

Semiannual conferences were an important and popular part of Church life in Germany in 1939 and throughout most of the war. Mission conferences were common before the war but could not be held later in the war because of restrictions in travel and resources. Each district held semiannual conferences and each branch held from two to four conferences each year. In addition, Sunday School and other auxiliary conferences were prominent events. The largest events were district conferences; some lasted from Friday through Sunday and included concerts, dances, and performances by choirs, orchestras, and theatrical groups. These were exciting affairs that drew hundreds of members who in turn often brought their nonmember friends.

German Latter-day Saints as Citizens under Hitler

Adolf Hitler and his National Socialist (Nazi) Party came to power in January 1933. In August 1934, German president Paul von Hindenburg died, and Hitler combined the offices of chancellor (which he had acquired legally) and president. By 1935, he outlawed the Communist Party and neutralized all other political parties, which gave him control of the parliament (Reichstag). He also won the loyalty of the German military by strengthening the army and the navy and establishing an air force—all in contradiction to the Treaty of Versailles, which had severely restricted the German military following World War I.

In Hitler's Third Reich, Latter-day Saints in Germany and Austria (which was annexed by Germany on March 12, 1938) were expected to be model citizens just as all other Germans. In other words, Saints were to be Germans first and to have no secondary allegiance. Nazi

Fig. 2. The Selbongen Branch building was constructed in 1929. During World War II, this was the only structure owned by the Church in Germany. The Polish name of the town is Zelwagi, and the building is currently owned and used by the Catholic Church. (Deseret News, *1938*)

Party programs were developed for every member of society old enough to say "Heil Hitler!" By 1936, everybody was encouraged—and often strongly pressured—to join the appropriate Nazi organization; there were distinct groups for men (Sturmabteilung), women (Frauenbund), boys (Hitlerjugend), girls (Bund Deutscher Mädel), athletes (Sportbund), truck drivers (Kraftfahrerkorps), teachers (Lehrerbund), and so forth. Each group had its own uniform and insignia. It was difficult to avoid every one of them; nevertheless, many adult Latter-day Saints were able to slip by without associating with the party, often by making excuses about spending their free time in some kind of humanitarian service.

The two prevailing faiths—Catholic and Protestant—comprised more than 95 percent of the German population in that era. Many smaller churches also existed in Germany but were not considered to be large enough to warrant concern; Latter-day Saints fell into this category. The two major churches were too powerful to be successfully attacked by the Nazi Party, while the smaller ones (commonly called "sects") were disregarded by both the government and the common people. The small number of Latter-day Saints in the Third Reich (just

over thirteen thousand among a population of eighty million) may have been an advantage in this regard because Church units were never large enough to attract attention. Indeed, in many cases, their meeting rooms were located in *Hinterhäuser*, or buildings behind main structures. Signs identifying the existence of the Church were usually small and unobtrusive. One usually had to be an insider to know that the Church existed in a given town or city.

One of the most visible ways in which a citizen could perform his or her civic duties was in the military. Perhaps as many as 1,800 Latter-day Saints in Germany and Austria performed active military service between 1939 and 1945, though few ever volunteered. Many more served in reserve units, including hundreds who had served in the German army in France or Russia in World War I. There was no provision for civil service as an alternative to military service in Hitler's philosophy, and there was no tolerance for anyone who wished to declare himself a conscientious objector.[7]

Community service was common among citizens in Nazi Germany, and Church members were often consistent and willing participants. They collected used winter clothing for soldiers at the front, dutifully stood in line to receive their ration cards, hurried to fight fires and rescue buried victims after air raids, and took refugees into their homes when other housing was not to be found. Of course, those functions were carried out by Germans of all religious persuasions who simply believed in helping because it was the right thing to do.

In a negative sense, being a good citizen in the Third Reich also included assisting the government in identifying and apprehending those persons who were considered enemies of the state—principally Jews. Several eyewitnesses interviewed in connection with this study remembered scenes of destruction after the "Night of Broken Glass" (Reichskristallnacht,

November 9–10, 1938), when organized Nazis raided Jewish stores and invaded Jewish homes. Some eyewitnesses later saw Jewish neighbors and friends being taken away in trucks, but—as most Germans of the day—had no idea what terrible treatment awaited those Jews under the secret German program termed the "Final Solution of the Jewish Question" (the murder of European Jews). Some Latter-day Saints decided for one reason or another that obedience to Hitler and his state was not required of a good member of the Church. Several of these Saints died in concentration camps, and several more spent time there.[8]

THE SOCIOECONOMIC STATUS OF LATTER-DAY SAINTS IN THE THIRD REICH

As they had for decades, Church members in the Hitler era belonged for the most part to the lower middle class. Many men were skilled laborers of the artisan classes, having learned a trade through an apprenticeship lasting from two to four years. A small number were masters in their trades and crafts. In only a few cases were Latter-day Saints in management positions, and there were few, if any, professionals such as physicians, attorneys, or teachers. For example, mission supervisor Herbert Klopfer was a translator and office worker, while his counselors Richard Ranglack and Paul Langheinrich worked in a hotel and in a government genealogical research office respectively.

Several members owned their own shops, such as Walter Krause, a carpenter in the Frankfurt/Oder Branch, and Friedrich Birth, a glazier in the Schneidemühl Branch. Several were small entrepreneurs, including Fritz Fischer, whose modest fleet of trucks and wagons transported manure from the streets of Berlin to the countryside, and Fritz Lehnig of the Cottbus Branch, who ran a wholesale vegetable business. Rare was the Church member who enjoyed a high rank in business or industry, as did Fritz Mudrow of the Berlin Schöneberg Branch (an administrator in the national labor force) and Karl Binder of the same branch (an engineer and manager in an armaments plant in Berlin).

Because the gospel had been preached primarily in the cities in Germany, very few Latter-day Saints in the Nazi era were farmers. It was simply too difficult to travel to church on Sundays from far away. (The branch in Selbongen, East Prussia, is a marked exception.) Although many Latter-day Saint families lived in multistory apartment buildings, they often rented garden space at the edge of town and kept animals such as chickens and goats. On the other hand, stories of dogs and cats are not common; no eyewitnesses recalled problems with feeding or protecting pets.

According to the testimonies of surviving eyewitnesses, most Latter-day Saint women were homemakers. When the German economy experienced boom years in the late 1930s, great emphasis was placed on occupational training for girls in the schools. Most teenage Latter-day Saint girls prepared for gainful employment in the Hitler era while their mothers often remained in the home. However, the war compelled a change in status for many of the homemakers when they were required by the government to assume jobs vacated by men who were drafted into the military. Most such jobs were in the blue-collar sector.

Very seldom did a Latter-day Saint family own a single-family dwelling. Only a few were wealthy enough to employ domestic servants, own an automobile, or have a telephone in the home. Most had indoor plumbing, but families often shared a restroom at the end of the hallway with their neighbors. Eyewitness stories about carrying water from the neighborhood well are common, and that necessity became more common as city water lines were destroyed.

Ration Coupons and Shortages in Wartime Germany

As in most nations heavily involved in World War II, ration coupons were an integral part of life in Germany even before the war began in 1939. Restrictions on most food and luxury items were constant. Specialty items generally disappeared from public view. Standing in lines to redeem food coupons took up large portions of the day, and families often split up to accomplish the task: the mother went to the butcher, one child to the baker, another child to the greengrocer, and so forth. However, a ration coupon was no guarantee that the item was actually available. It was a common occurrence that a store ran out of the item and the owner came out to announce to those still in line that there was no more of the foodstuffs they wanted—or he simply closed the door and hung out the *geschlossen* (closed) sign.

Toward the end of the war, the German government accomplished near miracles in keeping food distributed equitably throughout the country. Still, ration lines became ever longer, and stories are commonly told of women who refused to leave the lines when the air-raid sirens sounded; they preferred to believe that the raid would not come to their neighborhood, which allowed them to complete their purchases and feed their families. Essentially all eyewitnesses who lived in large cities in Germany and Austria reported that they had enough food until the very day the enemy arrived in their neighborhood. At that point the food system broke down totally and starvation threatened their existence.

Transportation in the Third Reich

Germany's public transportation systems were excellent during the Nazi period, built for densely populated areas where personal automobile ownership was a rarity. Latter-day Saints often tell of traveling to Church meetings on the bus or the streetcar, but some chose the longer walking time because they lacked money for the streetcar. Railroad service across the Reich featured only steam locomotives, but some traveled at very high speeds, and timetables were strictly observed during the first years of the war. Latter-day Saints report that there were no general restrictions on travel away from home during most of the war years, though some trains were full of troops, which meant that civilians had to wait for later connections. Travel by train often took longer than usual as water and coal supplies waned, tracks and bridges were destroyed, and various branches of the government and the military competed for the use of an ever-decreasing number of trains.

When attacks from the air and invading armies caused the destruction of the trains and the tracks, schedules were obviously interrupted and travel became unreliable. People rode in whatever conveyances were available, often in boxcars or cattle cars. During the final year of the war, the railroads frantically conveyed fresh soldiers to the front and wounded soldiers and refugees to the rear. According to eyewitnesses, it was no longer necessary to purchase tickets; instead, passengers fought their way onto the trains—many climbed through windows to get in. Refugees were often compelled to discard their luggage in the scramble to board a train.

Because they were prime targets for attacks, most railroad stations had air-raid shelters. Trains moving down the tracks or standing on sidings were under constant attack during the last year of the war, when the German Luftwaffe (air force) could no longer provide sufficient defense. Many Latter-day Saints were in trains attacked by fighter planes and several lost their lives in such attacks.[9] At the end of the war and for months afterward, people rode trains under dangerous circumstances; sitting on the roof, standing on the running boards, or clinging to other parts of the train were common means of riding along.

By the end of the war, bus and streetcar transportation had been seriously interrupted or curtailed in most German cities. Now and then, a streetcar would run for a few blocks, then passengers would get off and walk down the line for a few blocks, where the service would continue again. In cities with subway systems (*Untergrundbahn*, or *U-Bahn*), some of the lines survived below the streets and U-Bahn stations were commonly used as air-raid shelters.

Of the few Latter-day Saints who owned automobiles or trucks, most used them in association with businesses. Many of those vehicles were destroyed in air raids. During the last days of the war, surviving personal automobiles were usually seized by the government, the military, or the invaders; personal property was no longer protected.

Eyewitnesses recalled walking long distances from home to school and church; walking times of more than one hour in one direction were not uncommon. For persons in good health, walking was no hardship in Germany in those days. Indeed, many branch outings involved *wandern*, the tradition of walking all day through forests outside of town and enjoying a picnic along the way. Some eyewitnesses told of being baptized in forest ponds, and branch members walked up to an hour each way at all seasons of the year to witness the ceremonies.

Schools in Nazi Germany

The complex and respected German school system, which dates back to the 1870s, was expanded and improved during the early twentieth century. However, Allied air attacks did not spare schools; programs were often interrupted,

abbreviated, or cancelled, and graduations were routinely postponed. Some schools in larger cities served double duty, accommodating children from bombed-out schools in split sessions. Many LDS eyewitnesses recalled that the official school starting time was delayed by an hour or two on any morning following a night interrupted by an air raid.

Several eyewitnesses recalled having teachers who were enthusiastic Nazi Party members (all teachers employed by the state were required to join). Some told of singing the "Deutschlandlied" (German national anthem) or the "Horst-Wessel-Lied" (the official Party hymn) every morning. Others recalled that army-like inspections were conducted to insure the students' clothing was in order, their hair combed, and their fingernails clean, and that punishments were administered when an order was not followed.

Entire classes of school children were sometimes moved from larger cities to rural areas as part of the children's evacuation program (see "Kinderlandverschickung" in the glossary). Many teachers were sent with their homeroom classes to a distant small town to continue instruction away from the air raids. When schools were damaged or transformed into hospitals later in the war, the children were often pleased at first. Later, however, they learned of the disadvantages of a lack of formal instruction.

Religious instruction was provided for Catholic and Protestant students for the first eight grades of public school. Latter-day Saint children were allowed to choose between these two religions (where both were available) or to not attend at all. There are no reports of programmatic persecution of LDS students in public schools, though confrontations with fanatic Nazi teachers did occur now and then.

Even before the war, most German students left public school after the eighth grade to pursue an apprenticeship or employment. Few continued formal education, with less than 10 percent planning on attending university. The great majority of LDS youth did not or could not pursue higher education.

AIR RAIDS OVER GERMANY

As early as the first week of the war, Polish airplanes attacked cities in the German Reich. By 1941, British air raids were launched against most large German cities—especially in the western part of the nation. When the United States joined the war in the European Theater in 1942, the Allied bombing campaign became better coordinated and a standard procedure was developed: the British Royal Air Force conducted their raids under cover of night and the American Army Air Corps flew during the day. In some cities, air raids were rare, perhaps even unique. In others, especially where critical war industries were located, raids were more frequent. During 1944, the most important cities were subjected to raids every week. Because many large cities in Germany were just a few miles apart, enemy airplanes flying in one direction of the compass had to be considered to be on their way to one of several cities. Alarms were sounded in all possible target cities; in many communities, false alarms were more frequent than actual attacks.

Even in large cities, Germans seldom had access to official, heavy concrete bunkers for refuge from enemy attacks. In large cities, many bunkers were constructed in parks, in or near railroad stations, and near large intersections. Still, nowhere were there enough bunkers to shelter everyone. Typically Germans simply sought refuge in their own basements. Of course, those basements had not been constructed to protect people from five-hundred-pound "blockbuster" bombs, but residents did what they could to fortify the ceilings and

walls of their basements. In most cases, entries and exits were through the main hallway or stairway serving the entire building. Shelters in a variety of public buildings and even large private or commercial buildings were clearly marked as *Luftschutzraum* or *LSR* and were open to all (see the Zwickau Branch chapter).

Air-raid warnings were announced by civil defense officials with loud, wailing sirens. Three different signals were used: one to announce a possible attack, one for a probable or imminent attack, and one for the actual arrival of attackers over the city's air space. The interim between the first and the last alarms was from ten to twenty minutes or more. Thus there was usually time for people to find shelter, even if away from home. Proof positive of a pending strike was seen in the form of illumination flares dropped above the target by advance enemy airplanes. Called *Christbäume* or *Weihnachtsbäume* (Christmas trees) by the Germans, these flares were visible from miles away and heralded death and destruction. Civil defense units sometimes responded by burning decoy flares to mislead the attackers.

Every neighborhood had an air-raid warden. Wardens were sometimes auxiliary policemen, but most often were low-ranking members of the Nazi Party. When the air-raid sirens sounded, it was their job to see that people vacated their apartments, public buildings, and streets and sought refuge in the shelters. They also reminded people to close their blinds or turn off their lights to achieve total blackout. Heavy fines were levied against violators of this safety standard. It was also the air-raid wardens' responsibility to see that all entries to shelters were closed and locked when the final siren was heard. Persons not yet in shelters were then on their own to find alternative places of protection. For a variety of reasons, some people chose to stay in their apartments rather than go to the shelter. In reality, the chances of survival were almost equal wherever they were. On the streets, however, they could be killed by enemy bombs as well as by shrapnel from friendly antiaircraft guns used to shoot down the attackers.

Latter-day Saint eyewitnesses tell of preparing for air raids the same way their neighbors prepared. All but the smallest children were expected to carry a valise or a suitcase with the most important survival items as they descended into the basement or hurried down the street to a public shelter. One of the parents usually carried the most valuable family documents, including genealogical papers, family photographs, and books of scripture. Most brought a change of clothing and enough food for the next few hours. There was little time to worry about what was left behind.

Life in the typical air-raid shelter was little more than survival. Some tried to sleep (which was usually impossible because of the noise), while others prayed, read newspapers, or played cards (if there was enough light to do so). Parents tried to entertain or comfort their children. Some sat on chairs, others on the floor—usually in rooms that lacked proper heating or cooling systems. Most were exhausted from lack of sleep and wanted only to return to their homes.

Three means of self-defense were practiced everywhere people gathered in private shelters. First, because apartment houses in most cities were built with no space between them, the basements of any two adjacent apartment buildings usually shared a common wall. Residents were instructed to make a hole in the wall (*Mauerdurchbruch*) large enough for an adult to crawl through.[10] If the exit of one basement was blocked, the people could escape through that wall into the next basement by simply removing loose brick or temporary wood structures. Another standard feature in each shelter was one or more barrels of water; if

fires had broken out close to the escape route, each person could soak a blanket in the water and put it over his or her head to prevent suffocation or burns as he or she exited the shelter. Finally, the contents were removed from the attic of each house to provide less material for combustion and to make it easier to find and remove incendiary bombs. Such bombs often penetrated the roof and came to rest on the floor of the attic. The timer fuses usually did not initiate fire for several minutes, allowing residents who kept supplies of sand and water in the attic to smother the bombs before they began to burn or to douse smaller fires before they spread.

When the all-clear siren sounded, air-raid wardens moved to evacuate the shelters as fast as possible. The main purpose of this was to prevent the occupants from suffocating in the shelters when smoke became thick or firestorms ensued. In crowded neighborhoods with tall apartment buildings, fires that started in the upper floors soon spread downward and to adjacent buildings. The oxygen feeding those fires was sucked out of the environment, making it hard to breathe. The upward rush of the air to the fire felt like wind and gave rise to the term *firestorm*. People emerged from the basements and ran down the street in search of open spaces where air was more plentiful. A technical description of firestorms is provided by author David Irving in a police report from the city of Hamburg:

> An estimate of the force of this fire-storm could be obtained only by analyzing it soberly as a meteorological phenomenon: as a result of the sudden linking of a number of fires, the air above was heated to such an extent that a violent updraft occurred, which, in turn, caused the surrounding fresh air to be sucked in from all sides to the centre of the fire area. This tremendous suction caused movements of air of far greater force than normal winds. In meteorology the differences of temperature involved

are of the order of 20° to 30° C. In this fire-storm they were of the order of 600°, 800° or even 1,000° C. This explained the colossal force of the fire-storm winds.[11]

Following air raids, the fortunate people were those who emerged from the shelters to find that there had been no attack at all. It was also a relief to learn that the damage done was to structures blocks away and that one's own home was intact. However, this relief was often dispelled by the sound of another alarm siren a few hours later.

CULTURE AND ENTERTAINMENT IN NAZI GERMANY

Despite the privations of the war years, motion picture theaters, opera houses, dance halls, and bars stayed open until they were destroyed or their utilities were cut off.[12] New movies were released and new hit songs were heard over the radio. Newspapers were printed in many cities until the day the Allied invaders arrived. Soccer games were played and citizens went ice-skating, swimming, and hiking. Some Germans and Austrians even continued to take vacations (without leaving the country) for the first few war years. Birthday parties took place, christenings and weddings were celebrated in local churches, and clubs maintained their regular activities as long as possible. Local and national governments did their best to sustain the lifestyle of their citizens during the war and were remarkably successful in the effort. Of course, when the war came to an end and the conquerors ruled, life was reduced to mere subsistence, and entertainment was no longer a priority.

THE END OF PEACETIME

When World War II began on September 1, 1939, the majority of Germans believed that Germany's cause was just and that victory was likely if not certain. Many Latter-day Saints were of the same belief. But it is possible that members of the Church in Germany realized before other Germans that the war was not a just cause and that defeat and invasion were possible if not probable. This must have been a frightening prospect. Several decades ago, Douglas F. Tobler was told by several German eyewitnesses that they believed the prophecies of the Book of Mormon, namely, that any people fighting against the inhabitants of the promised land (North America) were doomed to ultimate failure. Those eyewitnesses must then have had terrible premonitions when Germany and the United States exchanged declarations of war in December 1941.

EDITORIAL COMMENTS

In chapters in which an eyewitness provided a single interview or document from which several quotations are taken, it may be assumed that all quotations and information attributed to that eyewitness were taken from the same source. This allows the elimination of hundreds of repetitious footnotes.

Some interviewees anglicized their names after immigrating to America. (For instance, the name Müller became Mueller.) This book will use German name spellings when referring to experiences that occurred in Germany and anglicized spellings when referencing interviews and other sources conducted or obtained in the United States. This seeming inconsistency is not meant to confuse the reader, but to show proper respect to the people who have shared their stories.

Precise details regarding the sufferings of Latter-day Saints in the following pages have been summarized or even suppressed in some cases. Sufficient allusions are made to the fact that what happened was often much worse than expressed in my descriptions. The presentation of gruesome detail serves no worthy purpose in this book. It is not my goal to emphasize the morbid, the heinous, the perverse, or the inhumane. What the Saints of the East German Mission experienced during World War II was often so terrifying and hideous that the reader may believe the many eyewitnesses who stated simply that "there are no words that could adequately describe what happened." Of course, no such generalizations or simplifications have been made where quotations have been taken from interviews and written eyewitness accounts.

NOTES

1. Douglas F. Tobler, interview by the author, Lindon, Utah, July 25, 2008.

2. Gilbert Scharffs, "Mormonism Holds On during the World War II Years," in *Mormonism in Germany: The History of the Church of Jesus Christ of Latter-day Saints in Germany* (Salt Lake City: Deseret Book, 1970), 91–116.

3. Excellent examples of the few published autobiographies are those of Werner Klein (Landsberg Branch, Schneidemühl District), Karola Hilbert (Berlin Neukölln Branch, Berlin District), and Gerd Skibbe (Wolgast Group, Rostock District).

4. See the stories of Anton Larisch (Görlitz Branch, Dresden District and Halberstadt Group, Leipzig District), Alfred Bork (Stettin Branch, Stettin District), and sister missionaries Renate Berger (Königsberg Branch, Königsberg District) and Helga Meiszus Birth Meyer (Tilsit Branch, Königsberg District).

5. Presiding Bishopric, "Financial, Statistical, and Historical Reports of Wards, Stakes, and Missions, 1884–1955," CR 4 12, 257.

6. Hitler's Germany had about 80 million inhabitants in 1939 and was roughly the size of the state of Texas.

7. The Jehovah's Witnesses in Germany (known as die Ernsten Bibelforscher) publicly opposed military service and as a group became inmates of prisons and concentration camps.

8. See the stories of Elisabeth Elsa Jung Süss (Chemnitz Center Branch, Chemnitz District) and Harald Damasch (Danzig Branch, Danzig District).

9. See the chapters on the Tilsit and Annaberg-Buchholz Branches for examples of such losses.

10. David Irving, *The Destruction of Dresden* (London: William Kimber, 1963), 42.

11. Ibid., 162.

12. The Berlin Opera House was destroyed and rebuilt twice during the war. No attempt was made to restore it after the third time it was bombed and burned out.

German sailors burying comrades on an island in Greece.

GEDENKBUCH
(MEMORIAL BOOK)

For the Lord suffereth the righteous to be slain that his justice and judgment may come upon the wicked; therefore ye need not suppose that the righteous are lost because they are slain; but behold, they do enter into the rest of the Lord their God. (Alma 60:13)

One of the original goals of this study was to compile a list of German and Austrian Latter-day Saints who did not survive World War II. When estimates by previous investigators suggested that approximately 550 LDS soldiers and 50 LDS civilians had lost their lives in the two German missions, serious questions emerged.[1] Were not the majority of branches located in large cities—the principal targets of Allied bombing attacks? Would not civilian Church members and meetinghouses also lie beneath the sights of the enemy bombardiers? Would it not be logical to suggest that civilian Saints were killed by invading enemy ground troops? If in fact all of the members of the Church units in areas later annexed by Poland and the Soviet Union were driven from their homes, could it not be assumed that some of them would not survive a trek of hundreds of miles to the west, often made in the dead of winter?

From written sources and eyewitness interviews, we have compiled a *Gedenkbuch* (memorial book) with more than six hundred names from the East German Mission. For each person, every attempt has been made to show the birth date and place; marriage date and place; spouse; death date, place, and cause; baptism and confirmation dates and places; priesthood ordinations; and military rank of the deceased. This Gedenkbuch information is included in the "In Memoriam" sections found at the end of each chapter. Photographs have been collected of several of the Latter-day Saints who did not survive the war.

Who is included in the memorial book? The initial goal was to determine which Latter-day Saints died as a direct consequence of the war (what the Germans refer to as *Kriegseinwirkung*). However, it soon became evident that in many cases it was not possible to state whether the death of a certain individual was or was not connected to wartime events or conditions. For example, several diseases, such as typhus, which otherwise would have been rare, were prevalent toward the end of the war. Minor illnesses sometimes caused the deaths of persons who spent a good deal of time in cold and dank air-raid shelters or out in the open after becoming homeless. The lack of qualified medical personnel and medical facilities certainly contributed to a general decrease in the quality of health care and thus an increase in mortality. Persons who died of heart attacks or strokes may have had their conditions deteriorate more rapidly when hurrying to an air-raid shelter or upon receiving news of the death of a soldier. In short, it was decided that no cause of death—including old age or senility—would be excluded from the list of LDS persons who died during the war years.

Each Latter-day Saint who died is found listed in the branch to which the person belonged on September 1, 1939 (except for the few who relocated during the war years). The personal data collected from Church records and eyewitnesses have been compared to public genealogical data bases, such as the LDS International Genealogical Index, Ancestral File, and Pedigree Resource File. In many cases, multiple sources offer conflicting data, especially when it comes to name spelling variations and place names.

Who is not included in the memorial book? A great many Latter-day Saints in Germany and Austria in the war era were not married to Church members. Many adult women were the only members of their families to have been baptized. They lost non-LDS husbands, parents, and children, who are not included in our compilation. For example, Erna Kaiser of the Stuttgart Branch documented no fewer than twenty-four close relatives who were killed in the war, only six of whom were Latter-day Saints. Thus, the sufferings of the Saints regarding the loss of life in their families was in many cases greater than is reflected in the lists of branches shown in this volume.

Some of the Latter-day Saints who died were inactive and possibly unknown to other branch members. It is possible that several hundred such persons should be listed here, but there is no way of knowing who they were because nobody in the branches knew of their demise.

Finally, we were hesitant to include persons shown in branch records as *vermisst* (missing) or *verschollen* (disappeared). Many of those Saints likely perished under the mountains of rubble resulting from catastrophic air raids over big cities, but no proof of this is available. If the truth were known, there might be more than one hundred persons in this category. Some persons listed as missing may have been driven from their homes, sought refuge elsewhere or simply lost contact with the Church.

The details shown in the "In Memoriam" section of each chapter do not represent original genealogical research. Entries include data supplied by eyewitnesses, descendants, and friends, taken from branch membership records and from the following public sources:

www.familysearch.org:

Ancestral File (AF)

International Genealogical Index (IGI)

Pedigree Resource File (PRF)

www.volksbund.de: This Web site is maintained by a society dedicated to the preservation of German war graves from the two world wars. The language is German. Searches can be made by the name of the soldier or the place of birth. Some women and civilians are included in this database.

Other abbreviations used in the Memorial Book lists include:

CHL: Church History Library of the LDS Church

FHL: Family History Library of the LDS Church

The names of persons who provided genealogical data are also found in citations.

Note

1. Gilbert Scharffs, *Mormonism in Germany: The History of the Church of Jesus Christ of Latter-day Saints in Germany* (Salt Lake City: Deseret Book, 1970), 116.

MAJOR EVENTS
OF WORLD WAR II

Compiled by Zach Alleman

1939

August

23   The Nazi euthanasia program begins. By the end of the war, seventy thousand mentally and physically disabled Germans are killed.

24–26   American LDS missionaries are evacuated to Denmark and the Netherlands.

28   Food ration cards are introduced in Germany. Meat, dairy, sugar, eggs, bread, cereal, and fruit are limited.

September

1   Germany invades Poland.

2   Willy Klappert of the Frankfurt am Main Branch is the first German LDS soldier to die.

3   Great Britain and France declare war on Germany.

29   Germany and the Soviet Union formally divide up Poland.

October

1   Royal Air Force (RAF) airplanes drop propaganda leaflets over Germany.

November

12   Clothing ration cards are issued in Germany.

23   Jews in German-occupied Poland are ordered to wear the yellow Star of David on their outer clothing.

27   German "Aryans" are given twelve months to divorce their Jewish spouses.

1940

January

11   German citizens suffer from coal shortages.

February

13   Thomas E. McKay appoints Herbert Klopfer as supervisor of the East German Mission.

April

9   Germany invades Denmark and Norway.

27   Heinrich Himmler issues orders for the construction of a concentration camp at Auschwitz.

27   German women ages fifteen to forty are required to register with the Employment Ministry.

May

10   Germany invades the Netherlands, Belgium, Luxembourg, and France. Winston Churchill becomes British prime minister.

19 The German ports of Hamburg and Bremen are bombed by the RAF.

20 German forces reach the English Channel.

26 British forces start the Dunkirk evacuation.

31 A shortage of doctors causes viruses to spread among the German people.

June

5 German forces launch an attack into France proper.

14 German forces enter Paris.

22 France surrenders to Germany.

26 Germany's meat ration is cut to fourteen ounces per week per person.

July

Hermann Goering, second to Hitler in the Nazi hierarchy, gives Reinhard Heydrich the authority to carry out preparations for a "final solution of the Jewish question" throughout German-occupied Europe.

August

13 The Battle of Britain starts.

25–26 The RAF conducts its first air raid on Berlin.

September

15 The German Luftwaffe launches a major attack on London.

17 Artur Axmann, the new German youth leader, decrees that all Hitler Youth ages fourteen to eighteen in areas vulnerable to air raids must attend air-raid training on Sunday mornings.

27 Germany, Italy, and Japan sign the Tripartite Pact.

1941

February

12 German Lt. General Erwin Rommel arrives in Tripoli in North Africa.

March

2 German forces enter Bulgaria.

24 Rommel launches his first offensive in North Africa.

April

2–6 German forces cross Hungary to invade Yugoslavia and Greece.

May

4 Hitler delivers his "Thousand-Year Reich" speech.

7 Joseph Stalin assumes premiership of the Soviet Union.

24 The German battleship *Bismarck* sinks Britain's battle cruiser HMS *Hood*.

27 The British Royal Navy sinks the *Bismarck* in the North Atlantic.

June

22 Operation Barbarossa begins when German forces invade the Soviet Union.

July

9 German forces capture three hundred thousand Soviet troops near Minsk.

10 Stalin assumes the role of commander-in-chief of the Red Army.

12 Britain and the Soviet Union sign a mutual assistance treaty.

August

1 The focus on the Wehrmacht and the armaments industry leaves German citizens without replacement parts for cars and other forms of transportation.

September

1 All German Jews over the age of six are ordered to wear a yellow Star of David with the word *Jude* written on it.

8 German forces lay siege to Leningrad.

October

2   In Operation Taifun, Germany starts the drive on Moscow.

31 German workers are required to "volunteer" to donate twenty-five reichsmark a week from their wages.

November

22 The German raider *Atlantis* is sunk.

December

7   Japanese forces attack Pearl Harbor.

8   The United States declares war on Japan.

11 Germany and Italy declare war on the United States.

19 Hitler assumes command of the German *Heer* (Army).
Only women are serving as missionaries in the East German Mission.

1942

January

14 German submarines attack shipping vessels off the U.S. East Coast.

26 The first contingent of U.S. troops to reach Europe arrives in Northern Ireland.

February

28 The use of cars for anything but work is banned in Germany.

March

17 Branches throughout Germany celebrate the Relief Society centennial.

19 A gas chamber is first used on human beings at Auschwitz-Birkenau.

21 Severe penalties, including sentences in concentration camps, are announced to deter German citizens from making unnecessary journeys by rail.

May

30–31 The RAF conducts a thousand-airplane raid on Cologne.

June

4   Mass evacuation of Cologne takes place.

July

4   U.S. bombers fly their first mission in Europe.
British bombers begin attacking Germany's second-largest city, Hamburg, continuing for four straight nights and causing a firestorm that kills thirty thousand civilians.

August

23 German forces reach Stalingrad.

October

27 Helmut Hübener of the Hamburg-St. Georg Branch (West German Mission) is executed in Berlin for treason.

November

19 Soviet forces counterattack at Stalingrad.

1943

January

14–23 Allied leaders hold the Casablanca Conference.

27 U.S. bombers conduct the first all-American raid on Germany.

28 All German men between ages sixteen and sixty-five and all women between ages seventeen and forty-five are to be mobilized for military employment.

30 The RAF conducts its first daylight raid on Berlin.

February

2   The German Sixth Army surrenders at Stalingrad; there are 295,000 casualties, including Karl Albert Göckeritz, president of the Chemnitz District.

Hans and Sophie Scholl are arrested on the Munich University campus for distributing pamphlets for the White Rose resistance group.

March

3   Friedrich Biehl, former supervisor of the West German Mission, dies in a fire in Russia.

May

31   Meat rations in Germany are cut to nine ounces.

June

13   German forces in North Africa surrender to the Allies.

July

7   Allied forces invade Sicily.

24–30 RAF bombings reduce Hamburg to rubble.

25   Benito Mussolini is overthrown and arrested.

August

17   Regensburg and Schweinfurt are destroyed in air raids.

September

3   More than one million citizens are evacuated from Berlin in one month.

October

13   Italy joins the Allies and declares war on Germany.

23   Martin Werner Hoppe, president of the Breslau District, dies in a field hospital in the Soviet Union.

November

20–22 The office of the East German Mission in Berlin is destroyed in air raids occurring on successive nights.

1944

February

20–27 Allied air forces launch the "Big Week" air raids over Germany.

March

6   U.S. bombers attack Berlin for the first time.

30–31 Nuremberg is bombed.

June

6   (D-day) Allied troops land in Normandy, France.

July

20   Claus Graf Schenk von Stauffenberg attempts to assassinate Hitler.

22   Herbert Klopfer, supervisor of the East German Mission, is reported missing in action on the Eastern Front.

September

10   Himmler orders that the families of all deserters be executed.
     German civilians begin the evacuation of eastern German provinces.

11   U.S. forces cross the German border near Aachen.

15   U.S. forces take the city of Nancy in Alsace-Lorraine.

25   Hitler calls up remaining sixteen- to sixty-year-old males for military service.

30   Germany's rationing of fish and meat drops to three ounces per person per week plus one-third of an ounce of egg.

October

5   All German hospitals are put under military control.
     German sixteen-year-olds are called up for military service.

November

28   Soviet forces cross the Danube River and approach Austria.

December

16   The Battle of the Bulge commences in Belgium and Luxembourg.

1945

January

Millions of German refugees begin the trek west by land and across the Baltic Sea.

Latter-day Saint refugees begin to gather in the Langheinrich home in Berlin and the Lehnig home in Cottbus.

15   The Battle of the Bulge is concluded; the Allies prevail.

16   Soviet troops liberate the Auschwitz extermination camp.

28   Soviet forces enter the German province of Pomerania.

30   The German hospital ship *Wilhelm Gustloff* is sunk in the Baltic Sea by a Soviet submarine and thousands of German refugees perish.

February

1   Soviet forces establish a small bridgehead over the Oder River east of Berlin.

9   "Fortress Königsberg" surrenders to the Red Army; district president Max Freimann is one of several Latter-day Saints who disappear there.

British and Canadian forces penetrate the Siegfried line and reach the Rhine River.

12   German women between the ages of sixteen and sixty are declared eligible for Volkssturm (home guard) service.

13–14   Allied air forces carry out the firebombing of Dresden.

March

5   U.S. forces enter Cologne.

German boys sixteen and older are sent into combat.

5–6   Chemnitz is destroyed by Allied airplanes.

7   U.S. forces cross the Rhine River at Remagen.

19   Herbert Klopfer, supervisor of the East German Mission, dies as a POW in the Soviet Union (this will not be known until 1948).

20   U.S. forces take Saarbrücken and Zweibrücken.

27   U.S. forces capture Frankfurt am Main.

April

5–14   Soviet forces take Vienna, Austria.

10   Allied forces enter the city of Hanover.

12   Franklin D. Roosevelt dies in office; Harry S. Truman becomes U.S. president.

15   British forces liberate Bergen-Belsen concentration camp.

16   Soviet forces start the final assault on Berlin.

17–20   U.S. forces capture Nuremberg.

19   Christian Heck, former supervisor of the West German Mission, is killed near Bad Imnau in southwest Germany.

22   U.S. forces cross the Danube River.

29   U.S forces liberate Dachau concentration camp.

Hitler designates Karl Dönitz to succeed him as president and Martin Bormann as chancellor.

30   Hitler commits suicide in his underground bunker in Berlin.

May

2   Berlin is surrendered to Soviet forces.

6   "Fortress Breslau" surrenders to the Red Army.

The Dresden District holds a spring conference in Dresden; Russian artillery fire is heard in the distance.

7	In Reims, France, Alfred Jodl signs the surrender of all German forces.
8	(VE Day) In Berlin, Wilhelm Keitel signs the surrender of German forces. At least 60 percent of the Saints in the East German Mission are homeless.
14	Heber J. Grant, President of The Church of Jesus Christ of Latter-day Saints, dies in Salt Lake City.

June

| 5 | The Allies (France, Great Britain, Soviet Union, United States) occupy Germany and Austria in four zones. |

July

1	American troops evacuate territory conquered in eastern Germany; Soviet troops move in.
	East German Mission leaders are granted use of the Wolfsgrün Castle near Zwickau and send LDS refugees to live there.
	Mission leaders make the first of two trips through the Soviet Occupation Zone to assess the status of the Saints of the East German Mission.

Fall

The first LDS refugees arrive in Langen near Frankfurt am Main and establish a colony.

1946

February–November

Elder Ezra Taft Benson visits the Saints in Europe and arranges for the distribution of welfare supplies from Salt Lake City.

1947

The only surviving LDS branch east of the new German-Polish border is in Selbongen (formerly East Prussia).

1950

The last surviving LDS soldier returns from a Soviet POW camp.

Mission and District conferences (such as this one in Schneidemühl) often attracted more than a thousand members and friends during the first few years of the war. (W. Kindt)

EAST GERMAN
MISSION

The home of the East German Mission was a stately villa at Händelallee 6. Across the street to the south was the famous Tiergarten—Berlin's answer to New York's Central Park. The Siegessäule (Victory Tower), one of the famous landmarks of Germany's capital city, was just two hundred yards to the southwest. From his office on the main floor, Alfred C. Rees of Salt Lake City presided over the East German Mission. In the summer of 1939, the mission included all of Germany east of the Elbe River and portions of Saxony to the southeast of the river (see map). Officially founded on January 1, 1937, the mission had a population of 7,601 members in 1939 and was one of the largest missions (by population) in the world at the time.[1]

The decade of the 1930s was a time of resurgence in the East German Mission. The wave of emigration of Latter-day Saints from Germany following World War I had diminished many branches and even led to the demise of some. However, Hitler's Third Reich produced a revitalized economy by 1935, and Germany had become a fine place to live—at least for the great majority of Germans. The work of about seventy full-time LDS missionaries was supported by loyal members. Convert baptisms were common, and most

meeting facilities were in excellent condition.[2] In 1938, a huge four-day conference was held in Dresden; the printed conference program indicates that all Church programs and organizations existed and were functioning very well among the thirteen districts and seventy-two branches of the mission. According to the mission secretary, "Approximately a thousand saints and friends from all over Eastern Germany came together and made the conference a wonderful success."[3] From that standpoint, it was an excellent time to be a Latter-day Saint in Germany.

Perhaps the most public success achieved by President Rees during his seventeen-month tenure was the publication of a lengthy article in the Berlin edition of the *Völkischer Beobachter* (*People's Observer*), the official newspaper of the Nazi Party. Under the title "In the Land of the Mormons," the article emphasized certain perceived similarities of the Church and Hitler's new Germany.[4] For example, whereas the LDS Church had suffered persecution at the hands of the residents of Ohio, Missouri, and Illinois, Germans had been forced to suffer under the humiliating stipulations of the Treaty of Versailles that ended World War I. The appearance of the article and the invitation to President Rees to write it offers some

Fig. 1. The districts of the East German Mission when World War II began.

evidence that the Church was not totally at odds with the Third Reich at that time.

However, the growing tension in European politics in the late 1930s began to be felt throughout the mission. The German government had instituted universal military conscription in 1935 and more and more male members of the Church were seen in uniform. The German army marched into the demilitarized Rhineland in 1936 and was involved soon thereafter in the Spanish Civil War. In March 1938, Germany annexed Austria. On September 14 of that year, rumblings of war caused concern among Church leaders in Salt Lake City, and they ordered an evacuation

of the American missionaries from the two German missions. Those in the East German Mission headed quickly to Copenhagen, Denmark. Mission records included this statement: "During the absence of the Elders from their fields of labor, local members were called upon to take over their offices, which they did with integrity and earnestness. The call came, then they answered."[5] When it turned out that the German occupation of the Sudeten territory in Czechoslovakia earlier that month did not lead to armed conflict, the missionaries of the East German Mission left Copenhagen and returned to their assignments by October 6.[6] During the 1930s, the greatest problem caused

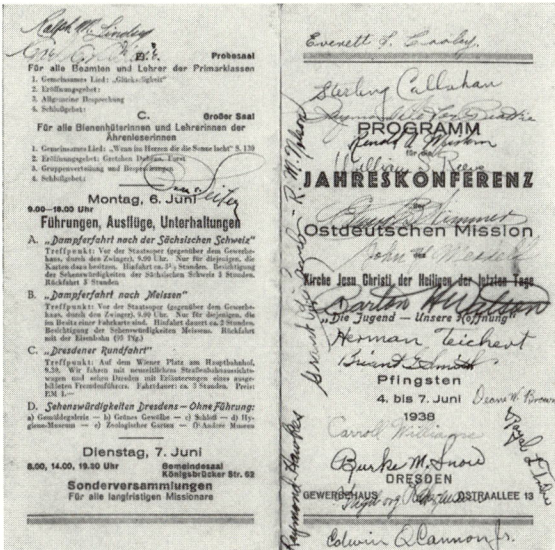

Fig. 2. Program from the 1938 Dresden mission conference. (W. Andersen)

by the German government for the Church was the dissolution of the Boy Scouts. Under the Nazi concept of *Gleichschaltung* (bringing all organizations into line with party goals), Latter-day Saint branches were required to discontinue all Boy Scout troops so that the boys could be inducted into the Hitlerjugend (Hitler Youth). This development was a great disappointment to the young men of the Church.[7]

On Friday, September 30, 1938, a new meeting schedule became effective in the East German Mission. Named the "Weekly Hour Meeting," this plan stipulated that the Relief Society, the MIA, the Genealogy Association,

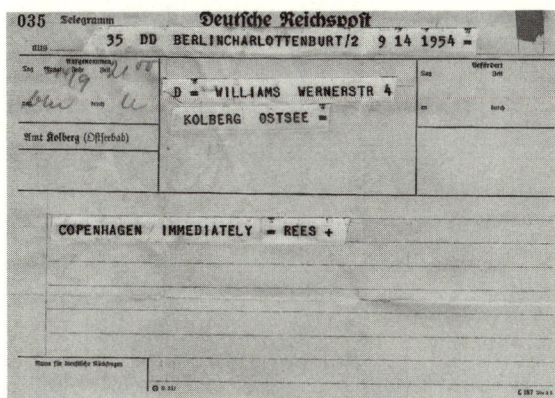

Fig. 3. Elders Williams and Andersen received this telegram in Kolberg on September 14, 1938. (W. Andersen)

the Gleaner and Beehive girls, and the priesthood were to meet once a week simultaneously and at the same place and then repair to their respective classes, where a special committee directed the program.[8] It is not known whether this scheduling change was suggested due to the lack of missionary support in the branches.

East German Mission[9]	1939	1940
Elders	385	419
Priests	191	194
Teachers	237	255
Deacons	429	429
Other Adult Males	1,281	1,228
Adult Females	4,385	4,328
Male Children	372	392
Female Children	347	373
Total	7,627	7,618

With Germany preparing for war in 1938, security was high, and foreigners such as American missionaries were in a position to see things that might be of interest to politicians and military experts in other countries. Adventuresome missionaries at times photographed military scenes, apparently unaware of ways in which their actions could be construed. On May 18, 1939, President Rees issued the following warning:

> We have again received official notice that taking photographs is a dangerous practice on the part of foreigners. We have already been asked to keep our kodaks in our trunks. This is again to advise you that I shall not be responsible for what may follow any breach or disregard of this request. I hope our obedience will be immediate, willing and lasting.[10]

He also instructed his missionaries to avoid all trade in foreign currencies, such as purchasing Polish zloty with German marks.

The growth of the German military in the years before the war required the induction of many members of the Church from all over Germany. It is possible that some members

Fig. 4. The mission leaders and office staff in 1940. From left: missionaries Erika Fassmann, Johanna Berger, and Ilse Reimer. Behind them: first counselor Richard Ranglack, mission supervisor Herbert Klopfer, and second counselor Paul Langheinrich.

were not enthusiastic about the presence of army, navy, and air force uniforms in the meetings, which may have led to this instruction from President Rees on April 8, 1939:

> If the organizations to which our young or older brethren belong do not require that they appear Sundays in uniform, they should be asked to dress in civilian clothes when coming to meeting and participating in ordinances. If, however, they are required to wear [the] uniform, they should not be denied the right or the privilege to participate in any of the activities of the priesthood to which they belong.[11]

In May 1939, the East German Mission held its last missionwide conference before the war. The theme was "The Trumpet Sounds for the Last Time." Such phrases were already common among the members of a church whose

very name suggested that the return of the Savior Jesus Christ was imminent. However, it seemed to Berlin district president Richard Ranglack that hardly any of the members understood the deeper meaning of that motto.[12] Perhaps he believed that some of the calamities prophesied for the latter days were soon to be experienced in Germany.

On July 31, 1939, Alfred C. Rees was officially released as the president of the mission. His successor was Thomas E. McKay, then serving as the president of the Swiss Mission in Basel. President McKay's instructions were to move to Berlin to take charge of the East German Mission, while temporarily remaining the president of the Swiss Mission.[13] With appropriate enthusiasm, Alfred C. Rees informed his missionaries of the change in leadership: "It is a source of deep satisfaction to know that those who stand at the head of the church, and who speak in the name of the Lord, have chosen President Thomas E. McKay to preside over this mission."[14]

The tenure of President McKay in the East German Mission was not a long one because on Friday, August 25, 1939, a telegram arrived from Elder Joseph Fielding Smith, who was touring Germany and was in Frankfurt am Main at the time. All foreign missionaries serving in Germany and Austria were to leave immediately for the Netherlands or Denmark.[15] The next day, Wynn S. Andersen, a missionary from Brigham City, Utah, and a member of the mission office staff, sent a telegram to each pair of missionaries with the appropriate instructions.[16]

"I was in the mission office when the evacuation message came in," recalled Richard Ranglack. American missionaries were released as branch leaders and worthy German brethren were set apart. "I will never forget those days." His story continued:

Thomas E. McKay was so worried about the Church in Germany. [He] transferred the responsibility for the East German Mission to Elder Herbert Klopfer, then the [Church's] interpreter and translator, with Elder Richard Ranglack as first counselor and Elder Paul Langheinrich as second counselor.[17]

After all of the missionaries were evacuated, President McKay returned to Basel.[18] Before leaving the Berlin office, he designated Herbert Klopfer as the mission supervisor. Brother Klopfer's title and duties were described in detail in a letter he received from President McKay on February 13, 1940. The central message was as follows: "All communications to the Presiding brethren and saints in the mission should go out over your name as mission supervisor." (The German term was *Missionsleiter*.) He was to be paid a full-time salary, select two assistants, advise President McKay of major decisions, maintain contact with the leaders of the West German and Swiss Missions, and send a weekly letter to President McKay.[19]

To underscore Brother Klopfer's appointment as the mission supervisor, President McKay appended a letter to be sent to the Saints in the mission: "To notify them of your call, your responsibility, and your authority. They will then know that you are acting in complete co-ordination with the authorities here and that what you do and say is official."

Born in Werdau, Saxony, in 1911, Elder Klopfer had served a full-time mission in eastern Germany and was barely twenty-eight years old when called to lead the mission. A faithful servant of the Lord, he had served as a full-time employee of the Church in foreign language correspondence and translation since 1933. In this capacity, he moved to Berlin from his hometown. He had excellent English skills (a result of living and working with American missionaries) and had interpreted for visiting General Authorities of the Church. This he did so well that people would ask him how long he had been in Germany; they thought he was an American who spoke better English than German.[20]

As mentioned, Richard Ranglack and Paul Langheinrich were chosen as his counselors. Both were experienced Church leaders and both proved equally dedicated in their service during and after the war.

The mission home on Händelallee 6 was a stately structure of three stories, sandwiched between similar structures. Much of its space was rented out by the Church.[21] Brother Klopfer moved into the home in September 1939 and lived on the main floor with his wife, Erna, and two sons, Wolfgang (Herbert) and Rüdiger.[22] The mission office had space on the same floor. The sister missionaries (all native Germans) lived on the top floor and male missionaries were housed in the basement. Other (non-LDS) families lived in other apartments. According to young Wolfgang Herbert Klopfer: "From the living room there was a balcony that looked out to the front of the house, right into the Tiergarten. My friend and I used to jump off of it with umbrellas as mock parachutes. It was fun, but my friend broke his legs doing that."

One of the last men serving full time in the East German Mission when the war began on September 1, 1939, was Richard Deus of Breslau (now Wrocław, Poland). Called as a traveling elder in March of that year, the husband and father of three was released in the spring of 1941 when he was drafted into the German army. Erika Fassmann of Zwickau was called as a missionary in 1940 and was one of five young women who served for at least two years during the war. The others were Edith Birth, Irmgard Gottschalk, Johanna Berger, and Ilse Reimer.

As Sister Fassmann recalled, "We did everything for the mission, because the brethren were all gone. We traveled to the district conferences and taught the sisters of the Relief Society, young women, and Primary. We were not allowed to tract, so we always worked in the office when we were in Berlin."[23] Sister Fassmann remembered traveling as far as Königsberg, Danzig, Breslau, and Dresden to attend and speak at district conferences. Despite the confusion of wartime railroad schedules and trains that often seemed to have room for troops only, she was somehow always able to secure railway tickets.

One of the last things Thomas E. McKay did as the president of the East German Mission was to extend a mission call. On January 1, 1940, he sent a letter to Ilse Reimer of the Kolberg Branch (Stettin District), asking her to come to Berlin in March. She accepted the call to work in the mission office at Händelallee, where she was to live with other sister missionaries.[24] By the time Sister Reimer arrived in Berlin, President McKay had returned to Basel, Switzerland.

Edith Gerda Birth recalled the following about her service in the mission office:

> The greatest need was for lesson material for all the organizations. In my diary I wrote about the many manuals we had to type and to print, the manuals for the Sunday School and Primary, genealogy, gospel doctrine class, the monthly *Sonntagsgruss*, etc. We had a little printing press in one room of the office, which was always in use. . . . All these printings we had to pack and take to the post office in a little hand wagon.[25]

Under Brother Klopfer's capable leadership, meetings continued with district presidents and priesthood groups, and district conferences were held for the general membership. Fulfilling his calling became a personal challenge for

- 1941 -

Fig. 5. Leaders of the East German Mission met in the office at Händelallee 6 in 1941 with the district presidents and the sister missionaries. Mission supervisor Herbert Klopfer and four of the thirteen district presidents lost their lives in the war.

28

Brother Klopfer when he was drafted into the army in 1940. Fortunately, he was stationed in Fürstenwalde (about forty miles east of Berlin) for the next three years. As a paymaster, he was able to take the train home to see his family on weekends and to travel to Church conferences in other cities. His counselors also visited him several times in Fürstenwalde to transact mission business and receive instructions.[26] Elder Klopfer wrote articles for Church publications and received visits from his wife and sons while in Fürstenwalde. On several occasions Sister Klopfer in the mission office transferred messages from her husband to Thomas E. McKay in Salt Lake City.

After the Japanese attack on Pearl Harbor on December 7, 1941, mutual declarations of war were issued by several nations. Because Japan and Germany had commenced a military alliance when the former declared war on the United States, Germany was required to follow suit. When that occurred, all communications between the Church leadership in Salt Lake City and the East German Mission leaders in Berlin were discontinued. The Saints in Germany were on their own.[27] During the absence of Brother Klopfer, counselors Richard Ranglack and Paul Langheinrich redoubled their efforts to maintain contact with district and branch leaders. Brother Klopfer was sometimes able to use an office telephone from his post in nearby Fürstenwalde, but otherwise wrote weekly letters to his counselors with advice and instructions.[28] Periodic meetings were held in Berlin with the district presidents, who traveled by rail from as far away as two hundred miles.

The German invasion of Poland on September 1, 1939, initiated a war that eventually meant the deaths of tens of millions of people. Latter-day Saints in Germany were not spared. The first known death was that of Willy Klappert of the Frankfurt am Main Branch in the West German Mission, who

Fig. 6. Hard at work in the mission office (from left): Johanna Berger, Erika Fassmann, and Ilse Reimer. (I. Reimer Ebert)

died on September 2.[29] For many years, issues of the Church publications in Germany had listed notices of members who died—civilians and soldiers alike. *Der Stern* (established in 1869) served both German missions, but its publication was interrupted in 1942. Thereafter, the mission office in Berlin issued first the *Sonntagsgruss* (*Sunday Greetings*), then the *Sonntagsblatt* (*Sunday News*). Over time, the quality of the publications suffered due to wartime shortages: only coarse paper was available, and photographs could not be included.

In the absence of Herbert Klopfer, Brother Ranglack represented the Church on several occasions in investigations conducted in the office of the Gestapo (the secret state police) in Berlin:

> Heavenly Father put the words in my mouth so that I was able to answer questions concerning our church. I was especially asked about our tenth article of faith, our position towards the *N.S.D.A.P.* [Nazi Party], membership in the party, Hitler youth, bearers of the knight's cross, [and] more. The singing of songs that contained the word "Zion" was prohibited. I was also asked concerning our meeting halls, conference mottos, the gathering of Israel, the American Church, our views about the war. I had [the] responsibility [to see] that all the sermons given were of [a] purely religious nature.[30]

In early 1941, the *Sonntagsblatt* featured the membership populations for the East German

Mission (see introduction). Accompanying comments indicated that 101 children were blessed in 1940, 44 children of record were baptized, 45 adults were baptized, 73 members died, and 121 had married.[31]

"It was our intention to keep the work of the Lord alive in Germany, to strengthen the faith of the members, and to see to it that the brethren remained active," reported Brother Ranglack. "We held district conferences in each district twice a year from 1940 through 1944 . . . and were able to travel all over the mission." He and Paul Langheinrich even traveled once to Czechoslovakia, visiting with the Saints in Prague and Brünn for four days each.[32]

Sister Ilse Reimer provided the following description of a day in the life of the sister missionaries in the mission home during this time:

Erika [Fassmann] and I usually got up at 6:00 A.M. and enjoyed the fresh morning air of the Tiergarten. When Erika slept in a bit, I practiced handstands in another room. I was

Fig. 7. Missionaries Johanna Berger (left) and Ilse Reimer in the garden on the rooftop of the mission home. (I. Reimer Ebert)

pretty good at that, even though I had not been on the school gymnastics team. Then we had a simple breakfast. From seven to eight we were to study the standard works of the Church. We worked in the mission office from 8:00 A.M. until 6:00 P.M., with a one-hour break for lunch. . . . Every missionary had her specific duties. Sometimes several of us worked on the same project. My assignment was to analyze the monthly statistical reports submitted by the district presidents.[33]

"There were highlights for us missionaries when we visited with the brethren at the district conferences, which were still held," wrote Edith Birth. "All the members looked forward to the district conferences. These conferences strengthened our testimony and kept us together and gave us support to stand up for the teachings of Jesus Christ."[34]

Ilse Reimer also enjoyed the district conferences, but speaking to large audiences was not one of her favorite assignments. Her talks were to be twenty minutes in length. The only way she felt confident in giving such long talks was to memorize each one in its entirety.[35]

A mission conference was held in Berlin on Sunday, June 1, 1941. That evening, Karl Göckeritz, president of the Chemnitz District, noted in his diary that the conference was held in the *Lehrervereinshaus* (teachers' union hall) in downtown Berlin and that 1,400 members and friends were in attendance.[36] Representatives of the West German Mission also came from Frankfurt am Main to participate in the conference. Christian Heck was the first counselor to West German mission supervisor Friedrich Biehl and Anton Huck was the second counselor. Elder Biehl was on active duty in the army at that time.[37]

In February 1943, Herbert Klopfer wrote a letter to his brethren in the mission leadership detailing their responsibilities in his absence. The letter was written from the mission office and began thus: "During the period of my prolonged absence and due to the hindrances caused thereby for the leadership of the mission, I would ask that my elders called to serve as mission leaders observe the following directives." He then provided instructions in twelve specific topics, such as historical reports, communications with district and branch leaders, publications, finances, and relations with the West German Mission. It is not impossible that Elder Klopfer had a premonition that he would soon no longer be able to carry out his duties as mission supervisor.[38]

On February 25, 1943, Richard Ranglack of the mission leadership issued instructions to all units that no copies of the *Sonntagsgruss* should be sent to military personnel. It read in part, "Due to increased restrictions in the use of paper and by order of the Army High Command, we have received the message that no religious literature may be sent to soldiers in the field."[39] Brother Ranglack requested that branch leaders and families alike give strict heed to this order. Despite the restrictions on printing, mission leaders were successful in finding private printing companies to produce German-language hymnbooks, portions of *Jesus the Christ,* and several copies of the Pearl of Great Price, as well as small tracts.[40]

After twenty-five months of service, Sister Ilse Reimer was released from her mission in April 1942. She later wrote, "I would very much have liked to stay longer on my mission. . . . It was one of the most beautiful times of my life."[41] Engaged to marry Fritz Ebert, an elder in the Stettin Branch, she compiled her final reports then boarded the train for the trip home to Kolberg (Stettin District).

As Germany's capital city came under increased attack from the enemy (the U.S. Army Air Corps by day and the Royal Air Force by night), Brother Klopfer moved his family to his hometown of Werdau in early 1943, where they lived with both sets of grandparents.

That fall, the East German Mission home at Händelallee fell victim to the attacks. On the evening of November 21, 1943, Erika Fassmann was the only missionary in the building. She remembered:

> On this evening I was totally alone in the office. I again disregarded the alarm (we missionaries usually did that because we believed the Lord would save us—the brethren scolded us more

Fig. 8. Missionary Johanna Berger in front of the mission home (I. Reimer Ebert). All of the buildings behind her were destroyed in the war, as can be seen in the 2007 photograph below (fig. 9). (J. Larsen)

31

than once for doing so). Then I heard the bombers coming and they apparently were heading right for [the neighborhood of] Händelallee. Suddenly the huge wood [front] doors were blown into the building. I hid in the kitchen and prayed for protection. Then I wondered where I could seek refuge. In the office we had a huge table on which genealogical papers—family group records—were stacked in tall piles. I told myself: "If the Lord protects anything at all, it will be these papers." So, I dove underneath the table. Then when the bombs stopped, I grabbed all of the papers and ran out of the building. All of the buildings around me were on fire. The moon was red and the sky on fire and I thought it was the end of the world.

Sister Fassmann recalled feeling relieved that the mission home had escaped destruction. However, the next morning, Richard Ranglack and Paul Langheinrich insisted that they evacuate the building. They spent all day moving mission property to the Langheinrich home at Rathenowerstrasse 52, about one mile to the north. By evening, only the personal possessions of the sister missionaries and some of the property left behind by the Klopfers were still in the building. The inspiration received by the brethren was right; the bombers returned that evening, and the mission home was completely destroyed.

Young Wolfgang (Herbert) Klopfer recalled that his father was on furlough at the time. He

Fig. 10. The ruins of the mission home (circled at upper left) at Händelallee 6 as shown in an Allied reconnaissance photograph of March 1945. To the right is one of Berlin's most famous landmarks —the Victory Tower, in Tiergarten Park.

had picked up his wife in Werdau and from there traveled to the mission home late on November 21. However, they had forgotten the key to the mission office and went on to the home of Brother Ranglack to spend the night. Had they remembered the key, they may have sought shelter in the basement of the building when the bombs fell the second time. Sister Klopfer told her son that she and her husband later visited the site and only the walls were standing. In the ruins they found the office safe with the tithing funds; the coins had melted from the heat of the fire and flowed out of the safe to form a small pool of metal. The only item recovered from the ruins was a small teapot with its lid. Just after the Klopfers left the ruins, several delayed-action bombs exploded and leveled the surviving wall remnants. Again they narrowly missed being killed.

The discouraging scene on November 22, 1943, was later described by Richard Ranglack: "The next morning we stood before the burned-out building. The feelings that came over us naturally gave way to tears. Now we had to start over. Our energy and courage would come from a higher source."[42]

From November 1943 until after the war, the mission office was housed in the apartment of the building in which the Langheinrich family lived. One by one, more apartments in the five-story building were vacated and Brother Langheinrich was quick to appropriate them for the missionaries and an increasing number of LDS refugees. They arrived from points as close as neighborhoods in Berlin and as far away as Königsberg, East Prussia. At the conclusion of the war, there were at least thirty members of the Church living in the building.[43]

Junior officer (Sergeant) Herbert Klopfer, the supervisor of the East German Mission, visited his family for the last time while on furlough in November 1943. Soon after, he was transferred to Denmark where he had

a remarkable experience on the Sunday be-
fore Christmas. A young girl in the Esbjerg
Branch later wrote the following account to
Sister Klopfer:

> Last night I visited the branch. There was
> a German. And even though we hated all
> Germans, we learned to love this man. He
> spoke to the congregation in English, because
> we could not stand to listen to German, and
> William Orum Petersen from Copenhagen,
> who was present, translated. Your husband re-
> lated how only a month ago he lost everything
> he had, and the mission home had been de-
> stroyed, but that he was thankful that his wife
> and children were in safety. He then gave tes-
> timony of the truthfulness of the Church. It
> was wonderful to see a man in the uniform we
> hated, who spoke with so much love for us. He
> was happy to be among the Saints.[44]

The mission supervisor next served in
France as a paymaster then was transferred to
the Eastern Front. By then (the summer of
1944), the German army was retreating from
the Soviet Union and was just a few miles from
the fatherland. In early October, a letter arrived in the home of Erna Klopfer in Werdau
informing her that her husband was missing in
action. Part of the letter written by the company commander reads as follows:

> It is my difficult responsibility to inform you that
> your husband, Junior Officer Herbert Klopfer,
> has been missing in action since July 22, 1944.
> . . . The division was surrounded on July 17.
> . . . A rescue mission was executed but was suc-
> cessful for only a few of the surrounded units.
> . . . I know how terrible it must be for you to
> not know the precise fate of your husband and
> I regret not being able to provide more details.
> Although we must consider the possibility that
> your husband was killed during the attempt to
> escape the encirclement, we can still hope that
> he will return home when the war is over.[45]

In Brother Klopfer's absence, Max Jeske was
called to serve as a counselor to Richard Ranglack,
now the de facto mission supervisor. Eventually,
it was learned that Brother Klopfer had perished

in a squalid hospital near Kiev, Ukraine. His son,
Herbert, explained how they learned what actually became of the mission supervisor:

> Another soldier in his company made a con-
> scious decision on the nineteenth of March,
> 1945, when he saw my father die; he made a
> note of the date and made a decision that if he
> were to make it out alive he would look up my
> mother and tell her that he was an eyewitness to
> my father's passing. He didn't know whether he
> was going to make it out, but in 1948, which
> is three years after the war ended, he was al-
> lowed to walk out of Ukraine to go home to
> his wife and on his way home he looked us up
> in Werdau and gave my mother the news that
> he was an eyewitness. That's the first informa-
> tion we had received in five years as to what ever
> happened to our father.

Without the report of this dedicated comrade, the death of Herbert Klopfer may have
never been confirmed.

Brother Ranglack narrowly missed being drafted into the Berlin police force on
February 3, 1945—one of the most difficult
days of his life. Concerned about his Church
responsibilities, he feigned an illness, and the
military physician classified him as unfit for
duty. That same day, his family's apartment
and the hotel where he worked were both destroyed in an air raid. Fortunately, he and his
family were able to move into an apartment in
the building where Paul Langheinrich lived.[46]

In March 1945, Paul Langheinrich allowed
Erika Fassmann Müller to go home to her
parents in Zwickau. (She had married Rudi
Müller of Danzig five months earlier.) She
had requested permission to participate in the
celebration of her parents' twenty-fifth wedding anniversary, but was not yet released as a
missionary.

On April 21, 1945, the invading Russian
army began to work its way through the streets
of Berlin in an agonizing battle that eventually cost the lives of nearly 350,000 civilians

and soldiers (German and Soviet).[47] As the enemy approached his neighborhood, Paul Langheinrich was already hosting about thirty members of the Church in his apartment house. In her diary, missionary Helga Meiszus Birth of the Tilsit Branch in East Prussia recorded the arrival of mothers and children from January through April. In summary, she made this pronouncement: "Rathenowerstrasse 52 has become the place of refuge for the Saints."[48]

Despite the challenge of feeding and protecting the refugees, Paul Langheinrich devoted some time to the entertainment of the children. On April 25, 1945 (the day the Soviets completed their encirclement of Berlin), he used the mission mimeograph machine to reproduce under the title *Kinderpost* some fanciful poetry and art for the children of the Lehnardt, Schneider, and Winkler families living in the same building. One of his poems read,

> Listen up! You children, when your parents complain in this very worrisome time, help them through your obedience to bear it well and always be ready to help. A child can bring sunshine into the home, sunshine for his parents, and the neighbors, young and old, will be gladdened as well.[49]

Brother Langheinrich concluded this edition of the *Kinderpost* with a reminder that the children should pray for their country, for the soldiers, and for all of the refugees who were suffering.

The invaders reached the Langheinrich's neighborhood on April 28, three days before the city surrendered and ten days before the war officially ended.[50] As the sound of enemy artillery fire became audible, Brother Langheinrich probably wondered how he could protect the members of his household—mostly women and children. The day before, about three miles to the south, Ingrid Bendler and her mother, members of the Schöneberg Branch in central Berlin, had discovered an abandoned

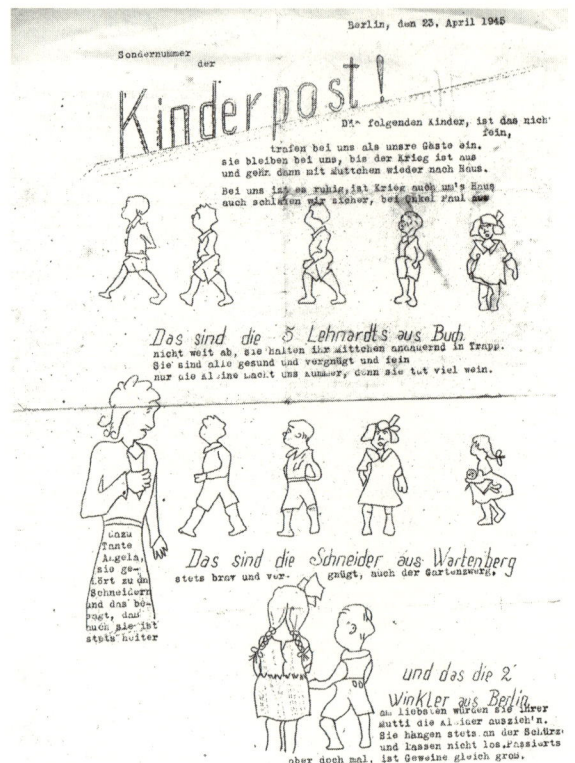

Fig. 11. Paul Langheinrich was the editor of the Kinderpost. (R. Winkler Heidler)

government warehouse full of food. The building had just been opened to the public and they joined other desperate civilians in taking whatever food they could carry. Ingrid felt the urge to deliver food to the Langheinrich home, despite her mother's protests:

> My bike was really loaded and it was hard to keep the balance. Never before had I gone through Berlin in this direction. Shooting was very heavy and I had no idea where the front lines were. I remember turning into a burning street. People would come out of there and ask where it was not burning; they were confused. Listening to that still small voice that I had heard before, I would go right into those burning streets, make a [correct] turn and was safe. I remember turning at the most unusual places and finding my way over broken bridges. To my great surprise I found the mission [Langheinrich] home real easy. . . . Had there not been a living testimony based on previous experiences and the knowledge that there is a God who guides and directs us and answers prayers—food would never have reached twenty-four hungry people [in the Langheinrich home] under enemy fire.[51]

34

Fig. 12. Roger P. Minert at the door to the apartment building that housed the Langheinrich family, the mission office, and many LDS refugees at the end of World War II. (J. Larsen 2007)

The final defensive bastion in Berlin was the eight-story antiaircraft Tower G that stood just north of the city's famous zoo, barely one thousand yards from Händelallee 6. When Tower G surrendered, the battle for the Reich capital was over.[52]

With the city's surrender, Berlin became a madhouse of unbridled terror, with Soviet troops committing unspeakable atrocities against the citizenry. No female was safe, and the Langheinrich home was just another target. On May 4, 1945, Brother Langheinrich relied on a political ruse and posted a sign by the door saying "American Church Office." The ruse was successful in turning away marauding soldiers who respected the name of their ally in the war against fascism. On at least one occasion, he stared down a Russian soldier who apparently wished to enter the building with evil intentions. Nobody living in the Langheinrich apartment house was molested.[53]

From the mission office, principally one room on the floor where the Langheinrich family lived, Brothers Ranglack and Langheinrich administered the affairs of the mission. They were assisted by missionary Helga Meiszus Birth and several young women refugees, such as Renate Berger of Königsberg and Angela Patermann of the Berlin East Branch. The young women spent many hours proofreading genealogical documents that were to be forwarded to Salt Lake City. Eventually, they began recording the whereabouts of Saints who were bombed out of or evicted from their homes.

When it was too dangerous to walk to their place of meeting (the Moabit Branch rooms had survived), the residents of the Langheinrichs' apartment house at Rathenowerstrasse 52 held Church meetings at home. Helga Meiszus Birth's very detailed diary includes the names of persons who gave talks, taught lessons, and offered prayers. A general prayer circle was conducted each morning at 8:00 and each evening at 8:00.

On May 11, 1945—three days after Germany surrendered—the mission records indicate that Sister Angela Patermann of the Berlin East Branch was called as a missionary and assigned to work in the mission office.[54] The leadership of the East German Mission clearly did not miss a beat as they contemplated how best to continue the work of the Lord amid the desolation and confusion of conquered and occupied Germany. "We had three goals," recalled Richard Ranglack, "to find the members who had been driven from their homes, . . . to call full-time missionaries, . . . and to find a larger facility for the mission home."[55] By the end of the year 1945, all three goals had been totally or substantially achieved. Mission leaders calculated that at least four hundred members of the Church in the East German Mission had perished and hundreds more were missing.[56]

During the summer of 1945, the office of the East German Mission was established anew in a fine building in the southwest Berlin suburb of Dahlem.

Fig. 13. On several occasions, Soviet soldiers stormed up this staircase of the Langheinrichs' apartment house at Rathenowerstrasse 52 in search of victims and booty. (A. Laemmlen Lewis, 2009)

NOTES

1. Presiding Bishopric, "Financial, Statistical, and Historical Reports of Wards, Stakes, and Missions, 1884–1955," CR 4 12, 257; The Church of Jesus Christ of Latter-day Saints, *Der Stern,* final no. for 1939–1941.

2. The Church owned only one building in the mission—the modest chapel built for the branch in Selbongen, East Prussia, in 1929. The building still stands but ceased to serve the Church when the last members quit the town in 1974.

3. East German Mission Quarterly Reports, 1938, nos. 26–27, East German Mission History.

4. A copy of the newspaper, dated April 14, 1939, is in the possession of Clark Hillam, a veteran of the West German Mission.

The most prominent feature of the article is a large photograph of the Salt Lake LDS Temple.

5. East German Mission Quarterly Reports, 1938, no. 40.

6. Ibid.; Wynn S. Andersen, interview by the author, Brigham City, Utah, October 19, 2006.

7. During the years 1925 to 1934, the Church's *Der Stern* magazine often featured photographs of branch Boy Scout troops. The importance of the program to the Church in Germany, Austria, and Switzerland was apparent.

8. East German Mission Quarterly Reports, 1938, no. 40.

9. Presiding Bishopric, "Financial," 1938; *Sonntagsblatt* (unpublished), no. 4, January 26, 1941; private collection.

10. Alfred C. Rees to missionaries of East German Mission, May 18, 1939, no. 7; trans. the author; Germany Berlin Mission, "Manuscript History and Historical Reports," LR 2428 2. See the history of the Kreuz Branch, Schneidemühl District, for the story of a specific event that may have precipitated this warning. See also Terry Montague's *Mine Angels Round About: Mormon Missionary Evacuation from West Germany 1939* for a similar problem that occurred in Saarbrücken ([n.p.: Roylance, 1989], 6).

11. Alfred C. Rees to missionaries of East German Mission, April 8, 1939, no. 5; trans. the author.; Germany Berlin Mission, "Manuscript History and Historical Reports," LR 2428 2.

12. Richard Ranglack, autobiography (unpublished), 1; private collection. He does not claim to have understood it himself.

13. Thomas E. McKay to missionaries of East German Mission, August 17, 1939, no. 12; trans. the author; Germany Berlin Mission, "Manuscript History and Historical Reports," LR 2428 2.

14. Ibid. August 15, 1939, no. 11.

15. Montague, *Mine Angels Round About,* 25–26. Church leadership in Salt Lake City called Hugh B. Brown in London and requested that he call the West German Mission office in Frankfurt. Mission secretary Elder John R. Barnes contacted President Wood and Elder Smith in Hanover with the news. They flew to Frankfurt immediately and instructed the mission staff to contact all missionaries with the evacuation order on August 25. Apparently, Elder Smith contacted President McKay with the same message at the same time.

16. Because he sent the message, Andersen does not have a copy of the telegram. However, he has a copy of a similar message sent in September 1938, when the missionaries were evacuated the first time. They returned to Germany from Denmark in October 1938.

17. Ranglack, autobiography.

18. Thomas E. McKay left Berlin in December 1939 and returned to Switzerland. From there he left for the United States in April 1940 (Wolfgang [Herbert] Klopfer, memoirs [unpublished]; private collection; Douglas F. Tobler, interview by the author, Lindon, Utah, November 5, 2007).

19. Thomas E. McKay to Herbert Klopfer, February 13, 1940; East German Mission History, CR 27, 140, Church History Library.

20. Herbert (Wolfgang) Klopfer, interview by the author, Salt Lake City, November 3, 2006.

21. See map of downtown Berlin.

22. Wolfgang officially changed his first name to Herbert after immigrating to the United States.

23. Erika Fassmann Mueller, interview by the author, Salt Lake City, February 3, 2006.

24. Ilse Reimer Ebert, autobiography (unpublished), 16–17; private collection; trans. the author.

25. Edith Gerda Birth Rohloff, "Life Is a Gift from God" (unpublished history, about 2003), 20; private collection.

26. Ranglack, autobiography, 2.

27. The same was true with the office of the West German Mission in Frankfurt am Main.

28. As reported by his son, Wolfgang (Herbert) Klopfer, memoirs.

29. Frankfurt-Main Branch, member records, FHL microfilm no. 68791, no. 298 (book I), Family History Library.

30. Richard Ranglack, "Bericht" (unpublished history); private collection.

31. *Sonntagsblatt*, no. 4, January 26, 1941; private collection.

32. Ranglack, autobiography, 2. The office of the Czechoslovakian Mission was also closed prior to the war and the few Saints there had no leadership at all. The city of Brünn is now call Brno.

33. Ebert, autobiography, 17.

34. Edith Gerda Birth Rohloff, autobiography (unpublished), 21; private collection.

35. Ebert, autobiography, 18.

36. Karl Göckeritz, diary, 1909–43; private collection; trans. the author.

37. Mission supervisor Friedrich Biehl was killed in the Soviet Union in March 1943 and his successor, Christian Heck, was killed in South Germany in April 1945. Anton Huck was the supervisor of the West German Mission at the end of the war.

38. Herbert Klopfer to mission leaders (Richard Ranglack, Paul Langheinrich, Friedrich Fischer), February 20, 1943, East German Mission History. He signed the letter as the Missionsleiter.

39. Eberhard Werner of Leipzig has an original copy of this message.

40. Ranglack, autobiography, 2.

41. Ebert, autobiography, 19.

42. Ranglack, autobiography, 2.

43. Wolfgang Kelm, interview by the author, Hurricane, Utah, October 9, 2006.

44. As cited by Herbert Klopfer, memoirs. He indicated that his father risked being called a traitor for fraternizing with the Danish and even took off his pistol belt while in the Esbjerg Branch meetings.

45. Unnamed company commander to Erna Klopfer, September 27, 1944, East German Mission History; trans. the author.

46. Ranglack, autobiography, 2.

47. Cornelius Ryan, *The Last Battle: The Classic History of the Battle of Berlin* (New York: Simon & Schuster, 1995), 520.

48. Helga Meiszus Birth, diary (unpublished), April 21, 1945, 3; private collection; trans. the author.

49. *Kinderpost*, mimeographed sheet (unpublished); private collection.

50. Ingrid Bendler, memoirs (unpublished); private collection.

51. Ryan, *The Last Battle*, 514.

52. Birth, diary, 8.

53. Armin Langheinrich, interview by the author, Salt Lake City, December 15, 2006.

54. East German Mission Quarterly Reports, 1945, no. 104.

55. Ranglack, autobiography. Ranglack continued: "When I look back on those years, . . . I have to say that I could never have found the energy to do those things without the help of my brethren, without the help of the Lord, or without praying to the Lord." Richard Ranglack was officially called as the president of the East German Mission by Ezra Taft Benson on March 20, 1946, and released by George Albert Smith on June 16, 1947 (via letters issued from the Church offices in London and Salt Lake City, respectively).

56. According to research supporting this book, the total number of members of the Church in the East German Mission who died as a result of World War II was 605 (see conclusion).

Hoffnung Israels
(D 82)

J. L. Townshend

Wm. Clayson

1. Hoff-nung Is-raels, Zi-ons Hee-re, Kin-der vom ver-
2. Seht des Satans fin-stre Hee-re, zahl-los wie der
3. Kämp-fe treu-lich nur für Zi-on, zück' das Schwert wohl
4. Bald ist dann die Schlacht zu En-de, macht-los je-der

heiß'-nen Reich, seht, der Hauptmann gibt das Zei-chen; vor-wärts
Sand am Meer! Hoff-nung Is-raels, vor-wärts, kämp-fe; nie-mand
ob dem Feind! Je-der Streich ent-waff-net Geg-ner, je-der
Sün-de Sohn. Vor-wärts, vor-wärts, tapf-re Ju-gend, denn dir

Chor

jetzt zur Front sogleich!
raubt den Sieg dir mehr!
Schritt uns mehr ver-eint.
winkt des Siegers Kron'!

Hoffnung Israels, ste-he auf; treib' den Feind mit

Macht zuhauf! Wachet, be-tet, kämpft vereint, weichen muß euch jeder Feind!

Gesangbuch

15

All over Germany, the Saints were asked to avoid singing hymns featuring such words as "Israel" and "Zion." This page from the hymnal of Evelyn Horn Preuss shows the hymn "Hope of Israel" with the number crossed out. (E. Horn Pruess)

BERLIN
DISTRICT
East German Mission

The capital of Hitler's Germany was a metropolis of 4,321,000 people in 1939.[1] Indeed, Berlin was home to more members of the LDS Church than any other city in the Reich. There were six branches in the city, and four more outside of town completed the Berlin District of the East German Mission.

In the heart of the historic province of Brandenburg, the Berlin District stretched north to the border of Mecklenburg, northeast to Pomerania, southwest to Potsdam, and due west to Rathenow. From the center of the district, it took about ninety minutes to reach Eberswalde and Rathenow by train. There was also a group of Saints meeting in Leest, just six miles west of Potsdam.

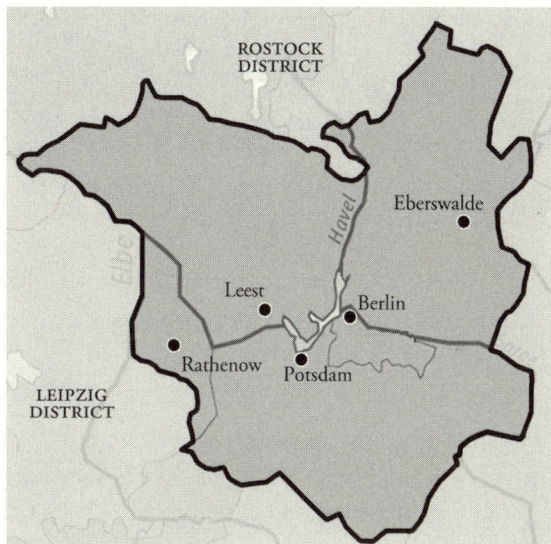

Fig. 1. *The Berlin District included ten units of the Church in and around the capital city.*

Berlin District[2]	1939	1940	1941	1942
Elders	73	75		
Priests	30	31		
Teachers	38	41		
Deacons	61	56		
Other Adult Males	193	192		
Adult Females	776	775		
Male Children	62	62		
Female Children	36	42		
Total	1,269	1,274	1,186	1,291

The 1,270 members in the district constituted 17 percent of the entire mission population. Just prior to World War II, Richard Ranglack of the Berlin Moabit Branch was serving as district president. When he was called as first counselor to mission supervisor Herbert Klopfer after the evacuation of the American missionaries, he was replaced by Friedrich (Fritz) Fischer of the Berlin Center Branch.[3] "My father was very busy as the district president and had lots of Church work to do. . . . He traveled all over the mission on the train. The Church paid his tickets," recalled his son Helmut.[4]

Fig. 2. A district priesthood meeting held in 1941 in the Berlin Center Branch rooms in the Hufelandstrasse.

Fritz Fischer was a remarkable missionary. In 1918, he had become acquainted with The Church of Jesus Christ of Latter-day Saints while living in Berlin. He took the message of the restored gospel back to his home town of Selbongen, East Prussia, where he was instrumental in bringing dozens of relatives and friends into the Church and establishing a new branch there.[5]

A district conference was held in Berlin every spring and fall through the end of 1944, according to Richard Ranglack.[6] Several members recall attending district conferences in the Lehrervereinshalle (teachers' union hall) in downtown Berlin.[7] From mission notes it is clear that all Church programs were being carried out in the district, including genealogical research and recreational activities.

As is told in the individual histories of the branches in the Berlin District, several meeting rooms were destroyed by 1945, and branch leaders were compelled to seek out new and temporary meeting places. Most of the unmarried men and young fathers in the district were drafted into the military, and many of the mothers left the city with their children to find less dangerous places to live. Entire LDS families moved away after losing their homes or when offices and factories were moved to rural locations and employees were required to move with them.

By 1944, Berlin was under constant attack from the air—by the British by night and the Americans by day. By the time the city was conquered in May 1945, approximately 150,000 Berlin civilians had lost their lives, and more than one million had left the city.[8] At least half of the members of the LDS branches in Berlin were still there to witness the hopeless battle fought by the harried German defenders against the invading Red Army. When the dust settled, more than one-third of the dwellings of Berlin were no longer inhabitable.[9]

Fig. 3. Major Church locations in Berlin in 1939: 1 = mission office; 2 = Langheinrich home; 3 = Moabit Branch; 4 = Center Branch; 5 = East Branch; 6 = Neukölln Branch; 7 = Schöneberg Branch.

The Air War over Berlin, 1939–45	
Air-raid warnings	389
Air raids	approx. 300
Residential units destroyed	36%
Total structures destroyed	21% (West Berlin), 15% (East Berlin)
Rubble from destroyed structures	Estimated 98 million cubic yards (75 million cubic meters)
Public air-raid shelter space available	approx. 25%
"Battle of Berlin" (from the air) lasted from 21 November 1944 to 25 March 1945 (British Royal Air Force and American Army Air Corps)	33 air raids 9,100 airplanes in action 500 airplanes shot down 4,000 civilian deaths 340,000 homes destroyed 400,000 people homeless

Civilians killed 1939–1945	52,000
Civilians killed spring 1945	Estimated 100,000
German soldiers killed spring 1945	Estimated 50,000–75,000
Russian soldiers killed spring 1945	Estimated 100,000
Women raped spring 1945	20,000 to 100,000

The battle for Berlin ended at the Zoo Flak Towers (Schöneberg Branch territory), while the formal surrender of Berlin took place in an apartment in Karlshorst (Neukölln Branch territory), where field marshal Wilhelm Keitel signed for the German Army High Command. Despite the sufferings and destruction of the war, five LDS branches in the city were alive and functioning at the end of the war. The four branches outside of the city were substantially weakened but were all holding meetings again by the end of the summer of 1945.

Notes

1. Cornelius Ryan, *The Last Battle: The Classic History of the Battle of Berlin* (New York: Simon & Schuster, 1994), 26.

2. Presiding Bishopric, "Financial, Statistical, and Historical Reports of Wards, Stakes, and Missions, 1884–1955," CR 4 12, 257.

3. Fritz Fischer was known as *Käsefischer* (the Fischer who deals in cheese), while a man named Karl Fischer in the Berlin East Branch was known as *Mistfischer* (the Fischer who deals in manure). Both terms were used affectionately among the members.

4. Helmut Fischer, interview by the author in German, Leipzig, Germany, June 2, 2007; summarized in English by the author.

5. Karl A. Keller, "Enthusiasm Is His Motto," *Instructor*, April 1956, 100–101. See also the chapter on the Selbongen Branch in this history.

6. Richard Ranglack, autobiography (unpublished); private collection.

7. Horst Schwermer, interview by the author, Salt Lake City, December 8, 2006.

8. Ryan, *Last Battle*, 520.

9. Felix Escher, *Luftbildplan Berlin, 1945* (Berlin: Bien & Giersch Projektagentur GmbH, 2004), 6–7.

Fig. 4. Fritz Fischer was the president of the Berlin District throughout World War II. (Instructor)

Berlin Center Branch

The heart of Germany's capital city of Berlin was the district called Mitte (Center). This part of town featured the majority of the city's governmental, historical, and cultural sites. The most famous street, Unter den Linden, ran from Brandenburg Gate east to the Spree River, where the palace of Germany's former emperors stood. All of this territory was included in the Berlin Center Branch of The Church of Jesus Christ of Latter-day Saints, as were the suburbs Prenzlauer Berg, Friedrichshain, and Weissensee.

Berlin Center Branch[1]	1939
Elders	10
Priests	5
Teachers	11
Deacons	12
Other Adult Males	49
Adult Females	154
Male Children	15
Female Children	11
Total	267

The Center Branch met in rooms on Hufelandstrasse, several blocks east of Alexanderplatz. Helmut Fischer recalled the rooms that were in the second Hinterhaus (a row of houses behind buildings lining the street):

> Our church rooms were in a factory building in the Hufelandstrasse 45, second Hinterhaus. We had a sign on the street with the Church's name. You went through two buildings, then upstairs [to the third floor]. There was a long corridor with the restrooms on the right, two classrooms, then a door, then the main meeting room. "The Glory of God Is Intelligence" was embroidered on the pulpit; then [there were] the usual pictures of Jesus.[2]

Helmut estimated the Sunday attendance at perhaps one hundred persons. With priesthood and auxiliary meetings held on various afternoons or evenings in the week, "we were constantly going to church," he recalled.

The Fischer family lived in the Weissensee suburb of Berlin and had to walk about a half hour to church. Helmut's father was Fritz Fischer, the president of the Berlin District throughout the war years. He was known as the Käsefischer (cheese Fischer) because of his employment at a company where cheese and other milk products were manufactured.[3] Brother Fischer used the public transportation

Fig. 1. Elder Cannon and Brother Alden with a picture of Adolf Hitler in 1938. (H. Kupitz)

Fig. 2. Adolf Hitler greets a crowd of well-wishers from the balcony of the Chancellery Building in downtown Berlin. (H. Kupitz)

system nearly every Sunday to visit one of the ten branches in the district.

When Helmut was ten years old, the German army attacked Poland:

> We were on school vacation when the war began, at our grandmother's place in the country. . . . I can remember hearing about it from the radio. It did not affect us that much at the time. . . . My parents talked very little about politics. We were trained to accept that stuff [National Socialism, etc.]. We kept the laws of God, so we had no problems with the laws of the land. . . . I don't remember anybody speaking about Hitler in church or praying for him.

The Fischer family had lived in an apartment house on Gustav-Adolf-Strasse since 1935. In an air raid in 1943, the upper floors of the building were hit, and a fire began. Brother Fischer saw the fire from the roof of the factory where he worked a few blocks away and quickly mobilized his colleagues to hurry to the home. While they removed some of the family's furniture from the building, others fought the fires upstairs. According to Helmut, "The neighbors lost their stuff and were angry that we had help getting our stuff out." The Fischer family found a new apartment just around the corner, where they lived until long after the war.

Roswitha Würscher was born in 1940. Her earliest memories were of the constant air raids. On several occasions, she saw the "Christmas trees" (illumination flares dropped by lead planes to mark the target) in the sky. "I really didn't know what they meant," she admitted. The family used their own basement as the air-raid shelter: "The door to the basement was under a carpet, and then we put a table on top of that. We went down there when the raids came."[4]

The fact that little children did not understand the full significance of war, air raids, and death is evident from this story told by Roswitha:

> I remember seeing something black lying on the street. I had no idea what it was, so while my mother was not paying attention to me, I ran over there to stare at it. It was the body of a person who burned to death. Then my mother saw me and pulled me quickly away.

As a schoolboy, Helmut Fischer had gone with his classmates to see the exterior of the concentration camp at Sachsenhausen near Oranienburg (just north of Berlin): "They were trying to educate us. It was interesting to see those places from the outside. The prisoners were POWs or criminals. We were really not told what was going on there."[5]

The meeting rooms of the Berlin East Branch at Frankfurter Allee were destroyed early in the war, and the branch moved around several times. By 1944, the branch members could no longer find rooms for their meetings, and it was decided that they should meet with the Center Branch. By that time, several members of both branches had lost their lives in the war or had moved away from the catastrophic conditions in Berlin.

The church rooms on Hufelandstrasse were eventually damaged in an air raid and much of the furnishings and branch property were lost. A school nearby served as the next meeting place until some rooms in a factory near the Friedrichshain Park became available.

On the ground floor, below the defunct church meeting rooms at the Hufelandstrasse address, the swimming pool and spa facility had survived the air raids. The last convert baptisms into the Church during World War II took place there. According to observer Heinz Kupitz, "My Aunt Elisabeth Tirsche and Anita, Gisela, and Wolfgang Kelm were baptized, and we stood around holding candles." In the words of Wolfgang Kelm (born 1932), who was twelve at the time:

It was decided to forgo the customary permission from the father and husband of baptismal candidates and baptize [my family] before the world came to an end. At this time the Russian armies stood at the gates of Berlin, awaiting the order for the final assault on the capital of the crumbling Third Reich. So on February 25, 1945, in the little pool in that factory building in Berlin, my mother, my sister, and myself were

baptized by one Friedrich Wernick. The water was 7 degrees Celsius [44 degrees Fahrenheit]. Even though I was young, I did not like the cold water much.[6]

Since 1942, Helmut Fischer had been an apprentice in a dental technology program. Due to his very small stature, he was not a favorite of his supervisor, "a 150 percent National Socialist who didn't like little guys." Barely sixteen years old, Helmut was still in that laboratory in March 1945 when his Hitler Youth company was mustered into service to man antiaircraft batteries with women and girls. When he reported for duty on April 20, Hitler's birthday, the Soviet Army was at the outskirts of Berlin. The night before the city surrendered (April 30–May 1), the commander of Helmut's unit told them to make their way to their homes as best they could. From their location by the Victory Column in the middle of the Tiergarten Park, Helmut needed to cross rivers and canals where the bridges had been destroyed.

Helmut was captured by the invaders before he had a chance to reach home or to exchange his Hitler Youth uniform for civilian clothing. Because of his military appearance, he was classified as a soldier and marched through several towns toward the east. On the way toward Landsberg, about seventy-five miles east of Berlin, he ran into a member of the Spandau Branch, a Brother Nöske:

I recognized him from different meetings, so I went up and told him who I was. He had Church books with him, so we talked about that in the evening. Then they [their Soviet captors] took his books and threw them into a big pile [to burn them].

Helga Meiszus Birth (born 1920) of the Tilsit Branch had been serving as a missionary since October 1944. She was assigned to the mission office, which was housed in the apartment building where the family of Paul

Langheinrich (second counselor to the mission supervisor) lived. Sister Birth, a war widow, kept a detailed journal during the last month of the war and recorded these remarks on Sunday, April 22, 1945:

> I decided to visit the Center Branch with Brother Langheinrich and Brother Patermann. . . . It took more than an hour to get to the meetinghouse. We did not find anybody there. A direct hit by an artillery shell had made a hole in the wall of the main meeting room and the damage to the room's contents was extensive. One of the members had already tried to clean up the mess but was interrupted in the attempt. That part of town was under such heavy artillery bombardment that the members could not get to the meetings.[7]

Roswitha Würscher remembered the end of the war on May 8, 1945: "I heard on the radio, 'The war is over!' and my first thought

was 'Can I go out and play now?' Of course I could not because the Russians were all over. The word went around that the Russians were good to children, so my brother and I went out [to look for food]."

From one day to the next, the population of Berlin began a hand-to-mouth existence, and Roswitha Würscher learned various tricks of procuring food (such as appearing to be very ill or sneaking onto unguarded supply trucks). While the branch members hungered and tried to keep out of the way of their Soviet oppressors, they found time to gather for Church meetings, often in the homes of members.

Young Helmut Fischer had been moved by train (in a cattle car, as was the prevailing mode of transportation for prisoners of war) as far east as Stargard in Pomerania. Fortunately, he was never sent to the Soviet Union. Due to

Fig. 3. The Kaiser Wilhelm Memorial Church in downtown Berlin in about 1940. Zoologischer Garten is Berlin's famous zoo. The church was destroyed in the same attack that hit the mission home. (H. Kupitz)

his small stature, he was classified by a German doctor as "category four: undernourished" and released from captivity, "Refugees were everywhere. I found a spot on top of a train back to Berlin. On July 18, the day after my father's birthday, I was home, and they were thrilled. My mother was so scared for me. They had no idea where I was."

The Fischer family had been fortunate to survive the invasion of the Red Army. While enemy soldiers ransacked the Fischer apartment, the family hid in the basement and were thus spared vandalism and assault. Brother Fischer's business was needed by the conquerors, so his employment was secure. With the war over, the Fischers joined other survivors of the Berlin Center Branch and met to continue their worship services. In general, the war had extracted a heavy toll from the Berlin Center Branch.

IN MEMORIAM

The following members of the Berlin Center Branch did not survive World War II:

Friedrich Wilhelm Barthel b. Prossmarke, Sachsen, Preußen 8 Mar 1870; son of Friedrich Barthel and Friederike Schulze; bp. 23 Oct 1939; conf. 23 Oct 1939; d. stomach cancer 16 May 1943 (FHL Microfilm 68809, book 2, no. 59; IGI)

Gloschard (husband) k. in battle (Würscher-Bartsch)

Wilhelmina Göring b. Gross Dombrowa, Woischnik, Schlesien, Preußen 22 May 1852; dau. of Matheus Göring and Rosina Bahn; bp. 10 Jun 1910; conf. 10 Jun 1910; d. 9 Aug 1942 (FHL Microfilm 68809, book 1, no. 64; IGI)

Anna Hedwig Gretzbach b. Berlin, Brandenburg, Preußen 19 Apr 1885; dau. of Erdmann Johann Gretzbach and Marie Lier; bp. 22 Aug 1899; conf. 22 Aug 1899; m. 11 Mar 1912, Max Jätsch; d. 3 Jun 1941 (FHL Microfilm 68809, book 1, no. 95; IGI)

Heinrich Carl Haberland b. Zeipen, Breslau, Schlesien, Preußen 16 Mar 1881; son of Carl Haberland and Johanna Sohn; bp. 28 Jun 1913; conf. 28 Jun 1913; m. 12 Oct 1903, Olga Kaliebe; d. 10 Jan 1941 (FHL Microfilm 68809, book 1, no. 72; IGI)

Helene Hallas b. Lorensdorf, Landsberg/Warthe, Brandenburg, Preußen 29 Ma 1909; dau. of Walentin

Hallas and Franziska Kupeler; bp. 14 Apr 1924; conf. 14 Apr 1924; d. 30 May 1942 (FHL Microfilm 68809, book 1, no. 77; IGI)

Günter Heinz Rudi Hirsekorn b. Berlin, Brandenburg, Preußen 6 Aug 1919; son of Heinrich Albert Wilhelm Hirsekorn and Bertha Auguste Dorothea Kähler; bp. 6 Jun 1933; conf. 6 Jun 1933; ord. deacon 4 Feb 1934; k. in battle 9 Sep 1942 (FHL Microfilm 68809, book 1, no. 341; IGI)

Johanna Luise Ernestine Hoffmann b. Thiergarten, Wohlan, Schlesien, Preußen 8 Nov 1865; dau. of Wilhelm Friedrich Hoffmann and Johanna Vierveg; bp. 8 Sep 1928; conf. 8 Sep 1928; m. Berlin, Brandenburg, Preußen 12 Jan 1910, Heinrich Beck; d. heart ailment Berlin 12 Jun 1943 (FHL Microfilm 68809, book 1, no. 14; IGI)

Helmut Gustav Hustadt b. Wuppertal, Elberfeld, Rheinland, Preußen 28 Jun 1910; son of August Hustadt and Louise Hause; bp. 27 Jun 1931; conf. 27 Jun 1931; ord. deacon 3 Sep 1933; d. wounds 20 Aug 1942 (FHL Microfilm 68809, book 1, no. 318; IGI)

Marie Betti Helene Kowalewski b. Stettin, Stettin, Pommern, Preußen 26 Apr 1898; dau. of Friedrich Kowalewski and Selma Schroeder; m. —— Radtke; d. old age 1943 (CHL CR 375 8 #2458, 1378–79)

Hans Joachim Krickhuhn b. Demmin, Pommern, Preußen 25 Oct 1922; son of Hermann Johann Joachim Krickhuhn and Margarete Zerull; bp. 9 Oct 1932; conf. 9 Oct 1932; ord. deacon 31 Oct 1937; non-commissioned officer; k. in battle Marlaz, Reval, Estonia 19 Feb 1943; bur. Tallinn-Maarjamäe, Estonia (FHL Microfilm 68809, book 2, no. 53; IGI; www.volksbund.de)

Hermann Wilhelm Krickhuhn b. Demmin, Pommern, Preußen 25 Oct 1922; son of Hermann Johann Joachim Krickhuhn and Margarethe Zerull (IGI); bp. 28 Aug 1937; conf. 28 Aug 1937; ord. deacon 26 Apr 1942; seaman; k. in battle 7 or 8 Apr 1945; bur. Leese Military Cemetery, Germany (FHL Microfilm 68809, book 2, no. 56, IGI; AF; PRF; www.volksbund.de)

Werner Alwin Franz Pegelow b. Berlin, Brandenburg, Preußen 24 Dec 1912; son of Hermann Pegelow and Auguste Becker; bp. 12 Apr 1924; conf. 13 Apr 1924; m. 5 Sep 1934, Gertrud Marie Otto; private; k. in battle Ilino-Wjasma, Russia 10 Oct 1941; bur. Ilino-Wjasma (FHL Microfilm 68809, book 2, no. 35; IGI; www.volksbund.de)

Max Otto Stoerhaas b. Schwedenhöhe, Bromberg, Posen, Preußen 11 Feb 1911; son of Wilhelm Stoerhaas and Meta Arehan; k. in battle 1943/44 (CHL Microfilm no. 2458, form 42 FP, Pt. 37, 726–27; IGI)

Pauline Traugott b. Oberlauterbach, Sachsen 11 Sep 1856; dau. of Christian Traugott and Margarethe Sperl; bp. 19 Jul 1921; conf. 24 Jul 1921;

m. —— Goldmann; d. old age 1941 or 1945 (FHL Microfilm 68809, book 1, no. 62)

Heinz Johannes Samuel Vielstich b. Kreuz, Pommern, Preußen 5 Dec 1923; son of Karl Friedrich Vielstich and Frieda Margarete Hildegard Quolke; bp. 11 May 1932; lance corporal; d. Greece 8 Jul 1943; bur. Dionyssos-Rapendoza, Greece (IGI; www.volksbund.de)

Jared Nephi Friedrich Vielstich b. Kreuz, Pommern, Preußen 29 Oct 1925; son of Karl Friedrich Vielstich and Frieda Margarete Hildegard Quolke; bp. 29 Oct 1933; private; d. 6 km south of Wlodawa, Bug, Poland 22 Jul 1944; bur. Pulawy Military Cemetery, Poland (IGI; www.volksbund.de)

Kurt Herbert Erwin Vielstich b. Kreuz, Pommern, Preußen 1 Oct 1915; son of Karl Friedrich Vielstich and Frieda Margarete Hildegard Quolke; bp. 5 Apr 1927; lance corporal; d. Braye, Chemin-des-Dames, France 5 Jun 1940; bur. Fort-de-Malmaison, France (FHL Microfilm 245291; IGI; www.volksbund.de)

Luise Marie Völlmer b. Frankfurt/Oder, Brandenburg, Preußen 25 Feb 1896; dau. of Marie Völlmer; bp. 12 Jul 1916; conf. 12 Jul 1916; m. Berlin, Preußen 12 Nov 1921, Erich Franz Will; 2 children; d. Berlin 21 Mar 1943 (FHL Microfilm 68809, book 1, no. 273; IGI)

Erich Otto Wiese b. Berlin, Brandenburg, Preußen 20 May 1917; son of Emma Wiese; bp. 20 Jun 1925; conf. 21 Jun 1925; d. 9 Nov 1944 (FHL Microfilm 68809, book 1, no. 259; IGI)

Erika Giesela Will b. Berlin, Preußen 31 Aug 1923; dau. of Franz Erich Will and Marie Luise Völlmer; bp. 20 Jul 1932; conf. 20 Jul 1932; d. Berlin 22 Feb 1941 (FHL Microfilm 68809, book 1, no. 275; *Sonntagsgruss*, no. 14, 6 Apr 1941, 56; IGI)

Erich Alfred Winter b. Stettin, Pommern, Preußen (IGI) 5 Jul 1895; son of Hermann Winter and Helene Pfahrkraft; bp. 25 Jun 1927; conf. 25 Jun 1927; m. 15 Apr 1922, Elisabeth Marie Daniel (div.); d. mental illness 1940 (FHL Microfilm 68809, book 2, no. 5; IGI)

Dietmar Alexander Würscher b. Berlin, Preußen 11 Nov 1941; son of Otto Karl Würscher and Kasimira Viktoria Cwiklinski; d. diphtheria 8 Jan 1945 (Würscher-Bartsch; IGI; FHL Microfilm 68809, book 2, no. 96)

Gerhard Wilhelm Würscher b. Berlin, Preußen 29 Sep 1921; son of Otto Karl Wuerscher and Kasmira Viktoria Cwiklinski; bp. 5 Aug 1930; k. in battle Iwan See, Naswa Fluss, Pakalowo, Tschernosem, Russia 22 or 24 Jun 1944 (Würscher-Bartsch; IGI; www.volksbund.de)

Udo Joachim Würscher b. Berlin, Preußen 6 Oct 1925; son of Otto Karl Wuerscher and Kasimira Viktoria Cwiklinski; bp. 15 Sep 1934; k. in battle 24 Jan 1945; bur. Wieszowa, Poland (Würscher-Bartsch; IGI; www.volksbund.de)

NOTES

1. Presiding Bishopric, "Financial, Statistical, and Historical Reports of Wards, Stakes, and Missions, 1884–1955," CR 4 12, 257.

2. Helmut Fischer, interview by the author in German, Leipzig, Germany, June 2, 2007.

3. The term differentiated him from Karl Fischer in the East Branch, who was known as the Mistfischer ("manure Fischer"). He owned a company that collected and disposed of manure with a fleet of horse-drawn wagons and trucks.

4. Roswitha Würscher Bartsch, interview by the author in German, Berlin, Germany, August 21, 2006.

5. What was going on there was, of course, the official incarceration of Jews and other undesirable civilians (criminals). Many thousands would be put to death or die of various causes before the camp was liberated by the Russians in April 1945.

6. Wolfgang Kelm, autobiography (unpublished, 1997), 15; private collection. Wolfgang's father was in the German army at the time, and his whereabouts could not be determined.

7. Helga Meiszus Birth Meyer, diary (unpublished), April 22, 1945, 3; private collection; trans. the author.

BERLIN EAST BRANCH

At the onset of World War II, the Berlin East Branch met at Frankfurter Allee 307. As Heinz Kupitz (born 1931) recalled, the rooms that the members had renovated were on the third floor of a four-story factory building. It was the first building next to the corner of Postkammerstrasse. There was a main meeting room, a classroom off to the side, and three more classrooms located in the main building on the street.[1] According to Hans Joachim Arndt (born 1933), there was an old pump organ in the main meeting room, and somebody initiated a campaign to replace it with a pipe organ if enough money could be donated.[2]

Berlin East Branch[3]	1939
Elders	20
Priests	6
Teachers	8
Deacons	12
Other Adult Males	34
Adult Females	164
Male Children	15
Female Children	4
Total	263

Fig. 1. Aaronic Priesthood holders of the Berlin East Branch during a meeting in the Primary room. (H. Kupitz)

Luise Winkler (born 1915) added these details to the description of the rooms:

> It was in a Hinterhaus at that address, and there was a factory building in front of it. There was a long room with a podium in it. Then there was a corridor, and on the left side there was a room for the little children.[4]

One of the largest branches in Germany in 1939, the Berlin East Branch had territory that extended from the east-central portion of the city to the eastern edge of town. The branch observed the common meeting times—Sunday School at 10:00 A.M. and sacrament meeting at 6:00 P.M. Most members went home for Sunday dinner then returned for the evening meeting. Some members traveled as long as two hours to church one way and were usually invited to dinner with local families between meetings.[5] Priesthood and auxiliary meetings were held during the week, as were Primary, MIA, and choir practice, according to Luise Winkler.

Regarding the number of persons who attended the East Branch on a regular basis, Annamarie Fischer (born 1926) stated that perhaps as many as two hundred persons came. "I was the kindergarten leader back then, and I had twelve children in my class."[6]

The late 1930s represented for most Germans something akin to a golden age. However, such was not the case for the Jews who still lived in Germany on November 9, 1938 (the great majority had already fled the Reich). Charlotte Baade Fischer (born 1903) recalled what became known as the "Night of Broken Glass," when Jewish persons and property all over the country were subjected to vandalism and assault:

> The Jews could find no peace then. The show windows of the shops were shattered that Saturday evening. When we went to church the next day, Sunday morning, the sidewalks were covered with glass. It was a horrible sight. The shops had been plundered, their owners driven out or imprisoned. We never got the whole story—just what we could see with our own eyes.[7]

As the persecution of the Jews escalated in 1939, the preparations for war also picked up speed, though many Germans were not aware of the developments.

"We were on vacation at the home of my grandmother out in the country," recalled Annamarie Fischer, "when all of the church bells began to ring. We didn't know why. It was usually for a wedding or because somebody [had] died in small towns. Then we found out there was a war, but we had no idea what it involved."

Hans Böttcher (born 1913) served a full-time mission in the southern districts of the East German Mission. Following his mission, he worked as a machinist for Winger & Co.

in Berlin. On September 1, 1939, he received a draft notice, but was rescued from the military by his employer, who argued that his work was critical to the war effort. This move kept Hans out of the army for another year. In the interim, he married his sweetheart, Ilse Franke, in Chemnitz.[8]

Hans Böttcher was drafted again in January 1942. With his unit, he moved slowly toward the Eastern Front, walking much of the seven hundred miles through East Prussia, Poland, Ukraine, and Russia. On three occasions, he was spared what could have been death at the front. First, he was shining the boots of his commanding officer when a bullet missed his head and struck his left thumb. On another occasion, he fell into a bomb crater at night and severely injured his knee. The third time, he contracted pneumonia. In each case, the injury or illness required hospitalization, and he

was removed from the front for a time. When he returned to the front after the knee injury, he learned that his unit had suffered numerous casualties. After his bout with pneumonia, he returned to the front to find that his unit had been essentially wiped out in a Soviet counter-offensive. "Again I was taken away by the Lord at the right time," he later explained.

When the war began, Hans Joachim Arndt's father was in a reserve army unit and was reactivated immediately. Stationed first in Berlin, he was later sent to the Eastern Front, Romania, Czechoslovakia, and finally Norway. He returned to his family after a short incarceration by the British in 1946. According to Hans Joachim, "I really had no father for seven years—from 1939 to 1946."

Gerhard Kupitz (born 1923) recalled that certain branch cultural events, such as the Christmas party and the annual Relief Society

Fig. 2. Members of the Berlin East Branch on Mother's Day, 1939. (H. Kupitz)

bazaar, were continued during the first year or two of the war. After that, the trappings for such activities were simply not available. As branch secretary, Gerhard took part in the ward teaching program that assumed a new purpose: locating branch members following air raids.

As the war progressed, more and more young men of the Berlin East Branch left for military duty. One of the first to lose his life was Kurt Vielstich (born 1915), who wrote these lines to members of the branch back home on June 4, 1940:

> It looks like we will see action soon. I don't know if I will ever see home again. Should I never come back, should I die for my people and my Führer, then I know that I will have done my duty. If we do not meet again on earth, then it will be in the hereafter. Give my best to the branch members.[9]

Kurt lost his life the next day in the German offensive against France.

Little children generally did not understand why air raids against Berlin took place, but they knew what terror was. As Christa Schmelter recalled:

> I was a very emotional child, and every time we were bombed and down in the cellar I would just fall to pieces and get hysterical. . . . The SS came in one time and wanted to fit us with gas masks, and I wouldn't let them put a gas mask on [me]; I just screamed and hollered and so they left me alone after that.[10]

It was 1941 when bombs left the apartment of the Willy Schmelter family uninhabitable. Daughter Christa remembered being evacuated to the home of her grandmother in the village of Berkenbrück on the Spree River, southeast of Berlin. For a time, Willy continued to travel to work at the Siemens factory in Berlin. As the district Sunday School president, he also traveled most Sundays in order to visit the ten branches in the district. According to Christa, "My father was straight gospel-oriented, not political, . . . [but] he would listen to the BBC all the time. [The radio was] on the wall furthest away from the next apartment." Willy Schmelter was drafted into the German army in about 1941.

Soon after the war began, the Berlin East Branch meeting rooms at Frankfurter Allee 307 had to be evacuated. The company producing munitions on the upper floors needed room to expand, thus the branch began to hold meetings in a building on Thaerstrasse. There were several classrooms there, including the foyer.

It was about that time that one of the few Church members in Germany who had been endowed in the temple lost her life. Sister Gonitzke had lived in Salt Lake City during the 1930s but returned to Germany to be with her family. In 1941, an air raid struck her home. The bomb that sheared off the façade of the building detonated in the basement where she had taken refuge and killed her along with her neighbors. After the attack, Mr. Gonitzke was seen by Heinz Kupitz; he was still sitting in his easy chair next to the heater by the apartment's inside wall and had to be rescued by firemen. Heinz's brother, Gerhard, reported that branch members had hoped to identify the body of Sister Gonitzke by her temple garments, but they were not successful.

Fig. 3. Several members of the Berlin East Branch. Access to the meetinghouse at Frankfurter Allee 307 was through the portal at the center background of this photograph. (H. Kuptiz)

That same year, the Kupitz apartment on Frankfurter Allee was damaged by bombs. Fortunately the damage could be repaired in those days because skilled workers and building materials were still available. According to Gerhard Kupitz, the family had a much better heater when the repairs were finished.

Gerhard Kupitz would normally have been inducted into the Reichsarbeitsdienst in 1940. However, as a technical draftsman working for a war-critical industry, he was exempt from national service until 1941, when a Wehrmacht draft notice arrived at the Kupitz home. "I would never have volunteered if they had not drafted me." Gerhard's basic training took place in occupied Poland. "I was a good marksman, but I was convinced that if I did not try to kill other people, I would get out of the war all right."[11]

On the Eastern Front, Gerhard Kupitz was responsible for drawing maps of the German positions so that artillery units in the rear could avoid hitting their own men up front. The maps had to be done well and to scale. The duty was dangerous but kept him out of the fighting for the most part.

Paul Radeke (born 1908) was drafted by the Wehrmacht in November 1940. A master watchmaker, he was then the district Sunday School president and had served as the branch

Fig. 5. Berlin East Branch members coming from distant homes arrived at this subway (U-Bahn) and commuter train (S-Bahn) station close to the meetinghouse. (H. Kupitz)

president before the war. He left his wife, Elsa, sons Jared and Dieter, and baby daughter, Evelin, in the care of his parents and Elsa's parents. Fortunately for the family, Paul was first stationed in Rathenow, less than two hours by train to the west. Despite the short distance from home and a few Sunday visits, Elsa missed Paul very much. From February to December 1941, she wrote him at least fifty-three letters and seven postcards.[12] Every one of the documents expressed a longing to have him home again. She also discussed family, church, and domestic issues in those letters. Here are samples of the content during that year (when conditions at home and on the battlefield were still quite good for Germany and its citizens):

February 4: I went to the Hufelandstrasse to check out an apartment. It was four flights up, so I didn't even look at it. There will be another place for us somewhere else.

April 4: I don't know when we can come see you [in Rathenow]. They say the trains are all full these days. So it won't be easy to travel with the children and the luggage. . . . I will go to the station next week to check on the details. I will probably start the trip from Lehrter Station because the trains start empty there. By the time they get to Alexander Square, they are already full. The local trains have room for anyone. If I take an express train, I have to have special authorization.

Fig. 4. An informal gathering of young adults of the Berlin East Branch. Note the swastika flag in the right corner. (H. Kuptiz)

Fig. 6. The family of Paul and Elsa Radeke. (E. McMillan)

April 18: I am writing to reassure you that we are all right. Last night we spent three hours in the basement [bomb shelter]. Our [antiaircraft] guns were firing hot and heavy. I haven't heard of any specific damage around here.

April 27: [At city hall] I asked about a larger coal allotment and a crib [for Evelin]. They can't provide those now, but should be able to soon. One of the officials (the one I like) was angry about the fact that your employer cannot come up with at least 10 marks a month to support us. The official says that at your salary, your employer made lots of money off of your work.

May 8: I visited the Berlin Center Branch on Tuesday evening. . . . I take advantage of every opportunity of talking with [district president] Fritz Fischer about your release [as district Sunday School president].

August 12: We survived last night quite well. The alarm began at 12:30, and the all-clear was sounded at 2:05 A.M. In ten minutes all of us were dressed and ready. The children had gone to bed at 8 P.M. so they already had some good sleeping time. Dieter heard the alarm first and got up immediately. I had the clothes all laid out and ready so it went very fast. The baby woke up just as I put her into the wagon, but she was really good. At 1:15 A.M. the Schulze family went downstairs, and I asked Mr. Schulze to help me carry the wagon. He came up as soon as he had carried his wagon downstairs. We waited on the stairs. By the time we went down, we could hear some dull thuds in the distance. Everybody thought it was the sound of bombs landing.

August 16: I am sick of the war and everything connected with it. This endless waiting is

terrible. Sometimes I could just go insane, but then the crisis passes and all is calm again.

August 19: Received two inquiries regarding our apartment. Yesterday people came twice to see it. . . . I looked at a three-room apartment near the Friedrichsfelde Station. It is in a new building and has a bathroom and costs only 60 marks. It is not expensive but a bit far from our garden [in Hohen Neuendorf]. What do you think?

September 30: Today we were informed that last week it was announced in the Berlin Center Branch that you had been released [as district Sunday School president].

November 2: No news about an apartment yet. I looked at one at Frankfurter Allee 305 last week. A four-room apartment is available, but it costs 100 marks rent [per month]. . . . Lots of apartments are becoming available every day. All were rented by Jewish families. The Jews have to move out on short notice. They are being sent to Lietzmannstadt. They can take only 100 marks and fifty pounds along. Everything else is to be sold at auction.

Bertold Patermann had moved with his family from Deutsch Rasselwitz, Silesia, to Berlin in 1939. An employee of the national railroad system, Brother Patermann was called as the president of the Berlin East Branch and served until the branch joined with the Berlin Center Branch in the spring of 1945.[13]

In the early 1930s, Karl Fischer (born 1902) had established a company for the transfer of manure from Berlin city sites to locations out of town. By 1942, his operation was prospering and involved a truck, several horse-drawn wagons, and a number of employees. Brother Fischer was affectionately known as the Mistfischer (manure Fischer) in contrast to Friedrich Fischer, district president and member of the Berlin Center Branch, the Käsefischer (cheese Fischer). Karl Fischer and his wife, Charlotte, had four sons when the war began. In 1942, they were encouraged to

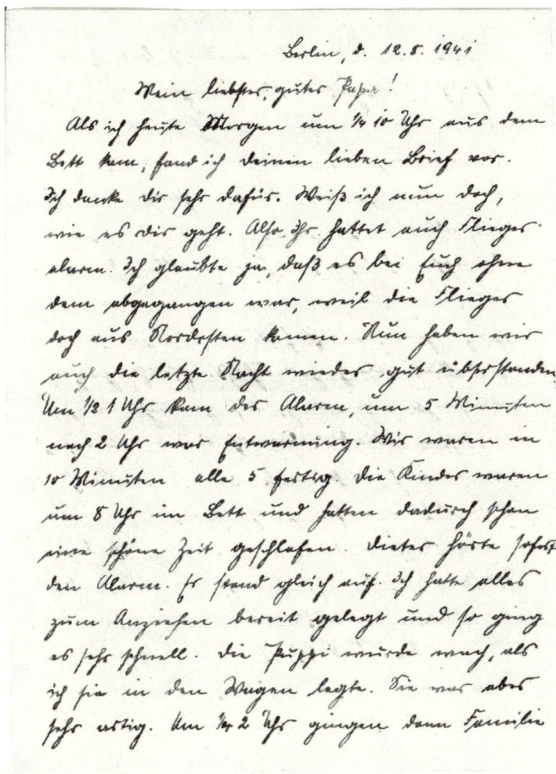

Fig. 7. One of the sixty cards and letters written by Elsa Radeke to her soldier husband, Paul, during the year 1941; she addressed him as "Papa" and signed as "Mother." (E. McMillan)

send their sons away from Berlin, and thus Hans and Fred (born 1933) went to Austria.[14]

Young Hans Fischer wrote home to describe their life near Linz, and the report was quite discouraging. He and Fred worked hard on the farm, lived in an unfriendly Catholic environment, ate from a common soup bowl, and were generally homesick. The Fischers had a telephone in their home (a rarity in those days), so Hans called home: "Pick us up! We can't stand it anymore!" Sister Fischer immediately took a train to Austria to bring them home. For the next few years, the Fischer boys lived in the home of their grandfather, Friedrich Baade, in Leest, just southwest of Berlin. They went home to their parents in Berlin on weekends when conditions permitted.[15]

Günter Buchta (born 1922) was initially drafted into the German navy in 1940, but his employer was able to have the order deferred on the basis of Günter's employment in steel fabrication, a war-critical industry. In 1942, following two months of training in diesel and steam-engine maintenance, he was stationed in Bremerhaven, Germany, on the North Sea coast. While there, Günter was on guard duty along the harbor one night from midnight until 2:00 A.M. Upon reporting to his superior officer at the conclusion of his watch, he was told, "Buchta, button your coat!" He was missing a button, but did not understand how that had happened until he was on duty again from 6:00 A.M. to 8:00 A.M.: "I was walking along [the same path] and saw something shiny laying there. I picked it up and found my button." A piece of shrapnel falling from the sky had apparently just missed his head and torn the button from his uniform.[16] In January 1943, he was transferred to Le Havre, the large Atlantic port and naval base in France.

Karl Winkler and Luise Böttcher had married in 1938. He was drafted several times before becoming a full-time soldier in 1942. That Christmas, he was home with his wife and two children (born 1939 and 1941), but the parting scene was very sad (see photograph, page page 54). Just a month later, Karl was killed. His widow recalled the circumstances:

> My husband died in January of 1943. An officer saw when my husband was shot and told my brother [Hans Böttcher], who then helped to bury him. And my brother gave immediate notice to our parents. We also received an official letter from the [Nazi] Party a few days later. We also got two savings books, each with 100 reichsmark for my children because my husband had fallen on the anniversary of Hitler's coming to power [January 30, 1933]. I received support from the state and did not have to work during the war.

Karl Winkler's daughter, Renate, was just a little girl when Berlin was being bombed on a regular basis, but she vividly recalled one odd incident that occurred when the family hurried downstairs to the apartment building's air-raid shelter:

> Downstairs in the basement there was a couch. My little brother sat down there and felt something very hot. A shell fragment had come in through the window just before we entered the room. If we had been there a few moments earlier, something bad might have happened. That was a testimony to us, and the [Primary] teacher later talked to us about how our Heavenly Father had protected us. I will never forget that.[17]

In July 1943, Luise Winkler was instructed by the city government to leave Berlin with her two children. Because they had relatives in Waldenburg, Silesia, they inquired at the mission office and learned that there was a small group of Saints in that town. Sister Winkler described their experience in the following words:

> We visited the branch in Waldenburg every Sunday while we were there. We had to take the street car. It was very small with only twenty people in two small rooms. The branch president came from Hamburg. I was responsible for the children and the singing, and I also took the children of my cousin (who was not a member) to church with me. Once, we went to Breslau for a conference. We stayed until September 1944 then returned to our apartment on Seestrasse in Berlin.

Barely twelve years old in 1943, Heinz Kupitz was assigned with his Hitler Youth comrades to go through his neighborhood after air raids to identify homes that had been damaged and to help rescue people from the shelters. Years later, memories associated with that service were still quite distinct:

> One time a bomb went right down into the subway station at Frankfurter Allee. I had to help dig [the civilians] out. One guy was screaming his head off from pain. They gave him a shot and finally we got him out. The sewer line was broken and we had to work through that stuff, and the stench was terrible. We learned later that the man died on the way to the hospital.

Fig. 8. Karl Winkler last saw his children at Christmas 1942. (R. Winkler Heidler)

Hans Joachim Arndt recalled the following:

> I was ten in 1943, and through school programs I was inducted into the Hitler Youth. We got to wear uniforms, and different parts of the uniform indicated different accomplishments. For example, we got a dagger if we passed a physical agility test, and then you had a strap diagonally across your chest.

That year, Hans Joachim Arndt's mother took him and his younger brother away from the Reich capital to the relative safety of the small town of Freiberg in Saxony, where they awaited the end of the war.

Christa Schmelter did not recall having church services in her grandmother's house in the country. With her father gone in the army, there was no priesthood holder anywhere near. However, religion was ever present:

> My mother would never go anywhere without her scriptures. . . . Grandma had her Bible and her scriptures. With all that turmoil, . . . we prayed all the time. We never ate unless we prayed. I do remember praying with my mother while we were traveling and while my dad was gone.

The British and Americans instituted a concentrated program of air raids over Berlin in November 1943. Charlotte Baade Fischer was across town near the Berlin Zoo when the first bombing began (probably on November 21). With short stops in shelters and stints of walking where public transportation was out of order, her trip home across central Berlin (about five miles) was a true odyssey. At the same time, her ten-year-old son, Fred, narrowly escaped death as he made his way home. As Sister Fischer wrote years later, "That evening both of us could have died and no one would have known where we ended up."[18]

As the air war left more and more of Berlin's neighborhoods in ruins, it became increasingly difficult to disregard the damage. Young Jared Fischer (born 1936) clearly recalled some gruesome street scenes:

Fig. 9. Most apartment buildings in Berlin were five to six stories tall, as in this photograph of Frankfurter Allee near the Kupitz home. (H. Kupitz)

Our parents didn't let us look at dead people. They said, "Just keep going. Don't look at them." Once on the Frankfurter Allee by the overhead [S-Bahn] tracks, some of the five-story buildings were totally destroyed by bombs, and everybody in the basement was killed—about thirty people. [Rescuers] couldn't get them out of the rubble for weeks. They didn't have the equipment we have today. . . . [Frankfurter Allee] is a four-lane street at that point. We had to walk by on the other side, and people covered their faces because of the awful smell. You can't lose that smell from your memory.[19]

On patrol duty in the North Sea in the summer of 1944, Günter Buchta was aboard a small boat (120 feet long by 26 feet wide) as one of a crew of twenty-eight men. Armed with only a 20-millimeter antiaircraft gun, the vessel was not designed for combat. It was on this boat that Günter patrolled what was soon to be the landing site for the Allied invasion of France. On June 4, 1944, they left a point slightly west of what would become Utah Beach. They proceeded east to a place called Port-en-Bessin, near what would soon become Omaha Beach, where they spent the night of June 4–5. Then they made their way gradually east to the port of Le Havre where they docked just a few hours before the largest invasion in history began on June 6. Just one day earlier, Günter's boat was sitting precisely where more than 100,000 Allied soldiers intended to land. Survival would likely have been impossible.

June 20, 1944, two weeks after the D-day landing, Günter's boat was attacked by fighter planes. One of the planes that fired a rocket made a direct hit on the engine room. Reacting instinctively, Günter quickly made the ten steps up to the deck and jumped over the side. "In one minute the whole thing was gone. We lost our ship," he recalled.

In 1944, Hans Böttcher was assigned to the artillery training range at Wildflecken in Bavaria, not far from his wife, who was living in her hometown of Chemnitz. She was able to visit him at Wildflecken. "It seems as if our love for each other grew in the time we were separated and of course with the insecure outlook of the chance of seeing each other ever again," he later wrote. By that time, they had a son and a baby daughter. After a short stay at the artillery range, Hans was sent to Italy.

Christmas 1944 was a very nice time for Hans in Italy. Although the winter weather was severe, the American army observed a cease-fire for the holiday, and Christmas Day was bright and shiny. Hans later wrote that the experience "was a drastic contrast to last year's Christmas holidays in Russia. But as soon as the holidays were over, the fighting continued." He recalled when news came that the Soviet Army was invading Germany from the east, the Americans and British were invading from the west, and Germany was being surrounded: "We felt like [we] were wasting our time, energy and lives for a lost cause."

As happened with so many schoolchildren in the Reich capital, Heinz Kupitz and several of his classmates were sent with their teacher to safety in a small town just east of the Neisse River—about one hundred miles southeast of Berlin—in the fall of 1944. The peace and quiet that was supposed to facilitate their education did not last long. On January 29, 1945, they were instructed to return to Berlin. A Polish farmer took the schoolboys on a wagon with rubber tires and delivered them to the railroad station in Frankfurt/Oder. From there, they took the train home to Berlin, where they arrived in time to experience the last days of Hitler's thousand-year Reich. While away from home, Heinz had not had any contact with the Church.

On about August 10, 1944, Gerhard Kupitz was in camp in Romania, not far from Odessa and the Black Sea, when the following event occurred:

I was just brushing my teeth early in the morning. . . . I had my shorts on, no shirt or shoes. I heard one of our Stuka [dive-bomber] planes coming toward us. Suddenly there was an explosion. . . . Apparently a Russian flak gun shot at him and the round hit a tree or the roof of the building I was in. Some of the shrapnel hit me in the arm. And that was one of the greatest blessings I could have had because [now] I was out of the real war. . . . I grabbed my arm to stop the bleeding, and then I ran to find a doctor. He said that I had a fracture.

Gerhard was put on a train for Vienna, Austria, but did not arrive there for three or four weeks due to the confusion in transportation schedules and attacks by partisans and by enemy aircraft. "We were in a cattle car with straw for a bed. The pus attracted flies, and it was not fun. [Before we arrived in Vienna] my bones grew back together." During the next few months, his arm healed, but he developed trouble walking. Doctors could not identify the problem, so they sent him to a succession of hospitals; he ended up back in Germany, in Dippoldiswalde near Dresden. In January 1945, it was determined that he was suffering from diphtheria and would likely have died in another two weeks had the illness not been diagnosed.

In January 1945, Willy Waldhaus, an elder in the Königsberg Branch, fled with his family before the invaders. Upon their arrival in Berlin, they were taken in by the Kelm family, who had been friends of the Church for several years and were well-known among members of the Berlin East Branch. Frau Kelm and her two children had wished to be baptized since before the war, but her husband had refused to give his consent. While he was away in military service, she took her children to church with no risk of familial strife. As her son, Wolfgang (born 1932), later wrote, "It never occurred to us not to go [to church on Sunday]." Indeed, they were sad when they lost the opportunity, as he learned on the Sunday following the devastating air raid of February 3, 1945:

> There was no public transportation in operation, so we set out early to walk to the meeting room on top of some building on Thaerstrasse. After walking for over an hour through the still burning ruins of Berlin we arrived at our destination, only to find it in ruins too. Young as I was in years [twelve], I had a feeling of great loss. The Church was literally gone out of my life.[20]

Angela Patermann recalled the destruction of the Berlin East meeting rooms in these words:

> One Sunday, when the people came to church, my father [the branch president] said, "You all go home as fast as you can." Many asked, "Why, why?" "I don't know why I have to tell you this." The meetings hadn't even started yet. He told the ones who came late, "We'd better go to the underground [station]." Just when we got to the station, the alarm went off, and the first bomb fell on the building we met in. The whole thing was gone.

According to former branch president Paul Radeke, the losses in that air raid included "furniture, membership records, tithing records, the branch history," and other items that could not be restored.[21] Again the branch moved, but this time they joined with the Berlin Center Branch in the Hufelandstrasse, which necessitated another half hour's travel for many branch members. Heinz Kupitz recalled that perhaps fifty or sixty persons from the Berlin East Branch attended meetings with the Berlin Center Branch.

Wolfgang Kelm had fond memories of Willy Waldhaus, who assumed the spiritual leadership of the Kelm home while Mr. Kelm was away in the army. As Wolfgang recalled:

> He was the first person in the Church that I ever knew that actually would teach the gospel in the home. You know we had family home evenings with this man, and I didn't have a father in the Church. . . . Before we went to the bomb shelter at night, when the night raids came, we always had our prayer before we went down with him. . . . It was a fast prayer, but it always was there.[22]

Fortunately, the Church was not totally gone from the life of Wolfgang Kelm because he was baptized along with his mother and his sister, Gisela, in late February 1945. Mission leader Richard Ranglack had decided that Mr. Kelm's permission was not needed to baptize his wife and his children "before the world came to an end."[23]

As the winter came to a close in early 1945, Hans Böttcher's unit was captured by the advancing American army in northern Italy. In a relatively comfortable prison camp, he came into contact with an American officer who was also LDS. Hans was taken aback when the American shook his hand, because fraternization between American captors and German prisoners was still forbidden. "He seemed to be a Jack-Mormon, because he was smoking," Hans recalled. Hans attended religious services with German Lutherans, including an Easter service where the pastor did not show up. He was secretly hoping for the opportunity to speak, and it actually came his way. He conducted "a Mormon service with a strict Mormon sermon, but they all liked it very much and asked me to do it again."

The air raid of February 26, 1945, hit the eastern Berlin neighborhood where the Karl Fischer (Mistfischer) family lived. Brother Fischer had dug out a bomb shelter for the family behind their home, and it was there that Sister Fischer had sought refuge with her son Hans and a domestic maid named Inge Reinhardt. One bomb landed about seventy-five feet away and uprooted a huge pear tree. An incendiary bomb actually pierced the wall of the shelter and came to rest just inches behind Sister Fischer:

About 10 centimeters (4 inches) further and I would have had it in my back. . . . Now we had to get out of the shelter. The dirt that landed on our shelter door was so much that we could not open it. Now three of us pushed against the door and it finally opened. . . . There were many fires. Our house also started to burn. First I went into the attic to put out the fires that were still very little. . . . We started to take furniture to the yard.[24]

In the confusion, Sister Fischer gave up trying to fight the fire, but her husband arrived a few minutes later and extinguished the flames. That night the family slept in employees' quarters next to their horses' stalls and were again driven out by fire. They escaped with only a few of the possessions they had saved from their home. In early April, Sister Fischer took her sons to Leest to live in the home of her father, Friedrich Baade, where they remained until after the war.

For young children, life in Berlin during World War II was not all terror, suffering, and death. Little boys still found ways to amuse themselves. Such was the case with Lothar Vielstich (born 1937). He was seven when his mother moved the family from the Lichtenberg suburb of Berlin to Hohen Neuendorf (just northwest of the metropolis). There they were given space in the vacation house owned by Paul Radeke. As Lothar recalled:

> We had a favorite oak tree. . . . We would sit up there and watch the planes literally go over into Berlin by the hundreds. . . . We would see some of the dogfights up there. We would see planes getting shot down. . . . I remember one time a German fighter got shot down, he came down on the parachute, and some Russian plane came up right next to him and shot him down right out of the air. . . . From the looks of it, he did not survive. . . . [Once] an English fighter plane started opening fire on us sitting in that tree. I think he probably mistook us for an antiair-craft gun or snipers.[25]

Paul Radeke's assignment near Berlin had been a very safe one for three years, but in

Fig. 10. The cottage of the Radeke family on their garden property in Hohen Neuendorf. (E. McMillan)

January 1945, he was sent to Frankfurt/Oder, where he joined the forces attempting to stop the Red Army's advance on Berlin. In April, he was taken captive and sent east. At about that time, his son of eighteen months, Gerd, died of a childhood disease. Because coffins were not to be had in Berlin at the time, a grandfather procured an empty fuse box from the army, and the child was buried in Hohen Neuendorf. Paul did not learn of his loss until he was released from a POW camp in Poland in September. He had been suffering so severely from kidney stones that he was classified as unusable for labor and sent home.

One of the last major air raids over Berlin took place on Sunday, March 18, 1945. The alarms interrupted Sunday School, and the members of the Berlin Center/East Branch made their way to the shelters. Those members who went out after the attack to see if their homes were still standing would probably not make it back for sacrament meeting, so the Kelms stayed at church. Whereas there was a very good attendance

Fig. 11. Gerd Radeke died just weeks before the war ended and was buried in an old army fuse box. (E. McMillan)

in the morning, Wolfgang remembered only a handful still there in the evening. He could not recall what was said, but a distinct impression was made:

> Until the day I die, I will see the picture of my burning hometown through the window of the meeting hall. While utter chaos was outside, there was peace inside. Whoever conducted the meeting asked for bread to have the sacrament and someone produced a sandwich. It was dismantled, and the sacrament was administered.[26]

Martin Nöske had been employed in the management of the Berlin public transportation authority but was demoted when it became known that he had socialist political leanings. Thereafter, he was a common streetcar operator and often allowed Heinz Kupitz to ride gratis. He called the boy by his middle name, Nephi, which irked young Heinz. In the last days of the war, Heinz and Brother Nöske ran into each other in a government food storehouse that had been opened to the local populace. As Heinz recalled, "Outside of the building he was shot and killed by fighter planes. I saw his body after that. He was buried in a mass grave by the Samaritan Church."

Just days later, Heinz was persuaded by Herr Herzog, his Hitler Youth leader, to serve as a messenger, using his bicycle to make his way through the streets:

> One day I was in the Rigaerstrasse, and an artillery shell landed, and I was hit. The shrapnel blew out my front tire and hit me in the leg. I pushed my bike to the neighborhood command post, and Herzog told me to go home and get my wound treated. So I went home and burned my Hitler Youth uniform in the heater. That was very lucky because the Russians arrived the very next day.[27]

In April 1945, Sister Schmelter took her daughters and made her way from Berkenbrück to her sister-in-law's home in nearby Sieversdorf. The Red Army came through at that time, and Sister Schmelter disguised her seventeen-year-old daughter as an old woman to protect her from assault. Each night of the trek, they sought refuge in a barn. On one occasion, they approached a farm that appeared to be abandoned. In the barn and in the house, the Schmelters found the bodies of several local residents hanging from the rafters. "I don't know if they committed suicide or if somebody else [killed] them," Christa later explained.

During the last week of April 1945, the Red Army moved through the Kelms's neighborhood in eastern Berlin. The soldiers stole valuables from the residents and terrorized the women. One of the leaders of the East German Mission, Paul Langheinrich, lived just north of the Tiergarten Park in western Berlin. During the first months of 1945, he had invited members of the Church to move into the apartment house in which his family lived because several apartments had been vacated by fleeing Berliners. Fearing worse treatment at the hands of the conquerors, Sister Kelm decided to leave her apartment in an area under Soviet occupation and take her children across town to the Langheinrich home. Her guests, the Waldhaus family, went along. It was April 25, 1945. To reach their goal, they needed to go through the enemy lines from behind and possibly pass through the thin line of German defenders in central Berlin. The small group of harried refugees worked their way through downtown Berlin for fully six miles then across the huge square in front of the Lehrter Railroad Station. At that point, they were actually between the Soviet army and the German army. Wolfgang Kelm later described their perilous situation:

> After the square was crossed and the artillery fire became more intense, we all decided to take a quick breather in some doorways that had a little overhang for protection. [Willy Waldhaus] came into the same doorway with [his son] Günter and myself. The next [artillery shell]

Fig. 12. Members of the Primary of the Berlin East Branch.
(H. Kupitz)

exploded in the street and we left the doorway
to find the others. Willy stumbled and fell. . . .
The adults went [back] to look for him. He was
still at the doorway, hit by shrapnel and died
shortly thereafter. When he was hit, he stood
directly in front of me.[28]

Willy Waldhaus had traveled hundreds of
miles to bring his family to safety, only to die less
than one mile from refuge at the Langheinrich
home and just a few days before the end of the
war. The Kelm family experienced the end of the
Battle of Berlin and the defeat of Germany
while living at Rathenowerstrasse 52 as part
of a veritable Latter-day Saint refugee colony.
When the fires were out, the shooting had
stopped, and the dust had settled, they decided
to return to their apartment in eastern Berlin.
As Wolfgang later recorded:

It was time to go home. Richard Ranglack, who
was the mission [supervisor] at the time and
lived in the same house, called us in and gave
each of us a blessing and turned us loose. We
walked through streets still littered with bodies,
back to [the suburb of] Lichtenberg. There we
found our apartment in order and not broken
into. Now the pieces had to be picked up. This
represented the end of the only world I had ever
known: The Third Reich![29]

The Patermann family also accepted Paul
Langheinrich's invitation to leave their home in
eastern Berlin and go to the Rathenowerstrasse
on April 21, 1945. "It was sort of a Mormon

colony," recalled Angela Patermann. Two
weeks later, Brother Langheinrich posted a
sign by the door saying "American Church,"
and by doing so, probably kept many marauding enemy soldiers away. However, as successful as Brother Langheinrich was in defending
the inhabitants of the apartment house, there
were some frightening moments. Angela remembered one harrowing event:

I was on the balcony with three girl missionaries. . . . Some Russians saw us and they came
up. When you came into the [Langheinrich]
apartment, there were several doors to the living room and the bedrooms. They came in and
looked and looked everywhere because they
were looking for us girls. There was a big double
door to the room we were in, and they did not
see that door. They went by, back and forth, and
couldn't see any doors, and then they left.

When the war ended on May 8, 1945,
Günter Buchta was still patrolling the coast of
the North Sea off Germany. His commander
took the boat to Amsterdam, where it was surrendered to the Allies. Under Canadian command, they returned to their route along the
North Sea coast, transporting soldiers and
equipment to Wilhelmshaven in Germany.
Günter was fortunate to be released on August
8, 1945. He dug peat moss in northwest
Germany for two months and then made his
way home to Berlin. When he finally saw his
mother, she was forty-nine years old but had
snow-white hair, "probably from all of the worrying," he suggested.

In the summer of 1945, Hans Böttcher
was in a prison camp near Pisa in northern
Italy. Somebody showed him the program
printed for a religious service held in Pisa in
which a certain Hans Karl Schade was a singer.
Recognizing the name of his friend from the
Dresden Altstadt Branch, he enlisted the help
of the local pastor to establish contact with
Hans Karl. When the reunion took place,

We were both overjoyed to see each other here in Italy among those 100,000 German POWs, . . . probably the only Mormons in this part of the country. . . . We immediately took off . . . to find a place, quite away from people, to be able to kneel down and pray. And that is just what we did. We poured our heart out before the Lord for opening the way to see each other. Then we were reporting each other's experiences.

Eventually, an LDS American army chaplain named Braithwaite located Hans Böttcher and drove him in a Jeep to Sunday meetings held by American LDS soldiers. As Hans later wrote, "I did not get very much of what was said, but oh it felt so good to hear old familiar tunes and prayers and a spirit that I had not been able to feel for a long time . . . and I took the courage to get up and give my testimony."

Hans Böttcher was released by his American captors in 1946 and traveled home to join his wife, Ilse, in Chemnitz. His children looked on him as a stranger and called him "uncle" (a term of familiarity for any adult male). Nevertheless, he was in very good health after serving at the Eastern and Italian fronts, and his family had survived the air raids at home. After nearly five years, they were together again to stay.

"My father was gone for nine years," recalled Christa Schmelter. Her story continued:

We didn't know for three years whether he was dead or alive. [One day] my mother decided she had to know one way or another. She fasted and prayed for three days, and at the end of the three days, there came a knock at the door, and a couple came, and they had a bouquet of chrysanthemums. And they asked if she was Mrs. Schmelter, Willie's wife, and she said, "Yes!" and he said, "These are from Willie, and he's okay. Don't worry, he's alive." That was about 1947.

Willie Schmelter returned to Berlin from a Soviet prison camp on December 21, 1949.

The Berlin East Branch was one of the largest and strongest in the East German Mission in 1939 and would prove itself to be equally

Fig. 13. *A street scene from central Berlin at the end of the war.* (H. Kupitz)

robust in the first few years following the end of the war.

In Memoriam

The following members of the Berlin East Branch did not survive World War II:

Alma Gonitzke ——— b. circa 1905; m. Hugo Ernst Gonitzke, 1 child; k. air raid Berlin, Preußen 1945 (R. Seehagen; FHL Microfilm 25775, 1935 Census; IGI)

Hedwig Auguste Wilhelmine Dittrich b. Charlottenburg, Berlin, Brandenburg, Preußen 20 May 1866; dau. of Valentin Dittrich and Auguste Wilhelmine Ullricke Krohne; bp. 15 Jul 1931; m. Berlin, Brandenburg, Preußen 25 Apr 1893, Karl Friedrich Wilhelm Mueller; 2 children; k. air raid Berlin 15 Mar 1945 (CHL Microfilm no. 2458, form 42 FP, pt. 37, 726–27; IGI)

Gonitzke b. Berlin, Preußen abt 1941; son of Hugo Gonitzke and Alma ———; d. illness Berlin 1943 (R. Seehagen)

Emmi Bertha W. Heise b. Ziebuehl, Guestrow, Mecklenberg-Schwerin 18 Sep 1878; dau. of Heinrich Friedrich Heise and Wilhelmine Ottilie Brodowski; bp. 24 Jan 1924; m. Kirchgrubenhagen, Guestrow, Mecklenberg-Schwerin 26 Oct 1900, Heinrich Kempa; 3 children; d. Berlin, Preußen 13 Dec 1943 (LDS Census)

Friedrich Jordan b. Spitzen, Ostpreußen, Preußen 2 Nov 1867; son of Jakob Nitschmann and Anna Jordan; bp. 24 Sep 1930; ord. teacher; m. Liebstadt, Ostpreußen, Preußen 14 Jun 1892, Bertha Grolms; 10 children; d. Berlin, Preußen 5 Nov 1942 (IGI)

Hans Gerhardt Klettke b. Posen, Posen, Preußen 8 Sep 1918; son of Edmund Ludwig Klettke and Salomea Antkowiak; bp. 11 Dec 1926; m. Berlin, Preußen 12 Jul 1942; noncommissioned officer; d. 2 km NW of Heilsberg, Ostpreußen, Preußen 4 Feb 1945 (A. Langheinrich; FHL Microfilm 271380; IGI; www.volksbund.de)

Paul Karl Lehmann b. Berlin, Preußen 7 Feb 1895; son of Karl Lehmann and Marie Zimmermann; d. May 1945 (CHL CR 375 8 #2458, 726–27)

Wilhelm Heinrich Meister b. Herzogswalde, Brandenburg, Preußen 7 Nov 1862, son of Johann Wilhelm Meister and Karoline Wilhelmine Jahn; bp. 26 May 1909; m. 1891 Berlin, Brandenburg, Preußen, Minna Helene Anna Korth; 2m. Sep 1923 Berlin, Auguste Pauline Bertha Hoffmann; d. 5 Oct 1941 (FHL Microfilm no. 245231 1930/1935 Census; IGI)

Johann Anton Metzeltin b. Berlin, Brandenburg, Preußen 27 Nov 1889; m. Emma Marie Hiszbach; bur. 25 May 1941 (FHL Microfilm no. 245232 1930/1935 Census)

Moritz Heinrich Eduard Noeske b. Schivelbein, Pommern, Preußen 4 Dec 1888; son of Gustav Reinhold Noeske and Ida Hulda Maria Elise Klatt; bp. 16 Aug 1924; m. Berlin, Brandenburg, Preußen 1913, Auguste Emilie Diebel; d. 22 Apr 1945 (IGI)

Else Albertine Rosalie Utech b. Stettin, Pommern, Preußen 14 Dec 1891; dau. of Wilhelm Karl Heinrich Utech and Caroline Christine Albertine Friederike Kuehl; bp. 19 Aug 1922; m. Köpenick, Berlin, Brandenburg, Preußen 5 Dec 1914, Paul Karl Wilhelm Meyer; d. 30 Apr 1945 (IGI)

Johanna Maria Louise Utech b. Stettin, Pommern, Preußen 19 Dec 1895; dau. of Wilhelm Karl Heinrich Utech and Caroline Christine Albertine Friederike Kuehl; bp. 12 Mar 1923; k. by Soviets 30 Apr 1945 (IGI; Waltraud Meyer Dierking)

Richard Heinrich Wilhelm Utech b. Stettin, Pommern, Preußen 18 Sep 1901; dau. of Wilhelm Karl Heinrich Utech and Caroline Christine Albertine Friederike Kuehl; m. 22 May 1926, Frieda Emma Martha Borosch; 1 child; d. Berlin, Preußen 1 Mar 1944 (IGI)

Wilhelm Heinrich Karl Utech b. Görcke, Pommern, Preußen 10 Jan 1863; son of Carl Friedrich Anton Utech and Johanna Maria Luise Miller; bp. 19 Sep 1925; ord. elder; m. 16 Oct 1891, Caroline Christine Albertine Friederike Kuehl; 6 children; d. Köpenick, Berlin, Preußen 13 Sep 1939 (*Stern*, no. 19, 1 Oct 1939, 307; IGI)

Karl August Winkler b. Berlin, Brandenburg, Preußen 19 Nov 1908; son of Heinrich Winkler and Wilhelmine Danowski; bp. 11 Jul 1924; conf. 11 Jul 1924; ord. deacon 3 Jun 1934; ord. teacher 10 Nov 1935; m. 28 May 1938, Luise Cäcilie Emma Böttcher; 2 children; d. Ewlanowo, Eastern Front 30 Jan 1943

(FHL Microfilm 68809, no. 88; IGI; Standesamt Berlin-Wedding #3461)

Erich Hermann August Zoschke b. Berlin, Brandenburg, Preußen 31 Aug 1914; son of Hermann Bernhard Carl Zoschke and Maria Ernestine Ligowski; bp. 30 Jun 1923; m. Sweden 28 Feb 1941, Maerta Alfrida Kristina Karlsson; corporal; MIA Stalingrad 1 Jan 1943; declared dead 31 July 1949 (Arndt; IGI; www.volksbund.de)

NOTES

1. Heinz Kupitz, interview by the author, Salt Lake City, March 17, 2006.
2. Hans Joachim Arndt, interview by the author, Sandy, Utah, August 25, 2006.
3. Presiding Bishopric, "Financial, Statistical, and Historical Reports of Wards, Stakes, and Missions, 1884–1955," CR 4 12, 257.
4. Luise Böttcher Winkler Sy, interview by the author in German, Leipzig, Germany, June 2, 2007; summarized in English by Judith Sartowski.
5. Gerhard Kupitz, interview by the author, Taylorsville, Utah, March 3, 2006.
6. Annamarie Fischer Moritz, telephone interview with Jennifer Heckmann, May 7, 2008; unless otherwise noted, audio version or transcript of the interview in the author's collection.
7. Charlotte Baade Fischer, autobiography (unpublished), 7; private collection; trans. Hans Fischer. November 9, 1938, was actually a Wednesday, but the broken glass was likely still there the following Sunday.
8. Hans Max Boettcher, autobiography (unpublished); private collection.
9. Karl Vielstich, letter to his family; private collection.
10. Christa Schmelter Spilker, interview by the author, Salt Lake City, February 9, 2007.
11. His hero in the matter of nonaggressive behavior was Jacob Hamblin, a Mormon pioneer and settler of Santa Clara, Utah.
12. Those letters are in the possession of his daughter, Evelin Radeke McMillan, who shared them with the author.
13. Angela Patermann Buchta, interview by the author, Salt Lake City, August 9, 2007.
14. Charlotte Baade Fischer, autobiography, 8.
15. Hans Fischer, interview by the author, Midway, Utah, March 26, 2006.
16. Günter Buchta, interview by the author, Salt Lake City, August 9, 2007. He still has the button as well as a piece of shrapnel taken from his back on a different occasion.
17. Renate Winkler Heidler, interview by the author in German, Leipzig, Germany, June 2, 2007; summarized in English by Judith Sartowski.
18. Charlotte Baade Fischer, autobiography, 10.
19. Jared Fischer, telephone interview with the author, April 11, 2006.

20. Wolfgang Kelm, autobiography (unpublished), 15. The account of Angela Patermann (above) regarding the destruction of the Thaerstrasse rooms is likely more correct in its date, namely, 1944.

21. Paul Radeke, report; private collection.

22. Wolgang Kelm, interview by the author, Hurricane, Utah, October 9, 2006.

23. Wolfgang Kelm, autobiography, 15. See also the account of the baptism in the Berlin Center Branch chapter.

24. Charlotte Baade Fischer, autobiography, 11–12.

25. Lothar Vielstich, interview by the author, Salt Lake City, July 12, 2007.

26. Wolfgang Kelm, autobiography, 15.

27. Soviet soldiers often interpreted any uniform with a swastika as being associated with the German military. Thus, many of the Hitler Youth were killed or made prisoners of war.

28. Wolfgang Kelm, autobiography, 18.

29. Ibid., 18–19.

BERLIN MOABIT BRANCH

The Moabit neighborhood of Berlin is located approximately one and a half miles north of the Tiergarten Park, or two and a half miles northwest of the city's center. Church meetings were held at Birkenstrasse 53, in the Hinterhaus.[1] According to Armin Langheinrich (born 1926), there was a large meeting room upstairs that included a stage and an organ. "There was a bakery below, and the aroma was wonderful," he recalled.[2]

Berlin Moabit Branch[3]	1939
Elders	14
Priests	9
Teachers	11
Deacons	13
Other Adult Males	40
Adult Females	158
Male Children	11
Female Children	8
Total	264

Moabit Branch member Wilhelm Werner (born 1916) was in uniform well before the war began. He served in the Reichsarbeitsdienst for seven months of 1938 then was drafted into the Wehrmacht. As a member of a reconnaissance battalion, he was one of the first German soldiers to cross the border into Czechoslovakia during one of Hitler's infamous "bloodless conquests." As Wilhelm later wrote:

> The occupation of Czechoslovakia was uneventful. . . . My unit drove over the border [from Silesia] and moved without hindrance to the territory that we were assigned to take. . . . We were in Czechoslovakia for about 6 to 8 weeks. In no time we were back in Potsdam [by Berlin] where we were treated like kings and people welcomed us with flowers and parades.[4]

On September 3, 1939, Wilhelm's unit moved from Silesia into Poland. Within a month, Germany's war against Poland was successfully concluded, and Wilhelm was back in Berlin.

Shortly after the war started in 1939, the Moabit Branch moved into rooms at Boyenstrasse 8. Sigurd Sadowski (born 1934) remembered that in order to get to the meeting rooms, branch members had to go through one building and past one inner courtyard to a Hinterhaus that had previously been an automobile repair shop. The first rooms were a foyer, a cloakroom, and restrooms, and then came a large meeting room with seats for perhaps ninety persons. Pictures of Jesus Christ, Joseph Smith, and the Salt Lake Temple were the principal decor in the meeting hall.[5] The corner of the room was later damaged by a bomb, but Church meetings were held there all through the war.

"The war started on my birthday. I was thirteen," recalled Armin Langheinrich. He had been in the Jungvolk since he was ten. "We learned Hitler's biography. . . . Sometimes we had to rattle [the details] off. Then we learned things similar to Boy Scouts and made knots and things. "We had bicycle tours in the nearby forest." He later became the treasurer for his Jungvolk group. He did not recall receiving any kind of military training nor missing any church meetings due to Hitler Youth activities.

Armin did not begin to learn a trade at age fourteen but instead passed challenging academic examinations and was admitted to a secondary school in 1941. His school was located only ten minutes from the mission home at Händelallee 6, so after school he often went there to help with office duties. One of his favorite tasks was to collate pages of instruction manuals. "We laid out the sheets we had printed on ditto machines . . . around the table and over couches, and then marched around putting the pages in order." His father, Paul Langheinrich, was the second counselor to mission supervisor Herbert Klopfer.

Albert Sadowski moved with his family from Dresden to Berlin Moabit in 1939, where he became branch president. The family lived

in an apartment at Schwarzkopfstrasse 3, about twenty minutes walking time from church. In 1940, Albert was drafted into the air force but was released again after eighteen months because he had a work assignment in a critical war industry. The factory was secret and located underground.[6]

Early in the war, Sigurd Sadowski's school was destroyed in an air raid. As usual, the children had all been sent home when the sirens began to wail, so nobody was in the school at the time. Sigurd later wrote:

> For the schoolchildren this was both a moment of tremendous sadness and reserved joy. We were terrified that all of us could have been in the classroom when it was destroyed. On the other hand, it is a very effective way to legitimately miss a few days of school.[7]

In September 1942, at the age of eight years, Sigurd was baptized a member of the Church. "I vividly remember my baptism," he recalled. "It occurred on a cold rainy day. The

Fig. 1. Berlin's parade avenue, Unter den Linden, decked out for the 1936 Olympic Games. (H. Kupitz)

water was warmer than the outside air. The actual baptism took place in a lake outside of Berlin. My father baptized me and Brother Garland confirmed me."[8]

During the invasion of France in the spring of 1940, Wilhelm Werner again saw action—this time it was too close for comfort when his communications unit came under fire from French artillery. He quickly crawled underneath a vehicle and later recalled what happened:

> I could see and hear shells exploding around us. Then I felt a heavy thump, and all courage left me. Hot water and gasoline began raining down on me. In no time I was lying in a puddle. I rolled out from under the vehicle to see what had happened and found it in flames. Everything we possessed was burning, including my triple combination of scriptures. People said that a guardian angel was with me. . . . I know that the preserving care of God was exercised.[9]

During the summer and early fall of 1941, Wilhelm Werner's tour of duty took him through several southeastern nations: Yugoslavia, Bulgaria, Romania, and Greece. He enjoyed easy times and good companions, but then life became challenging again. Germany had invaded Russia in June, and Wilhelm's unit was sent first back to Potsdam, then to the Soviet Union, where they arrived in time for the harsh winter of 1941–42.[10]

Kurt Lehnardt, his wife, Mathilde, and their young children (four boys and a girl by 1943) made their way to Boyenstrasse 8 from the distant northern suburb of Buch. They began the trip at seven o'clock in the morning, in order to be punctual for Sunday School at ten. One of the sons, Rüdiger, remembers how his father made many visits to members who were frequently absent from the meetings—perhaps as many as thirty members each month.[11]

Mathilde Lehnardt was the mother of infants all through the war. What was a difficult time for anybody in Berlin was especially challenging for her as she tried to keep her children safe and healthy—often in the absence of her husband, who managed a power plant near their home. On May 7, 1941, their fourth son, Detlef, was born in the Moabit Hospital. At the time, air raids over Berlin were common, and just one day after Mathilde brought her infant son home, the maternity wing of the hospital that they had just left was destroyed by bombs.[12]

Even very little children knew the procedures to follow when the air raids over Germany's capital city became so frequent that a night without one seemed too good to be true. According to Rüdiger Lehnardt,

> When we went to bed, after us five children undressed, we had to fold up our clothes and put them on the piano: five little piles of clothes and shoes. Mother would slap us awake in the middle of the night when the sirens came, when

Fig. 3. Wilhelm Werner (third from left) enjoyed his short stay in Greece in 1941. (W. Werner)

65

bombers came, and then we'd have to run, put on our clothes, and line up with our shoes; we didn't know how to tie our shoes since we were too little. So, my mother would tie our shoes for us. My dad had made a box, kind of like a serving tray with handles on it for my little sister, who was only a six-month-old baby, and so it was kind of like a baby bed that could be carried. My mom and dad would carry that. We all had our gas masks and a little backpack. Then it was always, "Hurry, hurry, hurry! The bombers are coming!" So we would run down the stairs.

On several occasions, the family emerged from a bomb shelter to see buildings burning and collapsing in the immediate vicinity.

Although the Langheinrich family's apartment on Rathenowerstrasse was not damaged, Maria Langheinrich remembered some problems: "Sometimes, when we came back to the apartment after an air raid, we found that the stovepipe in the kitchen had been knocked loose [by air shock waves] and there was soot all over the kitchen. It was terrible to clean up. That happened several times."[13]

Armin Langheinrich's schooling was interrupted by service to his country. His entire class of schoolboys was drafted as air force assistants and assigned to operate antiaircraft batteries at Humboldthain in north-central Berlin—one of the city's three huge flak towers. The boys manned the light antiaircraft guns at the lower turrets.[14] Armin recalled,

"I saw [the Americans] coming, two thousand airplanes up there!" Regarding the conditions at Humboldthain, he explained:

We had to live in those towers with the regular air force personnel, the antiaircraft people . . . and in the morning the teacher came. When it was summer, we would sit out on the grass outside for class. And sometimes we hoped for the air raid, so we could get out of class. . . . You know how young people are, we were stupid.

On May 28, 1943, Paul Langheinrich's daughter, Maria, married soldier Erhard Wagner of the Annaberg-Buchholz Branch (Chemnitz District). They were first married officially in the city hall of Annaberg-Buchholz. As part of the ceremony, the mayor formally presented them the standard gift from the government—a copy of Adolf Hitler's book *Mein Kampf*.[15] Then the couple went to the Moabit Branch meeting rooms where Friedrich Fischer, the president of the Berlin District, presided over a Church wedding ceremony. Because Erhard had only enough furlough for the wedding, there was no honeymoon at the time. He returned to his unit in France while she went to her father's home in Berlin. They would not be together again until he visited her in Berlin at Christmastime that year.

In the Soviet Union, Wilhelm Werner was in and out of combat situations for several years. As he would later write, "It seemed my fate to

Fig. 4. The Lehnardt family in Buch in October 1944 (from left): Kurt, Heidi, Mathilde, Everhard, Fritz, Rüdiger, and Detlef. All survived the war in good condition. (R. Lehnardt)

Fig. 5. Armin Langheinrich took this photograph of his classmates at their antiaircraft battery in northern Berlin. (A. Langheinrich)

be present when good comrades were either wounded or killed." On one occasion, his favorite lieutenant was hit in the abdomen by a large piece of shrapnel. The wound was severe, and there was nothing the soldiers could do to help the man: "That day I lost a good friend. His death cut deep into my soul. A young, promising life was lost, and we were all helpless." Shortly thereafter, Wilhelm was wounded when a small piece of shrapnel penetrated his left thigh. "After a tetanus shot and a few days behind the lines for rest, I was back at full duty."[16]

One of the saddest days for the Moabit Branch involved the Werner family. At the Eastern Front, Wilhelm Werner received a numbing telegram on December 26, 1943: "Mother, Ingeborg, Franziska killed by bombs. Come home. Father." All members of the Church, Wilhelm's mother and his two sisters (both recently married) had died of asphyxiation in an air-raid shelter. Wilhelm was allowed to return home to attend the funeral that had been delayed by the fact that the bodies of so many air-raid victims awaited burial. A huge entourage of 400–500 members of the Church in the Berlin District attended the service. Following the funeral, Wilhelm returned to the Eastern Front. However, four months later, he was sent home to recover from depression. The war was beginning to take its toll on him.[17]

At home on Rathenowerstrasse, Maria Langheinrich Wagner remembered how her father, Paul Langheinrich, kept constant vigil during air raids. He stayed in the attic in order to locate and neutralize incendiary bombs as fast as they landed. From the roof, he threw them down to the street. In the attic, where some bombs had penetrated the roof, he dunked them into buckets of water or buried them in sand. According to Maria, he was the neighborhood hero.

By the summer of 1944, Maria Langheinrich Wagner was expecting her first child.

The government and her parents encouraged her to move to her husband's hometown of Annaberg, far from the dangers of Berlin. She found an apartment on Wohlsteingasse, and her son was born there that summer. They were fortunate to stay in that apartment for the remainder of the war.

In 1944, Armin Langheinrich was eighteen years of age and was drafted into an armored unit. He learned Morse code to communicate with tank crews. During the confusion of the last few months of the war, he and other recruits were constantly shifted from place to place. From Guben on the Neisse River, he was sent to the Eastern Front in January 1945. Then they moved west to Zwickau in Saxony, then north to Magdeburg near Berlin. The next move found them on the Western Front near Belgium; then they moved back into Germany to the town of Selters. Having been promised weapons with which to fight the invading Allies, they moved north to Hamburg, Rendsburg, and finally to Denmark for a week. The promised weapons were never supplied.

In December 1943, the Lehnardt family of Buch awaited their fifth child. Mathilde later wrote of her emotions at the time:

> At first I didn't like [being pregnant] at all. Four children and the war. We as members of The Church of Jesus Christ of Latter-day Saints believe that the spirits are waiting to be born on the earth. We shared the opportunity to experience earth life to as many spirits as possible. It wasn't easy, but this belief strengthened me, and I awaited the baby's arrival eagerly. . . . When the nurses told me that it was a girl, I could hardly believe it.[18]

In February 1944, Kurt Lehnardt sent his wife and their five children east to Kreuz to escape the danger of air raids over Berlin. Mathilde and her five children arrived there after a long railroad journey and were greeted by several members of the Church. When

Fig. 6. Armin Langheinrich in the uniform of a Flakhelfer (assistant antiaircraft gunner) during the winter of 1943–44. (A. Langheinrich)

local authorities tried to send her to a farm family out of town, she resisted, wishing to stay in town and attend church in the Kreuz Branch. Fortunately, branch president Arnold Schmidt came to her aid and insisted that she be given quarters in Kreuz. She and her children stayed there for six months.[19]

As a boy in Berlin, young Sigurd Sadowski was well aware of the possibility of dying in an air raid. On one occasion, an incendiary bomb penetrated the roof and the ceiling of the family apartment, landing on their sofa. The timer had not yet set off the fuse, so his father quickly grabbed the bomb and threw it out the window. When it ignited in the street, he said, "Well, the angels were watching us tonight."

On several occasions after 1943, the Moabit Branch sacrament meeting was interrupted by air-raid sirens. Once, the branch president offered the benediction and then everybody ran for home or the nearest air-raid shelter. Sigurd Sadowski made it home just in time:

> It took us about ten minutes, running with fear in our minds and hearts, before we arrived home. We lived on the fourth floor of an apartment house. I had reached the second floor when a bomb exploded just outside our apartment house. The impact threw me and my brother Udo down half a flight of stairs and we both crashed into a wall. Wood splinters, glass, plaster, and dust were flying all around us.[20]

Mathilde Lehnardt did not wish to make the long journey from Buch to church on Sunday without her husband, but he was usually assigned a weekend shift at the power plant, and she had to go alone. On one Sunday in 1944, a massive air raid occurred, and she wondered how to get her five children home in safety. Along their way, they saw that homes were burning and the commuter railroad station had been destroyed. Walking several miles farther than usual, the Lehnardts reached the Pankow railroad station and were able to ride a few miles to Buch. "My sweet children were so good," Mathilde wrote. "No one cried, even though they were hungry and tired." Following that harrowing experience, Sister Lehnardt held Sunday School with her children at home.[21]

On July 20, 1944, Adolf Hitler narrowly escaped an assassination attempt when a bomb was placed in his conference room at Rastenburg, East Prussia. All over Germany, the news gave rise to either outrage or (premature) celebration. Wilhelm Werner wrote about that event: "August [July] 20, 1944, an attempt was made to kill Hitler. We were jubilant, celebrating because he was dead." Wilhelm also recalled how the jubilation subsided when it was learned that the Führer had survived the assassination attempt.[22]

Renate Berger (born 1930) and her mother from Königsberg, East Prussia, arrived in the Langheinrich home on January 28, 1945. Renate's father, Theodor Berger, had sent them

Fig. 7. The remains of the huge antiaircraft tower at Humboldhain in Berlin as they appeared in 2008.

to Berlin, while he was required to remain and defend Königsberg. The LDS colony at Rathenowerstrasse 52 continued to grow over the next three months, and it is clear from eye-witness statements that a wonderful spirit of co-operation and charity prevailed in the building, despite the fact that Germany's downfall was a foregone conclusion and death a real possibility.[23]

In the last year of the war, the Sadowski family dealt with extraordinary challenges, as described by son Sigurd:

> Four months before the war ended, my father deserted [the mine] position. He returned home, where he remained always on the lookout, antici-pating that he would be a target of the *Gestapo* [secret police]. He was always on the move to avoid detection—on flat roofs, in chimneys, at-tics, basements, and storage areas. It seemed to me that he received divine protection.[24]

Fortunately for Albert Sadowski's wife, Ericka, she and her children had at least spo-radic assistance from Albert as the Red Army approached, attacked, and conquered Berlin.

Somehow, Brother Sadowski found a way to serve in the Moabit Branch presidency while hiding from the police during the last months of the war. He was in great danger because fanatical Nazis were executing deserters and defeatists in broad daylight in an attempt to inspire the German populace to greater resis-tance against the invading Allied armies.

Sigurd Sadowski was ten in April 1945 when the street fighting in Berlin reached his neighborhood. One day, he was standing in the entry hall of their apartment building and witnessed an unforgettable event that was both horrible and comical:

> A German soldier made a desperate dash across the street to enter our main hallway. He man-aged to make it inside our hallway, then in-stantly fell dead right next to where I was stand-ing. As I carefully looked around the corner from our entrance, I saw a smiley-faced Russian giving me the "OK" sign. His "OK" signal to

me was his way of communicating that he knew he had shot and killed this German soldier who had died right at my feet. This Russian soldier was a sharpshooter.[25]

The frightful sight and smell of corpses during and after the Battle of Berlin were com-monplace in the memory of Sigurd Sadowski. Despite his youth, he was involved in the grue-some task of burying soldiers and civilians who had lain dead for days. His father was still hid-ing from the Soviets in order to avoid being taken prisoner; he only emerged now and then to help protect the women and feed families in the neighborhood. It was a daunting task.

In the apartment house at Rathenower-strasse 52, Paul Langheinrich (functioning at the time as the first counselor in the mission leadership) had invited Latter-day Saint refu-gees to live in the apartments of those who had fled the city. By the end of the war, approxi-mately thirty Saints lived in what was essen-tially a Church dormitory. The building also housed the East German Mission office, several sister missionaries, and the family of the mis-sion leader, Richard Ranglack. As the war came closer to his house, Brother Langheinrich be-came a local hero to the Saints by gathering food from many different and unexpected sources.[26] The Saints remained in that building until they located other housing in the summer of 1945.

In Rendsburg in northern Germany, Armin Langheinrich and his comrades were informed in early May that Hitler was dead.[27] They were instructed to immediately revert to the stan-dard military salute rather than the Hitler sa-lute they had been using ("We hated the Hitler salute," he explained).[28] Then they were trans-ferred to the naval center in Kiel on the Baltic Sea. Eventually Armin ended up as a prisoner of war under the British but was released to-ward the end of the summer of 1945. By means of creative transportation, he returned home by his birthday in September to parents who had no idea if he was even alive. Armin Langheinrich was blessed to see less combat as a soldier on two fronts than he had seen as a flak gunner at home in Berlin.

On April 20, 1945, the Lehnardt family accepted Paul Langheinrich's invitation to move into the LDS refugee colony at Rathenowerstrasse 52. They made their way downtown and were received warmly. The next day, Kurt went home, planning to bring more of their clothing to the Rathenowerstrasse. However, when he arrived home, the Red Army was already there; the enemy soldiers detained him, and he did not see his family again for a week.[29]

Rüdiger Lehnardt first saw an enemy soldier from a window in that building. He later said this about the incessant bombings in the last ten days of the war, "It's a complete miracle—I feel very blessed not to have been killed during those last days of the war."

The last Sunday meeting of the Moabit Branch before the war ended took place on April 22, 1945. Helga Meiszus Birth, a member of the Tilsit Branch serving as a missionary since October 1944, recorded the following in her diary:

> Nobody was certain if there would be church meetings today. I got dressed and headed for the North [Moabit] Branch. It was raining very hard on us as we walked. The terrifying noise of the flak accompanied us to church. Nobody was there except for Brother Ranglack, Brother Langheinrich, Brother Newer, two sisters, and me. For the first time ever, our meeting began late because we waited for more members to arrive. Werner [Ranglack] came and had to substitute as the organist. Even though we were few in number, the spirit was strong. "Where two or three of you are gathered in my name, I will be with you."[30]

On Friday, April 27, 1945, Renate Berger began a diary. Years later, she explained why she did so:

> My mother made me write a journal during the last few days of the war. There was nothing for us to do but to think about the horror that was to come upon us, and pray. We had been through so much and lived with the reality of death for the last 6 years. . . . Now my greatest fear was not dying but falling into the hands of Russian soldiers. So here we were, and the Russians were coming. We prayed. Our fate was in God's hands. I was 17 years old.[31]

What Renate wrote survived and constitutes a monument to the faithfulness of the members of the LDS refugee community at Rathenowerstrasse 52. The following are just a few of the entries she made in her diary from April 27 to May 10, 1945:

> Friday, 27 April: Great anxiety rests over all of us. The brethren suggested to come together in prayer and fasting. We prayed for strength and protection as we face the uncertainty of things to come.
>
> Saturday, 28 April: Helga [Meizsus Birth] and I spotted the first 2 Russian soldiers as we looked out a window. The first ones we saw were Mongols and a frightening sight to behold with guns in their arms and knifes [sic] in their mouths.
>
> Werner Ranglack told me in the afternoon that I would have to give a lesson during Sunday School tomorrow. I did not have much time and had to block out everything around me and focus on studying and preparing.
>
> Sunday, 29 April: Sunday School started at 11:00 A.M. 29 adults and 13 children were in attendance. . . . While we were conducting Sunday School, the city was under air attacks, heavy and frequent with increasing intensity. We could hear the by then familiar sound of falling bombs. . . . The ground would shake with each hit. I cannot believe that we are still alive. Are we destined to survive? . . . Then at 4:00 p.m. it was time to meet again for sacrament meeting. 32 attended.
>
> Monday, 30 April: Angela [Patermann] and I took care of the children today. We prayed with them and kept them busy so they would not focus on what was going on outside. It was not an

easy job. . . . We did not receive daily miracles of loaves and fishes but somehow we always had enough to get by. Today we had all the ingredients to make candy. So that is what we did.

Tuesday, 1 May: We had Relief Society in the afternoon. Marie Ranglack gave the lesson. Now during this time all the shooting and heavy artillery fire had stopped. It was very peaceful when all of a sudden a bomb exploded in the building next to ours. The air pressure was so strong that we were thrown off our chairs. Shell fragments came flying through the windows. It was a miracle that no one was hurt. It took our breath away. Another close call!

Wednesday, 2 May: Could it be? Word spread through the neighborhood that the war has ended. We were at PEACE! . . . We did not feel a jumping up and down kind of joy. . . . Will we see our fathers, husbands, and sons again?[32]

[Late tonight] We were startled when Elsa Langheinrich suddenly opened our door and said: "Children, the Russians are coming!" What now? We quickly dressed. During that time 3 Russians were already in the kitchen, and we heard them going from room to room. . . . [There was no room under the bed.] So we crawled into bed and covered ourselves with a big feather bed and then we waited. . . . Then the door opened and we heard steps coming to our bed. We were sweating "blood and water"; then someone lifted the feather bed. We were horrified. When I opened my eyes I saw Brother Patermann standing there. What a joy it was to see his smiling face. . . . We said a prayer of thanks before we went to sleep.

Thursday, 3 May: Helga and I were proofreading genealogical records. We did not accomplish much, just acted silly and giggled all afternoon and consumed at least 1 pound of candy. It was good to be able to laugh again.

On May 11, Mathilde Lehnardt and her five children made the trek from the Langheinrich apartment building back home to their northern suburb of Buch. It was a walk of about six miles that they accomplished in five hours, including an adventuresome crossing of the extensively damaged Fenn Street bridge. Their

home had been taken over by Russian soldiers, so Kurt had to put his family up in an abandoned apartment for a few weeks. However, the war was over, and the Lehnardt family had survived it intact.[33] According to son Detlef, "Our home had been only slightly damaged when an incendiary bomb plummeted through the roof into the apartment. Fortunately, neighbors were able to quickly break down the door and throw the bomb out of the window before a fire could break out."[34]

Moabit Branch members gathered from their hiding places in the basements of bombed-out buildings as well as from various parts of the continent. The Saints who had survived the ordeal gave credit to God for their deliverance. Although the war had taken many victims from among the membership of the branch, the survivors looked forward to better times.

One day after Germany surrendered and the war officially ended, Wilhelm Werner became a prisoner of war of the Soviets. His unit had survived until the end, mainly because the invaders bypassed his position on the coast of the Baltic Sea as they moved quickly toward the Reich capital. Over the next few months, Wilhelm's captors moved him around East Prussia and finally to a POW camp near Moscow, Russia. It was difficult to become accustomed to life in such a camp, where survival was the primary concern and all of the comforts of life appeared to have been carefully removed. Regarding conditions in the camp lavatory, for example, he wrote the following description years later:

Into the seating platform there were about twenty-five round holes to accommodate nature. These were small enough that we couldn't fall in. There were no doors on the side and no roof, allowing snow, ice, rain, wind, and sun heat to invade our facility. Openly exposed derrieres had to adjust to the prevailing climatic conditions. Other sanitary conveniences were hard to come by, or were nonexistent. If there

Fig. 8. By the end of the war, the apartment house at Rathenow-erstrasse 52 housed several refugee LDS families. (J. Larsen, 2007)

was any kind of bashfulness, shame, or humiliation, those feelings were completely suppressed during our confinement.[35]

From 1945 through 1949, Wilhelm Werner lived in various POW camps in central Russia, where he worked constructing buildings and highways. On several occasions, he became seriously ill and remained ill for months on end. One bout of diarrhea tortured him for six months. "There are no words to explain how dreadful my circumstance was. I was loosing [sic] weight and was already as thin as a beanstalk."[36] With minimal medication and care, he somehow survived each illness.

As horrible as Wilhelm's living conditions were in the Russian POW camps, the mental torture was worse, especially after four full years of incarceration. He later described it in these words:

Mental torture was considered worse than the physical tortures. The Russians nurtured mental stress by maintaining a state absent of surety: What am I doing? What's happening? Did [other soldiers who left the camp] go

home? That was the system.[37]

Finally, in November 1949, Wilhelm Werner was released from prison and transported to Germany. Arriving in Berlin on November 13, he underwent a medical examination and was given some money. He also received some canned food with the brand name Deseret.

Fig. 9. Wilhelm Werner as a prisoner of war in Russia in about 1948 (W. Werner)

"That means we were beneficiaries of LDS Church aid for the war refugees of World War II," he concluded. He noted the stark contrast between East Berlin (the Soviet Occupation Zone) and West Berlin (occupied by British, French, and American forces):

In the West, people were building, the lights came on, rubbish was removed, the city cleaned-up, restaurants were open, and movie houses were running. The streets in the East were full of rubbish, and the lights were still out, making the ruined buildings dark and uninviting. There was a very obvious difference between the progress made in rebuilding the West versus the East.[38]

Wilhelm made his way to Spandau, a suburb at the far northwest edge of West Berlin. Turning his back on East Berlin and communism, he found himself a job with the West Berlin police. A new life began for Wilhelm Werner.

In Memoriam

The following members of the Berlin Moabit Branch did not survive World War II:

Karl Hubert Allin b. Friedland, Schlesien, Preußen 6 Sep 1890; son of Joseph Allin and Louise Auguste Wiesner; bp. 6 Jun 1925; d. 1944 (CHL CR 375 8 #2458, 726–27; IGI)

Otto Bauer b. Biskupitz, Posen, Preußen 12 May 1918; son of Philipp Bauer and Luise Wilhelmine

Kuhn; bp. 16 May 1931; conf. 16 May 1931; ord. teacher 6 Sep 1936; ord. priest 4 Dec 1938; m. Berlin, Preußen 10 Mar 1941, Vera Giehr; k. in battle Eastern Front 15 Dec 1941 (FHL Microfilm 68809, no. 3; IGI)

Emilie Ottilie Bengs b. Sandwinkel, Brandenburg, Preußen 28 Jun 1875; dau. of Karl Bengs and Karoline Pfahl; bp. 25 Apr 1925; conf. 26 Apr 1925; m. Berlin, Brandenburg, Preußen 5 Jun 1897, Hermann Heinrich Schadewaldt; 5 children; m. 11 Jan 1938, Heinrich Krüger; d. starvation Berlin 8 or 9 Oct 1945 (FHL Microfilm 68809, no. 42; IGI)

Johanne Elfriede Boenke b. Stettin, Pommern, Preußen 7 Oct 1904; dau of Wilhelm Boenke and Klara Mueller; m. —— Lehmann; 6 children; k. Berlin, Preußen Feb 1945 (CHL Microfilm no. 2458, form 42 FP, Pt. 37, 1949: 1378–79; IGI; FHL Microfilm 271386, 1935 Census)

Theodor Wilhelm Bogda b. Deuswitz (?), Pommern, Preußen 2 Dec 1883; bp. Berlin, Preußen 4 Aug 1921; conf. 4 Aug 1921; ord. teacher 11 Feb 1925; m. Agathe Pikowski (div.); 1 child; d. 20 Jun 1941 (FHL Microfilm 68809, no. 107; FHL Microfilm 25726, 1930 Census; IGI)

Kurt Franz Botz b. Berlin, Preußen 18 Sep 1930; son of Erwin Botz and Elise Heuer; bp. 17 Sep 1938; conf. 17 Sep 1938; d. wounds 8 Jul 1945 (FHL Microfilm 68809, no. 7; IGI)

Wilhelmine Danowski b. Rudwangen, Sensburg, Ostpreußen, Preußen 28 May 1871; dau. of Luise Danowski; bp. 21 Apr 1933; conf. 21 Apr 1933; m. Berlin, Brandenburg, Preußen 22 Apr 1898, Heinrich Winkler; m. 12 Jun 1919, Johann Wieczorek; d. heart attack 5 Nov 1942 (FHL Microfilm 68809, book 2, no. 143; IGI)

Käthe Dorothea Emma Dühnisch b. Heidelberg, Baden 6 Feb 1874; dau. of Wilhelm Dühnisch and Dorothea Übe; bp. 1 Oct 1926; conf. 1 Oct 1926; m. 4 Feb 1894, Philipp Klein; d. 1942 (FHL Microfilm 68809, no. 108; IGI)

Erika Liselotte Durlach b. Berlin, Brandenburg, Preußen 15 Sep 1919; missing as of 1943 (CHL Microfilm no. 2458, form 42 FP, pt. 37, 730; FHL Microfilm 25758, 1935 Census)

Helene Meta Eglinski b. Torgelow, Pommern, Preußen 24 Oct 1885; dau. of Luis Ferdinand Eglinski and Louise Graubaum; bp. 20 Oct 1914; conf. 20 Oct 1914; d. 24 Jul 1940 (FHL Microfilm 68809, Book 1 no. 47, book 2, no. 24; IGI)

Johanna Pauline Fischer b. Bernstadt, Namslau, Schlesien, Preußen 11 Apr 1860; dau. of Johann Gottlieb Fischer and Anna Rosina Stolper; bp. 28 Aug 1925; conf. 28 Aug 1925; m. Breslau, Schlesien, Preußen 24 Nov 1891, Anton Domina; 3 children; d. Berlin, Preußen 9 Mar 1942 (FHL Microfilm 68809, no. 120; IGI)

Johann Heinrich Galand b. Langmichel, Gerdauen, Ostpreußen, Preußen 13 Jun 1888; son of Friedrich Johann Galand and Karoline Dreske; bp. 9 May 1936; conf. 9 May 1936; ord. deacon 20 Dec 1936; ord. teacher 6 Feb 1938; ord. priest 11 Sep 1938; ord. elder 5 Oct 1940; m. Berlin, Brandenburg, Preußen 2 Aug 1914, Helene Wilhelmine Kontusch; 1 child; m. 24 Oct 1925, Luise Auguste Wilhelmine Hübner; private; d. wounds Ellcom, Rheden, Gelderland, Netherlands 26 or 27 Mar 1945; bur. Ysselsteyn, Netherlands (FHL Microfilm 68809, no. 102; IGI; www.volksbund.de)

Otto Karl August Gennrich b. Tempelburg, Preußen 17 Mar 1886; son of Gustav Gennrich and Wilhelmine Schwiede; d. 1944 (CHL CR 375 8 #2458, 726–727)

Paul Greth b. Elbing, Westpreußen, Preußen 19 Apr 1917; son of Otto Greth and Elly Mewes; bp. 1 Feb 1936; conf. 2 Feb 1936; d. wounds Russia 1941 (FHL Microfilm 68809, book 2, no. 39; IGI)

Alfred Erich Emil Gretzbach b. Berlin, Brandenburg, Preußen 14 Mar 1888; son of Erdmann Gretzbach and Marie Lier; m. 11 May 1921; k. in battle (CHL Microfilm no. 2458, form 42 FP, pt. 37, 726–27; IGI)

Emil Paul Karl Jaekel b. 21 Feb 1909; son of Clara Luise ——; MIA as of 1948 (CHL Microfilm no. 2458, form 42 FP, pt. 37, p. 730; FHL Microfilm 271365, 1935 Census)

Paul Fritz Jaenicke b. Berlin, Preußen 8 Jul 1914; son of Paul Jaenicke and Wilhelmine Ebert; d. lung ailment 1945 (CHL CR 375 8 #2458, 726–727)

Werner Konrad Günther Kelm b. Görke, Pommern, Preußen 20 Apr 1908; son of Reinhold Kelm and Dora Rossmann; k. in battle 14 Oct 1941 (CHL Microfilm no. 2458, form 42 FP, pt. 37, 726–27; IGI)

Gertrud Kniepert b. 1920 (calculated); missing 1945 (CHL Microfilm no. 2458, form 42 FP, pt. 37, 730; IGI)

Hans Jürgen Kochan b. 18 Aug 1924; son of Willi Kochan and Auguste Bertha Mai; MIA Bjelgorod, Russia 1 Jan 1942 (CHL Microfilm no. 2458, form 42 FP, pt. 37, 730; FHL Microfilm 271380, 1935 Census; www.volksbund.de)

Heinrich Ludwig Herrmann Wilhelm Krüger b. Teterow Mecklenburg 19 May 1865; son of Heinrich Krüger and Johanna Friederike Kruse; bp. 17 Sep 1938; conf. 17 Sep 1938; ord. deacon 3 Sep 1939; ord. teacher 4 Aug 1940; m. 11 Jan 1938, Emilie Pfahl; d. brain disease 2 May 1944 (FHL Microfilm 68809, no. 41; IGI)

Edith Elfriede Elsa Löchel b. Berlin, Brandenburg, Preußen 17 Aug 1915; dau. of Willi Meissner and

Emma Löchel; bp. 29 Apr 1930; conf. 29 Apr 1930; d. lung ailment 11 Nov 1941 (FHL Microfilm 68809, book 1, no. 146, book 2, no. 84; IGI)

Emilie Auguste Ottilie Lueck b. Jägersdorf, Germany 3 Sep 1881; dau. of Gottfried Lueck and Louise Tischler; m. —— Schroeder; d. 2 Apr 1945 (CHL CR 375 8 #2458, 726–727)

Adolf Mosny b. 19 Dec 1895; MIA as of 1948 (CHL Microfilm no. 2458, form 42 FP, Pt. 37, 730; FHL Microfilm 245238, 1930/35 Census)

Rudolf Hermann Fritz Müller b. Berlin, randen-burg, Preußen 8 May 1899; son of Anton Hermann Waldemar Müller and Anna Marie Auuste Tietz; pb. 26 Mar 1927; conf. 26 Mar 1927; lance corporal; m. Berlin 18 Dec 1925, Agathe Marie Frisch; k. in battle Kgf. Dnjepropetrowsk 15 Dec 1945 (volksbund.de; IGI)

Johanna Anna Elisabeth Neher b. Züllichau, Brandenburg, Preußen 2 Apr 1912; dau. of Friedrich Neher and Emma Zacharias; bp. 8 Sep 1922; conf. 8 Sep 1922; m. 31 May 1933, Hans Schulz (div.); m. 11 Nov 1940, —— Schröder; d. consumption 14 Sep 1941 (FHL Microfilm 68809, book 1, no. 159 and 226, book 2 no. 136; IGI)

Heinz Fritz Johann Neugebauer b. 23 Jan 1916; son of Fritz Hermann Neugebauer and Hedwig Maria Martha Wanke; ord. deacon; MIA Russia 1941 (CHL Microfilm no. 2458, form 42 FP, pt. 37, 730; FHL Microfilm 245241, 1925 Census)

Ingeborg Helene Otto b. Berlin, Preußen 10 Apr 1921; dau. of Hermann Otto and Ernestine Schreiber Werner; bp. 26 Jun 1930; conf. 26 Jun 1930; m. Berlin 14 Jul 1943, Kurt Paul Noeldner; k. air raid Berlin 16 Dec 1943 (FHL Microfilm 68809, book 2, no. 99; W. Werner; IGI)

Margarete Franziska Otto b. Berlin, Preußen 2 May 1923; dau. of Hermann Julius Rudolf Otto and Ernestine Wilhelmine Marie Werner; bp. 25 Jul 1931; conf. 25 Jul 1931; m. Berlin 26 Jun 1943, Friedrich Wilhelm Schiege; k. air raid Berlin 16 Dec 1943 (FHL Microfilm 68809, book 2, no. 100, W. Werner; IGI)

Franz Paszotta b. 11 Dec 1906; son of Johann Paszotta and Agnes Hahn; MIA as of 1948 (CHL Microfilm no. 2458, form 42 FP, pt. 37, 730; FHL Microfilm 245252, 1930 Census)

Walter Hermann Karl Pegelow b. Berlin, Brandenburg, Preußen 7 Aug 1904; son of Hermann Pegelow and Auguste Becker; m. Charlotte Josephine Liebe; k. in battle 25 Apr 1945 (CHL Microfilm no. 2458, form 42 FP, Pt. 37, 726–27; IGI)

Johann Peter Adalbert Pommerering b. Plietnitz, Westpreußen, Preußen 29 Apr 1867; son of Gottlieb Pommerering and Justine Radke; ord. priest; m. Charlottenburg, Brandenburg, Preußen 13 Feb

1897, Eveline Berta Vogel; m. Elise Bertha Eva Vogel Sauermilch; 1 child; k. Apr 1945 (CHL CR 375 8 #2458, 1378–1379; FHL Microfilm 245255, 1930 Census; IGI)

Ida Helene Emilie Popp b. Wobesde, Pommern, Preußen 18 Nov 1865; dau. of Franz Ludwig Popp and Karoline Johanna Dorothea Voss; bp. 20 May 1908, conf. 20 May 1908; m. 19 Mar 1903, Franz Reinhard Benjamin Harder; k. air raid 4 Sep 1943 (FHL Microfilm 68809, book 1, no. 82, book 2, no. 50; IGI)

Wilhelmine Rosalie P. Rozosch b. Oppeln, Schlesien, Preußen 9 Nov 1850; dau. of Joseph Rozosch and Wilhelmine Silodzei; bp. 14 Jul 1921; conf. 14 Jul 1921; m. —— Mirsching; d. old age 21 Jan 1942 (FHL Microfilm 68809, book 2, no. 90; IGI)

Marie Henriette Schippke b. Wohlau, Schlesien, Preußen 17 Apr 1876; dau. of Wilhelm Schippke and Auguste Kindler; bp. 25 May 1913; conf. 25 May 1913; m. —— Adler; d. 30 Mar 1942 (FHL Microfilm 68809, book 2, no. 1; IGI)

Ernestine Wilhelmine Schreiber b. Rankau, Riga, Latvia 6 Aug 1890; dau. of Friedrich Schreiber and Ernestine Wilhelmine Mohr; bp. 21 Jun 1924; conf. 21 Jun 1924; m. Wilhelm Werner; m. 20 Jul 1920, Hermann Julius Rudolf Otto; k. air raid Berlin, Preußen 16 Dec 1943 (FHL Microfilm 68809, book 2, no. 98, W. Werner; IGI)

David M. Joseph Schulz b. Berlin, Brandenburg, Preußen 24 Apr 1892; MIA as of 1948 (CHL Microfilm no. 2458, form 42 FP, Pt. 37, 730; FHL Microfilm 245260, 1935 Census)

Gertrud Margarete Schulz b. Berlin, Brandenburg, Preußen 3 Mar 1892; dau. of Karl Schulz and Ida Lehmann; bp. 30 Oct 1922; conf. 30 Oct 1922; m. Berlin 25 May 1925, Otto Mannek; 1 child; d. Berlin 16 Aug 1942 (FHL Microfilm 68809, book 2, no. 86; IGI)

Wilhelmine Karoline Schulz b. Zurübbchen, Gumbinnen, Ostpreußen, Preußen 25 Feb 1866; dau. of Mathes Schulz and Wilhelmine Zackoet; bp. München, Oberbayern, Bayern 27 May 1907; conf. 27 May 1907; m. 30 Dec 1896, Karl Blonski; d. 1 Jun 1940 (FHL Microfilm 68809, book 2, no. 13; IGI)

Anna Julie Martha Tetzlaff b. Kischefko, Samta, Posen, Preußen 22 Jul 1868; dau. of Michael Tetzlaff and Pauline Orlowska; bp. 26 Jan 1924; conf. 27 Jan 1924; m. Tarnowka, Posen, Preußen 27 Feb 1892, Heinrich Robert Holz; 8 children; d. lung disease Berlin, Preußen 22 Oct 1942 (FHL Microfilm 68809, book 2, no. 59; IGI)

Reinhold Herbert Otto Walter b. 12 Jul 1912; MIA as of 1948 (CHL Microfilm no. 2458, form 42 FP, Pt. 37, 730; FHL Microfilm 245293, 1935 Census)

Ernestine Wilhelmine Marie Werner b. Ramka, Riga, Latvia 6 Aug 1890; dau. of Johann Friedrich Werner and Ernestine Wilhelmine Schreiber; bp. 21 Jun 1924; m. Berlin, Brandenburg, Preußen 20 Jul 1920, Hermann Julius Rudolf Otto; 2 children; k. air raid Berlin 16 Dec 1943 (IGI)

Kaethe Elisabeth Westphal b. Tilsit, Ostpreußen, Preußen 15 Jan 1909; dau. of Friedrich Westphal and Johanne Mansch; m. —— Knobloch; d. liver operation 1941 (CHL CR 375 8 #2458, 726–27)

Notes

1. East German Mission, notes, September 1, 1938, LR 2428 2, Church History Library.
2. Armin Langheinrich, interview by the author, Salt Lake City, December 15, 2006.
3. Presiding Bishopric, "Financial, Statistical, and Historical Reports of Wards, Stakes, and Missions, 1884–1955," CR 4 12, 257.
4. William Werner, *The Trail of a Common Man: William Werner's Story.*
5. Sigurd Sadowski, interview by the author, Sandy, Utah, November 21, 2006.
6. Sigurd Sadowski, autobiography (unpublished), 4; private collection.
7. Ibid., 9.
8. Ibid., 10.
9. Werner, *Trail of a Common Man*, 50.
10. Ibid., 55–59.
11. Rüdiger Lehnardt, interview by Erin C. Collins and Jennifer Heckmann, Orem, Utah, June 9, 2006.
12. Mathilde Petersohn Lehnardt, "My History" (unpublished personal history, 1977), 25–26; private collection.
13. Maria Langheinrich Wagner, interview by the author, Sandy, Utah, April 14, 2006.
14. Allied authorities attempted to destroy the tower in 1947 but failed. It is open for tours today.
15. Germans who married during those years joke that they displayed *Mein Kampf* on the coffee table, but never read it, because it was considered to be a very boring book.
16. Werner, *Trail of a Common Man*, 66, 71.
17. Ibid., 80.
18. Lehnardt, "My History," 27. A family with five children in Germany at the time was by no means a rarity. However, children too young to care for themselves under wartime conditions represented a particular challenge to parents—mothers often cared for their children alone while the fathers were away at war.
19. Lehnardt, "My History," 30–31.
20. Sadowski, autobiography, 15.
21. Lehnardt, "My History," 33.
22. Werner, *Trail of a Common Man*, 81. Claus Graf Schenk von Stauffenberg, a trusted army officer, had placed a briefcase containing a bomb underneath the table in a conference room at the army headquarters near Rastenburg, East Prussia. Somehow Hitler suffered only superficial injuries. Von Stauffenberg and thousands of suspected accomplices were executed for treason during the next few months.
23. Renate Berger Rudolph, "Survival 1945" (unpublished manuscript); private collection.
24. Sadowski, autobiography, 5.
25. Ibid., 20.
26. See the East German Mission chapter.
27. This probably occurred on May 1, the day after Hitler committed suicide in Berlin.
28. The Hitler salute (right arm lifted straight forward and upward, with the palm down) was instituted in the German armed forces following the abortive attempt on Hitler's life at Rastenburg, East Prussia on July 20, 1944. This was a measure designed to promote greater loyalty to Hitler on the part of the soldiers.
29. Lehnardt, "My History," 35–36.
30. Helga Meiszus Birth Meyer, diary (unpublished), 2; private collection; trans. by Renate Berger Rudolph.
31. Renate Berger Rudolph, diary (unpublished); private collection.
32. German military authorities surrendered the city of Berlin on May 2, but the war did not end until May 8.
33. Lehnardt, "My History," 38–39.
34. Detlef Lehnardt, interview by the author, Provo, Utah, April 24, 2008.
35. Werner, *Trail of a Common Man*, 87.
36. Ibid., 91, 96.
37. Ibid., 103.
38. Ibid., 105.

BERLIN NEUKÖLLN BRANCH

The last Sunday of August, as we came out of sacrament meeting, we were met by an unusual sight. Marching down the middle of the street was a group of German soldiers, not in any parade uniform, but in combat clothes, singing as they went. People on both sides of the street went berserk. They waved, threw kisses, laughed, and sang with the soldiers. A current of excitement filled the air, making my own heart pound faster. . . . Everywhere I looked, happy faces beamed—until I looked at my mother. She gathered [my sister] Esther and me close to her, as if trying to protect us from the scene. "Here they are going to war, joyful and laughing. When they come home there will be nothing but misery."[1]

Such was the recollection of Karola Hilbert regarding the beginning of World War II in Berlin. She was nine years old on the Sunday in question—August 27, 1939—the day after the last American missionaries had departed the East German Mission for Copenhagen, Denmark. The Paul and Maria Hilbert family were members of the Berlin Neukölln Branch.

Berlin Neukölln Branch[2]	1939
Elders	10
Priests	3
Teachers	3
Deacons	6
Other Adult Males	9
Adult Females	79
Male Children	2
Female Children	4
Total	116

Paul Hilbert's employment with the government had required that he move his family from Leipzig to Berlin in 1938. He was pleased to be at work again, having spent five years without employment. As an artist working in oil and water colors, he had refused to join the Nazi Party in 1933, declaring boldly, "I have chosen whom I will serve, and his name is not Adolf Hitler but Jesus Christ."[3] Brother Hilbert had been the branch president in Leipzig for five years and the same calling awaited him in 1938 in the Neukölln Branch in Berlin.

The Neukölln suburb of Berlin was about three miles southeast of the center of the city and directly east of the main airport at Tempelhof. The Neukölln Branch territory extended due south and southeast to the edge of the metropolis, as well as through the suburb of Köpenick to the east. The meeting rooms in late 1938 were located at Hasenheide 119 (near Hermannplatz) in the first Hinterhaus. In early 1939, the branch moved to the Thomasstrasse. Karola Hilbert recalled the rooms in detail:

The first apartment house door you went through from the corner. The corner was a music store. At the first apartment house we went into the courtyard, and across from the courtyard, there was a building that was like a music hall. They used it for concerts and stuff, and they taught the students in the music store, but they had all kinds of instruments, and it was just perfect for us. The entrance to it was on the side of the big hall. You went right, and there was a stand big enough to put chairs on it and have a place where they could talk to the people, and then it was [a] long way to go to the back where we had the folding stairs set up. In the very back, as you look at it, to the right side there was a stair going down into two rooms. The first room was used as a classroom and cloakroom. Then in the next room we had the heating arrangements. There was kind of a heating oven that you had to put coal into and add water. It was a kind of radiator.[4]

The average attendance at meetings may have been seventy-five persons. The branch observed the usual meeting schedule, i.e., Sunday School at 10:00 A.M. and sacrament meeting in the evening. Priesthood and auxiliary meetings were held on Tuesday and Thursday evenings.[5]

Searching for an apartment for his family in 1938, Paul Hilbert was given three addresses to check out. He felt directed to select the apartment at Oppelnerstrasse 6. The inspiration helped save his family because the other two apartments were destroyed during the war.[6]

Paul Hilbert's daughter, Ursula (born 1923), was chosen as one of seven pupils of the eighth grade who were to receive special recognition. However, the school's principal, a member of the Nazi Party, dropped her name from the list because she was not a member of the Bund Deutscher Mädel.[7] At the age of ten, she had not joined the movement, explaining to the principal that she already belonged to a youth group, the Primary organization of her church.

The oldest Hilbert son, Arno, was already in the German army when the war began in September 1939. The second son, Horst (born

1919), was in the Reichsarbeitsdienst in service on the Island of Usedom when war was declared, and his unit was immediately drafted into the army. He spent the rest of the year constructing fortifications on the Baltic Sea coast but was given leave to return to Berlin for Christmas. It was there that he met and became engaged to Irene Buchta.[8]

Maria Hilbert was summoned to her daughter's school one day, where the principal explained to her that the name of her daughter, Esther, "is not suitable and brings a bad reputation to her. Is it possible for you to change the name 'Esther' to another one?" Sister Hilbert was not ashamed of having chosen a Jewish name from the Old Testament and simply requested that her daughter be addressed by her family name—Hilbert. The suggestion was accepted.[9]

Sister Hilbert was a staunch defender of the LDS faith and of her family. A few years earlier, she had been awarded the Nazi Party's Mutterkreuz, a medal given to mothers of five children of more. She was not a member of the Nazi Frauenbund (mothers' league) and never wore the medal.[10]

Sophie Wiesenhütter (born 1922) was a teenager when the war began. She recalled:

> We originally attended the Berlin East Branch, but then we moved to Köpenick, Frau-Hollestrasse 9 and became part of the Neukölln Branch. My mother was a faithful member. We had the Book of Mormon in our home, so she read to me and taught me how to pray. My father wasn't a member, but he didn't object to us attending church.[11]

Sophie and her mother needed ninety minutes to get to church; they walked to an S-Bahn station, rode for a while, transferred to another S-Bahn train, then walked a final stretch to the meetings in the Thomasstrasse.

Elisabeth Leupold had moved in 1939 with her non-LDS husband and her children to Köpenick in the Neukölln Branch territory.

Her daughter, Mary-Elizabeth (born 1932), was baptized in 1940 at Grünau in southeast Berlin, where the Dahme River flows into the Spree. Soon after that, she began a gypsylike existence that would last until after the war. Because of the danger of air raids over Berlin, Mary-Elizabeth was first sent by her parents to the eastern German province of Silesia, where she stayed for eight or ten weeks ("The people were cruel to me and beat me," she recalled). Then she went to Schweidnitz, Silesia, to live with two aunts and a grandmother, but things did not work out there either, and she returned to Berlin.[12]

In 1941, at age nine, Mary-Elizabeth Leupold was on the road again. This time she was sent to live with a family in Stroebel in Silesia. Again, the situation was not a good one, and she returned to Berlin. Stroebel was a Catholic community, which may have been a contributing factor in the failure of that experience.

In the early days of the war, young LDS men and women would get together in a southeastern Berlin neighborhood known as Grünau. As Sophie Wiesenhütter and Heinz Kupitz recalled, "Those were informal weekend get-togethers. We just went there and others showed up. You could always count on somebody being there. Activities at Grünau included picnics and walks." With the increasing distractions of the war, the Grünau outings ceased to take place.[13]

As the attacks on Berlin from the air increased in frequency, the Hilbert family developed procedures for reacting to the warning sirens. As Karola recalled:

> My suitcase and those of my sisters were packed and waiting by our bedsides. They contained extra clothes, genealogy, identification, ration cards, personal necessities—everything we could think of that might be required should

our home be demolished and we need time to resettle somewhere else.[14]

One day in about 1941, President Hilbert found an older sister in the branch hanging a picture of Adolf Hitler in the meeting room. In his kind manner, he explained, "Sister, this man has no place in our Heavenly Father's house, unless he repents and is baptized." The sister quietly took the picture down. Paul Hilbert, an artist, later painted a sign and hung it on that same spot. It bore the text of Doctrine and Covenants 88:119: "Establish a house, even a house of prayer, a house of fasting, a house of faith, a house of learning, a house of glory, a house of order, a house of God."[15]

The German army attacked the Soviet Union in June 1941. President Hilbert, whose family had already suffered because of his lack of support of Hitler, was visibly upset. "That fool Sergeant [sic] Hitler is fighting the whole world! We've won a few battles, and the [enemy] will win the war. No country can survive battling on all her fronts."[16] According to Latter-day Saint eyewitnesses, many Church members in Germany were of the same mind as this branch president.

On the morning of January 6, 1942, Maria Hilbert awoke at 4:00 A.M. and was inspired to pray intensely for her son, Horst, who was in the Soviet Union. After two hours of fervent prayer for his safety, she awakened her daughters and told them what had happened and asked them to remember that day and time until they heard from him. Two weeks later, a letter arrived from Horst with this story:

Two weeks ago I was in a horrifying situation. With another comrade I was assigned to an outpost early in the morning between 4:00 and 6:00, when the enemy opened fire. We both could not leave or hide ourselves, and the shooting got more and more intense. At that moment, facing any second death, with tears in my eyes, I turned to my comrade and said to him, "I think my mother is praying for me." At

that very moment, while I turned, a bullet hit at stomach height a nearby pole. I followed the direction and found out that if I had not turned to speak with my comrade, the bullet would have hit and killed me.[17]

In 1942, Mary-Elizabeth Leupold's parents sent her away from Berlin again, this time in connection with the Kinderlandverschickung (the children's evacuation program that was organized through the schools).[18] She had recently been accepted into a college-preparatory school, and her entire class was evacuated. The first trip took Mary-Elizabeth and her classmates to Bautzen in Silesia and the second trip (also in 1942) to Bansin on the Baltic Sea. The latter experience turned out to be memorably positive: "We swam in the [Baltic Sea] the whole summer and had a wonderful time."[19]

Fig. 1. The family of Paul and Maria Hilbert in Leipzig in 1936—shortly before they moved to Berlin. (Roper and Reece)

Unfortunately, she had no contact with the Church while she was away from her family.

In 1943 Mary-Elizabeth Leupold was again on the way to a town far from the terror of Berlin. This time, her class was sent to Glebce, Poland, in the Carpathian Mountains. While there, she had a medical emergency and was sent back alone to Berlin. When the crisis was over, her mother put the eleven-year-old on the night train to return to Poland. Mary-Elizabeth recalled the confusing trip:

> The train was filled with soldiers, and I was supposed to go to Warsaw and transfer [there] into another train and then transfer to another train and [finally] get to where I was supposed to go. After four hours the train stopped and everybody had to get off except military. . . . So I was standing there at 2:00 A.M. with my little suitcase, not knowing where to go. Finally, I found a conductor. He said, "Quick, get on the train on track 4!" I jumped onto the moving train and . . . eventually arrived where I was supposed to be.

After about twelve more hours, Mary-Elizabeth reached her destination. During the last leg of the trip, she had fallen asleep, fallen over, and gotten a sizable bruise on her head. Fortunately, even little children could travel alone in safety on the German railway system in those days.

Still another trip away from home awaited young Mary-Elizabeth Leupold a year later. She was again sent away from Berlin with her classmates, this time to Taus in Czechoslovakia. It was by then the summer of 1944. With the Red Army approaching from the east a few months later, transportation became very disorganized, so the teachers decided to take the pupils back to Berlin. What should have been a trip of eight hours became an excursion of four days. Every train carrying military personnel or supplies had priority, and the train carrying the school children was constantly pushed onto a siding track to wait. They arrived home in November.

The first of two tragedies experienced by the Wiesenhütter family occurred in the summer of 1942. Their son, Heinz Alfred, had been serving on the Eastern Front. One day, the parents received a letter from his company commander stating that he had been sent on a mission to take supplies to another unit and had never returned.

The second tragedy suffered by the Wiesenhütter family occurred on December 9, 1943. In the words of daughter Sophie:

> We sat in the living room and talked until all of a sudden my mother cried out and fell to the floor. . . . A metal piece had come through the roof, through the ceiling, and hit her. I was sitting next to her in our living room when she was hit. It cut her arm and the leg too; it just hit her in the side. . . . She bled horribly, and we took her to the hospital and she lived just a couple of days. . . . She was conscious through this. She was just moaning and moaning. It was a terrible shock. Then my dad and I were alone.

The Wiesenhütters had chosen not to go to the basement that evening because the illumination flares had been dropped over a neighborhood miles away in northern Berlin, and the sound of the bombs was likewise quite distant. What hit Sister Wiesenhütter was likely a piece of metal torn from a British airplane by antiaircraft fire.

In September 1942, after avoiding death in several combat situations near Stalingrad, Russia, Horst Hilbert was finally granted leave to return to Berlin for three weeks. While there, he married his sweetheart, Irene Buchta, on September 19. An unofficial ceremony was held at church under the direction of Friedrich Fischer, the president of the Berlin District. As Horst later recalled, "It was a wonderful time, having been so close to death, being so close to the beloved wife, and my family. Only too soon, on October 2, 1942, I had to return to the Eastern Front. It was heartbreaking."[20]

In 1943, branch president Paul Hilbert's place of work was moved south to Thuringia, and he bade a sad farewell to his family, promising them that they would be safe if they stayed in their home. He was not released as branch president; in his absence, first counselor Peter Garg directed the affairs of the Neukölln Branch. Although most of the younger men were away from home in military service, there were enough priesthood holders to officiate in the branch. As Ursula Hilbert later recalled:

> We had one man blessing the sacrament who was ninety-two years old. We really respected and loved and honored him. Because there were no young men there, we girls helped him clean up, washing, drying, and putting away the little glasses. That's what we did with "Brother Erdmann," and he came every week and blessed the sacrament.

On August 14, 1943, Horst Hilbert must have thought that his good luck at avoiding death and injury at the Eastern Front had come to an end:

> I was standing at a somewhat elevated railway track, talking with a friend, Otto Becker. Suddenly I saw a big flame to my right, maybe 10 feet away. Then I felt like having evil smoke pressed into my mouth and felt a hard blow on my right side. When I tried to assess my situation, I found myself lying on the ground with a terrible pain, all at the same time, in my head, right arm, shoulder, breast, stomach, and hind part. And blood was streaming all over me. I had been hit by a mortar shell. Otto Becker got one piece of metal in his neck and was killed instantly. I got about 30 pieces, and I was luckier.[21]

The Germans were in retreat, but fortunately two comrades picked Horst up and carried him back to an aid station. He was eventually transported to Erfurt, Germany, where he recovered from his wounds in about six weeks. He spent the next year as a howitzer instructor, far from the front.

Maria Hilbert and her daughters tried to keep their home in Berlin functioning as wartime conditions became more challenging. "We girls had our bath every Saturday night because we wanted to be clean for church on Sunday," recalled Ursula Hilbert. The cast-iron tub was in the bathroom, and hot water was added as they took turns. The routine was complicated because their home teacher always visited on Saturday nights. The girls did not want him to know what they were doing in the adjacent room as each went through the bathing process, so they had to be especially quiet. "We always wished that he would come on Friday night instead," Ursula explained.

By late 1943, the war was beginning to affect attendance at the meetings of the Neukölln Branch. Men went off to war, families who were bombed out left to find other housing, and mothers with small children sought safety in rural settings. Sophie Wiesenhütter remembered other reasons for declining attendance:

> There were quite a few people who stayed away during Hitler's time because they were afraid that they could die. They wanted to have their names stricken from the record. I remember we had a duplicating machine [at church], and a kind of newsletter was printed out and sent to the ward [branch] members. And one Sister Odin wrote some letter [back] because she didn't want them sent to her.

At some point during the air war against the city of Berlin, the Leupold home in Köpenick received a direct hit from an incendiary bomb. It penetrated the roof and came to rest in the baby's crib. The family was in the basement shelter at the time, but Mr. Leupold was able to locate the bomb and remove it before it could start a major fire. As the attacks increased in frequency, the Leupold children had ample opportunities to collect pieces of shrapnel from the streets. As Mary-Elizabeth explained, "We had a little cigar case, so we took them to school and we traded them; you know kids. It actually is amazing when I think about how you adjust to your environment, to what's going on." As has been seen, it was a rare occasion when the little girl was in Berlin.

All through the war, Ursula Hilbert prayed that her family would survive the conflict. Once, she felt inspired to begin genealogical research on her family. As she later recounted:

> Every free minute I would write to different [parish offices] and then fill out family [group] sheets and pedigrees. When the alarm went off, I [would take] my package of genealogy with me [to] the basement. I believed having my ancestors' desires to be redeemed [would] protect me and my family from bombs and sudden death.[22]

The life of teenage girls such as the Hilberts in wartime Berlin was not one of parties, dates, and other entertainment. Many dance halls and movie theaters had been damaged or shut down as the citizens were encouraged to sacrifice for the *Endsieg* (final victory). Having young men as partners was very rare. In short, fun activities were not daily fare. At the office where Karola Hilbert worked, the atmosphere became more and more subdued. Concerned about Nazi spies in the area, she dared not discuss the war (and her hopes that Germany would lose). As she complained to herself,

> This isn't right! I'm just becoming a young lady; I should be happy and eager to talk and make new friends. It's all wrong; it's all Hitler's fault. Hitler! The very name [makes] me feel as if someone [was pouring] icy water over my head during the middle of a hot day.[23]

One of the members of the Neukölln Branch was a rarity among German Latter-day Saints: she was a half-Jew, the wife of a Brother Heber. When he was drafted into the German army, she continued to attend church. As time passed, she expressed her concerns to branch leaders that if her husband were killed in battle, she could expect to be rounded up as part of the Nazi program to rid Germany of all Jews. Certain trustworthy members of the Neukölln Branch then joined in an effort to provide food and housing for Frau Heber for about the last six months of the war.[24]

It was Christmas Eve 1944 in the Leupold home. Mary-Elizabeth's father brought home a Christmas tree, and the family decorated it as best they could. Just as they sat down to dinner, the sirens went off, and they heard bombs falling. With no time to reach the shelter ten minutes away, they went straight to the basement. Mary-Elizabeth described what happened next:

> During the next few hours the walls of our basement shook; the floor underneath our feet rolled from the explosions in the air and the ground. At one point we felt that our house had been hit. My father went outside to check what was happening and reported that several houses in our neighborhood were burning. A crashing airplane had shaved off the chimney of our house.

When the family finally emerged from the basement, they found the windows broken and cold air rushing through the home. The dinner was cold and covered with dust and dirt that had fallen from the ceiling. At that moment of deep discouragement, a brother cried out, "Our Christmas tree! Come and look!" In the midst of the destruction, the Christmas tree had remained untouched. They lit the candles and sang "Silent Night, Holy Night." According to Mary-Elizabeth, "Hope swelled deep inside me. Suddenly I knew that somehow, sometime in the future, peace would again be restored to earth."

For some people, the terror and confusion of air raids was too much to bear. Such was the case with Sister Latschkowski, the mother of three little boys, after an air raid on February 3, 1945. Karola Hilbert and her elder sister, Esther, had worried about this mother whose husband was away in the army, so the sisters hurried to her apartment after bombs landed in the neighborhood. Karola recalled the incident as follows:

> What a chaotic scene met our eyes! The house around her was on fire, and the walls were so hot the light green paint was blistering; yet she sat on the bed in total bewilderment, shaking her head, her hands turned upward on her lap in a helpless gesture. "What shall I do? What shall I do?" she sobbed again and again.[25]

Karola and Esther found two of the Latschkowski boys, and their dazed mother finally mumbled that the third was in a hospital. With the building burning around them, the sisters got the family out. Joined by their sister, Ursula, they returned to the Latschkowski apartment and were able to fill several sheets with household items before the smoke drove them away and the building was gutted by fire.[26]

By early 1945, the British and the Americans were bombing Berlin several times a day. Under those conditions, it was very difficult to collect food from the various specialty shops. To expedite the procedure, Sister Leupold gave ration coupons to several of her children and left them in lines at different stores. She would then make the rounds and take over in line when it came time for her to make the purchase.

The date February 26, 1945, was etched in the memory of Ursula Hilbert for years. As air-raid sirens announced the approach of American bombers, she tried to join her sister Edith in her company's shelter but arrived too late. Everywhere she looked, the streets and businesses were empty, and she could see squadrons of airplanes "like tiny birds in groups." Desperate to find a shelter in a local building, she suddenly ran into a young man who yelled, "Miss, we have to find shelter at once; the airplanes are above us!" Seconds after the two had found a shelter, the bombs began to explode nearby. When somebody came looking for the man who had rescued

her, he was nowhere to be seen. Huddling in the packed air-raid shelter, Ursula offered what she thought would be her last prayer, asking forgiveness for her sins and saying good-bye to her parents and her siblings.[27] Regarding the mysterious young man, she stated, "I can tell you, this was one of the Three Nephites who came and took my hand—he had a fine, warm hand—and ran with me to a safe place."

On many occasions, the Hilbert girls had listened as their mother prayed that they would not be at home if their apartment house were ever struck by bombs. As an apparent answer to those prayers, Sister Hilbert and her daughters were in church on Sunday, March 18, 1945, when the neighborhood suffered extensive damage. Buildings all around were on fire, as were the apartments above theirs, but courageous neighbors put out the fire.[28]

In the spring of 1945, Horst Hilbert was again in a combat unit, closer to the invading American army than to the Soviets, whom every German soldier feared. He was eventually able to surrender to "three Yanks" in a jeep and for him, the war was over. He spent much of his prison time in a camp near Remagen on the Rhine River. Because of his ability to speak English, he was treated better than the average German soldier.[29]

When the Soviet armed forces approached Berlin, they announced to the public through leaflets dropped by airplanes that they were coming to liberate the German people from Hitler's dictatorship and from facism. It was soon painfully clear that the term *liberate* did not apply. According to Ursula Hilbert:

> Those days of liberation of whom and what, I don't know which, brought every day new excitement. Liberated from Nazism, bombing, air raids, now starvation and horror, no food and water, living with enemies in town, broken homes physically and spiritually, this was overnight called the liberation.[30]

The Leupold family lived at the edge of the woods on the eastern boundary of the Köpenick suburb. Elisabeth Leupold and her children were some of the first Berliners to see the Red Army soldiers who fought their way into the area on April 21, 1945. Mr. Leupold was in the center of Berlin, serving as a soldier, and was away from home for twelve terrifying days. Huddling with her three children (ages five to eight) in a local bunker, Sister Leupold watched as enemy soldiers stole watches and other valuables from the neighbors. They then took the young women out to assault them, giving the other women and children a few moments to escape, which they did. As Sister Leupold later recalled:

> In terror everyone pushed to get away from the bunker. We knew, once the officers were satisfied, the rest of the men would fall over us. Outside the bunker the battle was raging. Bombs were exploding around us. It was like hell, fires burning, bombs exploding. Many of the fleeing lost their life. I ran and ran holding on to my children trying to reach safety. . . . We stepped over dead bodies everywhere. We finally found a place to stay. Everyone opened their home to strangers.[31]

In her rush to escape the bunker, Sister Leupold lost sight of daughter Mary-Elizabeth, who was barely thirteen years old. She had fallen in with refugees heading west, away from the Soviet troops, and thus began yet another trip away from home. Her route took her to the south. "I walked for 18 days, 20 or 30 km a day. . . . I ended up at a little village at the lower Alpine mountains," Mary-Elizabeth explained. Finding refuge on a Bavarian farm, she became a common farmhand and worked there for six months. It was there that she encountered the American army and saw her first black man: "I saw his glistening teeth, and I was scared to death."

Next to killing or capturing German soldiers, the main objective of the Soviet conquerors seemed to be the abuse of German women and girls. Karola Hilbert later recalled the mood in the Neukölln Branch:

> I can remember the April fast meeting in 1945 in Thomasstrasse. It was the last fast meeting before the war ended, and we had a special fast as a [branch]. We had heard so much about Russian atrocities, and we were afraid—we didn't know how much was propaganda or truth—but we prayed and fasted that the girls and the women in the branch would be protected, that they would not be defiled. I remember for the closing song, Edith had chosen "The Spirit of God." And we girls knew and sang the cadence to it. When we sang, we were not singing alone; there were angels with us. And we were not the only ones that heard it; everyone heard it. That was the last fast meeting we had, and none of those that fasted were defiled.[32]

The concerns in the heart of a faithful Latter-day Saint mother would have been much like those of any other mother in Berlin in April 1945. Maria Hilbert prayed constantly for the safety of her four daughters, ages fifteen to twenty-three. She may have heard that several LDS women had already been victimized by the invading soldiers. In any case, she was prepared to give her life in defense of her daughters if need be. Paul Hilbert was still in Thuringia, a province far to the south. He had not been able to visit his family for a very long time. As the war drew to a conclusion, he had no way to call them or write to them.

On April 25, 1945, the first Soviet soldiers came down Oppelnerstrasse, where they encountered only slight resistance. Sister Hilbert and her daughters were hiding in the basement with other residents of the building. Suddenly, the Soviets stormed into the basement, searching for German defenders; they found none. The soldiers left, and the Hilberts congratulated themselves on their good fortune. However, several hours later an enemy soldier returned, approached the Hilberts in their basement hideout, and stared intently at Edith. He seemed bent on having his way

Fig. 2. The ruins of the Anhalter railroad station. Most of Berlin's many railroad stations were destroyed by the end of the war. (R. Minert, 1973)

with her. Maria Hilbert calmly instructed her daughters to leave the building with her. "I had never seen Mother so horrified," recalled Karola. "Her face was drained of any color. Her eyes were wild with fright. Her fragile frame moved with speed and skill as she ran ahead . . . trying to keep herself between Edith and the soldier." The situation became critical, as Karola related:

> When the soldier managed to move between them, Mother forced herself in front of Edith again. At last, in frustrated anger, the soldier slammed his machine gun against Mother's chest. A short grunt escaped her, as if the gun had taken her breath away. He made wild angry gestures, babbling in Russian, but we all understood what he meant. If Mother moved again, he would pull the trigger without hesitation. . . . In this desperate situation, another soldier came into the courtyard. Black fear poured like tar into my chest as I realized that together they could accomplish their desire. But then I looked at the second soldier's face. His whole countenance shone as if he were a heavenly being, and in that moment I believe that he was.[33]

The second soldier spoke in low tones to the first, who slowly lowered the barrel of his weapon until it was pointing at the ground. Maria Hilbert and her daughters used the pause to race back into the basement. They had escaped a most terrifying situation. For the next few weeks they lived in their apartment

upstairs. Horst, the second son, had told them months before that invading soldiers were usually too tired to climb stairs to look for victims. This prediction turned out to be correct, and the women were safe from that point on. Of course, they almost never ventured outside of their apartment for the next month.[34]

When the invaders arrived in the Wiesenhütters' neighborhood in Köpenick in April 1945, Sophie was quick to find a hiding place:

> I was down in the basement. We had a little pile of coal and some old sacks then, and it was dark since the electricity was out. I hid behind that pile of coal and covered myself with some old sacks. [The soldiers] went through the house, and my father was there. The first thing they always asked was, "Where is the woman?" He said, "There is none." If they had come near, they would have shot him. I was quiet. They came down and stood right next to me, but it was dark, and they didn't see me, and I certainly didn't make a noise. They knew we were still there. It was a miracle.

Five days after their escape from the bunker and marauding Red Army soldiers, Sister Leupold and her children returned to their home that had been vandalized and desecrated. Her eldest daughter, Mary-Elizabeth, was still missing. Sister Leupold recalled that the conquerors demanded a week later that she vacate her home:

Fig. 3. Maria Hilbert faced the daunting challenge of protecting her four daughters from the conquerors of Berlin in the spring of 1945. (Roper and Reece)

Immeasurable despair came over me. I decided that the Russians would find only corpses when they came in the morning. But God, whom I thought had forgotten me, showed his mercy. He sent me a young sister from the Church who stayed with me all night. Her mother had been killed by a bomb a few years earlier, and I had taken her under my wing. She was searching for me to find out if we had survived. Now she was there to save me and my children. She wept and assured me that God will help. The next morning came and with it a miracle. My husband came and also brought some food. . . . I am still ashamed that I lost my faith. My God had again saved me. I should have known that there is no need so great that God cannot heal.[35]

Sophie Wiesenhütter and her father were evicted from their home in Köpenick for three months while Soviet officers were quartered there. For a time, Sophie lived with the Leupold family and had to walk miles and miles to work. During the day, it was relatively safe, but this was not the case after dark:

I was almost home, maybe ten minutes [away], and there came a group of Russians soldiers, maybe eight or ten. And they surrounded me, and I stood in the middle, and they had a flashlight. It was dark; the streetlights didn't work. And I just stood there, and they looked me over, said something, and let me go, which was unheard of. So that was a second miracle. I had some more. We really, truly were protected.

The Hilberts and other members of the Neukölln Branch breathed a sigh of relief when they learned in June 1945 that their district was to be part of the American occupation sector in Berlin. The border of the Soviet sector was the Spree River—a mere three blocks east of the Hilberts' apartment on Oppelnerstrasse.

Eventually, Horst Hilbert was transferred by the American army to the British at Wickrath, Germany, and released in the fall of 1945. He returned home in time to witness the visit of Elder Ezra Taft Benson, who had come to Berlin as part of his welfare mission in 1945.[36]

Mary-Elizabeth Leupold was finally reunited with her family after the war. In reviewing the events of the end of the war, she came to this conclusion:

Looking back at that time, I find that I was taken away from the battlefield and the Soviet invasion in a very strange and mysterious way. . . . I was spared all this [suffering]. . . . For the next six months as a thirteen-year old girl I was completely unprotected. . . . There was nobody in charge of me; no one knew I existed except for the farmer and the people in this little village. If someone had killed or raped me, no one would have been held accountable for it. Yet nothing happened to me. . . . Why I was shielded from suffering real harm while so many others were not, I do not know. Yet the fact is that I was. A loving God had held his protective hand over me.

All of the Hilberts, the Leupolds, and most of their friends in the Neukölln Branch had survived the war. Ursula Hilbert later explained the best method of survival: "You had to stand on your own testimony when you stayed [in Berlin]. There was no other way of doing it. We had to stand together in our branches; we were all friends, and we had to strengthen each other."

In Memoriam

The following members of the Berlin Neukölln Branch did not survive World War II:

Sophie Anna Jasinski b. Berlin, Brandenburg, Preußen 12 Dec 1897; dau. of Ludwig Jasinski and Auguste Wilhelmine Luise Bandelow; bp. Berlin 1 Dec 1923; m. Berlin 13 Oct 1917, Heinrich Hermann Alfred Wiesenhütter; 1 child; d. injuries suffered in air raid Köpenick, Berlin, Preußen 9 Dec 1943 (S. Wiesenhütter Ranglack; IGI)

Egon Alfred Jepp b. Schoenlanke, Pommern 7 Apr 1926; son of Emil Jepp and Marie Minna Emma Kaiser; MIA in Dec 1944 (CHL Microfilm no. 2458, form 42 FP, Pt. 37, 1949 list: 1382; FHL Microfilm 271369, 1930 Census)

Latschkowski, Infant k. air raid (K. Hilbert Reece)

Rosalie Emma Schöfer b. Riegersdorf, Schlesien, Preußen 10 Dec 1901; dau. of Karl Schoefer and Anna Pauline Huhndt; bp. in Schweidnitz, Schlesien, Preußen 10 Dec 1925; epileptic; k. euthanasia 1942 (M. Leupold Fowler; IGI)

Siegfried Wendt b. 17 Dec 1916; son of Marie Martha Griesbach; ord. deacon; MIA at age 33 (CHL Microfilm no. 2458, form 42 FP, Pt. 37, 1949 list: 1382; FHL Microfilm 245296, 1935 Census)

Walter Karl Emil Zietz b. Berlin, Brandenburg, Preußen 6 Feb 1909; son of Emil Karl Zietz and Elfriede Johanna Clara Eckstein; bp. Berlin 26 Jun 1929; m. Schweidnitz, Schlesien, Preußen 4 September 1930, Wilhelmine Pauline Hundt; 2 children; k. in battle near Moscow, Russia 4 Dec 1941 (M. Leupold Fowler; IGI)

NOTES

1. Patricia R. Roper and Karola H. Reece, *We Were Not Alone: How an LDS Family Survived World War II in Berlin* (Salt Lake City: Shadow Mountain, 2003), 12.

2. Presiding Bishopric, "Financial, Statistical, and Historical Reports of Wards, Stakes, and Missions, 1884–1955," CR 4 12, 257.

3. Roper and Reece, *We Were Not Alone*, 2.

4. Karola Hilbert Reece, interview by the author, Payson, Utah, April 22, 2006.

5. Ursula Hilbert Wendel, interview by the author, Bountiful, Utah, April 7, 2006.

6. Ursula Hilbert Wendel, autobiography (unpublished manuscript, about 1970), 3; private collection

7. See the description of the Bund Deutscher Mädel program in the introduction.

8. Horst Kurt Hilbert, "It Is a Long Way to Freedom" (unpublished personal history), 2–3; private collection.

9. Wendel, autobiography, 7.

10. The Mutterkreuz had three varieties, designed for the recognition of mothers of five, seven, and nine children.

11. Sophie Wiesenhütter Ranglack, interview by the author, Murray, Utah, July 13, 2006.

12. Mary-Elizabeth Leupold Fowler to the author, June 29, 2006.

13. Heinz Kupitz, interview by the author, Salt Lake City, March 17, 2006.

14. Roper and Reece, *We Were Not Alone*, 56.

15. Ibid., 31–32.

16. Ibid., 33. Hitler (a native of Braunau, Austria) finished World War I at the rank of corporal. Thus he was often sarcastically referred to by his opponents as the Austrian corporal.

17. Ursula Hilbert Wendel, autobiography, 6; spelling errors have been corrected.

18. See the description of the Kinderlandverschickung program in the glossary.

19. Mary-Elizabeth Leupold Fowler, interview by the author, Provo, Utah, May 5, 2006.

20. Horst Kurt Hilbert, "It Is a Long Way to Freedom," 20.

21. Ibid., 13–14.

22. Ursula Hilbert Wendel, autobiography, 13.

23. Roper and Reece, *We Were Not Alone*, 51

24. Karola Hilbert Reece saw Mrs. Heber in a German store in Utah in 1957; her husband had also survived the war.

25. Roper and Reece, *We Were Not Alone*, 81.

26. Ibid., 80–83. Two weeks after the war ended, Sister Latschkowski showed up at the Hilbert apartment with her three sons. Again mentally confused, she showed them the baby in the carriage and said, "He might be dead." He was. Sister Hilbert and Brother Garg buried the child outside a church cemetery nearby.

27. Ursula Hilbert Wendel, autobiography, 11–12.

28. Ibid., 13.

29. Horst Kurt Hilbert, "It Is a Long Way to Freedom," 20–21. He stated that 220,000 prisoners were at the Remagen camp. He was most likely in the infamous Sinzig camp, just two miles south of Remagen. In that camp, prisoners were classified as "disarmed personnel" rather than prisoners-of-war and thus not treated in accordance with the Geneva Convention. Tens of thousands of prisoners (including women and children) died at Sinzig, where there were no structures to house the prisoners. See James Bacque, *Other Losses* (London: Macdonald, 1990).

30. Ursula Hilbert Wendel, autobiography, 17. The Soviets bragged about having "liberated" the people in East Germany. Soviet troops remained there until 1990.

31. Elisabeth Schoefer Leupold, autobiography (unpublished), 13–14; private collection.

32. Sophie Wiesenhütter Ranglack was also in church that Sunday and corroborated the story.

33. Roper and Reece, *We Were Not Alone*, 121.

34. Ibid., 122f.

35. Elisabeth Schoefer Leupold, autobiography, 14–15. The young woman was Sophie Wiesenhütter.

36. Horst Kurt Hilbert, "It Is a Long Way to Freedom," 22.

BERLIN SCHÖNEBERG BRANCH

Covering most of the southwest portion of metropolitan Berlin, the Schöneberg Branch may have been the most expansive of the six branches in the capital city. On the north, it included the mission office at Händelallee 6 and the Tiergarten Park. At the southwest extreme, it bordered the Brandenburg-Potsdam Branch.

Berlin had experienced a veritable golden age in the 1930s. Under the National Socialist government, the country's economy had blossomed and its international status had also prospered. The Olympic Games of 1936 had invited the world to a Berlin that featured impressive new structures along broad avenues.

Wolfgang (Herbert)[1] Klopfer was born in this Berlin in February 1936—just as the Winter Olympic Games began. His earliest memories are of this huge city with its superb transportation system, parks, forests, and lakes. His family lived in the mission home at Händelallee 6, and the beautiful Tiergarten Park began literally across the street from the picture window of the Klopfer apartment. Herbert remembered that

> the huge city park [Tiergarten] provided unlimited opportunities for childhood fun and outdoor recreation. A playground of sandboxes amidst a forest of beautiful trees and wide open green areas suitable for all kinds of ball games was so close to home that we could see our home from where we were playing and hear our mother calling for us from our balcony. It was a quiet neighborhood . . . a country environment [that] made life in the big city very happy and satisfying.[2]

The Klopfer family attended church in the Schöneberg meeting rooms at Bülowstrasse 82 in the first Hinterhaus. Ingrid Bendler (born 1926) and her mother were also members of that branch. While the Klopfers could walk about one-half hour to church, the Bendlers came from an upscale neighborhood near Grunewald, far to the west, and needed public transportation to get to Bülowstrasse in about an hour. Ingrid remembered the rooms being on the fourth floor in a building that she was not proud to invite a friend to visit. The average attendance was about forty persons.[3]

Schoeneberg Branch[4]	1939
Elders	5
Priests	3
Teachers	1
Deacons	3
Other Adult Males	18
Adult Females	97
Male Children	2
Female Children	6
Total	135

Ingrid Bendler was the only person of her age in a branch with very few children. Fortunately, Fritz Mudrow, the branch president, took her under his wing and gave her many opportunities to serve:

> I was a Sunday School teacher when I was twelve. The Klopfer boys were in my class. . . . [President Mudrow] tried to keep me busy. Almost every Sunday, I had to stay at the back door and greet the people coming in. And he would have me give a poem, sing a song, something just to keep me going.

At the age of ten, Ingrid was inducted into the Jungmädel program of the Hitler Youth. She enjoyed the association with other girls, the activities, the trips, and the events that required the girls to miss school. The uniform was "a white blouse, blue skirt, brown jacket, and a black neckerchief. . . . When I was 15, I was not interested in that program any more and I didn't participate any longer. There was never any pressure to join the [Nazi] Party or be active in the Hitler Youth."[5]

Young Herbert Klopfer recalled the early part of the war:

> For a young person that was exciting. For the first two years the war had been reasonably easy for us. Even though we were constantly bombed and had to spend many nights in the basement." The mission home was just a few blocks from the business district of western Berlin, and the air raids in the neighborhood were very frequent.

A common pastime among elementary school children in large German cities was collecting pieces of shrapnel after bombing raids. As he later explained about the ways little boys had fun during the war, "Numerous splinters of grenade shells and fragments of bombs accumulated all over our street and in the park as they fell from the air. These were favorite 'toys,' but also extremely dangerous because of their very sharp and cutting edges."[6] The children usually kept their collections in shoe boxes and traded them on the school playground.

In 1942, a number of young adults moved into the Schöneberg Branch. These included sisters Inge and Fränzi Otto, each of whom married a soldier soon after their introduction in the branch. According to Ingrid Bendler, "We really celebrated those weddings, we danced all night. We came home at six in the morning and all of us showed up at ten o'clock for Sunday School." Another new member of the branch, soldier Wilhelm Werner, was ten years older than Ingrid, but they spent every evening of his three-week furlough together, and he became her first love.[7]

Ingrid Bendler was in school during the first four years of the war. Following her graduation from business college in the spring of 1943, life became a bit more challenging, as she was called upon for government service. Her mandatory Pflichtjahr (year of duty) assignment placed her in a private home as a nanny for essentially no pay. However, she had Sundays off and was able to attend church. When the attacks on Berlin increased in frequency and severity, the family moved out of town, and Ingrid's term of duty ended ahead of schedule.

Herbert Klopfer remembered air-raid alarms as often as twice each night. Whether in the basement or in their living room, his mother, Erna, gathered her sons close, and they prayed. Sometimes the sister missionaries who lived upstairs joined them:

They did not want to leave us alone. We huddled together, listening to the engines of enemy airplanes and hearing and feeling the rattling of windows and the detonations of bombs bursting nearby. Our hearts were filled with prayers, always hoping that the next bomb would again pass us up.

In early 1943, mission supervisor Herbert Klopfer (a soldier on active duty) followed the government's recommendation to move his family out of Berlin. During one of his furloughs, he took them and some of their property to the home of his parents in Werdau, Saxony, four miles west of Zwickau. His wife, Erna, and their two sons would live there for the next seven years. All four of the boys' grandparents lived under the same roof, as did their aunt.[8]

The Klopfer family's move to Werdau was providential. On November 21, 1943, bombs damaged the mission home on Händelallee in

Fig. 1. Mission supervisor Herbert Klopfer and his family celebrated the first Christmas of the war in their apartment in the mission home. Erna Klopfer's parents (Brother and Sister Hein) joined them for the occasion. Note the blackout curtain rolled up at the top of the window. (I. Reimer Ebert)

Berlin. Brother Klopfer's counselors, Richard Ranglack and Paul Langheinrich, mobilized members of the Church to move most of the mission office property to the apartment house in which Brother Langheinrich lived. This was inspired action because everything the Klopfers had left behind during their move to Werdau was lost the very next night when the mission home was totally destroyed by phosphorus bombs.[9]

On November 9, 1943, Ingrid Bendler was drafted into the Reicharbeitsdienst and sent to Költschen (east of Berlin):

> We had to wear a uniform, live in barracks, and help the farmers in a little farm community. . . . I cleaned the stables, helped with the harvest and threshing. I also helped with making sausages. . . . There was a daily fight with the geese . . . I liked to learn how to bridle the horses."[10]

It must have been an interesting and exhausting life for a city girl, but Ingrid was pleased to be away from the big city that was being pulverized from the air on a regular basis. In an apparently contradictory sense, she later suggested that it would have been better to be in Berlin than in the countryside: "It is just so much easier to be in the middle of things and experience them yourself than to be far away and imagine how bad it would be."[11]

Less than a month of her term in the Reichsarbeitsdienst had passed before Ingrid Bendler learned of the death of her dear friends, Inge and Fränzi Otto, and their mother—victims of an air raid. The funeral was "heartbreaking" and left her with a "downright lost feeling." Their burial was in a mass grave.[12] Wilhelm Werner (a half brother of Inge and Fränzi) had come from the Eastern Front to attend the funeral. He and Ingrid were engaged to be married before he left, but the two did not meet again until his release from imprisonment in Russia in 1949.

Fig. 2. A branch outing in the forest in the early years of the war. (I. Bendler Broughton)

The air raids eventually reached the Bendlers' neighborhood, and even when the bombs missed their house, the air pressure of nearby detonations shattered their windows. Ingrid's father worked hard to replace the glass in those windows. While most people in that situation simply covered the window frames with cardboard or wood, Mr. Bendler used glass-wire until he could get real glass, which he did several times a week. He simply refused to give up, insisting, "That's what the enemy wants; they want us to give up." During one attack, Ingrid's mother was hiding in a basement, and the woman sitting next to her was killed. Sister Bendler was "very shook up. Her nerves were shot."[13]

Herbert Klopfer told of several occasions when his parents were nearly killed, even after leaving Berlin. Once they were on the train from Berlin to Werdau. Just five minutes after the train departed the main station in Leipzig, the city was hit in a massive attack that took the lives of several thousand people, many of whom were trapped in railroad cars inside the main station.[14]

In 1944, Ingrid Bendler was informed that her term of duty with the Reichsarbeitsdienst had been extended by one year. She was asked to become a leader and to make the service her career. However, because she was totally cut off from the Church under those circumstances, she turned down the offer. The government responded with an unofficial punishment— assigning her to be a school teacher in East Prussia. This put her very close to the invading Soviet Army.

In Fröhlichshof, East Prussia, Ingrid was given charge of a class of eighty pupils from six to fourteen years of age. Without any formal teacher training (a total of three days), she had several wonderful experiences in elementary education and became a favorite among the farming population in that small town. One experience was not connected to school but was closely related to the standards of morality taught to her by a faithful mother and her teachers in the Schöneberg Branch:

> While I was teaching school in East Prussia, the [Waffen-]SS, that was the elite group of German [soldiers] came through the village. They were all very good-looking young men. They were strong and intelligent. All of them were handpicked. They would come to my door and try to conquer me. I had befriended a very nice shy young man; he told me that all the guys had a bet going . . . that I could not withstand their charms and [would] go to bed with them. . . . I was true to Willy [Werner] and stayed with the teachings of the Church. So I fought them off and I won. Had I been permissive, I would probably have lost the guidance of the Spirit.[15]

After spending Christmas 1944 with her parents in Berlin, Ingrid returned to Fröhlichshof where she heard terrifying rumors of Soviet atrocities committed on German soil.

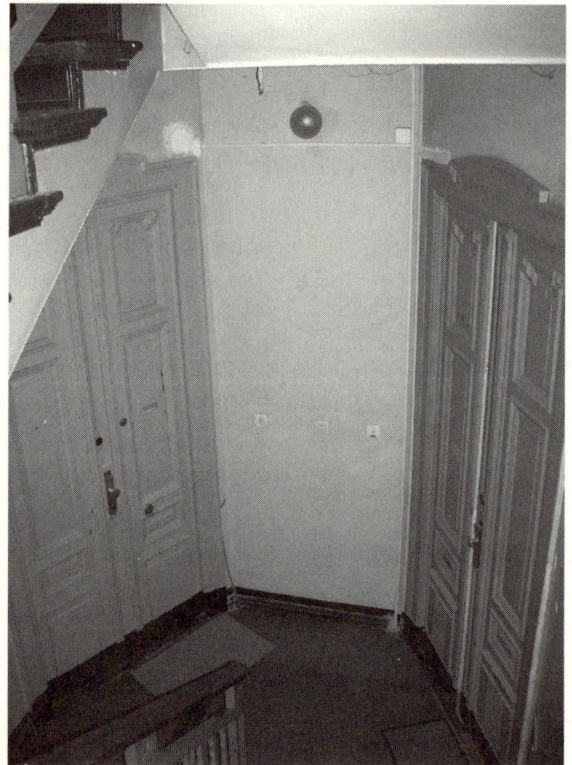

Fig. 3. The typical Berlin apartment house in 1939 was built about 1900. It was five stories tall with twelve-foot ceilings and two apartments per floor.

She contacted the local military commanders to express her fears and was allowed to leave on January 18, 1945, traveling with the army to the provincial capital of Königsberg. There she was able to squeeze into a train with several thousand people desperate to go west. The trip to Berlin usually took ten hours, but under the confusion of the time, it took Ingrid three days and three nights to get home.

Back in Berlin, Ingrid worked in an office where she dispensed ration stamps. When the Soviet invaders approached the city, they dropped flyers to convince the citizenry that resistance was futile. Artillery shells were soon bursting near the ration stamp office, but Ingrid and the staff continued to work: "When the firing and shelling would get too close we would duck a little, but never could or would we leave our desks, those ration stamps needed to be protected. People wanted to get everything they were allowed to receive."[16]

Ingrid's father was a carpenter employed by the city, so he took his family to city hall, where they stayed for the next few weeks in relative comfort. Mr. Bendler had been mustered into the Volkssturm but simply laid down his rifle one day and walked away from the fighting. He felt that dying under those circumstances would be senseless.[17] The carnage everywhere in Berlin was shocking and depressing. Ingrid remembered seeing a dead horse in the street and local residents hurrying to cut hunks of meat from the carcass. In a worse situation, she witnessed the following:

> While crossing a very busy intersection, I would always see a flat—very dirty piece of cloth that looked like a piece of uniform. It was no bigger than a pillowcase. There was a sweet sickening smell at the spot. We crossed it many times. One time a neighbor of mine investigated and kicked this cloth with his foot. Out came a finger with a crunched-up wedding ring. No one could ever think this was a human being. It must have been a soldier who was run over by

a tank. A clean-up crew picked this "leftover" human being up in one shovel, it was unrecognizable. This was a powerful lesson. Men are nothing by themselves. To literally see a human being reduced to a shovelful of nothing was a sobering experience. It reinforced in me the feeling of dependency to my Father in Heaven. I never felt important after that.[18]

Erna Klopfer and her sons experienced the end of World War II in the relative safety of the small town of Werdau, but her husband, the mission supervisor, had been reported missing in action the previous September. She did not learn of his fate until an emaciated soldier released from a POW camp in the Soviet Union in September 1948 knocked on her door in Werdau. He reported having been at Herbert Klopfer's side in a squalid camp near Kiev, Ukraine, when Brother Klopfer passed away on

Fig. 4. "To the residents of Berlin: Berlin is surrounded! . . . Any attempt to defend yourselves is totally futile." This flyer was dropped over the city by Soviet planes in the last week of April 1945. (R. Berger Rudolph)

91

March 19, 1945. Brother Klopfer's health had deteriorated due to hard labor in a salt mine.[19]

The battle for Berlin ended on May 2, 1945, the day before Ingrid Bendler's nineteenth birthday. In the rubble of the Reich capital, she still went to church, though it now took two hours to walk—one way. She later wrote the following about the Schöneberg Branch at the conclusion of World War II:

> Most everyone had lost everything. That didn't seem to matter. We rejoiced in being together. More and more members would come out of the ashes. Since we still had Sunday School in the morning and sacrament meeting in the evening I just stayed there all day. We rejoiced in being with each other and to see how many of the Saints had survived. Everyone had a story to tell. We were happy to be alive. All our relatives made it through the ending of the war. My brother and family was [sic] o.k. also.[20]

IN MEMORIAM

The following members of the Schöneberg Branch did not survive World War II:

Gerhard Bellmann b. Chemnitz, Chemnitz, Sachsen 11 Aug 1897, son of Wilhelm Bellmann and Marie Lippmann; sergeant first class; k. in battle 10 Apr 1945; bur. Costermano, Italy (CHL CR 375 8 #2459, 1034–35; www.volksbund.de)

Gerd Gustav Hermann Burkhardt b. 24 Jul 1920; son of Wilhelmine Marie Precht; bp. 20 Jun 1930; Luftwaffe corporal; shot down 26 Feb 1941; bur. Landeseigener Cem., Neukölln, Berlin, Preußen (*Sonntagsgruss*, no. 19, 11 May 1941, 76; FHL Microfilm 25733, 1930 Census; IGI)

Heinz Bernhard Hillig b. Limbach, Germany 25 Mar 1911; son of Bernhard Hillig and Marie Flohr; k. in battle Poznan, Poland 1942 (CHL CR 375 8 #2459, 1014–1015; www.volksbund.de)

Auguste Wilhelmine Holz b. Gross Hoppenbruch, Ostpreußen, Preußen 18 or 28 Jun 1862; dau. of Gottlieb Holz and Wilhelmine Priess; bp. 8 Aug 1925; m. —— Jaske; d. senility 18 Oct 1939 (CHL CR 375 8 #2458, 1939 data; FHL Microfilm 271366, 1930/35 Census; IGI)

Karl Herbert Klopfer b. Werdau, Sachsen 14 May 1911; son of Max Alfred Klopfer and Marie Hedwig Schaller; bp. 22 Jun 1923; ord. elder; East German

Mission Leader Aug 1939-; m. Beuthen, Brandenburg, Preußen 22 May 1934, Erna Luise Hein; 2 children; d. field hospital near Pushka, Kyev, Ukraine, USSR 19 Mar 1945 (H. Klopfer; letter from CO, CHL CR 27140; IGI; FHL Microfilm 271380, 1935 Census)

Walter Oskar Kramer b. Berlin, Preußen 10 Feb 1877; son of Johann Kramer and Louise Beck; m. Olga Wagner; k. air raid Chemnitz, Chemnitz, Sachsen 5 Mar 1945 (CHL CR 375 8 #2459, 1034–1035)

Heinz Paul Wilhelm Mueller b. Königsberg, Ostpreußen, Preußen 7 Jan 1902; son of Paul F. Müller and Bertha Kopenhagen; d. 13 Nov 1939 (CHL CR 375 8 #2460, 416–17)

Olga Wagner b. Marienberg, Germany 10 Feb 1877; dau. of Louis Wagner and Marie Mann; m. Walter Oskar Kramer; k. air raid Chemnitz, Chemnitz, Sachsen 5 Mar 1945 (CHL CR 375 8 #2459, 1034)

Walter Hugo Wolf b. Spandau, Berlin, Preußen 30 May 1890; son of Heinrich Wolf and Elisabeth Graneberg; m. 10 May 1919, Martha Marie Anna Nickel; 2 children; d. wounds Spandau 18 May 1949 (CHL CR 375 8 #2459, 1014–15; IGI)

Leonhard Zander b. Aachen, Rheinland, Preußen 9 Dec 1864; son of Johannes Zander and Elisabeth Kutsch; bp. 13 Sep 1919; ord. priest; ord. elder; m.; d. Berlin, Preußen 11 Feb 1941 (*Sonntagsgruss*, no. 10, 9 Mar 1941, 40; FHL Microfilm 245307; IGI)

NOTES

1. After arriving in the United States in 1951, he changed his first name to that of his father, Herbert Klopfer, the supervisor of the East German Mission from 1939 to 1945. See the East German Mission chapter.

2. Herbert Klopfer, "Childhood in the Big German City of Berlin [1936–1943]" (unpublished personal history), 3; private collection.

3. Ingrid Bendler Broughton, interview by the author, Kaysville, Utah, February 16, 2007.

4. Presiding Bishopric, "Financial, Statistical, and Historical Reports of Wards, Stakes, and Missions, 1884–1955," CR 4 12, 257.

5. Ingrid Bendler, autobiography (unpublished), 11; private collection.

6. Klopfer, "Childhood," 4.

7. Bendler, autobiography, 14.

8. Klopfer, "Childhood," 4.

9. See the East German Mission chapter for additional details about those two nights.

10. Bendler, autobiography, 14.

11. Ibid., 16.

12. Ibid., 16. The two Otto girls had married just months before their death. By the end of the war, their husbands had also been killed.

13. Ibid., 17.
14. Klopfer, "Childhood," 5.
15. Bendler, autobiography, 25.
16. Ibid., 27.
17. Ibid., 26.
18. Ibid., 33.
19. Klopfer, "Childhood," 6. Part of the remarkable report was that the soldier had gone first to Berlin, where by coincidence he had learned that the family was living in Werdau.
20. Bendler, autobiography, 33.

BRANDENBURG-POTSDAM BRANCH

O n Sunday, August 14, 1938, a special meeting was held in Potsdam, Germany, to open a branch of the LDS Church there. Mission president Alfred C. Rees presided, and Richard Ranglack, president of the Berlin District, was also in attendance. Edward B. Wimmer, a missionary from the United States, was called to be the branch president. The attendees included thirty-two members and friends.[1]

Potsdam-Brandenburg Branch[2]	1939
Elders	2
Priests	2
Teachers	0
Deacons	1
Other Adult Males	14
Adult Females	29
Male Children	5
Female Children	0
Total	54

The establishment of the Potsdam Branch is evidence of the growth that characterized the Church in Germany in the late 1930s. Potsdam lies just twenty miles southwest of the Reich capital at Berlin. Approximately 113,000 residents called Potsdam their home in 1939.

The new branch prospered in Potsdam; the records of the East German Mission show the following entry for Sunday, October 16, 1938:

Fig. 1. The Brandenburg-Potsdam Branch members posed for this photograph in 1941. (I. Bendler-Broughton)

"At the opening meeting of the new Potsdam Branch hall, twenty-five Saints and fourteen friends were present. The new hall was located at Kaiser Wilhelm Strasse 28."[3]

Friedrich Fischer, first counselor in the Berlin District presidency, and two sister missionaries also attended. No description of the meeting rooms is available.

While the Potsdam Branch members were striving to maintain and improve their presence in that city, things were not going as well in the city of Brandenburg, fifteen miles to the west. The mission presidency found it necessary to take the following action on Sunday, December 10, 1938: "The Brandenburg Branch, Berlin District, was dissolved. The members were transferred to the Potsdam Branch books, bringing the total membership in Potsdam to fifty-four."[4]

As of this writing, no survivors of the Potsdam Branch could be located for interviews.

In Memoriam

One member of the Brandenburg-Potsdam Branch did not survive World War II:

August Adolf Liedtke b. Mahnsfeld Ostpreußen, Preußen Apr 1859; son of Karl Ludwig Liedtke and Caroline Wilhelmine Buchholz; bp. 4 Apr 1904; ord. elder; m. Mansfeld, Ostpreußen, Preußen 8 Oct 1882, Auguste Koesling; 7 children; d. stroke Potsdam, Brandenburg, Preußen 17 Nov 1939 (*Stern*, 1 Jan 1940, no. 1, 15; IGI)

Notes

1. East German Mission Quarterly Reports, 1938, no. 35, East German Mission History.
2. Presiding Bishopric, "Financial, Statistical, and Historical Reports of Wards, Stakes, and Missions, 1884–1955," CR 4 12, 257.
3. East German Mission Quarterly Reports, 1938, no. 44.
4. Ibid., 10.

EBERSWALDE BRANCH

Located forty-five miles northeast of Berlin, Eberswalde was a city of approximately thirty thousand inhabitants in 1939. It was the home to a very small branch of the LDS Church, established in 1934. Ursula Jawureck moved with her parents, Johannes and Herta Jawureck, from Pomerania to Eberswalde in 1932, where they became acquainted with the Church through the Zaar family. Years later, Ursula recalled the rented meeting rooms used by the Church at Schicklerstrasse 11:

From the street, we went through a portal of the main building, across the courtyard, then into the Hinterhaus. We went up a spiral staircase outside, into the foyer that was about fifteen by twenty feet in size. There was a space for leadership meetings behind the table that we used for a pulpit. It was just a table with chairs and a tablecloth. The children's class was in the foyer—all of the children together. There were only a few of us. We met there from 1934 through the end of the war.[1]

Sunday School was held in the morning and sacrament meeting in the evening. The members went home between the meetings. Approximately twenty persons were in attendance on a typical Sunday during the first few years of the war.

A prominent family in the Eberswalde Branch was that of the branch president, Hermann Bünger, a letter carrier by trade. He went to church early every Sunday morning in order to heat the rooms. "Somehow he always came up with enough coal to do that," recalled Ursula Jawureck. "His family always cleaned the rooms but never took credit for it. The children had piano lessons so that they could play the pump organ for us. Brother Bünger wore the same suit every Sunday for years, and he gave a talk and a lesson every Sunday."

Eberswalde Branch[2]	1939
Elders	1
Priests	0
Teachers	0
Deacons	3
Other Adult Males	4
Adult Females	11
Male Children	2
Female Children	2
Total	23

The general minutes of branch meetings show an interesting statement inserted following the entry for October 1, 1939:

Sacrament meetings were held regularly during October and November [1939]. Because of the war, several missionaries and brethren have been drafted, causing frequent changes in branch leadership and several gaps in the records regarding meetings.[3]

Wartime conditions caused a change in the meeting schedule, according to the minutes recorded on December 10, 1939: "The members have agreed to change the starting time for sacrament meetings to 3:00 P.M., due to the blackout regulations caused by the current war."[4]

During the first few years of the war, branch activities continued as before. For example, on July 9, 1941, a Sunday School excursion took place. According to branch records, "Eleven persons participated, and the hours went by all too fast. It is the general consensus that we need to do this again soon."[5]

The average attendance at sacrament meetings in the latter years of the war was fewer than twelve persons, but once in a while the group was much larger. For example, following the sacrament meeting on March 15, 1942, there was a centennial celebration for the Relief Society. As reported in the branch

minutes, "The words and deeds of the [founding] women were memorialized in poems and talks. Those women showed the way for the next generation of service. Twenty-one persons attended the celebration."[6]

Johannes Jawureck did not allow his wife to be baptized until after the war, but he granted his daughter, Ursula, permission to join the Church just before her twelfth birthday. The baptismal ceremony took place in the city's lake, the Bachsee, on September 12, 1942. Ursula later described the event in these words:

We gathered at the market place then walked together to the lake for this little outing. It was cold, but the sisters wrapped me up in blankets when I got out of the water. We didn't have to do it in secret. Brother Dröhner confirmed me, and I will never forget the event.

According to the branch minutes, the baptism of Ursula and two other members was originally scheduled for August 16. However, several problems arose, and the ceremony was postponed. The start of the Relief Society meeting that day was delayed for one hour due to an air-raid alarm. Then there was no longer time to walk ninety minutes to the baptismal venue and back before the visitors from Berlin would have to leave town. Thus the Relief Society meeting was postponed, and the members walked to the baptismal venue but found that there were too many people bathing in the area to allow for the proper spirit for the ceremony. The members prayed and were directed to try again a month later.[7]

Shortly after her baptism, Ursula was inducted into the government's Jungmädel program along with all of the other girls in her school class. However, because of her apprenticeship, she was not required to join the League of German Girls when she became fourteen. Her father, not a member of the Church, belonged to the National Socialist Party. Ursula did not remember any conflict between the

Party and the Church at home or in school, nor did she recall any discussion of politics during Church meetings: "Brother Bünger said that we would put ourselves into the hands of the Lord and politics was not part of our church life. He was very careful about that."

Life in Eberswalde during World War II was relatively peaceful. The city had no critical war industry and was thus spared attacks from the air until the last year of the war. The Eberswalde Branch continued to meet on Sundays without interruption. Because there were so few priesthood holders in the branch, visitors from the district presidency and the mission office were frequently in attendance. Shortages and rationing did not allow for as many branch parties and celebrations as had been held before 1939, but the branch members remained a tight group during the war and helped each other through the privations. An average of six members of the Eberswalde Branch attended semiannual district conferences in Berlin.

Johannes Jawureck was drafted just after the war started and was gone the entire time with the exception of a few furloughs. In his absence, his wife, Herta, and his daughter, Ursula, were able to remain in their apartment and had enough food to sustain themselves. When Eberswalde was attacked from the air toward the end of the war, many homes were destroyed, but neither the Jawureck apartment nor the branch meeting rooms were damaged. No members of the branch lost their homes during those air raids.

The last entry in the branch general minutes written during the war states, "On April 2, 1944 a fast and testimony meeting was held. Regular sacrament meetings were held under local leadership on April 9, 16, 23, and 30, with an average attendance of six members."[8]

As the Red Army drove toward Berlin in April 1945, they found the city of Eberswalde prepared to surrender without any resistance. However, in a vain attempt to stop the invaders from taking the city, the German air force attacked the old core of the city and destroyed it.[9]

Ursula Jawureck had been told in school that the Red Army soldiers would put out the eyes of German children. At fourteen, she was terrified. Her mother had been told to leave town and flee to the west, but they had no place to go. Herta Jawureck helped her daughter disguise herself as an older woman, hoping to spare her the terrible fate that befell so many German women and girls at the hands of marauding Soviet soldiers: "For two or three weeks I could not wash my face or hair. I smeared my face with soot." Ursula's fears were soon on the verge of becoming reality, as she will never forget:

> Many of us were in the Engels' house. We were all hiding together. A Mongolian came by and wanted me to go with him. He was really drunk. I was only fourteen years old, and I was shaking with fear. All I could say in my prayer was, "Dear Heavenly Father, Dear Heavenly Father." I couldn't get past that.
>
> The house was really big, a villa really. He took me away, and I screamed, "Mommy, Mommy, Mommy!" And she yelled back, "Go with him or he will kill us all!" and I thought, "What kind of mother is she?" but later I realized that she had to do that to spare the rest of them. Then the soldier told me to take off my clothes, and then he lay down. I undid my top two buttons, then buttoned them up again, and did that back and forth so that he could see that I was doing something.
> Meanwhile I continued to pray, "Dear Heavenly Father, Dear Heavenly Father." I was so rattled that I could not think of anything else to say. Then I heard him breathing; he had fallen asleep, so I got out of there. When I got back, they asked if he had hurt me. "No, he's sleeping." The next morning the soldier woke up and went looking for me. He searched for me in the living room and the kitchen. My mother covered me up with a blanket. He didn't find me.

The war did not end officially for two more weeks, and the terror in Eberswalde continued for Ursula Jawureck and her mother. On one occasion, they were again hiding in the basement of the Engel villa. The Soviets had broken the windows a few days before and water stood a foot deep in the basement. Despite the cold water and the glass on the floor, members of the branch knelt in prayer and begged for deliverance. As Ursula later explained, "The house door was open, and Russians could have just come in. So we prayed that the Lord would make the Russians blind so they couldn't see us. The entire episode was terrifying. I was shaking the whole time, and I thought I'd never survive it all."

Herta Jawureck was spared violation because she had been kind to a Russian prisoner of war in previous months. He took it upon himself to protect her when his comrades arrived. Johannes Jawureck was still a prisoner of war somewhere; toward the end of 1945, he appeared at their home in Eberswalde in relatively good health. Ursula recalled the following:

> After the war when we went back to the church rooms, the spiral staircase had been removed and the pump organ was gone. The building was still there and was not damaged. So we didn't have meetings for a while. Then the brethren came from Berlin and tried to find the whereabouts of every member. So we started to have meetings in the living room of Sister Zaar.

Fortunately, President Hermann Bünger had not been required to serve in the Germany army and thus was able to remain in Eberswalde to direct branch activities until shortly before the conquerors arrived.[10]

In Memoriam

The following members of the Eberswalde Branch did not survive World War II:

Hermann August Karl Felger b. Schulzendorf, Brandenburg, Preußen 7 Apr 1859; son of Johann Friedrich Felger and Hanna Charlotte Friederike Richter; bp. 7 Aug 1933; m. Marie Klamann; 2 children; m. Eberswalde, Brandenburg, Preußen 6 Mar 1894, Liesette Marie Anna Prinzler; 1 child; d. Eberswalde, Brandenburg, Preußen 17 Jan 1941; bur. Eberswalde 22 Jan 1941 (*Sonntagsgruss*, no. 11, 16 Mar 1941, 43; IGI)

Paul Otto Bruno Friedrich b. Eberswalde, Brandenburg, Preußen 28 Nov 1899; son of Bruno August Friedrich and Berta Auguste Elisabeth Schilsky; m. 15 Jun 1923; d. 21 Nov 1940 (CHL Microfilm LR 2481 11, 130; IGI)

Felon Hermann d. 17 Jan 1940 (CHL Microfilm LR 2481 11, 131; IGI)

Hermine Elwine Auguste Klamann b. Brunow, Oberbarnim, Brandenburg, Preußen 25 Dec 1863; dau. of Karl Klamann and Friederike Sachtleben; bp. 2 Jul 1932; conf. 2 Jul 1932; m. 2 Aug 1885, Oskar Lehmann; d. stroke 28 Oct 1940 (FHL Microfilm 68809 no. 51; IGI)

Helene Johanna Eliesabeth Lemke b. Greifenhagen, Pommern, Preußen 17 Apr 1878; dau. of Wilhelm August Karl Lemke and Johanna Elisabeth Fransiska Baltzer; bp. 29 Aug 1928; conf. 29 Aug 1928; m. Eberswalde, Brandenburg, Preußen 7 Apr 1906, Karl August Gustav Martin Glaevcke; 1 child; d. suicide Eberswalde, Brandenburg, Preußen 24 Apr 1945 (FHL Microfilm 68809 no. 50; IGI)

Liesette Marie Anna Prinzler b. Salzmünde, Sachsen, Preußen 10 Feb 1862; dau. of Heinrich Karl Prinzler and Liesette Hecklau; bp. 12 Jul 1930; m. Eberswalde, Brandenburg, Preußen 6 Mar 1894, Hermann Karl August Felger; d. Eberswalde 19 Jan 1942 (IGI)

Notes

1. Ursula Jawureck Schieleit, interview by the author in German, Eberswalde, Germany, June 8, 2007; summarized in English by the author.

2. Presiding Bishopric, "Financial, Statistical, and Historical Reports of Wards, Stakes, and Missions, 1884–1955," CR 4 12, 257.

3. Eberswalde Branch, general minutes, 125, LR 2481/11, Church History Library.

4. Ibid., 126.

5. Ibid., 133.

6. Ibid., 137.

7. Ibid., 139.

8. Ibid., 146.

9. City of Eberswalde's official Web site, http://www.eberswalde.de/Historie.1337.0.html.

10. He fled to the west with his family and eventually settled in Celle in West Germany.

LEEST GROUP

There were two dozen organized small groups of Church members in the East German Mission in 1939. These groups were scattered all over the mission territory and generally consisted of one family each, with a few of their neighbors and friends. One such group was organized in Leest, twenty-two miles southwest of Berlin. The closest official branch was in Potsdam, six miles away. The story of the Leest group during World War II is both heroic and tragic.

The core of the Leest group was the Baade family. Friedrich ("Grandpa") Baade had joined the Church in the 1920s and had taught his children the gospel. The only other priesthood holder in the group was Michael Kolbin, the husband of Friedrich's daughter, Emma. He was born in Russia, but after being captured during the First World War had chosen to stay in Germany. The Kolbin family lived on the main floor of the Baade home, while the Baades lived upstairs.

The religious life of the Saints in Leest centered on the Baade home. Anna Frieda Martha Wolf, the only survivor of the group as of this writing, later recalled the setting:

> We held our meetings in the Baade home with perhaps a dozen persons. We used the largest room; it was about twenty by twenty-five feet in size. . . . We started at about 9:00 A.M. with sacrament meeting for one hour, then Sunday School. We little kids went into the kitchen for our class, and the older members stayed in the living room.[1]

The Autobahn (national highway) ring around metropolitan Berlin passed very close to Leest, and an eminent domain ruling cost the Baade family some of their land. According

Fig. 1. The Baade home in Leest as it appeared during World War II. (H. Fischer)

to Anna Wolf, Grandpa Baade "really suffered" from this development and was not a supporter of Hitler or the Nazi Party. His attitude may have attracted negative attention to the tiny group. Anna recalled the following:

> Sometimes we had visitors [government officials] in our meetings. [They] came to the house, greeted with "Heil Hitler," said that they were there to investigate the activities, then just listened and left—no disturbance, no interruption. They behaved very correctly.

As the war drew to a close, another of Friedrich Baade's daughters, Charlotte Fischer, brought her children from eastern Berlin to live in the Baade family home in Leest. With gasoline being close to impossible to find, she took a horse-drawn wagon belonging to her husband's business and traversed the twenty-two miles to Leest despite dynamited bridges and the confusion of a Berlin that would soon be conquered by the Red Army. Shortly after they arrived in Leest, Charlotte Fischer's sons saw enemy soldiers for the first time.[2]

One night, Hans Fischer (a Baade grandson born in Berlin in 1931) heard somebody pounding on the door of the Baade home. A Russian man who was working for the Fischer business in eastern Berlin answered the door and was confronted by Russian soldiers. He apparently told his countrymen that there were no German soldiers on the property. Satisfied, the soldiers left the home in peace—for the time being.

"The war had been hard on us, but we had been protected," recalled Anna Wolf. But the following weeks were a time of terror for her. She had married just weeks before the war began, but her husband (not a member of the Church) had been in the German army for years, and when the war ended in May 1945, his whereabouts were not known. The residents of Leest may have believed that when the fighting ceased, life would be easier for them. However, conditions under military occupation were worse than before. Anna Wolf gave this account of happenings in that little town:

> You can hardly believe what they did. Night after night, the Russians stole our stuff, killed people, and attacked women. I was still rather young in those days.[3] One of the sisters in the group [her husband was related to Grandpa Baade] was raped so many times [she was the only one], and we just could not help her.[4] We kept one window open all the time to listen for the Russians coming. We all got together in the village and talked about how we would defend ourselves against the Russians. . . . Well, I sat up by the window watching for them to come. I gave the signal with my whistle then everybody hid. Then the Russians stormed into our house, broke all of our windows, and looked for women to rape.

On one occasion, Anna was chased by enemy soldiers. She escaped them in her home and ran down Leest's only street, screaming at the top of her lungs. "Where did I run to? Grandpa Baade!" Friedrich Baade and his son-in-law blocked the entry of the home to prevent the soldiers from pursuing young Anna.

This may not have been the only time when Grandpa Baade made himself unpopular with the Soviet occupation troops. As soldiers ransacked homes in Leest and terrorized the populace, he did what he could to protect his home, family, and friends.

Anna believed that the soldiers' anger toward Grandpa Baade and other residents incited a terrible act of revenge, recounted by Hans Fischer:

> The war had been over for two or three months [by August 12]. Three Russian soldiers pulled up to the house in a jeep. One stayed in the jeep, and the other two came into the house and started taking clothing, watches, and anything else that they wanted. My grandpa had built that house himself; he finished it in 1900. He was so upset with these soldiers that he walked

Fig. 2. Friedrich Baade was laid to rest in the church cemetery in nearby Töplitz. (H. Fischer)

99

out to the jeep with a pencil and a piece of paper and wrote down the license plate number. He wanted to report them, because the Russian soldiers could get in trouble for doing that. When the Russian in the jeep saw what my grandfather was doing, he took out his pistol and shot my grandfather.

Grandpa Baade was carried into his home mortally wounded and died a few minutes later. But the tragedy that befell the founder and leader of the Latter-day Saint group in the small rural community of Leest did not herald the end of the Church there. The surviving Baades and their friends continued to hold Church meetings and remained loyal to their Heavenly Father.[5]

In Memoriam

Only one member of the Leest Group did not survive World War II:

Karl Friedrich August Baade b. Neu Töplitz, Brandenburg, Preußen 13 Dec 1867; son of Carl Ludwig Baade and Christiane Wilhelmine Wittenbecher; bp. 27 Aug 1927; m. Alt Töplitz, Brandenburg, Preußen 22 Oct 1893, Anna Elisabeth Ruhr; 6 children; shot by Soviet soldier, Leest, Brandenburg, Preußen 20 Aug 1945 (H. Fischer; IGI)

Notes

1. Anna Frieda Martha Wolf Touchard, interview by the author in German, Potsdam, Germany, August 21, 2006; summarized in English by the author.
2. Hans Fischer, interview by the author, Midway, Utah, March 26, 2006.
3. Anna Wolf was twenty-six years old at the time.
4. Her name was Anna Ruhr Meyer, according to Anna Wolf.
5. Just a few yards from the Baade home, a tiny but beautiful LDS meetinghouse now stands as a quasimemorial to the faithful Saints of Leest.

Rathenow Branch

If we had only been able to come to Salt Lake City before the great war, we could have missed those twelve terrible years that we now would like to forget." This statement written in 1958 could have been made by thousands of Latter-day Saints who experienced Hitler's Third Reich.[1] The writer, Gerda Hille Hubrich, was essentially the mother of the Rathenow Branch from 1936 until her immigration to the United States.[2]

Gerda Hille was born in Glienick, near Berlin, in 1918. In 1935, she married Fritz Hubrich in Guben on the Neisse River. Both were recent converts to the Church.[3] Their first son, Ralf, was born in Guben in 1936, and soon thereafter the family moved to Rathenow, a town fifty-five miles directly west of Berlin. Fritz had been a weaver in Guben but found work with the Emil Busch Company in Rathenow as a mechanic. He stayed there until he was sent to war. The Hubrich family expanded the Latter-day Saint population in Rathenow because they brought Gerda's mother and sister with them from Guben, and several Hubrich sons were born in Rathenow.

Rathenow Branch[4]	1938
Elders	3
Priests	1
Teachers	1
Deacons	1
Other Adult Males	11
Adult Females	37
Male Children	3
Female Children	2
Total	59

The Hubrichs remembered holding Church meetings in various schools as well as in the homes of members. According to mission records, the meetings were being held in the Hubrich home at Paul Nitzsche Strasse 24 in January 1943.[5] Their living room measured about fifteen by eighteen feet. There were seats for most of the older members, while the younger ones sat on the floor; attendance varied from ten to twenty persons. Sunday School was held in the morning and sacrament meeting in the evening, just as was done in larger branches.

Fritz Hubrich had been ordained to the priesthood by district president Richard Ranglack and was eventually called to be branch president. There were few other priesthood holders, and by the end of the war none were at home; thus the branch could not have a sacrament service as part of their meetings.

The general minutes of the Rathenow Branch show the following entry dated September 30, 1946, written by Fritz Franke:

In January 1943 I was drafted into the army, as was branch president Fritz Hubrich in May of the same year. The Rathenow Branch was thus devoid of leaders until 1 August 1943, when Brother Fritz Kuefner of the Berlin Spandau Branch was called to lead our branch.[6]

In 1943, Fritz Hubrich was drafted into the Wehrmacht and sent to the Eastern Front. He had no scriptures in his possession, never attended a meeting of the Saints or took the sacrament, and never met another Latter-day Saint soldier. He was completely isolated from the Church while he was on active duty, but he said his prayers every day. Serving as a radio operator, he witnessed the retreat of the German army from the Soviet Union back to the fatherland. One of his major combat experiences was the German attempt to rescue troops encircled by the enemy near Minsk.

Like most members of the Church, Sister Hubrich was not spared the terror of attacks from the air on the civilian population in German cities. She recalled:

One of the most dreadful days of my life was in April, 1944, when our city was for the most part destroyed by bombers. I lay with my new baby boy [Winfried] in bed, too weak to get around. The bombs fell all around us. We could see them explode through the window and expected every minute to be the last one. I prayed aloud for help as our house rocked back and forth and some of our neighbors' houses blew to pieces. Every second we thought our house would be the next one destroyed.

To temporarily escape further air raids in Rathenow, Gerda Hubrich traveled east to Silesia with her children. They stayed in that part of Germany for three months in what Sister Hubrich called "a small village safe from all of the horrors of war."

Far from home, Fritz Hubrich watched as several partisans were rounded up one day in the spring of 1945. He was ordered to shoot the partisans (which was legal under international law), but instead he directed his fire at the trees above. The officer in charge was angry at him for not obeying the order, but no penalty was administered. "Life didn't mean anything at the time," Fritz later recalled.

The advancing Red Army conquered Rathenow in April 1945 without significant resistance. Much of the town had already been destroyed. As in other areas under their

Fig. 1. The members of the Rathenow Branch gathered for this photograph in 1937. (G. Hubrich)

control, the conquerors quickly set out to enjoy the spoils of war. Sister Hubrich was a mother of three boys at the time, but she and her fifty-five-year-old mother were equally desirable targets of marauding soldiers. From late April through much of May 1945, Gerda kept her three sons close by her side. At the same time, she was being guarded by her own mother:

My mother would sit by the door, [Russian soldiers] came in drunk, and then they would see my mother . . . holding a candle sitting there, and the Russians said "Come, Frau!" My mother was very smart and said, "Frau not here, Frau in other house!" The women in the next house said the same thing. This happened for fourteen days.

At about that time, Fritz Hubrich's unit had retreated into Germany before the Soviet advance and he was about one hundred miles away from his family. He was eventually captured by the enemy and forced to dig his own grave. Gerda told his story:

Just before they were to shoot him, some German prisoners went by and after much pleading he was allowed to go with them. He escaped but was soon recaptured. Again he escaped without being harmed. This happened again; he was beaten a little and shot at a number of times, but he came through it all.[7]

Feelings of depression over the lost war and the terror of imminent assault at the hands of marauding conquerors was enough to drive thousands of German citizens to suicide. It can hardly come as a surprise that a Latter-day Saint mother would consider such a way out of the suffering. Gerda Hubrich had escaped her incarceration in a village just south of

Fig. 2. A view of the Hubrich home in Rathenow in 1940. (G. Hubrich)

Fig. 3. Gerda and Fritz Hubrich with their sons Ralph and Wolf Dieter in 1939. (G. Hubrich)

Rathenow and was walking the four miles to her own home with her sons and her mother. Along the way she paused by a small lake, "intending to end our troubles by drowning." She later recalled telling them, "Boys, let's go into the lake, and then we'll be with our Father in Heaven." Taking her life and the lives of her sons seemed to be the only way out of their misery. However, "my children screamed, and my mother said, 'God has protected us this far, and we will trust that He will continue to do so.' And this He did."

Within two days of this near tragedy, a disheveled Fritz Hubrich arrived in Rathenow to a wife who had nearly ended her life. The joyous reunion dispelled worry about the pending destruction. "Did they touch you?" he asked of his wife, knowing full well what Red Army soldiers were doing to women all over eastern Germany. He was happy to learn that his wife had escaped such brutal treatment.

The Hubrichs returned to a home inhabited by enemy soldiers but undamaged. They begged to be allowed in but were turned away. Fortunately, a place was found for them in bombed-out Rathenow. Nine months later, the family was finally allowed to occupy their home again. Just a few weeks after World War II concluded, branch president Fritz Hubrich welcomed the surviving Saints to worship services in the home of one of the member families. The Church was alive and would prosper in Rathenow.

In Memoriam

The following member of the Rathenow Branch did not survive World War II:

Walter Karl Neumann b. Rathenow, Brandenburg, Preußen 27 Mar or Nov 1933; son of Walter Friedrich Max Newmann and Else Frida Vogel; bp. 27 Nov 1941; d. pneumonia 27 Feb 1945 (CHL Microfilm LR 7336 11, General Minutes of Rathenow Branch; IGI)

Notes

1. Gerda Hille Hubrich, Church News, *Deseret News*, August 9, 1958, quoted in Dorothy South Hackworth, *The Master's Touch* (n.p., 1961), 254.
2. Gerda Hille Hubrich and Fritz Hubrich, interview by the author, Salt Lake City, June 27, 2007.
3. As of this writing, Fritz Hubrich may be the oldest surviving former branch president of the East German Mission during World War II.
4. Presiding Bishopric, "Financial, Statistical, and Historical Reports of Wards, Stakes, and Missions, 1884–1955," CR 4 12, 257.
5. East German Mission, "Directory of Meeting Places" (unpublished manuscript, 1943); private collection.
6. Rathenow Branch, general minutes, CHL, LR 7336 11.
7. Hackworth, *Master's Touch*, 257.

Spandau Branch

The modern Berlin suburb of Spandau was an independent community until it was incorporated into metropolitan Berlin in 1920. Located at the far northwest corner of the Reich capital, it was home to a branch of the LDS Church that met in rooms rented at Neue Bergstrasse 3 in the first Hinterhaus—a venue the Saints enjoyed long before, during, and after World War II.

Spandau Branch[1]	1939
Elders	4
Priests	2
Teachers	5
Deacons	3
Other Adult Males	15
Adult Females	53
Male Children	4
Female Children	0
Total	86

Born in 1925 to parents who had joined the Church just the year before, Rudi Seehagen recalled the layout of the rooms:

It used to be Hülsebeck's Building Company. My first wife's parents or grandparents were related to the Hülsebeck family; that's why we were able to rent the rooms there. There were stalls for horses and storage space for equipment and materials; the offices were above that. The company was no longer in business, so we renovated the rooms. You went through the front building's foyer then through a double gate then to the left and up the stairs. There were two rooms, and we removed the middle wall; that was our main meeting room. To the left was a smaller room for Relief Society or priesthood meetings. Then upstairs there were two classrooms (a total of four rooms).[2]

Rudi recalled seeing about thirty to forty people in church on a typical Sunday. Sunday School began at 10:00 A.M., with sacrament meeting at 5:00 or 6:00 in the evening.

Wolfram Dittrich (born 1928) recalled details of the seating in the chapel: "The large room had about seven rows of chairs with about ten chairs in each row. The branch presidency was seated on the rostrum."[3]

Walter Kuefner (born 1933) recalled going to church early on Sunday in the winter season in order to heat the rooms. Traveling to church from the town of Staaken to the west (an hour's trip), it made for a very early start to his Sunday.[4]

The Spandau Branch meetings continued with only one interruption throughout the war. An unidentified inactive member told her

Fig. 1. The mothers of the Spandau Branch in about 1940. (R. Seehagen)

husband, an army officer, about their rooms in the Neue Bergstrasse. He decided to requisition the rooms for storage. Horst Schwermer and district president Fritz Fischer went to the army office and explained their need for the rooms and suggested other places the army could store their equipment. The use of the rooms for Church meetings was restored with only one Sunday lost.

One of the rare changes in Church practice in Germany during war was the exclusion of songs that included words such as *Zion* and *Jehovah*. "That was too Jewish," recalled Rudi Seehagen. "Sometimes we forgot and remembered only when the word came up in the song. Well, it didn't cause any problem. At least not in our branch."

A variation of the ward teaching program was practiced in the Spandau Branch during the war. Rudi Seehagen was assigned to accompany Willy Knoll in visiting a total of thirteen families who lived over a wide area. Rudi remembered how they rode their bikes to communities as far away as Kladow (six miles to the south) and Niederneuendorf (four miles to the north). They were not able to visit all of the families every month.

Helga Abel was born in Spandau to Latter-day Saint parents in 1922. At the age of ten, she was inducted into the Jungvolk, the first phase of the Hitler Youth program (as was done all over Germany through the schools). It was a good experience, as she recalled:

I was singing and doing fun things, so they asked me to join the Jungvolk, and it wasn't long before I was in charge of my group. And we had outings, and we would sing (I loved to sing), and we would go camping. At that time we didn't have Primary, but we had the Jungvolk.[5]

When she turned fourteen and was invited to join the League of German Girls (BDM), her mother put her foot down and denied Helga permission; it would interfere with

Church meetings. During a neighborhood Nazi Party meeting in about 1936, Helga's name was brought up as one who should be blacklisted because of her refusal to join the BDM. Fortunately for her, a non-LDS man, a Mr. Singer, whose wife was a member of the Church, stood up for her and instructed the other party members to leave Helga Abel alone. "He saved my neck," she claimed.

Born in 1915 in Königsberg, East Prussia, Horst Schwermer had already served as a communications specialist in a German army cavalry unit for two years and had moved to Berlin. In the spring of 1938, he went to the city center of Berlin to attend a Latter-day Saint district conference. On the way, he noticed a very pretty young lady in the streetcar. She turned out to be Helga Abel, the girl selected to officially welcome mission president Alfred C. Rees and his wife to the conference and to present them with flowers. "That's how I found out that she was Helga Abel of the Spandau Branch," Horst explained.[6] At the time, Helga was only sixteen years old. Horst was an employee of the Lufthansa Airline Company of Berlin.

When she was seventeen, Helga Abel completed her schooling. She had wanted to study pedagogy and become a teacher, but the war had begun and some personal choices were no longer possible. She went to work instead as an assistant to an oral surgeon and stayed in his employ for several years. Toward the end of her tenure—August 30, 1941—she and Horst Schwermer were married. As Horst recalled:

> The church wedding took place in our church; Brother [Fritz] Fischer, our district president, was officiating. I picked Helga up from her parents' apartment in a white wedding carriage drawn by two white horses. After the

Fig. 2. Helga Abel and Horst Schwermer were married in the Spandau city hall. Note the portrait of Adolf Hitler in the background. (H. Schwermer)

wedding [at the city hall], we went to Lesky's photographer to have a picture taken.

There was no honeymoon for the Schwermers, but soon after the wedding Horst was accepted as a student at a technical college in Berlin and was able to stay at home until he was reactivated in the armed services in 1943. Until then, he served as a counselor to branch president Willy Knoll. The Schwermers' first son was born in a Berlin hospital. As Helga later recalled:

> The doctor was very unhappy with women that had babies because he had seen in Hamburg where people were on the street delivering babies and nobody could take care of them. Then part of the hospital got bombed and burned out. [My baby] was eleven days old when I left Berlin.

As the air raids over Berlin increased in frequency and severity, the city government urged mothers to take their children out of town. Helga Schwermer took the train east with her infant son, Jürgen, and found a place to live near the port city of Stettin. Before leaving home, she had offered to allow another Latter-day Saint family to live in their apartment.[7] Arriving in Stettin, she had to walk for ninety minutes to her new home—one small room in the home of some very nice farm people. "When I look back, I don't know how we did

it. [Jürgen] was only eleven days old, and I walked an hour and a half."

Despite wartime conditions, there were ways for children to entertain themselves. Walter Kuefner was one of many who collected shrapnel fragments after air raids. As he later explained, "We gathered them for how big they were and how new they were. If they were already a little bit rusty, they weren't from last night. If they were shiny, [they were new]."

Wolfram Dittrich recalled the event that caused his family to move from the Berlin neighborhood of Schöneberg to Spandau in 1942:

> I will never forget what happened in the night that our home was bombed. . . . Many houses stood in a row, and in the back we had a yard. Behind our home was a high school in which a bomb fell that night. We sat in our basement, and my brother was so scared because of the air pressure and the noise that he wanted to run away. I grabbed him at the last second. My mother owned a laundry in our building, and behind her working area was our apartment. The walls stood askew, and we could not live in it anymore. For this reason, we had to leave Schöneberg. The furniture was intact, but the walls threatened to collapse.

During the war, it was still important for young people like Wolfram Dittrich to progress in school. As the attacks on Berlin and its suburbs increased, schools were damaged or destroyed. School populations doubled up or held split sessions in some neighborhoods. As he later explained:

> The most difficult thing for us was that the schools were also attacked after 1942. When some schools were already severely damaged and could not be used anymore, we had school either in the mornings and some classes in the afternoon because that was the only time that was available.

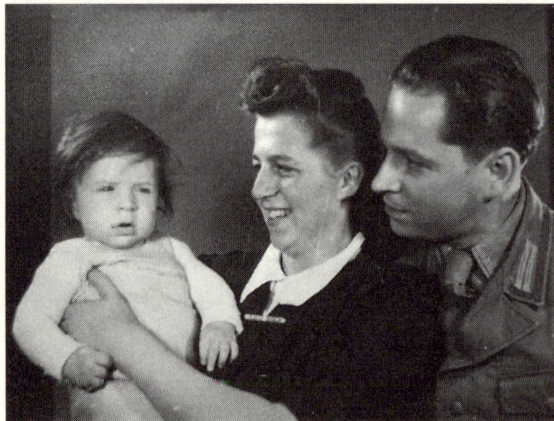

Fig. 3. Helga and Horst Schwermer with their son Jürgen. (H. Schwermer)

Rudi Seehagen was too young to serve in the military until the latter half of the war, so he continued to attend church with his family in the Spandau Branch. After completing public school at the age of fourteen, he began an apprenticeship as a porcelain painter in the Royal Prussian Porcelain Works in Berlin. This proved to be fortuitous because it later kept him out of the Reichsarbeitsdienst (RAD) for perhaps a year. "We were completing a special commission of porcelain for Adolf Hitler, and I was granted a one-year reprieve," he explained.

Spandau was a prime target for attacks by the American and British air forces. Huge factories there produced electronic equipment and tanks. During the air raids over Spandau, minor damage was done near the Seehagen home, but Rudi did not recall that any branch members lost their homes. Some of the windows in the meetinghouse burst from the air pressure of bombs exploding close by, but the building remained fully usable throughout the war.

Erich Gellersen, a native of the Stade Branch near Hamburg in the West German Mission, joined the Spandau Branch early in the war. As an aeronautical engineer, he had been transferred to Spandau by his employer, the BMW Company. Following every air raid, he rode his motorcycle around town, trying to locate members and learn how they had fared during the attack.

Out in the Pomeranian countryside northeast of Berlin, Helga Schwermer could see the lights of the fires after Allied air raids over the major Baltic port city of Stettin. On one occasion she murmured to herself, "They [the Nazis] want to build a victory on these ruins!" Next door was the family of a high-ranking officer, whose wife apparently heard Helga make what was considered to be a defeatist statement. She told her husband and the situation soon became critical. Helga recounted:

I don't know if it was the next day or two days later, I got called to [report to] the high Nazi party official. And he gave me hell. . . . "Do you

know that I should send you to a concentration camp?" And I said, "But I have a baby," and I don't remember what he answered to that, but I was just shaking. And then I was standing in the doorway, holding Jürgen, and he said, "You can think that [defeatist idea], but don't you ever say that out loud again." So if he had been a convinced Nazi, I would have been in a concentration camp.

Because they lived too far from a concrete air-raid bunker, Fritz Kuefner dug a hole in the yard by the family home in Staaken. He put some logs across it and piled sand on top. According to his son, Walter, "It was more of the real thing; you could see what was happening up there. You could see the airplanes and the explosions. You could sometimes see a plane being hit and the people jumping out with their parachutes." Being that close to the action, however, could be scary. Walter recalled worrying that the Americans who parachuted from the planes would be hiding along the way to school the next day. "The minute they came down, they were captured, but we kids didn't know that [at the time]."

Horst Schwermer was reactivated by the military in 1943. Sent directly to the Balkans, he served as a communications officer in a motorized infantry unit. "My vehicle was always right behind the lead one. They called us the 'fire engine of the Balkans' because we were always rushed from hot spot to hot spot. Our territory included Yugoslavia, Bulgaria, Romania, Greece, and Albania," Horst explained.

Helga Schwermer returned from Stettin to Spandau with her son in 1944. The Soviets were pushing toward German territory, and it was no longer safe near Stettin. Back home, she was living next door to her parents and enjoyed their support, as well as her husband's ongoing income from the Lufthansa office (though Horst was away in the army). She even belonged to a club of ten to twelve young wives

Fig. 4. The Seehagen family about 1941. Rudi is behind his parents. (R. Seehagen)

who went to the same air-raid shelter together on a regular basis.

By 1943, the Reich war effort needed every healthy young man. Rudi Seehagen's exemption was not extended that year, and he was inducted into the Reichsarbeitsdienst. He served with a work unit for three months along the coast of Estonia. Following his release from the RAD, he enjoyed a few days at home before his draft notice arrived. He reported to the local Wehrmacht office and was asked which branch of the military he wished to serve with. Rudi reported having had a serious accident that nearly cost him a foot a few years earlier and requested to be assigned to any unit but infantry. Three days later he was in uniform and on his way to Kobel near the former Polish border for basic training. From there his unit was transported to partisan territory in Russia where conditions were dangerous. It was soon clear that Rudi Seehagen's request to serve anywhere but in the infantry was not to be fulfilled. As he recalled, "When the army advanced, we were in the vanguard; when they retreated, we were the last to abandon the position. I was never wounded because my Heavenly Father always protected me, but some of my comrades were hurt."

Because many German soldiers routinely drank alcohol and smoked, Latter-day Saint soldiers were often under pressure to do the same. Rather than give in, Rudi Seehagen

traded his cigarette rations for other food items and successfully resisted temptation. He also avoided another problem: stealing. When his buddies raided local farms and stole food from the Russian inhabitants, Rudi did not go along. He already had enough to eat, thanks to his cigarette trades.

Horst Schwermer also enjoyed the advantages of observing the Church's standards for health, as was evident from an incident at Easter, 1944. His unit had moved into Hungary, and he stopped one Sunday for a drink with his buddies at a country inn:

> The boys ordered a beer, and I ordered a glass of milk. This was my national drink. And the boys got their beers, and it took a little longer for me to get my milk, and when it came [the host] had a big plate and a big piece of cake on it and a glass of milk. So when the boys said, "Oh my gosh, that will cost you," I said, "It doesn't matter, but it will taste good." And then [the innkeeper] came to collect the money from all the

Fig. 5. Rudi Seehagen made this sketch of his temporary quarters in Russia in 1944. (R. Seehagen)

boys. "Okay, how much do I owe you?" I asked him. "Nothing, you are my guest."

Because the Reich was becoming desperate for soldiers, Wolfram Dittrich was only in the RAD for two months at the age of sixteen before he was drafted into the army and trained in tank warfare. Wolfram's unit was then sent to the front to stop the British advance in northwest Germany. "My entire unit consisted of sixteen-``year-olds," he recalled. "In Rheine at the river Ems we first met the British in combat, and after a short time, only twenty-four of us were still alive." He was soon a British POW and barely seventeen years of age.

Walter Kuefner was only eleven years old when the Red Army surrounded Berlin in April 1945. Despite his youth, he was trained to defend the fatherland. He recalled: "Just before the end, I was trained to shoot a *Panzerfaust* [bazooka]. There was a captured English tank about one hundred feet from our trench, and we were supposed to hit it in our training." Fortunately, he was never forced to use the weapon in combat and did not participate in the fight against the invaders.

Horst Schwermer had been fortunate to attend meetings in the Spandau Branch for much of the war (a rarity among young Latter-day Saint men in Germany). In early 1945, he was sent to the Eastern Front, which at the time was already on German soil—just fifty miles east of Berlin. Horst found an opportunity to meet with the Saints in the Frankfurt/Oder Branch, where a Brother Butkus presided over the meetings. Because many of the members had already fled from the approaching Red Army, attendance was sparse. All during the war, Horst, a priest in the Aaronic Priesthood, carried his scriptures.

Horst Schwermer's thirtieth birthday, April 29, 1945, came just nine days before the end of the war. At the time, he was part of the

agonizing retreat of a decimated German army trying to slow the final Soviet drive toward Berlin. He dispatched two successive messengers to tank squadrons at the front, but both failed to return. Therefore, he found a bicycle and set out to deliver the message in person. While talking with the tank crews in the dead of night, he suffered a grievous wound:

> I was sitting on my bike, my right foot on the ground, the left one still on the pedal. And then I felt something, and I fell on my face. And I tried several times to get up, and fell down again. And then I reached down with my hand, and I found out, yes, there was nothing below the [left] knee.

A round fired by a Soviet tank had severed his leg. During the hours that followed, Horst lay on the ground and worried about bleeding to death. His first impression was to ask his comrades to shoot him rather than leave him to the enemy. Then he prayed, asking his Heavenly Father, "Why me?" The response was, "You know why!" Then he prayed that his family (now including two sons) might be protected. He never lost consciousness, and when the sun came up the next morning, he was discovered by German soldiers, who loaded him into their car. During the evacuation, the Soviets overtook the group, and they became prisoners. The invaders had relatively good medical personnel, but Horst was placed at the last of the line, and the supply of ether was nearly gone when it came time to operate on his leg. "I took one good, deep breath [of the ether] but was conscious again before they finished."

On March 16, 1945 (seven weeks before the war ended), Rudi Seehagen was one of thirteen soldiers cut off from the main German force by the advancing Red Army:

> We had held up an entire battalion of Russians for hours. When we ran out of ammunition for our rifles, we used our small arms. Our lieutenant wanted to commit suicide, but I talked him

Fig. 6. The Seehagen family sent this letter to Rudi in the Soviet Union in 1944, but it was returned as undeliverable ("Zurück!"). He could not be located at the time. (R. Seehagen)

out of that. I told him he might get home someday, otherwise the Russians might do the job for him [kill him]. We destroyed our guns so the Russians could not use them. We used up our last ammo; then we stood up and put our hands in the air. The Russian's political officer shot one of our officers immediately; then he told his soldiers to pursue our retreating army. They didn't want to because they were so scared of our army, so he shot five or six of his own men.

Being a prisoner of war was no privilege, but Rudi Seehagen was at least alive. During the next three weeks, he was given almost nothing to eat, and his only source of water was snow. He had no mattress to sleep on and preferred a flat board to the bare ground. On one occasion, the prisoners were being transported to the east by train and were attacked by German fighter planes. Rudi and his comrades dropped to the floor in the aisles while bombs landed to either side of the train. "When we got up, we found that the seats had holes from the shrapnel. I was protected all of the time."

In contrast, Wolfram Dittrich was treated very well by his British captors. Although he was moved about constantly from camp to camp, he was always allowed to leave the camp for a few hours now and then.

The plight of a young mother with an absent husband was a sad one in Germany in 1945. After the Red Army conquered Berlin, Helga Schwermer and other women in her neighborhood were herded into a large house

and ordered into the basement. Soviet soldiers came by constantly to pick out women for their entertainment. They had taken the women's identification papers and used them to call out the names of their next victims. Helga described the situation:

> Every time they would rattle their keys and come into the basement to get another woman, I would take Jürgen and put him on my lap and say, "We're sick," and try to scare them off. And young girls age twelve from this group, [after they were assaulted] they killed themselves. They went in the nearby [pond] the next day.

Until July, 1945, Horst Schwermer remained in the infirmary of a Soviet prisoner of war camp recovering from the loss of his leg. He had developed gangrene, and a second amputation was needed; his entire left leg was lost, but his life was saved. During his recuperation, his wife, Helga, was fortunate to learn of his whereabouts, as she recalled:

> A German woman who had worked in a Russian prison hospital came to Spandau and told me that my husband was in a Russian prison camp and she was supposed to tell me. I think she might have said that he was an amputee, which at that time sounded wonderful because that meant he was alive!

Determined to learn of the condition of her husband, Helga first sent her father to the Soviet POW camp in Salow (100 miles north of Berlin) to see Horst. Then she and her mother undertook the dangerous journey through territory occupied by the Soviet Army, where sexual assault was a constant threat. After spending the night on the floor of a local farmhouse, the two women sneaked up to the fence surrounding the prison camp and gave the guards some milk, bacon, and cigarettes. Moments later a medical officer appeared and instructed them to wait there. He came back with a nurse's uniform for Helga to wear, which ruse enabled her to pass the guard station and enter the camp. The tension was high, as she recalled:

> I'm sure I must have been shaking, because they looked at the passport, and they looked at me, but they let me go through. And then I went to [Horst]. . . . He was only skin and bones. But he was one of the few soldiers that hadn't cut his curly hair.

In July, Horst was released from prison. He had shrunk from 180 to 96 pounds, and the Russian medical personnel decided that he would not survive the trip to the Soviet Union. He was driven to a railroad station and boarded a train to Berlin. The sight of the devastated city, American soldiers, and the sound of music from the rubble elicited an emotional response: "I cried and cried. On one of the sticks [crutches], I had tied a piece of bread, and on the other end I had tied my triple combination." He was denied entry to the streetcar because he had no money. Fortunately, a kind woman bought him a ticket, and he rode from downtown Berlin across town to Spandau and a glorious reunion with his wife, Helga, and his two sons.

While thousands of German soldiers were imprisoned in Russia until 1949 and many as late as 1955, Rudi Seehagen was blessed to be released very early from that miserable existence. He had not been allowed to write even one letter home to the parents who had been told that he was missing in action. On October 31, 1945, he was set free in Frankfurt/Oder, just seventy miles from Berlin. Due to the sporadic railway traffic, he needed fully three days to get to the Reich capital that had been bombed beyond recognition. He remembered his homecoming vividly:

> The next morning was Sunday [November 4, 1945], and I found my way home by streetcar and subway. I only weighed eighty-six pounds at the time, so I had trouble going up and down the stairs to the trains. When I got off the last streetcar, I ran right into a sister from our branch who was on her way to church. While I went on home, she hurried to church to tell my father I had returned. He had been Sunday School president for years, and very faithful, but that day he told everybody: "You stay here and have Sunday School; I'm going home to see my son!"

On New Year's Day of 1946, Wolfram Dittrich was released from his captivity under the British near Stade (across the Elbe from Hamburg). He eventually rejoined his parents, who had moved to a town north of Berlin. As he later explained:

> Being home in Falkensee again was wonderful, except that the Russians were there. They occupied many of the houses and that was not pleasant. Back in the branch, I realized that not many things had changed. The members who were there before and during the war were also still attending and doing well.

The members of the Spandau Branch had been very fortunate during the war. Despite their proximity to critical war industries and to the Reich capital, and despite the ferocious battle in which the Red Army conquered the metropolis, the meeting rooms and members' apartments still stood when the smoke and the dust cleared. Following Germany's official capitulation on May 8, 1945, life in the Spandau Branch went on as before.

According to Helga Schwermer, "I wouldn't call it a hard life [in 1945]. We didn't know any better. I still had my parents, I knew [my husband] was alive, and sure, we were hungry, but everybody was—you weren't any different. And we still went to church every Sunday."

In Memoriam

The following members of the Spandau Branch did not survive World War II:

Horst Willy Franz Knoll b. Spandau, Brandenburg, Preußen 7 Oct 1924; son of Wilhelm Richard Paul Knoll and Emma Anna Emilie Zastrow; bp. 4 Nov 1932; k. in battle Russia 9 Dec 1943 (R. Seehagen; IGI)

Heinz Werner Konrad Schulze b. Spandau, Brandenburg, Preußen 7 Mar 1938; son of Konrad Heinz Werner Schulze and Marie Margarete Emilie Purann; d. diphtheria Berlin, Preußen 11 Jan 1944 (R. Seehagen; IGI)

Konrad Heinz Werner Schulze or Schumann b. Spandau, Brandenburg, Preußen 12 Feb 1915; son of Reinhold Adolf Konrad Hoffmann and Clothilde Emilie Frieda Schumann; bp. 22 May 1922; m. Spandau 4 Jan 1937, Maria Langner or Purann; 2 children; corporal; k. in battle near Stalingrad, Russia 14 Nov 1942 (R. Seehagen; IGI; www.volksbund.de)

Johann Erich Tobler b. Berlin, Brandenburg, Preußen 26 Dec 1891; son of Johannes Paul Gustav Tobler and Hulda Ottilie Brebach; bp. 15 Apr 1925; m. Berlin 29 Feb 1936, Carola Elisabeth Thiemer; k. in battle Spandau, Berlin, Preußen 22 Apr 1945 (CHL Microfilm no. 2458, form 42 FP, pt. 37, 1949 list: 1378–79)

Hermann Ernst Albert Vogler b. Bredereiche, Brandenburg, Preußen 3 Jul 1891; son of Hermann Ernst Albert Vogler and Friederike Charlotte Hagen; bp. Spandau, Brandenburg, Preußen 17 Apr 1924; m. Belzig, Zauch, Brandenburg, Preußen 9 Jul 1918, Anna Auguste Uebe; 2 children; k. in battle Spandau, Brandenburg, Preußen Apr or May 1945 (R. Seehagen; IGI)

Auguste Zastrow b. Sabow, Pyritz, Pommern, Preußen 25 Apr 1869; dau. of Friedrich Zastrow and Friedricke Bludorn; bp. 10 Oct 1910; d. Berlin, Preußen 13 Oct 1939 (*Stern* no. 23, 1 Dec. 1939, 372; IGI)

Notes

1. Presiding Bishopric, "Financial, Statistical, and Historical Reports of Wards, Stakes, and Missions, 1884–1955," CR 4 12, 257.

2. Rudi Seehagen, interview by the author, Sandy, Utah, March 9, 2006.

3. Wolfram Dittrich, telephone interview with Jennifer Heckmann in German, January 25, 2008; summarized in English by Judith Sartowski.

4. Walter Kuefner, interview by Michael Corley, Salt Lake City, February 22, 2008.

5. Helga Abel Schwermer, interview by the author, Salt Lake City, December 8, 2006; see the description of the Jungvolk and Bund Deutscher Mädel programs in the introduction.

6. Horst Schwermer, interview by the author, Salt Lake City, December 8, 2006.

7. When Helga Schwermer returned from Stettin, she found it difficult to get the visitors to leave the apartment, because the air raids over Berlin were beginning to take a serious toll on housing space.

Fig. 7. Surviving priesthood holders of the Berlin District gathered for a conference in the rooms of the Center Branch in the late summer of 1945. (S. Sadowski)

BRESLAU
DISTRICT
East German Mission

In 1939, the Breslau District was the third largest in the East German Mission. The district territory extended from the modern German-Polish border east and south to the 1939 border of Germany. The city of Breslau (now Wrocław, Poland) is about 225 miles from Berlin. In 1939, the city was the home to three branches of Latter-day Saints: Breslau Center, Breslau South, and Breslau West. Three other cities also hosted branches in the district: Liegnitz, Schweidnitz, and Schlegel.

Fig. 1. The branches of the Breslau District in the province of Silesia.

Breslau District[1]	1939	1940	1941	1942
Elders	50	49		
Priests	31	35		
Teachers	25	24		
Deacons	63	61		
Other Adult Males	106	109		
Adult Females	428	435		
Male Children	53	55		
Female Children	52	56		
Total	808	824	824	830

Before and during most of World War II, Martin Hoppe was the president of the Breslau District. According to the history of the East German Mission, President Hoppe held a special meeting with the presidencies of the three Breslau branches on January 24, 1939. In that meeting they discussed ways and means of improving the genealogical work in the district.[2] On March 5, 1939, Herbert Gulla of the Breslau West Branch was appointed first counselor to President Hoppe and Fritz Michael of the Breslau Center Branch became the second counselor.[3]

Martin Hoppe had served as a full-time missionary in the German-Austrian Mission.

He was drafted shortly after the war began and is seen in uniform in nearly all photographs taken during district and mission conferences through 1942. Somehow he found time to translate into German portions of the book *Jesus the Christ* by James E. Talmage. His translation was printed in 1943 by the East German Mission and sent to each LDS soldier in the field as a Christmas present.[4]

"My father spoke several foreign languages," explained Werner Hoppe years later. "He spoke fluent English, French, Russian, and several other languages. His occupation was business—specifically accounting. In the army, he worked as a translator at a prisoner of war camp with British soldiers." Brother Hoppe was stationed not far from Breslau, which made it possible for him to come home often on weekends. His son recalled that he sat on the rostrum with branch leaders and was usually in uniform.[5]

President Hoppe was transferred to the Eastern Front in 1942, still working as a translator. In October 1943, Martin Hoppe was wounded—shot through the lung while attempting to rescue a comrade. He wrote to his wife from a field hospital of his condition, and she wrote back to him on October 24:

> My dear Martin,
> Yesterday I received your letter from the field hospital and was very shocked. Please write again and tell us how you are doing. I hope that you will be sent back to Germany as soon as you are well enough to travel. It is odd that you had to flee.[6] You will have to tell us all about that later. Please take care of yourself so that you can recover fully.

Gertrud Hoppe could not have known that her husband had died the day before she wrote her letter. One month later, she received a long letter from Herbert Klopfer, supervisor of the East German Mission and a former missionary companion of Martin. His message reflected

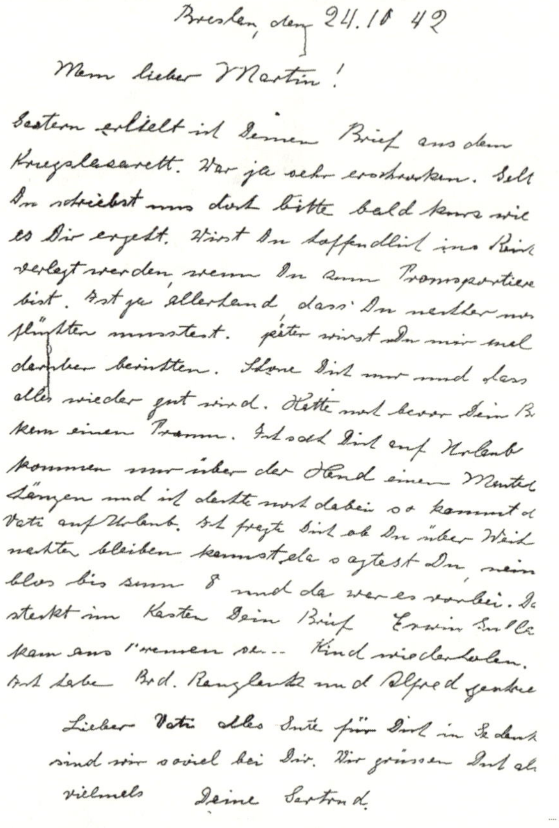
Breslau, den 24.10 42

Mein lieber Martin!

Gestern erhielt ich Deinen Brief aus dem
Kriegslazarett. War ja sehr erschrocken. Gelt
Du schreibst uns doch bitte bald kurz wie
es Dir ergeht. Wirst Du hoffentlich ins Reich
verlegt werden, wenn Du zum Transportieren
bist. Ist ja allerhand, dass Du nochmal
flüchten musstest. Später wirst Du mir mal
darüber berichten. Schone Dich nur und dass
alles wieder gut wird. Hatte mal bevor Dein B.
kam einen Traum. Ich sah Dich auf Urlaub
kommen nur über der Hand einen Mantel
hängen und ich dachte noch dabei so kommt d.
Vati auf Urlaub. Ich fragte Dich ob Du über Weih-
nachten bleiben kannst, da sagtest Du, nein
blos bis zum 8 und da war es vorbei. Da
steckt im Kasten Dein Brief. Erwin [illegible]
kam aus [illegible] [illegible] Kind wiederholen.
Ich habe Br. d. Ranglack und Alfred [illegible]

Lieber Vati alles Gute für Dich in Gedanken
sind wir soviel bei Dir. Wir grüssen Dich [illegible]
vielmals Deine Gertrud.

Fig. 2. By the time Gertrud Hoppe's letter arrived at the field hospital in Russia, Martin had already died. (L. Hoppe)

the sadness that must have been felt throughout the Breslau District and the mission. Some extracts of his letter dated November 29, 1943, are as follows:

> Dear Sister Hoppe,
> Two weeks ago, I came home on leave and learned from your sister-in-law in Zwickau that your husband had been wounded. While the news saddened me, I was all the more grieved to read that your husband, my brother, one of my best friends and fellow worker in the Church, had died of his wounds. . . . The dearest person God has given you on this earth has been taken from you and your children. But the Almighty who gave Brother Hoppe such a faithful and brave wife and mother of his children knows why He allowed your husband to die in this war. . . . My dear Sister Hoppe, I wish you and your children and your relatives in Breslau God's blessings and comfort. I wish you good

health and the assistance of the good people there during your time of grief. . . .
Your brother in the gospel
Herbert Klopfer

Martin Hoppe's successor as district president was Fritz Nestripke. It is clear from reports sent to the mission office that all programs of the Church were functioning well in the Breslau District at the time World War II broke out. Brother Nestripke apparently carried on in good faith as well. Richard Ranglack, first counselor to the mission leader, wrote that a district conference was held in Breslau twice each year through 1944.[7]

In January 1945, Adolf Hitler declared that all major cities in eastern Germany were to be turned into "fortresses" that would be defended to the last man. Women and children were to be evacuated, and all males ages fourteen (Hitler Youth) to seventy (Volkssturm) were to be impressed into service to halt the advance of the Red Army.

On March 8, 1945, General Hermann Niehoff took over as the commander of "Fortress Breslau" and issued instructions that included phrases typical among fanatic Nazi Party leaders as the war drew to a close:

> I expect that every soldier within this fortress is fully aware of our situation and will fulfill his duty to the utmost. . . . You are not only fighting for yourselves and your wives and your children, but for Breslau, the heart of Silesia, the strongest bulwark of the Reich against the red flood from the east.[8]

Despite a lack of equipment and supplies, the German defenders did indeed keep the Red Army out of Breslau until May 6, 1945. Later that year, the Soviets withdrew; the Allied nations had transferred the entire region to Poland.

Although many LDS families and individuals had fled the province of Silesia during the war, significant numbers were still in Breslau a full year after the war ended. Elder Ezra Taft

Fig. 3. This letter was sent to Gertrud Hoppe by the Wehrmacht office in Breslau, along with Martin's military service book. (L. Hoppe)

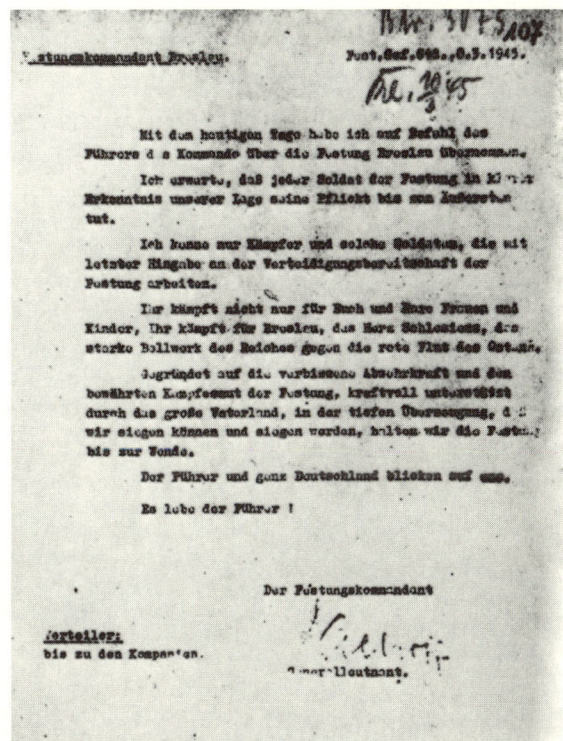

Fig. 4. General Herrmann Niehoff clarified the status of "Fortress Breslau" in this letter dated March 8, 1945.

Benson was touring Europe on a Church welfare mission and arrived in Breslau in 1946 to hold a conference with the surviving Saints. During the meeting, he was asked whether the Saints should leave the region. Heinz Koschnike was in attendance on that occasion and reported the following:

> He told us that the gospel had to be preached in Poland as well. We stared at each other. We then told him that we wanted to live among Germans, to move to Germany. We didn't want to stay in Poland. He said that he would inquire of the Lord and that we would meet again tomorrow. The next day he said that he had an answer from the Lord. We were to leave, and he would go to Warsaw to arrange it all. We would go to Frankfurt am Main. We didn't want to go to the Russian Zone in Germany. Which other zone was not important.[9]

In the summer of 1946, several cattle cars were used to transport Latter-day Saints from Breslau to Germany by rail.[10] By the fall of 1946, the Polish government had completed the forced evacuation of ethnic Germans westward to the Soviet occupation zone. The refugees were usually given one day's notice of the transfer and were allowed to take with them only what they could carry. Other property was simply to be left behind, including business interests and money in bank accounts. As far as The Church of Jesus Christ of Latter-day Saints was concerned, all branches of the Breslau District simply ceased to exist by the end of 1946.

NOTES

1. Presiding Bishopric, "Financial, Statistical, and Historical Reports of Wards, Stakes, and Missions, 1884–1955," CR 4 12, 257.

2. East German Mission Quarterly Reports, 1939, no. 53, East German Mission History.

3. Ibid., no. 55, 58. The conference in question involved a planning meeting on February 19, to which 233 members and friends came.

4. Herbert Klopfer to Gertrud Hoppe, November 29, 1943; private collection; trans. the author.

5. Werner Hoppe, telephone interview with Jennifer Heckmann, June 10, 2008.

6. The German phrase used suggests that Martin had to get himself off the field of battle without assistance, rather than be carried off by medics. The letter is in the possession of Martin Hoppe's son, Lienhard.

7. Richard Ranglack, autobiography; private collection.

8. A copy of the letter is seen in Herbert Michaelis, "Die Endphase des 2. Weltkrieges und seine Folgen," in *Der 2. Weltkrieg: Bilder Daten Dokumente* (Gütersloh, Germany: Bertelsmann, 1968), 613.

9. Heinz Koschnike, interview by the author in German, Bischofswerda, Germany, June 7, 2007; summarized in English by Judith Sartowski.

10. As it turned out, the Breslau Saints were not taken to Frankfurt as planned. Officials in the Russian occupation zone in eastern Germany did not allow them to pass through that territory. They were resettled in the towns of Rammenau and Bischofswerda near the Czech border.

BRESLAU CENTER BRANCH

Four months after World War II began, the East German Mission records showed the Breslau Center Branch having a total of 168 members. Thus it was the smallest of the three branches in Breslau, the capital city of Silesia, where approximately 550,000 people lived in 1939. Although there were challenges living in a huge city dominated by Catholics (60 percent) and Protestants, Latter-day Saint eyewitnesses felt that the impersonal character of a German metropolis allowed for tiny religious groups to be overlooked. Consequently, they were not bothered.

The Center Branch met in rented rooms at Sternstrasse 40, a short distance northeast of downtown. The territory covered by the branch was essentially the section of Breslau north of the Oder River.

As was often the case in Germany, the branch met not in the main building on

Sternstrasse, but in the first structure behind that building. Churchgoers passed through a large portal of the main building, crossed an interior courtyard, then entered the first Hinterhaus. Irmgard Gottschalk (born 1920) recalled that the branch rented rooms on two floors of that building.[1]

Breslau Center Branch[2]	1939
Elders	11
Priests	3
Teachers	2
Deacons	11
Other Adult Males	24
Adult Females	100
Male Children	8
Female Children	9
Total	168

Nearly 60 percent of the members of the Breslau Center Branch were adult females. This was not at all unusual in the branches in Germany. Indeed, the proportion of adult females in the Breslau District was 53 percent and in the entire mission 57 percent.[3]

The East German Mission records show the following entry for Sunday, March 12, 1939: "Herbert Neumann is appointed president of the Breslau-Center Branch, with Paul Franz as first counselor and Paul Fiedel as second counselor."[4]

Irmgard Gottschalk had served her Landjahr back in 1934. At the age of fourteen, she spent six months on a farm on the island of Usedom in the Baltic Sea. She enjoyed the work there but noticed the lack of religion under those circumstances: "It was a nice time for girls our age, but nobody put much emphasis on religion and such things." There was no

Fig. 1. Relief Society sisters of the Breslau Center Branch (I. Gottschalk Müller)

branch near Usedom, so Irmgard could not attend church until she returned to Breslau.

The Gottschalks were one of the many German families who were opposed to war. When the German army invaded Poland on September 1, 1939, Irmgard recalled hoping that there would be no war: "Many people were against what was happening but nobody could say anything; you had to be careful. It was a dull feeling that we had." Her two brothers were drafted right away. "It was not a nice feeling to see them leave," she recalled.

Irmgard Gottschalk was twenty-one and had finished her training as a saleswoman in 1941, when district president Martin Hoppe discussed with her the possibility of serving a mission. At the end of the second year of the war, there were no men left as full-time missionaries in the East German Mission. Proselytizing had been curtailed, but there was plenty of administrative work to be done in Berlin. The Gottschalk family lacked the funding for mission service, but President Hoppe promised to provide the money—30 reichsmark per month—through the Breslau District. The final hurdle was conquered when Irmgard was able, in compliance with government requirements, to find a young woman to assume her position at work.[5]

When an epidemic of diphtheria and scarlet fever hit Breslau in 1941, two of the children of Georg and Julianna Baron were infected: Gisela (born 1933) and Renate (born 1937) were quarantined in a large hospital. Renate also contracted German measles and remained in the hospital for six months. They eventually recovered, but many children in the same hospital did not.[6]

Georg Baron was drafted into the German air force and sent to Czechoslovakia. He was fortunate to take his family with him to the large eastern city of Olomouc (German: Olmütz). When he was transferred to Vienna,

Fig. 2. This picture was taken at the wedding of Herbert Gottschalk. (I. Gottschalk Müller)

Austria, in 1942, his family stayed in Olomouc and were still there when the war ended. Brother Baron was trained as a radar operator. One day, his unit was divided in half, his group being sent to France and the other to Russia. He later learned that essentially all soldiers in the other group had perished.[7]

"I remember my first three years in school," recalled Renate Baron:

The girls would sit on one side and the boys on the other. Every morning the first greeting was "Heil Hitler," and we had to stand straight as arrows while we sang [the national anthem] "Deutschland, Deutschland über alles." Discipline was everything, and we were punished if we misbehaved. . . . Two types of punishment I remember were standing in the corner facing the walls, and having a pencil placed on the backs of my hands while holding my hands palms down on the edge of my desk. If the pencil fell off, you would receive further punishment.[8]

Life in Czechoslovakia was very pleasant for Julianna Baron and her three daughters. Renate recalled fondly their walks through the parks of Olomouc. The country was to a great extent immune from the ravages of war; it was one of Hitler's prewar "bloodless conquests" and was considered occupied territory by the Allies. In other words, the country was preserved by both friend and foe. Renate later summed up their situation: "Our family was very lucky to live in Czechoslovakia towards the end of the war because the country was spared extensive bombing at the time when Germany was being demolished."[9] However, conditions were about to change.

On December 17, 1943, Irmgard Gott-schalk was released as a full-time missionary and returned to Breslau. She married Heino Müller of the Danzig Branch of the Church on March 1, 1944. She then moved into the home of her parents-in-law in Danzig, where her husband was employed in submarine construction. Heino was drafted into the Waffen-SS in September, and Irmgard remained in his parents' home.

In early 1945, the Müllers took Irmgard, their daughter-in-law, and fled Danzig when the Soviet invaders approached. They were fortunate to secure passage on a refugee ship that took them westward. Then they rode the train south to Zwickau, where they met up with Erika Fassmann Müller, another daughter-in-law who was also Irmgard's former missionary companion. Thanks to their emergency preparations, Irmgard's mother and a brother and sister were already in Zwickau. The Gottschalks were then taken in by the Suhrmanns, a Latter-day Saint family in the nearby Werdau Branch.

In the early spring of 1945, Julianna Baron had a strong impression to take her children west into Germany. She had not heard from her husband for six months, but she had learned that their home in Breslau had been totally demolished in an air raid and that her mother-in-law had perished in her basement. They began to make their way west and were allowed to ride on a farm trailer pulled by an old tractor. Not many days had passed before they were overtaken by Russian infantry. When she was about to be taken away by a soldier, Sister Baron produced a birth certificate showing that she had been born in Ukraine. The soldier left her in peace. Unfortunately, that good treatment was offset by poor treatment

on the part of German soldiers nearby who wondered if she was a traitor. They insisted that she had even spoken Russian with the invaders. As Renate later recalled, "Soon thereafter they told us that there was no room for us on the trailer. There we stood beside a road somewhere, Mother and her three little girls."[10]

The Baron odyssey was far from over. Thousands of German refugees were streaming through Czechoslovakia toward the German border. Along the way they passed heartbreaking scenes of destruction, suffering, and death. The greatest dangers were starvation and hostile action by Czech partisans. Indeed, on one occasion, partisans attacked a train in which the Baron family was traveling, but German soldiers defended the civilians. At the German border, Julianna Baron was shocked to learn that she was not allowed to cross. Their baggage was not ransacked or stolen, but they were forced to return east to Olomouc, a distance of 250 miles.[11]

In Olomouc, the four females of the Baron family were personae non gratae. As Germans, they were fortunate to have any kind of housing at all and were given secondary status when it came to ration coupons. Fortunately, Sister Baron's Ukrainian heritage helped her avoid the torture inflicted upon German women by marauding Soviet soldiers. She found work in a candy factory, and the girls learned Czech while playing with the native children. They were blessed and happy, but two important components of their life were missing: they had last heard from their father, Georg Baron, in 1944, and since late 1941 the family had been totally isolated from the Church.

In 1946, a letter from Georg Baron finally reached his family in Olomouc. Assuming that the German status of his family prevented the delivery of many previous letters, he addressed the next in French and had a comrade post the letter in Switzerland. The tactic worked, and after two years his family in Olomouc learned that he was alive. Later that year, Julianna Baron proved to Czech authorities that her husband was living near Frankfurt, Germany, and she was finally allowed to travel there with her daughters. The family then settled in Langen, where they became members of a thriving community of Latter-day Saint refugees.[12]

Looking back on her wartime experiences, former missionary Irmgard Gottschalk Müller made this statement (reflecting the sentiments of many Saints):

> I always saw things from the gospel perspective. We had the holy scriptures and the prophets. Whenever we had the possibility, we looked for the Church and held meetings so that we could strengthen each other's testimonies.

By the time the Baron family arrived in Germany, no members of the Center Branch were still living in Breslau (by then Wrocław, Poland); The branch had ceased to exist.

In Memoriam

The following members of the Breslau Center Branch did not survive World War II:

Herbert Hermann Görlitz b. Breslau, Schlesien, Preußen 27 Apr 1913; son of Hermann Paul Görlitz and Marie Anna Schlichting; bp. 2 Feb 1924; m. 7 Jan 1939; artillery gunner; d. hit by a train 12 Nov 1939; bur. Birkenfeld, Germany (*Stern* no. 24, Christmas 1939, 387; IGI; www.volksbund.de)

Kurt Heinz Gottschalk b. Breslau, Schlesien, Preußen (IGI) 12 Nov 1921; son of Karl Paul Gottschalk and Klara Reitzig; bp. 14 Jun 1930; k. in battle Krakow, Poland 31 Dec 1941; bur. Krakow Military Cemetery, Poland (Gottschalk, IGI; www.volksbund.de)

Walter Herbert Gottschalk b. Breslau, Schlesien, Preußen 1 or 31 Dec 1922; son of Karl Paul Gottschalk and Klara Reitzig; bp. 28 Feb 1931; m. 27 May 1944; k. in battle Vorwerk Ignatki, Poland 24 or 31 Dec 1941 or 1944 (Gottschalk, IGI)

Johannes Daniel Wilhelm Juras b. Breslau, Schlesien, Preußen 18 Sep 1921; son of Rudolf Ewald Juras and Meta Anna Raschke; bp. 25 Aug 1933; d. 29 Dec 1942. (IGI)

Kurt Fritz Erich Kobel b. Breslau, Schlesien, Preußen 27 Mar 1910; son of Karl Hermann Emil Kobel and Anna Pauline Vogt; bp. 5 Mar 1921; m. Breslau

Fig. 3. The Gottschalk brothers, Heinz (left) and Herbert (right), were two of the many Breslau Center Branch members in uniform. (I. Gottschalk Müller)

3 Nov 1932, Mrs. Anni Kobel; soldier; k. in battle 1942 (*Sonntagsgruss*, no. 2, 18 Jan 1942, 8; IGI)

Robert Wilhelm Mathias Erwin Krause b. Breslau, Schlesien, Preußen 14 Aug 1917; son of Ernst Wilhelm Krause and Lina Martha Schlichting; bp. 24 Sep 1927; corporal airman; d. flying a raid over England 19 Jan 1941; bur. Cannock Chase, Great Britain (*Sonntagsgruss*, no. 20, 18 May 1941, p. 80; IGI; www.volksbund.de)

Notes

1. Irmgard Ruth Gottschalk Müller, interview by Michael Corley in German, Salt Lake City, February 15, 2008; summarized in English by Judith Sartowski.
2. Presiding Bishopric, "Financial, Statistical, and Historical Reports of Wards, Stakes, and Missions, 1884–1955," CR 4 12, 257.
3. East German Mission Quarterly Reports, 1939, no. 58, East German Mission History.
4. Ibid.
5. By law, healthy employees in wartime Germany were only allowed to quit if they could provide a replacement worker. See the East German Mission chapter for information about Irmgard's service in the mission office in Berlin.
6. Renate Baron Nebeker, "Renate's Story" (unpublished autobiography), 2; private collection.
7. Ibid.
8. Ibid.
9. Ibid., 3.
10. Ibid.
11. Ibid., 4–5.
12. Ibid., 6–7.

BRESLAU SOUTH BRANCH

The Friedrichstrasse ran east–west through the Schweidnitzer Vorstadt area of Breslau. The Breslau South Branch rented rooms in house number 32 of that long street, and the branch territory was essentially the southern part of the city. Manfred Deus (born 1930) and his sister Katharina (born 1933) recalled that the meeting rooms were in the main floor in what had previously been office space. Heinz Koschnike (born 1930) added these details:

> We had the entire main floor. There was a corridor between small classrooms and the main meeting room. From the main room, there were two more classrooms behind it. We had restrooms and a cloak room on the other side. The decor was very simple, but we had a very impressive picture of Jesus Christ at the end of the room behind the stage (raised platform).[1]

Breslau South Branch[2]	1939
Elders	11
Priests	9
Teachers	7
Deacons	18
Other Adult Males	21
Adult Females	114
Male Children	18
Female Children	12
Total	210

Priesthood and Relief Society were the first meetings held on Sunday mornings, followed by Sunday School at 10:00 A.M. and sacrament meeting in the evening. Primary and MIA were held on Tuesday, the former in the afternoon and the latter in the evening.[3]

The typical attendance at meetings in the early war years was about one hundred persons, according to Annelies Hendriok (born 1923). For her and the youth of the branch, church involved much more than regular worship services. "I especially liked the dances that the youth group of our branch organized. And the plays that my mother made us perform were always very nicely done."[4]

According to Manfred Deus, priesthood service began in one's early years:

> Since the Aaronic Priesthood was in charge of cleaning the building and making the building ready for church services, in the wintertime I had to go there between six and seven o'clock in the morning and fire up the coal stoves; we had a big one in the chapel and separate coal stoves in two of the classrooms.

In July 1938, President Heber J. Grant visited Breslau. According to young Heinz Koschnike:

> I saw a prophet of the Lord for the first time, and he made a distinct impression on me. He really liked children and took the opportunity to speak to the children. We all met in the Breslau Center Branch meeting hall. He blessed us all, and he blessed the rooms there, and attendees wondered about that specific blessing. He said that these rooms would survive as the meeting place for the Saints.

Reactions among Latter-day Saints regarding the treatment of Jews in Hitler's Germany varied, as is evident from eyewitness statements. For example, Richard Deus (born 1903) was not a friend of the Nazi Party. He voiced concerns about the path Germany was taking under Hitler when a nationwide campaign of violence against the Jews left its mark on Breslau. On November 9, 1938, Nazi thugs looted Jewish businesses and invaded apartments as part of what came to be called the "Night of Broken Glass." The next morning, Brother Deus went out to inspect the damage. As his son, Manfred, recalled:

> He had the company car, and we drove through the city, and I saw the synagogues burning and

[Jewish] businesses destroyed. . . . I remember my father saying that the Jewish people are not members of our church, but they are still the people that are favored by the Lord. He said this is the beginning of the end of the Hitler regime because Heavenly Father would not tolerate that.

Only eight years old, Heinz Koschnike also had vivid memories regarding the Night of Broken Glass:

A brother in our branch whom I shall not name was standing right behind me on November 9, 1938, during the Reichskristallnacht. I was an eyewitness to the destruction of the synagogue in Breslau and saw how the Jews were standing out in the street weeping. I was touched by that. I then saw this elder of the church, but he told me that I should be ashamed about being sympathetic to the Jews. "You are a German boy," he said. I went home crying because I was so disappointed. My mother asked me what was wrong, and I said, "I'm not going to church with you anymore. What they teach us there is wrong." She had a difficult time explaining to me what was what. She said that people have their personal opinions.

To actively support Jews meant risking personal safety. For example, Rudolf Nolte (born 1926) recalled that his father, Franz Nolte, was accustomed to dealing with Jewish merchants. As a police officer, he once needed a pair of boots made and decided to have the work done by a Jewish cobbler who was already in a concentration camp. Somehow he arranged to have the Jewish man issued a pass to leave the camp to see his family. The Gestapo found out, and Franz Nolte was taken to court. Convicted of illegally supporting Jews, he was sentenced to a prison term "until the end of the war and five years thereafter." He actually served only one year of his sentence (six months in each of two concentration camps—Dachau and Auschwitz), but he lost his occupation.[5]

Fritz Neugebauer, Breslau South branch president, was born in 1892 and served in World War I. Perhaps his war experiences

Fig. 1. Richard Deus met Church President Heber J. Grant (left) in Breslau in 1938. Brother Deus was the only full-time male missionary in the East German Mission when the war began. (M. Deus)

soured him on politics. According to his daughter, Ingeborg (born 1926):

My father was never interested in any political happenings and did not want to participate in a party. My father always tried to conduct his life in a way that the Church approved. On Sundays, he was supposed to go and work on air-raid shelters, but he usually pretended to be sick so that he could fulfill his calling as a branch president.[6]

Annelies Hendriok had dreamed of being a pediatrician. However, because her father had worked for a Jewish firm before the war, he had lost his job and was unemployed. Thus, the money Annelies needed for medical school was not available. Her mother insisted that she be trained as a hairdresser, which she did for three years.

World War II began on September 1, 1939, with the German invasion of Poland. During the first week of the conflict, one or two minor air raids occurred over Breslau, about seventy-five miles from Polish territory. Little damage was done, and there would be no more attacks on the city until 1945.

When the war began, Elisabeth Wanke, (born Elisabeth Bräulich in 1919) had been a member of the Church for only two years. She had married Helmut Wanke, a priest in the Breslau South Branch, in 1938, and the branch had given them a big party, but there had been no time for a honeymoon. Helmut worked for the government, promoting sports and recreation programs in small towns near Breslau and enjoyed the use of an automobile for his work. That employment ended when he was drafted the day the war started. Fortunately, he was first stationed in Breslau and was allowed to visit his young bride quite often for the first year.[7]

The family of Richard and Gertrud Deus lived on Wielandstrasse, about twenty minutes from church on foot. Richard Deus was called in March 1939 to serve as a traveling elder and assigned to work in the Dresden District. He left his wife and four children to serve the Lord as a full-time missionary. In August, when all foreign missionaries were withdrawn from Germany, Richard was the only male missionary left. He served for two more years, part of the time in the Königsberg and Zwickau districts. He wrote the following for the *Sonntagsgruss*, the mission newsletter, in November 1940:

> Wherever I went I was accepted by the government and the people. In the eyes of the members of the Church I saw great joy whenever we elders visited them. Often, their small apartments were rearranged to make room for an extra bed, or they would even make a whole room available for cottage meetings for us. After being fed spiritually, the members went out of their

way to provide food for the body also. Many times it was a great sacrifice for them.[8]

"I was baptized exactly on my eighth birthday—October 7, 1939," explained Hartmut Wegner (born 1931). "It was done at night, in secret if you will, in the Oder River."[9] The family of Oskar and Hildegard Wegner lived in the suburb of Brockau. A short train ride of ten minutes brought them to the main station in Breslau, and it took another ten minutes on foot to reach the meetinghouse of the branch.

By 1940, Annelies Hendriok had finished her training as a hairdresser, but she still longed to work in medicine. She had made the acquaintance of a Lutheran pastor who worked in a hospital, and one day she sought him out. He arranged for her to begin working at the hospital. This upset Annelies's mother, who had gone to great lengths to find her daughter a position for training in one of the finest salons in Breslau. Nevertheless, Annalies began a two-year program in nursing in a local hospital and worked as a nurse for the duration of the war.

When he turned ten years old in 1940, Manfred Deus was inducted into the Jungvolk along with his classmates. "We were kind of forced to attend the meetings, because your ration cards depended on being certified by that organization that you attended and supported the activities."

Ingeborg Neugebauer also felt pressure from the local government in connection with the Hitler Youth program. Her father, branch president Fritz Neugebauer, did not support her attending Bund Deutscher Mädel activities. The result of this noncooperation was that Ingeborg's final grade in the training program she completed was reduced one full grade. Other than this penalty, she did not recall any conflicts between Hitler Youth activities and the branch meetings.

"My mother was a feisty woman," recalled Ursula Kundis (born 1937). She told the Hitler Youth leaders that if they marched on Sunday, her son would not march with them. On one occasion, she went to collect her husband's military pay and greeted the officials with "Guten Morgen!" rather than "Heil Hitler." When chastised for not using the official greeting, she responded "I'm sorry. The only person I will ever hail is my Father in Heaven." A hearty "Heil Hitler!" was yelled at her as she left the office.[10]

The Hitler Youth association was not attractive to young Hartmut Wegner. "I was not boy scout material," he later explained. Fortunately for him, his school was destroyed, and he attended split sessions in another building. With classes running from 2:00 until 7:00 P.M., there was no way for him to attend the Jungvolk meetings. "I was never inducted in the first place, which made me happy." School was not always easy for Hartmut, who recalled, "At one point we all had to declare what religion we were. Of course, everybody laughed in a very harmful sort of way when I said what I was because they associated this with American Westerns of some kind." However, he did not recall being seriously persecuted because of his faith.

Young Heinz Koschnike had no difficulties being the only Latter-day Saint boy in his neighborhood or in the public school. He was a good student in general but also in the required religion classes. He recounted the following experience:

Across the street from the school there was a candy store. I would go there quite often, and the lady owner once said, "You know, you are different from the other children who come here. What is going on? Why do you behave differently?" I told her about my upbringing, and I told her about my faith in God. Years later, God brought us to Bischofswerda [as refugees], and we were visiting a sister in a small town nearby.

She invited lots of neighbors to her house for a cottage meeting. There were three older persons I baptized there. They were the owners of the candy store in Breslau.

During the war, some Latter-day Saints admired Adolf Hitler and wished to express that admiration publicly. Heinz Koschnike described an incident he witnessed in the rooms of the Breslau South Branch:

One day I came into the priesthood meeting room where we had a large, really impressive picture of Jesus Christ smiling. I saw this brother standing on a chair replacing that picture with a large picture of Adolf Hitler. He took the Christ picture down and hung up the Hitler picture. Then Georg Zelder protested and asked, "What do you think you are doing here? Take it down or I will!" Then the other brother said, "If you do that, I will have the Gestapo here in thirty minutes, and you will be on your way to a concentration camp." Brother Zelder then climbed up on the chair and switched the pictures. Then he said, "So, Brother, do what you think is right, but don't forget that you are a member of the Church of Jesus Christ." The man didn't report Brother Zelder.

"We quite often had people from the Nazi Party come in and sit and listen to what was going on [in the meetings]," according to Manfred Deus, "They were usually sitting on the back row. We knew who they were because all of the members were known." Manfred also remembered that hymns containing the word *Zion* were to be avoided during those instances and the Book of Mormon was quoted less often because of the notion that this was an American church.

The government instituted the rationing of food and other items of daily consumption just days before the war began. "We purchased our food with ration coupons every Saturday," recalled Ruth Nolte (born 1915):

But we usually ran out before the week was over. We would take a potato, mash it, make it into patties, put various ingredients on it, bake it in our coal stove, and it sort of looked like cookies. I would take those to school. Sometimes mother couldn't make her potato salad because we had no potatoes. She would grind herring, mix it with some mayonnaise, and spread it on bread. At that age, fifteen or sixteen, you were always hungry.

The Wehrmacht caught up with Elder Richard Deus in early 1941, and he was drafted. After being trained as a medic, he was sent to the Eastern Front, where the German offensive had begun in June 1941.

Under German government policy, a soldier's wage was equal to what he was paid as a civilian before being drafted. In the case of Richard Deus, this was a serious problem. Because he had been paid nothing as a missionary for the two years before his induction, the army was not obligated to pay him anything at all. It took a substantial effort on his part to get the army to pay him for the support of his wife and four children. Eventually he was granted the minimum pay. At home, his wife was called to be the district Relief Society president. This required her to leave home on Sundays to visit other branches, and on occasion her children went to church alone.

Rudolf Nolte finished eighth grade in 1943. During the school year, his entire class of boys was trained in the operation of an antiaircraft battery near the town of Kraftborn. "We practiced loading and unloading the gun," he recalled. While there, the boys were visited by their schoolteacher for lessons twice a week. That fall, Rudolf began a term of six months in the Reichsarbeitsdienst program.[11]

Rudolf was drafted into the army in March 1944 at the age of seventeen and was initially trained in everything from bridge construction to mine laying. By the time he was eighteen, he was enrolled in an officers training program in the city of Rathenow, west of Berlin. While there, he attended meetings with the branch.

Fig. 2. A group of Saints met in the Nolte home at Christmastime 1943. (R. Nolte)

He was a deacon at the time and carried a copy of the Pearl of Great Price.

In 1944, Richard Deus developed blood clots in his knees and could not bend his legs. He was sent to an army hospital in Breslau, where he stayed for about four months. His family was allowed to see him there. When he had recovered enough to serve again, he was sent to Italy, where the climate was milder.

Manfred Deus recalled visiting the Liegnitz Branch, about one hour to the west of Breslau, to provide priesthood services in the absence of worthy brethren there. He took the train there with Carl Aeppin. In addition to assisting in the sacrament service (sacrament meeting was the only meeting held in Liegnitz at the time), Manfred played the reed organ and gave a talk each week.

In August 1944, three weeks after his fourteenth birthday, Manfred found a draft notice waiting for him. As a new Hitler Youth member, he was to report for duty at the railroad station the next day. With only one and a half days of training with a rifle, he was sent to dig trenches around the city for the defensive troops. At the time, Manfred was the secretary of the Sunday School. He recalled that one hundred or more persons attended on a typical Sunday. The attendance percentage was calculated based on a branch population of 250.

Elisabeth Bräulich Wanke was the Primary president for two years during the war. Because Wednesday was traditionally a short day at school, Primary meetings were held after school on those afternoons.

As the war dragged on, conditions in Breslau grew worse, and bad news became a weekly if not a daily reality. However, the members of the Breslau South Branch continued to serve the Lord. Heinz Koschnike later recalled:

There were no interruptions in our meeting schedules right up to the end. Of course, we had mostly older people there. The testimonies we heard in those days were really spiritual. We stuck together like never before. We prayed and wept together. The Lord was with us.

Annelies Hendriok saw her family being pulled apart as the war progressed. Her mother, who was employed at a local army post, was sent to Belgium. Her father—too old to be on active military duty—was sent to the Soviet Union, where he worked in materials management. Her brother was drafted into the Waffen-SS, and her sister was in the Reichsarbeitsdienst. Annelies was alone in Breslau and was saddened by the fact that "our entire family was in all kinds of different places."

As could be expected, the war did not prevent young people from falling in love. Indeed, in some aspects, the war may have expedited the process. Annelies Hendriok recalled how several young men in the three branches of the Church in Breslau were interested in her: "They would often ask me to marry them so that they could return to the front with a little bit of hope." However, her soldier brother very strictly warned her against making any hasty decision. The advice was good, given the high rate of death among the young men of the Breslau branches.

At her work, Ingeborg Neugebauer met a fine soldier who had lost an arm in the Soviet Union and was assigned to training programs. His name was Paul Gildner. He was not a member of the Church but attended meetings with her now and then. They were married on September 16, 1944. As she later recalled:

We were married in the civil registration office, and later we also had a celebration in our branch house. The entire branch attended. We rode in a white, horse-drawn carriage to our branch building. We even had a red carpet that they had laid down in the entrance to the branch rooms, and we had some golden chairs that we sat on.

Paul Gildner was a God-fearing man who eventually gave up his Sunday soccer games (having only one arm did not diminish his love for the sport) to attend church with his wife. Nevertheless, Ingeborg felt that some members of the Church were disappointed that the branch president's daughter had married a non-LDS man. Her mother was more accepting, saying that Ingeborg's husband replaced the son she had lost in the war. The newlyweds found an apartment in the same building in which her parents lived.

By the late winter of 1944–45, the meeting rooms of the Breslau South Branch at Friedrichstrasse 32 had been destroyed. The same was true of the rooms used by the Breslau West Branch. The surviving members of the three branches in the city all gathered in the rooms of the Center Branch at Sternstrasse 40. Heinz Koschnike recalled that the members,

Fig. 3. The Glaubitz family of the Breslau South Branch. (S. Glaubitz Bellersen)

who were once surprised at the blessing pronounced on these rooms by President Heber J. Grant in 1938, now recognized that the blessings were literally fulfilled (see above).

The Wanke family was together in East Prussia for Christmas 1944. Just after New Year's Day, Elisabeth heard a voice one night saying, "You have to leave on the seventeenth!" Nobody was in the room but her husband and her daughter, who were sound asleep. The next morning she informed her husband of the message. He believed that she should stay, and they argued, but she stood her ground, insisting that she must heed the voice and return to Breslau. She left for Königsberg on January 17. The train scheduled to take her back to Breslau was cancelled because the advancing Red Army had cut off the route. Elisabeth was expecting her second child, so she sought out the station's Red Cross service. A nurse put her on another train just before it was opened to the crowds of teeming refugees. Had she left a day later, she would have been stranded in Königsberg. She was not yet safe, however, because her train was fired upon by the Soviets, and the trip westward via Posen was anything but pleasant. She arrived home in Breslau just in time to be ordered out when the city was declared a fortress. However, her father, Albert Bräulich, was very ill and her mother, Emma, would not leave him. Elisabeth decided to stay, telling her

Fig. 4. Breslau South Branch members in 1944 (R. Nolte)

127

mother, "I'm not going to leave. I've seen what happens on those trains. If I'm to die, I want to die at home." They all stayed in Breslau.

By 1945, the Breslau South Branch had already lost a number of its unmarried men and fathers in the war. A memorial displaying the names of the fallen was painted on the wall of the main meeting room. According to Heinz Koschnike:

> To the right and the left [of the chapel door] we had the Iron Cross. Within the crosses we had the names and dates of the men in beautiful handwriting. One of the older men did the artistic work, Brother Zelder. He had only three sons. The government took his third son from the front to the interior after the first two were killed so that he would be safer, but an attack on the airfield where he was stationed killed him. But Brother Zelder never complained and never lost his testimony. He found his comfort in God, and he radiated this power in his testimony and his spirited talks.

Manfred Deus remembered counting twenty-three names on the wall by the end of the war. The Deus children left Breslau before their father's name could be added to the branch memorial.[12]

Hartmut Wegner recalled one of the last meetings of the Breslau South Branch in January 1945. "We lined up all of the chairs (there were no pews) in the room in which we held sacrament meetings. We all knelt, each one in front of a chair, and a very heartfelt, highly emotional prayer was sent up: Should we leave or should we stay?" Later, the Wegner family held a council and decided they should leave—except, of course, for Brother Wegner, who was required to stay and defend the city.

With the Red Army approaching Breslau, the local Nazi Party district leader, Karl Hanke, declared Breslau a "fortress" that must be defended to the last man. In January 1945, he gave orders that women and children who

Fig. 5. Breslau South Branch Mother's Day photo. (S. Glaubitz Bellersen)

wished to leave must do so immediately, but all men were required to stay in the city.

"We didn't suffer at all until the Fortress [January 1945]," recalled Elisabeth Bräulich Wanke. There was still enough food, fuel, electricity, and water for the city's residents. By then, her daughter was five years old.

On January 2, 1945, Rudolf Nolte completed a two-week furlough at his home in Breslau. Originally bound for the Eastern Front, he was detained as part of the force to defend the city against the Red Army that was approaching rapidly. "Our company served a one-block area of apartment houses, a distance of three streets away from where I had lived for almost seventeen years," he later wrote. Wounded on March 2, he spent the rest of the war in a hospital. When he recovered, the conquerors shipped him east to perform reparations labor.

Paul Gildner was not allowed to leave Fortress Breslau, but he was able to send his wife, Ingeborg, to live with his parents in Langenbielau, a few miles out of town. In February, he was released from Breslau, he picked up his wife at his parents' home, and they found passage on a train heading west to Dresden.

Heinz Koschnike was old enough in 1945 to be a member of the Hitler Youth, but he found ways to avoid involvement. When his school comrades were sent to defend Breslau against the besieging Red Army, Heinz found work that offered him an exemption:

> Fritz Neugebauer had a teamster business, and he had to take supplies up to the front and the civilians. He told me to come help him so that I would not have to go to the front. I never had to use a weapon. We were on the road constantly to deliver stuff. Of course we were under fire quite often. But we were [Church] members working together. We prayed together every day, and the Lord protected us.

One day in January 1945, Heinz was on his way home when the air-raid sirens sounded. He ran into the cellar of a nearby apartment building to wait out the attack. He described what happened:

> I had this strong feeling that I should leave the cellar immediately. The people there demanded that I stay because the all-clear had not yet been sounded. Despite their demands, I left the cellar immediately and hurried down the street. Suddenly I felt the air pressure from an explosion behind me and knew that something had happened. I turned around and saw that the building where I had been in the cellar had received a direct hit and had collapsed. I started to cry because God had saved my life.

By February 1945, the Red Army had fought its way to within two blocks of the Bräulich apartment, so Elisabeth and her parents were ordered by the police to move toward the center of the city. Elisabeth's brother-in-law, branch president Fritz Neugebauer, brought his team and wagon around and moved the family's belongings. The ride through the city center was an adventure, as Elisabeth later recalled:

> You wouldn't believe how scared those horses were when the artillery [shells] hit the big buildings! Oh, the noise! Uncle Fritz had a hard time [controlling] the horses, especially when we went over a great big bridge over the Oder River. I was afraid they would go over the railing and jump down [into the river]. . . . I was pregnant at the time. My little girl and I were sitting next to Uncle Fritz up front. . . . It was a flatbed trailer. Mother and a friend [were in the back and] held on to the luggage.

The Bräulich family was assigned a nice apartment, where they stayed until several months after the war. Since parting with her husband on January 17, Elisabeth had no idea where he was. In March, her daughter was born. Elisabeth walked forty-five minutes to the hospital, where she was given a bed in the basement. The nurse gave her an injection to expedite her labor, but used the wrong drug. Her labor lasted ten hours.

Ursula Kundis was only eight years old when the bombings of Breslau became frequent. She remembered her mother making "air-raid cookies" that she always kept ready to take to the basement when the alarms went off. As Ursula later recalled, "The neighbors would say, 'Mrs. Kundis, would you pray with us? You know how to do it.' And so we would pray together." On one occasion, they were surprised when residents of the adjacent house—some of whom were injured when the house collapsed—escaped through a hole in the wall into the basement where the Kundis family sat.[13]

Anna Frieda Sowada responded to the call to evacuate Breslau in early February 1945. She put her daughter, Mary (born 1939) on a sled, wrapped her up in a blanket, and said good-bye to her husband ("I'll catch up with you," he replied). Breslau women were told that they would be returning to the city as soon as the invaders were driven back. As it happened, they did not return, but were put on a train heading west, ending up in a small town in Bavaria in southeastern Germany.[14]

Gertrud Deus believed that she needed to stay in Breslau in order to assist single sisters in the city's three Latter-day Saint branches, but she was then persuaded that her own family's safety was perhaps more important. Moments after packing up to leave Breslau and locking the door to their apartment, Gertrud turned around and went back. "What are you doing, Mom?" her children asked. "I forgot my genealogical papers!" was the reply. Manfred recalled that it was twelve degrees below zero when they loaded their belongings onto a sled for the trip to the railroad station. The train headed slowly west, with no specific destination. Along the way, their only source of water was snow

gathered by passengers when the train stopped. Stops were frequent, and the journey to Görlitz that would normally have lasted about three hours ended up taking three days.[15]

In Görlitz, the Deus family got off of the train and stayed with friends. They had been told that they would be returning to Breslau after the Red Army was driven back, but such optimism was unfounded. After two weeks in Görlitz, they headed farther west to the city of Dresden, arriving there on February 11. Two days later, the worst air raid in Europe during World War II took place there. Tens of thousands perished in the firebombing of that industrially insignificant city crowded with refugees. Fortunately, Gertrud Deus had found a place to live with friends on the outskirts of Dresden. They were not harmed, but the air pressure from the exploding bombs broke the windows of the home in which they were staying.[16]

Oskar Wegner sent his family west on his wife's birthday—January 22, 1945. Fortunately, he was able to follow them just a week later, having been classified physically unfit for military duty. He caught up with them in Wallenberg, just a few miles south of Breslau. From there they proceeded by truck and train to Bavaria.

Ruth Nolte and her mother had been evacuated from Breslau and arrived in the Dresden main station at precisely the wrong time—just hours before the firebombing on February 13 and 14. They accidentally met Ruth's sister, Ilse, and her sister-in-law, Iffa, in the station and they all sought refuge in the basement shelter. After the first attack at 10:00 P.M. on February 13, they left the shelter and crossed the river into Dresden Neustadt. There they listened to another attack two hours later. The next day, they walked through the devastated city to the main station to locate their luggage, but it had all burned. With only the clothes on their backs, they found a train to

Fig. 6. The Breslau South Branch choir. (M. Sowada)

take them west to Chemnitz and south to Annaberg-Buchholz.

Ingeborg Neugebauer Gildner was yet another member of the Breslau South Branch who experienced the firebombing of Dresden firsthand. She later vividly recalled what she saw that terrible night:

> During the attack on Dresden, we saw animals [from the zoo] running around [town] and people in the streetcar had died because of the air pressure of the bombs. They looked like they were only sleeping. Fires burned in the city but not where we were. There were planes shooting at the people trying to flee. It was horrible. Everything was in chaos.

Richard Sowada (born 1905) was not as fortunate. He too had arrived in Dresden just a day or two before the firebombing, having left Breslau with his sister and his mother. Later, members of the Deus family reported seeing Brother Sowada in Dresden at the home of some Church members. When the air-raid alarm was sounded, the Deus family and the Sowadas went to different shelters, and Richard Sowada was never seen again. It was eventually assumed that he perished in the attack; he was declared legally dead as of February 14, 1945.

The Soviet siege of Breslau was characterized by an incessant artillery barrage. When it was too dangerous to be in the streets, members of the South Branch held worship services in their apartments. According to Heinz Koschnike, "The word was circulated each week that meetings would be held the next Sunday in the apartment of Brother or Sister so-and-so."

The last church meetings in Fortress Breslau that Elisabeth Bräulich Wanke could recall were held in the apartments of member families. According to her:

Fig. 7. Richard Sowada was the popular choir director in the Breslau South Branch. (M. Sowada)

> Every Sunday afternoon, even when the bombs were falling all the time, it was quiet and we could have sacrament meeting. And we had one deacon, and he would pass the sacrament. And Uncle Fritz [Neugebauer] was a very positive and very faithful member. And he would always give us encouragement that the Lord will protect us there, [from] the shooting or the bombing. Uncle Fritz would interrupt the speaker and we would sing a song really loud so we couldn't hear [the artillery]: "Master, the Tempest Is Raging" or "Jesus, Lover of My Soul."

With the capitulation of Fortress Breslau on May 6, 1945, the conquerors entered the city to find that they had been held at bay for eleven weeks by old men (the Volkssturm) and Hitler Youth. Heinz Koschnike remembered the declaration made by his mother, Clara Maria, at the time: "The power of the priesthood kept them out. Normally, it would have been a simple thing for them to storm the city against such weak resistance."

Latter-day Saint women in Breslau were as attractive to Soviet soldiers as any other German women. Thus it was only a matter of time before Sister Koschnike found herself in serious danger. In the words of her son Heinz:

> A drunken soldier came into our house and wanted to get my mother. As a young boy [age fourteen] watching this, I could not just stand

there and let it happen. I ran outside and pled to the officer in the street (he was watching out over the entire campaign). His heart was softened, and he came into our house and ordered the drunken soldier out of the room. That is how my mother was saved from this shameful fate.

In their Bavarian village, the Wegners experienced the entry of French troops on April 20, 1945. They were relieved when nobody made any serious attempt to stop the invaders. For them, the war was over. Over the next few months, they made a trek through various parts of the country, ending up in Herne in northwestern Germany. According to Hartmut, "My father's first concern was always to establish contact with the Church wherever we were. . . . This was our lifeline. If we could find a branch, we would have a connection with somebody." The Latter-day Saint branch in Herne was probably pleased to welcome the Wegner family.

When the war ended, Mary Sowada and her mother were living with two Catholic nuns in a small Bavarian town. Over the next few months, they were housed in filthy barracks with hundreds of refugees and countless rats and were then sent to northern Germany. They began a new era of life in Braunschweig in the British Occupation Zone.

In the ruins of Dresden, Gertrud Deus was invited by Church members to move into an empty apartment. When the Soviets entered the city in May, the locals thought the invaders were Americans and came out to greet them. When they learned the true identity of the soldiers, the women all ran for safety. Sister Deus did her best to hide her sixteen-year-old daughter, Gisela. On one occasion, a Russian soldier saw Gisela go into the house and tried to find her. He could not find his prey but came back several times to look for her. According to Katharina, "He would just stand there [in the street] and stare at the house because he could swear that he saw [my sister] go in there."

Richard Deus had spent very little time with his wife and his four children since being called as a missionary in March 1939 and as a soldier in 1941. On April 23, 1945, just two weeks before the end of the war, he was killed in action against the American army in northern Italy. His wife and children had essentially lived without him for more than six years.

When the war ended, Ruth Nolte and her mother were in Annaberg-Buchholz in Saxony (south of Chemnitz). Because they had relatives in the city of Hanover, they were allowed to travel to that city, located in the British occupation zone. The trip took two months. "The hardest thing about the war was that so many people died," Ruth later recalled. "You didn't think much about dying or being killed, but when it was over, you surely were glad to be alive!"

Just before the war ended, Paul Gildner was assigned to a training facility in Salzburg, Austria, and was able to take his wife, Ingeborg, along. He found her in Dresden shortly after the firebombing of February 13 and 14, and they took the long train ride south through Czechoslovakia to Salzburg. It was there that their first child was born a few months later. Then the Gildners located the LDS branch in Salzburg and joined with seven members of that branch to hold meetings. Paul Gildner was baptized a member of The Church of Jesus Christ of Latter-day Saints in June 1945—one of the first postwar converts in Germany.

Fig. 8. Richard Deus was killed in Italy two weeks before the war ended. (M. Deus)

132

Several months after Germany surrendered, the Allied occupation officials in Austria began to send refugees back to their own homes. Ingeborg and Paul Gildner faced the frightening prospect of returning to Breslau, already in Polish hands, and looked for a way west. Fortunately, one of the American soldiers serving in Salzburg had been a missionary in Germany, and he produced the papers the Gildners needed to move to the west and into the American occupation zone.

Hartmut Wegner's family did not return to Breslau. Their home had been destroyed, and they had lost all of their property, but more importantly (according to Hartmut years later), "we lost our identity, because our ancestors . . . had been there from the seventeenth century."

The Breslau apartment house in which the Kundis family lived was eventually bombed out. As Ursula recalled, "We had a piano, it was the only piano in the building. [Mother] could see some [piano] keys in the rubble, and that was it for the house." Sister Kundis was expelled from Breslau with her family in December 1945 and, after living in refugee camps, was finally reunited with her husband in Bremen, West Germany, in 1946.

On July 2, 1946, Elisabeth Bräulich Wanke was compelled to leave Breslau with her children and her parents. Still uninformed of her husband's whereabouts, she was eventually given a place to live in distant East Frisia, not far from the Netherlands in northwestern Germany.

In June 1946, Rudy Siebenhaar (born 1929), a native of Breslau, was able to escape from a Soviet prison camp and make his way carefully back to Breslau. On a Saturday afternoon he went to a black market gathering, where he watched two German girls trying to trade porcelain items for food. When their attempts to communicate with the Poles broke down, Rudy intervened and helped them get more for their valuables. He asked if they could

meet there the next day, but they said that they would be attending church. "What kind of church?" he inquired. "We are Mormons," was the response.[17]

Rudy recognized the name of the Church from an encounter with another POW a few months earlier. He had heard the story of the Prophet Joseph Smith and agreed to join the girls for church meetings the next day. The surviving Saints in Breslau all met in one group, in a deaf-mute school building right around the corner from Rudy's apartment. He was converted and baptized on August 13, 1946.

Branch president Fritz Neugebauer was eventually transported to Holthusen in East Frisia (northwest Germany) and went from there to Wilhelmshaven, where he established contact with the Church again. His wife also escaped to the west to be reunited with him, but his mother died in a refugee camp along the way in Czechoslovakia.

About one year after Rudolf Nolte was sent to the Soviet Union, camp guards found and destroyed his copy of the Pearl of Great Price. "I had a testimony," he later wrote, "but I had no religious affiliation or training for years." All he ever thought about in those days was when he would be allowed to go home.

Since December 1941, the East German Mission had no contact with Church leadership in Salt Lake City. In the months immediately following the war, the new branch president in Breslau wrote many letters to Salt Lake City to ask for guidance. Apostle Ezra Taft Benson arrived in Breslau in the fall of 1946 as part of his mission to ascertain the status of the Church members in Europe and to distribute welfare supplies. Heinz Koschnike was there and remembered the gathering well:

> One day in 1946 [Elder] Benson came to our apartment with two American officers, all Mormons. He talked to us in a special meeting. I met President Benson in person. He told us

that the gospel had to be preached in Poland as well. We stared at each other. We then told him that we wanted to live among Germans, move to Germany. We didn't want to stay in Poland. He said that he would inquire of the Lord and that we would meet again tomorrow. The next day he said that he had an answer from the Lord. We were to leave, and he would go to Warsaw to arrange it all. We would go to Frankfurt am Main. We didn't want to go to the Russian Zone in Germany. Which other zone was not important.

Shortly thereafter, the evacuation of the surviving Saints from Breslau began. They included "about one hundred people, mostly women and children, and about twenty men," according to Rudy Siebenhaar. Heinz Koschnike put the number at closer to two hundred persons. They were shipped in cattle cars to the west. The company was delayed at the new Polish-German border for at least a week, during which the following happened, according to Heinz:

> At the border, we would go up the hill from where the train was standing and have our meals. We called it Mormon Hill, and we had a church service each evening. And Polish people came from the town nearby to join us. More and more of them came. They loved the music, etc.

The plan to take the Saints to Frankfurt in the American occupation zone was thwarted when the Soviet officials refused to allow the Saints to pass through their occupation zone. The refugees were split into two groups and sent to the neighboring towns of Rammenau and Bischofswerda in the province of Saxony in the Soviet occupation zone. The refugees quickly found the Saints in Bischofswerda and went to church the next Sunday. As Heinz recalled:

> On Sunday we went to church. That was in a Hinterhaus, and there was a winding staircase. Those older sisters who had prayed [that priesthood holders would come] were so thrilled to have their prayers answered and they greeted us with tears. There were too many of us to even fit

in the rooms. There were about one hundred of us. That was in September 1946.

As a prisoner of war in the Soviet Union, Rudolf Nolte endured terrible conditions. He was often given only bread and watery soup amounting to no more than five hundred calories a day and was almost always assigned hard physical labor lasting twelve hours. As he later recalled, he once tried to steal some sugar:

> I noticed an empty sugar sack and proceeded to scoop a little bit of sugar into my can. I was caught and thrown in the prison for five days without food or bedding. It was in the month of March, and we had worked all day in rainy, snowy weather. So I had to cover myself with a wet overcoat. The bunk had only three planks, too small to support me. There I lay, freezing and hungry and isolated from the world. I could have died of pneumonia, and no one would have known or cared. Finally, on the last day of my confinement, I was served a bowl of watery soup. It tasted so good!

When it came time to be released, Rudolf Nolte told his Soviet captors that he was from Hanover. By that time, Breslau, Germany, had become Wrocław, Poland, and he was afraid that his captors would detain him even longer. He was finally reunited with his family in Hanover in 1948. His father, Franz Nolte, had been drafted late in the war and was reportedly buried in a mass grave at a prison camp near Moscow, Russia.

In 1954, Elisabeth Bräulich Wanke received word that her husband, Helmut Wanke, had been officially declared dead. By that time, she had probably been a widow for nine years.

With the exodus of fall 1946, the Breslau South Branch disappeared into history.

In Memoriam

The following members of the Breslau South Branch did not survive World War II:

Rudolf Erwin Baron b. Breslau, Schlesien, Preußen 8 Aug 1917; son of Alfred Fritz Baron and

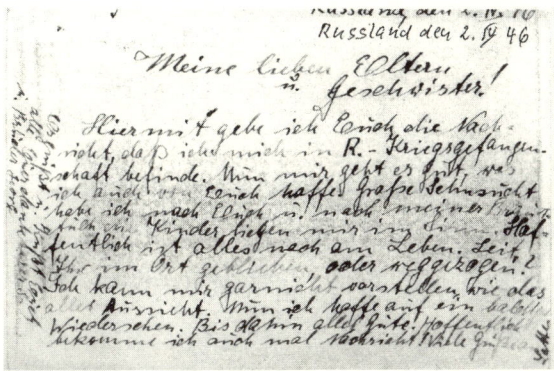

Fig. 9. Georg Janitschke wrote this card to his parents in 1946 from a POW camp in Russia. His greatest desire was to be reunited with his family. He died in a POW camp in 1947. (S. Glaubitz Bellersen)

Metaclara Caecilie Antoine Kosalek; bp. Mar 1934; m. Dresden, Dresden, Sachsen 20 Jun 1942, Erika Margareth Heine; non-commissioned officer; d. at San. Kp. 409 8 Apr 1945; bur. Baltijsk, Russia (IGI; www.volksbund.de)

Martha Anna Maria Bruma b. 1 Mar 1872 Breslau, Schlesien, Preußen; dau. of Johann August Anton Bruma and Christiane Schmidt; bp. 6 May 1922; m. Breslau 29 Sep 1892, Johann Franz Wanke; 10 children; d. Hohenelbe, Czechoslovakia 27 Apr 1945 (Neugebauer-Gildner; Bräulich-Wanke-Terry; IGI)

Richard Fritz Deus b. 10 Feb 1903 Breslau, Schlesien, Preußen; son of Karl August Ernst Deus and Auguste Johanna Rosalie Mintschke; bp. 3 Aug 1918 Breslau; ord. elder; m. 24 Dec 1926 Breslau, Gertrud Anna Pfeiffer; 4 children; traveling elder in East German Mission 1939–1941; non-commissioned officer; k. in battle San Benedeto, Italy 23 Apr 1945; bur. Futa Pass, Italy (M. Deus; IGI; www.volksbund.de)

Georg Albert Franke b. Breslau, Schlesien, Preußen 8 Apr 1906; son of Helene Franke; ord. teacher; d. 8 Jan 1940, Breslau; bur. Breslau 10 Jan 1940. (*Sonntagsgruss*, no. 41, 10 Nov 1940 n.p.; IGI)

Bruno Augustin Glaubitz b. Breslau, Schlesien, Preußen 3 Sep 1904; son of Augustin Petrus Glaubitz and Klara Korpus; m. Breslau 30 Mar 1929, Margaretha Frieda Janitschke; 3 children; d. Stalingrad, Russia 1 Jan 1943 (IGI)

Georg Karl Janitschke b. Breslau, Schlesien, Preußen 10 Feb 1915; son of Augustin Janitschke and

Fig. 10. Georg Janitschke (S. Glaubitz Bellersen)

Johanna Torke; bp. 2 Feb 1924; staff corporal; d. as POW Novosibirsk, Russia 20 Jul 1947 (Glaubitz-Bellersen; IGI; www.volksbund.de)

Alfred Wilhelm Koska b. Breslau, Schlesien, Preußen 11 Feb 1918; son of August Koska and Anna Rosina Walde; bp. 21 Feb 1926; d. 30 Jun 1944 (IGI)

Wilhelm Max Koska b. Breslau, Schlesien, Preußen 22 Mar 1916; son of August Koska and Anna Rosina Walde; bp. 6 Dec 1924; m. 27 Oct 1939; lance corporal; d. Krasnyj field hospital 625, Russia 9 Aug 1941; bur. Krasnyj, s.w. Smolenzk, Russia (*Sonntagsgruss*, no. 2, 18 Jan 1942, p. 8; IGI; www.volksbund.de)

Werner Lothar Neugebauer b. Breslau, Schlesien, Preußen 11 Mar 1924; son of Fritz Hermann Neugebauer and Hedwig Maria Martha Wanke; bp. Breslau 3 Sep 1932; corporal; k. in battle Osscha, Smolensk, Russia 26 Oct 1943; bur. Orscha, Belarus (Neugebauer-Gildner; IGI; www.volksbund.de)

Franz Nolte b. Bernterode, Sachsen, Preußen 23 Mar 1885; son of Heinrich Nolte and Elisabeth Schneider; bp. 11 Dec 1920; m. Breslau, Schlesien, Preußen 13 Nov 1913, Margaretha Elisabetha Leibner; 4 children; 2m. Anna Katharina Ibold; corporal; d. Soviet POW camp 6 or 11 May 1945 (R. Nolte; IGI; www.volksbund.de)

Paul Schmikale b. Nangesinawe, Wangersiuawa, Preußen 30 Aug 1880; son of August Schmikale and Luise Elisabeth Mueller; bp. 24 Sep 1928; ord. elder; m. Breslau, Schlesien, Preußen 20 Aug 1904, Emillie Anna M. Siegmund; 2 children; d. Breslau 10 Jan 1940 (*Sonntagsstern*, no. 26, 28 Jul 1940 n.p.; IGI)

Richard Karl Arthur Sowada b. Breslau, Schlesien, Preußen 23 Feb 1905; son of Karl Josef Sowada and Maria Theresia Hedwig Breuer; bp. 20 Oct 1940; m. Breslau 29 Dec 1937, Anna Frieda Bollach; 1 child; k. in air raid Dresden, Dresden, Sachsen 13–14 Feb 1945 (Sowada; IGI)

Gustav Gerhard Heinrich Walter b. Breslau, Schlesien, Preußen 25 Jul 1917; son of Gustav Hermann Walter and Elisabeth Martha Goebler; k. in battle (IGI)

Helmut Paul Johann Wanke b. Breslau, Schlesien, Preußen 19 Oct 1911; son of Johann Franz Wanke and Martha Anna Maria Bruma; bp. 6 May 1922; ord. priest; m. Breslau 28 Oct 1938, Elisabeth Maria Bräulich; 2 children; MIA Bischofsburg, Klackendorf, Mensguth, Seeburg, Wartenburg 1 Jan 1945; ruled dead 31 Dec 1945 (Bräulich Wanke Terry; IGI; www.volksbund.de)

Arthur M. Weiss b. Breslau, Schlesien, Preußen 14 Jul or 20 Aug 1914; son of Bertha Christiane Oriwall; ord. deacon; lance corporal; d. Lipowik Russia 10 May 1942 (Bräulich Wanke Terry; IGI; www.volksbund.de)

Erwin Josef Zelder b. Breslau, Schlesien, Preußen 26 Nov 1924; son of George Arthur Kurt Zelder and

Pauline Auguste Fruehauf; bp. 27 May 1933; d. Breslau 22 May 1944 (IGI)

Herbert Georg Kurt Zelder b. Breslau, Schlesien, Preußen 15 Sep 1914; son of George Arthur Kurt Zelder and Pauline Auguste Fruehauf; bp. 2 Oct 1922; m. Oels, Schlesien, Preußen 16 Sep 1939, Erika Auguste Emma Heinrici; d. Jul 1944 (IGI)

Paul Gerhard Zelder b. Breslau, Schlesien, Preußen 2 Dec 1922; son of George Arthur Kurt Zelder and Pauline Auguste Fruehauf; bp. 26 Feb 1931; non-commissioned officer; d. 20 Sep 1944; bur. Allensteig, Austria (IGI; www.volksbund.de)

NOTES

1. Heinz Koschnike, interview by the author in German, Bischofs-werda, Germany, June 7, 2007; summarized in English by the author.

2. Presiding Bishopric, "Financial, Statistical, and Historical Reports of Wards, Stakes, and Missions, 1884–1955," CR 4 12, 257.

3. Manfred Deus and Katharina Deus Siebenhaar, interview by the author, Sandy, Utah, March 9, 2006.

4. Annelies Hendriok Szeszeran, telephone interview with Judith Sartowski, April 9, 2008; summarized in English by Judith Sartowski.

5. Rudolf Nolte and Ruth Nolte, interview by the author, Sandy, Utah, November 21, 2006.

6. Ingeborg Neugebauer Gildner, interview by the author in German, Munich, Germany, August 9, 2006.

7. Elisabeth Bräulich Wanke Terry, interview by the author, Salt Lake City, November 17, 2006.

8. Richard Deus, "As a Traveling Elder—On the Road," *Sonntagsgruss*, no. 43, November 24, 1940; trans. Manfred Deus.

9. Hartmut (Hart) Wegner, telephone interview with Jennifer Heckmann, April 9, 2008.

10. Ursula Kundis De Haan, interview by Rachel Gale, Salt Lake City, June 29, 2007.

11. Rudolf Nolte, "My Life Story" (unpublished personal history, 2004); private collection.

12. The number of fatalities in this account does not match the number of soldiers shown at the end of this chapter. It may be that names of soldiers of all three Breslau branches were included in the memorial.

13. See the description of such escape holes in the introduction.

14. Mary Sowada, interview by the author, Salt Lake City, November 17, 2006.

15. Hitler Youth (boys ages 14–17) were required to stay in Breslau. Manfred stayed but wore civilian clothing.

16. See the Dresden Altstadt chapter for details on the firebombing of that city.

17. Rudy Siebenhaar, interview by the author, Sandy, Utah, March 9, 2006.

BRESLAU WEST BRANCH

With 265 members, the Breslau West Branch was the tenth largest in all of Germany in 1939. The meetings rooms were located at Westendstrasse 50 in the western suburb of Breslau known as Nicolai-Vorstadt. Werner Hoppe (born 1934) later described the setting:

> The branch building was interesting; it was located above the movie theater. It was a big hall that smelled of beer and smoke, but we cleaned it up. We had classrooms and restrooms. The room may have been used for other things during the week. We entered the room from the back. There were no pews, just chairs. There was a stage. We had to do a lot of cleaning. We always met in those rooms throughout the war. I do not recall any damage to the building; if it happened, it was after we left [in 1944].[1]

Ruth Gottwald (born 1929) recalled the following about the rooms there:

> We had lots of activities there because the room and the stage were large. And we had district conferences there. Primary and MIA were held during the week. We had sports and lots of stuff. It seemed like there was something going on [at the church] every day.[2]

Breslau West Branch[3]	1939
Elders	16
Priests	16
Teachers	11
Deacons	17
Other Adult Males	46
Adult Females	134
Male Children	12
Female Children	13
Total	265

Kurt Mach (born 1915) was interested in flying, so he joined a flying club in the 1930s.

He also qualified for a driver's license—a rarity in those days. In 1935, Hitler's government expanded the Reichsarbeitsdienst program and introduced universal military conscription. Kurt was the perfect candidate for national service. He spent six months of 1936 building roads and planting trees in a beautiful section of his native province of Silesia before being drafted into the air force in April 1937.[4]

During his basic training term, Kurt was stationed in Nordhausen (north-central Germany) and was pleased to join with the very small group of Latter-day Saints in a basement apartment to worship when his schedule permitted. "A marvelous spirit filled the seven to eight members there," he later wrote.

In August 1939, the month prior to the beginning of World War II, Kurt was injured on the job and classified as unfit to fly. This led to an assignment with air traffic control, and he was initially stationed near the German-Soviet demarcation line in occupied Poland. Engaged since 1939, he was granted permission to marry on May 30, 1940. The civil registrar was actually a farmer who performed the service voluntarily. His conduct was so unpolished that "we had a hard time suppressing our laughter." His bride was Elisabeth Nowak, not yet a member of the Church, and they had little time to celebrate: Kurt was called back to duty prematurely because Germany had launched several offensives in western and northern Europe.

Kurt was to have shipped out to France in June 1940, but he contracted an infection in his hands while handling munitions and remained near home in Breslau-Zimpel for treatments for the next six months. In 1941, his health deteriorated and he was released from the military but immediately assigned to civilian service with the air force. By the end of that year, two monumental things had occurred: his wife had given birth to a little girl,

and Germany had attacked the Soviet Union. Kurt was grateful to be home with his family.

As the war entered its third year in late 1941, members of the branch wished to preserve the memory of their fallen soldiers. According to Werner Hoppe, "I remember a memorial, a large poster, with the names of the brethren killed during the war, displayed in our meeting rooms. We kept holding meetings all the time [my family] was there, but there were fewer and fewer men in attendance."

Young Werner Hoppe was baptized in the Oder River on his eighth birthday—August 28, 1942. His entire family attended the ceremony, along with a few members of the branch. Soon thereafter, his father, district president Martin Hoppe, was transferred to the Eastern Front, where he continued to serve the Wehrmacht as a translator.

Ruth Gottwald experienced a personal tragedy in 1943. As she later explained:

> My father was not a member of the Church. In 1943, he apparently deserted and came home and didn't want to be in the army anymore. So he was at home for a few weeks, then they took him to the prison at Landsberg/Warthe and executed him by firing squad. His mother was allowed to visit him there and was told that he was to be shot. They refused to take me there to visit him because they didn't want me to be exposed to the situation. They didn't want me to be ostracized at school. They told me that he refused to eat toward the end but just smoked cigarette after cigarette. He just didn't want to be a part of it anymore.

His death left Ruth and her mother on their own to survive the last two years of the war.

As the air raids over Breslau began to make the city a very unsafe place to live, Ruth Gottwald and her mother sought refuge in the basement of the building where Sister Paula Hubert lived. Ruth recalled studying the Book of Mormon in that basement. The Gottwalds' apartment building survived the war, but their windows all burst from the air pressure caused by the exploding bombs, and there was an enormous bomb crater right in front of the building.

The health problems that left Kurt Mach unfit for active military duty were not severe enough to spare him from serving in the fruitless effort of repelling the Red Army's invasion of Germany that began in late 1944. He was drafted in November and sent to a defensive position about twenty miles from Warsaw, Poland. Later, he was sent to Czechoslovakia to be trained in the use of antitank weapons. From there he was able to visit his family in Breslau from January 11 to 13, 1945. Six days later, he returned to the Eastern Front and was captured there by the Soviets.

In the late summer of 1944, Gertrud Hoppe took her three children and left Breslau,

Fig. 1. *Youth of the Breslau West and Breslau Center Branches (front row from left: Brunhilde Hoppe, Werner Hoppe, Renate Müller, Bruni Deus; middle row: Rudi Nolte, Manfred Deus, Joachim Müller; back row: Werner Nitschke, Edith Müller). (W. Hoppe)*

following the city government's recommendation that women take their children to safer locations. For several months, the Hoppes lived with relatives in a small town near the Polish border. In January 1945, they returned to Breslau, just in time to join the exodus of civilians from the city that was soon surrounded by the Soviets. A train then took Sister Hoppe and her children through Czechoslovakia to Austria.

In January 1945, Kurt Mach's wife, Elisabeth, was informed that all women and children were to leave Breslau. While she was gathering a few critical items in her basement, she had left her little girls in the apartment upstairs. Suddenly, she heard a voice say, "Go upstairs!" but she looked around and nobody was there. Twice more the same message was audible and seemed to be more urgent. She dropped everything, raced up two flights of stairs, and found her baby daughter choking on a piece of cotton. As she later recalled:

> With lightning speed, I tore the stuff out of her mouth and she took a deep breath. I was paralyzed with fear but recovered quickly. I lifted her from the carriage, held her in my arms, and wept. . . . All I could say was, "Thank you, dear Lord, thank you, dear Lord."[5]

Trying to board an overcrowded train heading west, Elisabeth Mach was pushed back by desperate crowds of refugees. Nobody was willing to help her get the stroller into the train. At one point, three-year-old Karin was nearly pushed under the wheels of the train. When the train was about to depart, Elisabeth Mach was still standing there with two little daughters. Fortunately, the conductor learned of her dilemma. He was able to find a spot in a different car and helped her load the stroller into the train. They made their way to Weisswasser, near Torgau on the Elbe River, where they waited for word from their father, Kurt.

Fig. 2. The Martin Hoppe family of the Breslau West Branch. (L. Hoppe)

The Gottwalds delayed their departure from Breslau until it was too late. Ruth had been serving coffee and tea to refugees at the main railroad station, and she and her mother were not prepared to leave the city by train. They then chose the next best option, as she later explained:

> We had a sleigh that we loaded up and got out just before the city was totally surrounded. There was so much snow. We went about 45 minutes into the forest outside of town. We saw many people who had hanged themselves in the trees. My mother said that we couldn't survive in those conditions, so we returned to the city.

Ruth Nestripke (born 1925) also tried to leave Breslau with the first wave of evacuees. She was especially offended by the political leaders who provided no means of transportation and no suggestions as to where to go:

> When we asked the political bosses where we should go and how we should transport ourselves, they mocked us with the response: "You have feet! Or would you prefer that we carried you?" They called us *Volksschädlinge* [public liabilities] because we didn't want to leave and therefore hindered their attempts to defend the city. . . . [They threatened that] whoever didn't leave the city by the next day at 10:00 A.M. would be shot on sight, but that didn't work, either.[6]

Temperatures approached zero, and many who left town froze to death, while others simply gave up any hope of fleeing and returned to the city.

Back in Breslau, living conditions steadily deteriorated. One day, as enemy fighter planes sprayed bullets through the streets, Ruth Nestripke and her aunt ran inside a dairy store for shelter. Ruth fell down, reached for her aunt, and clung tightly to her. When the danger was past, she found that she was holding on to a dead German soldier. "You can imagine what I thought when I saw his face that reflected suffering and death," she recounted.[7]

A few weeks later, Ruth was hit by shrapnel from Red Army artillery. The metal left a hole nearly two inches in diameter on one side of her thigh and nearly three inches on the other side. Fortunately, Brother Zelder from the Breslau South Branch came by and was able to secure medical treatment for her. "I ground my teeth together because the pain was so intense, but I didn't want my dear mother to worry about me."[8]

Ruth Nestripke had to be taken to see the doctor every day for weeks because the wound did not heal. One day, he told her that she had to work to straighten her leg or else she would lose her ability to do so; the metal had torn her tendon. Shortly thereafter, she was looking out her window when a party official saw her and yelled: "Why aren't you out building street barricades?" "I'm wounded!" "That's what they all say!" he retorted. She was not surprised when a few minutes later, a soldier came by to arrest her but realized the error and quickly left with the excuse, "I'm just following orders."[9]

Stranded in Breslau, the Gottwald women were put to work helping to defend the city. Ruth described the situation in these words:

> We had to help dig out trenches for the soldiers. They retreated bit by bit and that was really scary. . . . Any time there was a pause in the bombing, people hurried to the stores to try to get something to eat. Then the dive bombers

139

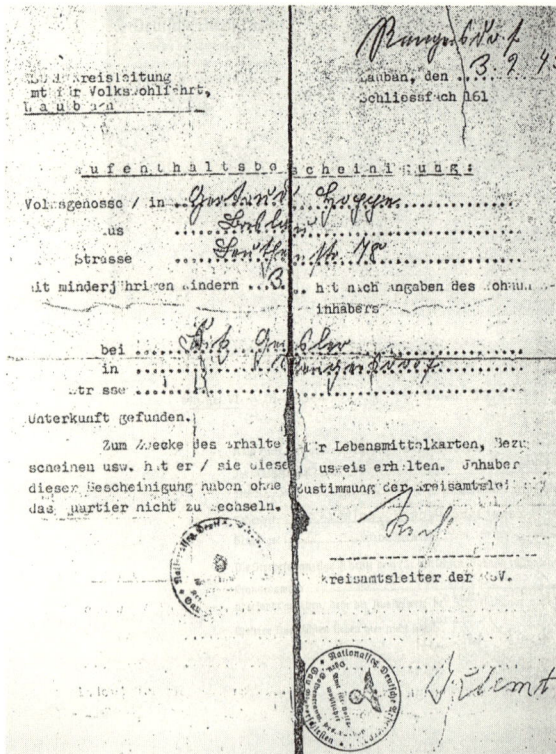

Fig. 3. *This certificate was issued in 1945 to the widow Gertrud Hoppe in support of her request for food ration stamps. (L. Hoppe)*

came and shot people in the streets. We didn't dare go outside. . . . Outside there were dead people all over and huge piles of rubble.

By March 1945, the Gottwalds were living downtown and had lost all contact with the Breslau West Branch on Westendstrasse.

By the time the city capitulated on May 6, 1945, many of the buildings had been reduced to rubble. What happened when the Red Army entered the city was, according to Ruth Nestripke, "worse than what we went through during the siege. The Russians were like animals. In fact, they were worse because they disregarded all intelligence and reason." The Polish came later and continued to rob and assault the civilians. In many cases, they evicted people from their homes with as little as ten minutes' warning.[10]

In October 1945, the Gottwalds were evicted from their apartment by the new Polish government. "Overnight we had to leave. We had one afternoon to pack and the next morning we had to leave." They took the train west to Liegnitz, then began a disorganized exodus west to Germany. Traveling with them was an uncle who was looking for his family along the way. When they reached Muskau at the new Polish-German border, they were detained. Ruth recounted the events years later:

At Muskau one morning (it was dark, about 5:00 A.M.) a man showed us the way to cross the border secretly. We were caught by two Russians, and they took my backpack. I had 500 marks rolled up in a blanket, and they took that and they took my uncle's last blanket. My uncle had some Church books and some paper money in the books. They took us to a guard station and kept the books overnight. They asked if those were Church books, and they gave them back the next morning. They didn't find the money. Then we walked to the border, through the no-man's-land, and my uncle started to sing: "O Babylon, O Babylon, we bid thee farewell!"

Once back in Germany, the Gottwalds made their way to Cottbus to join the colony of refugee Saints at the Fritz Lehnig home. There was no room for them there so they were sent to the new Church refugee colony at Wolfsgrün, south of Zwickau. Looking back on their terrible experiences in Breslau at the end of the war, Ruth said:

We never doubted God. That was our salvation, our faith. He protected us. I had grown up in the Church and was blessed. I just kept hoping that we would survive, and he saved us. We always believed in God. . . . The Church was our only salvation. What would we have done without the Church?

Following a bout with dysentery that lasted three months, Kurt Mach was close to death in a Soviet prison camp. Thirty-five to fifty German prisoners were dying of diseases in that camp every day, but death was also the punishment for anybody attempting to record their names. With the end of the war on May 8,

Fig. 4. Rudi Nolte in the uniform of the Reichsarbeitsdienst. (C. Kleist Nolte)

1945, transfers of the prisoners to points farther east began. By September, Kurt was in Pulavy but was considered so unfit for physical labor that he was released by his captors. On September 29, he began the trek home. He somehow survived (although other Germans were dying in great numbers around him) and made it to eastern Germany.

Like millions of other Europeans, Kurt searched in many offices in the Soviet occupation zone for information about his family. After finding employment in Sömmerda, he began writing letters to relatives to learn the whereabouts of his wife and his daughters (Karola was born in 1944). On December 4, 1945, he received a card informing him that they were in Torgau, a few hours to the north. The reunion was a bit confusing, as he recalled: "Of course I was a changed man. Just a week before my release, they shaved me bald again. We had lost all of our possessions, but we were alive." He then took his family back to Sömmerda.

After arriving in Austria, Getrud Hoppe was fortunate to find a group of Austrian Latter-day Saints in Haag am Hausruck near Salzburg. The family stayed there for four years then moved across the border into Germany. Looking back on those times, daughter Brunhilde Hoppe decided that she was glad to have been just a young girl during the war: "I was glad that I was not an adult or a mom in the war years because it would be especially hard if you had children then."

By the fall of 1946, all of the surviving members the Latter-day Saint Breslau West Branch had left the city, which would thereafter be called Wrocław, Poland, and the branch disappeared into history.

In Memoriam

The following members of the Breslau West Branch did not survive World War II:

Anna Pauline Galle b. Sacherwitz, Breslau, Schlesien, Preußen 19 Sep 1849; dau. of Gottfried Galle and Johanna Theresia Schmidt; bp. 12 Jun 1908; m. Christian Lerche; 8 children; d. senility 29 Nov 1939 (CHL CR 375 8 #2458, 1939 data; IGI)

Mannfred Hendriock b. Breslau, Schlesien, Preußen 3 Aug 1926; son of Walter Fritz Hendriock and Lisbeth Frieda Auguste Bollach; k. in battle Russia 2 May 1945 (R. Nolte; IGI)

Martin Werner Hoppe b. Breslau, Schlesien, Preußen 10 Oct 1906; son of Otto Martin Paul Hoppe and Emma Anna Ida Schwarz; bp. 15 Dec 1914; m. Nov 1933; 4 children; Breslau District President; corporal; d. Krgsl. 926 mot. Uman, Ukraine, USSR 23 Oct 1943 (A. Langheinrich; IGI; www.volksbund.de)

Karl August Kruber b. Schmograu, Schlesien, Preußen 6 Jan 1875; son of Johann Gottlieb Kruber and Christiane Skupin; bp. 10 Jul 1927; m. Breslau, Schlesien, Preußen 21 Feb 1910, Emilie Anna Marie Winkler; 5 children; d. cancer Breslau 30 Sep 1939 (CHL CR 375 8 #2458, 1939 data; IGI)

Johanna Pauline Moschinsky b. Olschina, Posen, Preußen 19 Feb 1848; dau. of Karl Moschinsky and Friedricke Drescher; bp. 26 Jan 1910; m. —— Pola; d. Spalitz, Breslau, Schlesien 3 May 1942 (FHL Microfilm 271394, 1935 Census; IGI)

Richard Alfred Pola b. Spahlitz, Oels, Schlesien, Preußen 19 Oct 1910; son of Ernst Wilhelm Pola and Pauline Mosch; bp. 13 Sep 1920; m. 30 Jun 1941; d. 1 Jul 1941 (FHL Microfilm 271394, 1935 Census; IGI; AF)

Renate Susanne Runge b. Bürgsdorf, Kreuzburg, Schlesien, Preußen 17 Nov 1914; dau. of Paul Wilhelm Runge and Marie Goy; bp. 6 Jun 1925; d. in childbirth Breslau, Schlesien, Preußen 5 May 1941; bur. Breslau-Mochbern 8 May 1941 (*Sonntagsgruss*, no. 23, 8 Jun 1941, p. 92; IGI)

Fritz Alfred Uebrick b. Kaltenbrunn, Schweidnitz, Sachsen, Preußen 20 Mar 1909; son of Paul Johann Übrick and Erna Pauline Klammt; bp. 28 May 1921; lance corporal; d. POW Frolowo, Russia 10 Jul 1944; bur. Sebesh, Russia (F. Tietze; FHL Microfilm 245289, 1925/30 Census; IGI; www.volksbund.de)

Hermann Walter b. Saint Petersburg, Russia, USSR 9 Feb 1896; m. Doberan, Livland, Estonia, USSR 6 Jul 1922, Ursula Kliefoth; 2m. Berlin Lichtenberg,

Preußen 5 Dec 1939, Sigrid Hansen; d. Berlin 7 Jan 1945 (SLCGW; IGI)

Anna Maria Weiss b. Ober Struse, Schlesien, Preußen 24 Mar 1884; bp. 6 May 1922; m. —— Wolf; d. Breslau, Schlesien, Preußen 20 Mar 1941 (*Sonntagsgruss*, no. 20, 18 May 1941, p. 80; IGI)

Christiane Johanna Zwilling b. Malian, Schlesien, Preußen 6 Jun 1873; dau. of Karl Friedrich August Zwilling and Pauline Juliane Seifert; bp. 7 Jul 1909; m. Breslau, Breslau, Schlesien 24 Apr 1899, Friedrich Karl Richter; 6 children; d. cholera Breslau 29 Jun 1945 (IGI; PRF)

NOTES

1. Werner Hoppe, telephone interview with Jennifer Heckmann, June 10, 2008.

2. Ruth Gottwald Richter, interview by the author in German, Aschersleben, Germany, May 31, 2007; summarized in English by the author.

3. Presiding Bishopric, "Financial, Statistical, and Historical Reports of Wards, Stakes, and Missions, 1884–1955," CR 4 12, 257.

4. Kurt W. Mach, autobiography (unpublished, 1965); private collection.

5. Elisabeth Nowak Mach, autobiography (unpublished); private collection.

6. Ruth Nestripke Dansie, journal, 6–7, MS 9556; Church History Library; trans. the author.

7. Ibid., 9.

8. Ibid., 10–11.

9. Ibid., 16–17.

10. Ibid., 22–23.

LIEGNITZ BRANCH

The city of Liegnitz, Silesia (now Legnica, Poland), was about one hour by train directly west of the provincial capital of Breslau and seventy miles east of the modern German-Polish border. The majority of the populace of that area of Silesia was Catholic.

Recalling his days as a member of the Liegnitz Branch, Werner Rosemann (born 1920) stated, "It was a small branch, but they were very good people."[1]

It was a tradition among LDS branches in Germany that activities in small branches were supported and attended by members of larger branches nearby. This was the case in Liegnitz, as is evident from the mission history that shows the following entry: "Sunday, 28 August 1938: The young people of the Breslau Branch went to Liegnitz to attend a special 'Youth Day' meeting there."[2] At the time, there were no more than five male youth and no more than three female youth; thus any youth activity in Liegnitz, the second-smallest branch in the district, would have been blessed to include visitors from other branches.

Liegnitz Branch[3]	1939
Elders	2
Priests	1
Teachers	0
Deacons	4
Other Adult Males	3
Adult Females	28
Male Children	1
Female Children	3
Total	42

The Rosemann family lived at Feldstrasse 23, just around the corner from the meeting rooms of the branch at Schützenstrasse 32. As was so often the case with LDS branches in Germany, the Liegnitz Branch rented rooms in a Hinterhaus in the interior of the block. Members had to pass through the main building on the street and across the courtyard to the building behind it, where a sign indicated the presence of the Liegnitz Branch: *Kirche Jesu Christi der Heiligen der Letzten Tage.* The rooms upstairs were not very large, but, according to Werner, "They were always very clean. We had a pump organ, but I do not recall any specific decorations."

According to Karl Rudolph Hallmann (born 1921), "One large room was on the second floor and another room was on the third floor. We held our Sunday meetings on the second floor and district meetings on the third floor. . . . We had thirty to forty chairs in the room."[4] Regarding the membership of the branch, Karl explained that "we had mostly newly baptized members or sisters whose husbands were serving in the military. The attendance fluctuated due to the conditions of the war or illness among the members. We had a wonderful spirit in the branch, although we had our complications and problems."

Just before the war began, Werner Rosemann completed an apprenticeship as a gardener in Parchwitz. He rode his bicycle to that town, about twelve miles from Liegnitz. "Everybody I dealt with knew about my association with the Church. There was never any problem with that. Even in school or in the military, I could—and did—talk freely about my religion."

When the war began on September 1, 1939, Karl Hallmann was serving with the Reichsarbeitsdienst stationed somewhere between Breslau and Berlin. "I fulfilled my service there without having any problems," he later explained. In those days, the boys of the Reichsarbeitsdienst did not know that a draft notice would likely be waiting for them when they were released and returned home. Nevertheless, war must not have been very attractive because (according to Karl) "the young people were not very fond of the idea of becoming soldiers someday."

Rather than wait to be drafted, Karl volunteered. Hoping that the war would be over soon, he calculated that by going into the army immediately following his year in the Reichsarbeitsdienst, he could minimize the interruption the military service would cause in his occupational training.

Just before Germany launched its monumental assault against the Soviet Union in June 1941, Werner Rosemann was drafted. He spent the rest of the war on the Eastern Front, in the northern sector near Finland and the besieged city of Leningrad. "I was trained as a marksman, but I am certain that I never shot a man. Things were pretty quiet on that end of the front, and my own life was never seriously endangered."

Karl learned that membership in the Church could be a hindrance to one's military career. As he explained:

> I was sent to Finland. I got a very good evaluation and was therefore promoted to be an officer. As soon as they found out which church I belonged to, they contacted Berlin to find out everything about me. Later, my commander received a letter saying that I could not be promoted because I belonged to a church whose headquarters were in the United States because Germany was at war with the United States. Another reason they mentioned was that in our Church, Jews could become members, and this did not agree with the standpoint of the government.

Later, Karl was sent to his hometown of Liegnitz for additional training. Fortunately, he was never in a combat situation and thus was never wounded. However, he stated that "danger was always just around the corner during the war."

Karl somehow avoided becoming a POW. He was fortunate to ride back to Germany on a train and even sat in a passenger car. He later admitted, "I was very lucky; the rest of the people [on the train] had to lie on the floor. Other soldiers had to walk home with bleeding feet."

During his time in military service, Karl did not have any contact with other Latter-day Saint soldiers. "There were not many who were soldiers and everybody was serving in a different area. There was no possibility of attending a sacrament meeting or going to church—it was just not common." Regarding the spiritual survival of Church members he knew during the war, Karl made the following statement: "If one had a testimony of the gospel, it was not difficult to keep it; but if one had no testimony or only a weak one, it soon became a problem and one had to leave the Church."

In the confusion of 1945, when the German army was in full retreat before the Soviet invasion, Werner Rosemann also somehow avoided being taken prisoner. He ended up walking all the way to Bavaria, a state in the far south of Germany, where he found employment as a gardener again. He had attempted to return to Liegnitz, but this was not possible because the territory had become part of Poland.

By the summer of 1946, Werner Rosemann's parents along with all other members of the Liegnitz Branch who had not previously fled the city were compelled by the new Polish government to leave. When they left, they were required to abandon almost everything they owned and to start a new and impoverished life in Germany. The Liegnitz Branch disappeared from the face of the earth.

In Memoriam

The following members of the Liegnitz Branch did not survive World War II:

Richard Erich Artur Jung b. Liegnitz, Schlesien, Preußen 21 Jun 1891; son of Johann Karl August Jung and Auguste Louise Helbig Geisler; bp. 9 Apr 1928; ord. deacon; ord. priest; m. Liegnitz 3 Feb 1921, Elly Gertrud Liesbeth Korge; 1 child; d. Kandalakscha, Russia 24 Apr 1946 (IGI)

Emma Pauline Schneider b. Löwen, Schlesien, Preußen 27 Mar 1878; bp. 25 Feb 1928; m. ——— Urbas; d. Liegnitz, Schlesien, Preußen 11 Jan 1941 (*Sonntagsgruss*, no. 23, 8 Jun 1941, p. 92; IGI)

Notes

1. Werner Rosemann, interview by the author, Bountiful, Utah, June 21, 2007.
2. East German Mission Quarterly Reports, 1938, no. 36, East German Mission History.
3. Presiding Bishopric, "Financial, Statistical, and Historical Reports of Wards, Stakes, and Missions, 1884–1955," CR 4 12, 257.
4. Karl Rudolph Hallmann, telephone interview with Jennifer Heckmann, January 29, 2008.

Schlegel Branch

The town of Schlegel in Silesia was about fifty miles south of Breslau, just fifteen miles from the border of Czechoslovakia. Situated in the Neuroder mountain range, the town had a population of about four thousand in the years preceding World War II. Among Catholic and Protestant neighbors, a small branch of Latter-day Saints also called Schlegel its home.

Schlegel Branch[1]	1939
Elders	2
Priests	0
Teachers	1
Deacons	2
Other Adult Males	4
Adult Females	10
Male Children	2
Female Children	1
Total	22

The history of the East German Mission mentions the branch in Schlegel only once before the history discontinued in early 1939: on Sunday, June 12, 1938, a branch conference was held in Schlegel.[2] As of this writing, no eyewitnesses were available to tell of other events in the branch or the lives of the members of the Church in Schlegel, Germany.

No members of the Schlegel Branch are known to have lost their lives in World War II.

Notes

1. Presiding Bishopric, "Financial, Statistical, and Historical Reports of Wards, Stakes, and Missions, 1884–1955," CR 4 12, 257.
2. East German Mission Quarterly Reports, 1938, no. 25, East German Mission History.

SCHWEIDNITZ BRANCH

The city of Schweidnitz is located about twenty-seven miles southwest of Breslau. Prior to the war, the town had a population of about thirty-five thousand people, the majority of whom were Catholic. The Latter-day Saint branch there met in rented rooms in a factory building at Bauhofstrasse 3. As in most branches in Germany, Sunday School started at 10:00 A.M. and sacrament meeting was held in the late afternoon or evening. According to Christa Zietz (born 1935):

> We had the whole upstairs floor. One large room was used for sacrament meetings and another large room for recreation. There were also other smaller rooms and closets. There were [usually] between thirty and forty people in attendance. . . . We always had a picture of Jesus. And one thing I remember very well: in front of the pulpit there was writing which said "The Glory of God Is Intelligence."[1]

Schweidnitz Branch[2]	1939
Elders	6
Priests	3
Teachers	1
Deacons	8
Other Adult Males	12
Adult Females	50
Male Children	10
Female Children	9
Total	99

From the recollections of Ursula Anders (born 1920):

> It took about an hour to get to church, which we did twice each Sunday, even in bad weather. Sometimes I got to church soaked to the skin. I could take my bike to church during the week but not on Sundays.[3]

The Schweidnitz Branch consisted of just a few large families. The surnames Anders, Burkert, Heilich, Köhler, König, Pöpel, Radon, Schöfer, and Zietz were well represented there.[4]

Ursula Anders had never joined the Hitler Youth. "None of my siblings did. It just wasn't our thing," she recalled. On September 1, 1939, war broke out. Ursula expressed her reaction to the news in these words:

> I was surprised to learn that Germany had attacked Poland. I was in the store when I heard that our army had marched into Poland. We had no warning. Then it was over in sixteen [twenty-one] days. I thought it was horrible.

Ursula's father was a blacksmith at the army post in Schweidnitz and was never drafted into the army. The family lived at Schlageterstrasse 20, about an hour's walk from the church. Fortunately, the home was not damaged during the war.

Christa Zietz's father, Walter, was drafted in 1940. "It was frightening to know that my father was in harm's way," Christa recalled, "He came home twice, and the third time he promised that he would come home when I started school [first grade], but he did not make it." Brother Zietz was only thirty-two years old when he was killed in battle just outside Moscow, Russia, on March 4, 1941.

According to the prevailing custom for mourning a family member, Wilhelmine Zietz was expected to wear black for one year. "I think my mother went longer," recalled Christa. In an attempt to cope with her grief, she took her two young girls to a forest ninety minutes distant to pick wild strawberries, raspberries, blueberries, and mushrooms. On one unforgettable occasion, they were next to a huge oak tree that was suddenly struck by lightning and burst into flames. Terribly frightened, they were nevertheless saved by their Heavenly Father's protection, according to Christa.[5]

Fig. 1. The Schweidnitz Branch shortly before the war. This photograph was taken in the cultural hall. (C. Zietz Simmons)

Fig. 2. Walter Zietz (left) and his brother Adolf in about 1940. Walter was killed near Moscow. (C. Zietz Simmons)

The Schweidnitz Branch experienced both member and convert baptisms during the war. "My baptism was on October 4, 1940, in the forest, at 8:00 p.m.," recalled Walli Pöpel. Her story continued:

It was at a reservoir outside of town. There were about ten of us and one adult [to be baptized]. [The adult] went into the water but came out fast because it was too cold for him. I thought he was a chicken and I said so, so I was the first. There were some sharp stones below and it hurt. But when I came out of the water, I felt so clean and so peaceful and that I was a good person. From then on I was not going to cause my mother any problems—but that didn't last long! Then we had a towel wrapped around us, and we walked all the way home, several miles.[6]

As part of their calling as "town missionar-ies," Elders Köhler and Burkhardt (members of the Schweidnitz Branch) knocked on the door of the Neumann family in 1941. Ilse Neumann was at home with her six children and sent the men away. However, they returned a few weeks later, and this time, Frau Neumann listened to their message. Her husband, Werner Bruno Neumann, was half Jewish and did not join the Church. Ilse was baptized with their two eldest children, Ingeborg and Horst, later that year. In 1942, daughter Brigitte (born 1934) was baptized. She recalled the event in these words:

When we all walked to the baptism, I was so excited. My mother was there and the [Church] brother who wanted to baptize me. It started raining, and I became angry and did not want to go through with the procedure anymore. The brother took his coat and put it around me because he knew how I felt. I wanted it to be the most beautiful day, and it was raining. I was baptized in the Weisstritz River. It was very cold, [but] as soon as I came out of the water, everything was different—I felt warm and welcome.[7]

Ursula Anders had finished school and completed an apprenticeship as a salesperson before the war began. She also participated in a course with the Red Cross and was a busy young lady when she became engaged to a soldier:

> I married in October 1942. He was Herbert Jagusch, a nonmember. We had a wedding dinner at home. My grandfather was there and siblings of my husband. We had a big dinner that we fixed ourselves. The wedding was in the civil registry office; nothing was done at church. Six months later (March 1943) he was killed in Russia. . . . We had no children. I was informed by a soldier who brought a letter from my husband's commanding officer. My husband was a messenger and was constantly moving up and down along the lines.

"It is indescribable being a widow after just six months," she explained. "I had told my husband about the Church, and he said that he would attend when he came home." Despite this devastating loss, during her year of bereavement, Ursula moved on with her life and became a full-time nurse, serving alternately in Schweidnitz and Breslau for the remainder of the war. Her memories of work as a nurse were vivid:

> They brought soldiers to us straight from the field hospitals. At the front, they were given lots of drugs, then we had to stop that when they came to us. One guy was screaming for drugs, but my boss told me that we couldn't give him any. So I gave him some placebo pills and his pain went away. I was gone for six months, then came back, and he was still there. He had my picture by his bed because he believed that I had healed him.

With the weapons of war ravaging the bodies of soldiers on many fronts, nurses needed nerves of steel to assist in putting those bodies back together. It appears that Ursula Anders was up to the task: "I really enjoyed being a nurse. . . . It was not psychologically difficult to be around those men because I could help them."

Stationed in Schweidnitz on Christmas Eve 1944, Ursula was in a Catholic hospital working the night shift. As she later reported, "There was a chapel where ten men had been put up, and they wanted to have a Christmas Eve mass. One man there was from France. He was in a wheelchair, and they rolled him in. Then they took him out because they said that he didn't belong there." Some inappropriate attitudes prevailed even at Christmastime.

National Socialist attempts to raise youth loyal to the government did not wane during the war. For example, Walli Pöpel was inducted into the Jungvolk in 1943 at the age of ten, along with her classmates at school:

> I really enjoyed the Jungvolk. I liked the marching, singing, and sports. We had competition in a large stadium. I excelled in every sport. In Schweidnitz we had a huge celebration and a local [Nazi] Party Jungvolk leader organized a huge stadium full of youth doing those routines with flags and ribbons.

Christa Zietz had no problems in school because of her religion. In fact, conditions were fairly pleasant for her in 1943:

> I remember my second grade teacher very well. She was the wife of the pastor of the Protestant church in Schweidnitz. She was very nice and kind to me. Her daughter was my best friend. I remember we made a pact that I would go to her church with her one Sunday and the next Sunday she would go to my church with me.

Her friend's elder brother appeared in church one Sunday and quietly observed a testimony meeting. Before leaving, he stated that he was very impressed and wished that he could feel the same way. He had simply come to see what his younger sister was experiencing.

Life in Hitler's Germany in the early years of the war was still relatively good for millions of Germans but not for people such as Walter Neumann, who had one Jewish parent. His daughter, Christa (born 1938), later recounted some of his trials during the war:

> Our father had to wear the Jewish star, and he was often taken away from home.[8] In those cases, my mother and Brother Heilig [the branch president] went and got him out from wherever he was. He was also often fired from his job, and it was difficult for him to find new work. People put an earring in his one ear because they wanted to make fun of him. The day our father was supposed to get baptized, he was sent into the water to find a deep spot that would work for his height. He could hardly breathe because of his heart condition, and they let him out again. Several times, they tried to baptize our father but there was always something that went wrong.

Frida Pöpel was left with four little children when her husband, Herbert, went off to war. According to their daughter, Walli:

> My father was unemployed since 1933 or 1934, so when the war started, he was drafted right away. He was in the air force. [During the war] we would see him once a year for a few days, then we took him to the train station to say good-bye, and we never knew if he would be coming back.

Räder müssen rollen für den Sieg! (Railroad wheels must roll to victory!) was the slogan of the German national railway system in World War II. However, that was only part of the story. Another part was the enormous relief effort needed to care for people on the long train rides west, as millions tried to evade the oncoming Soviets. Walli Pöpel and her Jungvolk friends were recruited to help feed the refugees streaming through Schweidnitz. She later described her work in these words:

> I worked at the train station to make sandwiches for the refugees. We made them in a big hall, using the *Kommissbrot* [dark army bread], and it was hard to chew. We made them and put them in baskets; then we went through the neighborhood to hand them out. Because we went down our own street, we stopped in our homes and gave some sandwiches to our family. And I ate one myself and ate a bit while we were making them. I was really hungry. That was in January 1945.

During the last months of the war, the conflict came ever closer to the relatively quiet town of Schweidnitz. Christa Zietz recalled one specific incident clearly:

> Our city was bombed heavily every day; we practically lived in the basement of our house where the bomb shelter was located. . . . I remember one Sunday, we had been to church, all had been calm, and we were sitting down to eat our Sunday dinner when there was a lot of noisy crashes, and flames of fire appeared outside our living room windows. The house was shaking, and we had a hard time going down into the bomb shelter. We had to hold on to the banister very hard or we would have fallen down the staircase. At first we thought that we had been hit, but we found out later that a house across the street had been hit instead. It felt like the end of the world had come. It was a surprise attack; it happened without any warning.

Ursula Anders was in Breslau when the word came that the invaders were about to surround the city. She later described the attempts made by the hospital personnel to evacuate patients from the city:

> We had to carry them [several were amputees] a long way to the railroad station. We saw a train that was reserved for officers, but I said, "We are putting our wounded on that train, and the officers can wait." When we were done loading the wounded, there was no room for the officers!

That train was the last to leave Breslau before the city was surrounded. Arriving in Berlin late that night, they survived an air raid, but Ursula had gained a few months' time before the war would catch up to her again.

Frida Pöpel took her four children and fled Schweidnitz on January 17, 1945. According to her daughter, Walli:

We went to the train station. Our friends had a fourteen-year-old son who was supposed to stay and fight with the Volkssturm, but we put him in woman's clothing, and he climbed over the fence to get on the train. We got fourteen people in the compartment. We were so crowded that the little children slept up above in the luggage racks.[9]

Sister Pöpel and her four children rode the train from Schweidnitz southeast to Prague. Walli explained what happened next:

The city [of Prague] was overflowing, so [officials] gave us some bread and water and sent us on to [Germany]. But that city was also overflowing, so we went on to Regen in the Bavarian Forest, where they put 200 of us in a school auditorium. There my mother had her fortieth birthday on February 22. It took us that long [since January 17] on the train without any bathing or washing. We did not change trains. Our train made it safely through while two other trains [of Schweidnitz refugees] were attacked by airplanes. We had plenty of Mormons in our train; they were all Schweidnitz Branch people. The branch ceased to exist when we left.

Frida Pöpel and her children ended up in the small Bavarian town of Abtschlag, seven miles from the German-Czech border. Living and working on a farm, they had no idea whether Herbert Pöpel was still alive. Fortunately, Walli could later tell of their reunion:

My father found us in Abtschlag when he came home in 1947. He hadn't seen us for three years. He found us through the Red Cross. . . . He had eaten better as a POW in France than we did [in Germany]. He drank wine even for breakfast. When he saw how we were starving and living in Germany with piles of destruction all around us, he wanted to take us and go back to France.

According to Christa Neumann, her family left Schweidnitz on February 23, 1945:

We left together with many people from the branch. We had already tried to leave our homes before, but then we went back. [That] morning, we [Saints] all met. Some of the families from the branch were already gone and used other opportunities to leave the city. The first thing

we did was to say a prayer together. Then, we walked to Kreuzwitz, a small place, because our [Schweidnitz] train station was destroyed and no train left from there. We waited for a long time, and it was very cold.

When they finally boarded the train, they were taken into Czechoslovakia. After a few weeks of confusion and partial starvation, the Neumanns (fortunately, an intact family) arrived in the large city of Plzen in western Czechoslovakia. The war was nearly over, and they were all imprisoned by the Czechs. For three weeks, they huddled in a small cell with forty other persons. Werner Bruno Neumann was then separated from his family, and Ilse was required to work in a nearby hospital. The children suffered from lack of food. Then the Americans (who had arrived in Plzen in late April) came to move them to another facility.

On her tenth birthday, April 21, 1945, Christa Zietz and her family were also evacuated from Schweidnitz. They traveled on a regular passenger train going south to the border of Czechoslovakia, where they were moved into a cattle car for the next phase of the trip. Then began what Christa would later call "that horrible journey through hell":

We were hated and persecuted, chased from one place to another, cubed up in pigpens and shot at [by partisans], exposed to the elements in bitter cold weather, where many people were physically abused and killed. Only through the protection of our Heavenly Father were we spared from that evil. We were starving and had to beg for food and water constantly.[10]

Christa's sister, who was four years younger, had broken her arm during the trip, and the family was nearly separated when Sister Zietz left the railroad station to find medical treatment for her daughter.

On April 21, the day the Zietz family left for Czechoslovakia, Ursula Anders was still in Berlin. It was on that day that the word went out that the invaders were about to complete their encirclement of the Reich capital. Ursula counted herself blessed to find a spot on a truck heading west. For the next two weeks, she and other refugees wandered west toward the Elbe River—sleeping in barns and begging for food. However, she found it impossible to cross over into what was believed to be friendlier occupation territory because the Soviets were carefully guarding the river. Eventually, an English truck gave her a lift across the river. From there she found transportation to Hamburg, but the city was devastated and its survivors were living in basements. Ursula moved on north to Elmshorn, where she found a budding new branch of the LDS Church.

Just over a month after the war ended, in June 1945, the Zietz family was sent home to Schweidnitz. They took a train to the border and then walked the rest of the way—about fifty miles. Shortly after their arrival, Christa and her grandmother were diagnosed with typhoid fever, to which the older woman succumbed on June 28. Wilhelmine Zietz was desperate to have her daughter hospitalized but had no money. One day, she was pushing ten-year-old Christa in a baby buggy toward the hospital, intensely praying about her need for money. "All of a sudden, she noticed something lying on the ground, and when she picked it up it was a wallet with exactly the amount of money in it that was needed," Christa later wrote.[11]

In the summer of 1946, the Zietz family members were required to either become Polish citizens or leave the country. They had already been thrown out of their apartment at Markt 14 at a moment's notice, losing most of their possessions. For this reason, it was not difficult to join with all of the surviving members of the Schweidnitz Branch in the decision to be deported to Germany. They were shipped to the East German town of Döbeln, Saxony, where

there was already a branch of the Church ready to take them in.

In June 1945, Ilse Neumann and her children were transported west from Plzen, Czechoslovakia, across the border into Germany. They were placed in the town of Windischeschenbach, just ten miles from the Czech border in the state of Bavaria. However, Walter Neumann was detained in Plzen and was never seen again. In 1948, the last of several inquiries was answered: Werner had died in a Plzen prison in 1946.

Ursula Anders's parents also chose deportation to Germany. They ended up in the town of Treuenbrietzen, north of Berlin, where their daughter did not see them again until 1947. By then a veteran army nurse and a young widow, Ursula looked forward to a better life after the war. For more than two years she had been mostly isolated from the Church: "I never saw Mormon soldiers in the hospitals. When I was not on duty (which was rare), I went to church in Breslau. I had a Book of Mormon with me until I fled Breslau." Through it all, she had remained faithful to the Church.

Almost all of the members of the Schweidnitz Branch made it safely west to what remained German territory. By the fall of 1946, the Latter-day Saint branch in Schweidnitz, Germany—renamed Swidnica, Poland—had ceased to exist.

In Memoriam

The following members of the Schweidnitz Branch did not survive World War II:

Herbert Jagusch m. 1942; k. in battle 1943. (Anders-Adolf)

Rosalie Emma Schoefer b. Riegersdorf, Neustadt, Ober-Schlesien 1 Feb 1905; dau. of Karl Schoefer and Anna Pauline Huhndt; bp. 27 Sep 1924; d. 1942. (Zietz-Simmons; IGI)

Walter Karl Emil Zietz b. Berlin, Brandenburg, Preußen 6 Feb 1909; son of Emil Karl Zietz and Elfriede Johanna Klara Eckstein; bp. 26 Jun 1927;

Fig. 3. Frida Pöpel was forced to flee Schweidnitz with her four children in January 1945. (W. Pöpel Sanger)

m. Schweidnitz, Schlesien, Preußen 4 Oct 1932, Wilhelmine Pauline Huhndt; 2 children; k. in battle Moscow, Russia 4 Dec 1941. (Zietz-Simmons; IGI)

NOTES

1. Christa Zietz Simmons, interview by the author, Manti, Utah, October 8, 2006.

2. Presiding Bishopric, "Financial, Statistical, and Historical Reports of Wards, Stakes, and Missions, 1884–1955," CR 4 12, 257.

3. Ursula Anders Wolf, interview by the author in German, Augsburg, Germany, August 7, 2006; summarized in English by Judith Sartowski.

4. List (unpublished, 2006); private collection; comp. Christa Zietz Simmons.

5. Christa Zietz Simmons, "Biography of Wilhelmine Pauline Huhndt Zietz" (unpublished personal history), 2; private collection.

6. Walli Pöpel Sanger, interview by the author, Provo, Utah, June 19, 2008.

7. Brigitte Neumann, Christa Neumann, and Ursula Neumann McKell, interview by Marion Wolfert in German, Salt Lake City, May 15, 2006; summarized in English by Judith Sartowski; transcript of interview in author's collection.

8. Since 1941, German law required all Jews to wear a yellow Star of David (about four inches across) on their outer clothing.

9. The standard passenger compartment in those days accommodated six persons.

10. Simmons, "Biography," 2.

11. Ibid.

WALDENBURG GROUP

The only information available about this group of Latter-day Saints came from one eyewitness—Luise Böttcher Winkler. She had been widowed in January 1943 and by 1944 was encouraged by the government to take her little children (born in 1939 and 1941) out of the city of Berlin to a safe location. She traveled to Waldenburg, Silesia, because she had been told that she could attend church meetings nearby. She later described the experience of being a Latter-day Saint in that small town:

> We visited the branch in Waldenburg every Sunday while we were there. We had to take the streetcar. [The branch] was very small with only twenty people meeting in two little rooms. The branch president came from Hamburg. I was responsible for the children and the singing, and I also took the children of my cousin (who was not a member) to church with me. Once, we went to Breslau for a [district] conference.[1]

Sister Winkler was determined to maintain contact with the Church even while away from home. She returned to Berlin in September 1944.

Nothing more is known about the members of the Church in Waldenburg.[2] It appears that no members of the group lost their lives in the war.

NOTES

1. Luise Böttcher Winkler, interview by the author in German, Leipzig, Germany, June 2, 2007; summarized in English by Judith Sartowski.
2. The town of Waldenburg is now known as Wałbrzych.

Fig. 4. Like this group of refugees, hundreds of Latter-day Saints from the Breslau District were forced to make their way westward in the dead of winter. (Deutsches Bundesarchiv, Bild 183-1990-0323-501)

CHEMNITZ DISTRICT

East German Mission

With a total of 1,051 members, the Chemnitz District was the second largest in the East German Mission at the end of the year 1939. The district consisted of six branches, all of which were situated in south-central Saxony. The city of Chemnitz, with two branches (Center and Schloss), had long been a bastion of the Church in eastern Germany. The city is located about 150 miles south of Berlin.

Because of the high concentration of Latter-day Saints in the area, the Chemnitz District territory was smaller than the Berlin District. Branches were located in Döbeln (twenty miles northeast of Chemnitz), Mittweida (ten miles north), Hohenstein-Ernstthal (nine miles west), and Annaberg-Buchholz (seventeen miles southeast).

Chemnitz District[1]	1939	1940	1941	1942
Elders	45	56		
Priests	32	22		
Teachers	42	43		
Deacons	54	54		
Other Adult Males	192	194		
Adult Females	596	599		
Male Children	41	46		
Female Children	49	48		
Total	1,051	1,062	1,058	1,022

In 1938, a mission directory showed that four small groups of Saints were also meeting in towns within the Chemnitz District:

Town	Host Family	Address
Geyersdorf	Wagner[2]	Hauptstrasse 92, main floor
Jöhstadt	Meyer	Innere Bahnhofstrasse 122
Schlettau	Hofmann	Markt 45
Walthersdorf	Petzold	Adolf Hitler Strasse 6, upstairs

Very little is known about those small groups of Latter-day Saints.

The East German Mission history has the following entry dated Sunday, May 29, 1938:

> On this and the previous day, the annual spring conference of the Chemnitz District was held in Chemnitz. Mission Pres. Alfred C. Rees, and the Elders of the district were in attendance. The choir, with the help of an orchestra, rendered some very beautiful musical selections. The meetings were well attended.[3]

Karl Göckeritz of the Chemnitz Center Branch was the president of the Chemnitz District. His counselors in early 1939 were Paul Langheinrich and Emil Heidler. Although a relatively young man (born in November

Fig. 1. The Chemnitz District was in the heart of the old Kingdom of Saxony in eastern Germany.

1909), President Göckeritz was called by one elder "the driving force in all of the branches in the district."[4]

President Göckeritz kept a diary for just more than a year, beginning in early 1941. He used a diary printed for the year 1936 and simply revised the date at the bottom of the page. The entries are very detailed and indicate a wide variety of family, church, occupational, and cultural activities. He even made frequent comments regarding the weather. The following are extracts from his diary:

Wednesday, March 19, 1941: Police monitored our building tonight regarding the blackout regulations.

Sunday, April 7, 1941: Very early wrote Church letters. Took Hannchen [wife Magdalena Johanna] and children to Center Branch. Train to Döbeln at 10:56. Gave talk and played music. On to Mittweida at 2:17. Visited Emmerlichs.

Rehearsal at church. Gave talk and played music. Home about 10:00 P.M.

Sunday, May 4, 1941: Conference. Went to church at 8:00 A.M. Everything is ready! Wonderful morning session. Superb decorations. Everything went very well. Choir practice. Solved all problems. Preparations for afternoon session. All went well. Then main session! 506 in attendance. Beautiful! Everything went well. The room was totally full! Gave one talk in each meeting and one prayer. Evening at home with Brother [Richard] Ranglack [from the mission office in Berlin]. Everything was wonderful!

Tuesday, May 20, 1941: Afternoon funeral service for soldier W. Opitz. Military ceremony. Very impressive! Evening in Central Theater for Paginini. Very nice. Heavy rain!

Saturday, May 31, 1941: Express train at 6:25 A.M. to Berlin. Great weather. In Berlin about 11:00 A.M. Walked to mission office. Met the people from the West German Mission: Brother and Sister Heck, Brother Huck, Sister Weipel, and Ilse Krämer. . . . Evening meeting at Hufelandstrasse [Berlin Center Branch]. Fine meeting!

Wednesday, June 25, 1941: Office work! Nothing special! Went to the dentist. In the evening wrote reports, then to Center Branch. Resolved various matters there. Rudi Seltmann killed in an accident near the Russian border.

Sunday, August 10, 1941: Took children to Sunday School early. Resolved some Church matters there. Rode my bicycle to Stollberg to take care of some matters there. Home with children. In the afternoon rainy weather! Took a nap. Then to Center Branch to speak with Brother Urban regarding members in Bohemia [Czechoslovakia]. Took care of some matters in Center Branch. Played [the piano] because nobody else was there.

Tuesday, September 2, 1941: Two hours of air-raid alarm during the night.

Friday, September 5, 1941: Held a baptismal ceremony. Six persons baptized, two confirmed. Very nice. Gorgeous summer evening!

Friday, September 12, 1941: In the evening to Center Branch. Construction work in upper room with Alfred Schulz, Oskar Bonitz, Lothar Cieslak. Really dirty work. Had a bath later.

Sunday, October 12, 1941: Got up at 6:00! It snowed during the night! To church at 7:30. Last-minute preparations for the conference! 8:00 presidency meeting. 10:00 morning session. Choir practice. Lunch. 2:30 Relief Society and priesthood meeting. 5:00 main session. All meetings had good attendance. I conducted three meetings and gave one talk. It certainly was a successful conference! Approximately 1,385 total attendance![5]

On October 17, 1941, the district presidency sent a letter to soldiers in the field:

Once again we have had a conference in the rooms you know so well, at Schadestrasse 12. Our district conference! Just as the earth has yielded the blessings of Almighty God through a fine harvest, so do we experience the goodness of our Heavenly Father in rich measure. . . . Although we cannot see you, we are still spiritually very closely connected with you. Just picture it: there was not an empty seat in the room. . . . As God lives, so lives His work. We greet you as loyal brethren in the gospel. Our fondest wishes accompany you. We ask the Lord every day to protect you, so that you may return in health to your homeland. May peace fill the earth very soon, so that all peoples may be joined in a righteous labor. . . . All of the branches you know are functioning as before: Annaberg-Buchholz, Chemnitz Center,

früh 6 Uhr auf! Es hatte nachts
etwas geschneit!
früh 1/2 8 i. Lokal - letzte Vorberei-
tungen f. d. Tagung!
8 Uhr Dis. Verslg.
10 " Morgenfeier
Chorproben - Mittagessen
14.30 - Frauentum - Priestertum
17.- " Hauptversammlung
alle Verslg. gut und ansprechend
3 Verslg geleitet - 1 Anspr.
es war bestimmt eine erfolg-
reiche Tagung! ca. 1385 Gesamt
anwesenheit!
12.
Sonntag, 11. Oktober 1936

Fig. 2. District president Karl Göckeritz wrote an enthusiastic entry in his diary regarding the district conference held on October 11–12, 1941. (H. Goeckeritz)

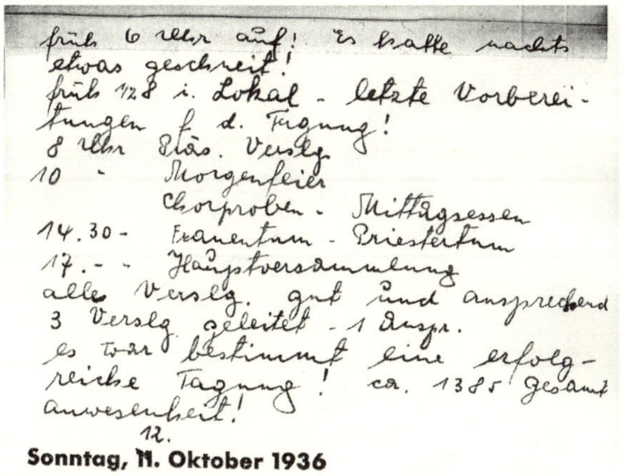

Schloss, Döbeln, Hohenstein, Mittweida. The wheel of truth continues to turn. . . . Be of the conviction that we are always thinking of you, though we may not write too very often. We too must respond to the call of duty here, as do you out there.

The back of the letter bore the signatures of forty-eight more members of the Chemnitz District.[6]

Karl Göckeritz did not know in October 1941 that his term as district president was nearing its end. Several diary entries of interest were yet to be made:

Tuesday, 28 October 1941: Air-raid sirens at 10:30 P.M. Very heavy antiaircraft fire. Ended about midnight.

Monday, 17 November 1941: Office work! Nothing special! Suffering from a very bad cold! In the evening a meeting of the elders. Fine meeting despite unsafe conditions.

Saturday, 22 November 1941: In the evening wrote a letter to all branches, then did night shift at factory. Mölders fell to his death somewhere near Breslau.

Monday, 15 December 1941: Went to town and bought a Christmas tree. Very difficult. Films are done. In the evening worked on reports at home. Heavy rain!

7 January 1942: In the evening to the Center Branch for a little Christmas party. Received notice that I am to report for military duty on 15 January.

15 January 1942: Worked in the office! Hannchen called to say that I don't have to report for military duty until 19 January 1942.

19 January 1942: Reported for duty at 8:00 A.M. at the post of Infantry Regiment 102 on Planitzstrasse. Assigned to second platoon of first company of reserve infantry in Chemnitz. Assigned a room. Issued uniform. Cleaned closet. To bed at 9:00 P.M. Twenty-nine men and two trainers in the room. Very cold!

Fig. 3. Karl Göckeritz (1909–43) was one of four current or former district presidents in the East German Mission who lost their lives in the war. (H. Goeckeritz)

Wednesday, 28 January 1942: The sergeant tells us that we will leave on Saturday for the Western Front—France.

30 January 1942: No special training. Had to get ready to move out. . . . In the evening one more visit from Hannchen and Papa and Emil Heidler and Paul Auerswald. At 5:00 P.M. Hitler gave a powerful speech.

The last entry in the diary of district president Karl Göckeritz is dated Saturday, February 14, 1942. By that time, he had been transferred not to France, but to Zwickau, a city just a few miles west of Chemnitz. He went to the movies that evening and saw the film *Über alles in der Welt*. In 1943, he was reported missing in action near Boldyrewka, Russia.[7] His successor was Emil Heidler.

Based on the testimonies of eyewitnesses, all six branches of the Chemnitz District of the East German Mission were still holding meetings when the war ended on May 8, 1945.

NOTES

1. Presiding Bishopric, "Financial, Statistical, and Historical Reports of Wards, Stakes, and Missions, 1884–1955," CR 4 12, 257.

2. See the Annaberg-Buchholz chapter.

3. East German Mission Quarterly Reports, 1938, no. 22, East German Mission History.

4. Johannes Jentzsch, "History of the Mittweida Branch" (unpublished history, about 1992); private collection; trans. the author.

5. Karl Göckeritz, diary, 1909–1943; private collection.

6. Karl Göckeritz to soldiers on active duty, October 17, 1941; private collection; trans. the author.

7. Harald Goeckeritz, interview by the author, Draper, Utah, February 17, 2006.

ANNABERG-BUCHHOLZ BRANCH

The twin towns of Annaberg and Buchholz are located seventeen miles south-southeast of Chemnitz and just six miles from the border of Czechoslovakia. Although geographically isolated in the Erzgebirge Mountains of Saxony, the branch there was strong and active.

Annaberg-Buchholz Branch[1]	1939
Elders	15
Priests	7
Teachers	11
Deacons	30
Other Adult Males	44
Adult Females	141
Male Children	13
Female Children	13
Total	274

The records of the East German Mission show several entries regarding the branch in Annaberg-Buchholz:

Friday, 1 July 1938: In order to repair the chairs in the Buchholz Branch hall, Chemnitz District, several special meetings were held to enthuse the saints to a united effort to raise money. The result was very good.[2]

Sunday, 17 July 1938: The Buchholz Branch, Chemnitz District, held a conference.[3]

Saturday, 6 August 1938: The Annaberg Branch choir, Chemnitz District, gave a very successful concert.[4]

Saturday, 8 October and Sunday, 9 October 1938: A branch fall conference was held in Annaberg-Buchholz; Herbert Klopfer [from Berlin] and Elder Roger A. Brown directed the conference.[5]

Sunday, 15 January 1939: The Annaberg-Buchholz Branch moved into a new hall. It was in the same building, but one flight higher.[6]

Sunday, 5 February 1939: An opening program was held in the new branch hall of the Annaberg-Buchholz Branch, Chemnitz District.[7]

Willi Schramm was the branch president. His daughter, Ruth (born 1929), recalled that the members of the branch came from many locations in the Erzgebirge Mountains:

> They came from all over. And they came in the winter, with their babies, walking! They had the babies wrapped in the baby carriage—it was just great! In fact, if you didn't come one or two Sundays [in a row], they [branch leaders] got after you.[8]

Erhard Wagner (born 1917) lived in the small town of Geyersdorf, just less than two miles east of Annaberg-Buchholz. "There were about 1,500 people in the town and six or seven Latter-day Saint families. We had about the largest percentage of membership of any town in Germany. The blood of Israel was very strong in our little town," he claimed.[9]

Erhard recalled that Relief Society and priesthood meetings were held just before sacrament meeting on Sunday evening, with MIA meetings on Wednesday evenings. "We walked back and forth to church twice every Sunday, one and one-half miles each way," he later explained. Erhard's sister, Alice (born 1926), remembered that the walk took an hour and that no bus was available to shorten the time. She also recalled attending Primary after school on Wednesdays and holding group meetings in Geyersdorf on Thursday evenings. She later explained, "We met in different homes. I was always so excited that I was able to go with my parents because I could learn more about the gospel."[10]

Ruth Schramm lived in Buchholz at Karlsbaderstrasse 19. From her home, she needed about fifteen minutes to go down the hill, across the bridge to Annaberg, up the hill and around the corner to the church rooms at Wilischstrasse 10. Regarding the facility, Alice Wagner later recalled, "We met in a big factory hall on the second floor. On the one side there were only windows, and on the other was a door to all the rooms we held the other meetings in."

Helga Martin (born 1931) recalled seeing pictures of Joseph Smith and Brigham Young on the back walls of the main meeting room. "There was a sign on the street side of the factory that said that we were the Kirche Jesu Christi der Heiligen der Letzten Tage."[11]

Sunday School was held in the morning, after which most of the members went home for dinner. They returned in the evening for sacrament meeting. Primary meetings were held on Wednesday afternoons after school. Ruth Schramm walked to church with her father on Sundays but went alone on Wednesdays. "It was a long walk, but it was safe in those days," she recalled.

In 1938, Erhard Wagner was drafted for two years of service in the German army. At the time, every young man in Hitler's Germany was required to serve the fatherland. In the summer of 1939, Erhard's father visited him at the camp in Leipzig where he was completing basic training and told his son what he had heard in BBC radio broadcasts in German from London. Erhard recalled the conversation:

> "Son, you're going to have war really soon. Hitler's starting a war." I told him, "Be careful, you have a Nazi living upstairs, and if he finds out [about the radio], you're gone. He's a 200 percent Nazi, that guy upstairs." Two weeks later, on a Sunday, we had to pack everything, march to the Polish border, and on the first of September we were right in [the action]. Nobody had any idea before.

Erhard Wagner had the dubious honor of moving across the border in the first hour of World War II—the German offensive against Poland. He was with an antiaircraft battery that followed close upon the heels of the infantry in the early morning hours of Friday, September 1, 1939. Although his unit marched past dead soldiers of both armies, there was little real resistance and Erhard's group never fired a shot. The Polish campaign ended in three weeks. From there, they loaded their artillery pieces onto railroad cars and headed westward.

On May 10, 1940, the German army crossed the border into Belgium, the Netherlands, and Luxembourg to begin an offensive that would result in the conquest and occupation of those three countries and eventually France to the south. Again, Erhard Wagner crossed the border on the first day of the campaign but saw no combat until May 19—his birthday—when his unit encountered resistance. "Oh, no, to-day's my birthday; maybe it's my last day," he

thought to himself. He survived the encounter and later had time to enjoy the sights in France. The next move took his unit to the demarcation line in Poland, where the Russians and the Germans had divided the conquered country in 1939. His enlistment term of two years soon elapsed, but there was no discussion of Erhard going home.

Ruth Schramm was one of two LDS children in her school of five hundred. "Can you imagine what I went through? Everybody else was Lutheran except one Catholic boy. There were a few boys who said, 'Rutha is a Buddha!' And Ruth didn't like that at all!"

Along with the rest of the girls in her school class, Alice Wagner was inducted into the Hitler Youth. In her recollection:

> There was a meeting once a week in the evening hours. We had to wear a skirt, a white blouse, and a jacket. It did not bother us. There were no meetings for the Hitler Youth on Sundays, and nobody in school picked on me because I was a member of the Church.

Fig. 1. The Annaberg-Buchholz Branch in the 1930s. (H. Martin Scharschmidt)

Fig. 2. Mother's Day in the Annaberg-Buchholz Branch during the war. (H. Martin Scharschmidt)

Wolfgang Scharschmidt (born 1928) was also in the Hitler Youth, but the program mattered little to him: "My father did not want us to go and encouraged us to stay home. I always found a reason not to go, and there wasn't any trouble when I stayed away."[12]

Erhard Wagner was trained in the use of one of the most effective and feared weapons of World War II—the German 88-millimeter howitzer. It could fire a projectile of about two feet in length and three inches in width nearly one-half mile per second. Erhard was responsible for determining the trajectory and the moment of fire. On one occasion in France, his battery of four howitzers shot down in one salvo three airplanes returning to England after a raid over Germany. Regarding his reaction to seeing enemy planes fall from the sky with no parachutes emerging from those planes, he recalled:

War is bad, but how can you feel real sorry about something like that when they come back after killing hundreds in our homeland? They did carpet bombing. Men, women, children, everybody got killed. That's terrible, you know. . . . We went right . . . to that place where the airplanes had [crashed], and I can't remember any cheering [about our victory].

In June 1941, the German army launched a massive assault against the Soviet Union. Again, Erhard Wagner was one of the first to cross the border into enemy territory. "When they told us that we were attacking Russia, we couldn't believe it. We were already fighting a front in Africa, and now we were fighting in the east. . . . It was foolish; we knew that."

One of the many Latter-day Saints who moved with the Wehrmacht into the Soviet Union in the summer of 1941 was Erhard Wagner's brother, Kurt, a deacon in the Aaronic Priesthood. In December of that year, he received a photograph of the children of the Annaberg-Buchholz Primary Association. He expressed his gratitude in a letter dated December 21, 1941:

Dear Sisters of the Primary,
Today I received the letter from little Hanna Scharschmidt. Please express to Hanna my deepest appreciation. I have looked at the photograph for a long time. It appears that only the children of faithful Saints are in this picture. Tomorrow it will be one-half year since

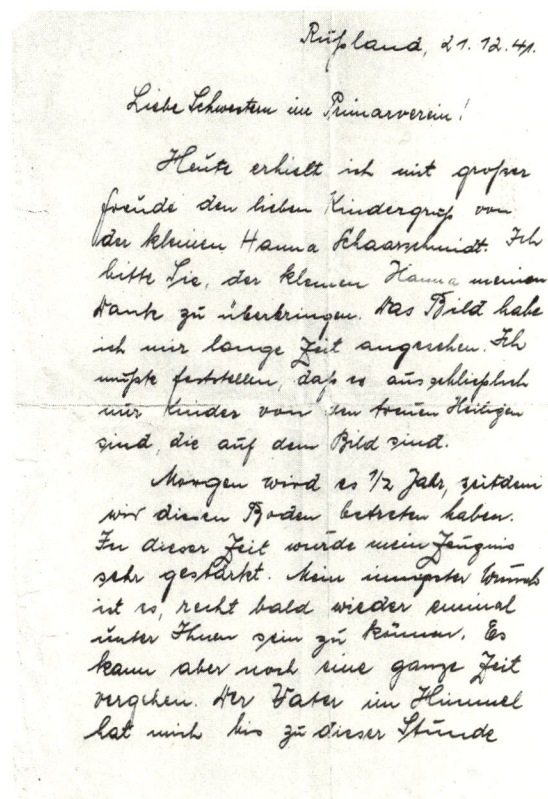

Fig. 3. Kurt Wagner wrote to the teachers of the branch Primary in December 1941. (A. Wagner Flade)

159

we entered this country. During this time, my testimony has been strengthened very much. My most fervent wish is to be among you again soon, but that may not be for a long time. My Father in Heaven has guided me through all of this and will continue to do so; of this I am convinced. . . . May you be blessed in your work.[13]

During a training session in 1941, Erhard Wagner was able to attend church in the Berlin Schöneberg Branch. It was there that he met and eventually fell in love with Marianna Langheinrich, the daughter of the second counselor in the East German Mission leadership. Over the next two years, they were able to spend a few days together and were finally married in his hometown of Geyersdorf in 1943. "The official gave us a copy of Hitler's book *Mein Kampf.* We buried it behind my house [in 1945] so the Russians wouldn't find it and think we were Nazis. It's still there," he explained years later.

Just before Christmas 1941, Erhard was in the Soviet Union, on guard duty at about forty degrees below zero. By the end of his watch, he had contracted such severe frostbite that "blood and water dripped down my chin and right away the skin was gone completely, and raw flesh." He spent the next nine months in five different hospitals in Latvia and Germany. "I was ready to take my life, believe me—that was so painful when I was wrapped up with a million lice underneath—itching, itching you can't imagine, and they gave me shots against that itching and then I felt better." When he finally returned to Russia in late 1942, he was told the sad tale of his unit's fate:

Two, three days [after I contracted frostbite] the Russian army got some reinforcements, more infantry, more tanks, more guns, more everything, and they broke through our line, we couldn't hold them. I know when I left that night we were 140 men strong, and eighteen men [were] left [after the engagement], and I wondered, "Would I not be alive today or

would I be among those eighteen?" The Lord was really on my side.

Christa Glauche and her father moved from Chemnitz to Annaberg-Buchholz after her mother died in 1942. Christa recounted her impressions of the new branch:

The branch [in Annaberg-Buchholz] was very strong at that time. It was all kept very simple, but in every branch I had been in, there was always a picture of Joseph Smith and Jesus Christ. This branch was larger than the one I had been in before.[14]

Georg Karl Richter (born 1908) had been married since 1932 and certainly did not wish to leave his family to become a soldier. However, the Wehrmacht had different plans, and he was drafted. After basic training in nearby Plauen, he was off to Russia in 1942. A deacon in the Aaronic Priesthood, he took the Bible with him everywhere he went.[15]

At Christmastime in 1942, Georg found himself and his comrades surrounded by Soviet troops. On Christmas Eve, they lit a candle and sang Christmas songs, believing that they could not possibly escape and would soon die. Then they prayed. Shortly thereafter, a German truck came by and they jumped aboard. Somehow the truck made it safely through both the Soviet and German lines. They were shot at but escaped unharmed.

That same year, Marianna Langheinrich Wagner left her parents' home in Berlin and moved to Annaberg near her husband's family. Her first child, Klaus Ulrich, was born there.

In early 1943, the Wagner family of Geyersdorf received heart-breaking news from the Eastern Front. Alice later explained their loss:

I had an older brother, Johannes Kurt Wagner, who was born on October 31, 1920, in Geyersdorf. He went missing in Stalingrad [December 1942–January 1943] while serving for the army in Russia. We received a letter stating that he was missing but never found out if he passed away. My brother was twenty [22] years old at that time, and he was a deacon. He was the secretary of the branch president.

In 1944, Erhard Wagner was sent to France and stationed near Cherbourg in Normandy, just a few miles from the beaches where the Allied forces landed on D-day, June 6, 1944. He was still having trouble with the skin on his face, so he was sent to another hospital some miles from the coast, just a few days before D-day. Again, he escaped combat with the enemy and was eventually stationed near Amsterdam in the Netherlands.

One day during the slow German retreat from Russia in 1944, Georg Richter was totally exhausted and simply fell down at the side of the road, unable to continue. When he came to, he found himself on the back of a truck. He later learned that somebody determined that he was still alive, and they loaded him onto the truck. He escaped death by a very slight margin.

Only sixteen years of age in 1944, Wolfgang Scharschmidt was needed by Hitler's Reich, which by then was facing certain defeat. Wolfgang was trained as an assistant antiaircraft gunner and sent off to western Germany. He explained that near the city of Essen, "the Americans came and I was taken prisoner and was brought to a large camp at Wesel. We didn't even have a roof over our heads and had

Fig. 4. Erhard Wagner's unit receiving artillery instruction in Potsdam in 1941. (E. Wagner)

Fig. 5. A 1938 priesthood meeting of the Annaberg-Buchholz Branch. (H. Martin Scharschmidt)

to sleep in a field—sometimes we even dug holes so we could be a little safer at night."

There were few attacks on Annaberg-Buchholz during the war, but quite often the route taken by Allied bombers was close enough that alarms were sounded and people rushed to the shelters. As in most towns, there were few official air-raid shelters, so most people sought refuge in their own basements. According to Ruth Schramm, "Even when they didn't attack our town, we still had to go down [to the shelter], and sometimes we wouldn't go down during the day. We watched, oh, how many planes were coming over us!"

The resilience of children is remarkable, even in wartime. As Helga Martin recalled, they went about their play. Alarms could be unnerving, but they did not worry much about the possibility of being killed in an air raid:

We lived in an area where there were not many attacks, and we were safer than in other towns. I did not live far from school and when the sirens blared, we were allowed to go home, and I also took other children home with me because their way home was longer than mine. When we played in the forest and we had an alarm, we were scared.

Alice Wagner did not have terrible memories of the air raids but recalled that on at least one occasion, a Church meeting was

161

interrupted so that the members could go to the basement. She saw bombers making their way across the skies to other targets and recalled seeing the red sky over Dresden and Chemnitz when those two cities were bombed and burning in early 1945. After the devastating attack on Chemnitz on March 5, refugees made their way to Annaberg, and the Wagners took in several of them.

As the war dragged on, Helga Martin worried more and more about her father:

> The most difficult thing was that my father was not home anymore. He was drafted by the Wehrmacht in 1942. In the beginning, he was close to home, but then they transferred him to a place further away. He was part of the retreat from Greece to Yugoslavia. We did not hear from him in over two years when he was missing. We received the notice in 1947 that he had died on September 15, 1945.

Toward the end of the war, Annaberg-Buchholz was attacked from the air and some damage was done to local structures. Ruth Schramm recalled her feelings at the time:

> One thing that I will never forget is our [town] church, our Lutheran church got bombed out, and it was gothic. And it was beautiful, that church. . . . When that was burning, that was absolutely awful. The steeple was one flame. And we stood there—it was early in the morning, three or four o'clock, and then when it finally fell over, we all cried. We really did.

Fig. 6. *The building at Wilischstrasse 10 as it appears today. (H. Martin Scharschmidt)*

According to Helga Martin, branch meetings were temporarily interrupted in the last few months of the war: "Our branch premises were used as a military hospital, and we could not hold our meetings, and we met at home, and the Methodist church allowed us to use their rooms, so we could at least have our sacrament meeting."

With the death and destruction visited on Germany, it can come as no surprise that some Saints became discouraged. Ruth Schramm recalled that one of her half sisters was terribly worried about her soldier husband:

> She said, "Dad, if he doesn't come home, I'm going to kill myself." And she had a four-year-old little girl, and my dad got really angry with her. But one thing she did, every Monday it was fast day for her. She fasted faithfully every Monday that he would come home. So, can you imagine, her faith was really . . . I shouldn't say shattered, but for a few weeks, she didn't go to church. But then she went back.

It was later learned that her husband had been killed when strafed by a fighter plane near Sevastopol, Russia.

For Erhard Wagner, the situation near Amsterdam was calm until April 1945, when Canadian troops attacked their position. By then, Erhard's unit had no ammunition left; they spiked their guns and simply tried to escape. However, there was nowhere to go; Erhard was wounded slightly and captured by the Canadians.

In their remote location in the Erzgebirge Mountains, the residents of Annaberg-Buchholz did not see enemy soldiers until the war was officially over. According to Ruth Schramm, "There were no [German] troops there, so there was no fighting. The Russians just moved in. I heard the commotion because [the streets were] all cobblestones."

The defeat of Germany was welcomed by many Germans who thought it meant the end of their sufferings. But some had staked all of their hopes on the success of the country, and the defeat was personally devastating. Christa Glauche recalled the reaction of her brother:

> There was one experience which I will never forget. My older brother wanted to be an officer and had already been a noncommissioned officer in charge of a company of soldiers. Just after the war ended, my brother came to Annaberg-Buchholz riding his bike. He carried a bazooka. He did not even know that the war had ended, and he was very surprised and cried bitterly. He remembered the six years that he and his friends had tried to survive this horrible time. I will never forget his crying because as an adult I had never seen him cry. He surrendered himself and was only taken prisoner for a little while by the Americans in [nearby] Schwarzenberg.

When the victorious Soviets came looking for women in Annaberg-Buchholz, Ruth Schramm and the other women in the house often crawled out a back window and hid in a shed. They always managed to elude their pursuers.

Even in the small town of Geyersdorf, the women were not safe from marauding enemy soldiers. Alice Wagner recalled a terrifying experience, in which she believed the hand of the Lord played an unmistakable role:

> One night, we were sitting at the dinner table eating our meal when we heard a terrible racket outside. We looked out the window and saw Russian tanks, Russian trucks, Russian motorcycles—Russians everywhere! My father said, "Let's get on our knees and pray that the Lord will not let anything happen to us." And he prayed, "Father in Heaven, blind these soldiers that they will not be able to see our house and protect us from the danger that threatens everybody in our neighborhood!" An hour and a half later we heard them coming out of the houses, getting into their vehicles and driving away. The next morning my girlfriend from school asked me if that wasn't the most horrible night ever. When I told her that they hadn't come into our house, she couldn't believe it. She told me that

Fig. 7. German soldiers inspect the ruins of a French plane downed by antiaircraft fire. (E. Wagner)

they were in every other house. They had raped her and her mother in front of their family.

Christa Glauche survived what could have been a life-threatening encounter with the occupation forces:

> I worked at the telephone central office, and the late shift usually lasted until 11:30 P.M. My co-worker and I walked from Annaberg to Buchholz, and there were some Russians who tried to threaten us. I said that I would tell their commanding officer what they tried if they did not stop. One soldier hit me and the day after, my face looked very different. But nothing else happened to us.

In summing up the behavior of branch members during the final years of the war and the aftermath, Christa stated, "All the members of the Annaberg-Buchholz Branch stayed close to each other during the last hard months of the war. They helped each other in every way." Eyewitnesses recalled that several Latter-day Saint families arrived as refugees from the East and were taken into already crowded living spaces: the Meier family from Königsberg, the Henkels from Frankfurt/Oder, and the Births from Schneidemühl.

In September 1945, Erhard Wagner was released by his Canadian captors and made his way home to his wife and son in Annaberg. He could claim to be one of the few German army veterans to march into enemy territory on the first day in all three major German offensives in Europe: Poland, France, and Russia. His wounds were healed, and all he wanted when he got home was to be with his family and to attend church. He had been totally isolated from the Church while at the front, having served continuously from 1938 to 1945. Then, in May 1946, he was called on a mission that lasted until October 1948.

Wolfgang Scharschmidt was released by his captors at the end of 1945. "I was able to go home while others were taken to Belgium or France to work [as involuntary laborers]. But I was not very tall so I was never very valuable to them." He was all of seventeen years old.

Georg Richter was taken prisoner by the French at the end of the war. After working in coal mines for four years, he was released and returned to his family in Annaberg.

In Memoriam

The following members of the Annaberg-Buchholz Branch did not survive World War II:

Erna —— d. from heart failure, 17 Aug 1940 (CHL Microfilm LR 1173 11, 107)

Brigitte Frieda —— d. difficult disease 24 Jan 1944 (CHL Microfilm LR 1173 11, 163)

Helmut Otto Goerner b. Zethau, Dresden, Sachsen 13 Nov 1912; son of Karl Julius Goerner and Martha Helene Boerner; bp. 8 Oct 1921; lance corporal; d. Ljubjatowa, southwest of Laura 1 Aug 1944; bur. Pulli, Estonia (IGI; www.volksbund.de)

Alfred Adelbert Hammerle b. Buchholz, Chemnitz, Sachsen 5 Apr 1920; son of Alfred Adelberg Hammerle and Klara Gertrud Nestler; bp. 30 Sep 1933; lance corporal; d. 17 Jun 1944; bur. Orglandes, France (A. Flade; IGI; www.volksbund.de)

Richard Hinkel b. Buchholz, Chemnitz, Sachsen 8 Sep 1888; son of Christian Theodor Hinkel and Hulda Grund; m. Buchholz 29 Jul 1922, Johanne Ziegloser; k. in a railroad train under attack by a fighter plane between Wolkenberg and Annaberg, Chemnitz, Sachsen 15 Apr 1945 (A. Wagner Flade; IGI)

Jean Kraemer b. Berlin, Brandenburg, Preußen 7 Mar 1909; son of Johannes Hermann Albert Kraemer and Emma Anna Raabe; bp. 22 Jun 1923; m. Berlin 16 Dec 1937, Auguste Konopatzki; 1 child; d. Mansky, Sachsen, Preußen 11 Mar 1944 (IGI)

Rudolf Johannes Kramer b. Buchholz, Chemnitz, Sachsen 8 Sep 1923; son of Felix Heinrich Kramer and Marthe Friede Mueller; bp. 17 Sep 1931; corporal; k. in battle Sanko, Russia 9 Nov 1943; bur. Sumy, Witebsk, Belarus (IGI; www.volksbund.de)

Rudolf Küler soldier; d. wounds Eastern Front 4 Apr 1942, age 34 (*Sonntagsgruss*, no. 12, 21 Jun 1942, 47)

Robert Lehrmann d. after a stomach operation 9 Dec 1941 (CHL Microfilm LR 1173 11, 107)

Herbert Karl Lindner b. Annaberg, Chemnitz, Sachsen 17 Dec 1923; son of Karl Rudolf Lindner and Hildegard Louise Groschopf; bp. 17 Dec 1931; d. 26 Nov 1942 (FHL Microfilm 271387, 1935 Census; IGI; AF)

Rudolf Eduard Martin b. Buchholz, Chemnitz, Sachsen 5 Feb 1901; son of August Eduard Martin and Emilie Sidonie Goeckeritz; bp. 10 Apr 1925; m. 29 Apr 1922, Clara Jung; corporal; d. POW camp 46, Bor, Yugoslavia 15 or 16 Sep 1945 (A. Flade; H. Martin Scharschmidt; CHL Microfilm no. 2458, form 42 FP, Pt. 37, 760; IGI; www.volksbund.de)

Bertha Mueller d. old age 19 Jan 1942 (CHL Microfilm LR 1173 11, 107)

Erich Pueschel b. ca. 1918; son of Kajotan Pueschel and Hedwig Krämer; k. in battle (IGI; Glauche-Schlünz)

Kurt Edmund Richter b. Buchholz, Chemnitz, Sachsen 2 Jun 1911; son of Edmund Karl Richter and Frieda Auguste Viertel; bp. 18 Jun 1921; ord. deacon; m. Buchholz 19 Oct 1929; d. Apr 1945 (IGI)

Walter Hans Roscher b. Annaberg, Chemnitz, Sachsen 22 Dec 1919; son of Venzenz Roscher and Marie Bertha Hofmann Schiller; bp. 6 Apr 1928; k. in battle Russia 1945 (A. Wagner Flade; IGI)

Helmut Paul Schaarschmidt b. Geiersdorf, Annaberg, Chemnitz, Sachsen 10 Feb 1913; son of Otto Paul Dostmann and Anna Maria Schaarschmidt; bp. 10 Sep 1926; m. —— Bastian; 1 child; d. Dresden, Dresden, Sachsen 17 Feb 1942 (A. Wagner Flade; IGI, AF)

Richard Willy Siebert b. Buchholz, Chemnitz, Sachsen 20 Aug 1908; son of Ernst Richard Siebert and Fanny Olga Auerbach; bp. 16 Apr 1923; ord. deacon; m. 5 Mar 1938; d. 1944 (A. Wagner Flade; IGI)

Paul Richard Teuchert b. Geiersdorf, Chemnitz, Sachsen 2 Jun 1877; son of August Julius Teuchert and Ernestine Gottlobine Breitfeld; bp. Annaberg-Buchholz, Chemnitz, Sachsen 5 or 15 Jun 1924; m. Geiersdorf 3 Sep 1905, Marie Emma Heinzmann; 2 children; d. stomach cancer Annaberg-Buchholz 30 Apr 1942 (I. Hinkel; D. Henkel Roscher; IGI; AF)

Willy Uhlig b. Reifland, Chemnitz, Sachsen 1 Dec 1905; son of Ernst Albin Uhlig and Hulda Minna Schaarschmidt; bp. 18 Jul 1914; m.; d. Russia 31 Jul 1949 (A. Wagner Flade; IGI, AF)

Johannes Kurt Wagner b. Geiersdorf, Chemnitz, Sachsen 31 Oct 1920; son of Paul Martin Wagner and Martha Elisabeth Hilbert; bp. 28 Jun 1929; ord. deacon; corporal; MIA Stalingrad, Russia end of 1942 (A. Langheinrich; A. Wagner Flade; FHL Microfilm 245291, 1930/35 Census; IGI)

Fig. 8. Kurt Wagner. (J. Flade)

Herbert Emil Zimmermann b. Buchholz, Chemnitz, Sachsen 16 Aug 1912; son of Karl Emil Zimmermann and Anna Martha Hermann; bp. 20 Sep 1924; ord. deacon; m. Buchholz 14 Oct 1939, Anna Marga Wolf; staff corporal; k. in battle south of Annenieki, Russia 4 Dec 1944; bur. south of Annenieki (A. Wagner Flade; FHL Microfilm 245307, 1930/35 Census; IGI; www.volksbund.de)

Notes

1. Presiding Bishopric, "Financial, Statistical, and Historical Reports of Wards, Stakes, and Missions, 1884–1955," CR 4 12, 257.
2. East German Mission Quarterly Reports, 1938, no. 31, East German Mission History.
3. Ibid.
4. Ibid., no. 35.
5. Ibid., no. 43.
6. Ibid., 1939, no. 53.
7. Ibid., no. 55.
8. Ruth Schramm Langheinrich, interview by the author, Salt Lake City, December 15, 2006.
9. Erhard Wagner, interview by the author, Sandy, Utah, April 6, 2007.
10. Alice Wagner Flade, interview by the author in German, South Jordan, Utah, February 10, 2006; unless otherwise noted, summarized in English by Judith Sartowski.
11. Helga Martin Scharschmidt, telephone interview with the author in German, February 15, 2008.
12. Wolfgang Werner Scharschmidt, telephone interview with the author in German, February 15, 2008.
13. Kurt Wagner to Primary leaders of Annaberg-Buchholz, December 21, 1941; trans. the author. Used with the kind permission of Alice Wagner Flade.
14. Christa Glauche Schlünz, interview by the author in German, Rostock, Germany, June 13, 2007.
15. Georg Karl Richter, telephone interview with Judith Sartowski in German, March 3, 2008.

CHEMNITZ CENTER BRANCH

In 1939, the population of the Chemnitz Center Branch was 469, making it officially the largest branch of The Church of Jesus Christ of Latter-day Saints in all of Germany. The city itself had about 375,000 inhabitants.

Chemnitz Center Branch[1]	1939
Elders	18
Priests	12
Teachers	12
Deacons	24
Other Adult Males	80
Adult Females	282
Male Children	16
Female Children	25
Total	469

The Center Branch rented two floors of a building at Schadestrasse 12, a few blocks south of the city's center. The rooms were located in the first Hinterhaus, and there were quite a few, according to Ilse Franke (born 1915): "The chapel was a long room and we could divide it into classrooms. There was a class in the choir seats on the stand."[2] Henry Burkhardt (born 1930) remembered a phrase painted above the podium: "The Glory of God Is Intelligence."[3] A sign on the outside of the building indicated the presence of the Church there.

Herbert Heidler (born 1929) remembered seeing a very large number of children (eighteen years and under) in the Sunday School "because the first ten rows were filled with children."[4]

Following the standard Sunday meeting format in Germany, Sunday School was held in the morning and sacrament meeting in the evening. At least one hundred forty persons attended meetings on a typical Sunday in 1939. Auxiliary meetings were held during the week—Relief Society and priesthood meetings on Monday at 7:00 P.M. and MIA on Wednesday, with choir practice on Thursday.[5] Ilse Franke fondly recalled her choir experience:

> We always had a choir, and I was in every one—children's choir, youth choir. I have sung all my life. My mother was the director. She always said, "You don't have a solo voice, but you are a wonderful head." She used the word *head* with the choir members. We had fifty voices one time, and sometimes we had a little orchestra—five pieces.

Because all of the Church programs were functioning in the branch, leadership meetings were also held. As Henry Burkhardt recalled, there was an advanced training class for the clerks before Sunday School on fast Sunday and a teacher improvement class every other Sunday from 9:00 to 9:45 A.M.

Just before World War II began, Ilse Franke was engaged to Hans Böttcher of the Berlin Center Branch. She had met him at the 1936 Olympic Games in Berlin, and then she waited while he served as a full-time missionary in and near Chemnitz. However, he was drafted into the German army soon after returning home in 1939, and their wedding was postponed. They finally married on December 8, 1939. The official ceremony took place in the civil registry office at city hall in Chemnitz, and the next day a Church service was performed in the chapel of the Center Branch, conducted by district president Karl Göckeritz. The Church service was informal because it had no legal validity in Germany in those days. The nearest

Latter-day Saint temple was in faraway Utah. Ilse recalled the event:

> We had no honeymoon. He had leave for five days, but it took two days to get to Chemnitz from Poland and two days to get back. My mother and my father would not let us sleep together the first night. The dinner included beef tongue—a delicacy in Germany, but my husband didn't like it.

Heinz Bonitz recalled hearing the news that Germany had attacked Poland on September 1, 1939:

> I listened to the radio when we heard that the Germans had gone into Poland. That is what I remember vividly. Nobody supported the idea of a war. My father had already served in World War I and my mother also. They knew what to expect.[6]

When the war began, Alfred Schulz (born 1899) prayed that as a husband and father, he would be spared military service. He was trained as an office worker and was pleased to be assigned to work at city hall. On several occasions, he was to accompany military units to the front, but his orders were changed each time, and he stayed home.[7]

Being a member of the Church caused problems in school for Brunhilde Falkner (born 1929) and her elder sister. The principal did not like Latter-day Saints, so Brunhilde's parents found it better to transfer their daughters

Fig. 1. Young people of the Chemnitz Center Branch in 1938. (R. Schumann Hinton)

to another school rather than to subject them to the principal's harassment. Unfortunately, a five-minute walk to school then became a twenty-minute walk.[8]

The Nazi Party's attempts to raise a generation of loyal youth involved the young people of the Chemnitz Center Branch as well. Reactions among Latter-day Saint youth varied, as is clear from the stories of several eyewitnesses. Just after the war began, Siegfried Donner (born 1930) turned ten and was inducted into the Jungvolk organization. "I liked it because of the uniform. I was plain, and it made me feel kind of powerful. I was into music, and I played a horn in the marching band. But my mother was against it, because I sometimes had duty on Sundays." However, things turned sour because Siegfried had long hair, and he was sent to work on a pig farm as a punishment. His mother, who suffered from a nervous condition, protested his treatment with the demand, "Don't I have any rights for my own boy?" When a Hitler Youth leader answered in the negative, she shouted, "You lousy jerk!" Only a statement from her physician explaining her nervous condition saved her from incarceration, as Siegfried explained.[9]

Thanks to his job of delivering about two hundred newspapers every day, Hyrum Cieslak (born 1930) was able to skip Jungvolk meetings. His father also saw to it that Hyrum never missed a Sunday church meeting due to Jungvolk activities. Fortunately, Hyrum did not suffer any consequences because of his absence.[10] Such passive resistance to Hitler's program of recruiting young people for his political purposes was common among LDS parents who sought similar excuses for their children.

Herbert Heidler was a member of the Hitler Youth but had an understanding with his adult leader regarding Sundays. He told the man that if there were Hitler Youth meetings on Sundays, he would not be in attendance. Herbert recalled that there was no training in

Fig. 2. Members of the Chemnitz Center and Schloss branches shortly before the war.

167

weapons, but some of the songs they sang had words suggesting violence.

Some boys recognized the subtle goals of the Hitler Youth. Henry Burkhardt explained that he "could see the problems. As part of the Hitler Youth, I came to understand the meaning and purposes of the Third Reich more and more. I promised myself that I would never be a member of the party."

Irene Härtel turned ten years old in 1941 and was inducted into the Jungvolk. One of the aims of the program was to teach German girls modesty and simplicity. Irene recalled, for example, that "I was not allowed to have a bow in my hair or wear earrings. . . . Hitler wanted a German woman or girl to have long hair tied in a bun."[11] The girls were also taught domestic skills on a regular basis and were required to render community service.

Johannes Lothar Flade (born 1926) turned fourteen in 1940 and was inducted into the Hitler Youth. He is one of many Latter-day Saint eyewitnesses who gave a positive description of the experience:

> I enjoyed myself. I was happy. I had a good time. Hitler Youth was just wonderful. I think it was on Tuesdays and Thursdays. [We did] mostly sports, and I was just excited about sports. I was very good. I could run fast, and I could throw far and jump far. . . . The only thing that I didn't do was meet on Sundays. They tried to threaten me, but I was so good in sports, they left me alone. I was already a leader at fifteen.

On New Year's Day 1940, Hans Böttcher showed up in Chemnitz for a surprise visit. He had been released from the army on special request by his employer, who managed a critical war industry in Berlin. He was in civilian clothing and would not say what he was really working on, but said instead that he made "refrigerator parts." He remained in Berlin the next two years, but his wife, Ilse, did not move there to join him. "I didn't want to

give up my nice apartment in Chemnitz and move my beautiful new furniture to that huge, scary city," she explained. Hans was still in Berlin when their first son, Hans, was born in Chemnitz on April 15, 1941.

On November 16, 1941, Henry Burkhardt's father, Richard, wrote one of many letters to his son Alfred ("Fred," born 1922) on the Eastern Front. The letter was returned by Fred's company commander when the young soldier was reported missing in action. The contents of the letter are typical among Latter-day Saint families in Germany during World War II:

> Dear Fred,
> Yesterday we received your fine letter of October 29–30, 1941. Thank you so much! We were so happy to receive it. It is our greatest joy that you are well and back with your comrades again! My dear Fred, we hope that you have been receiving all of the packages and letters we have sent. Mother has sent eight packages of 100 grams each. Have you received any of those? In the next few days, we'll put together a Christmas package for you. It is so tough to get stuff. Everything is confiscated for the army. . . . It seems that our bread ration coupons are consumed earlier each week. . . . It's terribly cold and stormy here right now. . . . In Sunday School they announced your greetings to everybody. And they all send their best wishes back to you. . . . I already told you that Erwin was wounded. I have been classified as fit for military duty again. So, everything's fine, right? Mother is so pleased that you have recovered. She was really worried about you. The boys are very busy, as always. And little Christa can now recite four-line poems. . . . Well, I have to close now. Best wishes from Mother, Papa, and your siblings.[12]

For most of the war years, there were only slight changes in the Chemnitz Center Branch. Brunhilde Falkner could not recall interruptions in the branch meeting schedule or any interference or persecution on the part of the government. "I can remember though that the word *Zion* was not allowed to be used in our songs

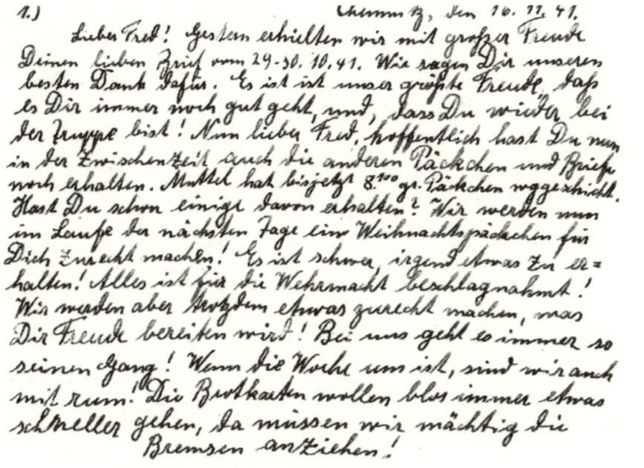

1.) Chemnitz, den 16. 11. 41.

Lieber Fred! Gestern erhielten wir mit großer Freude Deinen lieben Brief vom 29-30. 10. 41. Wir sagen Dir unseren besten Dank dafür. Es ist ist unsere größte Freude, daß es Dir immer noch gut geht, und, dass Du wieder bei der Truppe bist! Nun lieber Fred, hoffentlich hast Du nun in der Zwischenzeit auch die anderen Päckchen und Briefe noch erhalten. Mutti hat bisjetzt 8 Stück gr. Päckchen weggeschickt. Hast Du schon einige davon erhalten? Wir werden nun im Laufe der nächsten Tage ein Weihnachtspäckchen für Dich zurecht machen! Es ist schwer, irgend etwas zu erhalten! Alles ist für die Wehrmacht beschlagnahmt! Wir werden aber trotzdem etwas zurecht machen, was Dir Freude bereiten wird! Bei uns geht es immer so seinen Gang! Wenn die Woche um ist, sind wir auch mit rum! Die Brotkarten wollen bloss immer etwas schneller gehen, da müssen wir mächtig die Bremsen anziehen!

Fig. 3. The first page of the letter written by Richard Burkhardt to his son, Fred, in Russia in 1941. (H. Burkhardt)

or talks." This is consistent with observations made by eyewitnesses in other branches.

The members of the branch did their best to keep the rooms of the branch in the Schadestrasse in good order during the war. Sigrid Cieslak (born 1935) had the following recollection:

> Usually at the time of harvest, the members would bring vegetables from their garden, the biggest ones, and they were displayed. And I remember especially my mother, she always would have a flower arrangement from our garden every Sunday during the season.[13]

Many members of the Chemnitz Center Branch remembered the baptismal ceremonies that were held in the backyard of the Emil Heidler home at Helbersdorferstrasse 7. Herbert Heidler provided some detail:

> The basin in which we held baptisms was in our garden. It was just 10 meters [33 feet] away from our house and about 2 × 3 meters [7 × 10 feet] in size and about 1 meter [3 feet] deep. I was also baptized in this basin. Later in 1947, my father built an even bigger pool with the size of 7 × 3.5 meters [22 × 11 feet]. We baptized all year round.

Henry Burkhardt explained. "There were listeners in the branch, but our work was to proclaim the gospel." The term "listeners" refers to government officials. He recalled that branch president Paul Auerswald was once asked to hang the swastika flag in church, but he declined; he wanted to keep the Church and politics separate.

Some Latter-day Saints found it impossible to embrace Hitler and Nazism. Lothar Flade had the following to say about his father, Hans Emil Flade:

> My dad was not an anti-Nazi, because you couldn't afford to be that way. You would end up in a concentration camp. But he was a scriptorian, and when you understand the gospel, you know what's coming. About Hitler, he said, "This is the beginning of the end."

Lothar's mother and his elder sister were initially swayed by the mass events sponsored by the Nazi Party, but they did not join the Party. Eventually they learned that Hans Emil Flade was right about Hitler and the direction in which Germany as a nation was headed.

At city hall, a female colleague once accused Alfred Schulz of making public speeches (in church) against the Nazi Party. He did not mention what the informer believed he had said but wrote the following about his treatment:

> I was called in by the Gestapo and interrogated. I was able to prove that the allegations were false but was told that I must not associate myself with the Church any longer. I was to give up all callings in the branch. I spoke with the district president, and he advised me that this was in my best interest. Therefore, at the fall conference, I was honorably released from all of my callings.

In Nazi Germany, public statements criticizing the government could bring dire consequences. Such was the case with the family of Center Branch member Helmut Süss on September 2, 1942. Helmut's wife, Elsa Elisabeth Jung Süss, was arrested and accused of making treasonous comments. In response, officials of the government took the couple's three little children (Hanna and twins Edith and Eva) into custody and delivered them to an orphanage in Chemnitz-Bernsdorf. Years later, the matter was carefully studied by Sister Süss's brother-in-law, Wolfgang Süss (born 1927), who summarized the information he collected as follows:

A resident of the same apartment building had denounced my sister-in-law to the police for making so-called treasonous statements. On one occasion, she was reportedly in a milk store and had complained about the lack of milk for infants. My mother was standing right next to her daughter-in-law and personally heard that comment, whereupon she instructed her to be silent. We do not know whether the informant cited other so-called treasonous statements made by my sister-in-law. However, it may be assumed that she would not have been arrested for a single such comment. Elisabeth was then arrested, put in jail, and we were not informed of her whereabouts. Her husband, my brother Helmut, was a soldier in France at the time. Elisabeth had two children from a previous marriage: her son Werner was placed with a farm family and her daughter Inge was taken in by the Diakonissen Order. . . . Both parents

were allowed (under guard) to visit their children in November 1943, after which there was no more contact between the parents and the children or other family members.[14]

Hanna Süss, Elisabeth's youngest daughter, later recalled the day her mother was arrested: "My mother was taken away when we were home on my birthday in 1942. We were waiting for my siblings to come back from school so we could eat together. We did not have a chance to say good-bye to each other."[15]

According to Wolfgang Süss, his brother Helmut Süss was killed in France on September 5, 1944. Helmut's wife, Elsa Elisabeth, ended up in the Ravensbrück Concentration Camp near Fürstenberg (eighty miles north of Berlin), where she died on January 25, 1945. Wolfgang's mother was eventually informed of this in writing.

Regarding the charges against Sister Süss, her daughter Hanna later stated, "We never got

Fig. 4. Chemnitz Center and Schloss Branch members on an outing in 1940. (S. Donner)

anything in writing that explained why all of this happened."

Life at home in a large German city was not all privation and suffering in 1941. District president Karl Göckeritz, an office manager, found time to go to Haag am Hausruck in Austria for a summer vacation. He left home on July 6,

Fig. 5. Elisabeth Elsa Jung Süss died in the Ravensbrück Concentration Camp. (W. Süss)

1941, and was apparently gone for two weeks. While in Haag, he spent quite a lot of time with the Rosner family and other members of the LDS branch there. His diary entries give the impression that he left his family at home in Chemnitz.[16]

That same year, Irene Härtel's father was drafted into the Wehrmacht. She recalled the day he left their home in Jahnsdorf by Chemnitz:

My mother wept at home, and we took the sled and went down with my father to where he had to meet the others. We wept, and then our father was gone. When he came back for a few days of vacation once and wore his uniform, I cried that he would not be my father because he wore that [uniform]. I had never seen him in uniform before, and I will never forget that experience.

When the Wehrmacht unleashed its forces against the Soviet Union in June 1941, Alfred Schulz was immediately concerned, as he later wrote: "[Hearing about this] gave me a feeling of sadness. I had a kind of premonition, a worry that cannot really be described. . . . I could not believe that this would result in victory."

Ilse Franke Böttcher's husband was drafted again in 1942. His employment was no longer reason for an exemption when Germany

was fighting on fronts all over Europe and in Africa. Back at home, Ilse gave birth to a daughter, Margaret, in October 1942. For several months, she lived with her children in the town of Bischofswerda, about sixty miles to the northeast of Chemnitz. Then she went to a small town in Austria with her children and her mother. However, that did not last long because Hans came to Chemnitz on leave and Ilse hurried home to see him. Life for Ilse and her children continued to be a merry-go-round as she followed Hans to a gunnery range in southeast Germany for several months, then returned to Chemnitz when he was sent to Italy.

Daily life during wartime can be challenging and serious, but the normal emotions of young people do not disappear. For example, Lothar Flade was a youth of sixteen when he and two friends were preparing for a 1942 district conference by hanging a large sign over the stage in the Schadestrasse meeting rooms. He later wrote about the incident that occurred at that moment:

I heard the door open at the other end of the chapel. I turned around and saw three young girls enter. One of those girls [Alice Wagner of Annaberg] wore a blue dress and a blue hat. I will never forget it. Something happened to me as I was looking at this girl. I knew at that moment that I was looking at my future wife.[17]

Charlotte Popitz (born 1915) recalled her wartime wedding fondly:

I got married in 1942. In the morning, we went to the civil registration office [at city hall] and in the afternoon we rode in a wedding carriage because gas for a car was not available anymore. It was beautiful. The Chemnitz [Center] Branch was in the Schadestrasse. We met in a factory building, and the priesthood holders had decorated everything beautifully for our wedding. Brother Karl Göckeritz married us in the afternoon. The whole branch celebrated together. . . . The choir sang, and one brother sang a beautiful song.[18]

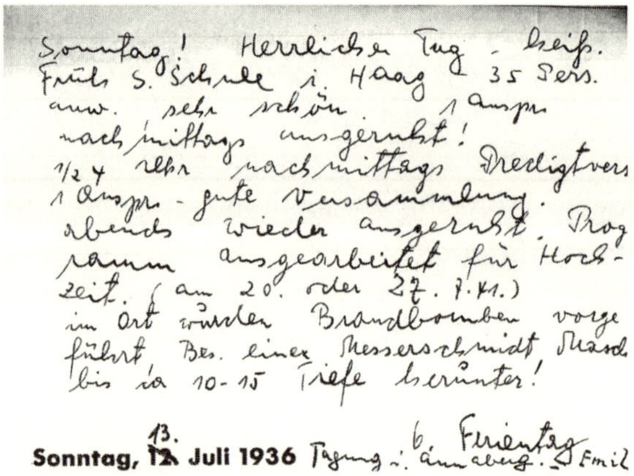

Fig. 6. District president Karl Göckeritz of the Center Branch enjoyed a nice vacation in July 1941. His diary entry indicates that he attended church in the Haag Branch in Austria. The diary was designed for 1936, so he had to change the dates. (H. Göckeritz)

Sister Popitz Ficker had little time to celebrate with her husband. He had been granted two weeks furlough and was then on his way back to Budapest, Hungary.

On August 28, 1939, Irene Härtel became a member of the Church:

> I was the baptized in the backyard of the Heidler family because they had a little pool. We took my father's motorbike, and we were not allowed to have three people sitting on it, but we went that way to my baptism, and I was sitting on the tank and my mother behind my father. We also got a little bouquet from [the Heidler's] garden, and I was confirmed in their living room. I remember it vividly. That day, other people were baptized also.

During the war, Siegfried Donner and his mother were mostly on their own. His father was a government employee and worked at aircraft production facilities such as Peenemünde, where the V-1 rocket was built. "He was hardly ever at home," Siegfried later explained, "My mother and I lived from whatever we could get. She even chopped up mice to feed to the chickens. If people had known, they wouldn't have eaten the eggs. And she faithfully paid her tithing. Both of my parents did."

Lothar Flade volunteered for service in the German armed forces. As a leader in the Hitler Youth, he knew that a draft notice was heading his way within months and that he was bound for a specific unit that did not interest him. Volunteering would allow him to join a unit of his choice, in this case the Waffen-SS. This he did in 1943.[19] Because the Waffen-SS troops were under the command of one of Hitler's closest comrades, Heinrich Himmler, the soldiers received much better care than common army soldiers. As Lothar later explained:

> By the time we got into Russia, I saw those poor slobs [regular army] walking along in 45 or 50 degrees below with the storm howling across the fields. I was sitting in a car. We had better food, better weapons. We never had to walk; they drove us every place. It was just wonderful.

By early 1944, Lothar Flade, though still seventeen, was already the leader of a platoon of soldiers in the communications corps. It was their job to lay and maintain wires providing communications among frontline units. Such units suffered heavy casualties, but Lothar was not wounded: "I was just lucky and the Lord took care of me." A few months later, he volunteered for duty elsewhere and was sent to Normandy in France.

In 1943, Leopoldine Cieslak followed the advice of city officials to protect her children from the ravages of war by sending them to live with relatives in small towns. Sigrid was sent to live with her grandmother in Riesa. She was to stay there until her father came home. Because her grandmother was not a member of the Church and there was no branch nearby, Sigrid was isolated from the Church until 1947, when her father finally returned from an American POW camp.

Hyrum Cieslak was sent to Rittmitz to live with a family on a dairy farm. There he continued his apprenticeship in dairy farming and joined the Wächtler family in attending church in the the Döbeln Branch, about four

Fig. 7. The Wächtler family in Rittmitz. (S. Cieslak Rudolph)

miles to the northwest. He did not return to Chemnitz until the summer of 1945.

The tension of air raids and impending death was still vivid in the mind of Susanne Flade Groebs (born 1915) when she described the situation years later:

> We spent a lot of hours in the basement of my parents' house. The sirens were always wailing, and it was horrible. We heard crashing all around, but nothing happened to us. . . . Nobody wanted to be alone during a raid, so they gathered together. You never knew if a bomb would fall on you. I never want to experience that again.[20]

As a young mother at home without her husband, Ilse Franke Böttcher was pleased with any kind of support she received. Her parents still lived in Chemnitz and helped where they could. Both of her children were born in a local hospital, and the state provided the usual incentives: she was awarded twenty marks (five dollars) each time she nursed a baby for the first six months.

Throughout the war, strict measures were needed to black out German cities at night. Siegfried Donner later explained how windows had to be totally covered so that not the slightest bit of light escaped. "They [the wardens] came and knocked on your windows [if they saw light]. If they came twice, you were in trouble. They thought you were trying to tell the British where we were."

One evening in 1943, Alfred Schulz came home under the usual black-out conditions and saw a glimmer of light from a window in the living room. Aware of the possible penalties for nonobservance of blackout regulations, he attempted to fix the problem. While doing so, he fell and broke several ribs. He spent the next five weeks recuperating in his apartment.

One of the most difficult aspects of air-raid alarms for Ilse Franke Böttcher was the fact that she had to go from the fourth floor of her apartment building to the basement with her two little children. It seemed that nobody in the building was able to help her. "We had to go to the basement, or they [the insurance company] would not pay if you were killed. But if you were dead, you didn't get the money anyway." Each time she left the apartment, she carried her most valuable papers with her.

In the village of Jahnsdorf, the Härtel family lived in an apartment house without a basement, thus when the alarm sounded, they walked (or ran) about a hundred yards to a restaurant called Der Felsenkeller. According to Irene, she was not scared that they would be killed:

> We always tried to wear as much clothing as possible in case we had to stay away from home for a long time. Sometimes, we had to go into the shelter up to twice or more a night, especially during the last year of the war. We were there a total of fifty times or more. When there was an alarm, we got our luggage that was already prepared and ran to the shelter. The luggage was packed only with necessities.

Several times, Irene hid with her mother and her siblings in a cave behind Der Felsenkeller. The cave went no more than a hundred feet into the mountain and would not likely have protected them if a bomb had landed close to the entrance.

On June 6, 1944, the Allies launched the largest invasion force ever assembled. Crossing the English Channel, they set more than 100,000 soldiers on the beaches of northern France in an attempt to breach Hitler's so-called Fortress Europe. A few days later, Lothar Flade arrived to join the defensive effort, having just come from the Soviet Union. One month later, the Germans had yielded ground to the Allied forces, where the war came to an end for Lothar, who was still only seventeen:

> When I woke up, I was lying in a hole. [The enemy] had overrun our position and machine-gunned us, and my friend was cut in half and lay there dead next to me. Then they threw one of those little grenades and knocked me out. When I came to, I couldn't see, and I figured out that I had blood running down into my eyes. I had a couple of pieces of shrapnel in my skull. I scraped them off and must have had a concussion. There was nobody around, so I started to walk to where the Germans were. I came to the edge of the forest, and I found three rifles pointing at me. . . . [The enemy soldiers] just looked at me, and I said, "I've got to take a leak." (I spoke English.) The Canadians began to laugh. I took care of my business, and then they led me away.

Charlotte Popitz Ficker had no children during the war, so she was employed and prayed for her husband to come home safely. His last furlough during the war was in 1944, after which he wrote to his wife a few more times. He told her that he was in Austria, then in southeast Germany, where he was a fireman and disarmed bombs. He was captured there by the Americans in the spring of 1945. Because he spoke English very well, he was given favored status among the German prisoners of war, meaning more food and more pleasant work assignments.

The air raids over Chemnitz left the Falkner family intact, but disease took a heavy toll. The year 1944 turned out to be very difficult for Brunhilde Falkner. "In January I moved to Zwickau because both my parents passed away in 1944 due to illness. My mother suffered

from cancer and passed away in January while my father had a heart condition and passed away in December." She moved in with her grandparents, who were not members of the Church. Brunhilde was pleased to belong to a good branch for the remainder of the war.

Throughout 1944, Alfred Schulz served the Reich in various administrative positions. For most of the year, he was in Potsdam by Berlin, but he also spent time in a very quiet and pleasant area of Russia. He was never in any danger. Late in the year, the call went out for all older men to report for duty in the Volkssturm (home guard). For the first few weeks, he was exempted due to his work at city hall, but he contributed by giving blood on many occasions. He also helped out in rescuing people from the ruins of bombed-out buildings.

As a student at the State Academy of Technology, Heinz Bonitz was exempt from military service for a time. He had already spent three months in the Reichsarbeitsdienst, working not far from Schneidemühl. By 1943, the fatherland needed him more as a soldier than as a student, so he was drafted. Following his training in Kolberg and in Teplitz-Schönau, Czechoslovakia, he was a lieutenant of artillery.

Just after the year 1945 began, Heinz was shipped across the Baltic Sea to the Kurland (the German name for the occupied Baltic States). He was wounded there by shrapnel on January 27, 1945. While he was recovering

Fig. 8. Chemnitz Center Primary children. (S. Cieslak Rudolph)

in a hospital in Latvia for the next month, his unit was moved across the Baltic to defend the German heartland. When he received new orders, he doctored the papers to show that he was to report to Stettin, then proceeded to the harbor in nearby Riga. With SS troops on the lookout for soldiers trying to leave the combat zone without authorization, Heinz needed some trickery to board a ship. He later described how this was done:

> I took off the insignia from my uniform to look like a common soldier and ran towards the ramp where they were loading [wounded] soldiers onto the ship. I grabbed somebody's legs and helped them carry him aboard. This is how I got onto the ship. . . . Then I hid in hopes that they would not find me. [About six hours later] the ship left the harbor.

In early 1945, Ilse Franke Böttcher took her children to Aue, about twenty miles south of Chemnitz, to live with her aunt and her uncle. By doing so, she missed the worst hours in the history of her hometown.

On Monday, March 5, 1945, the city of Chemnitz was the target of several massive air raids, and much of the city was reduced to rubble overnight. The first attack occurred just after noon, and another came in the early evening. It was then that what may have been the

single worst tragedy among Church members in Germany during World War II occurred. Bruno Fischer and his wife Johanna sought refuge in their basement. Their daughters Elisabeth and Erika happened to be there for a short visit, their soldier husbands being far from home. Erika Fischer Lohberger also had her two little boys with her. In addition, two elderly sisters from the Chemnitz Center Branch came from their apartments nearby to be with the Fischers. Survivors reported that the entire building was leveled by the direct hit of a large bomb. Apparently, everyone in the basement of that structure perished instantly—at least eight members of the Chemnitz Center Branch.

The death of the Fischer family was a trial for the Chemnitz Center Branch members. Charlotte Popitz Ficker recalled how she felt when she learned that they had been killed:

> I had known [the Fischers] and was extremely hurt when they died, and this was one time I doubted Heavenly Father. And I asked myself why Heavenly Father would let this happen. My mother reminded me how nice it was that this family was together again.

Charlotte's mother was referring to the fact that the husbands of the two Fischer sisters—Helmut Lohberger and Heinz Hänsel—were both killed in battle.

Herbert Heidler also had clear memories of that terrible night:

> I looked out of my window on the fifth floor and saw how all the bombs were dropped on Chemnitz. They dropped phosphorus and people burned alive. They ran to the next pond trying to extinguish the fire but when they came out [of the water] they were burning again just seconds later. They stayed in the water until somebody helped them to scrape off their skin. These were the most horrible scenes I had to witness.

During the night of March 5–6, Henry Burkhardt felt for the first time that he might die: "My life was seriously threatened. . . .

Fig. 9. Irene Härtel Schönfeld stands at the entrance to the small cave that was used as an air-raid shelter in 1945. The gate was added after the war. (J. Larsen, 2007)

I came out of the basement with a wet blanket over my head. That was the only time I thought I would not survive." As bad as things were, he recalled that the war taught him to be without fear.

Days after the attack on Chemnitz, Emil Heidler, acting president of the Chemnitz District, sent his son, Herbert, to inquire after the fate of the Fischers. On Sonnenstrasse in front of the ruins of the Fischer home, Herbert found the bodies covered up, already in a most hideous condition. He retrieved some personal items and conveyed them by bicycle to Bruno Fischer's surviving daughter, Hildegard, in Niederwürschnitz, about nine miles to the southeast.[21]

Siegfried Donner, who lived just a few streets away, also went to inquire about the Fischers and saw the bodies. They were badly burned and already covered with lime. Siegfried

then went looking for his best friend; Ludwig Fedelmann was not a member of the Church but a neighbor and a close school friend. His family had sought refuge in the basement of the school rather than at home, but they perished when the school was also reduced to rubble. The next day, Siegfried helped dig his friend out of the rubble, bloodied and dead.

Reiner Gröbs lived with his family in a suburb about four miles from downtown Chemnitz. He was not yet five years old at the time but years later still had distinct memories of the attack:

I remember the shock of the antiaircraft: Boom! Boom! Boom! Boom! And I remember after the raid was over . . . we climbed up to the upper story and opened the window. . . . Above the pine trees we could see the flames shooting up. [There were] four or five inches of new snow,

Fig. 10. Elisabeth Fischer and Heinz Hänsel were married in 1943. (E. Göckeritz McClellan)

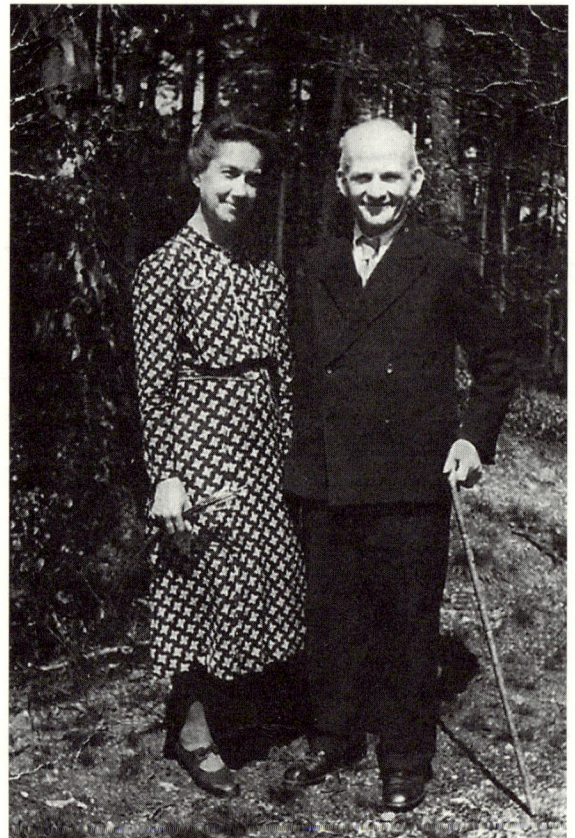

Fig. 11. Bruno and Johanna Fischer perished in their basement along with six other members of the Chemnitz Center Branch. (E. Goeckeritz McClellan)

and it was really kind of eerily beautiful, because the flames cast purple and orange and red and yellow shadows on the freshly fallen snow.[22]

Hanna Süss was living with her grandmother at the time. They had spent the night in a shoe factory across the street from the apartment. Later, they were taken to the fire station, where her grandmother discovered that one of the twins was missing in the confusion. Fortunately, the girl was found safe.

Young Karl Heinz Göckeritz (born 1935) recalled that in the aftermath of the air raid, an enemy airplane was found lying in the middle of the playground across the street from his home. He described the experience:

> It was right in the middle of the playground; . . . it didn't hit anything. In the morning when it got light, the police came, but before the police came, all the kids went over there. I was there too. The pilot was lying there dead. He just had one of those little hats on, like a little motorcycle helmet. Then the police came and covered everything up. He was lying outside the plane, but the plane wasn't on fire or anything. He must have just crashed straight down. Everybody took a piece of the airplane.[23]

From a farm in Hainichen, Hyrum Cieslak could see that Chemnitz was in trouble. As he later explained, "We saw the sky full of planes all day long." On a bike, he made the twelve-mile trip to Chemnitz to determine the status of his mother. Making his way through the rubble of the city, he saw "bodies stacked like cordwood." He learned that "neighbors had wondered why my mother had been so calm and did not seem to panic about all the people dying around her. She told them that she prayed. She invited everybody to pray with her and they did."

Among the many structures that disappeared under the bombs and the fires of that terrifying night were the rooms of the Chemnitz Center Branch at Schadestrasse 12. All of the

Fig. 12. Erika and Helmut Lohberger with their son Peter in about 1942. All three and son Heinz (born 1944) died in the war. (E. Goeckeritz McClellan)

Church property in the rooms was lost. Henry Burkhardt went there the day after the attack and described the situation in these words:

> We went to the branch house on March 6. It was still burning, and we could see how the piano and the organ had fallen from the upper floor to the main floor. Everything was gone. We did not have a meetinghouse anymore. . . . Then we held our meetings in little groups on Sundays because the Schloss Branch rooms were too small. The home teachers informed us where we should meet.

The Schloss Branch meetinghouse at Winklerstrasse had not been damaged in the attack. However, after the devastation of the city on March 5, many members were not able to get there, so they held meetings in apartments still intact. As Charlotte Popitz Ficker later recalled:

> We also held meetings in people's houses. Sometimes, there were fifty members in one room. People sat on the windowsills and on anything they could find. Even nonmembers attended who lived in the same house because they were interested in what we had to say. We did not have the sacrament in those meetings.

During most of the war years, the Härtel family of Jahnsdorf had taken a train and a streetcar on their way to church (a distance of six miles). These means were interrupted as a result of the March 5 air raid. As Irene remembered:

We had to walk [to church] after that. I remember one Sunday at the end of the war when we attended the [Schloss] Branch and we had to walk for three hours just to get there. The main hall was very small, and the younger people were asked to stand up and let the elderly sit down. We were young and stood up but had already walked all the way. My sister was very tired and sat down outside of the main room. Later, we found a shortcut to the Schloss Branch, and it did not take three hours anymore. On the way there, we sang songs or took a break to eat something. . . . [Between meetings] we stayed with other families [in town].

In late 1944, branch president Hans Emil Flade was asked by local Nazi Party leaders to assume the position of block air-raid warden. He declined the request, indicating that his job as the manager of a factory and his work for the Church left him no time to be the warden. His son, Lothar, later learned from his mother that his father had been called "a swine and all kinds of other things," but he had refused to yield. Two weeks later, Hans Emil Flade was picked up by the police and transported to Berlin to work on a rubble detail, helping to clean up the ruins of the Reich's capital city. He was essentially a political prisoner.

In early March, Heinz Bonitz left the ship that had conveyed him from Riga, Latvia, to Swinemünde, north of Stettin. While the SS detained him (which again could have been disastrous), the air-raid sirens began to wail, and he went down into a shelter. During the attack, "the building swayed so much that it felt like we were on a ship." Taking advantage of the confusion, he sneaked out and walked northwest toward Wolgast. There he was detained by police again but managed to escape and board a train south to Pasewalk, then east to Stettin. By some miracle, Heinz actually found his unit there.

Hitler's birthday, April 20, was always an occasion for bombastic radio announcements. Heinz recalled hearing a speech by Joseph Goebbels, the German propaganda minister,

Fig. 13. Hans Emil Flade died in Berlin in the last week of the war. (J. Flade)

in which he said something akin to this: "After this long and dreadful conflict, we will be able to place a laurel wreath on [Hitler's] head." The enemy was apparently not impressed by the message and began to shell Heinz's position; he was hit in the arm by shrapnel. Still able to walk, he headed for Stettin with a comrade, then decided not to seek a hospital there but continued westward. During the next two weeks, he slowly made his way west across the province of Mecklenburg, then north through Schleswig-Holstein to the city of Flensburg—just short of the Danish border.

On April 23, 1945—just two weeks before the German surrender—Johannes (Hans) Heidler was killed fighting the invading Red Army. His brother, Herbert, recalled the situation clearly:

We received notice of my brother's death. There was a boy whom we recognized as a friend of my brother. He told us how he was a witness when Hans was shot. But he also told us that they had to leave him because the Russians had already started a new attack. Since then, my mother always wondered if he was really dead or still alive and maybe taken by the Russians. This thought never left her, and she prayed for clarity in this matter. One morning, we woke up early and my mother was very happy. She told us how she had seen her son during the night in her bedroom. He was dressed in white, and he smiled at her, and she knew that he was happy, although he did not say anything to her.

When the Soviets encircled Berlin in late April, Alfred Schulz was caught in the city. As a Volkssturm soldier, he knew that his chances for survival were poor. He changed into civilian clothing but was still rounded up by enemy soldiers. While Germans were being executed right and left, he too was shot in the neck. Fortunately, the bullet missed a fatal target by mere millimeters, but he fell as if dead. He later wrote about the wound he suffered:

A nerve was separated, and I was paralyzed over half of my body. Later, it was determined that the fifth vertebra in my neck was destroyed and the sixth about seventy percent damaged. I was curious about the process of dying. Everything went black. . . . When I came around, I was lying on my back among many others. I didn't know if they were dead or alive.

During the weeks after the fall of Berlin, Alfred Schulz recovered enough to be able to walk a bit. Somehow, he was able to get a message out of the facility where he was held prisoner, and that message was later delivered by a missionary to his family back in Chemnitz. Eventually, Alfred was classified as unfit for labor and released to return to Chemnitz. "It was a glorious reunion," he explained. "The neighbors and the branch all welcomed me home with great joy."

As a POW in Scotland, Lothar Flade became a beneficiary of his father's good works. Before the war, Hans Emil Flade had warned a Jewish colleague of impending danger, so that the man was able to escape the Gestapo and immigrate to Switzerland. That same man later became an officer in the British army and recognized the Flade name. He located Lothar, told him the story, and stated, "If you are half the man your father is, I will help you." That help came in the form of a transfer to a POW camp in Texas, rather than in Canada.

In the summer of 1945, Ilse Franke Böttcher and her two children left Aue and returned to Chemnitz. Trying to find a place on the train back home for the three of them proved to be a major challenge, given the confusion at railroad stations all over Germany at the time. At one station, a woman conductor was quite rude to them but was scolded by Ilse's three-year-old son, Hans, who said, "You're just an old witch!" His defiant accusation brought about a change in the woman's attitude, and she found a way to get them into the train.

When World War II ended, Anni Franke exclaimed to her daughter, Ilse Franke Böttcher: "We've lost everything but you, and it doesn't matter. We're alive!" Ilse returned to Chemnitz with her children and found that most of the surviving Saints were meeting in the rooms of the Schloss Branch on Winklerstrasse.

Just after the war ended, Heinz Bonitz was able to attend church in the Altona Branch near Hamburg. During the summer of 1945, he secured official papers from the British occupational authority confirming his status as a free man. "I was never taken prisoner by anybody," he later recalled. By November, he could return to the Soviet occupation zone and his hometown of Chemnitz. Unfortunately, his mother had died just a week before, and he found his home destroyed. Heinz explained that his survival was due to a promise made by

President Heber J. Grant during his 1938 visit to Dresden: "He told us that whatever happened, we would not perish, but would come to Zion. I did not doubt that. I knew that the war could not stop that."

Many years later, Susanne Flade Groebs explained what happened to her spiritually during the war years when she worked hard to raise her son, Reiner, while her soldier husband was gone: "My testimony became stronger and stronger. I prayed that our Heavenly Father would 'deliver us from evil.'"

Regarding the entire war experience, Henry Burkhardt summarized his feelings in these words: "The gospel was the foundation on which we survived this time. I do not know how we could have survived without the gospel in our lives."

Herbert Heidler made the following remarks when he contemplated the attitudes of the Chemnitz Center Branch members at the end of the war:

> There was a family who had lost all they had, and the next morning they stood up in sacrament meeting and bore testimony and were grateful to be alive. Even the mothers who had lost their sons in the war stood up and were grateful for their lives. Somebody once said during a meeting, that

Fig. 14. The aftermath of the bombing in Chemnitz. (S. Wagner Flade)

we do not know the answer to everything and there will be tough situations, but we will one day know the answer to all of these questions.

Lothar Flade was in Texas—far from Europe—when the fighting ended. He was eventually moved from Texas to Arkansas, then to Alabama, then to Pine Bluff, Arkansas, where he worked in a munitions factory. In May 1946, he was given his release papers, sent to New York, and put on a ship for Germany. How great his disappointment must have been when the ship was not allowed to dock in Germany but was turned back to Rotterdam in the Netherlands. From there he was sent to Belgium. While he awaited his release, he nearly starved, losing sixty pounds. "They gave us nothing to eat. I went to the bathroom once in four weeks. I will never forget that," he explained.

By the late summer of 1947, Lothar had been moved back to England. After three years of no mail from home, he was still unaware of the fate of his family, but a letter from his sister finally reached him. She wrote that their father, political prisoner Hans Emil Flade, had been killed in Berlin on the last day of the war. Apparently he had been found dead with a piece of shrapnel embedded in his right forehead.

For more than four years, young Lothar had been isolated from the Church. A deacon, he had no scriptures, no opportunity to partake of the sacrament, no interaction with LDS soldiers—nothing but prayer. The first contact came in 1947. A relative had written to the office of Ezra Taft Benson in London and asked that a missionary be sent to visit Lothar. He was working in the beet harvest that fall near Cambridge when a letter arrived from Elder Benson. The missionary arrived just before Lothar was released, thus he never had a chance to attend Church services in England. He arrived in Chemnitz in late November 1947.

Shortly after the war, Charlotte Popitz Ficker learned that her husband was a prisoner of war under the Americans in southern Germany. Although he was less than two hundred miles away from Chemnitz, she could not visit him. He finally returned to her in 1950.

Regarding the way the Saints in Chemnitz reacted to the trials of wartime, Henry Burkhardt made the following observation:

> During this hard time of the war, inactive or less-active members of the Church came back and joined us again. Nobody became less active or fell away from the Church. We all looked for something to hold on to. We held our baptismal services in the little Chemnitz River or in a little basin provided by [the Heidler] family. The sacrament was passed in both Sunday School and sacrament meeting.

The Chemnitz Center Branch lost at least fifty of its members during World War II—more than any other branch in the East German Mission. Nevertheless, the survivors went right to work after the war to find a new place to hold meetings and to carry out the work of the Church.

IN MEMORIAM

The following members of the Chemnitz Center Branch did not survive World War II:

Paul Auerswald b. Neuschönburg, Zwickau, Sachsen 3 Jan 1894; son of Alban Auerswald and Hulda Emilie Meinhold; bp. 17 Sep 1927; conf. 17 Sep 1927; ord. deacon 2 Sep 1928; ord. teacher 2 Jun 1929; ord. priest 6 Apr 1930; ord. elder 19 Oct 1931; m. Chemnitz, Chemnitz, Sachsen 15 Feb 1916, Elsa Erna Tanzmann; 2 children; 2m. 16 Mar 1945; d. 1945 (CHL, LR 4326 22, no. 1; IGI)

Walter Bergmann b. Chemnitz, Saxony 1 May 1897; m. 29 Apr 1920, Marie Erna Neuschrank; 5 children; sergeant; d. POW camp, Deutsch-Eylau 31 May 1945; bur. Ilawa, Poland (Popitz Ficker; IGI; www.volksbund.de)

Richard Alfred (Fred) Burkhardt b. Chemnitz, Chemnitz, Sachsen 20 Mar 1922; son of Max Richard Burkhardt and Johanna Else Müller; bp. Chemnitz 18 Aug 1930; conf. Chemnitz 18 Aug 1930; MIA Dec 1941 by Leningrad, Russia (H. Burkhardt; IGI)

Lothar Alfred Cieslak b. Chemnitz, Chemnitz, Sachsen 11 Jul 1927; son of Alfred Otto Cieslak and Leopoldina Rosalie Ottilie Leibner; bp. 10 Aug 1935; k. in battle Western Front 2 Apr 1945; bur. Soldaten-friedhof Bensheim, Hessen (Hyrum Cieslak; IGI; www.volksbund.de)

Herbert Emil Derr b. Chemnitz, Chemnitz, Sachsen 22 Nov 1909; son of Emil Derr and Hulda Olga Spindler; bp. 11 May 1918; m.; seaman first class; k. in battle Clisson, Nantes, France 13 Aug 1944; bur. Pornichet, France (www.volksbund.de; IGI)

Fig. 15. Alfred (Fred) Burkhardt. (H. Burkhardt)

Ida Minna Eckhardt b. Gablenz, Chemnitz, Sachsen 14 Jul 1865; dau. of Karl Friedrich Eckhardt and Amalie Wilhelmine Gebhardt; bp. 29 Aug 1925; conf. 29 Aug 1925; m. Gablenz 27 Nov 1887, Markus Max Seifert; 9 children; d. stroke Erdmannsdorf, Chemnitz, Sachsen 29 Sep 1939 (CHL LR 1932 21, no. 179; IGI; AF; PRF)

Karl Falkner: b. Nurnberg, Mittelfranken, Bayern 14 Jun 1885; son of Paul Heinrich Falkner and Anna Katharina Lauterbach; bp. 14 Nov 1925; m. 1 Nov 1907, Ida Klara Taubert; 5 children; 2m. Chemnitz, Chemnitz, Sachsen 11 Sep 1926, Lina Ella Tierlich; 3 children; 3m. Helene Mehnert; d. illness Chemnitz 22 Dec 1944 (H. Falkner-Pippig; IGI; AF)

Bruno Max Fischer b. Oberwiesenthal, Chemnitz, Sachsen 15 Apr 1881; son of August Ehregott Fischer and Louise Auguste Seltmann; bp. 17 Mar 1923; conf. 17 Mar 1923; ord. deacon 9 Nov 1924; ord. teacher 25 Apr 1926; ord. priest 31 Aug 1931; m. Chemnitz, Chemnitz, Sachsen 29 Mar 1909, Johanna Emma Roggenbau; 4 children; k. air raid Chemnitz 5 Mar 1945 (E. Goeckeritz; CHL LR 1632 21, no. 131; IGI; AF)

Elisabeth Linda Fischer b. Chemnitz, Chemnitz, Sachsen 24 Apr 1919; dau. of Bruno Max Fischer and Johanna Emma Roggenbau; bp. 14 May 1927; conf. 14 May 1927; m. Annaberg, Chemnitz, Sachsen 13 Mar 1943, Joachin Karl Heinrich Haensel; k. air raid Chemnitz 5 Mar 1945 (CHL LR 1632 21, no. 136; IGI; AF)

Erika Johanna Fischer b. Chemnitz, Chemnitz, Sachsen 16 Jun 1916; dau. of Bruno Max Fischer and Johanna Emma Roggenbau; bp. 23 Jun 1924; conf. 23 Jun 1924; m. Chemnitz 30 Sep 1939, Albrecht Hugo Hellmut Lohberger; 2 children; k. air raid Chemnitz 5 Mar 1945 (CHL LR 1632 21, no. 135; IGI)

Emil Hans Flade b. Chemnitz, Chemnitz, Sachsen 18 Sep 1892; son of Ernst Emil Flade and Amalia Ida Schroeder; bp. 20 Jun 1925; ord. elder; m. Chemnitz 15 Jul 1914, Paula Hulda Musch; 2 children; police trainee; k. in battle Wedding, Berlin, Preußen Apr or May 1945 (J. Flade; www.volksbund.de; FHL Microfilm 25767, 1930/35 Census; IGI; AF)

Helmut Bruno Fleming b. Chemnitz, Chemnitz, Sachsen 12 Jul 1911; son of Bruno Paul Fleming and Flora Minna Hoeppner; bp. 12 Jul 1927; k. in battle 1945 (Popitz Ficker; IGI)

Waldemar Fleming b. Chemnitz, Chemnitz, Sachsen 29 Nov 1914; dau. of Bruno Paul Fleming and Flora Minna Hoeppner; bp. 5 Jun 1927; d. in asylum (euthanasia?) 1941 (Popitz Ficker; IGI)

Selma Liddi Froede b. Zug 4 Jun 1883; dau. of Emil Froede and Pauline Kinden; bp. 31 Jan 1920; conf. 1 Feb 1920; m. 7 May 1935, Fritz Junghanns; k. air raid 8 Mar 1945 (CHL, LR 4326 22, no. 201; IGI)

Joseph Johann Frohm b. Erlangen, Mittelfranken, Bayern 15 Oct 1862; son of Josef Haberich and Theresie Frohm; bp. 8 May 1907; conf. 8 May 1907; ord. elder 13 Oct 1929; m. Chemnitz, Chemnitz, Sachsen 12 Feb 1890, Minna Wilhelmine Prell; 2 children; d. old age Chemnitz 24 Mar 1942 (CHL LR 1932 21, no. 326 or 576; IGI; AF)

Helene Anna Frosch b. Dittersdorf, Germany 9 Feb 1878; dau. of Friedrich Frosch and Anna May; m. —— Herrmann; d. 6 Feb 1945 (CHL CR 375 8 #2458, 1394–95)

Karl Albert Göckeritz b. Lössnitz, Freiberg, Dresden, Sachsen 1 Nov 1909; son of Max Karl Goeckeritz and Minna Emilie Enderlein; bp. 2 Sep 1919; ord. elder; Chemnitz district president; m. 14 Mar 1934, Magdalena Johanne Derr; 3 children; MIA near Stalingrad, Russia Jan 1943 (Karl-Heinz Goeckeritz; Harald Goeckeritz; IGI)

Joachim Karl Heinrich Haensel b. Chemnitz, Chemnitz, Sachsen 11 Jun 1919; son of Karl Oscar Haensel and Flora Martha May; bp. 13 Oct 1927; conf. 13 Oct 1927; ord. deacon 1 Nov 1931; m. Annaberg, Chemnitz, Sachsen 13 Mar 1943, Linda Elisabeth Fischer; policeman; k. in battle Streindorf, Italy 12 Feb 1945; bur. Kranj, Slovenia (www.volksbund.de; CHL LR 1933 21, no. 76 or 356; IGI)

Erich Lothar Hauck b. Chemnitz, Chemnitz, Sachsen 24 Jan 1904; son of Emil Robert Haugk and Hulda Lina Leonhardt; bp. 24 Jul 1926; conf. 24 Jul 1926; ord. deacon 18 Feb 1929; m. 21 Apr 1934, Charlotte Elfriede Goeckeritz; k. in battle 23 or 25 Mar 1945 (CHL, LR 4326 22, no. 144; IGI; Popitz Ficker)

Martha Heymann b. Chemnitz, Chemnitz, Sachsen 18 Mar 1889; dau. of Franz Louis Heymann

and Johanne Christiane Friedericke Doelling; bp. 18 Mar 1910; d. 3 Dec 1941 (K. Göckeritz diary; FHL Microfilm 162783, 1935 Census; IGI; AF)

Erich Walter Hinkel b. Frankenstein, Chemnitz, Sachsen 24 Nov 1911; son of Karl Friedrich Hinkel and Bertha Emma Dietrich; bp. 15 Jul 1922; corporal; k. in battle 22 or 24 Apr 1945; bur. Bad Überkingen, Württemberg (CHL Microfilm no. 2458, form 42 FP, pt. 37, 1394–95; IGI; AF; www.volksbund.de)

Martha Helene Hoeppner b. Chemnitz 2 Dec 1887; dau. of Friedrich H. Hoeppner and Marie Helene Herzog; d. tumor 6 Mar 1945 (CHL CR 375 8 #2460, 258–59)

Elsa Elisabeth Jung; b. Waldheim, Chemnitz, Sachsen 12 Mar 1902; dau. of Ernst Emil Jung and Anna Helene Otto; bp. 22 Aug 1931; m. Chemnitz, Chemnitz, Sachsen 14 May 1927, Hermann Otto Tutzschky; 2 children; 2m. Chemnitz, Helmut Otto Süss; 5 children; arrested Chemnitz 2 Sep 1942; k. in Ravensbrück Concentration Camp, Ravensbrück, Brandenburg, Preußen 25 Jan 1945 (W. Süss; Popitz Ficker; IGI; AF; PRF)

Rudolf Kurt Lehmann b. Chemnitz, Chemnitz, Sachsen 17 Jun or Jul 1917; son of Ernst Kurt Lehmann and Marie Gertrud Leevig; bp. 5 Nov 1927; conf. 5 Nov 1927; ord. deacon 6 Mar 1932; m. 27 Feb 1941, Gertrud Elfriede Oberländer; lieutenant; k. in battle west of Gamasza, Hungary 6 Mar 1945 (CHL, LR 4326 22, no. 237; IGI; Popitz Ficker; FHL Microfilm 271386, 1930/35 Census; www.volksbund.de)

Ida Wilhelmine Loerner b. Leitz, Thüringen 20 Jun 1870; dau. of Karl Robert Loerner and Karoline Gutenberg; bp. 25 Apr 1925; conf. 25 Apr 1925; m. 2 Mar 1889, Hugo Schmutzler; d. weakness 18 Apr 1940 (CHL LR 1932 21, no. 295 or 545)

Albrecht Hugo Hellmut Lohberger b. Hohenstein-Ernstthal, Chemnitz, Sachsen 23 Aug 1915; son of Ernst Hugo Lohberger and Elsa Anna Mueller; bp. 7 Mar 1928; m. Chemnitz, Chemnitz, Sachsen 30 Sep 1939, Erika Fischer; 2 children; Senior Lance-Corporal or Private 1st Class (Obergefreiter); d. Russia OR Raczynk, Poland 23 Aug 1944; bur. Opechowo, Poland (Popitz Ficker; IGI; www.volksbund.de)

Heinz Jürgen Lohberger b. Chemnitz May 1944; son of Albrecht Hugo Hellmut Lohberger and Erika Johanna Fischer; k. air raid Chemnitz 5 Mar 1945 (IGI)

Peter Hellmut Lohberger b. Chemnitz, Chemnitz, Sachsen 7 Oct 1940; son of Albrecht Hugo Hellmut Lohberger and Erika Johanna Fischer; k. air raid Chemnitz 5 Mar 1945 (IGI)

Auguste Luisa Melzer b. Dresden, Dresden, Sachsen 13 Nov 1851; dau. of Karl August Melzer and Amalie Rudolph; bp. 6 Aug 1920; conf. 8 Aug 1920;

Fig. 16. Heinz Hänsel.
(E. Goeckeritz McClellan)

Fig. 17. Helmut Otto Süss.
(W. Süss)

m. 29 Jun 1890, Carl Gustav Hahmann; d. old age Apr 1945 (CHL LR 1632 21, no. 105; IGI)

Elsa Anna Mueller b. Hohenstein-Ernstthal, Chemnitz, Sachsen 22 Feb 1885; dau. of Ernst Louis Mueller and Wilhelmine Auguste Peenert; bp. 5 Nov 1927; m. Hohenstein-Ernstthal 24 Dec 1906, Ernst Hugo Lohberger; 5 children; 2m. 17 Nov 1923, —— Mueller; k. air raid Chemnitz, Chemnitz, Sachsen 5 Mar 1945 (IGI)

Emma Marie Muesch b. Sebastiansberg, Chemnitz, Sachsen 18 Dec 1884; dau. of Johann Anton Muesch and Karoline Sidonia Schlottig; bp. 24 Jul 1926; conf. 24 Jul 1926; m. 14 Dec 1929, Paul Kuehnel; d. intestinal cancer 25 Oct 1941 (CHL LR 1932 21, no. 187; IGI)

Martha Frieda Peter b. Ringthal, Mittweida, Sachsen 19 Aug 1901; dau. of Otto Friedrich Peter and Lina Bertha Leutert; bp. 10 Sep 1927; conf. 10 Sep 1927; m. Mittweida, Leipzig, Sachsen 24 Dec 1921, Martin Johannes Donner; 3 children; d. heart ailment Claussnitz, Leipzig, Sachsen 12 Dec 1940; bur. Claussnitz (*Sonntagsgruss*, no. 15, 13 Apr 1941, 60; CHL LR 1932 21, no. 208 and LR 4326 22, no. 55; IGI)

Johannes Gerhardt Poppitz b. Chemnitz, Chemnitz, Sachsen 2 Jul 1914; son of William Gerhardt Poppitz and Johanne Helene Baum; bp. 2 Jul 1922; MIA Russia 1944 (Popitz Ficker; IGI)

Edwin Alfred (Fred) Preissler b. Borstendorf, Chemnitz, Sachsen 30 Jun 1888; son of Ernst Emil Preissler and Anna Emma Richter; bp. 26 Jul 1923; conf. 26 Jul 1923; ord. deacon 9 Nov 1924; ord. teacher 25 Apr 1926; ord. priest 26 Mar 1928; ord. elder 1 Dec 1929; m. Borstendorf 9 Jul 1911, Maria Elsa Hunger; 5 children; d. Chemnitz, Chemnitz, Sachsen 22 Apr 1940 (CHL LR 1932 21, no. 139; *Sonntagsstern*, no. 17, 26 May 1940 n. p.; IGI; AF)

Kurt Alfred Preissler b. Chemnitz, Chemnitz, Sachsen 17 Mar 1913; son of Edwin Alfred Preissler and Marie Elsa Hunger; m. Chemnitz, Chemnitz, Sachsen

11 Dec 1937, Kaethe Hildegard Haehle; 1 child; k. in battle 1943 (Popitz Ficker; IGI; AF)

Ida Alma Reichel b. Obernhau (?), Germany 11 Jun 1868; dau. of August Reichel; m. —— Braumann; d. old age 24 Sep 1940 (CHL CR 375 8 #2458, 1394–95)

Anna Reissmann b. Geyer, Chemnitz, Sachsen 14 Aug 1866; dau. of Martin Reissmann and Auguste L. Dessauer; bp. 17 Mar 1926; d. 30 Jan 1940 (CHL CR 375 8 #2458, 1394–95)

Marie Helene Richter b. Chemnitz, Chemnitz, Sachsen 22 Feb 1877; dau. of Julius Richter and Clara Schubert; d. 8 Oct 1942 (CHL CR 375 8 #2458, 1394–95)

Heinz Otto Rieck b. Chemnitz, Chemnitz, Sachsen 28 Sep 1917; m. Chemnitz 4 Oct 1941, Rahel Regina Theodora Göckeritz; MIA near Leningrad, Russia 1 Jan 1944 (Popitz Ficker; IGI; www.volksbund.de)

Johanna Emma Roggenbau b. Chemnitz, Chemnitz, Sachsen 1 Feb 1889; dau. of Hans Friedrich Gustav Arnold Roggenbau and Emma Emilie Hunger; bp. 15 Oct 1921; conf. 15 Oct 1921; m. Chemnitz 29 Mar 1909, Bruno Max Fischer; 4 children; d. air raid Chemnitz 5 Mar 1945 (CHL LR 1632 21, no. 132; IGI; AF; PRF)

Guido Guenther Scheithauer b. Chemnitz 6 Oct 1922; son of Martha Marie Loose; k. in battle (Popitz Ficker; FHL Microfilm 245258, 1930 Census)

Martha Elise Schreiber b. Buchholz, Chemnitz, Sachsen 29 Feb 1912; dau. of Moritz Schreiber and Anna Martha Lang; d. diabetes 16 Jan 1945 (CHL CR 375 8 #2460, 258–59)

Markus Max Seifert b. Erdmannsdorf, Chemnitz, Sachsen 20 Mar 1864; son of Friedrich Fuerchtegott Seifert and Juliane Dorothea Emmerich; bp. 28 Jul 1930; m. Gablenz, Chemnitz, Sachsen 27 Nov 1887, Ida Minna Eckhardt; 9 children; d. Erdmannsdorf 18 Mar 1944 (IGI; AF; PRF)

Jutta Monika Süss b. Chemnitz, Chemnitz, Sachsen 15 Sep 1940; d. 2 Jun 1942 (W. Süss)

Helmut Otto Süss b. Chemnitz, Chemnitz, Sachsen 26 Feb 1913; son of Georg Walther Suess and Marie Agnes Lindner; bp. 3 Oct 1931; conf. 9 Oct 1931; ord. deacon 30 Nov 1932; m. Chemnitz 28 May 1934, Elsa Elisabeth Jung; 5 children; lance corporal; k. in battle Baumeles Dames, Doubs, France 5 Sep 1944; bur. Andilly, France (W. Süss; Popitz-Ficker; CHL LR 1933 21, no. 233 or 509; IGI, www.volksbund.de)

Elsa Erna Tanzmann b. Chemnitz, Chemnitz, Sachsen 2 or 25 Sep 1895; dau. of Kurt Reinhard Tanzmann and Liba Henriette Schumann; bp. 17 Sep 1927; conf. 17 Sep 1927; m. Chemnitz 15 Feb 1916,

Paul Auerswald; 2 children; d. lung ailment Chemnitz 9 Jan 1945 (CHL, LR 4326 22, no. 4; IGI)

Lina Ella Tierlich b. Gablenz, Chemnitz, Chemnitz, Sachsen 11 Feb 1900; dau. of Heinrich Franz Tierlich and Lina Anna Taubert; bp. 17 Mar 1926; m. Chemnitz, Chemnitz, Sachsen 11 Sep 1926, Karl Falkner; 3 children; d. Chemnitz 7 Jan 1944 (H. Falkner Pippig; FHL Microfilm 245258, 1930 Census)

Manfred Alexander Vettermann b. Chemnitz, Chemnitz, Sachsen 11 Apr 1916; son of Emil Max Vettermann and Emma Margarete Franke; bp. 10 Apr 1925; k. in battle in the West 5 Jan 1945 (Popitz Ficker; IGI; AF)

Walter Emil Vettermann b. Chemnitz, Chemnitz, Sachsen 7 Jul 1911; son of Emil Max Vettermann and Anna Margarete Franke; railroad policeman; k. on the Slutsk—Minsk Railway, Belarus 27 Jun 1944; bur. between Slutsk and Minsk, Belarus (Popitz Ficker; IGI; AF; www.volksbund.de)

Anna Marie Vogelsang b. Krumbach, Leipzig, Sachsen 9 Mar 1893; dau. of Karl Moritz Vogelsang and Auguste Theresia Thuemer; bp. 21 Oct 1919; conf. 22 Oct 1919; k. air raid Chemnitz, Chemnitz, Sachsen 5 Mar 1945 (I. Franke Böttcher; CHL LR 1632 21, no. 91; IGI; AF)

Amalie Auguste Wittig b. Zöblitz, Chemnitz, Sachsen 4 Jun 1867; dau. of Friedrich Moritz Wittig and Christiane Friedricke Uhlmann; bp. 2 Sep 1919; m. —— Claus; d. 11 Mar 1944 (CHL CR 375 8 #2458, 1394–95)

NOTES

1. Presiding Bishopric, "Financial, Statistical, and Historical Reports of Wards, Stakes, and Missions, 1884–1955," CR 4 12, 257.

2. Ilse Franke Böttcher, interview by the author, Idaho Falls, Idaho, June 10, 2006.

3. Henry Burkhardt, interview by the author in German, Leipzig, Germany, June 2, 2007; unless otherwise noted, summarized in English by Judith Sartowski, and audio version or transcript of the interview in the author's collection.

4. Herbert Heidler, interview by the author in German, Leipzig, Germany, June 2, 2007.

5. John (Johannes Lothar) Flade, interview by the author in German, South Jordan, Utah, February 10, 2006.

6. Heinz Albert Bonitz, telephone interview with Judith Sartowski, May 2, 2008.

7. Alfred P. R. Schulz, papers, 1921–1950, MS 8242, Church History Library.

8. Brunhilde Falkner Pippig, telephone interview with Jennifer Heckmann in German, February 15, 2008.

9. Siegfried Donner, interview by the author, Salt Lake City, February 2, 2007.

10. Hyrum Cieslak, interview by the author in German, South Jordan, Utah, January 17, 2008. Of course, not only LDS parents tried to keep their children from becoming involved in Hitler Youth activities. Many Germans were opposed to such programs for political, religious, or cultural reasons.

11. Irene Härtel Schönfeld, interview by the author in German, Jahnsdorf, Germany, May 29, 2007.

12. Richard Burkhardt to Fred Burkhardt, November 16, 1941; private collection; trans. the author.

13. Sigrid Cieslak Rudolph, interview by Michael Corley, Salt Lake City, January 17, 2008.

14. G. Wolfgang Süss, autobiographical report, April 22, 2006; author's collection.

15. Hanna Süss-Benten, interview by the author in German, Friedrichsdorf, Germany, August 7, 2006.

16. Karl Göckeritz, diary, July 1941; private collection; trans. the author.

17. John Lother Flade, autobiographical report; private collection.

18. Charlotte Popitz Ficker, interview by the author in German, Nuremberg, Germany, August 13, 2006.

19. See the description of the Waffen-SS (elite combat troops) in the glossary.

20. Irmgard Susanne Flade Groebs Staufenbeil, interview by Michael Corley in German and English, Salt Lake City, January 25, 2008.

21. See the Hohenstein chapter for additional details.

22. Reiner Gröbs, interview by the author, Salt Lake City, January 19, 2007.

23. Karl Heinz Goeckeritz, interview by Michael Corley, Salt Lake City, February 8, 2008.

CHEMNITZ SCHLOSS BRANCH

The Schloss (Palace) Branch was by far the smaller of the two Latter-day Saint branches in Chemnitz in 1939. It had 186 members of record, while the Center Branch had 469. The Schloss Branch was named after the palace sitting on a hill in the northwest section of the city. The address of the rooms rented by the Schloss Branch was Winklerstrasse 19, almost exactly one mile from downtown Chemnitz (the *Markt*).

Chemnitz Schloss Branch[1]	1939
Elders	8
Priests	5
Teachers	5
Deacons	11
Other Adult Males	45
Adult Females	101
Male Children	5
Female Children	6
Total	186

Fig. 2. Schloss Branch meetinghouse—the Hinterhaus at Winklerstrasse 19 as it appeared in 2008.

As was the case with so many other LDS branches in Germany at that time, the Schloss Branch met in a Hinterhaus on two floors. According to branch member Ruth Schumann (born 1928):

> There was one large room upstairs with dividers. Downstairs there was a cloakroom that could be used as a classroom. The rest of the downstairs was a plumber's workshop. The Bruno Schreiter family lived in the same building. They let the Church rent one of their rooms with a small balcony for a classroom for Sunday School, Primary, and Relief Society.[2]

Sunday School was the first meeting of the day, beginning at 10:00 A.M. Sacrament meeting was held in the evening. Relief Society and priesthood meetings were held on Monday evenings, MIA on Tuesday evenings, and

Fig. 1. Chemnitz District priesthood holders dressed to represent heavenly messengers and latter-day prophets for a program in 1938. (R. Schumann Hinton)

Primary on Wednesday afternoons after school. Thursday evenings were used for choir practice.

In a Chemnitz District conference of 1938, Hans Schumann helped some of the men to dress as Latter-day Saint prophets of the years 1830 to 1938. He and his sister, Marianne, used hair, wigs, and makeup from their parents' beauty parlor and barbershop. It took weeks to make the preparations. Ruth Schumann recalled that district president Karl Göckeritz, the only local member who owned an automobile, drove the actors one by one from the salon to the meetinghouse before the program.

Ruth Schumann was eleven years old when World War II began. Fortunately, Chemnitz was spared the sufferings inflicted on many German cities for most of the war. Ruth recalled having enough food to eat during the war, but dairy products were hard to find, and fruit became a rarity. Because of the fruit shortage, each child was given a vitamin C tablet in school every day.

Christa Glauche (born 1923) recalled a problem with politics in Germany during the war:

> My parents were not politically involved in anything. They were very active in Church, and therefore there was no time for any other activities. My mother's brother often talked about politics and my parents did not respond; my father got very anxious because he did not

like talking about this topic. My uncle was not a member of the Church.

Some Saints in Germany found it possible to express brotherly love regarding the enemy in wartime, as is clear from Christa Glauche's recollection of her mother:

> When the war started, my brothers and male cousins had to serve in the war, and my mother got sick because she was so worried about everybody. She also cried when a British ship was sunk because she always thought about how all the boys on the ship also had mothers waiting for them to come back home.

Christa Glauche's mother died in 1942, and Christa moved with her father to Annaberg-Buchholz, where she lived until 1946. They were welcomed into the large LDS branch there.

Ruth Schumann's father, Rudolf, was under pressure to join the Nazi Party. According to his son, Hans, he gave the party representatives this carefully worded refusal: "I never have broken any law of the land and I will never do that. However, I cannot join any party because I cannot offend any of my clients who belong to a different party or faith than I belong to. I will be neutral."

Air raids were not a serious problem in Chemnitz until 1945, but there were plenty of false alarms. On one occasion, the alarm went off during sacrament meeting. According to

Fig. 4. The typical Bollerwagen served many thousands of German refugees in the last years of the war. (C. Glauche Schlünz)

Ruth: "The choir was singing a very wonderful, comforting song from the ninety-first psalm, and the branch president said, 'We're not going to go to a shelter. We're going to stay right here.' And the planes went somewhere else. I do not believe that this was a false alarm."

The date March 5, 1945, will forever be etched in the minds of surviving Chemnitz residents. Ruth Schumann remembered that three attacks from the air occurred on that day. The Schumann home was damaged at about noon in the first attack; two bedrooms upstairs were destroyed, but the beauty parlor on the street level survived. The electrical and water systems were nonfunctional. At 8:00 P.M., another attack occurred, and the family hurried around the corner to seek refuge in the basement with the Schneiders. As Ruth recalled:

> It was horrible. It was terrible. My dad made me lie on the floor, and above me was my brother and my sister and my mom and my dad, and then he put his arms around us. After a while, Brother Schneider and my dad went upstairs and saw that everything was on fire, and they decided that we had to get out of there. There was snow on the ground and that helped against fires from incendiary bombs. That was on a Monday. The day before, Sunday, Brother Schneider (who was in the branch presidency) had said: "Brothers and Sisters, I don't know why I'm telling you this, but tomorrow morning I want you to check out your hand wagons

Fig. 3. A class of the Chemnitz Schloss Branch Sunday School in 1938. (R. Schumann Hinton)

[Bollerwagen or Leiterwagen], to see if they're all in working condition."

Brother Schneider was clearly referring to the preparations made by several million Germans who already had fled from or been driven out of the eastern territories invaded by the Red Army.

By Tuesday, March 6, several thousand people in Chemnitz had perished, and many thousands more were homeless, among them several members of the Schloss Branch who then put those little wagons to good use. The Schumanns headed out of town to Auerswalde, about five miles north of Chemnitz, where they had owned a vacation cabin ("a shack") for some years and were known among the neighbors. The Schumanns were still in their shack six weeks later when the war came to an end in that part of Saxony. As Ruth later related:

I looked out of the window, and I saw American tanks approaching from the other slope, across the river. . . . And my mother put out a white tablecloth on the clotheslines. And here came German soldiers. I think some of them were SS, and they said if my mother would not take in the tablecloth they would kill my papa. So we had to take it in. . . . Then the Americans started shooting at us.

The family left their shack and hid for a while. When the firing was over, they returned to find about thirty holes in the shack. "We would have either been killed or terribly wounded," Ruth claimed. The Schumann family eventually returned to Chemnitz, as did their son Johannes, who was released in 1946 as a prisoner of war in the Soviet Union.

The Schumanns were together, but Ruth recalled that many families could not be reunited: "I will never forget the messages written [often in chalk] on bombed-out houses, like: 'Mother, where are you? I am back and could not find you. Your son . . .' Other mes-

Fig. 5. Young singles and married couples of the Chemnitz Center and Schloss Branches in 1942. (R. Schumann Hinton)

sages were more encouraging: 'We are alive! You can find us at [address].'"

The meeting rooms on Winklerstrasse had survived the war and soon became the venue for the Chemnitz Center Branch as well. Until other rooms could be found later in 1945, consecutive meetings were held for the two branches. However, the windows had been knocked out and could not be replaced for some time. The members covered the window spaces with cardboard and wood. This made it very difficult to see when the power was out, so the members used candles to provide light to see their hymnbooks and to read the sacramental prayers.[3]

Despite the fact that both Chemnitz branches had suffered heavy losses in soldiers and civilians, both branches were active and determined to carry on in faith once peace was restored.

In Memoriam

The following members of the Chemnitz Schloss Branch did not survive World War II:

Emma Auguste Wilhelmine Albrecht b. Waldenburg, Chemnitz, Sachsen 3 Apr 1851; dau. of Friedrich Wilhelm Albrecht and Wilhelmine Heinicke; bp. 31 Jan 1920; conf. 1 Feb 1920; m. 26 Jan 1879, Franz Louis Beckmann; d. heart failure Chemnitz, Chemnitz, Sachsen 14 Apr 1941 (*Sonntagsgruss*, no. 22, 1 Jun 1941, 88; CHL LR 1933 21, no. 4; IGI)

Elfriede Liddy Barth b. Chemnitz, Chemnitz, Sachsen 22 Nov 1926; dau. of Reinhold Herbert Barth and Liddy Camilla Schlicke; bp. 31 Aug 1935; conf. 31 Aug 1935; k. air raid Chemnitz 5 Mar 1945 (Spieler; CHL LR 1933 21, no. [6 or 282] and LR 4326 22, no. 7; IGI)

Ilse Elfriede Barth b. Chemnitz, Chemnitz, Sachsen 25 Aug 1931; dau. of Reinhold Herbert Barth and Liddy Camilla Schlicke; bp. 24 Aug 1940; conf. 24 Aug 1940; k. air raid Chemnitz 5 Mar 1945 (CHL LR 1933 21, no. 235 or 511; IGI)

Selma Ida Beckmann b. Langenchursdorf, Chemnitz, Sachsen 5 Apr 1866; dau. of Johann Gottfried Beckmann and Caroline Wilhelmine Polster; bp. 15 Jan 1910; conf. 15 Jan 1910; m. 16 Aug 1891, Albin Stenzel; 1 child; d. heart ailment Chemnitz, Chemnitz, Sachsen 14 Jan 1941 (*Sonntagsgruss*, no. 6,

9 Feb 1941, 24; FHL Microfilm 245274, 1935 Census; CHL LR 1933 21, no. 138; IGI)

Paul Lothow Boehme b. Frankenberg 13 Jul 1894; son of Emil Jaukeojoll Boehme and Marie E. Jahn; bp. 14 Aug 1927; conf. 14 Aug 1927; m. 11 Oct 1924, Mowther Adelheit Zimmermann; d. accident 3 Sep 1943 (CHL LR 4326 22, no. 37)

Meta Ella Brueckner b. Geyersdorf, Annaberg, Sachsen 1 Aug 1898; dau. of Carl Emil Brueckner and Anna Auguste Meyer; bp. 14 Jan 1914; conf. 14 Jan 1914; lost 20 Jan 1941 (CHL LR 1933 21, no. [204 or 480]; IGI)

Johannes Emil Franke b. Chemnitz, Chemnitz, Sachsen 30 Apr 1910; son of Max Goers and Liddy Franke; bp. 6 Dec 1919; conf. 7 Dec 1919; m. —— Liesel; d. wounds inflicted by shrapnel 18 Jun 1942 (CHL LR 1933 21, no. 28; IGI)

Bertha Minna Glaesser b. Weißbach, Chemnitz, Sachsen 8 Oct 1860; dau. of Johann Gottlieb Glaesser and Johanne Caroline Nestler; bp. 9 Apr 1910; conf. 9 Apr 1910; m. Weißbach 18 Feb 1886, Robert Oswald Glaesser; 15 children; d. stroke Chemnitz, Chemnitz, Sachsen 14 May 1941 (CHL LR 1933 21, no. [52 or 328]; IGI; AF)

Johann Friedrich Max Godat b. Königsberg, Ostpreußen, Preußen 4 Feb 1881; son of Johann Friedrich Max Godat and Bertha Friederike Lindemann; bp. 31 Jan 1920; conf. 1 Feb 1920; m. Chemnitz, Chemnitz, Sachsen 7 Oct 1913, Anna Marie Schulz; d. heart failure Chemnitz 27 Feb 1942 (CHL LR 1933 21, no. 41; IGI)

Anna Marie Haubold b. Gablenz, Chemnitz, Sachsen 21 Apr 1889; bp. 16 Nov 1913; conf. 16 Nov 1913; lost 20 Jan 1941 (CHL LR 1933 21, no. [220 or 496]; IGI)

Johannes Heidler b. Chemnitz, Chemnitz, Sachsen 11 Jun 1927; son of Emil Heidler and Anna Maria Gleisberg; bp. 10 Aug 1935; conf. 10 Aug 1935; ord. deacon 14 May 1941; k. in battle 23 Apr 1945 (Puppitz-Ricker; CHL LR 1933 21, no. 71 or 347; IGI; AF)

Karl Gottfried Heinrich b. Lengefeld, Chemnitz, Sachsen 29 May 1900; son of Karl Albin Heinrich and Aurelie Jenny Graichers; bp. 8 Jul 1927; conf. 8 Jul 1927; ord. deacon 10 Jun 1929; ord. teacher 1 Mar 1931; ord. priest 1 Jul 1934; ord. elder 14 Jul 1940; m. Grosshartmannsdorf, Dresden, Sachsen 6 Aug 1927, Anna Lina Haertig; 3 children; d. nerve paralysis Chemnitz, Chemnitz, Sachsen 16 Nov 1944 (CHL LR 1933 21, no. 71; IGI; PRF)

Willi Hoehnl b. Chemnitz, Chemnitz, Sachsen 28 Dec 1918; son of Isidor Ambros Hoehnl and Ida Bertha Hoyer; bp. 15 Apr 1927; conf. 15 Apr 1927; m. Chemnitz 24 Dec 1940, Luise Schubert; 1 child;

d. tuberculosis 7 May 1940 (CHL LR 1933 21, no. 255; IGI; AF)

Johanne Charlotte Hunger b. Chemnitz, Chemnitz, Sachsen 6 Mar 1908; dau. of Ernst Hermann Hunger and Pauline Czaja; bp. 3 Feb 1934; conf. 4 Feb 1934; d. pneumonia 28 Sep 1940 (CHL LR 1933 21, no. 203; IGI)

Olga Lina Kaiser b. Hartmannsdorf, Chemnitz, Sachsen 8 Jul 1866; dau. of Ernst Gotthilf Rudolph Kaiser and Theresia Pauline Liebert; bp. 20 Dec 1922; conf. 20 Dec 1922; m. Hartmannsdorf, Chemnitz, Sachsen 18 May 1891, Ernst Bruno Nier; d. old age 6 Aug 1943 (CHL LR 1933 21, no. 128; IGI; AF; PRF)

Gerhard Heinz Kinder b. Chemnitz, Chemnitz, Sachsen 27 Apr 1920; son of Emil Adolf Kinder and Martha Hedwig Uhlig; bp. 23 Jun 1932; conf. 23 Jun 1932; k. in battle near Smolensk, Russia 18 Feb 1942 (CHL LR 1933 21, no. 90; IGI)

Helmut Kinder b. Chemnitz, Chemnitz, Sachsen 24 Nov 1911; son of Martha H. Uhlig; ord. deacon; k. in battle (W. Rohloff; A. Langheinrich)

Karl Gustav Kuehn b. Hermsdorf, Görlitz, Schlesien, Preußen 12 Oct 1866; son of Johann Friedrich Kuehn and Maria Rosina Muehle; bp. 29 Jan 1902; m. 18 May 1891, Anna Luise Auguste Hansche; 2 children; 2m. Leschwitz, Görlitz, Schlesien, Preußen 17 Nov 1895, Pauline Selma Hansche; 3 children; d. Leopoldshain, Görlitz, Schlesien, Preußen 25 Jul 1943 (IGI)

Karl Friedrich Gustav Kuehn b. Leopoldshain, Görlitz, Schlesien, Preußen 4 May 1909; son of Karl Gustav Kuehn and Pauline Selma Hansche; bp. 23 Oct 1917; m. 17 Nov 1933; d. 8 Mar 1944 (IGI)

Alma Martha Lang b. Buchholz, Chemnitz, Sachsen 4 Jun 1880; dau. of Karl Herm. Lang and Emilie Junghuas; bp. 25 Jun 1921; conf. 25 Jun 1921; m. 28 Jan 1905, Richard Moritz Schrieber; d. diabetes 16 Jan 1945 (CHL LR 1933 21, no. 152; IGI)

Karl Paul Langer b. Ehrenfriedersdorf, Sachsen 20 Jan 1867; son of Karl Hermann Langer and Wilhelmine Haenchen; bp. 15 Aug 1930; conf. 15 Aug 1930; ord. deacon 6 Dec 1931; ord. teacher 21 Aug 1933; ord. priest 16 Jul 1939; m. 16 Jan 1904, Anna Marie Seidel (div); 2m.; 3m.; d. heart ailment 1 Jan 1942 (CHL LR 1933 21, no. [109 or 385] and [281 or 641]; Karl Goeckeritz; IGI)

Anna Luise Lungwitz b. Kappel, Chemnitz, Sachsen 13 Sep 1884; dau. of Otto Bruno Lungwitz and Anna Marie Fritzsch; bp. 17 Sep 1921; conf. 17 Sep 1921; m. Chemnitz, Chemnitz, Sachsen 27 Dec 1907, Max Arno Glauche; 5 children; d. diabetes Chemnitz-Kappel, Sachsen 18 May 1942 (CHL LR 1933 21, no. 51; IGI; PRF)

Ewald Friedrich Mehner b. Oberweschnitz, Stollberg, Chemnitz, Sachsen 19 Jan 1869; son of

Gottlieb Mehner and Christine Caroline Richter; bp. 3 Feb 1914; conf. 3 Feb 1914; d. asthma Chemnitz, Chemnitz, Sachsen 7 Apr 1941 (*Sonntagsgruss*, no. 22, 1 Jun 1941, 88; CHL LR 1933 21, no. 117; IGI)

Friedrich Oswald Werner Morgenstern b. Leipzig, Leipzig, Sachsen 12 Mar 1918; son of Friedrich Oswald Morgenstern and Frieda Selma Anna Pertuch; bp. 8 May 1928; conf. 8 May 1928; soldier; d. found dead in hotel 19 Dec 1942 (CHL LR 1933 21, no. 116; IGI)

Frieda Selma Anna Pertuch b. Ortelsdorf, Chemnitz, Sachsen 2 Oct 1880; dau. of Adolf Hermann Pertuch and Amalia Wilhelmine Liebers; bp. 17 Dec 1910; conf. 17 Dec 1910; m. Niederlichtenau, Chemnitz, Sachsen 8 Nov 1903, Friedrich Oswald Morgenstern; 4 children; d. heart attack Chemnitz, Chemnitz, Sachsen 6 Feb 1942 (CHL LR 1933 21, no. 114; IGI)

Anna Hedwig Peter b. Efurt, Sachsen 31 Apr 1899; dau. of Johann Ernst Hermann Peter and Klara Hedwig Fischer; bp. 1 Nov 1924; conf. 1 Nov 1924; m. May 1935, Fritz Junghanns; k. air raid 8 Mar 1945 (CHL LR 1933 21, no. 135 or 479; IGI)

Christiane Karoline Petzold b. Pillmannsgrün, Voigtland, Sachsen 14 Jun 1853; dau.. of Carl Christian Petzold and Caroline Christiane Koelbel; bp. 12 Jun 1920; conf. 12 Jun 1920; m. Plauen, Sachsen 2 Jun 1877, Emil Ernst Mueller; 12 children; d. old age Waldenburg, Chemnitz, Sachsen 17 Nov 1941 (CHL LR 1933 21, no. 124; IGI)

Ernst Hans Pöcker b. Chemnitz, Chemnitz, Sachsen 19 Aug 1912; son Ernst Max Pöcker and Helen Klara Lindner; bp. 6 Oct 1923; conf. 7 Oct 1923; ord. deacon 5 Oct 1930; m. 31 Aug 1935, Fanny Elsa Weiser; soldier; k. in battle Russia 22 Jun 1941 (*Sonntagsgruss*, no. 28, 21 Sep 1941, 112; CHL LR 1933 21, no. 132; IGI)

Rose Ruthild Richter b. Chemnitz, Chemnitz, Sachsen 9 Jul 1927; dau. of Max Otto Richter and Rosa Gertrud Seipp; bp. 5 Sep 1941; conf. 5 Sep 1941; d. pleurisy 1945 (CHL LR 1933 21, no. 298 or 658; IGI)

Camillo Johannes Schoenfeld b. Limbach, Chemnitz, Sachsen 24 Nov 1913; son of Camillo Rinaldo Schoenfeld and Hedwig Helene Mueller; bp. 18 Sep 1925; conf. 18 Sep 1925; m. 9 Dec 1939; lance corporal; k. in battle Buimer, Bjelgord, Russia 18 Aug 1943 (CHL LR 1933 21, no. 167; IGI; www.volksbund.de)

Harold Joachim Schoenfeld b. Chemnitz, Chemnitz, Sachsen 19 May 1927; son of Camillo Rinaldo Schoenfeld and Hedwig Helene Mueller; bp. 31 Aug 1935; conf. 31 Aug 1935; k. in battle by Gueben 4 Mar 1945 (CHL LR 1933 21, no. 169; IGI)

Anna Marie Schulz b. Wiesenburg, Zwickau, Sachsen 18 Mar 1877; dau. of Hermann Benjamin Schulz and Marie Auguste Heydel; bp. 24 Sep 1917;

conf. 24 Sep 1917; m. Chemnitz, Chemnitz, Sachsen 7 Oct 1913, Johann Friedrich Max Godat; d. stomach problems Chemnitz 15 Mar 1942 (CHL LR 1933 21, no. 40; IGI; AF)

Anna Marie Seidel b. Ehrenfriedersdorf, Sachsen 27 Aug 1872; dau. of Karl August Seidel and Christiane Paule Haehnel; bp. 15 Aug 1930; conf. 15 Aug 1930; m. 16 Jan 1904, Karl Paul Langer (div); k. air raid Chemnitz, Chemnitz, Sachsen 5 Mar 1945 (CHL LR 1933 21, no. 110 or 386; IGI)

Kurt Erich Wagner b. Chemnitz, Chemnitz, Sachsen 5 Apr 1910; son of Ernst Bruno Wagner and Anna Lina Thomas; bp. 1 May 1920; conf. 1 May 1920; ord. deacon 18 Jun 1928; m. 25 Sep 1937; rifleman; k. in battle by Mekensia, Sewastopol, Russia 18 Dec 1941 (CHL LR 1933 21, no. 184; IGI; www.volksbund.de)

Marie Emilie Winkler b. Lunzenau, Chemnitz, Sachsen 14 Nov 1873; dau. of Robert Winkler and Auguste Freigang; bp. 21 Oct 1919; conf. 22 Oct 1919; m. 9 Mar 1902, Joseph Hamperl; d. 9 Dec 1940 (CHL LR 1933 21, no. 82 or 358; IGI)

NOTES

1. Presiding Bishopric, "Financial, Statistical, and Historical Reports of Wards, Stakes, and Missions, 1884–1955," CR 4 12, 257.

2. Ruth Schumann Hinton, interview by Jennifer Heckmann and Erin Clark, Lehi, Utah, June 23, 2006.

3. Similar lighting problems persisted in many branches in Germany at the end of the war. This practice likely gave rise to the rumor that German Saints were using candles (or even incense) at the sacrament table as part of some forbidden ritual. Some members propagating those rumors in foreign countries based the "forbidden rituals" on the fact that the German Latter-day Saints had been isolated from priesthood leadership in Salt Lake City for nearly four years.

DÖBELN
BRANCH

Located twenty miles north-northeast of Chemnitz, the city of Döbeln had a population of approximately twenty-one thousand when World War II began in 1939. The branch of Latter-day Saints in that town was very small, numbering only nineteen persons, thirteen of whom were adult women.

Döbeln Branch[1]	1939
Elders	0
Priests	1
Teachers	0
Deacons	0
Other Adult Males	4
Adult Females	13
Male Children	1
Female Children	0
Total	19

The Döbeln Branch held its meetings at Burgstrasse 15, in the first Hinterhaus, main floor. Young Fritz Wächtler (born 1936) described the setting:

> It was right among the businesses in Döbeln. We went to a short alleyway, and our meeting-house was in the [Hinterhaus]. . . . I believe we had three rooms, [the largest being] a sacrament [meeting] room that was also used as a Sunday School room.[2]

Sunday School began at ten o'clock and sacrament meeting took place in the afternoon. Fritz estimated the typical attendance at thirty people. As in most branches in the East German Mission, a number of friends also attended.

According to Fritz Wächtler, "Dad was a member of the party, but he didn't participate in any of the activities because he was working in agriculture. He was busy all day long. He didn't have time for government meetings." Johannes Wächtler was the branch president in Döbeln for many years. At one point, he was drafted and in uniform, but for only one week. His employer, an elderly man with a very large farm, appealed to the Wehrmacht and was successful in having Brother Wächtler classified as an indispensable agricultural employee. Thanks to his employer's intervention, Johannes Wächtler was fortunate to remain home for the duration of the war.

Rudolf Wächtler was not quite seventeen years of age in the summer of 1940, when he was approached by Karl Göckeritz, the president of the Chemnitz District and asked if he would be willing to serve a mission. As Rudolf later wrote:

> I said that I would have to talk with my father first. He responded that he had already done that and that I had my father's full support. I asked if I might have a week to consider the matter, and he said that he would ask me again in one week.[3]

On his way home—a distance of about six miles—Rudolf talked with his father and came to the conclusion that he would serve a mission. The call came from Berlin just after his seventeenth birthday.

Rudolf was ordained a priest when he received his mission call. He joined Richard Deus, a traveling elder, on December 4, 1940. They worked together in Zwickau for a month, in Plauen for three months, and in Naumburg for two months. While there, Brother Deus received his draft notice and went home to Breslau.[4] Rudolf Wächtler was then transferred to Demmin in Pomerania (north of Berlin). No other men were called into missionary service, so Rudolf worked alone. His mission lasted only until August 1941, when he was inducted into the Reichsarbeitsdienst and released as a full-time missionary.

In 1943, Hyrum Cieslak (born 1930) of Chemnitz was sent by his parents to live on a farm in Rittmitz. He joined the Wächtler family in attending church in the Döbeln branch and felt very much at home there. Soon he was asked to work with the Aaronic Priesthood boys.[5]

With the farmwork hindered by the severe shortage of male laborers, the Wächtler boys were often taken out of school and put to work in the fields. "We each had a team of oxen," Fritz explained. "We went out in the field and helped out on the farm."

Apparently the Döbeln Branch moved to different rooms during the war because Hyrum Cieslak clearly remembered a different setting:

Fig. 1. Members of the Döbeln Branch in 1940. (F. Wächtler)

We met in the Bäckerstrasse 12. Johannes Wächtler was our branch president. We met in one of the houses in the back. In the front building we had a small room for the Primary. Then we had to walk up the stairs to reach our main meeting room. We had a beautiful podium, an organ, and there may have been some pictures on the wall. . . . There were about twenty-five to thirty people in attendance.

During the final year of the war, refugees from eastern Germany (primarily the province of Silesia) began to stream through the Döbeln community. According to Fritz Wächtler, "We had to shorten our living space. We'd share with other people. Sometimes the kitchen had to be shared."

On May 6, the arrival of the Red Army appeared imminent, so Johannes Wächtler prepared his family to flee. Fritz later described the situation:

> We loaded a wagon up, with a team of oxen, all ready to go. We packed all night. . . . [The next morning] we started off, heading for the next town [west]. We got there and they said, "Go back! The Russians are here!" When we went back, we found out that [the Russians] had been watching us all night as we packed up. So we were actually surrounded. That was the day before the war ended. . . . So we just turned around and went back to our home.

By the time the excitement of war had subsided, the Wächtlers found themselves living in a small town the population of which had doubled due to refugees. The owner of the farm where the

Fig. 2. Priesthood holders of the Chemnitz District met in Döbeln during the war. (F. Wächtler)

family had their apartment was taken away and never seen again. Johannes Wächtler became the manager. Under the new government, the farm was split up into tiny parcels and given to individuals. During the summer of 1945, Brother Wächtler was instrumental in keeping many people alive when food supplies were woefully inadequate. Under those challenging circumstances, the Döbeln Branch had survived without any significant disruption of their meetings.

In Memoriam

Only one member of the Döbeln Branch did not survive World War II:

Erich Robert Märtig b. Döbeln, Leipzig, Sachsen 11 Oct 1914; son of Emil Robert Märtig and Anna Selna Hayne; bp. 10 Aug 1929; m. 31 Dec 1937; soldier; d. military accident 2 Nov 1939; bur. Döbeln 7 Nov 1939 (*Stern*, no. 24, Christmas 1939, 387; IGI)

Notes

1. Presiding Bishopric, "Financial, Statistical, and Historical Reports of Wards, Stakes, and Missions, 1884–1955," CR 4 12, 257.

2. Fritz Wächtler, telephone interview with Jennifer Heckmann, May 21, 2008; transcript or audio version of the interview in the author's collection.

3. Rudolf Wächtler, "East German Missionary Stories," in *Ostdeutschland auf Mission*, 215.

4. For more about Richard Deus, see the Breslau South Branch chapter.

5. Hyrum Cieslak, interview by the author in German, South Jordan, Utah, January 17, 2008; summarized in English by Judith Sartowski.

HOHENSTEIN-ERNSTTHAL BRANCH

The town of Hohenstein is nine miles directly west of Chemnitz in what is called the Ernstthal Valley in Saxony. With sixty-nine members in 1939, this was the third-largest branch in the district, serving members living in Hohenstein itself and in several surrounding villages.

Hohenstein Branch[1]	1939
Elders	2
Priests	1
Teachers	2
Deacons	4
Other Adult Males	16
Adult Females	40
Male Children	0
Female Children	4
Total	69

The Hohenstein Branch met in rooms in the first Hinterhaus at Logenstrasse 16. "We entered through two gates and then came into the courtyard where the building was," recalled Ilse Böhme (born 1925).[2] It was a manufacturing building, and the meeting rooms were on the main floor. The members did their best to make the rooms more compatible for worship services, according to this entry from the East German Mission history:

> Monday 5 Dec 1938: From this day on until December 17th, the Hohenstein Branch, Chemnitz District, was completely renovated and remodeled. All members took active part.[3]

This kind of renovation campaign was very common among Latter-day Saint branches in Germany.

Ilse Böhme and Eva Göckeritz (born 1934) both remembered an embroidery with the words "The Glory of God Is Intelligence" hanging from the pulpit that stood to the side of the chapel. The rostrum might have been one step up from the main floor. "We had some interesting classrooms," explained Eva, "The children all went together in the room where we had to walk around a factory boiler." Class was sometimes held in the courtyard as well. Attendance on Sunday may have been thirty to forty persons.[4] The MIA met on Tuesday evenings and the Relief Society on Thursday evenings.

Ilse Böhme recalled that the rooms were warm if there was sufficient coal, but as the war progressed, there was no coal to be found and the members had to wear their coats to stay warm.

Shortly before the war, Ilse became acquainted with the poor condition of Jews in Nazi Germany. Near the church was a camp full of Jews, as she recalled:

> I saw them being hurt and beaten. That was horrible. One time I said to a man from the SS, "If you raise your hand one more time to hurt these poor people, you will have me to answer to." He replied, "If you were not so young, I would report you right away, and you would be heading for a concentration camp."

Although expected to do so, Ilse Böhme did not join the Bund Deutscher Mädel when she turned fourteen. As she later explained, "I received threatening letters indicating that the police would come for me if I did not attend. But I responded that Sunday School was enough for me. I was the only girl in my class at school who did not go."

Georg Göckeritz, the president of the Hohenstein Branch, lived seven miles south of the city in a small town called Neuwürschnitz. Brother Göckeritz had moved there from Chemnitz to work as an accountant in the town's only factory, and he built a house for his family there. According to his daughter, Eva, it was quite a trip to church: "We had to walk for one hour, then we rode the trolley for forty-five minutes, then we walked another fifteen to twenty minutes. We left home at 6:00 or 6:30 A.M." The Neuwürschnitz neighbors called Georg Göckeritz "the running Mormon preacher" because he was always in a hurry to get to church and walked well ahead of his family.

The only time the Göckeritz family went to church during the week was for MIA, "because my dad was the teacher," recalled Eva Göckeritz. "MIA was a branch activity and everybody came." Primary was held during the week without the Göckeritz children, who had Primary meetings with their mother in Neuwürschnitz. Hildegard Göckeritz invited neighborhood children to join them, and the gatherings were quite popular.

Rosemarie Göckeritz (born 1939) recalled how her father, who had lost an eye at age sixteen, was drafted into the German army several times. As an accountant at a local factory, he was indispensable to his employer, a Herr Friedrich. Georg Göckeritz must have felt himself immune from military service because each time he was drafted, Herr Friedrich managed to have the call deferred. However, the employer's good graces had their limits, because Brother Göckeritz refused to join the Nazi Party and dared to argue with his employer on the topic of politics versus religion. One day he insisted that "I believe in God, and I believe in Jesus, and Hitler does not figure in what I believe."[5] For Herr Friedrich, that was the straw that broke the camel's back, and he made no attempt to protect his employee when the next draft notice came. Despite having only one eye, Georg Göckeritz was needed by the Reich. Fortunately, his handicap prevented him from receiving a combat assignment. He was sent to Lüneburg in northern Germany and was never in danger.

In March 1941, Georg Göckeritz came home on furlough. His wife recorded her thoughts about the event in her diary:

March 9, 1941: We have had such a fine time together. We all went for a walk this afternoon. Raimund constantly holds on to his Papa. Soon he will leave us again. I walked with him as far as the Luther beech tree and the moon was shining! It was harder than I thought it would be. But it must be this way. One last kiss, then we went our separate ways. May God grant that we may be reunited again soon.[6]

Eva Göckeritz turned eight in 1942 and was baptized in Chemnitz in the back yard of the Emil Heidler family home. The baptismal font was the concrete basin used by the family to catch rainwater. As she later reported, "I was baptized in that waterhole in the pitch dark. Most of the baptisms were done in secret. . . . My own mother wasn't there." Later on, baptisms were performed in an indoor swimming pool in Hohenstein. Eva Grossmann's father, Ernst (not a member of the Church), was an employee there and allowed the Saints to come in after hours for baptismal ceremonies.

According to the East German Mission record, the Hohenstein-Ernstthal Branch had moved to a new location by January 1943: Theodor Fritzsche Strasse 16. It is not known why the move took place.[7]

As Eva Grossmann recalled, there were several military industries in Hohenstein that attracted the attention of Allied bombers. On one occasion, an American or British airplane was shot down and crashed just down the street from the Grossmann home. On two other occasions, dive-bombers chased her and shot at her. Some of the Allied tactics were truly disturbing, she recalled, such as when the planes dropped "little dolls and pencils and stuff" that were actually trick incendiary devices. "When you touched the things, they would explode. A lot of children got killed or lost some of their [fingers]."[8]

There were not very many fun things to do in wartime, as Raimund Göckeritz (born 1937) recalled. Some activities such as soccer games took place on Sundays, but Raimund was not allowed to participate in them. His best friend lived just two houses away, but the alarms of potential air raids were a constant concern. Despite the terrible reality of it all, some aspects of war were fascinating, as he later explained:

> I still remember one time when a dogfight [took place] right in front of our house, and we watched [the pilots] shoot at each other. It was about three airplanes chasing one airplane. One got shot down. . . . We saw it from our house. It landed somewhere in the field.[9]

Ilse Böhme was married in the civil registry of the town hall on February 2, 1944. She was a bit young at the time but was certain that she would be ordered to work for the army if she did not marry soon. Her groom was Martin Friedrich Hengst, and they had only three days together before he had to return to his post. About a year later, he was captured by the Americans, and Ilse had no idea of his whereabouts for quite a while.

Georg Göckeritz eventually served three different stints in the German army. He left home for the third time on December 8, 1944. Little Rose Göckeritz (born 1940) clearly remembered that sad farewell. Again, Georg's wife, Hildegard, confided her feelings to her diary:

> It was hard to say good-bye, but with the Lord's help we will survive this. His last words were directed to his children. He is our most precious possession next to the gospel. . . . We all want to hold onto each other tightly, so that we can get through the worst. All year long, we have been able to go to Hohenstein to church and that has really been nice. May we be blessed to continue to do so.[10]

Fig. 1. The branch in Hohenstein-Ernstthal met in this Hinterhaus during World War II. (J. Larsen, 2007)

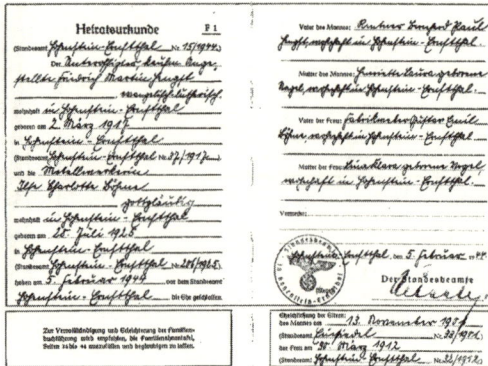

Fig. 2. The marriage certificate of Ilse Böhme and Friedrich Martin Hengst dated February 5, 1944. She is described as gottgläubig (God-believing). (E. Göckeritz McClellan)

In early 1945, several million Germans left their homes in the eastern provinces and fled to the west. Some of them came through Hohenstein seeking a place to live. The Grossmann family took in about a dozen relatives. As Eva reported, "We had only three big rooms and a little kitchen. It was pretty messy!"

Raimund Göckeritz's parents consistently prayed that the war would end soon, and they told their children that they believed that Germany could not win the war. Young Raimund repeated some of their statements in school, which could have caused serious problems had his teacher been a fanatic Nazi. Fortunately, he was not and took the time to caution the Göckeritz parents about what they said in the presence of their children.

In February 1945, a district conference was held in Chemnitz, and Ilse Böhme Hengst recalled the conclusion of the conference vividly:

> President Langheinrich [of the mission leadership] was there. At the end we sang "God Be with You till We Meet Again," and we all held hands. We had never done that before. Two weeks later they [many members in Chemnitz] were all dead.

Two weeks after the conference, on March 5, 1945, the city of Chemnitz suffered a catastrophic air raid. Late that night, Hildegard

Göckeritz and her daughters emerged from the basement of their Neuwürschnitz house and saw the red sky over Chemnitz, twelve miles to the northeast. Sister Göckeritz's parents, Bruno and Johanna Fischer, were members of the Church living in Chemnitz. Eva, then ten years old, later described her mother's reaction to what she imagined was going on in her hometown:

> I will never forget the look on my mother's face. I think she knew [what happened to her parents] because her face was bright red. . . . The next morning there were all these people coming [from Chemnitz] with their hair singed and their eyebrows, dragging little kids, and some of them had lost their shoes and clothes. It was really sad. And we were just hoping that our family would come too, but they didn't.

Day after day, no word came from Chemitz regarding the status of the Fischers. On March 10, 1945, Hildegard Göckeritz wrote of her concerns in her diary: "I still have no word from Chemnitz since the terrible attack on March 5. . . . If I didn't have the Church right now . . ."[11]

What she had feared the most became a reality on March 14:

> A sad day for me. Rudolf was here and brought the bad news from Chemnitz. My loved ones are all dead. Oh, I just can't believe that they're all gone. My dear parents, my dear sisters Elisabeth

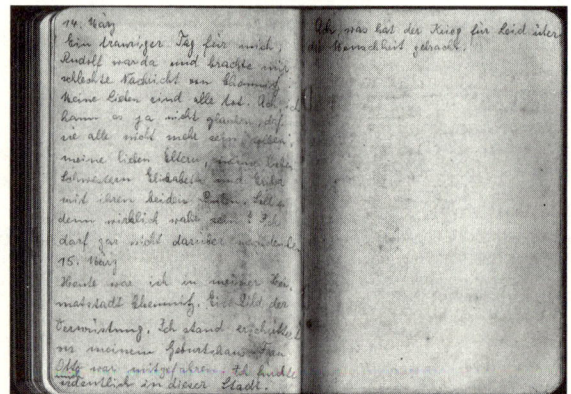

Fig. 3. On March 14, 1945, Hildegard Fischer Göckeritz wrote in her diary about the death of her parents, two sisters and two nephews in nearby Chemnitz. (E. Göckeritz McClellan)

and Erika, and her two little boys. Can it really be true? I dare not even think about it.[12]

She hurried to Chemnitz to see for herself and made this entry the next day:

Today I was in my hometown, Chemnitz. The picture of destruction. I stood devastated before the house in which I was born. Mrs. Otto went with me. I am really scared to even be in this city. Oh, what terrible suffering this war has brought upon mankind.[13]

In what may have been the single worst tragedy in the Church in Germany in World War II, eight Saints perished in the Fischer home in Chemnitz on March 5—six members of the Fischer family and two elderly sisters who had sought refuge in the Fischers' basement when the alarms sounded. Apparently, a direct hit had killed them all instantly.[14]

A few days later, Emil Heidler, a member in Chemnitz, rode his bicycle all the way to Neuwürschnitz. He told the family that he had personally seen the bodies of the Fischers, and he brought them some of their personal effects, including two purses. Eva later recalled:

The smell of the things was so terrible that we couldn't even bring them into the house. . . . First my mom put them on the back step, then the smell was so bad that we put them into a little greenhouse. When they finally aired out a bit, we brought them in. I don't know if we even kept them.

Georg Göckeritz was granted a furlough of two weeks to console his wife over her loss. Some neighbors tried to convince him to stay home—to not return to his unit—because the war was lost anyway, they said. He resisted the temptation to desert, knowing that it could cost him his life if he were caught; he dutifully returned to his unit in northern Germany.

The town of Hohenstein was spared great damage during the war, but there was at least one frightening occasion for Ilse Böhme

Fig. 4. Branch president Georg Göckeritz and his family just before he returned to military service in December 1944. (E. Göckeritz McClellan)

Hengst. In April 1945, "one last bomb was dropped next to our house. It left a hole big enough to build a new house in. I was thrown against the stove but I wasn't hurt."

Eva Grossmann's mother very nearly suffered the fate of a defeatist. One day in late April 1945, she went to the city hall to get money from her husband. She told a girl there that she needed to buy groceries soon because the American army was approaching the town. The girl reported her to the police, and Eva's mother was arrested. Eva (then thirteen years old) went along and was so upset by her mother's situation that the police chief scolded her sharply: "What are you crying about? Your mother is still alive, but she should be shot! You'll hear from us!" Fortunately, the Americans were indeed very close by. They entered the city and arrested the police chief before any action could be taken against Sister Grossmann.

In Neuwürschnitz the war ended with the arrival of the American army. They shelled the village for a while, and a few civilians were killed, but the Göckeritz home was not damaged. On the main street, somebody made a barricade of desks and chairs from the school in an attempt to stop the American tanks. Eva was the one to hang out a white sheet from their window to indicate that no resistance would be offered. "I remember that Hitler was still screaming over the radio, something about how we would still win the war."

"It was frightening," recalled Raimund Göckeritz. "We had never seen black people before, and most—I think about sixty per-cent—of the [American] soldiers were black, and they were big. . . . They went through all of our homes with their guns."

The Americans searched the Göckeritz home but left with only one item: the Mother's Cross that the government had awarded Hildegard Göckeritz for giving birth to six children for the Reich.

"My dad was captured by the British on April 29, 1945. I will always remember that date," explained Eva Göckeritz:

> They treated him like an animal, stole all of his valuables, etc. Then he was assigned to work in an office and he had a decent life. He had to write the orders for people to get released. One day the colonel said, "Why don't you write your own release order?" and so he did.

Eva and Raimund Göckeritz both recalled coming home from church one Sunday in the summer or fall of 1946 to find their father sit-ting in the kitchen. According to Raimund, the reunion was "heaven on earth; it was un-believable." The young Göckeritz family had survived the war, and their home was intact.

Eva Grossmann's father, Ernst, was in Czechoslovakia when the war ended. He avoided capture and sneaked across the bor-der into Germany, just a few miles from Hohenstein. When he arrived at his home just weeks after Germany's surrender, he was in excellent health. Eva's brother, Ernst Robert, was captured by the Soviets and did not return from the Soviet Union until 1949. She recalled seeing him approach the house on the final leg of his journey: "He came down the street re-ally slowly, and he had no shoes on, just old rags. He looked horrible, but he was alive." Regarding the Hohenstein Branch during the

war, Eva Grossman stated that "we kept very close and had good times." Her own family was richly blessed in that no close relatives died.

Looking back on her war experience, Ilse Böhme Hengst stated, "I had a testimony of the gospel. . . . We did not mourn concerning the war and our relationship to our Heavenly Father. We did not doubt that our Heavenly Father loved us."

In Memoriam

Only one member of the Hohenstein Branch did not survive World War II:

Friederike Wilhelmine —— b. 30 Jan 1861; bp. 18 Jul 1925; m. —— Gäbler; 1 child; d. Hohenstein-Ernstthal, Chemnitz, Sachsen 2 Mar 1941 (*Sonntagsgruss*, no. 15, 13 Apr 1941, 60)

Notes

1. Presiding Bishopric, "Financial, Statistical, and Historical Reports of Wards, Stakes, and Missions, 1884–1955," CR 4 12, 257.

2. Ilse Böhme Hengst, interview by the author in German, Ho-henstein-Ernstthal, Germany, May 29, 2007; unless otherwise noted, summarized in English by Judith Sartowski.

3. East German Mission Quarterly Reports, 1938, no. 50, East German Mission History.

4. Eva Göckeritz McClellan, interview by the author, Payson, Utah, April 3, 2007.

5. Rose Goeckeritz Groebs, interview by the author, Salt Lake City, January 19, 2007.

6. Hildegard Fischer Göckeritz, diary, March 9, 1941; private col-lection; trans. the author.

7. East German Mission, "Directory of Meeting Places" (unpub-lished manuscript, 1943); private collection.

8. Eva Maria Grossmann Donner, interview by the author, Salt Lake City, February 2, 2007. In the last few months of the war, the Allies enjoyed total air superiority over Germany.

9. Raimund Goeckeritz, interview by the author, Salt Lake City, March 3, 2006.

10. Göckeritz, diary, December 8, 1944.

11. Ibid., March 10, 1945.

12. Ibid., March 14, 1945.

13. Ibid., March 15, 1945. This was the last entry made before 1949.

14. See the Chemnitz Center Branch chapter for full details on the fate of the Fischer family. It is possible that more members of the Church perished in a single night in Hamburg in July 1943, but no details are available.

MITTWEIDA BRANCH

Located just ten miles north of Chemnitz, the town of Mittweida had about twnety-four thousand residents in 1939. Only twenty-three of them were members of The Church of Jesus Christ of Latter-day Saints. Church meetings were held in rented rooms at Max Beulich Strasse 10 at the time.

Mittweida Branch[1]	1939
Elders	1
Priests	1
Teachers	3
Deacons	1
Other Adult Males	3
Adult Females	12
Male Children	2
Female Children	0
Total	23

In a branch history written by Johannes Jentzsch, we find the following comments for the year 1939:

> The building in which we were holding our meetings, the "House of the German Laborer," was purchased by the city of Mittweida. They pressured us to leave based on the supposed need for renovations. Our meeting times were often changed and sometimes the meetings were cancelled. On September 24, a sacrament meeting was held at the home of Max Jentzsch in Weinsdorf [two miles northeast]. Finally, we found another meeting place for the branch, a little side building on Schulstrasse, across from the Fischte School. The owner was a Jewish man named Lässer. The average attendance at all meetings was twelve persons—four friends and eight members.[2]

Johannes Jentzsch recalled the branch conference held on October 15, 1939. District

president Karl Göckeritz presided and was asked if Germany would win the war. He replied, "Israel will win the war."

According to the branch history, Johannes Jentzsch was picked up from his place of work and taken into custody by the Gestapo in 1940. He narrowly missed being sent to the Buchenwald concentration camp, based on the charge that Latter-day Saint preachers told people to refuse to do work on Sundays during wartime.

The average attendance at meetings during 1940 was nine persons (seven members and two friends). By January 1941, the meeting rooms had moved to Heinrich Gutsche Strasse 7.[3] There is no information as to the reason for the move. The attendance at meetings in 1941 continued to decline. Mothers were required to join the general work force and thus miss meetings. The branch president, Max Jentzsch, had to walk or ride a bicycle from his home in Weinsdorf to Mittweida, though he still suffered from wounds received in World War I.

"I always enjoyed going to church, even though we had to walk for about a half hour. We did it twice on Sunday and also during the week," explained Reiner Lässig (born 1935).[4] His sister, Annemarie (born 1939), recalled how they held hands as they walked to church. Between Sunday School and sacrament meeting, they would visit their uncle and their grandmother.[5]

During the year 1942, members of the branch were again subjected to some harassment. For example, Max Jentzsch was told by a Nazi Party member that the Church would be "totally wiped out" when the war was over. Emil Heidler of the district presidency recommended that the sign "Kirche Jesu Christi der Heiligen der Letzten Tage" be removed from the building where the meetings were held. By the end of the year, the only brethren left at home were Max Jentzsch and Walter Lässig.

Despite the hardships of the war years, the average attendance at meetings had increased to thirteen (twelve members and one friend).

The report for the year 1943 begins with these words: "The war has taken a decided turn. On all fronts we are retreating." The members became more united under the stress, and the average attendance rose to seventeen members and friends. At times, the brethren could not attend and meetings were cancelled. Sacrament meeting was held immediately following Sunday School.

As a boy, Reiner Lässig went to the movie theater on occasion and recalled the following impressions:

> They always had a special news reel about the war, always saying how well [the soldiers] were doing. They never told us about the bad times toward the end of the war [or] when they were close to Stalingrad, when they had problems. They never told us about that.[6]

Reiner was baptized in a reservoir called the Stahlbecken just outside of Mittweida. It was 1944, and he was nearly nine years old.

Walter Lässig, Reiner's father, spent at least three years in the uniform of the Wehrmacht. His children later explained that he came home only twice. According to little Annemarie, "When my dad came to visit, I followed him around all the time. I think I even followed him into the bathroom because we never saw him very much, and we just wanted to get his attention while he was there."

Unofficial branch historian Johannes Jentzsch wrote that branch president Max Jentzsch was the only priesthood holder left at home during 1944, until Paul Emmerlich was released from the army. Sunday School still took place every week and sacrament meeting took place on thirty-four different Sundays during the year. The average attendance was again seventeen persons. Regarding the end of the war, the branch history reads as follows:

Fig. 1. The family of Ida and Otto Lässig. (R. Lässig)

On April 15 the enemy approached [Mittweida], so meetings were not held. The Americans took Mittweida without any fighting, but German defenders were in Weinsdorf, where branch president Max Jentzsch lived, and fighting took place there until the Russian army approached from Hainichen. On April 22, while the Jentzsch home was being hit by artillery shells, members gathered with Paul Emmerlich in Mittweida to hold a meeting at the usual hour.

Annemarie Lässig recalled the terror she felt when enemy artillery was heard near Mittweida:

> We woke up many times that night, and my mother grabbed us and ran down the stairs. We were down in the basement sitting together on a sled. My mother said a prayer. I remember the noise and the glass shattering, but she said a prayer, and we felt comforted that nothing would happen to us, but we were all pretty scared down there.

Young Reiner Lässig recalled how the American soldiers treated children during the two months they were in Mittweida as occupation forces. Two quite different experiences were unforgettable:

> I remember one whose name was Jim. I will never forget his name. He used to bring out his C rations . . . and packages from home and share them with us. He took us on jeep rides. But there was another American, an American Jew. I will never forget his face [with his] thick glasses. He would come out with C rations, . . . pour gasoline all over them, in front of the kids, and would burn them. . . . He hated Germans that bad. . . . But most of them were really nice.

Reiner's impression of the Soviet soldiers was also distinct years later. They arrived in July 1945 and conditions changed drastically: "Most of the time they didn't have shoes; they just had rags wrapped around their feet. Then the women had to hide. I don't blame the Russian soldiers [for their misdeeds]; they were so uneducated."

Fortunately, almost all of the members of the Mittweida Branch survived the war. As they came home one by one, the branch that had never given up was revived.

In Memoriam

The following members of the Mittweida Branch did not survive World War II:

Karl Moritz Laessig b. Wildenfels, Zwickau, Sachsen 30 Jul 1872; son of Hugo Oswald Laessig and Marie Christiane Werner; m. Schönau, Zwickau, Sachsen 9 May 1897, Ida Auguste Lauckner; 6 children; d. Wildenfels 11 Sep 1941 (IGI)

Alma Richter b. Lauter 22 Apr 1869; m.; d. 2 Mar 1944 (History of Mittweida Branch; FHL Microfilm 271402)

Notes

1. Presiding Bishopric, "Financial, Statistical, and Historical Reports of Wards, Stakes, and Missions, 1884–1955," CR 4 12, 257.

2. Johannes Jentzsch, "History of the Mittweida Branch" (unpublished history, about 1992); private collection; trans. the author.

3. East German Mission, "Directory of Meeting Places" (unpublished manuscript, 1943); private collection.

4. Reiner Lässig, interview by Michael Corley, Riverton, Utah, March 29, 2008.

5. Annemarie Lässig Ferrari, interview by Michael Corley, Riverton, Utah, March 29, 2008.

6. The German Sixth Army surrendered at Stalingrad, Russia, in February 1943. The loss of 295,000 men heralded the defeat of Hitler's Third Reich in the minds of many Germans.

The choir of the Chemnitz District.

DANZIG
DISTRICT
East German Mission

The Danzig District of the East German Mission was in a unique situation. Following World War I, Danzig was declared a Free City and thus was independent from Germany. Therefore, the city was the only part of the mission that was not in Germany. Danzig (now Gdańsk, Poland) is a port on the Baltic Sea. As a Free City with German-speaking inhabitants, it was positioned to serve both Germany and Poland commercially. South and west of Danzig was the so-called Polish Corridor, transferred from Germany to Poland in the Treaty of Versailles (1919) as an access to the sea, an arrangement that angered millions of Germans who lived in that region. Returning the Polish Corridor to Germany was a prime incentive for Hitler to conquer Poland in 1939.

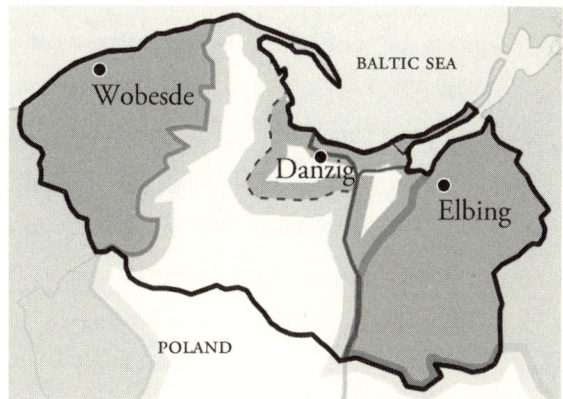

Fig. 1. *The Free City of Danzig was independent before World War II. German-speaking members of the Church in the Polish Corridor attended the closest branch in Danzig or in Germany.*

The Danzig District consisted of only three branches: Danzig, Elbing, and Wobesde. As a result of the confusing political boundaries, Wobesde (fifty-five miles to the west) was in the province of Pomerania in Germany, whereas Elbing (forty miles to the east) was in East Prussia, another German province. The disadvantages of the political situation of the Latter-day Saint branches in the district were evident in such incidents as the one recorded in the East German Mission History for Sunday, November 13, 1938:

> The fall conference of the Stolp [later Danzig] District was held in Danzig. Members of the Elbing and Wobesde branches could not attend, due to the fact that the "group" passport which

Danzig District[1]	1939	1940	1941	1942
Elders	13	14		
Priests	6	7		
Teachers	5	6		
Deacons	15	12		
Other Adult Males	53	30		
Adult Females	102	101		
Male Children	8	10		
Female Children	16	14		
Total	218	194	201	212

Fig. 2. Attendees at the district conference in Danzig on April 12, 1941, in front of the Danzig meetinghouse. (I. Reimer Ebert)

they had did not fulfill the requirements to enter the Free city of Danzig, even though they had previously been told that such a passport would be sufficient. In spite of this, an inspirational conference was held, at which Pres. Rees took active part.[2]

Emil Voge (born 1895) was called to serve as the president of the Danzig District in February 1938. He lived in Lauenburg, Germany—about forty miles west of Danzig. Each time he wanted to visit the branches in Danzig and Elbing, he was required to cross two or even three international boundaries (from Germany into Poland, then into the Free City of Danzig, then east into Germany [East Prussia]).

The last entry in the East German Mission History regarding the Danzig District is dated February 1, 1939. A meeting for district missionaries was held in the rooms of the Elbing Branch. Mission president Alfred C. Rees came

from Berlin, and other attendees came from branches in the Danzig and Königsberg districts. The record indicates that forty-five members and forty-nine friends attended the meeting.[3]

The tension along the German-Polish border had been emphasized and bemoaned by Nazi propaganda ever since Hitler came to power in 1933. The German dictator constantly demanded from the international community that the Polish Corridor be returned to Germany so that ethnic Germans living there would not be subjected to harassment by the Polish inhabitants of the region. The persecution was very likely not as intense as the German media represented it, but it was at least in some cases genuine. Rudi Seehagen (born 1925) of the Berlin Spandau Branch was in the region in 1938 and recalled the following incident involving Germans in Germany and in Poland:

In 1938, I was with the Hitler Youth for a week along the Polish border. The border was just a creek there. There was a former German village there. The Germans came from their village [in Poland] over to the creek across from us and sang German songs with us. The Polish police followed them and beat the people to get them away from us (and they beat women and children), and I saw that with my own eyes.[4]

The German army invaded Poland on Friday, September 1, 1939, but the armed conflict lasted only twenty-one days. For more than five years, Poland was under German military occupation. Danzig was again a German city, and Latter-day Saints traveling in and through the area no longer had any difficulties at border crossings.

In the fall of 1944, Soviet troops invaded East Prussia (the Königsberg District). A few months later, they approached Danzig. The members of the Danzig, Elbing, and Wobesde Branches who had not already fled to the west did their best to escape the enemy. By the summer of 1946, all members of the three branches of the Danzig District had left the area, and the Church no longer had any presence there.

NOTES

1. Presiding Bishopric, "Financial, Statistical, and Historical Reports of Wards, Stakes, and Missions, 1884–1955," CR 4 12, 257.
2. East German Mission Quarterly Reports, 1938, no. 46, East German Mission History.
3. Ibid., 1939, no. 55.
4. Rudi Seehagen, interview by the author in German, Sandy, Utah, March 9, 2006; summarized in English by Judith Sartowski.

DANZIG BRANCH

As the only branch of the LDS Church in the German missions that was not in Germany itself, the Danzig Branch was a novelty. The fact that the branch even continued to exist was a blessing, given the adjustments made to the German borders after World War I. The territory to the west and the south of the Free City of Danzig had been ceded to Poland, and the majority of the ethnic Germans living there had moved to German states to the east and the west.[1]

Danzig Branch[2]	1939
Elders	7
Priests	3
Teachers	3
Deacons	5
Other Adult Males	22
Adult Females	42
Male Children	4
Female Children	11
Total	97

The Danzig Branch was not very large but still the largest of the three in the Danzig District. With ninety-seven members, the branch was strong enough to support all of the auxiliaries and programs of the Church. As was often the case in German branches, the largest group was that of adult females (43 percent in this branch).

Hedwig Biereichel (born 1915) recalled meeting in several different schools during the 1930s, but the branch meetings took place at Damm 7 in the city's District IV when the war started. There were thirty to forty members in attendance at that time.[3]

The family of Hermann and Paula Lingmann lived on a small Baltic island near Danzig and operated a modest store there. Brother Lingmann was pressured to join the Nazi Party but declined. His daughter, Esther (born 1924), recalled the following incident:

> One day, the Jungvolk marched in front of our store, stopped there, and started singing *"Haut die Juden an die Wand"* [throw the Jews against the wall]. . . . My father stepped outside,

asked who the leader was, and when one boy stepped to the front, my father slapped him. He shouldn't have done that because the next day they did it again, but this time the police were there . . . waiting for my dad to come outside so they could arrest him. . . . Later on, the main leader of the party came and told my father sincerely that he would have to join the party or he would lose his customers.[4]

In 1939, Esther Lingmann was required to serve her Pflichtjahr for the government and was assigned as a nanny in a family with five children. She was only fifteen and looked much younger. Her mother accompanied her to the home where she was assigned to work. When the lady of house saw her, she said, "I have five children, and you're too young to help me!" Later, Esther was assigned to work with a different family, where she was allowed to leave at 4:00 P.M. each day. She was close enough to home to spend every night with her own family. Soon thereafter, she found employment in the Danzig shipyards.

Margarete Damasch Eichler (born 1906) was a young mother and the wife of an unemployed laborer as World War II approached. In her autobiography, she wrote of the political conditions in Danzig in the late 1930s: "There were many debates about [Hitler] in Danzig. About three-quarters of the population of our Free City of Danzig were against him."[5] Nevertheless, Hitler enjoyed a sizable following in Danzig, and Richard Müller (born 1926) recalled seeing and hearing many groups of uniformed Nazi Party members and Hitler Youth. "Later on, the Nazi movement in Danzig became stronger and stronger," he explained.[6]

The German army invaded Poland on Friday, September 1, 1939. Heino Müller (born 1922) recalled the day quite clearly:

We stood on the tops of our apartment houses and watched when the [German] dive-bombers attacked the Polish. . . . The Polish put some guns into a post office building, and a real fight broke out. It went on for two or three days before the Polish gave up and came out. . . . It was terrible! We didn't like it at all.[7]

The campaign lasted only three weeks and peace was restored. After nearly two decades as a Free City, Danzig was again part of the German Reich; all of the territory lost by Germany to Poland through the 1919 Treaty of Versailles was regained, and Adolf Hitler soon went there to celebrate the victory. To accommodate the Führer, local officials expanded a large hotel, but the expansion required the demolition of the Eichler home on Jopengasse. Sister Eichler unhappily spent a great deal of time searching for a new apartment. On the other hand, her husband, Ernst, had work again because the German war effort required many additional laborers in the Danzig harbor.[8]

"I saw Hitler in person twice," explained Richard Müller, "when he came to Danzig after the Polish campaign in September 1939 and in about 1942 or 1943, when he came to inspect submarine construction." The organizers of those visits saw to it that throngs of schoolchildren were lined up along the route to cheer Germany's Führer as he drove by.

Lilly Eichler (born 1932) turned eight in 1940 and was baptized in the Baltic Sea. "We

Fig. 1. The Müller family during the war: (top from left) sons Heino, Richard, and Rudi; (bottom) daughter Wilma and parents Katharina and Wilhelm. (W. Fassmann)

206

didn't have to do it in secret. There was no problem," she later explained.[9]

Charlotte Schulz Bever (born 1922) lived with her family in Zoppot, a small town about eight miles west of Danzig. She later described the effort required to attend Church meetings:

> From Zoppot to Danzig we had to take the train, and then we walked to the branch meetinghouse in the city center. This took us over one hour since we also had to walk to the train station [in Zoppot] and then again from the train station in Danzig to the branch rooms, which was a fifteen-minute walk. We could only attend church on fast Sunday since we did not have much money.[10]

Because they could not attend church meetings more than about once a month, Charlotte's mother worked hard to keep their faith alive in the home. As Charlotte later explained:

> My father did not have work but my mother always paid her tithing faithfully. She knew the Book of Mormon very well. During the winter time, when we were sitting with our backs to the oven, my mom and I sang songs out of the old hymnbook.

Hedwig Biereichel's husband was not a member of the Church, but in her opinion, "he was a better man than many of the members." He was drafted into the German air force ground crew soon after the war began. Their second child, a son, was born on April 6, 1940, and Sister Biereichel gave him the name Iwan, as she described years later: "My husband was gone when [Iwan] was born and was really angry when he came home and found out what name I had chosen." The civil registrar tried to talk her out of using a Russian name for her son, but she insisted, stating later that she had been inspired to name him Iwan (but she had no idea why). Later, she learned how the selection of her son's given name actually saved her life (see below).

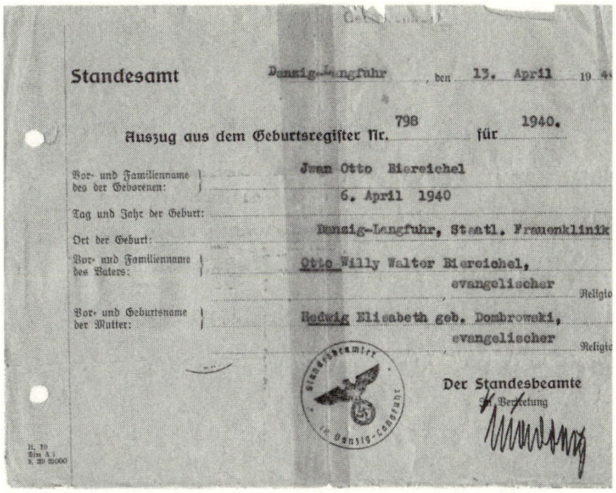
Standesamt Danzig-Langfuhr, den 13. April 1940

Auszug aus dem Geburtsregister Nr. 798 für 1940.

Vor- und Familienname des der Geborenen: Jwan Otto Biereichel

Tag und Jahr der Geburt: 6. April 1940

Ort der Geburt: Danzig-Langfuhr, Staatl. Frauenklinik

Vor- und Familienname des Vaters: Otto Willy Walter Biereichel, evangelischer Religion

Vor- und Geburtsname der Mutter: Hedwig Elisabeth geb. Dombrowski, evangelischer Religion

Standesbeamter in Danzig-Langfuhr

Der Standesbeamte
In Vertretung

Fig. 2. The birth certificate of Iwan Biereichel in 1940. The letter J represents I in the name of the child, and the civil registrar erroneously listed Hedwig's religion as evangelisch (Protestant). (I. Biereichel)

The meeting rooms at Damm 7 were apparently given up during the early years of the war because Hedwig Biereichel recalled meeting at Guttemplerloge later on. Unfortunately, the calamities of war followed them there: "Then everything was bombed out. . . . All the priesthood leaders were gone and nobody could bless the sacrament anymore. Relief Society was still held [for a while]. We did not see each other [much] anymore."

The records of the East German Mission indicate that at least one more move had occurred by 1943—to the address of An der großen Ölmühle 1. Richard Müller recalled that the building was used by some kind of antialcoholism association during the week and by the branch on Sundays. The structure did not survive the fall of Danzig in 1945.

In mid-war, Rose and Lilly Eichler were sent to the town of Wobesde, near the Baltic Sea about sixty-five miles west of Danzig. There they were safe from the air raids over Danzig and were privileged to live with a fine Latter-day Saint family—the Lawrenzes. The girls went to school and church in Wobesde and felt quite at home. When the Eichler family moved to a Danzig suburb, Lilly returned home to them. Rose stayed in Wobesde

Fig. 3. The Danzig Branch on Mother's Day, 1939. (L. Eichler Love)

because she was nearing the end of her public school tenure. She remained there until the late summer of 1945.[11]

An electrician by trade, Heino Müller worked in the Danzig shipyards in the construction of submarines. This critical war industry was Heino's ticket to civilian life. He reported to the draft board in 1940 for an examination but was exempted from military service. During the war, he was often the only young man attending church in the Danzig Branch. During these years, he also courted former missionary Irmgard Gottschalk of the Breslau Center Branch, and they were married on March 1, 1944.

Wilma Müller was attending a business school when the war broke out in 1939. She then found a job as a secretary but was paid less than 100 marks a month. Her father suggested that she join his company—the Kafemann Company at the Danzig shipyards. She made

the transition and was paid more than twice the previous amount. She was still working there in late 1942 when she became engaged to Emil Voge. They were married on October 20, 1942, and she was ready to leave Danzig to live in Lauenburg, Pomerania, but needed permission to do so. As she explained, "The law stated that nobody could walk away from the job unless they had a replacement." Her sister-in-law Irmgard was willing to assume her job, and Wilma was allowed to move to Lauenburg.[12]

All over Germany and Austria, individual Saints had to decide whether to support the Nazi Party or to avoid the issue. Most of the members of the Damasch and Eichler families were not in favor of Hitler, but a few members of the Danzig Branch joined the Nazi Party after Germany conquered the Free City in 1939. In fact, in early 1942, one of them denounced Margarete's husband, Ernst Eichler, to the Gestapo as a traitor. According to Sister Eichler's autobiography:

> Ernst was told the police had found out that he worked for the Americans. . . . He denied the charges and asked for an explanation. He was then cross-examined about his Boy Scout activities. . . . Ernst tried to explain that he was in charge of a pathfinder program. . . . [The police] intentionally tried to confuse him and catch him in a contradiction.

During the interrogation, Brother Eichler explained his patriotism based on the Church's Twelfth Article of Faith. He also explained his loyalty to Jesus Christ and unabashedly defended Christ as a Jew. After three hours, he was released and instructed simply to avoid the use of the term "Boy Scout."[13]

Lilly Eichler recalled how her father agonized about the political and military situation in the early war years. He would listen to the government propaganda in the radio broadcasts and pace across the floor. "He was just listening and shaking his head. He didn't say a word, [but] he was totally against it," Lilly recalled. As a youngster, she saw other people hanging out large swastika flags, and she thought that was exciting. "Why can't we have a flag?" she asked her mother. "Your father doesn't want that," was the response. Finally, Lilly was allowed to have "one of those tiny flags that you hold in your hand."

Harald Damasch (born 1905) was employed in an aircraft factory in Dessau in early 1942 when he carelessly mentioned to colleagues that Germany had little chance of winning a war against both the Soviet Union and the United States. He was arrested soon thereafter and spent several months in a concentration camp. His health was seriously damaged, and after he was released, he told his wife that he had been poisoned. He died shortly after returning to Danzig.[14]

According to Richard Müller, his father responded to the pressure of the Nazi Party in a very ingenious way. Instead of becoming a Nazi, he joined a different patriotic organization called the Reichskolonialbund—a league promoting the heritage of the German colonial territories in

Fig. 4. Hedwig Biereichel and her son, Iwan, in 1941. (H. Biereichel)

Africa before 1918. All Wilhelm Müller had to do to appear active in the league was distribute literature sent to him from the league headquarters in Berlin. This allowed him to keep the local Nazis at bay.

Hedwig Biereichel's husband served in the army in Berlin, northeast Germany, Paris, and Italy, where he was captured in 1943 by the Americans. Hedwig did not see him again until 1946. At home in Danzig, Sister Biereichel was not happy with Hitler's government or the Nazi Party. She told this story:

> I gave food to Russian prisoners working on the trash collection detail. I hid the food in my trash can. Sometimes I went outside to them and gave them the packages that I made so that they could hide it. I did it every week. I did enough things in contradiction to Hitler's instructions that they should have shot me fifty times. Somebody even reported me because of my son's name (Iwan).

Somehow, she always had a plausible excuse for her behavior.

During the war, Sister Biereichel attended church regularly with her children. According to her recollection, the Church suffered no persecution at the hands of the government, but officials attended the meetings at times, and hymns featuring the words *Zion* and *Israel* were not to be sung.

Toward the end of 1942, Wilma Müller Voge went to live with her new husband in the town of Lauenburg (now Labes, Poland), two hours west of Danzig and an hour south of Wobesde. Emil Voge was the president of the Danzig District. Because there was no branch in Lauenburg, the Voge family officially belonged to the Wobesde Branch (fifty-five miles to the west). However, it was more convenient for them to attend the Danzig Branch. Emil Voge, a master tailor, was a supervisor in the Zeek Company, which made military uniforms. Wilma later wrote about her service as a member of the Church in their isolated location in Lauenburg:

> When I left Danzig I had to be released from my church calling. We both wondered what the Lord wanted me to do in Lauenburg. After a few days I received a letter from the [mission] headquarters in Berlin calling me to be the historical and financial secretary for the Danzig District. They said that the calling had never been given to a sister before but because so many brethren were fighting in the war, they wanted me to do it. . . . We spent so much time together doing the Lord's work. We traveled together [to visit the branches] until two weeks before [our son] was born [on November 17, 1943].

When air raids began to strike Danzig on a regular basis, the residents found themselves spending more and more time in bomb shelters and basements. As was the case throughout Germany, if an alarm lasted until after midnight, the start of school the next morning was delayed by one hour. Years later, Lilly Eichler recalled the importance of the timing: "Sometimes [the alarms] ended five minutes before twelve, and we were mad because we were deprived of that extra hour of sleep." During air raids, the Eichlers usually went to the basement of a large government building nearby ("It was a nasty place!"). Often, Lilly's father did not go there with the family, being too far from home.

Many of the antiaircraft crews around Danzig consisted of schoolboys. Richard Müller was one of those boys in 1943 at the age of sixteen. With his friends, he was sometimes stationed at a battery for several days at a time. During that time, teachers would come from the school to give the boys their lessons in mathematics, chemistry, and other subjects. A year later, Richard served in the Reichsarbeitsdienst, but only for six weeks because his draft notice arrived on May 15, 1944.

By mid-September 1944, Richard Müller had finished his basic training in Munster near Hannover and was transferred into an Officer Candidate School. He had no desire to become an officer, but his father wrote to advise him to stay in such a program as long as possible, in order to stay out of combat zones. Wilhelm Müller also advised his son regarding standards of personal conduct, "If you keep the Word of Wisdom, if you keep yourself morally clean, nothing [bad] will happen to you." One very pleasant aspect of this training period was that Richard was able to attend church meetings ("At least Sunday School," he explained) in the nearby Celle Branch for five months.[15]

When his draft notice arrived in September 1944, Heino Müller realized that the Reich now needed him more as a sailor than as an electrician. Because he knew submarines inside and out, he assumed that he would be assigned to serve aboard one of those vessels. However, one day, a navy officer announced to the recruits, "I have the honor to hand you over to the Waffen-SS." Heino Müller had become a member of the elite combat troops under the personal command of Heinrich Himmler—one of the top men in Hitler's Germany.

Riding the train south to Prague for basic training, Heino prayed to his Heavenly Father, "No matter what happens to me, help me that

I don't have to hurt anybody or kill anybody!" His training was brief, a mere five shots from a rifle on the firing range. "The idea of these German troops being so well trained was a fairy tale by that stage of the war," he later explained. By October, he was a member of the famous SS Hohenstaufen Division, fighting the Americans who were advancing toward Germany. Assigned to the signal corps, Heino was in the thick of the fighting in Belgium when the Germans unleashed their final attack—the Ardennes Offensive that became known as the Battle of the Bulge. He escaped death on several occasions, such as the time when a huge piece of shrapnel landed near him: "It was about a foot long with sharp edges. If that had hit me, that would have been the end of me. It landed right at my feet."

By the time Heino Müller's battalion was pulled from the front at the Bulge, only one officer and about forty men were left of the six hundred who entered the battle. After a few weeks of rest in Germany, they were shipped to Hungary, where they attacked Soviet positions. Once during heavy artillery fire, Heino moved quickly from one crater to another, theorizing that the enemy changed his trajectory with every shot, such that the safest place would be where the last shell landed. Fortunately, his theory was correct.

In the first few weeks of 1945, the members of the Danzig Branch discussed what they should do as the Red Army approached the city. Branch president Willy Horn had received a letter from Paul Langheinrich (second counselor to the mission leader in Berlin) encouraging the Saints to evacuate the city right away and head west (which some branch members had already done). From Sister Eichler's recollection:

> When Brother Horn finished reading the letter, . . . he [said that he] thought that Heavenly Father would protect us from all the terrors of

the war, if we had enough faith in him. . . . He asked us to form a circle with the chairs. . . . We all knelt by the chairs, and Brother Horn offered a very humble and long prayer. When he was finished, he . . . told us to trust in the Lord and to return home with peace in our hearts—all would be well. A week later we heard that some of the members did not listen to his counsel but . . . left for the west. . . . Those of us who stayed behind experienced much agony and hardship.[16]

It would seem that Willy Horn's inspiration may have been in error on that occasion. In reality, those who rejected his recommendation and left the city right away were spared great hardship. Those who stayed suffered. There were disagreements on the issue even between spouses. For example, Brother Eichler decided that his family should remain in Danzig, though his wife did not agree.

Hermann Lingmann was required by the government to stay and defend Danzig, and his wife decided to stay with him. Thus only their daughter, Esther, boarded a ship in early March for the voyage to the west and safety from the invaders. Sitting in a coal hold of the ship, Esther heard odd sounds, and the lights went out. It was announced that the engine was having mechanical problems. Then word went around that the message was not true; the ship had struck a mine. A while later the ship hit another mine, and Esther went up on deck. There she found the sailors wearing life jackets—apparently ready to abandon their ship, which by then was listing to one side. Fortunately, they were close to a port, and another ship came alongside to rescue them. Eventually, Esther reached Wilhelmshaven in western Germany and was taken in by a local family for the next two weeks.

Hedwig Biereichel was still in Danzig when the Red Army entered the city in the spring of 1945. Her husband was already a prisoner of the Americans, and she had recently given birth to her third child. She was fortunate to be taken into her parents' home, but no place was safe after Danzig surrendered, especially for a pretty woman thirty years of age. As she later recalled,

> Once a soldier wanted to take me, and my father got in the way. He pointed his pistol at my father's chest and said, "If the woman doesn't come with me in five minutes, I'll kill the father." I was ready to go, rather than have my father killed, when an officer came through the door. Instantly, the soldier put his pistol away and denied that he had threatened us. The officer ordered the soldier out and promised us that this would not happen again. I was ready to kiss the officer's feet. I owed him my life.

In March 1945, the Soviet army entered Lauenburg. Wilma Voge's first son, Wilfried, was sixteen months old, and she was six months pregnant. When an enemy soldier found that Emil Voge had a paper with a swastika seal, the soldier decided that Emil was a Nazi and should be executed. A feisty young mother, Wilma jumped in front of her husband and declared, "You kill me and the boy first!" The shocked soldier left the house.

One evening, Russian soldiers entered the home Wilma was staying in and uttered the terrifying command, "Frau, komm!" A young officer intervened and sent the soldiers away. He returned on several occasions to save Wilma and her sons again, such as the night when several homes in the Voge neighborhood caught fire. The homes were built in rows and might all have burned down, but Wilma's protector gathered several other Russian soldiers and tore down part of the adjoining house to form a firebreak. Later, Wilma wrote, "We knew that the Lord had sent [that soldier] to protect us."

Unfortunately, their protector was not around when other soldiers came to take Emil Voge prisoner. As he was led away, he told his wife, "Our lives are in God's hands."

Ernst Eichler (born 1937) remembered the last few days before the invaders conquered

Danzig. His family lived in a small suburb on the outskirts of town, and German soldiers fought a hopeless defensive campaign against the Soviet onslaught:

> Every house except ours was destroyed. Ours was damaged by our own military. The Russians were advancing fast, and the German artillery lowered their guns so low, they shot right through the roof of our house. When the Russians came [closer], my dad would watch out of the window, he could tell they were coming. And we would go down in our shelter and hide. We could actually see the Russian army from our house.[17]

When the German defense of Danzig proved fruitless and the invaders entered the Eichlers' neighborhood, the family huddled in a hole Brother Eichler had dug beneath the basement. Ernst recalled the events of March 26, 1945:

> We heard soldiers walking around upstairs, you could hear their boots on the floor. We didn't hear anybody coming down, but my dad failed to engineer this bomb shelter very good; he didn't put ventilation in it. After about half an hour or so, we were running out of oxygen. And my dad carefully pushed the trapdoor up to let air in, and as soon as he got up, a rifle was coming down there. So somebody came down into the cellar looking but didn't know we were down there. But when my dad pushed the door up, the soldier made us all come out. My dad was taken prisoner. And then we had to leave. They forced us out.

Ernst Eichler was the fourth of five children. Those children were old enough at the end of the war to contribute to the effort of collecting food for the family. During the final months of the war, Ernst and his elder sister, Ellen, were sent by their mother to a farmer just outside of town. Their errand was to get some potatoes. Ernst told this story:

> We were heading on home carrying a bag of potatoes—there probably wasn't even ten pounds in it. My sister and I each had one hand on it; she

was three years older than me. Then the air-raid sirens went off, and we wanted to get to a shelter. We saw a Russian dive-bomber drop his bombs, then he swooped down right at us with a machine gun and shot the bag of potatoes out of our hands. [Ellen] dove into the bushes, and I did too, and then I lost her. I didn't know where she was. The potatoes were rolling all over the street. And I was crying, a seven-year-old boy, and I kept calling my sister, I said, "Ellen! Ellen!" And she wouldn't answer. She was in the bushes just a few feet from me. Finally she said, "Be quiet! They'll hear us and come back and shoot at us again!"

During the next few months, Hedwig Biereichel came to understand why she had been inspired to name her son Iwan. On many occasions when she attempted to procure food for her children, she ran into obstacles. When she displayed the boy's birth certificate, those obstacles were removed from her path. The Soviets and the Polish apparently assumed that she had chosen that name because she was a communist sympathizer.

In the summer of 1945, Wilma Voge gave birth to her second son, Nephi, in the house that nearly burned down. Fortunately, Emil had been released from a work detail just a few miles away and made it home for the event. There was no hospital nearby, and Wilma was assisted by a nurse who apparently did not observe proper hygiene practices. Wilma bled profusely and developed a fever. "How I ever lived through this I will never know," she later wrote.

By the time Richard Müller finished Officer Candidate School in March 1945, thirty of the fifty-six men had been eliminated from the program. Following successful completion of the course, he was sent to Döbeln in Saxony for training with rocket artillery. After three weeks in Döbeln, he was sent back to Munster. As a junior officer, he was given command of thirty men armed with bazookas. Their orders were to stop British tanks advancing along the Hamburg-Hanover Autobahn. While entrenched along the Autobahn, they had a curious experience:

> Some women SS guards from the Bergen-Belsen Concentration Camp were marching some female prisoners down the road. The prisoners looked terrible. When the guards saw my thirty men, one of them said, "Here is my chance to get some sex again!" and she started to take off her clothes. I was only eighteen and a half and had never seen a naked woman before. My knees went weak, and I prayed to my Heavenly Father: "Please, please help me!" Then I drew my pistol and threatened my men: "If any of you get involved with these women, I'll shoot you!" Of course, I had no intention to shoot them. Here were these well-fed SS women taking off their clothes, and over there were the prisoners looking like walking skeletons. Luckily, one of the women yelled, "Come on, we've got to get out of here!"

A few days later, Richard Müller's unit was caught between the invading Americans and the retreating Germans. As his unit fell apart in the confusion, he and his friend ran for the forest, trying to work their way to a safer environment. By April 27, they had surrendered to British soldiers and were taken to Belgium and put to work. On September 23, Richard turned nineteen and in accordance with camp tradition was allowed to eat all he wanted. He threw everything up a half hour later, because "my stomach just couldn't take it."

By April 1945, Heino Müller's Waffen-SS unit had retreated through Yugoslavia to Austria, where they encountered British troops coming from Italy. Heino knew that he was fortunate to surrender to the British, who understood that Waffen-SS soldiers were not the men responsible for the deaths of Soviet POWs or inmates of concentration camps. "That was the best thing that could have happened to me," he later explained. "If the Russians had captured us, I don't know if I could have gotten out alive."

Under first Soviet and then Polish occupation authorities, some Germans in Danzig were evicted while others were forced to stay. The Danzig Branch was torn apart in this confusion. For example, Margarete Eichler and her children became refugees for the next six months, subject to constant danger and privation. Sister Eichler later recorded her first thoughts in this new and insecure stage of life:

> We walked for hours and everybody was getting tired. We had not eaten anything for almost 24 hours. I thought of the pioneers [in the United States] and likened our situation to theirs, although they had to leave for their religious beliefs. They, too, had to leave many of their belongings behind, pushing heavy carts on uneven dirt roads into an unknown future. Heavenly Father comforted them and blessed them to make their load seem lighter. I hoped that Heavenly Father would help us too, and that all would be well in the end.[18]

A few days later, they escaped from a burning house but lost much of what little they carried with them, including all of Brother Eichler's family history documents. Sister Eichler's Book of Mormon was spared. Indeed, a few weeks later, an angry Red Army soldier took that book from Sister Eichler and tried to tear it up, yelling, "Hitler book! Hitler book!" Somehow, he was unable to destroy the book, and she concluded that an invisible force had prevented him from damaging her precious volume.[19] Braving conditions severe enough to crush weaker women, Margarete somehow kept her children and her mother-in-law (weakened by illness) alive and moving away from Danzig.[20]

As the Eichlers headed south, they left notes at every Red Cross station, seeking information about Brother Eichler. On one occasion, a man saw the note they posted and said that he knew where Brother Eichler was. It turned out that he had been shipped to the Soviet Union as a prisoner and then was released because he was very ill and his captors thought that he was dying. Sister Eichler found her husband in a squalid field hospital, covered with newspapers

and lying among corpses. As soon as he had recovered sufficiently, they headed west to Berlin and south to Saxony. In October 1945, they arrived at the Latter-day Saint colony at Wolfsgrün near Zwickau.

After Charlotte Schulz Bever was forced to leave Danzig, she headed west to Germany. She settled in Schwerin, north of Berlin, where there was no branch at the time. Fortunately, missionaries located her there soon after her arrival, and a branch was established.

In October 1945, the Voges were evicted from their home, and Wilma was subjected to additional suffering. She was bedridden the entire winter. With the arrival of spring, she was ready to leave what had become Poland. During the family's last trial, the evacuation to Germany, there was one last tragedy at the railroad station. She wrote this description:

> As we waited I was busy changing Nephi. We noticed that Wilfried had disappeared. I got almost hysterical, blamed my poor husband for not watching him. It was so bad, because the train was supposed to come shortly and we had to go with or without Wilfried. I was running, asking different people if they had seen a little boy. One lady said that she had seen a little boy with a book under his arm a few blocks away. Thank God, we found him before the train came. Another terrible thing happened. As we looked for Wilfried, someone took my husband's briefcase with all his genealogy. I thought my husband had lost his mind that day. I don't think he had ever recovered from the loss as long as he lived. Here he had lost many years' work. Only God knows what happened to his records.

In the summer of 1946, the Voge family arrived in Langen near Frankfurt am Main and became members of the growing Latter-day Saint refugee colony there.

Shortly after the Eichlers arrived at Wolfsgrün, the mission leaders in Berlin asked Brother Eichler if he would return to Danzig to help the remaining Saints evacuate that city and travel west to Germany. He reluctantly accepted the assignment (having nearly died just months before) and returned to Danzig. A trip that normally would take one day took three weeks.

Hedwig Biereichel remembered how Brother Eichler came back to rescue the twenty-two Latter-day Saints still in Danzig. At the time, only two priesthood holders, Willy Horn and Johann Kossin, were still in Danzig, and meetings were being held in the Horn home. Sister Biereichel told this story:

> The brethren sent me to get permission to leave Danzig and I used my lists of [Church] members to get permission. I told them that all the people (22 of them) were my family. We got the permission to go second class on the train. We left on a train on November 21, 1945—our seats were cushioned. Our railroad trip took us across the Oder River bridge at Küstrin. There was a Russian officer in every car so that the Polish would not rob us blind. We were put into the concentration camp at Dora-Mittelbau near Nordhausen. They had changed it into a refugee camp. . . . Later we went to the mission office in Berlin, and from there to Wolfsgrün.

Hedwig Biereichel later made her way to West Germany and was united with her husband in 1946.

The eldest Eichler daughters, Ruth and Rose, eventually joined their parents and siblings in Wolfsgrün, and the family was complete again. Their parents' agonizing wait was finally over.

Hermann Lingmann was captured by the Red Army but somehow managed to escape during the summer of 1945 and make his way to Glauchau. Soon thereafter, he received a telegram from his wife, who had been safely evacuated from Danzig. He found her and brought her to Glauchau, where they were given a nice apartment by city officials.

Richard Müller was released from his POW status in Belgium in mid-December 1945 and made his way directly to Celle. After six weeks

Fig. 5. Richard Müller, fourth from right, as a new Wehrmacht recruit. (R. Mueller)

there, he crossed the border into the Soviet Occupation Zone and found his parents living in a small town near Wismar in Mecklenburg. They were attending church in Rostock. From there, they joined the large colony of Latter-day Saint refugees assembled at Langen in the American Occupation Zone.

As a POW, Heino Müller was moved by his British captors to Northern Italy, where he worked as an electrician. During his incarceration, he and his comrades were told that there was no value in returning to Germany yet because in the ruined economy of the defeated nation, there would be no employment for them. He was finally released in June 1947 and made his way to Langen, where he joined his wife in the Latter-day Saint refugee colony. Regarding his short military career, he later made these comments:

> Sometimes people have problems because of the war. I never had any problems because I never did anything I had to regret. The Lord probably listened to me and arranged it so that I did not have to hurt anybody, shoot anybody, though I had the chance to do that. . . . I trusted in the Lord. I knew he would help me. I was so sure of it.

Looking back on the war years in Danzig, Lilly Eichler recalled that her family lived in a kind of cocoon. They concentrated on family and church and tried to forget the difficult things happening around them.

Fig. 6. Wilhelmine and Wilhelm Ruth. Sister Ruth died in child-birth in 1943. (K. Ruth)

Richard Müller later saw clearly how the Lord had blessed his family: "There was hardly any family in Germany who had three sons in uniform and all of them came home safely. None of the three of us got even a scratch."

For years, the Lingmann family held onto their hope that Johannes would return. Missing in action in Italy since April 1945, he was officially declared dead in 1960. Given the terrible sufferings of the members of the Danzig Branch, the fact that only ten of them are known to have died during the war is remarkable.

In Memoriam

The following members of the Danzig Branch did not survive World War II:

Wilhelmine Henriette Braatz b. Cetschau, Danzig, Westpreußen, Preußen 7 Oct 1899; dau. of Johann Edward Julius Braatz and Auguste Catharine Rieck; bp. Free City of Danzig 9 Aug 1934; m. Danzig 11 Aug 1934, Wilhelm Herbert Ruth; 2 children; d. childbirth Danzig 21 Aug 1943; bur. Danzig (Kurt Ruth)

Bruno Erich Damasch b. Danzig, Westpreußen, Preußen 3 Sep 1896; son of Georg Damasch and Johanna Olga Detloff; bp. 9 Sep 1904; m. 5 Jun 1930, Frieda M. Baumgart; 2m. 25 Oct 1941, Herta ——; MIA Danzig 1 Mar 1945 (IGI; www.volkbund.de)

Erich Harald Damasch b. Danzig, Westpreußen, Preußen 29 Sep 1905; son of Georg Damasch and Johanna Olga Detloff; bp. 11 Jul 1916; m. 27 Mar 1937; d. ill effects of concentration camp confinement Danzig Free City 12 Dec 1944 (M. Eichler; IGI)

Marie Amalie Friederike Enseleit b. Danzig, Westpreußen, Preußen 7 Dec 1854; dau. of Johann Enseleit and Juliana Henriette Wilhelmine Henriette Preuss; bp. 31 Oct 1904; m. Danzig 27 Oct 1876, Louis Theodor Müller; 10 children; d. Danzig Free City 25 Feb 1940 (*Sonntagsstern*, no. 17, 26 May 1940, n.p.; IGI)

Charlotte Marie Haeldtke b. Danzig, West-preußen, Preußen 20 Aug 1894; dau. of Richard Wilhelm Haeldtke and Clara Franziska Klose; bp. Aug 1920; m. Danzig Free City Sep 1919, Hermann Karl Wolf; 2 children; d. starvation Danzig Aug 1945 (IGI)

Robert A M Lau b. Danzig, Westpreußen, Preußen Feb 1869; son of Friedrich Lau and Augusta Rohr; bp. 20 May 1907; ord. teacher; m. Julianne Krauser; d. starvation Jun or Jul 1945 (FHL Microfilm 271385, 1930/35 Census; IGI)

Johannes Lingmann b. Schneidemühl, Posen, Preußen 18 May 1921; son of Herman August Lingmann and Paula Elisabeth Weller; bp. 29 Sep 1929; private; d. Apr 1945; bur. Costermano, Italy (IGI; www.volksbund.de)

Maria Katharina Otto b. Weichselmünde, Danzig, Westpreußen, Preußen 20 Apr 1864; dau. of Georg Otto and Katharina Cornelia Goergens; bp. 14 Sep 1924; m. Weichselmünde 18 Nov 1883, Johann Gottlieb Kossin; 12 children; d. lung disease Danzig Free City 21 Sep 1939 (*Stern* no. 20, 15 Oct 1939, pg. 323; FHL Microfilm 271381, 1930/35 Census; IGI)

Arthur Otto Sawatzke b. Danzig, Westpreußen, Preußen 27 Aug 1897 or 27 Sep 1899; son of Carl Otto Sawatzke and Minne Renate Holstein; bp. 4 or 10 Aug 1927; ord. teacher; m. Schönau, Danzig Free City 2 Aug 1927, Gertrud Marie Sawatzke; 4 children; d. as forced laborer Russia 15 Aug 1945 or 1946 (Sawatzke; IGI; FHL Microfilm 245257, 1930/35 Census)

Johannes Hermann Wolf b. Danzig Free City 1 Jun 1922; son of Hermann Karl Wolf and Charlotte Maria Haeldtke; bp. 1 Jun 1930; k. in battle Russia 24 Jul 1944 (H. Müller; IGI)

Notes

1. The modern Polish name of Danzig is Gdańsk.

2. Presiding Bishopric, "Financial, Statistical, and Historical Reports of Wards, Stakes, and Missions, 1884–1955," CR 4 12, 257.

3. Hedwig Dombrowska Biereichel, interview by the author in German, Hanover, Germany, August 6, 2006; unless otherwise noted, summarized in English by Judith Sartowski.

4. Esther Lingmann Vilart, interview by Michael Corley, Salt Lake City, April 24, 2008; unless otherwise noted, transcript or audio version of the interview in the author's collection.

5. Margarete Damasch Eichler, autobiography (unpublished, 1999), 57; private collection.

6. Richard Müller, interview by Michael Corley, Bountiful, Utah, March 14, 2008.

7. Heino Müller, interview by Michael Corley, Salt Lake City, February 29, 2008.

8. Rose Eichler Wood, "Biography of Rose Wood" (unpublished), 8–9; private collection.

9. Lilly Eichler Love, telephone interview with Jennifer Heckmann, April 2, 2008.

10. Charlotte Schulz Bever, interview by the author in German, Schwerin, Germany, June 11, 2007.

11. See the Wobesde Branch chapter for more about Rose's experiences in 1945.

12. Wilma Müller Voge Taylor, "Life Story" (unpublished autobiography, 1985); private collection.

13. Margarete Damasch Eichler, autobiography, 70–71. The Boy Scout program in Germany was dissolved by government order in 1934. The twelfth article of faith reads as follows: "We believe in being subject to kings, presidents, rulers, and magistrates, in obeying, honoring, and sustaining the law."

14. Eichler, autobiography, 60–61.

15. The Celle Branch was part of the Hanover District of the West German Mission. No other soldier from the East German Mission is known to have had a similar opportunity. Most were totally isolated from the Church while away from home.

16. Eichler, autobiography, 80–81.

17. Ernst Eichler, interview by the author, Spanish Fork, Utah, March 31, 2006.

18. Eichler, autobiography, 91.

19. Ibid., 100.

20. Ibid., 115.

ELBING BRANCH

The city of Elbing is located forty miles east-southeast of Danzig. To attend district conferences in the Free City of Danzig (the center of the Church district and German territory until 1919), Elbing Saints needed to cross an international border.[1]

Elbing (now Elblag, Poland) was a city of about sixty-five thousand people in 1939. Among them and living nearby were sixty-one members of The Church of Jesus Christ of Latter-day Saints. They held their meetings in the second Hinterhaus at Adolf Hitler Strasse 11. Young Meta Semrau (born 1924) recalled using a long but not large room as the chapel and having one other small room for a second class. She recalled that attendance at meetings may have been about twenty members and friends.[2]

Gertraude Bsumek (born 1937) lived with her family at Skaggerakstrasse 2. She recalled taking a long streetcar ride downtown to church. The family of Edwin and Ella Bsumek had moved to Elbing from Göttingen in western Germany in 1939 and immediately sought out the local branch of the Church.[3]

Elbing Branch[4]	1939
Elders	3
Priests	1
Teachers	2
Deacons	2
Other Adult Males	10
Adult Females	34
Male Children	4
Female Children	5
Total	61

Meta Semrau and her mother became members of the Elbing Branch when they moved to Marienwerder—about fifty miles to the south. They had moved from Westphalia in western Germany after the death of Meta's father. Because it took two hours to get to Elbing by train, the Semraus were not able to attend church very often. They were pleased that the missionaries came to visit them on occasion, but that ended in August 1939 when the missionaries were withdrawn from Germany. Later, Emil Voge (president of the Danzig District) came with his wife, Wilma, to visit the Semrau family in Marienwerder.

In 1938, Meta was fourteen and became a member of the League of German Girls (Bund Deutscher Mädel). About the experience she recalled:

We had to join, but it was the very best [experience] that I ever could have. We didn't talk about politics. We came together every week, and we sang songs, and we talked about all kinds of things—not about Hitler. We made nice trips to the mountains, which were very far away from Marienwerder, and we went on bike trips.

The war caused little stir in Elbing for several years, but family life was subject to significant interruptions. Meta Semrau's two older brothers were both drafted and were gone from home for much of the war. Gertraude Bsumek's father was drafted early in the war and came home only a few times before 1945.

As time went on and it became clear that Germany could lose the war and be invaded, people began to think more about their personal security. For example, Gertraude Bsumek described how they safeguarded their most important documents:

My mother had a baby stroller, in which she kept the critical documents for our family. She buried them down below [the baby], and that baby stroller, of course, went with us wherever we went because we had these little boys, my younger brothers. And that's where she hid the documents.

Meta Semrau recalled that the president of the Elbing Branch was a Brother Scherwinski. He was eventually drafted into the army and came home after losing a leg in combat.

Bad news came to the Semrau family as the third year of the war came to a close. Meta's brother Fritz (twenty-two years old) was killed in battle on August 24, 1942, near Wornisch, Russia. More tragedy befell the family two years later. The elder son, Wilhelm (twenty-eight), contracted malaria and was sent home to a hospital in Marienwerder. He died there and was buried in the late summer of 1944.

Soon after moving to Elbing from her hometown of Tilsit, Waltraut Naujoks Schibblack was called to be a Sunday School teacher. She was pleased that the branch there still held regular meetings; the Church and her faith constituted hope. As she recalled:

This was also a large branch, but much of the priesthood was gone [drafted] already. All the sisters were very active, and I felt much more of a friendship than in the Tilsit branch. . . . I can remember being able to attend a meeting every Sunday during the war.[5]

The Red Army first set foot upon German soil in the fall of 1944 in East Prussia—just 110 miles east of Elbing. Soon the government encouraged civilians to evacuate to the west. Waltraut Naujoks Schibblack recalled quite clearly how she learned of the evacuation of Elbing:

One day in January 1945, my husband got up from the dinner table and told me that we had to leave. The first six Russian tanks were already in Elbing at that time. I took only the little bag that I used to take with me into the air-raid shelter, and we left. It was January [1945]; we had to walk, and it was very cold. My mother-in-law was not a member of the Church, and she cried for a long time. She did not want to leave her beautiful home and her city. My husband told her that he would leave whether she came with us or not because he knew what would happen [when the invaders came]. She joined us.

Gertraude Bsumek recalled the circumstances surrounding their departure from Elbing:

I remember one day, the word went around the community, "Everybody from such-and-such neighborhood is to meet at this-and-that particular location." In different neighborhoods, all the people went to certain gathering places, as instructed. [City officials] told us the Russians were coming and we had to leave the city. Now, my father was in the army, so he was away. My mother was there, just with us little kids. I was only seven at the time, and my three brothers were all younger. So we packed up what we could and went to the gathering place. My aunt refused to go because she was pregnant, and her husband, my Uncle Paul, was one of those really loyal, never-say-die Germans who believed that they could keep the Russians out of town. It was October 1944.

Gertraude Bsumek tried to help her mother on their trek west. With the two youngest boys in the baby carriage, there was little room for family belongings. As a soldier at the front, her father, Edwin Bsumek, was not there to help. In fact, he had already been taken prisoner, and his family did not know where he was. When they left their apartment, Ella Bsumek and each of her children wore several layers of clothing, both because it was very cold and because it was a convenient way to carry more clothing for the journey. Gertraude described what happened next: "At the railroad station, they stuffed us into a cattle car, but there was no room to sit down. We traveled to the small town of Dahlen near Dresden to my Aunt Lidia, who was not very gracious about taking us in."

Shortly after their arrival in Dahlen, Ella Bsumek and her four young children were witnesses—albeit from a safe distance—to the firebombing that destroyed Dresden on February 13–14, 1945. According to Gertraude, "We could see the lights in the sky from the fires. And in the other direction, toward Leipzig, another huge city, when the bombers caused fires there, we could see that in the sky, too."

In the town of Marienwerder, people were leaving their homes and hurrying westward. Just to the west of town was one of the largest rivers in the region, the Vistula. Meta Semrau recalled that her family had often walked out to the river and looked west across the river to Poland. When it came time to leave town, that river very nearly stopped Meta and her mother from getting away before the enemy soldiers came. They had delayed their departure until January 1945 and found that as they approached the Vistula bridge, an army truck pulled up by them, and a German soldier said, "You're lucky we're still here. We'll take you across the bridge, and then we're going to blow it up to slow the advance of the Russians."

Making their way north toward Danzig, Meta and her mother were fortunate to find a succession of rides on army vehicles for five miles, then ten miles, then five miles again. They had left nearly all of their possessions back in Marienwerder and knew when they left that they would probably never see their home again. She later wrote, "It was a very, very sad day." They had heard refugees from farther east telling how the Soviets were destroying homes, and they had no desire to return to see what had happened. From Danzig, they tried to find a train to transport them farther west.

Meta Semrau and her mother always seemed to be just one step ahead of the invaders. They probably would not have survived the hectic journey west had they not been transported many times for short distances by the retreating German soldiers. One night, they knocked on the door of a farmhouse to ask for a bite to eat and the privilege of sleeping in the barn. The farmer's wife nearly turned them away but then paused and said, "Why not? After all, we'll probably be refugees like you very soon."

Meta and her mother crossed most of eastern Germany on their flight and ended up in the town of Stendal, about one hundred miles directly west of Berlin. It was there that the invading enemy arrived just one week before the end of the war. The Semrau family had survived the ordeal but had been totally cut off from the Church for four months. They had not escaped the war without sacrifice, but Meta and her mother recognized the hand of the Lord in preserving their lives, though her two brothers had lost theirs.

The first soldiers to enter Dahlen in April 1945 were Americans. However, they were soon replaced by Soviet occupation forces. Several officers chose the home of Gertraude's Aunt Lidia for their headquarters and evicted the inhabitants. Had Sister Bsumek been allowed to stay in that home, she would have been safe from marauding soldiers (who feared their officers). Instead, she moved out and found rooms with a Mrs. Pönitz close by. Now she had to be on guard against Red Army soldiers who were hunting for young women. Gertraude Bsumek was still a child at the time and did not understand the soldiers' intentions, but she did understand fear and physical danger:

> One day, a Russian officer tried to rape my mother. I was only seven, and I didn't understand what his purpose was, but I heard her screaming and raced upstairs and burst into the room and saw him with her on the bed. I began to pound him and hit him as hard as I could. Well, he jumped up and backed away and left. And later on, he actually came back and apologized for what he was doing. I was too young; I didn't know what all this meant.

As had happened so many times before, a smiling providence had provided a way for a young mother to escape unspeakable suffering. Another blessing came in the early return of Edwin Bsumek. His English captors had decided to release him after just a few months of incarceration. He was united with his family in September 1945. Several months later, the family was reunited with the Church.

From Elbing, Waltraut Schibblack, her husband, and her in-laws went northwest to Danzig, then west to Kolberg, and then to Stettin, where they were fortunate to find places on a military train to Berlin. They ended up in Bertelsdorf in western Germany, safe and sound.

By the summer of 1946, all of the surviving members of the Elbing Branch had left or been forced out of the area and had found new places to live several hundred miles to the west. The Elbing Branch had ceased to exist.

In Memoriam

The following members of the Elbing Branch did not survive World War II:

Ingrid Margot Herrig b. Elbing, Westpreußen, Preußen 30 Jun 1939; dau. of Paul Richard Herrig and Gisela Margot Martha Bsumek; d. whooping cough 27 Nov 1939 (CHL CR 375 8 #2458, 1939 data; IGI)

Fritz Gustav Semrau b. Nekla, Posen, Preußen 26 May 1920; son of Hermann Emil Semrau and Marie Martha Hildebrandt; bp. 14 Jun 1928; gunner first class; d. B. Stadniza, 10 km south of Semljansk, field hospital 239 24 Aug 1942; bur. Stadniza, Woronesh, Russia (Semrau; *Sonntagsgruss*, no. 20, Oct 1942, 80; IGI; www.volksbund.de)

Wilhelm Hermann Semrau b. 23 Oct 1916 Herne, Westfalen, Preußen; son of Hermann Emil Semrau and Marie Martha Hildebrandt; bp. 23 Oct 1924; d. malaria Marienwerder, Westpreußen, Preußen 1944; bur. Marienwerder (Semrau; IGI)

Notes

1. See the Danzig District Chapter for details on this confusing geopolitical situation.
2. Meta Semrau, interview by the author, Salt Lake City, October 27, 2006.
3. Getraude Bsumek Arndt, interview by the author, Sandy, Utah, November 10, 2006.
4. Presiding Bishopric, "Financial, Statistical, and Historical Reports of Wards, Stakes, and Missions, 1884–1955," CR 4 12, 257.
5. Waltraut Naujoks Schibblack, telephone interview with Jennifer Heckmann in German, February 15, 2008; summarized in English by Judith Sartowski.

Wobesde Branch

The members of the Wobesde Branch of The Church of Jesus Christ of Latter-day Saints must have felt quite isolated. Theirs was the only branch of the Church for miles in any direction, being about 130 miles east of Stettin and sixty-five miles west of the Free City of Danzig, the center of the Church district to which Wobesde belonged. To attend district conferences, the members from Wobesde had to first cross the border into Poland, then cross another border into Danzig. Jürgen Pawelke (born 1929) remembered making the trip to Danzig: "As we passed through the Polish Corridor, we had to close the windows and shut the blinds in the train."[1]

Wobesde Branch[2]	1939
Elders	3
Priests	0
Teachers	1
Deacons	5
Other Adult Males	3
Adult Females	21
Male Children	1
Female Children	3
Total	37

Jürgen described the setting for Church meetings at home in Wobesde:

At the beginning of the war in 1939, we met in Sister Marie Kutschke's home.[3] Her husband was not a member. She had a fairly large living room where we could all meet. At that time, our branch had 33 [37] registered members and about 45 people attended the meetings. We did not have a problem to find some space to sit, and we were all very comfortable. We held our meetings there until the end of the war. Our branch president was Hermann Heise. We had our Sunday School at 10:00 A.M. and our sacrament meeting at 6:00 P.M. on Sundays. We also held a teachers' improvement meeting, Relief Society, and Primary during the week—all at the Kutschke home.

Jürgen's sister, Brigitte (born 1935), recalled the following about the family's attendance at Church meetings:

In the morning, we had Sunday School and then in the evenings, our sacrament meeting. My parents made sure that all of their children went—there was no excuse. During the week, we held the other meetings, but I cannot remember that my parents went very often because we lived a little ways from the town.[4]

The fact that there were more persons attending the church meetings than were registered members of the Church may seem like

the results of an enthusiastic missionary effort. However, there was always the possibility that some of the visitors had ulterior motives. As Jürgen expressed later, "We also had to be careful because we were not sure if somebody was watching us or not. There were more people attending than were registered, and we never knew if those watching were friends or not."

In 1939 (when he turned ten), Jürgen Pawelke was inducted into the Jungvolk with his classmates, but he was not enthusiastic about the program. Fortunately, his work on the family farm (about one mile from town) prevented him from attending the meetings, and nobody caused him any trouble about that. His father had been drafted at the onset of the war, leaving Jürgen as the man on the farm, but his father was released very soon and came back to assist with the farm work. Their main daily task was to collect and transport 120 to 140 cans of milk (each about five gallons in volume) by wagon to Stolpmünde, six miles to the west.

The Pawelke family lived in an area populated by both Germans and Poles. To children unaware of politics and world events, it mattered little who was who. According to Brigitte, "As a child, I always played with my cousin, and we also played with the Polish children. We did not have any problems. The Polish had their own traditions when it came to playing, and we were also allowed to use what they had."

Conducting baptismal ceremonies was an adventure in the Wobesde Branch. According to Jürgen Pawelke, the members walked a mile or two to the coast of the Baltic Sea, and three persons waded out to a spot that was sufficiently deep. He explained: "The third person was there to prevent anybody being carried away by the current. Sometimes, young people would follow us and make fun of us, but we didn't have to do it in secret."

Jürgen participated in the religion course at school when he and his classmates approached

Fig. 1. Members of the Wobesde Branch in the early war years. (W. Kindt)

the age of fourteen, the age at which most Lutheran youth are confirmed in their church. The pastor who conducted the catechism course praised Jürgen and other Latter-day Saint youth, because, as Jürgen recalled, "we were his best students because we already knew everything he wanted us to learn." The pastor also commented that he wished he would see as many members of his church in his services as the Mormon branch president saw in his.

A small branch in Germany during the war had a bit more flexibility than a large branch when it came to scheduling meetings. Jürgen recalled the following:

> We had many activities in our branch. When there was nice weather, we went to a member's home that was close to a forest, and we held our Sunday School and our sacrament meeting in that forest. We never asked anybody for permission. We always sang hymns. At the beginning, we did not have any instruments, but my uncle had a violin with which he gave us the starting note. During the war, we also bought an organ, and I even received some lessons, and I tried to play some songs. Later, we had a sister from Danzig, Rose Eichler, who stayed with us, and she accompanied us during the war.

Rose Eichler (born 1930) had been sent to Wobesde as part of the general effort to evacuate children from Danzig as the air raids against the port increased in frequency and severity. She was quite happy in the little town

and enjoyed attending church with the branch there. "Meetings were held in Aunt Kutschke's house," she wrote. Her MIA teacher was a young lady named Gerda Hoeppner. "I just loved her. I always thought that she was so close to being perfect. When I was with her, it always made me feel that I wanted to be good and to improve myself."[5]

As was true with many rural communities in Germany, Wobesde did not suffer from the direct effects of the war until the last few months of the conflict. According to Jürgen Pawelke,

> We never had a disruption in our church meetings until the end of the war. The Russians came into our area on March 9, 1945, a Friday, and the following Sunday we did not have our meetings, but the week after that everything was back to normal. Wobesde was not damaged during the invasion. After that, our branch [leaders] advised the women to never go alone.

In the weeks following the arrival of the Red Army in Wobesde, the danger of women being assaulted was severe. According to Jürgen Pawelke, "We always hid about forty [women from Wobesde] at night since we lived on a farm a little ways from the town."

Rose Eichler visited her parents in Danzig one last time in early 1945. Her parents decided that she would be safer back in Wobesde, so she returned, making the entire trip by herself at the age of fourteen. As was true for the entire family, she was no more or less safe in either location. The danger she faced in Wobesde when the invaders arrived on March 9, 1945, was a kind of mental torture. For months, she lived in constant dread of physical abuse.[6]

Brigitte Pawelke was only ten years old when enemy soldiers stormed through the town. She probably had no idea why the soldiers ransacked the houses searching for women and girls, but she was frightened nonetheless:

> One night, I thought that I would not survive, when a Russian soldier broke open the door and

222

I was lying in bed. He told us that he wanted the girls to come with him and if we did not obey his command, he would do something horrible to us. The first thought that we had was to pray and each person said his or her own prayer. A little later, an officer came inside and threw the soldier out. He apologized for his behavior. I never forgot that experience.

Hiding in every possible nook or cranny, Rose Eichler and other members of the Wobesde Branch wept and prayed constantly as marauding Soviet soldiers searched for female victims among the local population. Time and again, Rose was within a few feet of disaster, and she soon concluded that chance was not the reason for her escape:

> The first time something like this happened, or the second time, or even the third, you could have thought this was coincidence that we were not found. But I'm certain this was not the case, for it happened over and over again. I'm sure that it was Heavenly Father who heard and answered our prayers.[7]

Rose and her friends became experts in stealth, quickly learning how best to escape the omnipresent soldiers. Although the women stayed inside two specific buildings for one month each, there were many occasions when they ran through fields of grain or sought refuge in the cemeteries "that the superstitious Russians" would not enter ("at night we were superstitious too, and we didn't want to go and hide there").[8]

During the summer of 1945, some of the Wobesde Saints contracted frightful skin conditions—likely a result of their poor food supply. Rose later wrote of the sufferings:

> We would break out with pus-filled blisters all over. I remember waking up one day and part of my hand was all covered with small, pus-filled blisters. Others had other types of sores all over them. And the Russians brought lice in, and we didn't know how to get rid of them. Somebody decided we would use kerosene oil and we put

that on our heads. It killed the lice all right, but it nearly killed us too![9]

When the Polish took over the territory around Wobesde, Rose and her friend Ruth Pawelke were forced to work as cleaning women in a police station. One day, they were beaten severely with a rubber club with apparently no provocation. The next day, they were able to attend a fast meeting with surviving Saints in a schoolhouse. Tears streamed down their faces as they bore testimony. "I can still feel that," Rose wrote years later:

> There was this feeling that we were completely in their power. They could take everything away from us; they could hurt us; they could beat us; they could even kill us if they chose to. But there was one thing they couldn't touch, and that was our faith.[10]

In the fall of 1945, Ernst Eichler was asked by the leaders of the East German Mission to return from Berlin to Danzig in search of Saints needing help to evacuate the area. As part of his dangerous rescue mission, he made his way to Wobesde where he found his daughter, Rose. Brother Pawelke took them by wagon to Stolp, where they boarded a train for Germany (in the meantime, Brother Eichler had gone off in search of other Saints). On the way, the Saints witnessed several terrifying events and a great deal of suffering. Finally arriving at the mission home in Berlin, they were welcomed and cared for then sent south to join the colony of Latter-day Saint refugees at Wolfsgrün, where Rose saw her mother for the first time in nearly a year. Soon, all of her sisters were located and the Eichler family was reunited.[11]

Just as other ethnic Germans living in and near Wobesde, the Latter-day Saints of the Wobesde Branch were soon expelled from what had become Polish territory in 1945. For the Pawelke family, the move took place on Jürgen's eighteenth birthday, July 27, 1947. The Polish

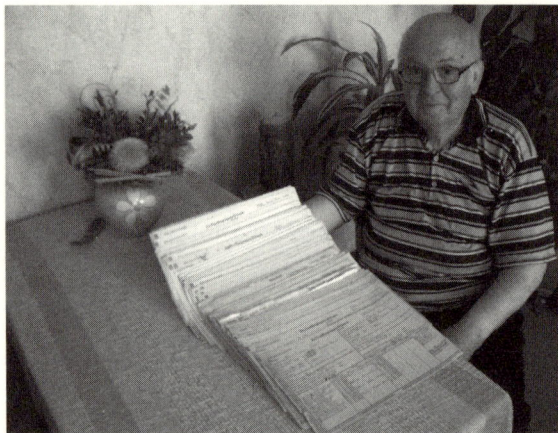

Fig. 2. Jürgen Pawelke holds the many family group records his mother took along when the family was forced to leave their farm in 1947. (J. Larsen, 2007)

mayor had informed the family the night before that they must prepare to leave. They dressed in several layers of clothing and took all of their Church literature. This included more than one hundred family group records prepared by a Brother Czerwinski of the Elbing Branch. The Pawelkes were sad to leave the farm that they had worked so long, but they had no choice. Life there had become intolerable.

"Even though the war was difficult, the Church was always a center of attraction for us," explained Brigitte Pawelke regarding the importance of the Church to its members. Brigitte was eleven when the order came to leave Wobesde. She recalled the process vividly:

> When we left, we were first taken to Stolp on a wagon pulled by horses. We could take whatever we could carry. Then we boarded a train in Stolp and stayed in a wagon that was used for animal transportation before. We had some straw and some blankets. It was a very long trip. We did not go through every station automatically. We had to wait before somebody let us through, and the food was terrible—if we even had any at all.

The Pawelkes rode the train to Germany, first to Forst on the Neisse River then to Anneberg by Torgau. With their departure, the Wobesde Branch passed into history.[12]

In Memoriam

The following members of the Wobesde Branch did not survive World War II:

Artur Fritz Ferdinand Gennrich b. Wobesde, Stolp, Pommern, Preußen ca. 1923; son of Albert Richard August Gennrich and Meta Elisabeth Puttkammer; bp. 8 Aug 1937; m. 1945; k. in battle 1945 (R. Eichler; IGI; J. Pawelke)

Erwin Franz Wilhelm Lawrenz b. Wobesde, Stolp, Pommern, Preußen 20 Apr 1922; son of Karl Max Wilhelm Lawrenz and Marta Herta Auguste Franke; bp. 8 Aug 1937; soldier 28th Jäger Division; k. in battle H.V. Pl. Utschno Sanko 5, Russia 18 Aug 1942; bur. Korpowo, Russia (*Sonntagsgruss*, no. 20, Oct 1942, 80; R. Eichler; J. Pawelke; IGI; www.volksbund.de)

Heinz Ewald Lawrenz b. Wobesde, Stolp, Pommern, Preußen 12 Jan 1921; son of Karl Max Wilhelm Lawrenz and Marta Herta Auguste Franke; soldier; k. in battle 1942 (*Sonntagsgruss*, no. 20, Oct 1942, 80; R. Eichler; J. Pawelke; IGI)

Horst Herbert Voge b. Schneidemühl, Preußen 15 Dec 1921; son of Emil Otto Voge and Alma Olga Riewe; bp. 15 Dec 1929; d. Lauenburg or Schneidemühl, Pommern, Preußen 20 Mar 1940 (*Sonntagsstern*, no. 17, 26 May 1940, n.p.; IGI; AF)

Notes

1. Jürgen Pawelke, interview by the author in German, Halberstadt, Germany, May 31, 2007 unless otherwise noted, summarized in English by Judith Sartowski.
2. Presiding Bishopric, "Financial, Statistical, and Historical Reports of Wards, Stakes, and Missions, 1884–1955," CR 4 12, 257.
3. According to official records, the branch was still meeting there in January 1943. East German Mission, "Directory of Meeting Places" (unpublished, 1943); private collection.
4. Brigitte Pawelke Prautzsch, telephone interview by Judith Sartowski, February 25, 2008; transcript/audio of interview in author's collection.
5. Rose Eichler Wood, autobiography (unpublished), 11; private collection.
6. Ibid., 15–16.
7. Ibid., 17.
8. Ibid., 18.
9. Ibid., 21.
10. Ibid., 22.
11. Ibid., 23–25.
12. The Polish name of Wobesde is Objazda.

DRESDEN
DISTRICT
East German Mission

With the sixth-largest district population of Latter-day Saints in the East German Mission in 1939, the Dresden District was located in the south-central area of the mission. The district's neighbors were the Chemnitz District to the west, the Leipzig District to the northwest, the Spreewald District to the northeast, the Breslau District to the east, and the country of Czechoslovakia to the south.

Dresden District[1]	1939	1940	1941	1942
Elders	44	47		
Priests	11	13		
Teachers	27	23		
Deacons	60	56		
Other Adult Males	124	130		
Adult Females	429	430		
Male Children	38	36		
Female Children	42	45		
Total	775	780	775	766

When World War II broke out in September 1939, the Dresden District consisted of branches in the following cities: Dresden, Freiberg (eighteen miles southwest of Dresden), Nössige (fifteen miles northwest), Bischofswerda (twenty-five miles northeast), Bautzen (forty miles northeast), and Görlitz (seventy miles northeast). According to the testimonies of eyewitnesses, there were two branches in Dresden by 1943: Altstadt (south of the Elbe River) and Neustadt (north of the river). When the war began, Max Hegewald of Freiberg was serving as the district president.

The East German Mission history includes an entry regarding the establishment of a new branch in Grosshartmannsdorf in January 1939. However, the mission membership records do not show any such branch at the end of 1939, and as of this writing, no surviving eyewitnesses from the Grosshartmannsdorf Branch have been identified.[2]

Max Hegewald was a bailiff for the city court in Freiberg. Born in 1897, he had served in

Fig. 1. The branches of the Dresden District.

Fig. 2. *The official announcement and invitation to the 1940 fall conference of the Dresden District. (K. Bartsch)*

World War I and lost an eye, thus making him unfit for military duty. According to his daughter, Judith (born 1924), he also carried in his skull a bullet that could not be removed, which was the cause of constant and severe headaches. "My father was a very steadfast man. During the war, the traveling for him [became] more difficult because he could not take public transportation that often anymore," Judith explained.[3]

Rudolf Hegewald recalled that his father was very busy as the district president. "He was very seldom in Freiberg. He visited all of the branches in the district and even went to district conferences as far away as West Prussia [Schneidemühl District] and East Prussia [Königsberg District]."

In 1944, the German government announced that all older men and men usually classified as unfit were to be inducted into the Volkssturm (home guard). President Hegewald thus found himself back in uniform but was fortunate to stay close to home and avoid combat in the final months of the war.[4]

Heinz Hegewald explained that his father was a member of the Nazi Party "due to his occupation. All government employees had to be members of the party." President Hegewald's sons did not recall that their father had any

Fig. 3. *The palace of the king of Saxony in Dresden stood as a burned-out ruin until the 1990s. (R. P. Minert, 1987)*

226

Fig. 4. Dresden's Frauenkirche was one of the many cultural monuments destroyed in the firebombing of February 13–14, 1945. (R. P. Minert, 1987)

interest in politics or participated in Nazi Party meetings. As far as they knew, his work as district president was never hindered by his occupation.

The mission records indicate that in January 1943, a group of Saints held church meetings in the small town of Rechenberg-Bienenmühle, about twenty-one miles south of Dresden as the crow flies and two miles from the Czechoslovakian border. There is no indication of how many members were living in the area, but it was likely the case of a family or two, and perhaps they were refugees from areas hit hard by the war. The address of the meeting place was Muldenthalstrasse 41.[5]

Despite the condition of Dresden after the catastrophic firebombing of February 13–14, 1945, a district conference was held there on Sunday, April 29, 1945. The rooms of the Altstadt Branch had been totally destroyed and those of the Neustadt Branch confiscated for refugee housing, so the conference was held in a Lutheran Church building in Neustadt. Both Margot Burde and Edith Schade had recollections of that conference. Both recalled attending the Sunday meetings while hearing the Soviet artillery and tanks in the distance. The invaders arrived in downtown Dresden the next day.

In light of the widespread destruction in that area of Germany, it is remarkable that when World War II came to an end, members of most of the branches in the Dresden District of the East German Mission still had a

place to meet and that meetings were still being held. After only slight interruptions caused by the victorious Allied armies in this region, the branches were alive and well and looking forward to better times.

NOTES

1. Presiding Bishopric, "Financial, Statistical, and Historical Reports of Wards, Stakes, and Missions, 1884–1955," CR 4 12, 257.

2. East German Mission Quarterly Reports, January 15, 1939, no. 53, East German Mission History.

3. Judith Hegewald, interview by the author in German, Schwerin, Germany, June 11, 2007; summarized in English by Judith Sartowski.

4. Rudolf Hegewald and Heinz Hegewald, interview by the author, Salt Lake City, January 19, 2007.

5. East German Mission, "Directory of Meeting Places" (unpublished manuscript, 1943); private collection.

BAUTZEN BRANCH

The city of Bautzen is located forty miles east-northeast of Dresden on the main railroad route from Dresden east to Breslau in Silesia. In 1939, the city had a population of about forty thousand people. The branch membership was only forty-nine persons when World War II began. It is interesting to note that nearly three-quarters of the members were adult females.

Bautzen Branch[1]	1939
Elders	2
Priests	0
Teachers	2
Deacons	1
Other Adult Males	6
Adult Females	36
Male Children	1
Female Children	1
Total	49

The meetings of the Bautzen Branch were held at Gerberstrasse 16 in the apartment of the Nikol family. Hermann and Martha Nikol had two sons and two daughters. Marianne (born 1922) recalled that her father was the branch president and the only elder still active after the first year or two of the war. Some members lived out of town, and transportation became increasingly problematic. "Sometimes we only had three or four people in our meetings," Marianne explained.[2]

On the other hand, Marianne told of holding meetings at other locations:

> We also met in some restaurants during the war. We had nice rooms until the missionaries left, then we lost those. We rented the back rooms of hotels or restaurants. One was in Nordstrasse [the Gewerkschaftshaus] and another was Gaststätte [restaurant] Spenke in Wendischer Graben [where we held meetings for some time].

The Nazi Party was not a positive factor in the life of the Nikol family. Hermann declined to join. According to Marianne, "Thanks to his opposition, I was denied a place in a higher school, or so a teacher told me." She instead attended business school for two years, during which time the war started.

Besides the absence of young men and the occasional tragic news from the battle front, the war did not come home to Bautzen until the last year. Marianne recalled shortages of food, but explained that ration cards were not used in Bautzen: "The merchants would run out of [certain items]; then they would tell us to come back when there was more." Other shortages were also apparent, such as in the world of entertainment. Marianne explained that dances were cancelled and movies were rare in her town.

From 1942 to 1945, Marianne was assigned to the staff of the regional Wehrmacht command office near Radebeul (northwest of Dresden). One of the privileges of the office was that she and her friend were allowed to issue themselves passes for public transportation until the firebombing of Dresden occurred on February 13–14, 1945. Marianne gave this account of conditions at the time:

> That night [February 13] we had to walk for ninety minutes to our apartment because the streetcars did not run. From there we could see the flares over the city. It was horrible. We watched as the planes attacked the city. . . . Then we saw the planes coming at noon [February 14]. It was really terrible. After the attacks, I saw the downtown. It was a catastrophe. You cannot possibly imagine how terrible it was. [Many] people were burned [to death], and the survivors had swollen red eyes from the smoke.

A few days later, Marianne used one of her self-produced passes to take the train home to Bautzen. Soon after her arrival, it was time for civilians to flee the city: the Red Army was approaching. Marianne's description of the family as refugees reflects reality for most Germans living in the path of the invaders:

> When we left, we took a Leiterwagen with some bags of clothing and bed linens.[3] We put our grandma with her heart condition on top, my three-year-old brother on her lap. My sister and my mother pulled the wagon, and I pushed. We left the city near the end of the war [April 1945]. . . . We walked from Bautzen [southwest] to Neukirchen and on to Bad Schandau [by the Czech border].

Near Bad Schandau, they encountered their father, Hermann Nikol, who had been inducted into the Volkssturm (where he was fortunate to be assigned noncombat duties). Brother Nikol told his wife and his daughters to go back to Bautzen as fast as they could; he believed that they would be safer there. They hurried through the night to complete the journey of twenty miles home. As they entered the city over an obscure bridge on the south side of town, they could see that many structures in Bautzen were still burning.

To their relief, Sister Nikol and her daughters learned that their home was intact—except for the damage done by enemy soldiers who had quartered there for several days. Marianne described their home in May 1945:

> Our windows were broken, but we were able to use our shutters to close the opening, and we could lock those. It was dark, but we were safe. We used wood and cardboard to cover the windows. We were very fortunate. Our cellar was cut out of stone and went back into the yard, but you couldn't tell it was there, so it had not been ransacked. My mother had put up lots of potatoes and bottled fruits, so we had food to eat when we got home.

Now and then, Red Army soldiers came to the door of the Nikol apartment. Because they seemed to have evil intentions, Marianne's aunt kept a constant vigil. She was fluent in both Russian and Polish and was therefore able to give them a good tongue-lashing whenever she felt that they were after her nieces. She did indeed save the girls from abuse.

With the war over in May 1945, the Latter-day Saint branch in Bautzen slowly came back to life. There is no record of any members of the Bautzen Branch losing their lives in World War II.

NOTES

1. Presiding Bishopric, "Financial, Statistical, and Historical Reports of Wards, Stakes, and Missions, 1884–1955," CR 4 12, 257.
2. Marianne Nikol, telephone interview with the author in German, June 26, 2008; summarized in English by the author.
3. The typical Leiterwagen was the size of a Bollerwagen, but had frames like a ladder (*Leiter*) rather than solid panel sides. Cardboard could be added to make the frame sides into panel sides. See the Halberstadt chapter for a photograph of a Leiterwagen.

BISCHOFSWERDA BRANCH

Members of the Bischofswerda Branch could attend district conferences in Dresden. The train ride took them twenty-five miles to the southwest in less than one hour. The branch was not large, but the Saints there had and exercised great faith in the Lord. For example, the following was reported in the history of the East German Mission:

> Mon 5 Dec 1938: Elder Otto Hass, president of the Bischofswerda Branch, Dresden District, was called to administer to an eight-year-old friend of the Church, who was sick with diphtheria. On the day following the administration, the child was completely recovered.[1]

Bischofswerda Branch[2]	1939
Elders	1
Priests	0
Teachers	1
Deacons	3
Other Adult Males	3
Adult Females	14
Male Children	4
Female Children	3
Total	29

In early 1939, the branch meetings were held at Brauhausgasse 1 in a Hinterhaus, with access from the Albertstrasse.

Unfortunately, the mission history after 1941 has not been preserved, and little else is known of the Bischofswerda Branch during World War II. Heinz Koschnike was the only eyewitness available at the time of this writing. He did not come to Bischofswerda until 1946, when he and his family were evicted from Breslau along with other members of the three LDS branches in that city. Government officials assigned them living space in Bischofswerda and in the neighboring town of Rammenau.

Heinz described how the survivors of the small branch welcomed the LDS refugees, who greatly increased their numbers:

> On Sunday we went to church. That was in a Hinterhaus, and there was a winding staircase. Those [three] older sisters who had prayed for us were so thrilled to have their prayers answered, and they greeted us with tears. There were too many of us to even fit in the rooms. There were about one hundred of us. That was in September 1946.[3]

The "three older sisters" mentioned informed the refugees that they had been praying for a long time for the Lord to send priesthood holders to their town. By the end of the war, fully one-third of the members of the branch had died. Thanks to the refugees, the Bischofswerda Branch had experienced a virtual rebirth.

IN MEMORIAM

The following members of the Bischofswerda Branch did not survive World War II:

Emma Martha Bellack b. Schmoelln, Bautzen, Sachsen 23 Dec 1879; dau. of Johann Carl Gottfried Bellack and Anna Marie Flachs; bp. 23 Oct 1927; conf. 23 Oct 1927; m. Bischofswerda, Bautzen, Sachsen 1 Aug 1903, Ernst Willi Sturm; 5 children; 2m. Bischofswerda 10 Aug 1918, Emil Gustav Max Boden; 1 child; d. typhus Bautzen, Bautzen, Sachsen 9 Dec 1941 (CHL CR 375 8, reel #2427, no. 69; IGI)

Otto Hermann Paul Hass b. Stettin, Pommern, Preußen 4 Sep 1867; son of Christian Friedrich Erdtmann Hasse and Caroline Dorothea Luise Schuenemann; bp. 25 Feb 1903; conf. 25 Feb 1903; ord. teacher 19 Nov 1903; ord. priest 13 Oct 1912; ord. elder 13 Sep 1914; m. Spandau, Berlin, Brandenburg, Preußen 19 Dec 1892, Anna Franziska Juliane Hinze; 6 children; 2m. Bischofswerda, Bautzen, Sachsen 5 Dec 1931, Johanne Gertrud Kettner; 2 or 5 children; d. exhaustion Bischofswerda 27 Jul 1942 (CHL CR 375 8, reel #2427, no. 52; AF; IGI)

Anna Pauline Hempel b. Wilthen, Bautzen, Sachsen 2 Nov 1879; dau. of Karl Hempel and Karoline Kaulfuss; bp. 29 May 1938; conf. 29 May 1938;

m. 11 Jan 1905, Karl Gustav Richter; d. accident 28 Jul 1944 (CHL CR 375 8, reel #2427, no. 68; IGI)

Hermann Paul Lange b. Plagwitz, Breslau, Schlesien, Preußen 23 Jan 1906; son of Karl August Lange and Anna Ida Klara Lehmann; bp. 17 May 1933; m. 28 Dec 1930; MIA 1944 or d. 1945 (CHL CR 375 8 2458, 1410; CHL 2458, form 42 FP, pt. 37, 1949 list: 1410–11; IGI)

Karl Otto Rudolf Quente b. Borau, Bautzen, Sachsen 2 Nov 1919; son of Otto Karl Quente and Johanna Gertrud Kettner; bp. 18 Aug 1928; conf. 18 Aug 1928; ord. deacon 7 Mar 1934; m. 19 Apr 1943, Martha Kuliberta Foswalde; MIA Russia 1942 or 1943 (CHL CR 375 8, reel #2427, no. 113; IGI; AF)

Kurt Walter Quente b. Bischofswerda, Bautzen, Sachsen 20 Nov 1920; son of Karl Otto Quente and Johanna Gertrud Kettner; bp. 31 Mar 1929; m.; d. 17 Mar 1945 (IGI)

Karl Gustav Richter b. Neukirch, Breslau, Schlesien, Preußen 29 Sep 1874; son of Karl August Richter and Christiane Beck; bp. 13 Jul 1941; conf. 13 Jul 1941; m. 11 Jan 1905, Pauline Richter; d. accident, 28 Jul 1944 (CHL CR 375 8, reel #2427, no. 88; IGI)

Erich Helmut Roethig b. Neugersdorf, Zittau, Bautzen, Sachsen 22 Oct or Dec 1919; son of Karl Erich Roethig and Frieda Elsa Gleitsmann; bp. 1 Nov 1927; m.; MIA 1944 or d. 4 Mar 1945 (CHL CR 375 8 2458, 1410; CHL 2458, form 42 FP, pt. 37, 1949 list: 1410–11; IGI)

Rudolf Johannes Schaarschuch b. Dresden, Dresden, Sachsen 5 Dec 1920; son of Richard Emil Schaarschuch and Martha Lina Rietschel; bp. 13 Jan 1929; conf. 13 Jan 1929; soldier; k. in battle near Stalingrad, Russia, 6 Sep 1942 (*Sonntagsgruss*, no. 1, 3 Jan 1943, 4; CHL CR 375 8, reel #2427, no. 77; IGI)

Heinz Erich Wolf b. Rauschwitz, Sachsen 23 May 1920; son of Erich Wolf and Elsa Selma Neumann; k. in battle Russia 14 Dec 1941 (CHL CR 375 8 2458, 744; CHL 2458, form 42 FP, pt. 37, 744–45; FHL Microfilm 245303, 1935 Census)

NOTES

1. East German Mission Quarterly Reports, 1938, no. 50, East German Mission History.

2. Presiding Bishopric, "Financial, Statistical, and Historical Reports of Wards, Stakes, and Missions, 1884–1955," CR 4 12, 257.

3. Heinz Koschnike, interview by the author in German, Bischofswerda, Germany, June 7, 2007; summarized in English by Judith Sartowski.

DRESDEN ALTSTADT BRANCH

Called the "Florence on the Elbe," the city of Dresden was truly a cultural gem in Germany in 1939. Famed internationally for its many museums and architectural monuments, the city was also known as the home of one of the most treasured brands of porcelain in Europe. The former capital city of the kingdom of Saxony, Dresden was a railroad center but otherwise had no military or industrial significance. The population of the city at the time was approximately six hundred fifty thousand.

Dresden Branch[1]	1939
Elders	18
Priests	2
Teachers	10
Deacons	20
Other Adult Males	79
Adult Females	203
Male Children	16
Female Children	17
Total	365

At the onset of World War II, the East German Mission records indicated the existence of only one branch of the Church in the city of Dresden. It was called simply the Dresden Branch, but was later referred to as the Altstadt (Old City) Branch. It is clear from eyewitness testimony that by 1942 or 1943, a second branch existed under the name Neustadt (New City) Branch. They will be treated here as two coexistent branches for most of the war. The official membership shown in the table above represents the only branch in the city at the end of 1939.

Elder Leo Van Gray of Pocatello, Idaho, was one of the last foreign missionaries to leave

Dresden before World War II began. The following entries in his diary reflect the tension felt by missionaries and Altstadt Branch members alike as peacetime drew to a close:

Thursday 24 August: The warning has come. Our trunks are to be packed and ready—in case. . . . Shortly after dinner the telegram came. After that I helped pack a stove into the Altstadt Church house.

Friday 25 August: The tension is surely growing tonight. Now things are beginning to move with fast rapidity. Never in my life have I seen things so quickly fired up. After a dinner at the Brux's a telegramm came to the house stating "Come Berlin Immediately Trunks Same Train." [Elders] McKay, Hawkes, and Montague was resting while I was writing a letter, but I immediately jumped on my bike and ran over to Mutties [Sister Schäckel] and told [Elders] Sorenson and Nuttal the sad news. The Rigby's had just left there, and I caught up with them at the German Hygiene Museum. They were very dissapointed. I went home and packed. All seven of us tried to eat at the house but were unsuccessful. . . . Went home and finished packing.

Saturday 26 August: Awoke early this morning. Everything seems to be a hustle and bustle here in Dresden. I went right out to Sister Dotters and picked up two white shirts she [had] washed for me. She was rather blue. Her husband left last night for the front. I came back to breakfast and the finals in packing. Went over to the Church house to get a Kodak for Montague and tell Sorenson to get a wagon. All trucks and horses have been confiscated this morning. We left Dresden at 12:54, arrived Berlin about 3:30.[2]

Annelies Höhle recalled that American missionaries had assisted members in renovating the rooms for the Altstadt Branch when the property was first acquired:

When we started, the missionaries were still here and helped with the construction and painting. Suddenly they were gone, and we thought, well, they will be returning soon. The branch house was dedicated in early September.[3]

Herbert Schröter recalled the departure of the American missionaries: "That was a really sad experience. They didn't want to leave Germany. They loved Dresden. . . . It happened so fast, they were gone, and the next Sunday we had no missionaries anymore. There was a lot of sadness."[4]

The rooms in which the Altstadt Branch met before the division were at Königsbrückerstrasse 62 on the main floor. Following the establishment of the Neustadt Branch, the Altstadt Branch found rooms to rent at Zirkusstrasse 33 (south of the river and just east of the downtown). The Neustadt Branch stayed on Königsbrückerstrasse, moving to number 93 (about one mile farther north).

Harald Schade (born 1930) described the rooms at Königsbrückerstrasse 62 as follows:

> Our branch met in an old restaurant. In the front there was a big grocery store and the other rooms were occupied by our branch. We had a big kitchen, an entrance hallway, the main hall with a podium, and an adjoining room. The choir sat in the first few rows on the main floor. We used the podium for a theatre club two or three times a year before the war. We had a picture of President Heber J. Grant hanging on the side wall. Above the podium there was a phrase painted: "The Glory of God Is Intelligence."[5]

The first meeting on Sunday mornings was priesthood meeting. Sunday School followed but was shortened on the first Sunday of the month to accommodate a fast and testimony meeting. Sacrament meeting was held at 6:00

Fig. 1. The chapel of the Altstadt Branch on Zirkusstrasse. The banner reads, "Truth will prevail." (K. Bartsch)

P.M. in the winter and 7:00 P.M. in the summer. There were approximately ninety people in church on Sundays. The full slate of meetings continued during the week, as Harald recalled: "We had Relief Society on Tuesday, and Monday nights we had Bible class. On Wednesday afternoons we had Primary and MIA in the evening hours. On Thursday nights we had our choir practice."

Herbert Schröter (born 1923) recalled a phrase from scripture on an embroidery hanging on the pulpit in the chapel: "'Be ye doers of the word, and not hearers only.' There was also a spiral staircase, and I remember trying to go down it to a room [in the basement] where we had our kindergarten. On the front of the building was a sign with the words 'Kirche Jesu Christi der Heiligen der letzten Tage' in black and gold."

The president of the Dresden Altstadt Branch throughout World War II was Willy Bohry.

The Schade family lived at Hindenburgufer 16 in the Altstadt. Harald Schade recalled that it took about thirty minutes to cross the Elbe and walk north to the church. Herbert Schröter often rode to church with his mother in his grandfather's car and arrived early. Between meetings on Sundays, Herbert and his mother enjoyed a good soup in a restaurant across the street or spent the time with other members of the branch.

Harald's sister, Edith (born 1919), served her Pflichtjahr from 1939 to 1940 in the home of a wealthy couple without children. Having graduated from a college preparatory school, she then applied for admission to a college for teachers. In an interview with the director, she was told that as a member of an American church, she had a very different worldview than the one espoused by Germany's government. Later, she received a letter from the ministry of education in Berlin stating that she could not be admitted to the program. "In this case," she

later explained, "it seemed to be a big disadvantage to be a member of the Church." She then found employment in a large company providing products for the military.[6]

On May 14, 1941, Max Schade (the father of Edith and Harald) passed away. After his death, his widow, Martha Schade, found a smaller apartment at Segnitzerstrasse 25 in the Neustadt. She and her children began to attend church in the Neustadt Branch.

Dieter Dünnebeil (born 1931) was baptized in the Elbe River. "We didn't have any other place to do baptisms," he explained. It was in a flood stage at the time (spring 1939), and he was a bit scared as he entered the water. "But they held on to me," he recalled.[7]

Annelies Höhle gave birth to a son named Winfried in 1942. He was born one month early and apparently showed signs of slow development early on. Sister Höhle had not heard of the Nazi program of euthanasia (so-called mercy killings) but was concerned that Winfried might be taken from her. She later described her fears:

> I had to be very careful that I never went anywhere with him where he might stand out. I didn't take him to get shots. . . . I just had to watch myself. I think still to this day that it was some sort of an inner voice telling me, "Don't go out with him." An inner feeling. And if I hadn't followed this voice, I might not have had Winfried for long. They probably would have taken him away.[8]

Herbert Schröter finished his activities in the Hitler Youth in 1941 at the age of seventeen. "We had been taught about the greatness of Adolf Hitler and how he was going to change Germany in four years' time." Then he was called into the Reichsarbeitsdienst and worked in Poland for eight months constructing an airfield. On October 6, 1941, he was drafted by the Wehrmacht and sent to Officer's Candidate School in Dresden. As he later explained:

Fig. 2. Herbert Schröter (left) running through the streets of Stalingrad under fire. This photograph was taken by his friend, who was killed minutes later. (H. Schroeter)

I was proud to be an officer cadet. I got a better uniform, better pay, better food, and I looked really nice. I was at an army post in Dresden Neustadt, not at the front like the rest of them. It lasted longer than basic training, because I had more learning to do to become an officer. And I went home every weekend, and I got to go to Church with my mother.

Herbert was still in training in Dresden when word came that his father, Bernhard Wilhelm Schröter, had been killed by partisans in the Soviet Union. "They sent his personal effects back [his money and pictures of the family] and told us that he had died for greater Germany," he recalled. By early 1942, Herbert was a lieutenant serving near Kiev, Ukraine. "At that time the German army progressed every day, we went forward and forward. . . . I fought in so many battles. . . . I was in the Sixth Army."

On November 22, 1942, the German Sixth Army was encircled in Stalingrad, and Herbert Schröter was in the middle of the city embroiled in bitter house-to-house combat. Just before Christmas, he was awarded the Iron Cross First Class for bravery, and the medal was presented personally by General Friedrich Paulus, commander of the Sixth Army. For the next few weeks, still wearing his summer uniform, Herbert endured temperatures far below zero and watched as his comrades lost ears, fingers, and toes to frostbite. By February 2, 1943, all attempts to reinforce the Sixth Army had failed and Field Marshal Paulus (recently promoted) had no option but to surrender the entire force. Some 70,000 German soldiers had been killed, and the Soviets counted 91,000 prisoners in what would become Hitler's greatest debacle of the war.[9]

As the German prisoners were being marched away from the ruins of Stalingrad, Herbert Schröter met a high-ranking officer who tried to convince him that they had essentially no chance of surviving. Herbert and a friend decided to take their chances of escape with the officer, and the three men moved bit by bit toward the side of the road. As the sun set, they dropped to the ground and tried to appear to be dead. Herbert's account continued:

> The last [Russian guard] walked by us and we looked around, nobody behind us anymore so we stood up . . . and walked back the way we came. The officer had a map and an idea about where the next village might be. It was peaceful, no shots, no nothing, just dark. . . . Then a jeep came toward us very slowly—an American jeep [produced for the Soviets]. What were we going to do? We lay by the side of the road and when they came by, we jumped up and jerked the doors open and pulled the men out. They were taken totally by surprise, speechless, not expecting anything like that. We told them to take off their coats and their guns and they were not rebellious. In the back of the jeep was a big sack of Russian bread. We made the Russians help us turn the jeep around, sliding it on the frozen road. Eric, the other soldier, knew how to drive the jeep so we headed west. But we had to be careful, because we might come upon some Germans, and they would kill us because we looked like Russians. Then a column of Russian vehicles with about fifty soldiers approached, and again we wondered what we should do. One driver stopped, rolled down his window, and spoke to us. Our driver knew a little Russian and said a few words in reply. The Russian told us that the German lines were about ten kilometers [six miles] ahead and that we shouldn't go that direction. Our man said, "Thanks for the information." They left and we drove on, stopping when we came to a forest. We made a fire and warmed up our bread. Then one man stood guard with the gun because the wolves there were really mean.

The next day, the three men abandoned the jeep and walked toward the west with the sun as their guide. After crossing territory that yielded no signs of life, they spent the second night without a fire. Fortunately, they found a haystack and crawled inside to sleep. The third night was also spent in a haystack, amid a landscape of desolation. In the late afternoon of the fourth day, they spotted some soldiers in white winter clothing on the horizon. Not knowing whether the soldiers were friend or foe, they moved very slowly in that direction until they could determine that the soldiers wore German helmets and carried German rifles:

> We ran toward them, opening our Russian coats to show them our German uniforms, while yelling "Don't shoot! We're Germans! We escaped from the battle of Stalingrad!" They took us to their commander who asked how we could have survived. We showed them our bread supply. . . . Then for three days we could eat, . . . mostly goulash and potatoes and gravy. It was really good. And we got new uniforms and stuff, and then they divided us up.

Back home in Dresden, most of the members of the Altstadt Branch were living a life still relatively free from hardship. In church, however, at least one thing was different: by January 1943, the meetings were being held at Zirkusstrasse 9. It is not known why the move took place, but city officials often confiscated large rooms to house homeless people.[10]

Throughout the war, the Latter-day Saints in Dresden were issued ration cards for food, as was the case all over Germany. Dieter Dünnebeil remembered that his family always had enough food. "You had to stand in line a lot when the stuff came in [to the stores], but it was organized." In fact, Dieter's family got by a little bit better than their neighbors, because they used their tobacco ration cards to trade for other food items. "Maybe it wasn't right, but what else could you do? You had to survive!"

In 1943, Paul Gräber sent his family from Berlin to a small town south of Dresden to live with relatives. Brother Gräber was in the

Fig. 3. Herbert Schröter (left background, circled) in the ruins of a factory during the battle of Stalingrad. (H. Schroeter)

army and wanted to know that his family was safe from the constant air raids plaguing the Reich capital. His wife and two daughters spent the rest of the war in Wittgensdorf, nine miles south of Dresden. Daughter Karin (born 1940) recalled that it took nearly three hours to get to Dresden to attend meetings in the Altstadt Branch. Because of the long trip, they could only attend one meeting each Sunday.[11]

Hitler Youth meetings took place at times on Sundays, but Harald Schade did not attend. His mother explained to the leaders that church meetings took priority, and fortunately there was no penalty for Harald's absence. In 1944, at age fourteen, he hoped to be accepted into a cavalry group of the Hitler Youth, but he was too small and was thus turned down.

Following his escape from Soviet captivity in February 1943, Herbert Schröter witnessed the gradual retreat that took the German army from deep inside Russia back toward the German Reich. It was an agonizing retreat and

the result—defeat for Germany—was clear to Herbert well in advance. In early 1945, he was taken prisoner by the Red Army in eastern Germany.

In what was likely the worst disaster to ever occur on German soil in a single twenty-four hour period, the city of Dresden was attacked by Allied airplanes on February 13–14, 1945. At the time, the city was literally overrun by thousands of refugees from the eastern German provinces, fleeing the invading Soviets. Many of the refugees were actually living in the streets, unable to find housing or still hoping to board a train for towns farther west. The justification for the attacks was the assumption on the part of the Allies that Dresden was a key railroad transportation hub and a staging center for troops to be sent to the east to oppose the Soviets. According to historian David Irving:

> By the beginning of February 1945, the capital
> of Saxony was . . . virtually an undefended city,
> although the Allied Bomber Commands might

236

well plead ignorance of this. In addition the city was . . . devoid of first-order industrial, strategic, or military targets-in-being.[12]

At 10:13 P.M. on February 13, the first British bombs were dropped on Dresden. Irving described the tactics employed against Dresden as follows:

> First the windows and roofs would be broken by high-explosive bombs; then incendiaries would rain down, setting fire to the houses they struck and whipping up storms of sparks; these sparks in turn would beat through the wrecked smashed roofs and broken windows, setting fire to curtains, carpets, furniture, and roof timbers.[13]

The second wave of Royal Air Force bombers flying at 20,000 feet released their loads over an already fiercely burning Dresden beginning at 1:24 A.M. on February 14. By the time the two RAF attacks had concluded, hundreds of bombs weighing as much as 8,000 pounds each had been dropped along with 650,000 incendiary bombs. A total of 1,400 aircraft had participated in the two attacks.[14] Rescue crews were summoned to Dresden from miles away and were already at work in the early morning hours of February 14. The city was in shock, and nobody could have imagined that the carnage was not yet over.

A member of the crew of the last British Lancaster bomber to drop its load over Dresden in the second attack later described the experience in these words:

> There was a sea of fire, covering in my estimation some 40 square miles. The heat striking up from the furnace below could be felt in my cockpit. The sky was vivid in hues of scarlet and white, and the light inside the aircraft was that of an eerie autumn sunset. We were so aghast at the awesome blaze that although alone over the city, we flew around in a stand-off position for many minutes before returning for home, quite subdued by our imagination of the horror that must be below. We could still see the glare of the holocaust thirty minutes after leaving.[15]

Just after noon on February 14—at 12:12 P.M.—the third attack began. This time it was the United States Eighth Air Force with a total of 1,350 Flying Fortresses, Liberators, and fighter escorts. The bombers dropped a total of 771 long tons of explosives on the burning city.[16] Following this bombing run that lasted only eleven minutes, American fighter planes raced low over the city, seeking out remaining targets of interest. Many concentrated their attacks on the banks of the Elbe River, where thousands of civilians had sought refuge from the flames and the smoke of the burning city.[17]

In their apartment house on the corner of Fürstenstrasse and Dürerstrasse (about one mile from the center of town), the Speth family heard the sirens at about 10:30 P.M. on February 13. A few minutes later, they huddled in their basement with their neighbors and felt the vibrations of bombs landing nearby. After forty-five minutes, they were relieved that they were still alive, and their apartment building was apparently intact. However, the power was out, and they decided to stay in the basement—a very wise decision, because within hours, the second attack began. Daughter Dorothea recalled the situation:

> It was a terrifying experience! But when the silence finally returned, we were still alive. . . . However, we were trapped in the basement. . . . The stairway, our [main] exit, was blocked by the fire. The only way out was a hole in our basement wall connecting the basement with the house next door.[18] . . . It was barely big enough to crawl through. We couldn't take anything with us. Our family and an older couple who lived on our floor managed to escape through this hole. Most of the homes in our area of the city were now destroyed or burning, and the few that remained would soon be on fire. We all realized that we needed to get away from the burning houses immediately![19]

Brother Speth began to lead the family (his wife and four daughters) directly north on

Fürstenstrasse toward the Elbe River, where they believed they would escape the fires and find better air to breathe. Suddenly, he changed directions and went east on Dürerstrasse. His wife, several yards behind, called to him to tell him to continue straight up Fürstenstrasse, but the rushing winds of the firestorm drowned out her voice. As she hesitated to follow him, preferring to take the wider street, a daughter admonished her with the words "Mom, let's follow Dad; he holds the priesthood!" Yielding to this advice, she hurried to catch up with her husband, who had turned north into the narrow Glückstrasse toward the river. A few minutes later, they were safe in one of the buildings of the Johannstadt Hospital and learned what could have happened had they gone down the wide Fürstenstrasse. Dorothea recounted that

> A neighbor lady entered the building. . . . [She and her husband] decided to walk straight down [Fürstenstrasse] to the river. Her husband . . . walked very quickly, leading the way, but she . . . could not follow so quickly and lagged behind. Suddenly she saw her husband burnt alive in front of her eyes. Unknown to anyone, liquid phosphorus from one of the bombs had covered the street. It could not be seen but was immediately ignited whenever anyone stepped on it. . . . If we had not followed our father, we would have walked right into that liquid phosphorus. I learned that night how important it is that we follow the priesthood.[20]

Dieter Dünnebeil's family lived in the suburb of Leuben, five miles southeast of the center of the city. They knew the routine when the air-raid sirens sounded: for years, they had taken their little bags and headed down into the basement of their apartment house. Nothing had ever happened before, and he was thinking that night, "Here we go again for nothing." The group huddling in their basement that night included the building's residents and many refugees as well. Later,

Dieter had a clear recollection of that tragic night:

> All of a sudden we heard from far away *boom, boom, boom*—explosions. We had only heard that once before, about two years earlier. We figured it wouldn't take long, maybe a half hour. Then the lights went out, and we knew it was serious. . . . That was around eleven o'clock, so we went to bed. Then at two o'clock, we again heard *boom, boom, boom*. The siren was right across the street from our apartment house, and it scared you out of your bed. Then we went downstairs again.

Dieter and his family were frightened by the smoke coming from downtown the next morning. American airplanes were also screaming past, searching out specific targets. There was no radio news, so they were unsure of what had happened. They did not go toward the downtown, "because we were scared now, too. We thought this was the end of the world. Nothing happened that serious before. So we just hung around, and we tried to get some more food, [you know] how you act in emergencies." Eventually, the Speth family (having spent the night in the Johannstadt Hospital) arrived at the Dünnebeil home and described the terror of the events that had taken place in their downtown neighborhood. Soon, several other LDS families, refugees from eastern Germany, were taken into the Dünnebeil apartment.

Christa Gräber (born 1934), Karin's older sister, was ten years old when Dresden was destroyed. She recalled that their mother got them out of their Wittgensdorf house when they heard the bombs fall and saw the lights of the fires from ten miles away. They hid in ditches near their home. Following the attack on Dresden, the Gräbers did not attend church for several weeks, and school ended for Christa for the year.[21]

The damage inflicted on Dresden surpassed that of any other aerial attack in Europe

1 Zeiss-Ikon factory
2 (5 miles to S.E.) Sachsenwerk factory
3 (9 miles to N.E.) Sachsenwerk factory
4 Siemens glass factory
5 Zeiss-Ikon (Goehlewerk) factory
6 Industrial Estate
7 Arsenal
8 Infantry Barracks
9 Friedrichstadt Marshalling yards
10 S.S. Rock bunker
11 Military Transport park
12 Air Zone Command H.Q.
13 Grailing cigarette factory
14 Yenidze cigarette factory
15 Central Telegraph Office
16 Löbtau gasworks
17 Neustadt gasworks
18 Wettin power station
19 Johannstadt power station
20 Oil store
21 Oil store (Shell)
22 District heating plant
23 Seidel & Naumann factory

Fig. 4. This map from Irving's The Destruction of Dresden *shows the degree of destruction in various neighborhoods. The black represents total devastation. (D. Irving)*

in World War II. Irving reported the destruction of 1,600 acres of city territory. Dresden city authorities exerted great efforts to identify the victims, but with so many refugees and transients in the city at the time, this task was daunting. The total killed was estimated at 135,000. Most of the bodies were buried in mass graves or incinerated in the streets in enormous funeral pyres. The downtown residential areas were obliterated, while the largest railroad stations, bridges, and the Neustadt army post survived with little damage.

Stories of horrific deaths are common and eyewitnesses reported seeing people as human torches emerging from basement shelters or jumping into the Elbe. However, due to the nature of firestorms, most victims died of suffocation. The flames from tall apartment houses along narrow streets needed oxygen to burn and sucked the air from the lungs of people close by. According to Irving, "Probably over seventy per cent of the casualties were caused by lack of oxygen or by carbon monoxide poisoning."[22] For days following the attack, entire groups of

civilians in air-raid shelters were found dead but in normal physical condition, the victims appearing as if they had simply fallen asleep.

Population of Dresden as of Feb. 1945	650,000
Estimated refugees in Dresden	300,000 to 400,000
Total estimated deaths on February 13–14, 1945	135,000
Homes totally destroyed	75,358
Homes badly damaged	11,500
Residential area destroyed	1,600 acres

Annelies Höhle later described the fate of the Altstadt Branch members and their meeting rooms:

[The church] was destroyed, yes. Actually, in the entire bombing, as far as I know, we lost only one sister. That was Sister Wiedemann, who lived in the center of the city, right downtown. The others all showed up after the bombing.[23]

One of Christa Gräber's vivid memories regarded conditions outside of Dresden in the weeks following the firebombing. She recalled diving into ditches on the way home when enemy fighter planes came around looking for people as targets. "I knew they were coming to shoot people, and I saw them, and we ran from our little street where we walked on, it was just a street, and threw ourselves in a ditch, and I did that many times."

The Red Army arrived in Dresden in the first week of May 1945. Residents had hoped that the Americans would get there first because rumors of Soviet misdeeds were daily fare among refugees from the east. Dieter Dünnebeil recalled that there was no fighting in his Dresden suburb of Leuben because German soldiers were intent on heading west to surrender to the Americans. Dieter's family was not harassed by the invaders, but he recalled hearing women in their neighborhood scream during the night. He remembered being happy to hear that Hitler was dead; at least the bombing would stop, he thought.

Looking back on the war, Dorothea Speth told how her family lost their home and nearly all of their material possessions. However, before the terrible air raid, living conditions had not really been bad:

> During World War II, we always had enough to eat, and we still had enough of a variety of things to eat. Things were rationed, but we still had enough sugar, we still could buy some chocolate, and we still had meat at least for Sundays or once during the week. We always had enough bread, and we always had enough potatoes. I never remember being hungry.[24]

In the summer of 1945, Paul Gräber returned from his service with the army. He had managed to escape capture and as such was one of the first Latter-day Saint soldiers to come home. However, he was suffering from a recent wound, having been shot through the mouth.

His daughter, Karin, recalled his sufferings: "I remember we sat down to eat and he always took stuff out of his mouth, always. Broken bone, broken teeth, splinters coming out of his mouth." Just three weeks later, Brother Gräber was dead. He had eaten some toadstools found in a local forest and died of poisoning.

Herbert Schröter spent part of his four years of Soviet imprisonment in Siberia. ("I didn't like that at all!") He was finally released on September 17, 1949, in Frankfurt/Oder. He had to show his release papers many times a day as he made his way back to Dresden, about 150 miles south. "When I got back to Dresden, I thought of that city quite like a child. I didn't recognize anything except the Elbe River. It was destroyed—nothing there anymore. I had to go through mountains of rubble." For nearly eight years, he had been away from home with no contact with the Church or other Latter-day Saint soldiers. As he later explained:

> When I went to war . . . my testimony was not strong. I knew the gospel was true. They told us that every Sunday. We read in the Book of Mormon and the Bible. . . . I don't know how I survived, but I prayed a lot. . . . I wasn't strong, but I gained my testimony in the war.

Dieter Dünnebeil remembered fondly the Altstadt Branch in wartime. "What kept us together was that we were like a family. We grew so close together and took every possibility and chance to be together, to see each other, and keep in contact."

At the time of the firebombing of Dresden, the Altstadt Branch probably had more than two hundred members of record. As of this writing, only two members are known to have perished during the attacks of February 13–14, 1945, but several more died from a variety of other causes.

In Memoriam

The following members of the Dresden Altstadt Branch did not survive World War II:

Theresia Amalie b. Waldenburg, Sachsen 31 Jul 1864; dau. of Carl Friedrich Paling and Christiana Theresa Berger; bp. 9 May 1929; conf. 9 May 1929; m. —— Ballmann (div.); missing as of 10 Dec 1948 (CHL, LR 2328 22, no. 174; FHL Microfilm 25717, 1930 Census; IGI)

Paul Balke b. Zeithain, Dresden, Sachsen 15 Feb 1892; son of Wilhelm Franz Balke and Emilie Ernestine Weser; bp. 14 Dec 1923; conf. 16 Dec 1923; m. 9 Aug 1924, Marta Waechtler; d. 24 Mar 1943 (CHL, LR 2328 22, no. 1; IGI)

Rudolf Erwin Baron b. Breslau, Schlesien, Preußen 8 Aug 1917; son of Alfred Fritz Baron and Meta Caecilie Antoine Kosalek; bp. 24 Mar 1934; conf. 24 Mar 1934; ord. deacon 17 Nov 1935; m. Dresden, Dresden, Sachsen 20 Jun 1942, Erika Steiner or Erika Margareth Heine; k. in battle 8 Apr 1945 (CHL, LR 2328 22, no. 177; CHL 2458, form 42 FP, pt. 37, 744–45; IGI)

Minna Erna Barthel b. Zongenberg, Thüringen 17 Sep 1911; dau. of Karl Barthel and Mina Boehme; bp. 21 Jul 1927; conf. 21 Jul 1927; missing as of 10 Dec 1948 (CHL, LR 2328 22, no. 2)

Klara Hedwig Brux b. Werdau, Zwickau, Sachsen 11 Dec 1867; dau of Adolf Brux and Anna Weidlich; bp. 20 Nov 1926; d. accident 14 Apr 1941 (*Sonntagsgruss*, no. 21, 25 May 1941, 84; IGI)

Marie Czekalla b. Mokan, Schlesien 9 Aug 1900; dau. of Franz Czekalla and Helena Schaum; bp. 31 Jan 1920; conf. 1 Feb 1920; missing as of 10 Dec 1948 (CHL, LR 2328 22, no. 10)

Karl Felix b. 1875; d. old age Dresden, Dresden, Sachsen 15 May 1941 (Schade-Krause; *Sonntagsgruss*, no. 24, 15 Jun 1941, 96)

Abraham Johannes Gommlich b. Wilschdorf, Dresden, Sachsen 28 Nov 1922; son of Max Paul Hermann Gommlich and Helene Martha Hegewald or Uhlig; MIA Stalingrad, Russia Jan 1943 (Heinz Hegewald; IGI)

Manfred Werner Gommlich b. Wilschdorf, Dresden, Sachsen 5 Aug 1925; son of Max Paul Hermann Gommlich and Helene Martha Hegewald or Uhlig; MIA Stalingrad, Russia Jan 1943 (Heinz Hegewald; IGI)

Max Paul Hermann Gommlich b. Rähnitz, Dresden, Sachsen 14 Dec 1900; son of Max Paul Hermann Gommlich and Klara Minna Mueller; bp. 21 Oct 1910; m. Raehnitz, Dresden, Sachsen or Wilschdorf, Dresden, Sachsen 27 Dec 1921, Helene Martha Hegewald or Uhlig; 2 or 3 children; MIA Stalingrad, Russia Jan 1943 (Heinz Hegewald; IGI; AF)

Klara M. Louise Herrmann b. Bülzig, Merseburg, Sachsen, Preußen 9 Aug 1869; dau. of Edward Herrmann and L. Knoblauch; bp. 7 Sep 1926; conf. 7 Sep 1926; m. —— Siegert; missing as of 10 Dec 1948 (CHL, LR 2328 22, no. 141)

Alfred Arthur Klemm b. Demnitz, Preußen 27 Feb 1883; son of Gustav Klemm and Auguste Schubert; d. old age 22 Sep 1941 (CHL CR 375 8 #2458, 1410–11)

Dora Liebsch b. Bautzen, Sachsen 24 Apr 1908; missing as of 1943 (CHL 2458, form 42 FP, pt. 37, 748; FHL Microfilm 271387, 1935 Census)

Johanna Gertrud Liepke b. Oberneukirch (?) 10 Feb 1898; dau. of Gustav Liepke and Ida Weber; bp. 20 Nov 1926; conf. 20 Nov 1926; m. —— Tietz; 2m. 3 Jun 1922, Hermann Buhr; missing as of 10 Dec 1948 (CHL, LR 2328 22, no. 153)

Willy Walter Marx b. Dresden, Dresden, Sachsen 6 Sep 1919; son of Rudolf Marx and Dora Elisabeth Scherfler; bp. 6 Jul 1938; conf. 6 Jul 1938; m. 19 Sep 1940, Edith Goldammer; d. 21 Nov 1941 (CHL, LR 2328 22, no. 86; IGI)

Amalie Auguste Mietsch b. Elsterwerda, Dresden, Sachsen 20 Jun 1863; dau of Karl Mietsch and Rosa Fichte; bp. 10 Sep 1923; conf. 10 Sep 1923; m. Mar 1889, Herrmann Boehme; missing as of 10 Dec 1946 (CHL, LR 2328 22, no. 180; IGI)

Johanna Pauline Niedergesaess b. Jenkwitz, Schlesien, Preußen 19 Jun 1858; dau.of Kurt Elschker and Johanna Charlotte Christiane Niedergesaess; bp. 19 Jun 1937; m. Meissen, Dresden, Sachsen 3 Feb 1894, Friedrich Wilhelm Stiefler; d. Dresden, Dresden, Sachsen 29 Jan 1941 (*Sonntagsgruss*, no. 11, 16 Mar 1941, 43; IGI)

Max Hermann Reschke b. Grosszschachwitz, Dresden, Sachsen 4 Aug 1907; son of Richard Paul Reschke and Emma Bertha Clara Dietrich; bp. 27 Sep 1921; m. 28 Oct 1933, Gertrud Frieda Lassmann; d. kidney disease 8 or 18 Oct 1939 (CHL CR 375 8 #2458, 1939 data; IGI, PRF)

Agnes Hildegard Rieger b. Dresden 2 Apr 1911; dau. of Joseph Rieger and Emma Worker; bp. 15 May 1924; conf. 18 May 1924; missing as of 1943 (CHL, LR 2328 22, no. 181; CHL 2458, Form 42 FP, Pt. 37, 748)

Max Emil Paul Schade b. Dresden, Dresden, Sachsen 19 May 1874; son of Karl August Leberecht Schade and Emilie Henriette Beckert; bp. 6 Oct 1905; ord. elder; m. Dresden 1 Oct 1907, Martha Clara Elisabeth Marx; 8 children; d. old age Dresden 14 May 1941 (Schade-Krause; *Sonntagsgruss*, no. 24, 15 Jun 1941, 96; CHL Microfilm MS 16596; IGI; AF)

Bernhard Wilhelm Schröter b. Grosswaltersdorf, Freiberg, Sachsen 9 Apr 1898; son of Julius Bernhard Schroeter and Marie Clara Daehnert; bp. Dresden, Sachsen 21 Oct 1922; ord. priest; m. Grosswaltersdorf 21 or 22 Sep 1922, Helene Martha Zöllner; 3 children; lance corporal; k. in battle Ramenje, Tschudowo, Russia 23 or 25 Nov 1941; bur. Ramenje, Tschudowo, Russia (Schroeter; www.volksbund.de; IGI; AF)

Elly Carlotte Schütze b. Dresden, Dresden, Sachsen 27 Nov 1913; dau. of Karl August Schütze and Marie Elisabeth Lehmann; bp. 4 Feb 1922; m. Herbert Thummler; d. as a result of air raid Dresden 13 Feb 1945 (Matt Heiss; CHL 2458, Form 42 FP, Pt. 37, 744–45; IGI)

Horst Georg Schulze b. 3 Dec 1908; son of Emma Louise Jungfer; ord. deacon; m.; MIA 1943 (CHL 2458, Form 42 FP, Pt. 37, 748; FHL Microfilm 245260, 1930/35 Census)

Hermann Helmut K. Fr. Sieber b. Dresden, Dresden, Sachsen 11 Jan 1907; son of Samuel Koch and Johanna Sieber; bp. 14 Dec 1923; conf. 16 Dec 1923; missing as of 10 Dec 1948 (CHL, LR 2328 22, no. 139)

Franz Ferdinand Helmut Speth b. Dresden, Dresden, Sachsen 30 Mar 1922; son of Joseph Speth and Frieda Hedwig Winkler; bp. Dresden 13 Oct 1930; ord. deacon; k. in battle Minsk, Bellarus, USSR 19 Mar 1943 (H. Schroeter, D. Speth Condie; G. Speth Kehaya; IGI; AF)

Selma Stuetzner b. 26 Aug 1874; bp. 16 Jul 1909; m. ——— Wiedemann; k. in air raid Dresden, Dresden, Sachsen 13 Feb 1945 (CHL, LR 2328 22, no. 183; Schade-Krause; FHL Microfilm 245299, 1930 Census)

Otto Weber b. Dresden, Dresden, Sachsen 18 Dec 1898; son of Karl Gustav Weber and Auguste Schubert; bp. 29 Jun 1910; conf. 29 Jun 1910; ord. deacon; ord. teacher 12 Sep 1920; ord. priest 3 Mar 1929; missing as of 10 Dec 1948 (CHL, LR 2328 22, no. 156; CHL 2458, Form 42 FP, Pt. 37, 748)

Max Zöllner bp. 1916; d. Dresden, Dresden, Sachsen 18 Oct 1940, age 65 (*Sonntagsgruss*, no. 45, 8 Dec 1940 n.p.)

NOTES

1. Presiding Bishopric, "Financial, Statistical, and Historical Reports of Wards, Stakes, and Missions, 1884–1955," CR 4 12, 257.
2. Leo Van Gray, diary, 1939; private collection.
3. Annelies Höhle and Ursula Höhle Schlüter, "Those Are Just Little Things," in *Behind the Iron Curtain: Recollections of Latter-day Saints in Eastern Germany*, ed. Garold N. Davis and Norma S. Davis (Provo, UT: Brigham Young University Press, 2000), 264. Because the records of the East German Mission show the Altstadt Branch meeting at Königsbrückerstrasse 62 as early as

September 1, 1938, the new construction mentioned by Sister Höhle was actually a renovation, and Leo Van Gray's record corroborates the activity.
4. Herbert Schroeter, interview by the author, Bountiful, Utah, June 21, 2007.
5. Harald Schade, interview by the author in German, Burg Stargard, Germany, June 10, 2007; unless otherwise noted, summarized in English by Judith Sartowski.
6. Edith Schade Krause, interview by the author in German, Prenzlau, Germany, August 18, 2006.
7. Dieter Duennebeil, interview by the author, Salt Lake City, May 4, 2006.
8. Höhle and Schlüter, "Those Are Just Little Things," 265–66.
9. Hellmuth Günther Dahms, "Der Weltanschauungskrieg gegen die Sowjetunion," in *Der 2. Weltkrieg: Bilder Daten Dokumente* (Gütersloh, Germany: Bertelsmann, 1968), 397. Total losses of the German Sixth Army may have been as high as 295,000 men.
10. East German Mission, "Directory of Meeting Places" (unpublished manuscript, 1943); private collection.
11. Karin Gräber Adam, interview by the author, Bountiful, Utah, April 18, 2007.
12. David Irving, *The Destruction of Dresden* (London: William Kimber, 1963), 76.
13. Ibid., 138–39.
14. Ibid., 146.
15. Ibid. The bomber in question had arrived ten minutes behind schedule and was therefore "alone."
16. Ibid., 154.
17. Ibid., 152.
18. See the description of this precaution in the introduction.
19. Dorothea Speth Condie, "Let's Follow Dad—He Holds the Priesthood," in *Behind the Iron Curtain*, 33.
20. Ibid., 35. The detail on the street names was provided by Dorothea's sister, Gisela Speth Kehaya, in a letter to the author on July 15, 2008.
21. Christa Gräber Zander, interview by the author, West Jordan, Utah, March 2, 2007.
22. Irving, *Destruction of Dresden*, 189
23. Höhle and Schlüter, "Those Are Just Little Things," 264. In reality, one other sister in the branch was killed that night.
24. Condie, "Let's Follow Dad—He Holds the Priesthood," 37.

DRESDEN NEUSTADT BRANCH

The Dresden Branch was divided in about 1942 to become the Altstadt Branch and the Neustadt Branch. Because no membership figures are available for branches of the East

German Mission after 1939, there is no way to know the membership of each branch at the time of the division. The total membership in the Dresden Branch when the war began was about 365.

Siegfried Dietze (born 1930) lived with his family in a northern suburb of Dresden. He recalled some difficulties with the National Socialists before the war:

> My father was persecuted by the Nazis in 1936 for doing business with the Jews, and I had to be removed from school because it was not safe, or so the teacher said. Once I was pushed into a swimming pool and almost drowned because the kids were told that I was a Jew friend, . . . so we had to move. And we actually moved to a place called Friedewald, which is just slightly outside the city of Dresden.[1]

Siegfried's sister, Erica (born 1924), later provided more detail about the problems her father experienced in his store:

> One day, my mother found a notice in the local newspaper, telling people to not go to my father's store because he was a friend to Jews. My father dealt with Jews because he got the best products from them. [The Nazis] were against us because of that. But it turned out that we had more business after that than before.[2]

During the war, Brother Dietze criticized Hitler within the walls of their own home. Erica recalled him saying, "How can we win this war when we have the whole world against us? That Hitler, he's crazy!"

The fact that Latter-day Saints were still active missionaries in wartime is evident from the story of the conversion of the Burde family of Dresden Neustadt. As daughter Margot Burde (born 1931) explained:

> We lived in a large apartment house, and there were three families living [on one floor]. And there was a soldier by the name of Heinz Bürger who gave my father the Book of Mormon. [Heinz] was a member of the Dresden Branch. . . . My father was always interested in the truth,

and he wanted to learn more about it. And also my mother. They were very religious people. So on October 18, 1941, my parents and I were baptized in the Elbe River. It was freezing cold. There were huge big cracks in the ice. I remember I slipped. . . . But, when I came out, I remember to this day how warm it felt. It was such a peaceful feeling, such a spiritual feeling.[3]

The Neustadt Branch met in rooms at Königsbrückerstrasse 93. Margot Burde provided the following description:

> There was a front building, and then it went down a little way, and there was one house in the middle, like a garden house. . . . We had one large room and that was the chapel and one room in the front. So we had two rooms, that little room was more like where Relief Society [sisters] met, and the priesthood holders, and the Primary, which we had during the week. There may have been thirty people in church on a typical Sunday—maybe more, counting the children.

"There was a sign out front showing the name of the Church and the times of the meetings," recalled Edith Schade (born 1919). "The rooms we used were previously a carpentry shop."[4]

The branch observed the traditional meeting schedule, with Sunday School in the morning and sacrament meeting in the evening. During the week, they met for Relief Society, Primary, MIA, and priesthood meetings. As Margot recalled, "We had old sisters teaching us in Primary on Wednesday afternoons. We loved them. We had fun times, even during the war."

At the age of ten, Margot and her schoolmates were inducted into the Jungvolk. They learned knitting and crocheting and sang lots of songs, especially patriotic songs. She was glad that the Monday meetings did not prevent her from attending church.

Richard Burde was an artist, a painter. Nevertheless, in Hitler's Germany, Brother Burde was valued more as an infantry soldier. In

Fig. 1. Dresden Latter-day Saints in 1940. (K. Bartsch)

France, Belgium, and Russia, he was fortunate to never fire his rifle at the enemy. However, he was away from his family almost constantly from the time he was drafted in 1940 to the spring of 1945.

The Burde family lived at Königsbrücker-strasse 41, just three blocks up from the Church. Margot spent her playtime with other girls of the branch, either at their homes or in church, "which was our second home anyway," she explained.

At the age of twelve, Siegfried Dietze was baptized by Karl Wöhe, the branch president, on August 29, 1943. "I was baptized in the Elbe River at six o'clock in the morning because we were not supposed to do anything in public," he later explained. His father was not very active in the Church, so Siegfried often walked to church alone, a trip that took him an hour and a half in one direction. "I stayed there all day long on Sunday. . . . [Between meetings] many of us young people would talk together, walk together, read together, and enjoy our friendship."

Harald Schade (born 1930) recalled that in the last year of the war, he was the only deacon available to pass the sacrament, and Karl Wöhe was the only elder attending meetings. Brother Wöhe worked for a newspaper and was on duty on Sundays now and then. He resorted to inviting inactive brothers to help out in his absence. Harald described the situation in these words:

> To get help, the branch president brought back inactive older men, usually elders, who could help us bless and pass the sacrament when our president had to work. One of them could not read anymore, so I knelt with him and read the prayer, and he recited it after me.[5]

During the war, Edith Schade developed excellent skills in typing and also became experienced in genealogical research. She assisted families in the branch and conducted research in church offices in the vicinity. She later recalled that on several occasions, she walked all the way to the town of Nössige (twelve miles to the west). "I remember walking two hours. . . . The branch was astonished that I took the time on my Sunday to go and help them."[6]

At the age of fourteen, Margot Burde was called to be a teacher for the six- to eight-year-old children. At first, she was disappointed to leave the class of her girlfriends, but she soon fell in love with her new calling:

> We had a lot of polkas and sang songs, and we did not have any visual aids like in America when you're teaching your Primary. No pictures, nothing. We just taught out of the Bible and out of the Book of Mormon. We had nothing to show. And the children—they just sat so still, they were so disciplined. They never went out to the toilet or went home or anything like that.

The terror of an air raid was still vivid in the mind of Erica Dietze when she gave this account of an attack on her neighborhood in 1944:

> There were fifteen of us in the basement. The bombs were already falling, and my dad said, "Everybody on the floor lengthwise! Open your mouth, because if a bomb hits us our lungs will rupture, and we'll be dead right away!" So we did that, and the bombs fell around us, and the house shook, and all of a sudden the biggest noise you could hear, a bomb fell directly on the house, and the whole house was on fire. And we were in the basement. Dad said, "Everybody up! Quickly!" Then we ran outside and jumped into a bomb crater made a few days earlier. There we waited until the air raid was over. We were safe, and nobody was hurt.

During the Christmas season of 1944, Martha Schade and her children worried about what to do with the Soviet army already on German soil. They packed a wagon and prepared to leave town, but Sister Schade had some last-minute concerns. Edith recalled the discussion:

> My mother asked us to pray with her one more time. She then said that Heavenly Father had protected our home so much that he must not want us to leave it behind now. We made the decision to stay and to [maintain] a place of peace and quiet for those who might come seeking help. That is what we did, and it was the right decision.

During the first weeks of 1945, refugees from eastern Germany began to stream into and through Dresden. Edith Schade recalled that some were Latter-day Saints, and the Schade apartment was soon full to overflowing:

> We did not invite them, and nobody asked us to take them in, but we did. They were all members—some from Görlitz and others from Bautzen. . . . Right before Dresden was attacked [on February 13], fourteen people slept on our floors. I think most of them stayed for about three weeks.

Many refugees passed the Burde apartment on Königsbrückerstrasse. Margot Burde described them as resembling "pioneers with handcarts. They filled the basement of our building when the air-raid sirens went off that night [February 13]. So many people!"

Just a week prior to the firebombing of Dresden, the residents still felt quite safe, having seen only one instance of bombs dropped on the city prior to that time. They believed that their city was of no military importance, so they must have been surprised to see the streets covered one day with papers dropped from the air with a cynical rhyme in German: "*Die Dresdner Zwerge kommen zuletzt in die Särge.*" Literally translated, it stated, "The Dresden dwarfs will be the last in the coffins." Margot Burde and other readers could hardly have imagined what the message would mean just one week later.

The infamous firebombing of Dresden, the "Florence on the Elbe," began late in the evening of February 13, 1945, and lasted through noon the next day, as described in the Dresden

Altstadt chapter. When the attacks began, Harald Schade was staying in the home of an older sister near the northern outskirts of town. He watched from afar as the city was set on fire and later gave this description:

> The city burned for at least three to four days. We did not have fire stations anymore, and there were no functional water lines left. Mother had stayed at home, so we went home [in the Neustadt] to find out what had happened to her. We found her in her bed, safe and sound. Our family home was not destroyed, but the air pressure burst the windows.

When the air-raid sirens began to wail on that fateful evening, young Peter Hans (born 1940) was living in Dresden Neustadt with his mother and had a good suggestion for her:

> I told my mother that we should kneel down and pray when the alarm went off on February 13, 1945. There was a lady who had told us that we should go into the basement with her. But we decided to go into the army post in Dresden Neustadt. We later saw that her house had been destroyed and that she had been killed. I have never forgotten it.[7]

Edith Schade had just finished assisting the Hubold family with genealogical research in their apartment in the southeastern suburb of Seidnitz when the first attack began. At the very periphery of the bombing area, that neighborhood suffered little damage during the first attack, but was hit hard two hours later. Edith had been trained in firefighting tactics and had heard of firestorms in other cities—where the fires sucked in so much oxygen that a wind was created—but she experienced it now for the first time when she went outside to assess the damage to the building:

> There was a hurricane-force wind blowing, and we could hardly stand. We made our way around the house to see if there were any more fires. The place looked like a battlefield. . . . Burning debris was flying through the air. We could not put out any of the ensuing fires because there

was no more water, and more and more burning objects were flying through the air and landing everywhere. . . . The fire and the wind became so furious that there was nothing more to do but go back into the apartment building.[8]

At seven o'clock the next morning, Edith Schade set out for home, wondering if her family in the Neustadt had survived. Despite being in very good physical condition, she needed five hours to negotiate the three miles through the rubble of the city. She passed along the eastern edge of the city center then crossed the damaged but still usable Albert Bridge. She had crossed the bridge many times before, but now the task was hazardous:

> Wherever I put my feet I felt danger, insecurity, and fear. When I finally had the bridge behind me, I looked down at the once beautiful grassy meadows that had formed the bank of the river. It was indescribable. Human bodies—or were they corpses?—lay everywhere. During the bombing, many people had run for the river—burning [human] phosphorus torches—hoping to save themselves in the water, but fighter planes had repeatedly come low over the river and strafed these helpless people. This was repeated the next day, and there lay the bodies.[9]

Most of the Altstadt was destroyed, and the damaged territory extended north across the river into the Neustadt for about one mile—to within one block of the Burde apartment. When Margot and her mother heard the all-clear sirens and emerged from the basement of their building after the final attack, they were greeted by scenes of horror. The fire and the smoke were so close that they threw water-soaked blankets over their heads to prevent suffocation. Many people were running from the flames and screaming, while a few began frantically to rescue residents trapped in basements.

Even little children can ask questions about the violence of war, as was the case when Peter Hans was near the Elbe River with his mother shortly after the attack:

After the big attack on Dresden, we also saw how German soldiers had jumped into the Elbe River to flee but how low-flying American planes still shot them, and that is how they were killed. I could not understand this as a little child. My mother held me in her arms, and only when I had gotten older did I slowly start to understand. I was so scared.

Siegfried Dietze lived far from the Dresden downtown, but was not spared a close-up experience with the firebombing. He was attending high school in Radebeul at the time, and the principal of his school sent the students downtown "to help the people in Dresden. No direction. No information. Just go help," he explained. They took the streetcar to the Neustadt, but police prevented them from entering the Altstadt. Siegfried began carrying suitcases for a woman with two children, when the American attack began just after noon on February 14. "We all panicked, and I panicked, and I just dropped the suitcases and ran. I was just barely fourteen years old."

Siegfried found shelter in a hotel basement but soon felt insecure and ran back out into the street. For a few moments, he stood next to a high retaining wall by a railroad bridge over the river. Just when it seemed that the last bomb had fallen, "something said to me, 'Run!' and I ran." Seconds later, one last bomb fell just above where he had been standing, and rocks rained down on him. His story continued:

> I fell down, of course, all of these incendiary bombs kept falling all around me, bombs that explode and started burning. And there were some other people lying around crying, and I didn't lie there too long, there were no bombs falling. It became a little quiet. I got up and I ran to the overpass behind me, and sure enough there was a little truck there with [the driver] saying, "Let's get out, let's get out!" . . . I tell you, the Lord saved me right there.

Although artist Richard Burde never fired his rifle at the enemy, he was close enough to the action on the Eastern Front in January 1945 to be shot in the knee, and he very nearly missed being taken on a hospital train heading back to Germany. He arrived in Dresden in serious condition just before the firebombing took place. Somehow word came to his wife that he was in a local hospital, and she and Margot hurried to visit him. She described the scene there—as all over town—as sad and chaotic: "So many soldiers were bleeding, and there was crying and screaming. It was awful!"

Because the precise bombing of the Allied airplanes had spared most of the Dresden suburbs, no members of the Neustadt Branch were killed. During that catastrophic air raid, the rooms of the Altstadt Branch at Königsbrückerstrasse 62 were destroyed, and the members of that branch who remained in the city joined with the Neustadt Branch. They held meetings only on Sunday evenings for the next few months. The windows of the rooms at Königsbrückerstrasse 93 were destroyed, and the members sat in cold rooms. Harald Schade recalled watching his sister, Edith, play the pump organ wearing gloves.

Following the firebombing, Harald and his mother lived without gas and electricity for several months. They had to draw their water from a well. Refugees streamed through the city as the war drew to a close. Some were Church members from the east who attended the branch meetings for a while, then moved on when they found places to live.

The devastated city of Dresden offered no resistance to the invading Red Army in the last week of the war, the first week of May 1945. As Harald Schade recalled:

> We heard artillery fire far away, then ever closer. One shell landed close to our house, and then suddenly they were there. No Russian soldier came into our house. We had heard about their deeds. We often heard women scream in the neighborhood, but the women in our house were spared. I was not sad when I heard that Hitler had died.

Margot Burde was closer to the action the day the Red Army arrived in Dresden. She later wrote that the surviving members of the Church were attending a district conference in a local Lutheran church because the rooms of the Altstadt Branch had been destroyed and those of the Neustadt Branch were filled with refugees:

> As we sat together worshipping the Lord, we heard the droning of the Russian tanks and artillery—the so-called "[Stalin] organs." They were approaching the city, but we went on with our conference. On Monday, May 7th, the Russians entered Dresden, and we saw some street fighting. . . . My mother and I watched from the window. We saw war going on in front of our eyes, soldiers shooting out of their windows.[10]

"It was May 7, 1945, and we were expecting the Americans to come," recalled Siegfried Dietze. His story continued:

> So I saw some tanks across from us going through a village which was maybe a mile away, and I shouted to my father, "The Americans are coming!" Of course, we didn't know that this wasn't the case, but an hour later a Russian soldier comes up to our house just dressed in leather pants and a leather jacket with a pistol in his hand and says, "Schnaps!" So my father gives him some liquor and some meat and puts the white flag out. . . . [There were] twenty-five Russians living in our house, sleeping overnight, raping [women]. . . . [They] took most of our stuff, my father's car, all of our bikes.

As fate would have it, after the fighting subsided, Soviet soldiers (apparently Mongolians) were parked in front of the door of the Burde apartment. Brother Burde was still in the hospital and therefore could not protect his family. When the soldiers began to loot the homes and attack the women and girls, Sister Burde braided her daughter's hair in an attempt to make her look substantially younger than her fourteen years. On one occasion, she hid Margot under a bed and was able to convince a soldier that he was mistaken in thinking he had seen another young girl in the building. The terror lasted at least a week and resulted in death for some, as Margot recalled: "Several girls were raped so many times that they died."

Not all experiences of Latter-day Saints at the hands of the invaders were tense or tragic. Edith Schade told of Soviet efforts to help the residents find food and other assistance. She called their actions "exemplary." "Most of the officers also spoke German, so we could understand them." At the same time, Edith and her sister were also realists who avoided walking around alone.

The Dietze store was out of business when the invaders came. The Soviets confiscated their three automobiles and their bicycles. Products were not to be had, so the family ceased business operations for a time. Regarding the thefts committed by the invaders, Erica later explained, "They don't tell you why, they just feel they are winning the war and everything belongs to them now."

The personal effects of Erika's brother Werner Dietze were returned to his family in Friedewald in February or March 1945. His parents had written him to report that they survived the terrible attack on Dresden, but the letter apparently arrived too late. He had been awarded the Iron Cross, Second Class on February 5. According to Siegfried, "My parents were totally devastated. Werner was supposed to come home two weeks later, but there was an attack by Russians, and he got shot in the stomach, and he bled to death."

When she recalled the spiritual condition of the Dresden Latter-day Saints during those perilous times, Margot Burde explained:

> Our Heavenly Father saved us and blessed us so much. Our prayers became more intense and our faith became unshakable. We were united in our faith. We as brothers and sisters did a lot of fasting and praying together. . . . We were such strong members of the Church. We were like a family.

Given the terrible carnage of the firebombing of Dresden, it is nothing short of remarkable that not one member of the Dresden Neustadt Branch is known to have died during that fateful night.

In Memoriam

The following members of the Dresden Neustadt Branch did not survive World War II:

Martha Louise Clauss b. Pirna, Dresden, Sachsen 30 Jun or Jul 1868; dau. of Franz Tobias Clauss and Wilhelmine Henriette Schramm; bp. 15 Jun 1934; conf. 15 Jun 1934; m. Dresden, Dresden, Sachsen 1888, Franz Foerster; 1 child; 2m. Dresden 18 or 28 Dec 1912, Karl Robert Jahn; d. old age Dresden 14 Sep 1943; bur. St. Paul's Cemetery 18 Sep 1943 (CHL LR 7093 21, no. 71; CHL LR 7093 22, 32; IGI)

Gustav Bruno Friedrich Dietrich b. Dresden, Dresden, Sachsen 10 Nov 1863; son of Arno Willibald Toepfer and Auguste Clara Dietrich; bp. 2 Jul 1927; conf. 2 Jul 1927; ord. elder 4 Sep 1932; m. Dresden 8 May 1863, Maria Theresia Kuehnel; m. Dresden 9 Feb or 11 Dec 1900, Minna Kamilla Doering; d. old age Kamenz, Sachsen 21 Oct 1943; bur. Kamenz 25 Oct 1943 (CHL LR 7093 21, no. 214; CHL LR 7093 22, 32; IGI)

Werner Martin Dietze b. Dresden, Dresden, Sachsen 5 Jun 1925; son of Max Martin Dietze and Hulda Liddy Bernhardt; bp. 11 Sep 1934; conf. 11 Sep 1934; k. in battle Riga, Latvia 25 Jan 1945 (CHL LR 7093 21, no. 229; IGI; PRF; S. Dietze)

Max Hermann Eggert b. Dresden, Dresden, Sachsen 26 Mar 1905; son of Arthur Karl Richard Eggert and Ida Ernestine Luise Steinert; bp. 11 Aug 1940; ord. deacon 25 Dec 1940; m. Dresden 22 Dec 1932, Marie Linda Goehler; 2 children; k. in battle Cadico, Futa Pass, Italy 18 Oct 1944 (IGI)

Ernst Kurt Gerlach b. Meissen, Sachsen 20 Oct 1900; son of Paul Gerlach and Marie Breitsche; bp. 21 May 1912; conf. 21 May 1912; m. 18 Jun 1932, Emma Kasselt; k. in battle 10 Feb 1945 (CHL CR 375 8 2458, 744; IGI)

Hermann Haschke b. Karbitz, Aussig, Böhmen, Austria 10 Jul 1892; son of Franz Haschke and Theresia Patzner; bp. 1 Oct 1929; conf. 1 Oct 1929; m. 31 Mar 1918, Hedwig Schreiner; d. heart attack 27 Mar or May 1941 (CHL LR 7093 21, no. 51)

Clara Wilhelmine Hoffmann b. Gelenau, Chemnitz, Sachsen 18 Aug 1859; dau. of Friedrich Christian Hoffmann and Christiana Wilhelmina Spielmann; bp. 8 Oct 1908; conf. 8 Oct 1908; d. old age 18 Mar 1942 (CHL LR 7093 21, no. 66; IGI)

Emma Bertha Hornauer b. Belyern b/ Torgau 22 Sep 1883; dau. of Friedrich H. Hornauer and Marie Winkelmann; bp. 1 Sep 1928; conf. 1 Sep 1928; m. 14 May 1937, —— Kunze; d. accidental asphyxiation 16 Jan 1940 (CHL LR 7093 21, no. 80; NG-IGI, AF, PRF)

Christine Eva Huertig b. Dresden, Dresden, Sachsen 31 Oct 1940; dau. of Reinhold Helmuth Huertig and Eva Marianne Schade; d. lung ailment 16 Sep 1941; bur. St. Mark's Cemetery, Dresden Neustadt, Dresden, Sachsen 20 Sep 1941 (CHL LR 7093 21, no. 207; CHL LR 7093 22, 26; IGI)

Anna Bertha Klaus b. Wachau, Radeberg, Dresden, Sachsen 15 Jan 1866; dau. of Friedrich August Klaus and Auguste Emilie Ziegenbalg; bp. 21 Mar 1925; conf. 21 Mar 1925; m. Wachau 16 May 1886, Julius Ernst Grossmann; 1 child; 2m. Radeberg, Dresden, Sachsen 3 Jun 1892, Ernst Phillip; d. old age 4 May 1940 (CHL LR 7093 21, no. 116; CHL LR 7093 22 23; IGI; AF)

Alfred Walter Lippmann b. Grosshartmannsdorf, Dresden, Sachsen 26 Oct 1918; son of Emil Hugo Lippmann and Alma Ida Eilenberger; bp. 23 Nov 1927; conf. 23 Nov 1927; k. in battle 8 May 1945 (CHL LR 7093 21, no. 95; CHL CR 375 8 2458, 744; CHL 2458, form 42 FP, pt. 37, 744–45; IGI)

Lina Matthes b. Oschatz, Leipzig, Sachsen 20 Dec 1869; dau. of Friedrich Wilhelm Matthes and Amalia Wilhelmine Franziska Wilsdorff; bp. 13 Nov 1925; conf. 13 Nov 1925; d. old age 6 Feb 1944; bur. Anne Cemetery, Dresden, Sachsen 11 Feb 1944 (CHL LR 7093 21, no. 99; CHL LR 7093 22, 33)

Gustav Adolf Merk b. Dresden, Dresden, Sachsen 6 Aug 1865; son of Hermann Richard Merk and Louise Ch. Dressler; bp. 2 Oct 1926; conf. 2 Oct 1926; m. 1 Apr 1891, Hedwig Polster; d. old age 4 Apr 1940 (CHL LR 7093 21, no. 100)

Johannes Georg Riedel b. Dresden, Dresden, Sachsen 31 Dec 1912; son of Karl A. Riedel and Priska M. Winkler; bp. 31 Oct 1926; conf. 31 Oct 1926; k. in battle 1944 (CHL LR 7093 21, no. 130)

Amalie Auguste Zumpe b. Karlsberg, Bautzen, Sachsen 17 May 1859; dau. of Louise Zumpe; bp. 26 Jun 1936; conf. 26 Jun 1936; m. —— Schneider; d. old age 22 May 1944 (CHL LR 7093 21, no. 143; NG-IGI, AF, PRF)

Anna Schwarz b. Grüna, Chemnitz, Sachsen 5 Sep 1868; dau. of Ernst Louis Schwarz and Auguste Vieweger; bp. 22 Aug 1908; conf. 22 Aug 1908; m. 29 Dec 1889, 1 Jun 1931, August Barth; 2 or 8 children; d. old age 11 Nov 1943 (CHL LR 7093 21, no. 195; IGI)

Bernhard Paul Simons b. Müllersbach (?), Gummersbach, Rheinland, Preußen 11 Aug 1867; son of Wilhelm Simons and Johanna Schreiber; bp. 16 Jul 1912; conf. 16 Jul 1912; ord. deacon 1 May 1921; m. 16 Mar 1888, Johanna Friederike Schreiber; d. heart attack 20 Sep 1942 (CHL LR 7093 21, no. 155; IGI)

Therese Stowwasser b. Zettlitz, Karlsbad, Böhmen, Austria 16 Apr 1888; dau. of Anton Stowwasser and Anna Schwengabier; bp. 3 Aug 1921; conf. 7 Aug 1921; m. 1 Jul 1905, Richard H. H. Trepte; d. heart attack 29 Mar 1941 (CHL LR 7093 21, no. 175; IGI)

Karl Emil Straube b. Kleinvoigtsberg, Dresden, Sachsen 11 Apr 1868; son of Karl Johann Straube and Amalie Auguste Naumann; bp. 16 Jul 1904; conf. 16 Jul 1904; ord. deacon 26 Jan 1921; ord. teacher 16 Apr 1922; ord. priest 6 Aug 1922; ord. elder 4 Sep 1932; m. 21 Mar or May 1895, Sophie Laura Elschner; 3 children; d. asthma Dresden Neustadt, Dresden, Sachsen 5 Aug 1941 (CHL LR 7093 21, no. 165; IGI)

Judith Ghemela Kulina Ulpts b. Dresden, Dresden, Sachsen 3 May 1932; dau. of Johannes Ulpts and Ghemela E. Strauch; k. in air raid Dresden 13–14 Feb 1945 (CHL LR 7093 21, no. 181; IGI)

Priska Meta Winkler b. Großenstein, Sachsen 22 Dec 1880; dau. of Moritz Winkler and Mathilde Schmidt; bp. 20 Nov 1926; conf. 20 Nov 1926; m. 3 Apr 1907, Karl A. Riedel; 1 child; d. lung ailment 19 Mar 1944 (CHL LR 7093 21, no. 129)

NOTES

1. Siegfried Dietze, telephone interview with Jennifer Heckmann, May 5, 2008; unless otherwise noted, transcript or audio version of tape in author's collection.
2. Erica Dietze Koch, telephone interview with Jennifer Heckmann, May 7, 2008.
3. Margot Burde Duennebeil, interview by the author, Salt Lake City, May 4, 2006.
4. Edith Schade Krause, interview by the author in German, Prenzlau, Germany, August 18, 2006; unless otherwise noted, summarized in English by Judith Sartowski.
5. Harald Schade, interview by the author in German, Burg Stargard, Germany, June 10, 2007.
6. It would have taken approximately four hours or more to walk the twelve miles. There is little wonder why the Saints in Nössige were grateful for Edith's efforts on their behalf. In her description of the frequent walks to church in the Königsbrückerstrasse, she said, "We all had healthy legs from walking so much."
7. Peter Hans, interview by the author in German, Planitz, Germany, June 3, 2007.
8. Edith Schade Krause, "The Dead Need No Water," in *Behind the Iron Curtain: Recollections of Latter-day Saints in East Germany, 1945–1989*, ed. Garold N. Davis and Norma S. Davis (Provo, UT: Brigham Young University Press, 2000), 5.
9. Ibid., 8.
10. Margot Burde Dünnebeil, autobiography (unpublished), 2; private collection.

FREIBERG BRANCH

Freiberg, located eighteen miles southwest of Dresden, was a key silver-mining town in the Erzgebirge Mountains and had a population of thirty-five thousand in 1939. The state of Saxony that included Freiberg was the home to more members of The Church of Jesus Christ of Latter-day Saints than any other state in Germany; the districts of Dresden, Chemnitz, Zwickau, and part of Leipzig had a total of twenty-three branches. More than 3,100 of the 7,608 Saints in the East German Mission lived in that relatively small area.

Freiberg Branch[1]	1939
Elders	17
Priests	4
Teachers	10
Deacons	17
Other Adult Males	20
Adult Females	96
Male Children	13
Female Children	13
Total	190

At the onset of World War II, the branch met in rented rooms in a Hinterhaus at Marienstrasse 4. Judith Hegewald (born 1924) later described how the Saints gained access to the rooms:

The front door [of the main building] was always open, and in order to reach the Hinterhaus, we just walked through the front door and then the corridor. We did not have a sign at the door saying that we met there. People lived in the front of the building, and when we walked through the corridor, we could see a garden on the left. On the right side we walked into [our rooms].[2]

Dorothea Henkel (born 1932) later recalled the arrangement of the rooms:

It was one big room that we remodeled; it used to be a factory. We had dances in there, we had meetings in there, we held everything in that one big room, and then we had three classrooms. And we had the cloakroom and one little room they used as a kitchen with a connection for a two-flame gas burner.[3]

Ingrid Henkel (born 1937), Dorothea's sister, recalled that the floors were oiled wood. "We could never sit on the floor when we were kids. We had to be very careful with our clothes. And we had no indoor toilets, just outhouses."[4]

Heinz Hegewald (born 1931) remembered specific decor in the chapel:

We had a wonderful picture of the prophet Joseph Smith (his profile) on the wall at the right of the congregation. And on the podium, we had a picture, a motif from the Bible. And also, we had a verse embroidered on the pulpit "Love one another." And on the right side of the chapel was a picture with Christ knocking on the door.[5]

Regarding the branch meeting schedule, Judith Hegewald recalled:

The first meeting was Sunday School in the morning, then we walked home and had some lunch and rested. In the evening hours, we walked back because sacrament meeting started at 7:00 p.m. After that meeting, we held our choir practice from 8:30 to 9:00.... During the week, we went to church two more times. We went for Relief Society and priesthood meeting and to MIA on a different [evening]. Primary was on Wednesday afternoon.

The family of Wilhelm Henkel lived on the northern outskirts of Freiberg in a suburb called Lössnitz, where the parents had built a two-story home in the 1930s at Schulweg 3F.

They walked about forty-five minutes to church twice each Sunday—for Sunday School in the morning, then home for dinner, then back to church for sacrament meeting in the evening.

Heinz Hoeke (born 1930) recalled an average attendance of perhaps eighty to one hundred twenty persons (in a room that could accommodate about one hundred fifty persons). According to his account, the branch choir always sat at the front of the room.[6] Paul Kleinert was the branch president during the war years.

With both LDS Primary and Jungvolk (the first phase of the Hitler Youth) meetings being held on Wednesday afternoons, Heinz Hoeke found a way to be punctual for both meetings: he simply wore his Jungvolk uniform to Primary.

Judith Hegewald was not allowed to join the Bund Deutscher Mädel. Although her father, district president Max Hegewald, was a member of the Nazi Party (as required by his employment at the court in Freiberg), he was not a supporter of the Nazi youth programs. Judith recounted what happened when BDM leaders came to the home to inquire about her absence: "My father explained that I would be needed at home helping to take care of my siblings [because] I was the second oldest."

At age ten, Dorothea Henkel was inducted into the Jungvolk program, along with her schoolmates. The activities included learning about the life of Adolf Hitler, folk dancing, handicrafts, collecting for the winter relief fund, making toys for poor people, marching in parades, and participating in athletic festivals. As she later recalled, "I sometimes missed meetings, but I didn't get in trouble because my father was gone [in the military] and my mother was pregnant, so I had to help my little sister."

The Hegewald brothers experienced some difficulties as members of the Jungvolk orga-

Fig. 1. The members of the Freiberg Branch just prior to the war.

nization. Rudolf (born 1930) recalled having some German youth meetings on Sunday:

> If possible, we would go after the Hitler Youth meeting to our sacrament meeting in our brown shirts and our belts across the chest and a knife at our side. And all we did was take the knife off and pass the sacrament in Hitler Youth uniform with the swastika armband.

For a while, things became very difficult for another Hegewald boy, Gerhard. According to Rudolf:

> My brother Gerhard and I were in the same meeting where there were about a hundred youth, and the leader pointed to us and said we were the saboteurs because we would go to church sometimes on Sunday instead of to the Hitler Youth meeting, and he mentioned to the mass of young people that he hoped that they knew what to do with the saboteurs.

Apparently the boys did "know what to do." Gerhard was beaten up soon after that meeting.

Dorothea's father, Wilhelm Henkel, was a shoemaker by trade. Toward the end of 1939, he received a mission call from Berlin but was prevented from serving when drafted into the German army in January 1940. With the exception of a few home visits on furlough, Brother Henkel was absent from Freiberg for most of the war. Dorothea recalled having to wait until she was nine years old to be baptized because she wanted her father to baptize her. The ceremony finally took place at Soldiers Pond near Freiberg on October 23, 1941.

Even in wartime, there was time to be a child, as Dorothea later described:

> We played all kinds of fantasy games and fairy tales; we didn't need lots of clothes to dress up in, just our imaginations. Just a scarf and a hat maybe; we just had great times. I wasn't a tomboy, but I played with the boys, climbed trees, jumped over walls, things like that.

Fig. 2. Former Freiberg branch president Wilhelm Henkel (right) as a soldier in Marseilles, France, in about 1942. (D. Henkel Roscher)

Fig. 3. Clemens Hegewald was killed in Russia in December 1942. (M. Hegewald)

Heinz Hoeke also had a good time as a child in Freiberg. He recalled playing soccer and enjoying all kinds of sports. He also played soldier ("I was always the commander!"). At the age of twelve, he was baptized a member of the Church in September 1942.

Judith Hegewald was inducted into the Reichsarbeitsdienst in 1942 at the age of eighteen and spent six months in the service of her country. While in Plauen, she received a letter regarding her brother, Clemens:

> The letter said that my brother had died, and I was allowed to go home for three days. They did not tell us how he died, but they sent a written letter. We wore black for a while afterwards. I wore a black ribbon around my arm over my uniform. My father gave a talk in sacrament meeting and wept terribly. . . . Even an entire year later, I dreamed of [Clemens] every night. He always smiled at me in those dreams, and he was happy. I cried a lot during that time, but it seemed like those dreams [came] to comfort me.

After her release from the Reichsarbeitsdienst, Judith went to work in Leipzig for the military for a time. Later, she accompanied her father, the district president, as he visited other branches. She explained, "He wanted me to meet somebody in the Church, so he took me with

him sometimes when he went to Görlitz. I met three young boys, but they all died in the war."

The Dzierzon family lived in Grossschirma, about five miles from the meetinghouse. They walked or rode their bicycles to attend church. During the war, Erich Dzierzon met a young lady who was a member of the locally dominant Lutheran church. He recalled:

> It was a case of love at first sight, and I told her that if we were going to be together then it would be best if we had one religion. She . . . accepted the gospel as soon as I told her about it. We were married during the war and our daughter, Gisela, was born during the war.[7]

Willi Dzierzon spent several years on the Eastern Front and wrote later that his life had been spared on several distinct occasions. Once he was sent with a message to the next village, and while riding his horse toward a long, low hill, heard a quiet but clear voice say, "Stop!" He stopped and examined the ground around him. A recent rain had exposed several antipersonnel mines to his view. "That was the first time my life was saved."[8]

On another occasion, Willi was again on horseback, approaching an abandoned concrete artillery bunker. The dirt road split, one track leading downward in front of the bunker and the other leading upward behind the bunker, both tracks uniting again on the other side. He later explained that he should have spared his horse the effort necessary to take the upper road but took the more difficult path anyway. Just as he was next to the bunker, an artillery round landed on the lower road exactly on the opposite side of the bunker, such that the bunker shielded him and his horse from the shrapnel from the shell. "I would have been killed or maimed," he later concluded.

Ingrid, the second Henkel daughter, recalled that her mother served as the Relief Society president of the Dresden District throughout the war. She took the train to visit other branches in the district, sometimes taking a daughter along. When Sister Henkel traveled alone, another woman in the branch looked after her children.

Rudolf Hegewald remembered very clearly the attack on Freiberg on October 7, 1944, "because it was my grandmother's birthday," he explained. They actually watched the attack from an upstairs window:

> We were sick and tired of air-raid warnings when nothing happened. All those years from '39 to '44, nothing happened to our little city, so we didn't listen to the sirens anymore. When the alarms would sound, we would just watch these bombers come, 30,000 feet or higher with the big condensation trails.

But on this day things were different. The boys watched bombs fall as close as three hundreds yards down the street. According to Rudolf, "The pressure of the explosions lifted the roof tiles, and they made a terrible noise, a clattering noise. We were down in the basement in a matter of seconds." After the attack, people all over town went out to survey the damage. "Some people had been decapitated by the explosions. It was a terrible sight."

Heinz Hoeke also recalled the attack of October 7 in vivid detail:

> We knew that the war had come home to Freiberg that day. I was at work and remember how the sirens began to wail. We first thought that nothing would happen because there had been alarms before. Then somebody said that bombs were falling, so we hurried down into the basement. If a bomb had hit the building, we would not have survived.

In the fall of 1944, a Russian laborer came to board with the Henkel family. At first, Sister Henkel, whose husband was still away in the military, was scared that the young man (about twenty-two, according to Dorothea) would be unclean and dangerous, but they learned otherwise. He turned out to be an opponent of Stalin

and swore that he would commit suicide if the Red Army caught up with him. He even attended church once or twice, Dorothea remembered.

As the war neared its end, refugees from eastern Germany streamed through Saxony on their way west. As Heinz Hegewald recalled:

> In our [church] meeting, we were asked to take some families in, and my mother, bless her heart, she was a true Christian, and even though there were eight of us at home, almost ten, with the parents and the grandma, she took in the Arndt family who had been bombed out in Berlin. We spared one room for this family—Sister Arndt and her sons, Hans Joachim and Dieter.

Latter-day Saint refugees came to Freiberg from far away. The Naujoks and Augat families of the Tilsit Branch in the Königsberg District (East Prussia) arrived in early 1945 and were put up in the church rooms at Marienstrasse 4. According to Heinz Hegewald, "They were always mothers and children. Never a husband or father. These were terrible times, but the Lord helped us."

As the Third Reich neared collapse in January 1945, Rudolf Hegewald witnessed something quite startling. He told this story:

> Let me give you another little experience I had concerning the destruction of the Jewish race in Germany. Often people ask us whether we knew. Well, I tell you, in 1945, in January, I saw a terrible picture I will never forget. Down our street, SS [soldiers] had surrounded about three hundred Jewish women, their heads shaven, and they herded them down the street with German shepherd dogs, just like cattle. And then I thought, "What is happening in Germany?" They couldn't kill them where they were, so they drove them farther inland, and this was the first time that I noticed that Germany had committed an unspeakable crime. I knew that the women were Jewish because they all wore their Jewish star [Star of David].

In early 1945, Dorothea Henkel became personally aware of the horrors of war, not because of attacks on Freiberg but because victims of the firebombing of Dresden were brought to Freiberg for treatment. She was in the hospital recovering from an appendectomy when Dresden was attacked on February 13–14. When the burned and injured filled the hospital, Dorothea was sent home to recuperate. She vividly recalled her reaction when the Dresden people arrived: "All those burned people, those injured people from Dresden. It was horrible! They brought a lady into my room; she was badly burned. It was terrible!"

Because she was sent home from the hospital early, Dorothea did not heal well. Her incision became infected, and the stitches would not come out properly:

> Sometimes I was really down, and then we had a home teacher come, and he gave me a blessing, and I went to the bathroom, and here I pulled another stitch out. That went from February till August—six months until that healed.

Rudolf Hegewald and his father, Max Hegewald, rode their bicycles to Dresden two weeks after the bombing

> To see what happened to the members, and we found the ones in the Altstadt—the old core of the city. The Altstadt was wiped out, and we saw the corpses still lying in the streets, and then they were shrunk, maybe that big [two feet], an adult (when they burn, they shrink), and they were black corpses, just lying in the street at that time—two weeks later.

Fig. 4. The Freiberg Branch met in rooms in the Hinterhaus attached to this structure throughout World War II. (I. Henkel Rudolph)

Hans Joachim Arndt was one of the few eyewitnesses to tell of military training associated with his time in the Jungvolk:

> Toward the end of the war, the last two months, they actually trained us in our Hitler Youth programs, how to use real weapons. We shot rifles, we learned how to throw grenades, they were telling us the usual slogans of "this is the battle to the bitter end," and they wanted us to be prepared for that.[9]

Fortunately, Hans Joachim and his schoolmates were never required to be soldiers in the lost cause of keeping the Soviet soldiers from conquering Freiberg.

Rudolf Hegewald recalled how the war directly threatened him during March and April of 1945, when Allied airplanes enjoyed total air superiority and flew over Freiberg looking for targets:

> After church, when we went home, we would have to look and know where the airplanes were. If we could see the airplanes, we assumed that they could see us so we would hide. If we didn't see the airplanes, then we would run from house to house to get home safely. And as a matter of fact as a young fourteen-year-old, I went out in the fields to see the dive-bombers better, and then if I saw them come, I would throw myself down and take some grass to cover me up so they wouldn't shoot at me. This is a vivid experience I had in 1945 right before the war ended.

"I was drafted into the Volkssturm [home guard] on April 15," recalled Heinz Hoeke. He reported for duty the next morning and was transported into the Erzgebirge Mountains. When they heard that their destination was Czechoslovakia, Heinz and several other boys had no desire to go there, so they jumped on a truck bound in a different direction. They had deserted, and if they had been caught, the consequences could have been fatal. Fortunately, the boys eventually were able to take a train back to Freiberg without being arrested.

Before the Red Army entered Freiberg, they fired on the city with their artillery, in response to the last German defensive efforts. Dorothea Henkel had gone to a local dairy to get a can of milk, and on her way home she narrowly missed injury when a piece of shrapnel landed next to her. "The next thing we knew, the Russians were coming out of the forest, so we hid in our cellar," she recalled. "Our neighbor across the street was a communist. He came out and greeted the Russians with open arms, and the Russians just looked at him and took his watch and walked off. It was funny." Heinz Hoeke remembered hearing the roar of the enemy artillery when he was on his way home from church on May 7. When the invaders entered the city the next day, there were twenty persons (mostly refugees) living in the home with Heinz's family. One day, they had a serious scare:

> A Russian officer came into our apartment, saw all of the young women, and told us that they were beautiful. Then he left. He must have told others, however, because that night many soldiers came looking for those women. They were hiding in the bathroom, so the soldiers did not find them.

As refugees, the Arndts of Berlin had few possessions when they were taken in by the Hegewald family. Hans Joachim Arndt recalled that they took great care to preserve certain personal documents:

> We had a collection of important documents we always [kept] with us. My mother actually stowed those underneath the seat of a four-legged stool. And this stool went with us everywhere we went. We carted it with us, and it had those documents stored in the seat. I remember, that's how we kept those things. I'm not sure whatever happened to the stool, but the documents survived.

Sister Henkel and her three daughters lived in the cellar of their home for three weeks, while the rooms upstairs were inhabited by thirty enemy soldiers. There were several frightening moments, but "the Lord took care of us," according to Dorothea. "We didn't have a war raging in our town like the bombing in Dresden, just a minor thing, but we had the Russians in our houses. Those were perilous times for everybody. But the Church was there. We could always go to church."

Some Saints believed that the end of the war meant the end of all of their problems. According to Rudolf Hegewald, "When the Russian army arrived, they came down our street—Gabelsbergerstrasse—and we hailed them as liberators. We were happy to have them in town. We could now finally sleep at night in our beds—no more air raids." Unfortunately,

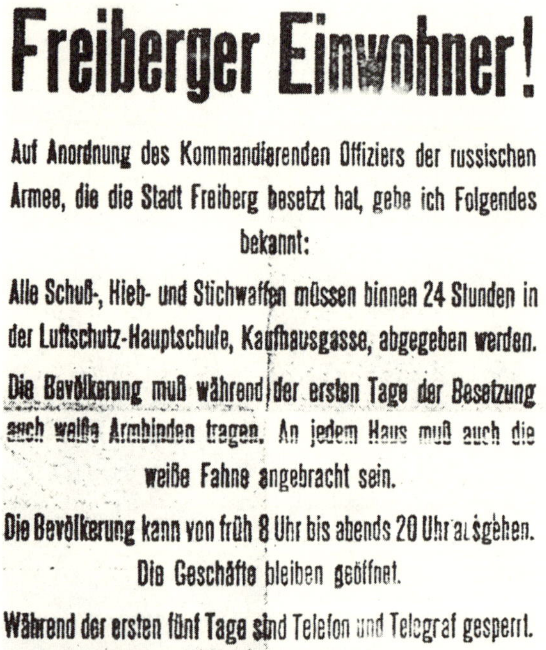

Freiberger Einwohner!

Auf Anordnung des Kommandierenden Offiziers der russischen Armee, die die Stadt Freiberg besetzt hat, gebe ich Folgendes bekannt:

Alle Schuß-, Hieb- und Stichwaffen müssen binnen 24 Stunden in der Luftschutz-Hauptschule, Kaufhausgasse, abgegeben werden.

Die Bevölkerung muß während der ersten Tage der Besetzung auch weiße Armbinden tragen. An jedem Haus muß auch die weiße Fahne angebracht sein.

Die Bevölkerung kann von früh 8 Uhr bis abends 20 Uhr ausgehen.

Die Geschäfte bleiben geöffnet.

Während der ersten fünf Tage sind Telefon und Telegraf gesperrt.

Alle Sabotageakte an Fabriken, Leitungen usw. sind verboten.

Fig. 5. "Residents of Freiberg! By order of the commanding officer of the Russian army that has occupied the city of Freiberg, I announce the following: All firearms, swords and military knives are to be surrendered at the main civil defense school at Kaufhausgasse within twenty-four hours. During the first days of the occupation, civilians must wear white armbands. A white flag must be displayed on every building. Civilians may be on the streets from 8:00 A.M. to 8:00 P.M. Stores are to remain open. During the first five days, telephones and telegraph machines are not to be used. All acts of sabotage against factories, utility lines etc. are forbidden."

Rudolf soon realized that "we had gone from the frying pan into the fire."

> [The soldiers] had permission from the Soviet commander to plunder and to rape and to do anything they wanted, and to steal, and so at nights, they would break into our apartments. We had to hide our sisters—we had four sisters—and our mother at nights. We would hide them in the garden, someplace in the bushes, because [the soldiers] would enter the houses and try to find females.

The reaction of Judith Hegewald, Rudolf's sister, to the invasion was more frightful:

> The Russians came in large groups with their tanks. It was horrible for us to see them walking up the Gabelsbergerstrasse. We were scared and did not know what would happen. They came by at night and went through houses searching for women. They also tried to come into our building. All of the families in our building stayed strong together.

Heinz Henkel described his impression of the common enemy soldier: "He was out to get three things: watches, bicycles, and women." Millions of Germans in the area occupied by the Red Army would agree with his assessment, but others would add many household appliances to the list of items stolen.

Once the war ended, members of the Freiberg Branch longed for the return of husbands, fathers, and brothers. Gisa Henkel (born 1943) was only four years old when her father, Wilhelm Henkel, returned from a POW camp in France in November 1947. It was a confusing event, as she later explained:

> He was skinny, but he was pretty healthy. I didn't know him. When he came home I was still in a crib. And he came home and my mom was so excited, and she came in—it was midnight, and he said, "Oh, look who's home!" And I said, "Yeah, an uncle!" And my mom said, "No, it's your dad!" And I said, "No, it's an uncle!" And over and over my mom said, "It's your dad!" and I said, "No, it's an uncle!" And my dad had a sa-

lami that he had gotten somehow, and he showed me the salami, and I said, "That's my dad!"

Wilhelm Henkel had been away from his family (except for a few short furloughs) for seven years and ten months.

Looking back over his life during the war, Erich Dzierzon stated:

> I served in the German army for seven war years, in Poland, in France, and in Russia, and came home without a scratch, which was a miracle. . . . During the war, I had neglected my church duties, and now that the war was over, I had to repent and make up for lost time.[10]

Erich's confession that he had neglected his church duties should not be judged harshly. The probability that a German soldier who was a Latter-day Saint would meet another soldier of the same religious affiliation was so low that stories of such meetings are very rare. Latter-day Saint German soldiers almost never served in areas where they could attend church and were usually totally isolated from the Church while in uniform.

Regarding the spiritual survival of the Saints in Freiberg during the war, Rudolf and Heinz Hegewald shared the following conclusions:

> The gospel was their anchor. That was the only thing they had to hang on to in order to survive. That is the truth. Even the destruction of Dresden and the killing of many members down there, it did not make the surviving members bitter. We all knew and had the testimony that they were in a better place now. We were under the influence of the old fashioned Mormons— the pioneers. This was typical German style— you hold on to the testimony, on to the gospel. There was no question about it.

In Memoriam

The following members of the Freiberg Branch did not survive World War II:

Anna Helene Eilenberger b. Großhartmanndorf, Dresden, Sachsen 3 Jun 1889; dau. of Ernst Louis

Eilenberger and Anna Marie Reichelt; bp. 27 Jun 1921; m. Großhartmannsdorf 3 May 1914, Bruno Hermann Baessler; 2 children; d. Gränitz, Dresden, Sachsen 21 Dec 1942 (IGI)

Ernst Louis Eilenberger b. Großhartmannsdorf, Dresden, Sachsen 29 Feb 1856; son of Karl August Eilenberger and Juliane Wilhelmine Bellmann; bp. 8 Nov 1911; ord. elder; m. Großhartmannsdorf 31 Aug 1879, Anna Marie Reichelt; 14 children; d. Großhartmannsdorf 20 May 1940 (*Sonntagsstern*, no. 21, 23 Jun 1940 n.p.; IGI; AF)

Ernst Heinrich Geistert b. Rudelstadt, Schlesien, Preußen 23 Oct 1849; son of Karl Gottlieb Jeremias Fehst and Beate Christiane Geistert; bp. 23 Apr 1905; ord. elder 1923; d. old age Freiberg, Sachsen 6 Sep 1939 (*Stern* no. 21, 1 Nov. 1939, 340; FHL Microfilm 25773, 1935 Census)

Clemens Carl Hegewald b. Freiberg, Dresden, Sachsen 18 Jan 1923; son of Max Otto Hegewald and Margarete Martha Uhlig; bp. 7 Nov 1931; soldier; k. in air raid Newel, Russia 16 Dec 1942; bur. Newel, Russia (Heinz Hegewald; www.volksbund.de; IGI)

Robert Herrmann Hegewald b. Cämmerswalde, Dresden, Sachsen 16 Sep or Nov 1871; son of August Wilhelm Hegewald and Emilie Wilhelmine Meyer; bp. 1 Jul or Aug 1919; ord. elder; m. Liddy Thekla Hemmig; d. Freiberg, Dresden, Sachsen 5 Apr 1941 (*Sonntagsgruss*, no. 22, 1 Jun 1941, 88; FHL Microfilm 162780 Census; IGI)

Hermann Heinrich Henkel b. Lietzen, Brandenburg, Preußen 19 Mar 1911; son of Friedrich Wilhelm Henkel and Auguste Marie Ruttke; bp. 29 Mar 1932; m. Frankfurt/Oder, Brandenburg, Preußen 15 Dec 1932, Frieda Marie Hofmann; 4 children; ord. elder; staff corporal; k. in battle Lenggries, Oberbayern, Bayern 30 Apr 1945; bur. Traunstein, Bayern (D. Henkel, G. Henkel-Hagen, D. Henkel Roscher; www.volksbund.de; IGI)

Johannes Walter Jakwerth b. Freiberg, Dresden, Sachsen 6 Dec 1922; son of Josef Jakwerth and Linna Emma Kasper; rifleman; k. in battle Rava Ruska, Galizien, Russia 25 Jun 1941; bur. Potelitsch Cemetery, Ukraine (D. Henkel; www.volksbund.de; PRF; IGI)

NOTES

1. Presiding Bishopric, "Financial, Statistical, and Historical Reports of Wards, Stakes, and Missions, 1884–1955," CR 4 12, 257.
2. Judith Hegewald, interview by the author in German, Schwerin, Germany, June 11, 2007; unless otherwise noted, summarized in English by Judith Sartowski.
3. Dorothea Henkel Roscher, interview by the author, Salt Lake City, April 14, 2006.
4. Ingrid Henkel Rudolph, interview by the author, Sandy, Utah, July 26, 2007.
5. Rudolf Hegewald and Heinz Hegewald, interview by the author, Salt Lake City, January 19, 2007.
6. Heinz Hoeke, interview by the author in German, Highland, Utah, February 10, 2006.
7. Erich Dzierzon, Gisela Dzierzon Heller, and Manfred Heller, "Gospel and the Government," in *Behind the Iron Curtain: Recollections of Latter-day Saints in East Germany*, ed. Garold N. Davis and Norma S. Davis (Provo, UT: Brigham Young University Press, 2000), 287–88.
8. Willi Dzierzon, "Some Faith-promoting Experiences in Russia," (unpublished manuscript, about 1949); private collection.
9. Hans Joachim Arndt, interview by the author, Sandy, Utah, November 10, 2006.
10. Dzierzon, Heller, and Heller, "Gospel and the Government," 287–88.

GÖRLITZ BRANCH

Seventy miles east of the city of Dresden, at the far eastern extent of the Dresden District, lies the city of Görlitz. In 1939, the town was situated on both sides of the Neisse River—the old part of town being on the west bank. The main railroad route from Dresden east to Breslau ran through Görlitz.

The Görlitz Branch of The Church of Jesus Christ of Latter-day Saints had 104 members at the time, making it the third largest branch in the Dresden District. Nearly two-thirds of the members were adult females.

Görlitz Branch[1]	1939
Elders	2
Priests	3
Teachers	3
Deacons	7
Other Adult Males	18
Adult Females	62
Male Children	4
Female Children	5
Total	104

Fig. 1. A celebration in the Görlitz Branch in 1938. (F. Larisch)

Lifelong Görlitz resident Ruth Baier (born 1917) recalled the seating arrangement in the rooms in which the branch met during the war at Emmerichstrasse 68:

> There always was one row with elderly sisters and then behind them sat the younger people and then came the youngest children. There were about 8–10 children and then 8–10 teenagers . . . there. This must have been about 35–40 people attending Sunday meetings.[2]

The branch observed the typical meeting schedule, beginning with Sunday School at 10:00 A.M. The members then went home for the noonday meal and returned in the evening for sacrament meeting. Relief Society, priesthood, and MIA gatherings were held on Wednesday evenings, with Primary meetings on Saturdays.

Helmut Habicht (born 1926) described the rooms in which the branch met:

> We had a main room in the highest floor of a former factory building. We also had four classrooms. During the war, the owner also allowed us to use rooms on the main floor of the building.[3]

When World War II began, Anton Larisch (born 1901) was the branch president in Görlitz. However, he had to be released when his employment with the Junker Aircraft Company required him to move in November 1939 to Halberstadt, northwest of Leipzig. His wife, Charlotte, and their children stayed in Görlitz. They would not be permanently united again until the last month of the war. In early 1940, Anton enjoyed two weeks at home. His diary entry for March 17, 1940, reads thus:

> Everything went as hoped for and this is my first Sunday at home with Mutti [Mother] and children. . . . The reunion was a great day of joy for us all. I arrived in the night from Thursday to Friday at 12:30 A.M. Friday evening we had a family night with the children. Later I went with Lotte to a late-night performance at the theater.[4]

For Anton, the months in Halberstadt (180 miles northwest of Görlitz) became years, but the government did not allow him to move his family to Halberstadt. Every time a six-month period of employment came to an end, he looked forward to returning to Görlitz, but each time his assignment at the Junker factory was extended. In early September 1940, he was allowed to leave Halberstadt and visit his family for ten days. He wrote in his diary that while he was at home in Görlitz, he repaired twenty pairs of shoes, pickled one hundred cucumbers, took his children to the movies, and went on walks with his dear wife, Charlotte.[5]

The life of the children in the Görlitz Branch was influenced in a very special way by two women who are seen in virtually all Primary photographs taken during the war years. Jutta Larisch (born 1938) wrote of these two devoted sisters with great reverence:

> [Baerbel Neumann] lived alone but was never alone. She was always seen in the company of children. She was the Primary president for many years. Her love and programs tied us all to the Church. She sold magazines for a living and must have left an invitation to children in every home she went to. She introduced many people to the Church. When she walked down the narrow sidewalks, there was never enough room for all the children who wanted to walk with her.[6]

About the other woman, Marietta Kulke Lehmann, Jutta wrote the following:

> She was the director of our Görlitz Branch children's choir. She had a lovely voice and [a] very

Fig. 2. The Görlitz Branch Sunday School in 1938. (H. Habicht)

attractive personality and a love for children. We wouldn't miss trudging through the snow on our thirty- to forty-five-minute walk to church in order to be there for the children's choir practice.

Unfortunately, under pressure from the government, the new Görlitz branch president, Felix Seibt, officially discontinued Sunday School attendance by children in early 1940. This must have been especially disappointing for sisters Neumann and Lehmann.[7]

Political programs such as the Hitler Youth were designed to include every child beginning at the age of ten. Therefore, despite physical challenges caused by a case of infantile paralysis, Helmut Habicht was inducted into the Jungvolk program and described his experiences as follows:

I was a member of the Jungvolk when I was ten years old, but the meetings did not interfere with our Sunday church meetings. For the most part it was a good experience because we . . . learned about our region, but as children we did not know what the aim of all this was. They did

not openly talk about Hitler and the government but there were hints of it. When I was fourteen years old, I automatically advanced to the Hitler Youth and also participated in some of the things they offered, but it also never interfered with our meetings.

Horst Sommer (born 1926) turned fourteen in October 1940 and joined the Hitler Youth. Because many Hitler Youth groups had a specific focus, Horst chose a group specializing in cavalry training. Due to the random assignment of recruits to the various branches of the military,

Fig. 3. The Görlitz genealogical research group during one of their wartime study sessions. (J. Schmidt Runnacles)

his training with horses was of little value to him when he was later drafted into the navy.[8]

The Jungvolk program was initially fun for Eberhard Sommer (born 1930), but as he attended more and more meetings, he found himself dissatisfied with the political drilling he experienced. "I detested saying '*Heil Hitler*' and really started doubting what they were teaching us."[9] He began to skip the meetings, preferring to spend his time swimming and boating on the river. He was picked up on several occasions by his leaders but was never severely punished.

On June 24, 1943, a Sunday, Eberhard was baptized in the Neisse River by President Felix Seibt. Eberhard's father (not yet a member of the Church) was away in the army and gave his permission in a letter. He had opposed Eberhard's baptism for several years, insisting that his son was not yet ready. Now he indicated that his son was prepared.[10]

In the first year of the war, Ruth Baier was engaged to marry Erich Hain, but his military service commitment prevented the wedding for several months. Finally, they married on August 6, 1940. She described this event years later:

> First, we went to the civil registration office [in city hall] and later had a little celebration with the entire branch. [Eric] got furlough for ten days for our wedding. Soldiers did not come home very often. We also did not go on a honeymoon because there was no money and there was not much to eat.

After Eric returned to his unit, Ruth continued to work with her parents in their beauty salon.

On December 29, 1941, little Vera Larisch (only fifteen months old) died of diphtheria. The diary entry recorded by her father, Anton Larisch, was predictably sad. He hurried home from Halberstadt to attend her funeral and ended up staying for two weeks to nurse his entire family back to health from various

illnesses. Despite his enthusiastic missionary efforts in Halberstadt (where he was working to revive a dormant branch and was serving as branch president), being away from his family was tearing Brother Larisch apart.[11]

As the war progressed and German soldiers were dying in Europe, Asia, and Africa, a woman in the Görlitz Branch received successive messages that her sons had been killed one by one. Ruth Baier Hein recalled how the branch members did their best to comfort this sister in her grief:

> Sister Else Wagner had lost three sons and a son-in-law. We held a ceremony to honor her sons. There was prelude music, singing, and talks given by people who knew the sons. Sister Wagner could not say anything—she was deeply moved. I think she later expressed her gratitude to everybody who helped. She was very strong in the gospel and never blamed or doubted Heavenly Father. She did not have much money and was not physically strong, but she was a devoted sister.

Horst Sommer was inducted into the Reichsarbeitsdienst in August 1943. However, the needs of the Germany military were so intense at the time that his one-year term of duty was shortened to three months, and he was drafted into the navy. He later described his reaction to the assignment:

> Serving in the navy was not my fondest wish. I was not thrilled to serve on a submarine. I thought that a hero could also be a man who said "no" sometimes. . . . Being in a submarine is like being inside a tank. There is no easy way to get out. . . . I was in a submarine for several hours [only one time] but was never on a real voyage.

Six decades later, Horst could still describe in great detail the process of exiting a submarine at depths up to six hundred feet.

Heinz Sommer (born 1921) was a mechanical engineer working at one of the two war factories in Görlitz. His employment exempted him from military service, but his younger brother, Eberhard, remembered later that Heinz felt guilty about being a civilian; other young men in the neighborhood were fighting and dying for their country while Heinz sat at work in his hometown. He finally gave in to local pressure and volunteered in 1943. He was assigned to the air force and did essentially the same thing in Italy that he had done back in Görlitz.

Heinz was killed in 1944. The official explanation was that he was fighting partisans in Italy. However, his brother, Eberhard, recalled hearing that Heinz was sitting at his desk designing motors for rockets when he was shot through the window by a partisan. The incident was never fully explained.[12] Eberhard was only thirteen at the time and had serious questions about the loss of his brother:

When my brother was killed, I asked the Lord why it could happen. I received a peaceful feeling about it. I remember my brother Heinz saying many times to me, "The gospel is true. Live the gospel—you will need it." It stuck with me. I knew what he meant.

In the fall of 1944, the Soviet army invaded eastern Germany, and the flight of millions of German civilians began. Fred Larisch (born 1934) was ten years old at the time, but later clearly recalled watching refugees stream past their house in Görlitz:

For months prior to our leaving, we saw horses and wagons and people walking in a continuous stream. Our street was like a highway. They were refugees, and we didn't know where they were coming from. They seemed to be in distress, not knowing where to go, but they were following continuous lines of refugees coming through, being sent by train into different areas. . . . Then all of a sudden, we found ourselves being refugees.[13]

"The war didn't really come home to us in Görlitz until the last few months," recalled Helmut Habicht, "Until then, life simply went on." Then the government asked women and

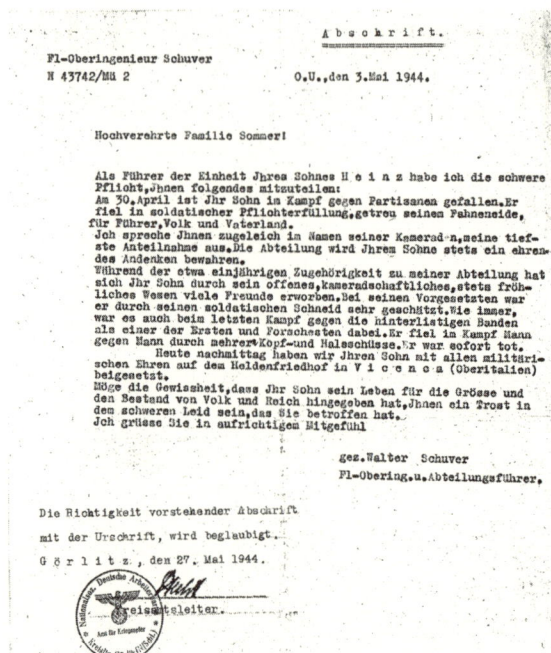

Fig. 4. The letter every family feared: "It is my sad duty to inform you that your son, Heinz [Sommer] was killed while fighting partisans on April 30 [1944]." (H. Sommer)

Fig. 5. Ruth Larisch was baptized by her father in the Neisse River in 1940. (F. Larisch)

children to evacuate the city. With the men away in military service and with Helmut exempt because of his paralysis, he had become the principal priesthood holder of the branch. "I had to bless and pass the sacrament and preside over the meetings," he explained. Fortunately, there were several other boys in the Görlitz Branch who were prepared to fill the roles of men within their families, such as Eberhard Sommer and Fred Larisch.

Fourteen-year-old Eberhard Sommer was asked by his mother to take charge of their departure from Görlitz. She told him that because he held the priesthood, he should make the main decisions, and she would follow. They boarded the last car of a passenger train standing in the Görlitz railroad station. Suddenly, Eberhard had the distinct impression that they had to get off the train, despite the fact that they had nice seats. His mother first resisted then yielded, and they moved to another car. The next morning, the train was attacked by dive-bombers, and the passenger car in which they were first seated was destroyed.[14]

Charlotte Larisch included the following statement in her autobiography: "On a Sunday morning in February, 1945, I gathered some clothes and pots and something to eat and put it in the baby buggy and set Gisela, who was almost two years [old] at that time, on top of it and walked with the children to the next town."[15] Thus began the exodus of Sister Larisch and her children from Görlitz.

Ten-year-old Fred Larisch recalled that while his mother pulled the baby carriage, he and his sister Ruth pulled the family's Leiterwagen.

> Our Leiterwagen was from three to four feet long and about eighteen to twenty inches wide. The sides were like a ladder, with ribs. The rear wheels were about sixteen inches in diameter and the front wheels were smaller. We put everything that we possibly could carry on that wagon.

With the Red Army approaching, things looked very bleak for Sister Larisch and her children. Not only did she have to find a way to leave town and protect her children, but her husband had been arrested in January (charged

Fig. 6. Members of the Görlitz Branch posed for this photograph in 1942. (F. Larisch)

with treason), and she had no idea where he was being held. However, conditions were about to change for the better, as she later wrote:

> In that time of sorrow and worry, a wonderful thing happened. The six weeks for Anton's arrest were over, and he was set free.[16] . . . He arrived at Görlitz at noon of the same Sunday that we left in the morning. He got his bicycle out of the cellar and tried to reach us. We did meet in [Löbau]; it was really a miracle because I did not know he was free and on his way to find us. . . . It seemed almost impossible for him to find us because he did not know where we went and there were so many refugees. When we met that day, we knew it was possible only through the help of our Father in Heaven.

Once they were reunited, the Larisch family made their way to Halberstadt.

Charlotte Larisch's sister, Johanna Schmidt (born 1927), wrote detailed descriptions of the sad plight of refugees in the last months of the war. Shortly after leaving Görlitz, she and her mother were in Bautzen, trying to get to Halberstadt to join Charlotte. It appeared that they were on their way when they were crowded into boxcars and the train pulled out of the station. In her own words:

> It was in the middle of winter, with no heat whatsoever in the boxcars, no washing facilities, no toilets, no food, absolutely nothing but thousands of people. . . . Nobody knew where we were going. The train stopped early in the morning so everybody could get out and stretch. After that, the train would stop every two or three hours to let us out and stretch, but then we were closed up again in the dark. That went on for three days and three nights in the dark and cold. Only once did we stop long enough to have some food cooked for us, and that was the only time we had something warm to eat. I can't describe the feeling I had on that train. I am sure that everyone on that train felt the total despair that I did. When the train stopped I would walk around by myself and just pray, and when we were back inside the train I sat on top of our hard suitcases that were in the handcart to wait for the next stop, but there was no room to stand up and move around.[17]

When the journey ended, Johanna learned that they were in Czechoslovakia—nowhere near Halberstadt and headed in the wrong direction. Fortunately, they made their way to

Fig. 7. The Görlitz Branch presidency during the war (from left): Kurt Lehmann, Felix Seibt, and Hermann Kulke. (F. Larisch)

Fig. 8. Bernhard Habicht, Heinz Sommer, and Gunter Wagner were all killed in combat. (H. Habicht)

Prague and from there found a train heading back into Germany. Her story continued:

> From there to the city of Halberstadt, we traveled under terrible conditions again for three days and three nights, changing trains thirteen times with no place to sit or sleep. . . . There was no way of knowing what the conditions would be like. I honestly don't know how we managed. . . . As we finally arrived in Halberstadt, we were greeted by an air-raid alarm.

Finally united with her sister, Charlotte Larisch, Johanna Schmidt enjoyed a little security, but her trials were far from over. On Sunday, April 8, 1945, what she called "a few peaceful weeks" came to an abrupt end; another air raid reduced nearly all of Halberstadt to rubble in a matter of minutes. Her nephew, Fred Larisch, was looking out the apartment window. Suddenly, he yelled that bombs were falling, and everybody raced to the basement of the apartment house. Johanna recalled the event:

> All around us the bombs exploded. This went on for about five to seven minutes, what seemed an eternity to us, and then all was quiet. . . . It was not long after that when we heard that next group of planes coming. . . . Nobody can imagine the horror that we felt as we sat there wondering if we were going to die. . . . This time it was a terrifying hissing sound, and the air pressure from the explosions was so strong that we felt as if our eardrums would burst. We could feel the whole house shaking. It was so terrible that I wished and prayed with all my heart that I could die. I even told the Lord, "Oh, please, let the house collapse on us and kill us instantly."[18]

Remarkably, the Larisch and Schmidt families survived the dreadful experience, as did all of the active members of the Halberstadt Branch.

When the American tanks rolled into the town of Langenstein (a suburb of Halberstadt) where the Larisch family lived in late April 1945, Anton went out to greet them. Because he had been studying English in night classes, he wanted to talk to them. According to Fred,

"My father was asking them if any of them were LDS. All of the tanks stopped then. We didn't find any LDS soldiers, but they gave us a lamb."

There were no air raids in Görlitz until the end of the war, according to Helmut Habicht. Then things happened in rapid succession, and he had to seek shelter on about twenty occasions. One bomb did strike the meetinghouse, damaging the Relief Society room, but the other rooms were intact. Finally, the government requisitioned the rooms for use as housing for refugees. By the time the war ended on May 8, 1945, the remaining members of the Görlitz Branch were holding meetings in the apartments of two families. A few weeks after the war ended, the members were allowed to use the rooms at Emmerichstrasse 68 once again.

When the invaders entered Görlitz, Ruth Baier Hein's mother decided to take a strong stand in the family's defense. As Ruth later recounted:

> We were home when the Russians first came into our house. My mother was very strong in her faith, and we were also. We prayed, and then the Russians did not steal any of our property. My mother approached them and asked firmly: "What do you want from us? My son-in-law helped Russian women, protected them while he was serving in Russia and shared his Christmas packages with them. What do you want from us now?"

The bold approach intimidated the soldiers, and they left the family in peace.

"I was not a prisoner until the war was over," recalled Horst Sommer:

> We were captured by the British in Schleswig-Holstein. Many [German prisoners] were taken to Siberia, since they needed workers there. I worked for a farmer near Nienburg on the Weser for about a year until 1946. The next few steps on the way home led me through Wanne-Eikel where I worked in a coal mine.

During the summer of 1945, Johanna Schmidt felt compelled to return to Görlitz to determine the status of her home. Her trip from Halberstadt took her through a devastated and defeated Germany. She walked and carried heavy suitcases part of the way. Arriving in Görlitz, she went straight to her home. As Johanna recalled:

> Oh, how it looked. Simply indescribable. I walked from one room to the next, and it was all just one big mess. There was not one piece of furniture that was not damaged or broken, and all of our clothes that we had left behind, as well as our mattresses, had been stolen. There had been a concentration camp about five minutes from our home, and when the prisoners there were released they naturally came into the homes and took what they needed and wanted. Nobody could really blame them for stealing, but they destroyed a lot too. . . . I walked through our garden and found pots and dishes broken, scattered all around.[19]

After cleaning up the home as best she could ("so that my mother would not have to see it like this"), she spent another week traveling back to Halberstadt.

Anton and Charlotte Larisch and Johanna Schmidt survived the immediate aftermath of the war in Halberstadt, though conditions there were deplorable. After five years of active attendance and missionary work in Halberstadt, Anton was set apart as the branch president there on June 1, 1945. A change in employment finally made it possible for him to take his family back to their hometown of Görlitz in February 1946.[20]

Horst Sommer finally arrived at home on June 30, 1946:

> My mother knew I was still alive, but she did not believe that I was actually standing in the house because she did not know when I was coming back. I didn't write to tell my mother that I was on my way home because in those days so many men were shipped to Russia without notice that she would have looked for me to come home, and I might have been on my way to Russia.

In reviewing his attitude as a Latter-day Saint under the harrowing circumstances of World War II, Helmut Habicht made this observation:

> I think I had a testimony of the gospel of Jesus Christ, and it did not change during the war. It

Fig. 9. Priesthood holders of the Görlitz Branch. Four of these men lost their lives in the war. (H. Habicht)

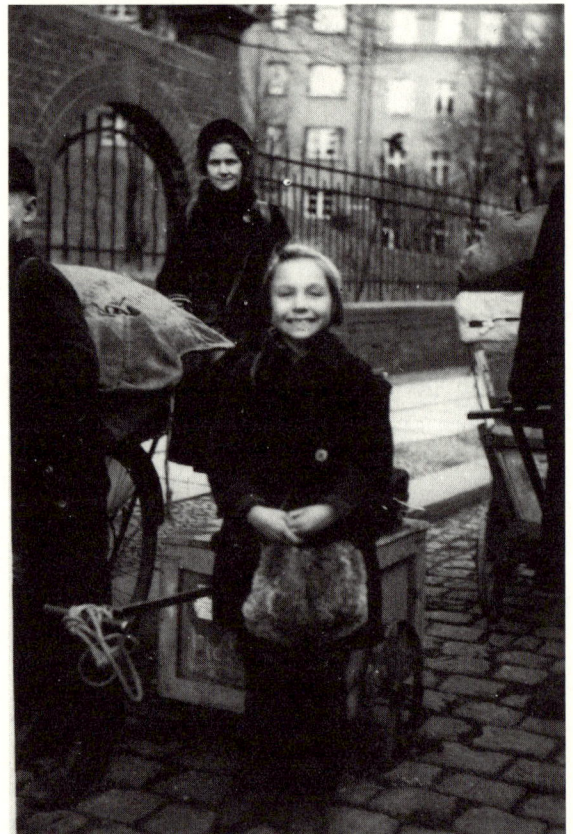

Fig. 10. Jutta Larisch was happy to be home again in Görlitz in February of 1946. (F. Larisch)

was strengthened because my father was not a member. My mother was a wonderful example of kindness and that was the gospel for me. . . . She was the ultimate example for me.

In Memoriam

The following members of the Görlitz Branch did not survive World War II:

Johanna Berger full-time missionary Berlin 1939–1941; m. ——— Groth; k. in air raid Hamburg 1943 (Larisch; H. Sommer)

Rudolf Bernhard Habicht b. Görlitz, Schlesien, Preußen 21 Mar 1924; son of Richard Ernst Friedolin Habicht and Emma Marie Rachak; bp. 30 Jul 1933; ord. priest; Waffen-SS corporal; MIA Eastern Front Dec 1944 (Habicht; FHL Microfilm 162769, 1935 Census; IGI)

Karl Gustav Friedrich Kühn b. Leopoldshain, Görlitz, Schlesien, Preußen 4 May 1909; son of Karl Gustav Kuehn and Pauline Selma Hansche; bp. 23 Oct 1917; m. 17 Nov 1933; d. Russia 8 Mar 1944 (Habicht; IGI)

Karl Gustav Kühn b. Hermsdorf, Görlitz, Schlesien, Preußen 12 Oct 1866; bp. 29 Jan 1902; m. 18 May 1891, Anna Luise Auguste Hansche; 2 children; d. Leopoldshain, Görlitz, Schlesien, Preußen 25 Jul 1943 (IGI)

Vera Sigrid Erika Larisch b. Görlitz, Schlesien, Preußen 4 Oct 1940; dau. of Anton Larisch and Charlotte Anna Luise Schmidt Larisch; d. diphtheria 29 Dec 1941; bur. Görlitz 31 Dec 1941 (Görlitz Branch History, Anton Larisch diary, 25; AF; IGI)

Hedwig Lehmann b. Görlitz, Schlesien, Preußen 5 Apr 1892; dau. of Hermann Lehmann and Emilie Sommer; d. old age 13 Jul 1944 (CHL CR 375 8 #2458, 744–45)

Kurt Lehmann b. Görlitz, Schlesien, Preußen 29 Jul 1908; ord. elder; k. in battle Penzig, Schlesien 17 Apr 1945 (G. Lehmann)

Ernst Friedrich Michalk b. Neupuschwitz, Bautzen, Sachsen 22 Nov 1919; son of Karl Traugott Michalk and Marie Martha Luecke; bp. 2 Aug 1929; m. 8 Jan 1944; d. 4 or 5 Mar 1945; bur. Kamp-Linfort Military Cemetery, Ger-

Fig. 11. Kurt Lehmann (H. Habicht)

many (Habicht; www.volksbund.de; IGI; AF)

Heinz Sommer b. Görlitz, Schlesien, Preußen 1921; son of Hermann Alfred Sommer and Else Böhme; ord. priest or elder; k. in battle northern Italy 30 Apr 1944 (W. Sommer; IGI)

Heinz Günther Wagner b. Görlitz, Schlesien, Preußen 28 Feb 1924; son of Johann Karl Wagner and Anna Elsa Lohse; bp. 30 Jul 1933; corporal; k. in battle 3 km west of Orlansk, Ukraine 28 Oct 1943; bur. Krassny-Bojez, Ukraine (H. Wagner; www.volksbund.de; FHL Microfilm 245291, 1935 Census; IGI; AF)

Fig. 12. Rudi Wagner (H. Habicht)

Hermann Heinrich Walter Wagner b. Görlitz, Schlesien, Preußen 7 Jan 1915; son of Johann Karl Wagner and Anna Elsa Lohse; bp. 13 Sep 1924; ord. teacher; k. in battle southeast of Metkowitschi, Russia 7 Feb 1944 (H. Wagner; FHL Microfilm 245291, 1935 Census; IGI; AF)

Wilhelm Rudi Wagner b. Görlitz, Schlesien, Preußen 1 Aug 1922; son of Johann Karl Wagner and Anna Elsa Lohse; bp. 27 Jul 1930; ord. teacher; k. in battle near Repky, Russia 12 or 14 Feb 1944 (H. Wagner; FHL Microfilm 245291, 1935 Census; IGI; AF)

Notes

1. Presiding Bishopric, "Financial, Statistical, and Historical Reports of Wards, Stakes, and Missions, 1884–1955," CR 4 12, 257.

2. Ruth Baier Hein, interview by the author in German, Görlitz, Germany, June 6, 2007; unless otherwise noted, summarized in English by Judith Sartowski.

3. Helmut Habicht, interview by the author in German, Görlitz, Germany, June 6, 2007.

4. Anton Larisch, diary, March 17, 1940, 7; private collection; trans. Ruth Larisch Hinkel.

5. Ibid., September 6, 1940, 16.

6. Jutta (Judy) Larisch Winkelmann to the author, letter, October 7, 2006; author's collection.

7. Because this kind of intervention is not mentioned by eyewitnesses, in other branches the ruling must have come from the city government.

8. Horst Sommer, interview by the author in German, Görlitz, Germany, June 6, 2007.

9. Eberhard Sommer, biography (unpublished), 41; private collection.

10. Ibid., 46.

11. Larisch, diary, December 29, 1941, 25.

12. Sommer, biography, 53.

13. Fred Larisch, interview by the author, West Jordan, Utah, November 10, 2006.

14. Eberhard Sommer, biography, 56.

15. Charlotte Larisch, "The Story of Anton & Charlotte Larisch," *The Announcer* (unpublished family newsletter, April 1971), 4; private collection. Anton Larisch had been arrested in Halberstadt (again and on the same spurious charges) and had been transferred to a prison in Berlin in January 1945.

16. See the Halberstadt Branch chapter for the story of Anton Larisch and his troubles with the law.

17. Kenneth Runnacles and Johanna Schmidt Runnacles, "Our Lives" (unpublished family history, about 1977), 52; private collection.

18. Ibid., 54.

19. Ibid., 58.

20. Larisch, "Story of Anton & Charlotte Larisch," 5.

NÖSSIGE BRANCH

The small town of Nössige is located fifteen miles west-northwest of Dresden in Saxony. The branch of Latter-day Saints living in and near Nössige during World War II had come into being mainly due to Jakob Christeler, a native Swiss, who owned a small farm there. Brother Christeler's children and grandchildren comprised the majority of the small branch. Other families joined the Church due to his missionary efforts as he sold dairy products in the towns around Nössige. According to Elsa Böhme (born 1922), "One day he visited my family, and they talked about the Church. [My family] later joined the Church."[1]

The family of Arno Rudolph lived in Semmelsberg, four miles east of Nössige. Son Georg Rudolph (born 1926) recalled his family riding bicycles for forty-five minutes to Nössige to attend meetings held in a large room in the building in which Grandpa Christeler lived on a large farm.[3]

Nössige Branch[2]	1939
Elders	2
Priests	1
Teachers	0
Deacons	6
Other Adult Males	3
Adult Females	14
Male Children	7
Female Children	0
Total	33

Another son, Jacob Rudolph (born 1930), added these details:

We came with our bicycles, and we left them [at the foot of the stairs.] There were steps that went up to the second floor. We came in the right where the kitchen was, and they had a little living room in there. It was a little home for the workers who worked on the farm.[4]

According to Jacob Rudolph, his family members could not be deterred from attending church on Sunday: "We went in bad weather, it made no difference. In the winter time we went on skis. But my parents still walked."

Sunday meetings (both Sunday School and sacrament meeting) took place in the morning in this small branch. On occasion, as many as thirty persons were in attendance.

Fig. 1. Jakob Christeler was the "founding father" of the Nössige Branch. He disappeared in Dresden in 1946. (G. Rudolph)

In the small town of Semmelsberg, the Rudolph children were not under great pressure to participate in Hitler Youth activities. Brother Rudolph simply explained to the group's leaders that his children were busy attending church and did not have time for additional meetings.

Jakob Christeler had spent a year or so living in Salt Lake City during the mid-1930s. He had taken genealogical documents along and was able to do ordinances in the Salt Lake Temple for many of his ancestors. When he returned to Nössige before the war, he was one of the very few endowed Latter-day Saints living in Germany.[5]

In a small town, a foreign or unknown religious group could be a matter of interest to the police. Elsa Böhme remembered that government agents visited meetings on occasion:

We knew that if there was a person we did not know [in the meeting], he was there to listen to what we had to say. They wanted to find out if we said anything against the government, but we didn't, and they left us alone.

Arno Rudolph and three of his four sons were eventually drafted into the German army. Brother Rudolph returned after just six months of duty in Czechoslovakia and was not required to serve again. "He was night blind," explained his son, Jacob. Two of the Rudolph boys lost their lives—Walter was killed near Stalingrad, Russia, and Herbert died in an accident while building a bridge in France.

During the absence of so many of their young men, life went on for the Saints of the Nössige Branch. In 1941, Jacob Rudolph was baptized. He recalled the event: "I was baptized in a pond a little bit outside of Nössige. My grandfather [Jakob Christeler] baptized me."

The Ludwig family had moved from Görlitz to Nössige shortly before the war, and Brother Kurt Ludwig soon became the branch president. His son, Herbert K. Ludwig, later wrote a long and very detailed account of his experiences

Fig. 2. The Nössige Sunday School on an excursion in 1938. (G. Rudolph)

in Hitler's Germany. His preface included the assertion that one could live under National Socialism without being a part of it. For example, he and his father were convinced that Hitler was leading the country in the wrong direction—a direction not sanctioned by God.[6]

Kurt Ludwig was drafted into the army at the beginning of the war but was fortunate to be released after a short tour of duty. While he was in the Wehrmacht, his son, Herbert, was the only son at home to run the farm and was therefore exempt from military service until his father returned. When Herbert finally became a soldier, he had these feelings:

> With all the pomp, music, parades, and talks, we finally did raise our hands and repeat the oath of loyalty and death; I felt helpless, forlorn! . . . What happened the next seven years in uniform to me I could fit in one sentence, "With the help of the Lord, I was preserved and returned home."

Herbert Ludwig's first year of duty was spent in the Soviet Union, where he was involved in the campaign to capture Moscow. Arriving in August of 1941, he experienced euphoric victories as the German army advanced quickly and steadily toward the Russian capital. However, as the German nation reveled in victories, what Herbert saw gave no cause for rejoicing. Here is his description of one battle:

> Picture a mile-wide valley with a small river meandering through the pasture, the road running along it, forest on both sides from three to five hundred yards from the road, when two almost identical columns of vehicles met up with each other. Ours consisting of twin and four barrel automatic 20 millimeter guns, and theirs of heavy machine guns two and four barrel on trucks mounted, and when they had rolled up the full lengths, ours being on full-alarm stations. Some one on our side gave the order to fire, the Russians never had a chance—destruction was total, bodies strewn all over trying to escape, some hanging out the truck windows with the trucks still on fire, others with the doors open had just fallen out, others on the way to the woods mowed down. Some trucks trying to escape being caught in the cross fire still burning, ammunition exploding; some were ripped apart, and so were people; a total destruction.

As with so many other LDS soldiers, Herbert's main concern was the possibility that he might be forced to take the life of another human being. On one occasion, he entered a dark house and found a Russian soldier lurking inside. They actually bumped into each other but neither had room to maneuver his rifle. Both raced for an exit, and each threw a grenade back into the room. Apparently, neither grenade killed anyone.

Herbert was constantly in combat engagements over the winter of 1941–42 and earned several medals for valor. He was the only member of his company not wounded or killed. However, on at least ten occasions, he came within inches of death or severe injury.

Fig. 3. The room in which the Nössige Branch held its meetings was reached via this staircase on the Christeler farm. (G. Rudolph)

270

Fig. 4. A wartime wedding is celebrated in the room used for worship services in the Christeler home. (G. Rudolph)

In his written account, the phrase "Thank you, Lord!" marks such specific events, as he constantly recognized the hand of God in saving him (and he admitted that there were probably other times when he was not aware of having been endangered and spared).

In early 1942, Herbert was in close combat in a small Russian village and was chastised angrily by an officer who noticed that he was not firing his rifle. In response, Herbert took careful aim and shot about two feet above the heads of enemy soldiers. A few hours later, he and a comrade were hiding behind the corner of a cottage when an artillery shell tore through the roof just two feet above their heads. He later described the lesson he learned:

An impression, or you could say a voice, which let me know for the rest of my life—"just as you had aimed" [two feet higher]. . . . How can I forget such a lesson? . . . Do unto others as you would have them to do unto you.

During his eight months in Russia, Herbert had experienced the German advance to within a few miles of Moscow and the retreat that followed. He had gone through hell, suffering in ways he could barely bring himself to describe in writing. His sentiments were likely those of many Latter-day Saints in the uniforms of many nations at the time:

How do you stay sane? How do you keep integrity? How do you keep the Word of Wisdom? Or the commandments? Well, you just do; you make up your mind, and you don't care about peer pressure or the opinion of your superiors. You will have plenty of opportunities to prove that you are loyal, dependable, physically better, and mentally more alert. You will be hated, admired, and commended for your guts; but above all you will walk ten feet taller (not stuck up) but for joy in knowing that you are sustained by the Lord. . . . How do you pray? As for me, very seldom aloud; but short and to the point. You feel closer than ever to Him.

After a short and relatively pleasant stay in France (interspersed with two furloughs at home), Herbert Ludwig was on his way to North Africa. He found it to be a totally different war featuring a clearly visible foe, very warm (but preferable) temperatures, and the presence of aircraft. Initially, Herbert and his comrades under the command of field marshal Erwin Rommel enjoyed clear victories against the British and the Americans, but the Allies eventually gained control of the region, and the German *Afrika Korps* was defeated and tens of thousands of prisoners taken. Herbert was soon on his way to the United States and experienced what would be known as paradise for German prisoners fortunate to be taken there for the duration of the war. He was sent first to a camp in Ellis, Illinois, arriving there in the fall of 1942.

The camp in Ellis offered better conditions for German prisoners than they had seen for years as regular soldiers. Herbert Ludwig described the POWs as "birds in the golden cage." He was fed well, treated with respect, and even paid for his labor (ten cents per hour by the Americans and three dollars per month from the German government through the Red Cross). He was allowed to write one card and one letter to Germany each month, and he received letters from home as well (with certain words blacked out by censors). He even received letters and packages from his Aunt Frances in Salt Lake City. An Uncle Herbert and an Uncle Willi actually visited him, as did Bishop Fred Busselburg from nearby Milwaukee, Wisconsin.

Georg Rudolph was in an apprenticeship program in Nössige when he was inducted into the Reichsarbeitsdienst on November 23, 1943. He served in that program near Warsaw, Poland. Just a week after returning to his family in Semmelsberg and to the Saints in Nössige, he was drafted into the Wehrmacht. It was already 1944, and he was sent to a unit near

Paris. Georg was very fortunate in his assignment, as he explained:

> I was trained to be a truck driver. There was an officer who always wanted to go to Paris, and he needed a driver, so he asked me, and I had many opportunities to see Paris. Oftentimes, as we drove through France, there were planes flying very low, and when they saw a car on the road, they started shooting at it. We tried to hide somewhere and often had to jump out of the car.

By early 1945, Georg was serving near Meissen, only a few miles from his hometown. His assignment had changed, and he was to monitor the artillery fire of the advancing Red Army; he and his comrades did so by placing microphones in the ground. As did thousands of other German soldiers facing the Soviets, Georg and his unit preferred to surrender to the Americans, so in April they cautiously made their way toward the Western Front, then only a few miles away. They were fortunate to be taken prisoner by the Americans not far from the city of Hanover.

As a common soldier with a very short tour of duty, Georg was a deacon in the Aaronic Priesthood. He never met another Latter-day Saint soldier while away from home, never had the opportunity to attend a Church meeting, and had no scriptures to read. The Lord blessed him, in that he was never in combat and thus never in serious danger. He was kept prisoner for only about six weeks and would have gone home right away, but this required that he cross the border from the British Occupation Zone into the Soviet Zone. He decided to work on a farm for a while and then joined with a friend from Leipzig. The two sneaked across the zonal border and made their way home. Georg Rudolph was able to celebrate Christmas 1945 with his family.

Sometime in 1946, Herbert Ludwig was sent from the POW camp in Illinois to New York City. He and his comrades were told that they were being released and shipped home. The transport ship passed the Statue of Liberty as it departed for France. Once there, the American promises of a quick trip home were violated. Herbert was sent to a camp in northwest France and forced to work in a coal mine. It was 1946 before he found a chance to escape and cross the border into Germany. With a comrade, he worked his way gradually north into the British Occupation Zone and from there across into the Soviet Zone. It was August 1946 when he finally caught sight of his home:

> One hour from home! Slowly I start walking, I want it to be dark when I arrived, a surprise. . . . I make the final turn from the hill down from where I had seen my home for awhile; as I turn in, a small, white wooden fence comes up; it had not been there when I left. Now I can see our kitchen window with light in it. Oh, my Lord, I see more. I see Father, Mother, and sister, my head swirls, can I make it without being seen? Down the road, into the yard, up the outside flight of stairs, into the hall. I rap at the door, can't stand the tension—"Come in," is the call from Father. I can't move. The door bursts open, my sister looks out, her mouth drops wide open. . . . "Oh, no, Herbert?!" . . . Father and Mother join in the embrace; do we need words? Happiness was never more true!!

One of the saddest events in the history of the Nössige Branch occurred in the summer of 1946. With his daughter, Jakob Christeler attended a district conference of the Latter-day Saints in Dresden. By then, he was an

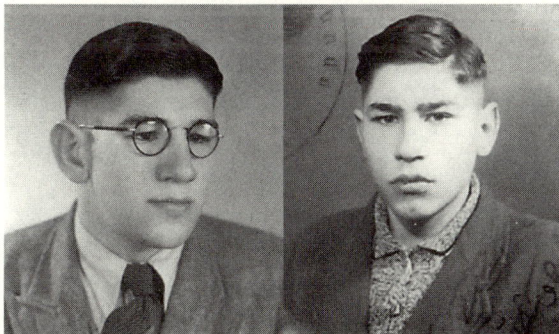

Fig. 5. Arno Walter Rudolph. (G. Rudolph)

Fig. 6. Alfred Herbert Rudolph. (G. Rudolph)

older man suffering from something similar to Alzheimer's disease. After the meeting, he and his daughter waited for a streetcar. When it arrived, she boarded, carrying his coat with all of his personal papers (it was a very warm day). Suddenly the streetcar pulled away before he could get on. By the time she could return to that location, he was nowhere to be found. All efforts to locate him were in vain, and he would have been unable to identify himself. Jakob Christeler simply disappeared.

Elsa Böhme summed up the sad experience of the war and her reactions in these words: "What helped me throughout this horrible time of war was the knowledge that we are Heavenly Father's children and that He loves us. He wants us to return to Him. I never doubted that He loves us although terrible things happened."

In Memoriam

The following members of the Nössige Branch did not survive World War II:

Jakob Christeler b. Sengg, Bern, Switzerland 16 May 1866; son of Christian Christeler and Susanna Katarina Tritten; bp. 7 May 1904; endowment Salt Lake Temple 20 Oct 1937; m. Possendorf, Dresden, Sachsen 15 May 1892, Minna Anna Kuettner; 6 children; disappeared Dresden, Dresden, Sachsen 7 May 1946 (IGI)

Alfred Herbert Rudolph b. Semmelsberg, Dresden, Sachsen 21 Jun 1923; son of Arno Arthur Rudolf and Rosa Frieda Christeler; bp. 9 May 1931; k. in battle France 20 Nov 1942 (George Rudolph; IGI)

Arno Walter Rudolph b. Nössige, Dresden, Sachsen 24 Apr 1916; son of Arno Arthur Rudolf and Rosa Frieda Christeler; bp. 26 Apr 1932; m. Krögis, Dresden, Sachsen 17 May 1941, Elli Liesbeth Beyer Ludwig; 1 child; k. near Stalingrad, Russia 31 Dec 1945 (George Rudolph; IGI)

Gottfried Walter Hommel b. Dresden, Dresden, Sachsen 12 Aug 1925; son of Johannes Bernhard Waechtler and Elisabeth Anna Hommel; bp. 5 Jul 1941; soldier; k. by mob near Nössige, Meissen, Sachsen 12 May 1945 (Fritz Waechtler; IGI)

Notes

1. Elsa Böhme, telephone interview with Jennifer Heckmann in German, February 8, 2008; unless otherwise noted, summarized

in English by Judith Sartowski, and an audio version of transcript of the interview is in the author's collection.

2. Presiding Bishopric, "Financial, Statistical, and Historical Reports of Wards, Stakes, and Missions, 1884–1955," CR 4 12, 257.

3. George Rudolph, interview by Michael Corley in German, Salt Lake City, January 17, 2008.

4. Jacob Rudolph, interview by the author, Salt Lake City, July 26, 2007.

5. At that time, the Salt Lake Temple was the closest temple to Germany.

6. Herbert K. Ludwig, autobiography (unpublished); private collection.

The family of Dresden district president Max Hegewald shortly after the war. One son had died as a soldier. (Hegewald)

HINDENBURG
DISTRICT
East German Mission

The Hindenburg District of the East German Mission of The Church of Jesus Christ of Latter-day Saints was the smallest district in the mission in both area and population. It was situated at the farthest eastern-central extent of Germany in 1939. There were only seventy-two members in three branches and one group in the district.

The city of Hindenburg was located at the eastern end of the territory. All of the branches were within just a few miles of the German borders with Poland and Czechoslovakia. The distance from Hindenburg to the office of the East German Mission in Berlin was 240 miles—a good day's journey by railroad in those days.

The Hindenburg District was organized just prior to World War II. The history of the East German Mission includes these details:

> Sunday, 10 July 1938: A special meeting was held in the Hindenburg Branch to organize the new Hindenburg District. Brother Martin Werner Hoppe, president of the Breslau District, presided. The branches of Hindenburg, Gleiwitz, and Ratibor were taken from the Breslau District and organized into the new Hindenburg District. Elder Ray D. Zollinger [a young missionary from the United States] was sustained president of the new district.[1]

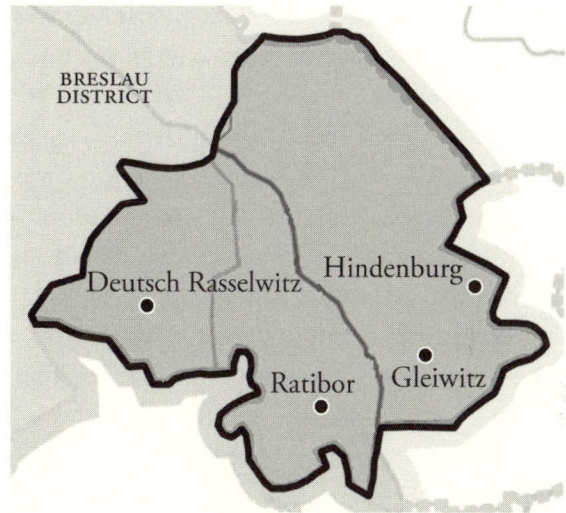

Fig. 1. *The branches of the Hindenburg District.*

On October 16, 1938, the first conference of the new district was held in the rooms of the Hindenburg Branch under the leadership of mission president Alfred C. Rees.[2]

In addition to the branch in the city of Hindenburg, there was a branch in Ratibor, twenty-four miles southwest of Hindenburg, and another in Gleiwitz, ten miles west. The name Gleiwitz is still associated with infamy because it was at the German-Polish border near Gleiwitz that Hitler's government staged an "attack" by Polish troops on a radio station.[3] The trumped-up affair was used as the justification for the invasion of Poland by German troops beginning on Friday, September 1, 1939.

Hindenburg District[4]	1939	1940	1941	1942
Elders	3	3		
Priests	4	4		
Teachers	1	1		
Deacons	3	3		
Other Adult Males	9	9		
Adult Females	41	43		
Male Children	6	7		
Female Children	5	5		
Total	72	75	79	79

No information regarding the Hindenburg District is found in the journal of the East German Mission after 1939. When a letter was sent by East German Mission leaders to all district presidents on August 12, 1941, no district president in Hindenburg was included among the addressees. It is possible that nobody was called to succeed Elder Zollinger, who was evacuated from Germany with the other American missionaries on August 25, 1939.

All of the Hindenburg District territory was ceded to Poland following World War II. After the Polish government forced the evacuation of German citizens from the region in late 1946, all traces of the presence of The Church of Jesus Christ of Latter-day Saints there were lost.

NOTES

1. East German Mission Quarterly Reports, 1938, no. 29, East German Mission History.
2. East German Mission Quarterly Reports, 1938, nos. 41–42.
3. It was later determined that the "Polish soldiers" were actually criminals from German prisons attired in Polish uniforms. All dead soldiers [prisoners] shown to the media had been executed by the SS and placed in positions that simulated combat.
4. Presiding Bishopric, "Financial, Statistical, and Historical Reports of Wards, Stakes, and Missions, 1884–1955," CR 4 12, 257.

DEUTSCH RASSELWITZ GROUP

Bertold Patermann joined The Church of Jesus Christ of Latter-day Saints in 1932, thanks to an enthusiastic man with whom Brother Patermann worked on the railroad. After his first wife died, Bertold married Kornelia Schiller, and she helped bring up his children in the new faith. The Patermanns formed the nucleus of the Church in the small town of Deutsch Rasselwitz in Silesia, just a few miles from the Czech border. The population of the town was about three thousand when World War II began.

"Later my father converted a neighbor lady and her daughter, who lived in the same house. That was our branch for a long time," recalled Angela Patermann.[1]

During the late 1930s, American missionaries were common visitors in the Patermann home. The town was predominately Catholic, but the neighbors did not seem to care about the tiny group of religious outsiders. "They didn't cause trouble because they thought we were nuts," according to Angela Patermann. There was no persecution of any kind.

The Patermann home at Neustädterstrasse 150 hosted all Church meetings in Deutsch Rasselwitz until 1939. Brother Patermann, a priest in the Aaronic Priesthood, conducted a sacrament meeting on Sundays. For larger meetings, such as district conferences, the small group took the train to Ratibor (eighteen miles to the southeast) or Hindenburg (thirty-five miles due east).

Just before the war started, Bertold Patermann was transferred to Berlin in connection with his employment with the railroad, which was a government entity in Germany in those days. This meant the effectual end of the Latter-day Saint group in Deutsch Rasselwitz. The Patermann family became members of the Berlin East Branch.[2]

The Polish government expelled all Germans from Deutsch Rasselwitz by the end of 1946, so it can be surmised that no Latter-day Saints were living there after that time. The name of the town was soon changed to Racławice Sldskie.

No members of the Deutsch Rasselwitz group are known to have lost their lives in World War II.

NOTES

1. Angela Patermann Buchta, interview by the author, Salt Lake City, August 9, 2007.
2. For more about the activities of the Patermann family, see the Berlin East Branch chapter.

GLEIWITZ BRANCH

In September 1938, the Latter-day Saint branch in Gleiwitz was meeting in rented rooms on the main floor at Oberwallstrasse 13.

"There were mostly women and children attending the meetings, but we could always count on everybody coming on Sundays. There were eight to fifteen people in attendance." Such is the recollection of Gerhard Ertel (born 1926).[1]

It is interesting to note that while there was an official branch in Gleiwitz, the year-end 1938 membership data available from the East German Mission show not even one holder of the Aaronic or the Melchizedek Priesthood. One wonders who presided over the meetings, baptized new members, or administered the sacrament. If the same was true here as in other small branches, district leaders and priesthood holders from other branches in the district visited on Sundays and performed such services.

Gleiwitz Branch[2]	1939
Elders	0
Priests	0
Teachers	0
Deacons	0
Other Adult Males	3
Adult Females	10
Male Children	0
Female Children	2
Total	15

As a teenager, Gerhard Ertel found himself in a challenging situation on Sunday mornings. He was a member of a brass band in the Hitler Youth and was to open a program at ten o'clock—precisely the hour when Sunday School began. After playing the opening march music in the movie theater, he sneaked out to attend Sunday School (four houses down the street). Just before noon, he sneaked back into the theater and was there when the lights went up again—ready to play more march music.

"In the Hitler Youth we were taught to be tough," explained Gerhard: "Once we hung a boy up in the tree and didn't get him down until the next day [unharmed]. That's what we were taught—to be fast and strict. . . . This education started when we were little children, and they could do anything with us and we would act it out."

The German radio station on the outskirts of Gleiwitz by the Polish border was the scene of the first altercation between German and Polish troops—at least in the reports given the German people. The fake attack of Polish troops on the radio station was used as the justification for the German invasion of Poland on September 1, 1939. The name Gleiwitz will long be associated with that infamous affair.

As in most eastern German cities, the war was far away from Gleiwitz after the conquest of Poland. According to Gerhard Ertel, Church meetings continued as before. Perhaps the branch even gained in numbers somewhat because a directory of the East German Mission showed that the Gleiwitz Branch meeting place had moved to Hüttendamm 4 by January 1943. There is no indication why the move was made or what the rooms were like at the new location.[3]

In 1944, Gerhard turned eighteen and soon was drafted into the armed forces. On April 4, he reported for duty and was assigned to the navy. There he had some choice of service and asked to be made a mechanic. He was shipped to the Baltic seaport of Lübeck and trained to work with torpedoes for submarines. Later, he prepared torpedoes to be shipped to Bremen where they were loaded into submarines.

Advance units of the Soviet army entered the city of Gleiwitz on January 20, 1945.[4] It is likely that some of the members of the Gleiwitz Branch had fled the city by that time. Gerhard Ertel's parents had remained and were treated relatively well by the conquerors.

Gerhard served in the navy barely a year before the British arrived in northern Germany and the war ended. Although he was a POW under the British, he did not feel like a prisoner because he was allowed to move about freely during the day. Nevertheless, he was far from Gleiwitz and totally isolated from the Church. He had no scriptures to read and never encountered another Latter-day Saint while away from home.

In the summer of 1945, Gerhard's parents left what had become Poland and moved west. Their first stop was Berlin, where they received instructions from mission leaders to travel south to the Latter-day Saint refugee colony at Wolfsgrün in Saxony. A few months later, they moved on to the American Occupation Zone and settled in another refugee colony of Saints—in Langen, south of Frankfurt am Main.

Gerhard Ertel located his family through correspondence and traveled from northern Germany to Langen to be reunited with them. He had never seen combat and had not been subjected to ill treatment as a prisoner of war. Looking back, he reached this conclusion: "What I had learned in the [Gleiwitz] Branch, I used and applied throughout my entire life, especially in the time when I was a soldier and did not have a connection to the Church. The teachers in the Sunday School and my mother taught me."

The Church of Jesus Christ of Latter-day Saints ceased to exist in Gleiwitz by the summer of 1946 at the latest. The Polish name of the town is now Gliwice.

In Memoriam

The following members of the Gleiwitz Branch did not survive World War II:

Renate Ingeborg Ertel b. Gleiwitz, Schlesien, Preußen 15 Oct 1941; dau. of Alfred Ertel and Bronislawa Franziska Schiller; d. Gleiwitz 23 Jan 1944 (Ertel; AF; IGI)

Anton Helios b. Groß Lagiewnik, Schlesien, Preußen 8 May 1900; son of Anton Helios and Rosalie Grabinski; bp. Gleiwitz, Schlesien, Preußen 18 Sep 1931; conf. 18 Sep 1931; d. 22 Sep 1942 (CHL, CR 375 8, no. 55; IGI)

Alfred Bernhard Kowollik b. Drahthammer, Schlesien, Preußen 18 Aug 1899 or 1900; son of Franz Kowollik and Vateska Gattys; bp. 21 Oct 1937; conf. 21 Oct 1937; m. 6 Oct 1924, Anna Gerszczyk (div.); home guard; d. Woloschilowgrad, Russia 8 Dec 1945; bur. Lugansk, Ukraine (CHL, CR 375 8, no. 56; www.volksbund.de)

Margarete Henriette Christiane Kruber b. Breslau, Schlesien 21 Dec 1910; dau. of August Kruber and Emilie Winkler; bp. 6 Dec 1924; conf. 7 Dec 1924; m. 28 Nov 1938 Erich Grau; missing (CHL, CR 375 8, no. 57)

Anna Maria Motyezka b. Groß Strehlitz, Oppeln, Schlesien, Preußen 4 May 1892; dau. of Josef Motyezka and Karoline Kowollik; bp. 9 Sep 1938; conf. 9 Sep

1938; m. 10 Sep 1919, Friedrich Jüttner; d. poisoning 17 Oct 1939 (CHL, CR 375 8, no. 38)

Liselotte Weigand b. Stettin, Pommern 4 Jan 1916; dau. of Philipp Weigand and Meta Katilius; bp. 31 May 1924; conf. 1 Jul 1924; m. 27 Jun 1936, Erich Gustar Prust; missing (CHL, CR 375 8, no. 58)

NOTES

1. Gerhard Ertel, interview by Jennifer Heckmann, Langen, Germany, August 14, 2006; summarized in English by Judith Sartowski, and audio version or transcript of the interview in the author's collection.

2. Presiding Bishopric, "Financial, Statistical, and Historical Reports of Wards, Stakes, and Missions, 1884–1955," CR 4 12, 257.

3. East German Mission, "Directory of Meeting Places" (unpublished manuscript, 1943); private collection.

4. David Irving, *The Destruction of Dresden* (London: William Kimber, 1963), 81.

HINDENBURG BRANCH

The city of Hindenburg, Germany, was located just east of Gleiwitz in the state of Silesia. The city had approximately fifteen thousand inhabitants in 1939, of whom only thirty-four were members of The Church of Jesus Christ of Latter-day Saints. Just before World War II began on September 1, 1939, the branch members met in rented rooms at Dorotheenstrasse 9 on the second floor. By early 1943, the meetings had moved to Dorotheenstrasse 94 in the home of a person or family named Czock.[1]

As of this writing, no surviving eyewitnesses from the Hindenburg Branch have been identified, nor have historical writings of deceased eyewitnesses come to light. However, it is fortunate that the records of the East German Mission in Berlin include several entries regarding the Hindenburg Branch:

Hindenburg Branch[2]	1939
Elders	2
Priests	2
Teachers	0
Deacons	2
Other Adult Males	6
Adult Females	17
Male Children	3
Female Children	2
Total	34

Saturday, January 1 [1938]: The Primary Association of the Hindenburg Branch held a program evening, which was attended by one-hundred and thirty-six persons.[3]

Sunday, February 20. A conference of the Hindenburg Branch Sunday School organization was held, attended by seventeen members and eleven friends.[4]

Thursday, February 24. The Hindenburg Branch Primary Association held a program evening, with ninety-three persons attending.[5]

Tuesday, March 8. Following the Breslau Conference, a special meeting was held in Hindenburg, with Miss. Pres. and Sister Alfred C. Rees as honorary guests. In attendance also were sixty-nine persons, forty-three of them friends [nonmembers].[6] The secret police in Hindenburg questioned the branch president about their Primary work and demanded a list of the branch members.[7]

Thursday, 25 August 1938: The Primary Association of the Hindenburg Branch held a very successful "Homecoming." When members and former members met, there were one-hundred and fifty persons present.[8]

Sun 8 Jan 1939: Gerhard Herud is appointed branch president and Karl Czerwinski first counselor.[9]

Tue 28 Feb 1939: After receiving notice that the rent on their hall was ended, and unable to find another branch hall for the time being, the members of the Hindenburg Branch attended religious services in Gleiwitz.[10]

Remarkably, for such a small branch—thirty-four members at the end of 1939—it seems that all of the Church programs in Hindenburg were functional before the war broke out. On several occasions mentioned above, there were far more friends than members in attendance.

There is no additional information regarding the inquiry made by the Gestapo in March 1938. One can only speculate about the reasons for an investigation into the activities of the Primary organization. All over Germany in those days, it was common for Latter-day Saint children to invite friends to go with them to Primary on Wednesday afternoons (Wednesday was the short schoolday in Germany). It may be that this was happening in Hindenburg as well and that neighbors wondered about what was being done in Primary meetings or who was in charge.

One has to wonder whether the loss of the Church meeting rooms in Hindenburg spelled the demise of the branch. Traveling even ten miles to Gleiwitz to attend meetings would likely have proved disadvantageous, given the increasing rarity of trains available for civilian travel during the war.

The Red Army invaded the Hindenburg District territory in January 1945; armored units rolled into Hindenburg against little resistance on January 20.[11] By the end of 1946, the new Polish government had forcibly evicted all German citizens, which can only mean that the Latter-day Saints in that city were gone by then and that the branch had ceased to exist. The name of the town was changed to Zabrze.

In Memoriam

Only one member of the Hindenburg Branch did not survive World War II:

Willy Emanuel Hadzik b. Kattowitz, Schlesien, Preußen 24 Mar 1920; son of Johann Hadzik and Anna Nowak; bp. 10 Feb 1935; conf. 10 Feb 1935;

d. POW camp Argos, Greece 16 or 17 May 1941; bur. Dionyssos-Rapendoza, Greece (CHL CR 275 8, no. 105; IGI; www.volksbund.de)

Notes

1. East German Mission, "Directory of Meeting Places" (unpublished manuscript, 1943); private collection.
2. Presiding Bishopric, "Financial, Statistical, and Historical Reports of Wards, Stakes, and Missions, 1884–1955," CR 4 12, 257.
3. East German Mission Quarterly Reports, 1938, no. 9, East German Mission History.
4. Ibid., no. 12.
5. Ibid.
6. Ibid.
7. Ibid., no. 26.
8. Ibid., no. 35.
9. Ibid., no. 51.
10. Ibid., no. 56–57.
11. David Irving, *The Destruction of Dresden* (London: William Kimber, 1963), 81.

Ratibor Branch

Located twenty-four miles from the seat of the Hindenburg District of the East German Mission, the city of Ratibor was just twenty miles north of the German-Czech border and thirty-five miles west of the German-Polish border. The branch of Latter-day Saints in this city was as isolated from the Church as it was from the rest of Hitler's Germany.

Ratibor Branch[1]	1939
Elders	1
Priests	0
Teachers	1
Deacons	0
Other Adult Males	0
Adult Females	13
Male Children	1
Female Children	0
Total	16

Due to a lack of eyewitnesses as of this writing, little is known about the Latter-day Saints in Ratibor. The mission directory shows that in late 1938, the meetings were held in the home of the Nawrath family at Gertrudenstrasse 37. Five years later, the same family hosted the branch for meetings at a different address: Gartenstrasse 14.

By 1946, virtually all ethnic Germans had vacated the territory, and any activities of the Church faded into history there.

No members of the Ratibor Branch—one of the smallest official branches of the Church in all of Germany—are known to have lost their lives in World War II. The Polish name of the town is Raciborz.

NOTE

1. Presiding Bishopric, "Financial, Statistical, and Historical Reports of Wards, Stakes, and Missions, 1884–1955," CR 4 12, 257.

Elder Ezra Taft Benson visited the Selbongen Branch on August 6, 1946, to arrange for the delivery of Church welfare supplies.

KÖNIGSBERG
DISTRICT
East German Mission

In 1918, the German Empire ceased to exist. A republican form of government was introduced, and the Treaty of Versailles took large portions of German territory and ceded them to other nations. When most of the province of West Prussia was given to Poland by that treaty, the province of East Prussia was totally separated from the rest of Germany (see map in introduction). Culturally and politically, East Prussia was isolated from the rest of Germany, surrounded by Poland, Russia, and Lithuania. The city of Königsberg (now Kaliningrad, Russia) was the historic capital of East Prussia and had been a stronghold of The Church of Jesus Christ of Latter-day Saints since the turn of the century.

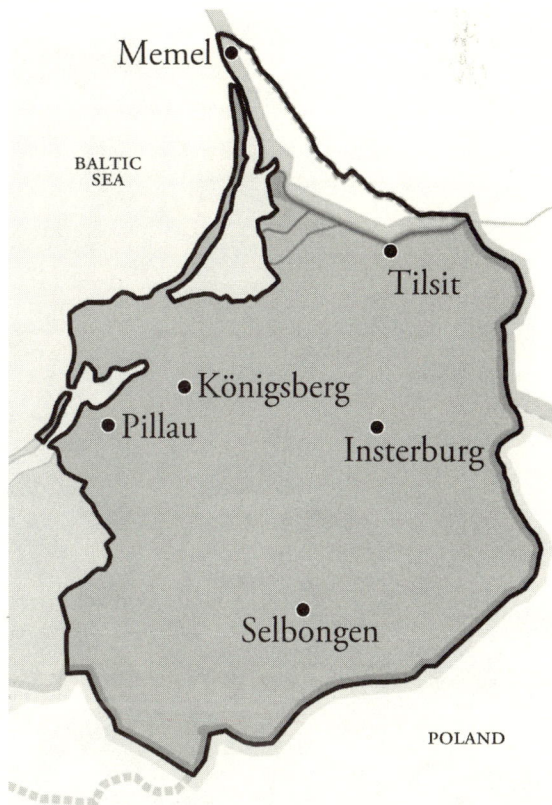

Fig. 1. *The Königsberg District was isolated from the rest of Germany.*

Königsberg District[1]	1939	1940	1941	1942
Elders	30	30		
Priests	8	20		
Teachers	23	25		
Deacons	41	38		
Other Adult Males	152	155		
Adult Females	424	430		
Male Children	41	49		
Female Children	52	58		
Total	771	805	800	798

The largest branch of the Church in the district at the end of the year 1939 was in the city of Königsberg itself. Other branches in the Königsberg District were located in Memel (fifty miles north), Tilsit (forty-two miles northeast), Insterburg (thirty-three miles

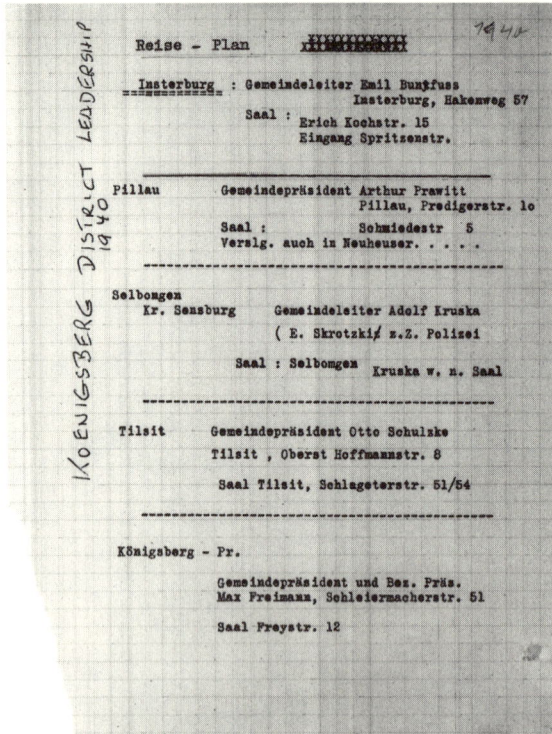

Fig. 2. Traveling elder Richard Deus typed this list of branches to visit in the Königsberg District in 1940. (M. Deus)

east), Selbongen (forty-five miles southeast), and Pillau (eighteen miles west). Each of the branches was within three hours of Königsberg by train. When leaders of the East German Mission wished to visit from Berlin, they had to cross the Polish corridor, then enter East Prussia (Germany) again—a distance of three hundred miles. It took about seven hours to reach Königsberg by train from Berlin.

The president of the Königsberg District throughout the war was Max Freimann of the Königsberg Branch. He served until his disappearance (along with several other Latter-day Saints) during the Soviet conquest of that city in April 1945.

Richard Deus (born 1903) of the Breslau South Branch, a full-time missionary, spent several weeks in the Königsberg District in late 1940. In an article he wrote for the Church magazine, *Der Stern*, he expressed his gratitude for the gracious manner in which he was received by the Saints during his tenure in East Prussia.[2]

Fig. 3. The priesthood meeting attendees during the district conference in Königsberg in October 1940. (A. Buntfuss)

District president Max Freimann was dedicated to his calling, as his daughters recalled:

Every other Sunday, our father visited a different branch. He never left on Saturday—always on Sunday very early in the morning. He often had to walk many miles in the worst weather. He came home tired, but he never complained about the work he had to do.[3]

According to President Freimann's son, Reinhard (born 1933), Max Freimann was called on by the city government to answer inquiries regarding the Church: "He was never a member of the [National Socialist] Party. Sometimes, he was summoned by the police and they asked him questions but nothing happened. . . . We [Latter-day Saints] were left alone."[4]

The records of the East German Mission in Berlin indicated that every district of the mission held a conference twice each year through the end of 1944. The conferences of the Königsberg District were always held in Königsberg on Friday through Sunday, or Saturday and Sunday in the later war years. The local Saints hosted members of the other five branches in their apartments. The Freimann sisters recalled how that worked: "They all slept on the floor and we managed to house [and feed] all the visitors." As in other districts, participants emphasized the fun the Saints had when they gathered for such spiritual feasts, cultural activities, and entertainment.

Inge Grünberg (born 1927) also recalled those semiannual events: "We had district conferences that were so well attended that we had nine hundred people or more, and sometimes there wasn't room to get everybody in."[5] The rooms at Freystrasse 10 were apparently large enough to accommodate sizable congregations.

The Red Army crossed the border into East Prussia (Germany) in October 1944. For the

Fig. 4. Gleaners and Beehives at a district conference in Königsberg on June 8, 1941. Irmgard Gottschalk and Erika Fassmann, missionaries from the Berlin office, are in the first row, second and third from left. (R. Berger Rudolph)

Fig. 5. (Top) This choir sang for the Königsberg District conference in September 1941. The banner reads, "The path to perfection." (I. Reimer Ebert)

Fig 6. (Bottom) Festivities at a Königsberg District conference in 1942. The banner reads, "Wake up and become a light!"

Fig. 7. Attendees at a district conference in 1942. District president Max Freimann is at the far left.

Fig. 8. The leaders of the Königsberg District met in the home of Max Freimann (seated center) in 1943. (Freimann)

first time, Latter-day Saint civilians were in danger of losing life and property to an enemy they could see face to face. Some Saints had already fled the region, and many more would do so before the invaders arrived in their towns. All of the branches of the Königsberg District had been substantially weakened by the time the 1945 New Year dawned, but all eyewitnesses still at home testified that Sunday meetings were held until the end of the war.

By the time World War II ended on May 8, 1945, more than 600,000 German citizens had fled East Prussia.[6] By the autumn of 1946, the northern half of the province had been ceded to Russia and the southern half to Poland. The remaining Germans had been forced to leave or to assume Polish or Russian citizenship. As far as can be determined, all members of the six branches of the Church in East Prussia who survived the war left the region, migrating to what is Germany today. All six branches were therefore discontinued, and the Church disappeared from the region until the 1990s.

Notes

1. Presiding Bishopric, "Financial, Statistical, and Historical Reports of Wards, Stakes, and Missions, 1884–1955," CR 4 12, 257.

2. East German Mission, *Sonnagsgruss*, December 1, 1940

3. Ruth Freimann Dietz, Ingrid Freimann Juras, and Irmgard Freimann Klindt, interview by the author in German, Salt Lake City, March 23, 2007; unless otherwise noted, summarized in English by Judith Sartowski.

4. Reinhard Freimann, interview by the author in German, Hanover, Germany, August 6, 2006.

5. Inge Grünberg Seiffer, interview by Jennifer Heckmann in German, Backnang, Germany, August 17, 2006; audio version or transcript of the interview in the author's collection.

6. David Irving, *The Destruction of Dresden* (London: William Kimber, 1963), 78.

Insterburg Branch[1]	1939
Elders	0
Priests	1
Teachers	1
Deacons	0
Other Adult Males	7
Adult Females	31
Male Children	0
Female Children	0
Total	40

INSTERBURG BRANCH

The city of Insterburg (now Chernyakhovsk, Russia) is located about thirty-three miles east of Königsberg, the capital of East Prussia. When World War II started on September 1, 1939, approximately fifty thousand people lived in Insterburg, only forty of whom were Latter-day Saints.

"Our branch was small, mostly a few old ladies and some children," recalled Käthe Braun (born 1925). "While I was there, we didn't have a Primary organization, MIA for young people, or Relief Society."[2] Because the membership of the Insterburg Branch was dominated by adult females (78 percent), and there were officially no elders in the branch at the onset of the war, priesthood leaders from

Fig. 1. Insterburg branch members outside of their meeting place. (R. Braun Fricke)

Königsberg came to visit and direct branch activities. Käthe recalled three of them: district president Max Freimann and his counselors, Emil Jenschewski and Brother Rzepkowsk—all from Königsberg.

The Insterburg Branch met in rented rooms at Erich-Koch-Strasse 15 on the main floor. Ruth Braun (born 1923), Käthe's sister, recalled that "we had a curtain in the middle of the room, separating it so the adults could have one side of the room and the children the other. We were just a few families." Albert Buntfuss (born 1926) recalled that one room measured about twenty by twenty-five feet in size.

Eyewitness accounts of life among the members of the Insterburg Branch come from two families—Braun and Buntfuss. Ruth Braun recalled that the branch president, a brother Jakulat, had passed away shortly before the war. The branch may have leaned upon visiting priesthood authorities for a while, but Alfred

Buntfuss recalled that his father, Emil Alfred Buntfuss, was the branch president during the war: "He blessed and passed the sacrament" (which he could have done while not yet an elder).[3] Sunday School was the first meeting of the day, but the branch likely held no meetings during the week in those days.[4]

About his father, Alfred Buntfuss recalled the following:

> Before the war, my father had to go to jail, and he was released four or five months later. A sister in the Church accused him because my father had told her husband that he could not have the priesthood. He was taken to prison because they thought he was a communist. . . . My father was against the regime. I knew that. We always listened to the English BBC radio station, though it was prohibited.

Ruth and Käthe's mother, Minna Braun, had been baptized in 1931. She was a very faithful member who was not ashamed to share the gospel with others. Käthe remembered how her

Fig. 2. Insterburg branch outing. (R. Braun Fricke)

Fig. 3. The chapel of the Insterburg Branch just before World War II. (A. Buntfuss)

mother always seemed to have a purse "stuffed full of missionary tracts." She handed them out to people on their way to church meetings—a walk of nearly one hour. Sister Braun was sad when the missionaries left, which happened with no warning on August 25, 1939. According to Ruth, "When [the missionaries] were gone, it seemed like everything was different and we didn't have any connection with Salt Lake City anymore."

At that time, Käthe Braun was living on a farm about two hours by train south of Insterburg. Having finished her schooling, she was required to do a Pflichtjahr (year of government service) on a farm. She and seven other girls took the place of farm boys who had been drafted. "Nobody was thinking about war then," Käthe recalled,

But we were close to the Polish border and suddenly things changed in our otherwise quiet neighborhood. Tanks rolled by, columns of soldiers in vehicles drove by. So many strange noises. This went on for about a week, then it was quiet again. This was a really scary time for us. We would all have rather stayed home with our families.

Käthe disliked farm work, so she was transferred to a different town to work as a domestic servant. She finished her year of service, then returned to Insterburg and found a job in a shop where uniforms were made. There she hoped to complete her occupational training.

Because her workplace was close to church, Käthe was given a key to the rooms and went there several times a week during her lunch hour to clean and dust so that things were in order for the meetings on Sunday.

Minna Braun's eldest son, Fritz Wilhelm Braun, may have been the lone priest in the branch in 1939. He was killed in battle on September 6, 1941, at the age of twenty-seven.

Fig. 4. Insterburg Saints posed for this photograph after holding their last meeting in 1941 at Erich-Koch-Strasse. The sign on the wall to the right displays the name of the Church. (A. Buntfuss)

His sister Käthe later wrote, "When the army informed us that [Fritz] was dead, my father [Wilhelm Braun] wept. It was the first time I had ever seen him cry. He sat at the table, and tears ran down his cheeks."

In his photo album, Alfred Buntfuss wrote the following caption for a photograph of the branch members that was entitled "The last meeting—1941":

> The end of the Insterburg Branch. The Mormons had been a thorn in the side of Hitler's government for some time. The missionaries were long since gone. Members were in the military. My father was sent to Norway to work at a wharf. The building had belonged to a Jew who was in a concentration camp. The building was declared structurally unsafe.

After this time, the family of Emil Alfred and Gertrud Buntfuss and one other family took the train west to Königsberg about twice a month to attend meetings. It was expensive and involved a lot of travel time. Ruth Braun went north to Tilsit about once a month to attend meetings there. She enjoyed spending time with the Schulzke family in Tilsit.

The Church was fortunately not yet defunct in Insterburg. Alfred Bork, a soldier and member of the Stettin Branch, was stationed close enough to Insterburg to attend Church meet-ings there. His diary reported the following on April 5, 1942:

> Visited the Insterburg Branch today at Spritzenstrasse. Not many members attended, but it was a wonderful time. Last week I searched for three hours before I found the meeting place.[5]

Brother Bork's record does not indicate whether the branch had found new rooms or if the meetings were being held in the home of a member. One week later, April 12, 1942, he sought out the branch again:

> No meeting today. Only every other week. Thanks to the war, there is no coal, at least not enough. And the branch leader comes from Königsberg. And there are so few members who attend. Today I visited the Sawatzki family at Cezilenstrasse 14.[6]

Apparently, the Saints in Insterburg were not about to give up on their church, despite no longer having an official meetinghouse. The January 1943 directory of the East German Mission showed that meetings were being held at Theaterstrasse 1 in the Jakulat home.[7]

Alfred Buntfuss was never an enthusiastic member of the Hitler Youth: "On the one hand the activities were a lot of fun but, on the other hand, I did not have a good feeling. I was the only Mormon in our Hitler Youth group." Being the only Latter-day Saint in the neighborhood was not always an honor to a little boy. "Sometimes, in school or in our neighborhood they made fun of me and called me Mormone-Zitrone [Mormon lemon], but they never said anything worse."

Boyhood ended for young Alfred in 1942. He went to Poland for a month of hard training under SS soldiers who had been wounded. After that, he was inducted into the Reichsarbeitsdienst. He was trained as a barber during the day and as an antiaircraft gunner at night. This was only the beginning of his service to the Reich. As he later wrote:

> After the Reichsarbeitsdienst, I went home but there was a letter on the table saying that I would be drafted in just three days. I actually wanted to pass my exam as a barber while at home, but there was not enough time. I was inducted and served in the navy. The basic training was in France, in the Vosges Mountains. I was to be a medic. After one month in France, I was transferred to a convent in the Netherlands. There were still monks living there, and we received training in every area—from surgery to how to treat the human body.

By June 1944, Alfred Buntfuss had completed his medical training and was now officially in the navy. He served aboard various ships in the North Sea and docked on several occasions in German-occupied Norway. Once he arrived late and missed the transfer to another ship. Using a few days of wait time, he managed to visit his father, who was stationed a few hours from the port. As Alfred later explained, "It was a remarkable experience for me and my father during those two days because we had not seen each other for such a long time."

As a navy man, Alfred was never in mortal danger, but he learned the importance of listening to the voice of inspiration. As he later explained,

> Once, we had a four-hour break, and I heard a voice telling me that I should not undress. I did not know how to respond, and the voice came again. Seconds later, the ship struck a mine, but we were lucky because it only affected one side. We stopped at the next harbor right away. They fixed the holes, and we went on. Two days later, the same thing happened to us. I had listened to the voice telling me to stay in my clothes. That night, when [our ship] sank, I was the only one not in my sleeping gear.

Käthe Braun finished her occupational training in 1943, but instead of seeking employment, she was assigned by the government to work at a munitions factory in Christianstadt

in western Silesia, hundreds of miles to the southwest. Her job was to monitor the readings on large boilers, and she worked twelve-hour shifts. With weekends free, she attended Church meetings in branches in Breslau and Liegnitz. Käthe remained at that location until the war ended.

In general, the citizens of Insterburg were relatively safe during the war because Germany's enemies—the Allied air forces—were too far away to attack the city. All of that changed in the fall of 1944, when the government suggested that evacuating Insterburg would be wise. Gertrud Buntfuss had to flee the city without the assistance of her husband or her son. She left her home shortly before Alfred returned on leave in October 1944 and was fortunate to make her way safely to the province of Mecklenburg (north of Berlin).

"We left with about a week to spare," Ruth Braun explained. She and her mother made the trek of one hundred miles to the west and south to the town of Preussisch Holland, at the very western border of East Prussia. They were there when the Soviets came through the region in early 1945.

In January 1945, Ruth Braun made her way to the Insterburg railroad station with lots of clothing and a small supply of food. She managed to get aboard a train overloaded with desperate refugees trying to reach Königsberg. Ruth planned to travel west with several other relatives. She said good-bye to her father at the station because he had been inducted into the Volkssturm and was required to stay and defend the city.

Ruth's party made it to the Baltic Sea coast at the port town of Pillau. During the harrowing trip, when it often seemed like they would not find passage across the Baltic, Ruth constantly prayed for deliverance. It was freezing cold, and food was scarce. The threat of being caught by the invading Soviets prevented any

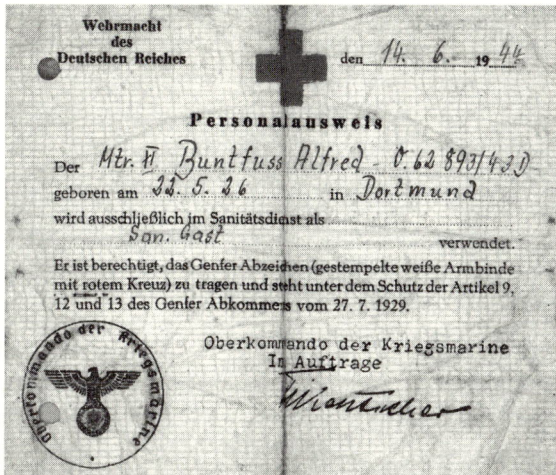

Fig. 5. Alfred Buntfuss was a certified medic. (A. Buntfuss)

feeling of safety or security. Finally, they were taken aboard the ship *Tatti* and found themselves sailing westward.

After a voyage of about three hundred miles, the ship docked at Warnemünde. The passengers were safe from the invaders for a time. From there, they rode the train west to the town of Elmshorn, north of Hamburg in the province of Schleswig-Holstein. In Elmshorn, Ruth watched as British troops drove through the streets in May 1945; there was no fighting. For Ruth Braun, the war was finally over. Soon a branch of the Church was established in Elmshorn for Saints who had been forced from their homes in the provinces of eastern Germany.

At work in the factory in Silesia since 1943, Käthe met a man named Willi Leupold, a fellow employee. He was fifteen years older but very polite and nice to her. In a few months, they became close friends, and by April 1945 they were married. She had by then lost all contact with her family in Insterburg. The Red Army was closing in on the factory, but she had Willi to protect her. They began walking west, hoping to reach the area where the American army was known to be. However, the Soviet invaders overtook them, passing them on the road in their rush toward Berlin.

In the confusion, Käthe and Willi reversed their travel and headed east, thereby passing the Soviets on the way. As moving targets, they avoided becoming civilian casualties.

Shortly after the war ended in May 1945, Polish soldiers arrived in Reichenau, where Käthe and Willi were living, and informed the German populace that they were being expelled from the country; Poland had been given that territory, and the new owners wanted the Germans out. The process was painful, as Käthe later wrote:

> Like cattle we were driven to a pasture. Old and young were thrown out of their homeland where generations of their ancestors had lived. What a tragic scene greeted our eyes. Old and sick people who could not walk were loaded into small handcarts. Grandfathers and grandmothers pulled or pushed the carts as we were organized into travel companies. Everywhere there were guards with bayonets. All of us were shocked at their brutality and could hardly understand what was happening. Thus began the great exodus.

When they reached the new German border, the Polish police told the refugees, "Don't come back!" Käthe and Willi Leupold then found a place to live just inside the Soviet Occupation Zone of Germany. In early 1946, Käthe learned that a branch of the Church was holding meetings in nearby Görlitz, and she joined them for a conference. After three years of sporadic attendance, she had a solid connection with her church again.

According to Käthe Braun Leupold, her mother was never able to leave Preussisch Holland. Under the poor living conditions of the time, she contracted polio and died there in August 1945. Wilhelm Braun survived the Soviet conquest of Insterburg and found his way to western Germany in 1946, where he was united with his daughter, Ruth. His son, Walter, had been taken to Russia as a forced laborer. Although his health was substantially

Fig. 6. Alfred Buntfuss as a sailor in the German navy. (A. Buntfuss)

weakened, Walter survived and returned to Germany in 1947.

After the war, Alfred Buntfuss was in a POW camp and happened to visit the office of a dentist who recognized his name. The man had recently treated Alfred's father, Emil, and allowed Alfred to use a radio to send a message regarding his father. Eight hours later, a response arrived indicating his father's whereabouts. They could not yet meet, but were allowed to talk on the telephone several times.

Alfred Buntfuss was a POW in the British Occupation Zone with duties that included clearing the North Sea of mines. He filled out a missing persons card on his father at the latter's last known location and to his surprise, Emil showed up one day at the camp gate. The missing persons card had functioned to perfection.

In 1946, Alfred and his father were both free and traveled to Mecklenburg to find Gertrud Buntfuss for a joyous reunion. According to Alfred, "It was such a great blessing for all of us." They were in the Soviet Occupation Zone and starvation was a way of life, but at least they were alive and together. The war was finally over for the Buntfuss family.

There were no Germans left in Insterburg by fall 1946. The small branch there ceased to exist.

In Memoriam

Only one member of the Insterburg Branch did not survive World War II:

Henrietta Amalie Braek b. Klein Genie, Gerdauen, Ostpreußen, Preußen 20 or 26 Aug 1869; dau. of August Braek and Amalie Lagnuke; bp. 23 or 29 Apr 1931; m. Adolf Hoffmann; 1 child; d. in flight 1944 or 1945 (IGI)

Notes

1. Presiding Bishopric, "Financial, Statistical, and Historical Reports of Wards, Stakes, and Missions, 1884–1955," CR 4 12, 257.
2. Käthe Braun Luskin, autobiography (unpublished); private collection.
3. Albert Buntfuss, interview by the author in German, Leest, Germany, August 31, 2006; unless otherwise noted, summarized in English by Judith Sartowski.
4. Ruth Braun Fricke, interview by the author in German, Hamburg, Germany, August 15, 2006.
5. Alfred Bork, diary (unpublished), April 5, 1942; private collection; trans. the author.
6. Ibid., April 12, 1942. Alfred wrote on June 6, 1942, that "Brother Repkowski" of Königsberg, whose family he visited that day in Königsberg, was the leader of the Insterburg Branch.
7. East German Mission, "Directory of Meeting Places" (unpublished manuscript, 1943); private collection.

Königsberg Branch

The historic capital city of the Prussian province of East Prussia was Königsberg, a center of science and culture for hundreds of years. Although it was far from the heart of Germany, this city was part of the national consciousness. It had been cut off from Germany after World War I but was not forgotten by Hitler's government in the 1930s. In 1939, the city had about three hundred thousand inhabitants.

Königsberg Branch[1]	1939
Elders	21
Priests	7
Teachers	17
Deacons	19
Other Adult Males	86
Adult Females	266
Male Children	19
Female Children	30
Total	465

Eyewitnesses report a large population of Latter-day Saints in the 1920s, but a wave of emigration had seen at least one hundred of them leave for the United States. There were as many as three branches of the Church in Königsberg shortly after World War I (1918). With 465 members, the Königsberg Branch was the second-largest in all of Germany in 1939.

The Königsberg Branch met in rented rooms at Freystrasse 12 on the main floor of the first Hinterhaus. Three daughters of district president Max Freimann—Irmgard, Ingrid, and Ruth—later stated that Church meetings were held at that same location throughout the war.[2] They described the rooms as follows:

> The rooms were in the Hinterhaus. When we went inside there was a small room that also led to the wardrobe and the restroom. The next room was the large room with a curtain and a podium for theater plays and other special occasions. Up some stairs, there was another large room and two or three classrooms. The choir did not stand on the rostrum but on the floor to the side. The room upstairs was large also, and we used it for some meetings when the room downstairs was too small.

Their younger brother, Reinhard Freimann (born 1933), added these details to the description of the facilities:

> There was also a sign that said that we were the Kirche Jesu Christi der Heiligen der Letzten Tage and people who walked past [the main building] could see that there was a church in the back building. We also had an organ in the largest room.[3]

The Freimann sisters recalled the following about the meetings:

> Sunday School started at 10 A.M. and after that we went home [and came back later for sacrament meeting]. We lived in the Schleiermacherstrasse 51. It was pretty far away. We could have taken the street car, but that would have cost too much money for the entire family, so we walked about forty-five minutes (one way) to church on Sunday. We had an attendance of two hundred people and more than one Sunday School class—up to four different ones.

As in other branches, auxiliary meetings were held on several evenings in the week and Primary on Wednesday afternoons.

In July 1939, Elder Joseph Fielding Smith visited Königsberg and presided over a district conference. Renate Klein (born 1930) was baptized in connection with the conference. "I was the newest member of the Church attending the conference, so I got to shake [Elder Smith's] hand." The Emil and Auguste Klein family had just moved from Königsberg to Bartenstein, about thirty-five miles to the south. Emil Klein was not a member, but supported his family in their Church activity. For example, he allowed his wife to pay tithing on his income because she had no income of her own. She and her daughters made it to Königsberg only to attend district conferences and a few other special occasions.[4]

"We had a good Relief Society and we had lots of training classes there. I never had any interest to go elsewhere to learn how to cook or to sew." Such was the recollection of Inge Grünberg (born 1927). She also had the following memories of Sunday School:

> When the opening exercises for Sunday School were over, we all stood up and the children on

Fig. 1. The family of district president Max Freimann in about 1937. (Freimann sisters)

the front row marched out (there was a tiny bit of a military spirit about it) to their classrooms. We had about 120–150 in church on a typical Sunday.[5]

Membership in the Bund Deutscher Mädel (League of German Girls) was a challenge for Inge Grünberg. However, as she later explained, there were ways to be both a good Latter-day Saint and a loyal member of the Hitler Youth group on Sundays:

> At 10:00 A.M., when we were starting our [Church] meetings, the BDM gathered and went to the movies. I went with them until we were seated in the theater and the lights went down. Then I sneaked out, changed my clothes, and put my BDM stuff in my bag and went to church. My friends didn't report me.

With his classmates, Reinhard Freimann was inducted into the Hitler Youth program when he turned ten. As he later explained:

> I was a member of the Jungvolk. I went every week to all the meetings that we had, but I can remember, I only went twice on a Sunday. The normal meetings were held on Sundays and that was a conflict but nobody complained about [my absence]. My parents did not state their opinions about the regime or politics in general. They remembered our [twelfth] article of faith, which states that we should accept our leaders and not work against them.[6]

Regarding the life of Latter-day Saints in Königsberg during the war, Inge Grünberg (born 1927) had these recollections:

> Our [Church] meetings continued as always. We were cut off from the Church in America and eventually we didn't get the *Stern* [Church magazine] any more. People lost their hymnbooks and scriptures when they were bombed out. We kept all of the Church traditions (celebrations, etc.) through the war the best we could.

Erika Jenschewski (1925) served her Pflichtjahr on a farm from 1939 to 1940. She was miserable on the farm, especially in the winter when she was required to run across frozen fields to procure food ration coupons. As she explained, "In those days women were not allowed to wear pants and dress warm. I was just screaming for cold, and when I came back, my feet were frozen. I had really bad frostbite all over." Erika wanted to be a saleslady but was not allowed to train for that work for several more years. She first had to learn domestic skills.[7]

Inge Freimann finished school in 1940 and planned to study clothing design, but was told, "Your plans can't be fulfilled. You must have forgotten that there's a war on." She was assigned to work in an office at the army post and learned office skills. "One day I found a letter on my typewriter; I was being sent to Böhmisch Chamnitz [Czechoslovakia] for a course in office skills for three months with twenty young women. I cried my eyes out because I had to leave."

Karl Margo Klindt of the Flensburg Branch was a sailor stationed in Königsberg, where he met Irmgard Freimann. For several years, they planned to be married, but his service in the navy resulted in delays. Finally, he received permission to marry after the German victory over Poland, and the wedding took place in Königsberg on December 30, 1939. Within a week, he returned to his unit.

Ruth Freimann (born 1921) fell in love with a man who had been a Catholic priest— Franz Holdau of Wuppertal in the Rhineland. He had arrived in Königsberg in 1942 and was already acquainted with the Book of Mormon. He attended branch meetings and became interested in Ruth. As she later stated, "He asked me if I would marry a man of another church, and I said, 'Never!'" He was baptized in November 1942. Soon they were engaged, and Ruth recalled the events connected with the wedding:

> We got married in the civil registry office [at city hall] first and then went over to the Church. We celebrated our wedding all night long. We

Fig. 2. The Königsberg Branch in 1938. (Freimann)

danced and had nice food. Every member of the branch attended, and I wore a white dress.

Like so many wartime weddings, this one left little time for a honeymoon. They visited Franz's parents in Wupperthal. By June 30, Ruth was back at home in Königsberg, and Franz was on his way to his Wehrmacht unit in Russia. Life as a new bride did not last long for Ruth Freimann Holdau. On August 3, less than two months later, Franz was killed near Ladoga Lake in Russia, leaving Ruth a widow.

Sigrid Klein (born 1932) was baptized in a secret ceremony in the Pregel River in Königsberg in the summer of 1941. It was a memorable event in her recollection: "It was at 5:00 A.M. I was wearing a white nightgown and got covered with oil. It was near the harbor and a tanker had leaked oil. I looked terrible! I don't know how they ever got me clean!"

The education of Germany's youth suffered in large cities during the war. Christel Freimann (born 1931) recalled interruptions in Königsberg: "We often missed school. When there was an alarm [while we were] in school, we went into the shelter. But when the school was destroyed, they told us to stay home until they found some other building that we could have class in."[8]

The sorrows associated with a father leaving his family to report for military duty represent an international phenomenon, and many Latter-day Saint families experienced this. Karin Kremulat (born 1938), recalled when her father left home:

> He did not volunteer, no, he wanted to stay with his wife and with his two little girls and he did not want to go at all. My mother would even say, "Do you have to go? Why don't you just stay with us? We can hide you." And he would say, "You have no idea what they would do to me. I have to go," and so he did.[9]

The last time Karin saw her father was at Christmas in 1943. Soon after that, he was reported missing in action. His wife, Louise

297

Schipporeit Kremulat, mourned her husband for several years. According to Karin, "[Christmas was] a very sad time for my mother because after that she would never want to have a Christmas tree. I remember in later years my sister and I would go and find our own because it was such a hard time for my mother."

Branch president Haase was a man of good humor, according to Erika Jenschewski:

> He was very concerned about the young people. He really taught us to live a clean life, and he made lots of parties for us so that we were together. He was a very fine member. He had parties in his home where the young people came. . . . He was almost blind, but he was funny, a good leader.

Just after the war started, Inge (another Freimann daughter) met Alfred Bork, a youth from the Stettin Branch who was stationed near Königsberg. He became a frequent visitor in the Freimann home and eventually received permission from Max Freimann to be engaged to Inge. However, like so many other soldiers, Alfred returned to the front, and his visits to his fiancée in Königsberg were rare.

Friedrich (Fritz) Haase had served as the president of the branch for several years when he was drafted and sent to Russia in 1943. His counselors, Fritz Bollbach and Emil Jenschewski, directed the meetings in his absence. Brother Bollbach was a student at the State Building School and worked in the construction of barracks for POWs in Königsberg. His work in a high-priority war industry made him exempt from military service for much of the war. On July 1, 1944, he was awarded a master's degree at the Institute for Vocational Advancement.

Bit by bit, the war was beginning to wear out the people of Königsberg. Irmgard Freimann Klindt recalled those days:

> Our lives became one of survival. We had ration cards to get food. We were allowed a little butter, some bread, and a few eggs. Life was very routine. We continued attending all the meetings at Church and tried not to think about the war.[10]

In 1943, air raids and false alarms became an increasingly frequent aspect of life in Königsberg. Gudrun Hellwig (born 1934) recalled how she reacted to the sirens:

> We had constant alarms and attacks. We went down to the basement during the night, and I had already developed a rhythm and got up every night at the same time, around 10:00 P.M., and left for the basement. We did not go to bed fully dressed, but everything was ready in case we needed to go.[11]

The war came home to Königsberg in all its brutality in 1944. The family of Theodor and Maria Berger were some of the city's first Latter-day Saints to lose their home. During the night of August 27–28, an air raid struck their neighborhood. Sister Berger and her daughter, Renate—the only ones at home—sought shelter in their basement. Maria later described the event in these words:

> Because fire raged all around us, a heavy iron door, our only way out, expanded and would not budge. We were trapped. Fear set in. The shelter was filled to capacity, and the air supply was limited. It is hard to describe the destruction we found when we finally were able to leave the shelter in the morning. The Cranzer Allee was a long, wide street. Every single house had collapsed and was enveloped in a blazing fire. The sea of flames created a big [wind] storm. Everyone tried to find their home site. We stood in total shock by the smoldering ruins of our house. In the rubble we found a small, engraved plate from our piano, the only sign that we once lived there. . . . We cleaned up and . . . went to church.[12]

The Bergers had lost everything, including the genealogy papers tracing Brother Berger's ancestry to the 1500s. Fortunately, the Bergers were taken into the home of Sister Marie Jenschewski that very day.

Fig. 3. Members of the Königsberg Branch on an outing during the war. (Freimann)

Little children were taught how to behave during air raids. Helga Kremulat (born 1937) had vivid memories of the procedures:

> We had these black shades that we had to put in front of the window. . . . We had to make sure that there was not any light coming through, so they wouldn't see where there were homes, when the airplanes would come over. . . . And we had to go down in the basement—because we lived farther upstairs—we had to have a little suitcase ready to take downstairs with our important papers. My mother had to take care of this.[13]

Inge Grünberg recalled similar experiences:

> When the air raids came, all six of the families in the apartment house were to gather in the basement as a shelter. Once, we decided that we wouldn't go down there. Then we discovered that all of the other people were sitting in front of our door and on the stairs. They said, "If you don't go to the basement, we won't either, because you pray. We want to be where you are." They hadn't learned how to pray.

Inge worked as an office staff member at an army post for the last few years of the war. On at least one occasion, she escaped disaster:

> Once my friend begged me to do her weekend shift so that she could be with her new husband. I did her shift and she did mine the next week so that I could celebrate my birthday. The next day I went to the office and found that it had been destroyed. My friend lay there, burned to death and a very small corpse. I was saved again by my Heavenly Father.

In late 1944, Emma Klein took her daughters, Renate and Sigrid, to Königsberg for another district conference. The city had just suffered a devastating air raid, and the Kleins viewed the ruins of the downtown as they rode the streetcar to church. When they told the driver they wanted to get off, he told them that there was nothing left in the neighborhood. Nevertheless, they got off and walked around the corner. According to Renate, "We saw that the [church building] was standing, but the house in front and the houses on either side were gone. And our building had those huge windows—not one window pane was broken."

The Freimann sisters recalled that during the attacks on Königsberg, people wanted to be in the same shelter as Max Freimann: "Many came into our basement because they knew that we would be protected. Our father prayed on those nights. Our father never forgot to tell anybody else that we were members of the Church."

Irmgard Freimann Klindt's husband, Karl Margo Klindt, was taken prisoner by the British shortly after the Allied invasion of Normandy in June 1944. As Irmgard explained, "I thought he was dead. . . . The German government thought he had deserted. . . . They wanted to put my father-in-law in prison for [hiding] him." With the help of a Danish uncle, it was finally learned that Karl was a POW in England.[14]

The meeting rooms at Freystrasse were confiscated by the National Socialist Party in December 1944. The branch was temporarily allowed to hold meetings in a nearby Protestant church. However, that lasted only two weeks because the Protestant church council retracted their invitation. Meetings were next held in the home of Emil and Marie Jenschewski.[15]

Leaders of the East German Mission understood that many of the Saints in the districts of eastern Germany would have to leave their homes if Germany were invaded by the Red Army. As Inge Grünberg recalled, "[Mission second counselor] Paul Langheinrich told us all in East Prussia to send a box with our important documents to a specific family in western Germany."[16]

In March, Inge Grünberg was allowed to leave the city. Her mother had already gone to Dresden and was there during the firebombing of February 13–14. Inge did not arrive until after that terrible event, as she explained:

> In March 1945, I made my way to Dresden to be with my mother. The bridges were destroyed, and I found a fisherman who took me across the Elbe and [I] paid him with cigarettes. I was there for only one day because I had to move on to Magdeburg to work at the army post. The officers were burning lots of papers there. I was to report there on March 21 and was worried that I would be called a deserter if I didn't show up.

Gudrun Hellwig did not recall a formal evacuation order for women and children in Königsberg, "But my father had already noticed that the wounded were taken out of the military hospitals, and then he decided that we had to leave also." He found the family a place on the train heading west to Pillau, a small port on the Baltic Sea. Gudrun recalled that military police removed men from the train at various stops, ordering them to stay and defend what had been declared "Fortress Königsberg." Gudrun's father, a streetcar driver, also remained in the city as a member of the Volkssturm.

During the last year of the war, a heroic and desperate effort was initiated to evacuate German civilians from the eastern provinces by boat across the Baltic Sea to northwestern Germany. This campaign involved hundreds of military and commercial ships as well as private vessels. By the end of the war, several million people had been transported across the Baltic. Gudrun's mother, Margarete Hack Hellwig, recognized this route as the simplest and fastest, and she and her daughter joined thousands of others hoping to secure a place on a ship. Gudrun remembered the terrible cold at the port:

> We then reached Pillau, and it was very cold—sometimes down to −20 degrees Celsius. We slept in a large room that night, and it was cold. The next morning I can remember standing at a pier and there was a large group of people.

. . . My mother had to concentrate so that she wouldn't lose me in that group. There were large ships and people were trying to board and there was luggage lying all over the ground.

Margarete Hellwig and her daughter were taken on a small craft from Pillau to Gothenhafen, where they joined a huge group of refugees on board the *Wilhelm Gustloff*. It was a transport vessel that still bore the markings of a hospital ship. Squeezing their way past other harried refugees, Gudrun and her mother found a spot in a hallway down below, next to the engine room where it was nice and warm. Then there came an announcement over the intercom that the ship was dangerously overloaded and that some of the passengers would have to disembark. Volunteers were sought urgently. Gudrun clearly recalled what happened next:

> My mother was always praying and at that moment she didn't have a good feeling; she told me that we would have to leave the *Wilhelm Gustloff*. I protested a bit because I was so tired and our spot was so warm. But she insisted, so we got off the boat.

Margarete Hellwig later described her feelings aboard the doomed vessel:

> All of a sudden, I became really scared. It seemed as if somebody wanted to push me out. I told my daughter, Gudrun, "I'm not staying in here, I've got to get out!" She answered, "Mommy, it's so warm, let's stay here!" "No, I'm not staying here, I have to get out!" I was so very frightened. So we moved to another ship.[17]

Sister Hellwig's decision saved their lives. They boarded a smaller vessel that left the harbor with the *Wilhelm Gustloff*. It was the night of January 30, 1945. Just after 9:00 P.M., the *Wilhelm Gustloff*, loaded with an estimated ten thousand passengers and crew, was attacked by a Soviet submarine. Struck by three torpedoes, the ship went down in about ninety minutes, spilling many of its passengers into the frigid waters of the Baltic. Only about 1,200

Fig. 4. The sinking of the Wilhelm Gustloff *on January 30, 1945, resulted in the deaths of thousands of refugees.*

passengers were rescued.[18] The sinking of the *Wilhelm Gustloff* was the worst maritime tragedy on record. Having been unable to sleep, Sister Hellwig watched the catastrophe from the deck of the trailing ship. She was convinced that their escape from death was due to the intervention of the Holy Ghost.

Maria Berger and her daughter, Renate, fled Königsberg on January 26, 1945, after receiving warnings from friends and neighbors. Learning that an important bridge along the land route to Berlin had been destroyed, they joined with three other women and headed for the Baltic Sea. They were unsuccessful in boarding the transport ship *Wilhelm Gustloff*, but found places aboard the smaller vessel *Maria Vissa*. When the ship made a stop in the Danzig harbor, the passengers learned that the *Wilhelm Gustloff* had been sunk. As Maria Berger later wrote, "We had tried so desperately to get on that ship. How grateful we were now, not to be among those who perished in the ice-cold waters of the Baltic Sea."[19]

The Bergers left the boat at Wollin and made their way by train to Berlin, where the Paul Langheinrich family took them into what was a growing Latter-day Saint refuge in the apartment house at Rathenowerstrasse 52. They spent the remainder of the war in that building and were given Church assignments that they gladly fulfilled.[20]

Desperation led Marie Jenschewski to employ a daring ruse to save her son, Helmut. At sixteen, he was not allowed to leave Königsberg, where boys of Hitler Youth age were required to defend the city against the invading Soviets. Fearing that he would not survive the conflict, Sister Jenschewski and her daughter, Erika, dressed the boy up as a girl. According to Erika, "We put a dress on him and he had a scarf around his neck and he looked very cute. So he got away with us. We left Königsberg on January 26, 1945. We had one suitcase for all of us and we had to ride in a cattle car." Of course, their father, Emil Jenschewski, was not allowed to leave Königsberg.

The Jenschewskis rode the train to Pillau, where they boarded a ship for Danzig. From there another train took them to Berlin. On the way, Marie Jenschewski was carrying tithing funds she was determined to deliver to the mission leaders. To ensure the money's safety, she had hidden it under her clothing. At the mission home on Rathenowerstrasse, she turned over the entire sum to the mission leaders. She was then instructed to take her children to Zwickau, where Church members would provide them a place to live. The Jenschewskis arrived there in February 1945 and were indeed treated very well by the members of the Zwickau Branch.

In early 1945, Louise Kremulat took her daughters Helga and Karin and left Königsberg with little time to spare. They had packed a wagon (a typical Bollerwagen measuring about four feet long, two feet wide, and two feet deep) and made their way to the railroad station. As Karin recalled:

> We were on the last train that left Königsberg, and it was supposed to take us to Austria. It never did. It went through Czechoslovakia and about [sixty miles] past Prague. The train stopped and was bombed. For some reason it was not going to Austria and everyone left the train—we were on our own. So we picked up our bundles and started walking.

Fortunately, their Bollerwagen somehow survived the railroad journey, and they loaded it for the trip north back toward Prague. Karin's story continued:

> We packed that Bollerwagen full and we pulled it. My aunt had one too, and we helped her pull it. I pulled the wagon about two hours and my mother and my sister helped with the other wagon and my aunt pushed the baby buggy, so it was really a pitiful sight.

Karin Kremulat turned seven years old the day the family entered Prague. It was May 8, 1945, the day Germany formally capitulated. At that point, however, their party of refugees was totally isolated—no German troops to defend them, no transportation to move them, nobody to feed them, but plenty of Czech freedom fighters and Soviet invaders to harass them. As Karin's older sister, Helga, recalled:

> It was very scary because sometimes the Russians would come on their horses and say, "If you're hiding any soldiers here, we're going to shoot you all." Of course, for me, it was very scary. My sister was a year younger, and she just kind of looked them in the eyes and thought, "Gee, this is exciting to see these Russians on their horses." My mother claimed that because my sister looked them in the eye, they left and let us alone.

From Prague, the women and girls made their way north into Germany, then west and north to the town of Milbergen near Minden, where the girls' grandmother was living. The war was over for Louise Kremulat and her daughters, but the search for her missing husband lasted for several years. Sister Kremulat sought information from government agencies and the Red Cross and carefully studied the lists of prisoners released from Soviet camps, but her husband was never heard of again.

Max Freimann was inducted into the Volkssturm and was gone much of the month of January 1945. His son, Reinhard, recalled that Brother Freimann was not freed from Volkssturm duty even long enough to accompany his family to the railroad station. He had to say good-bye at the streetcar stop then return to his post. As Irmgard Freimann Klindt wondered years later, "How could we have known that we would never see our father or our home again?"

As the Freimann family made their way west, Ruth and Irmgard managed to find their way to the Island of Rügen to visit Inge. From there, they backtracked to Demmin to meet their stepmother, Helena Freimann. The women then took a train to distant Flensburg, where they arrived in early February. They spent the rest of the war in peace and safety there.

Emma Klein left Königsberg with her two daughters and headed west. They traveled past Dresden, then south into Czechoslovakia. Emil Klein was required to stay in East Prussia

Fig. 5. *The Jenschewski family of the Königsberg Branch. The children in the back row (Edith, Kuno, and Erika) were members of Hitler Youth organizations. (E. Jenschewski Koch)*

but was able to get away before the war ended (due to a leg damaged in World War I, he was exempt from military service). He caught up with his family near Karlsbad, Czechoslovakia, at the end of February 1945. Sigrid Klein later recalled the reunion: "He arrived at midnight and we were thrilled. We wanted to hug him, but he said, 'Don't touch me! I have lice.' It didn't matter; we were happy to have him back again."

Just a few weeks after the end of the war, the Klein family began the trek northward back into Germany. They had been expelled from Czechoslovakia on short notice and began walking toward Chemnitz, pulling a two-wheeled cart with what belongings they could rescue. Along the way, Emil Klein told his daughter, Sigrid, something surprising: "You know, when we get back to a town where there's [an LDS] church, I'm going to be baptized." (He kept his promise and was baptized in August 1945.)

Arriving in Chemnitz, Emma Klein knew that a branch of the Church was nearby but had no idea how to find it. At the railroad station at 6:00 a.m., she spoke to a man who was sweeping the floor. He thought that she was looking for the Jehovah's Witnesses until she mentioned the name "Mormons." Then he said, "I'm not a Mormon, but I know one," and proceeded to give her the address of the family about two miles across town. Sister Klein went there alone and heard the same response again: "I'm not a Mormon, but I know one." This man gave her the address of the family of Richard Burkhardt, just a block away. The Kleins, who had been traveling with the Paulus family of five, were quite relieved to be taken into the Burkhardt home, and space was found for the Paulus family as well—nine persons in all. The Kleins were grateful that their own lives were spared, but they later learned that a total

303

of twenty-six close relatives had died in the war (none of whom were Latter-day Saints).

Toward the end of January 1945, Fritz Bollbach and several other men from the branch decided to leave Königsberg and make their way to the west. Knowing that they could easily be accused of desertion and executed for abandoning Fortress Königsberg, they cautiously walked toward Pillau on the Baltic Sea. They narrowly avoided arrest on one occasion but were eventually caught and inducted into the Volkssturm. With about one hundred other civilians, they heard these words from an officer of the SS: "Men, you are not prisoners; you are being inducted into the militia to defend our fatherland. Do not attempt to flee. The sentries are instructed to shoot if you do." The serious nature of the warning became shockingly real shortly thereafter when Fritz came upon a scene that filled him with deep sadness—the bodies of men accused of treason and desertion:

> The closer we got, the more horrible the view. On either side [of the road], men, soldiers, and civilians hung on large beeches [trees]. Most had a sign fastened on the chest with handwritten labels: deserter, absent without leave, cowardice in the face of the enemy, etc.[21]

Fritz was horrified that Germans would kill Germans while the Third Reich came crashing down around them. During March and April, Fritz was assigned first to drive a motorcycle and deliver messages, then to drive a truck to transport food and other supplies. As the Red Army advanced slowly toward the Baltic Sea coast and the masses of refugees grew larger and more desperate, Fritz saw ever-increasing degrees of violence. Desperation drove people to rash acts, as he witnessed on one occasion when a Soviet artillery shell injured two horses hitched to a wagon:

> Before we could do anything, some people were already cutting pieces of meat from the legs of the still living animals. It was [a] terrible sight. I believe that people were already eating the flesh while the horses were still alive.[22]

In late April 1945, Fritz managed to escape from his forced militia assignment by disguising himself as a railroad worker and sneaking aboard a tugboat that transported him to the Hela Peninsula. There he jumped aboard a ship that had cast off and was already three feet from the pier. He had risked execution for desertion but was finally on his way across the Baltic. The ship took him to Copenhagen, Denmark, where he was imprisoned by British soldiers. Fritz's short but harrowing military experience was over.[23]

Gudrun Hellwig recalled spending nearly a week on the Baltic Sea under foggy conditions. "Our ship was listing to one side so maybe it had been damaged too." They landed at the harbor of Kiel, Germany, and made their way inland. Being some of the first refugees to arrive in the rural province of Schleswig-Holstein, they had no problem finding a place to stay on a farm near Krummberg. There they waited out the end of the war, hoping to be united with their relatives.

The search for loved ones began even before the war ended, and Gudrun Hellwig remembered the scenes: "The husbands and wives looked for each other and wanted to find their families. They put up pictures and [wrote in chalk] names on walls so that people could see who was looking for whom." Eventually, they found Margarete Hellwig's sister and Gudrun's father; he had been released from a Soviet POW camp.

Some of the most detailed Latter-day Saint documents to survive World War II are the letters of Theodor Berger (born 1893), an elder in the Königsberg Branch. Like all men ages sixteen to sixty, Brother Berger was required to stay in Fortress Königsberg to defend the city against the invading Red Army, while the women and children were permitted to leave. On January 26, 1945, Brother Berger sent his family to Berlin to the home of Paul Langheinrich, second counselor to the supervisor of the East German Mission. He mailed several letters to his wife at the Langheinrich home from February 7 to April 2. The following excerpts from his letters provide insight into the condition of the men who were forced to stay and defend the city:[24]

February 7, 1945
Dear mother, where are you and Renate? I am still alive and well, am considered "military" and have to work at the *Zeugamt* [weapons arsenal].

February 14, 1945
We were under terrible artillery fire. Dead and injured covered the streets. I stayed calm and prayed to God to hold His protecting hand over me and especially to protect you. Should I die, I know it is His will. I have accepted the end. Königsberg is now surrounded but not hopelessly delivered to the Russians.

February 22, 1945
I would be so very happy just to know you are safe in Berlin or some other place.

February 25, 1945
The Russians have committed many atrocities. It can't go on much longer. The German army fights so hard to keep the city. Artillery fire keeps me awake, I can't sleep anymore. I am so grateful that you don't have to live through this.

March 1, 1945
I was paid on February 15. Money is now worthless, but I still want to pay tithing and will give it to Brother Freimann on Sunday night when all members will meet again. (There are fifteen of us left.) We do not know anymore which day of the week it is. Nothing matters!

March 5, 1945
The uncertainty is hard to endure. I hope it will not be a terrible end full of horror.

March 21, 1945
We hear that Berlin gets bombed daily. My heart aches for you. I wish I knew more about your fate. What does the future hold for us?

Even if we are reunited, our lives have been changed forever.

March 24, 1945
Good news, your letter arrived! I was so happy to hear from you. I am glad that you have a place to stay, that you are with friends and feel the Lord's blessings. We here will get together on Sunday and be with you in spirit and thank God that we are still alive. Please don't despair even when it gets hard to hold your head up high. Our faith in God will make us strong.

March 25, 1945
On Sunday, seven faithful members gathered together to worship. Present were: Brothers Freimann, Jahrling, Jenschewski, Seliger, and Berger, and Sisters Habermann and Hesske. It was comforting to talk about how we suffer, with families scattered everywhere not knowing from day to day if they are still alive and yet always hoping to be reunited again. I do believe that our Father in Heaven is with me and will shield me from pain and suffering. I pray daily for His mercy and hope that I can live to better serve Him. I am grateful to know that He does not withhold His blessing from any of His children who believe in Him. I feel a peace and quiet within even with bombs exploding around me. Should He call me, so be it. It will be His will.

April 2, 1945
Russian troops are closing in fast! Some members of the Church got together yesterday at Freimann's apartment. When I got there, I found a room full of friends: Brothers Freimann, Seliger, Jahrling and Wetzker, and Sisters Hesske, Habermann, Freimann, Kolbe, Fett, Schmidt, Seliger, and Martsch. It was a good time. We gained strength from each other and shed many tears. So you see, we are not alone. God is with His children even in this surrounded fortress. A turning point is near. We know something will happen soon. May the Lord bless you in Berlin. All is in His hands. To know God is with me keeps my soul quiet, and I get comfort from one special song I remember: "Ruh, Ruhe dem Pilger" [Peace to the Pilgrim].
Auf Wiedersehen!

It is most remarkable that the last message from Theodor Berger in Königsberg to his family in Berlin could actually be delivered after April 2, 1945. His letters represent priceless historical documents that attest to the devotion of the last surviving Latter-day Saints in Königsberg.

On April 9, the determined but hapless German defenders of Fortress Königsberg surrendered to the Soviets. The conquerors slaughtered many of the defenders—soldiers and civilians alike—and transported many others east to labor camps. Evidence suggests that not one of the Latter-day Saints mentioned in the Berger letters survived the fall of Königsberg. Berger family records show the date April 30, 1945, for Theodor Berger's death in Königsberg. In 1952, a German court ruling declared Max Freimann dead.

Shortly after the war ended, Maria Berger was assigned an apartment in Berlin for her daughters and her grandson. She began a new phase of life without her husband.

Inge Freimann explained that her fiancé, Alfred Bork, had planned to serve a mission before being drafted by the Wehrmacht. Now and then he wrote to her about prophetic dreams he had:

> He could always tell what would happen, and he would write me a letter before something terrible happened. I got a letter that he had sent on April 1 [from Königsberg], and he told me that he had dreamed of my mother (who had already passed away) and that they had been in a large field. She told him in that dream that they would see each other on Easter. The last letter that I received from him was sent on Easter. After that, I never heard from him again.

Alfred Bork disappeared in April 1945. Under the chaotic conditions in eastern Germany at the time, it can come as no surprise that the German army never reported him missing in action and the Soviets did not list him as a POW. Several years passed before Inge Freimann lost hope of seeing him again.

The war had been over for several months before Inge Grünberg's wanderings finally ended. From Magdeburg, she had moved west into the Lüneburg Heath in the British Occupation Zone and from there to Flensburg near the Danish border. There she met Helena Freimann and learned the fate of several of the Saints in Königsberg.

Fritz Bollbach eventually located his wife and daughters through Red Cross search services. They were living in the new Latter-day Saint refugee community at Langen, south of Frankfurt am Main in western Germany. In August 1946, Fritz was released by his British captors, made his way to the American Occupation Zone, and was set free. He arrived in Langen on a Sunday and found the apartment where the family lived. Two daughters were at home, while his wife and the youngest daughter were attending church.[25]

Karl Margo Klindt was released from a British POW camp in February 1946. When he returned to his wife in his hometown of Flensburg, he was very thin and emotionally sick.[26]

Emil Jenschewski was released from a POW camp in Russia in 1948 and made his way back to Germany. His daughter Erika later recalled how the reunion took place:

> He found out from the Berlin mission home where we lived. [At our apartment] he stood in front of me and I didn't recognize him. He said, "Didn't you know your father was so skinny?" His eyes were just sparkling. I looked at him and said, "You *are* my father." So he was [finally] with us.

Unfortunately, one family member could not be located: Son Kuno Jenschewski had disappeared during the defense of Berlin just days before the war ended. He was listed as missing in action.

With the conquest of eastern Germany at the end of World War II, the northern half

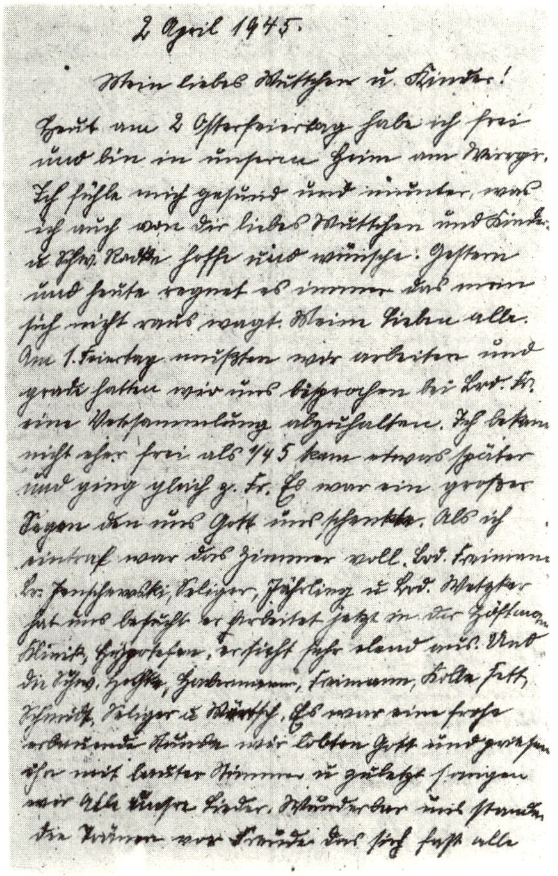

Fig. 6. Although Königsberg was surrounded by the enemy, this letter written by Theodor Berger on April 2, 1945, was somehow delivered to his wife, Maria, in Berlin a few days later. (R. Berger Rudolph)

of the province of East Prussia was ceded to the Soviet Union and with it the city of Königsberg (now called Kaliningrad). It is believed that all of the surviving members of the Königsberg Branch of The Church of Jesus Christ of Latter-day Saints had left the city or were expelled by the new Russian government by the end of 1946. Once a stronghold of the LDS faith, the city was devoid of the restored gospel for at least the next four decades.

In Memoriam

The following members of the Königsberg Branch did not survive World War II:

Theodor Reinhold Berger b. Trebnitz, Schliesien, Preußen 10 July 1893; son of Otto Berger and Karolina Messner; bp. Königsberg, Ostpreußen, Preußen

Germany 23 Aug 1924; conf. Königsberg 23 Aug 1924; ord. deacon Königsberg 28 Oct 1925; ord. teacher Königsberg 4 Aug 1930; ord. priest Königsberg 2 Apr 1933; ord. elder Königsberg 7 Mar 1937; m. Königsberg 23 Jun 1917, Maria Berta Bresilge; 2 or 4 children; MIA Königsberg 30 Apr 1945 (R. Berger Rudolph; www.volksbund.de; IGI)

Karl Herrmann Bollbach b. Groß Bajohren, Preussisch Eylau, Ostpreußen, Preußen 10 Mar 1872; son of Friedrich Ferdinand Bollach and Henrietta Wilhelmine Dunkel; bp. 25 Sep 1920; m. Uderwangen, Preussisch Eylau, Ostpreußen, Preußen 28 Nov 1897, Wilhelmine Dunkel; 3 or 5 children; d. Königsberg, Ostpreußen, Preußen Mar or Apr 1943 OR 7 May 1943 (Fritz Bollbach; FHL Microfilm 25726, 1930 Census; IGI)

Heinz Werner Freimann b. Königsberg, Ostpreußen, Preußen 2 Feb 1916; son of Max Gustav Freimann and Margarete Hedwig Krause; bp. 25 Jun 1924 Oberteich, Ostpreußen, Preußen; m. Königsberg 20 Jul 1940, Delila Zellmer; 2 children; sergeant major; d. H. V. Pl. D. 14 I. D., Braunsberg, Ostpreußen, Preußen 20 Feb 1945; bur. Braniewo, Poland (R. Freimann Dietz; www.volksbund.de; IGI; AF)

Max Gustav Freimann b. Taleiken-Jacob, Memel, Ostpreußen, Preußen 15 or 16 Dec 1888; son of Gustav Louis Freimann and Auguste Johanne Stolz; m. Königsberg, Ostpreußen, Preußen 9 Oct 1915, Margarete Hedwig Krause; 6 children; 2m. Königsberg 26 Mar 1932, Wanda Helene Maria Sommer; 1 child; ord. elder 3 Nov 1929; MIA Königsberg Apr 1945; officially declared dead 9 Sep 1952 (J. Juras; www.volksbund.de; IGI; AF)

Johanna Amalie Grudnick b. Taukitten, Königsberg, Ostpreußen, Preußen 29 Jan 1875; dau. of Friedrich Eduard Grudnick and Dorothea Wilhelmine Treptua; bp. 21 Apr 1923; m. Königsberg, Ostpreußen, Preußen 25 Oct 1898, Wilhelm Gottlieb Pokern; 6 children; d. Königsberg 10 Jun 1940 (FHL Microfilm 245255, 1930/35 Census; IGI)

Franz Helmut Holdau b. Wuppertal-Elberfeld, Rheinland, Preußen 5 or 7 Jun 1916; son of Franz August Holdau and Anna Heischeid; bp. Königsberg, Ostpreußen, Preußen 29 Nov 1942; conf. Königsberg 29 Nov 1942; m. Königsberg 5 or 12 Jun 1943, Ruth Ursula Freimann; rifleman; d. near Ladogasee, Russia 3 Aug 1943; bur. Michajlowskij, Russia (J. Juras; www.volksbund.de; IGI; AF)

Kuno Jenchewski b. Koenigsberg, Ostpreußen, Preußen 14 Apr 1926; son of Emil Gustav Jenschewski and Marie Amalie Blum; ord. priest; k. in battle Berlin, Preußen Apr or May 1945 (Marie Berger; Erika Jenchewski Koch)

Hans Gerhardt Klettke b. Posen, Posen, Preußen 8 Sep 1918; son of Edmund Ludwig Klettke and Salomea Antkowiak; bp. 11 Dec 1926; m. Berlin, Preußen 4 or 12 Jul 1942, Gerda Kuhn; non-commissioned officer; d. 2 km northwest of Heilsberg, Ostpreußen, Preußen 4 Feb 1945 (www.volksbund.de; IGI)

Rudi Heinz Knauer b. Königsberg, Ostpreußen, Preußen 14 Oct 1918; son of Gustav Hans Knauer and Auguste Hedwig Lindtner; bp. 25 Aug 1925 or 27 Aug 1927; ord. deacon; m. Königsberg 15 Jul 1943, Edith Erna Jenschewski; d. 30 May or Jun 1944 (FHL Microfilm 271380, 1935 Census; IGI)

Alfred Hermann Knop b. Königsberg, Ostpreußen, Preußen 15 Jun 1904; ord. priest; m. Herta Charlotte Hennig; 4 children; d. Königsberg 28 Apr 1941 (*Sonntagsgruss*, no. 23, 8 Jun 1941, 92; FHL Microfilm 271380, 1935 Census)

Ernst Rainer Otto Lemke b. Rauschen, Ostpreußen, Preußen 28 Jul 1944; son of Otto Ernst Lemke and Edith Lina Meyer; d. dysentery Cottbus, Germany 4 Aug 1945 (IGI)

Otto Ernst Lemke b. Fischhausen, Ostpreußen, Preußen 6 Mar 1909; son of Carl Hermann Lemke and Wilhelmine Rosine Gemp; bp. 6 Aug 1927; m. 18 Jun 1943, Edith Lina Meyer; 1 child; lance corporal; k. in battle near Alt-Radekow, Brandenburg 23 Apr 1945 (Berlin civil registry 3 Jun 1948; IGI)

Berta Marie Nitsch b. Borchersdorf, Ostpreußen, Preußen 10 Feb or Jul 1884; dau. of Carl August Nitsch and Henriette Mundzeck; m. Königsberg, Ostpreußen, Preußen Oct 1902, August Hermann Martin; 5 children; 2m. Otto Friedrich Riegel; 3 children; d. Königsberg 15 or 16 Apr 1941 (*Sonntagsgruss*, no. 22, 1 Jun 1941, pg. 88; FHL Microfilm 271403, 1935 Census)

Werner Walter Rzepkowski b. Königsberg, Ostpreußen, Preußen 17 Jan 1920; son of Richard Rzepkowski and Ella Friedericke Rock; bp. 18 Jun 1929; d. 1 Nov 1943 or 31 Dec 1945 (IGI; AF)

Kurt Rudolph Sprie b. Gutenfeld, Ostpreußen, Preußen 10 Nov 1906; son of Robert Emil August Sprie and Kaethe Bertha Ritter; bp. 13 Aug 1915; ord. teacher; d. 1943 (FHL Microfilm 245272, 1935 Census; IGI)

Siegfried Robert Konrad Paul Sprie b. Königsberg, Ostpreußen, Preußen 20 Jan 1925; son of Konrad Erich Sprie and Klara Frieda Sommer; bp. 15 Sep 1934; airman; d. Radymno, Jaroslau, Poland 22 Jul 1944 (FHL Microfilm 245272, 1935 Census; IGI; www.volksbund.de)

Harry Willi Waldhaus b. Königsberg, Ostpreußen, Preußen 2 Apr 1926; son of Wilhelm Karl Waldhaus and Gertrud Minna Kaminski; bp. 8 May 1937; soldier; k. in battle Olsany 10 Sep 1944 (W. Kelm; www.volksbund.de; IGI)

Wilhelm Karl Waldhaus b. Königsberg, Ostpreußen, Preußen 20 May 1901; son of Friedrich Waldhaus and Johanna Friedericka Lupp; bp. 24 Jul 1937; m. Königsberg 2 Dec 1922, Gertrud Minna Kaminski; 3 children: k. by artillery Berlin, Preußen 25 Apr 1945 (W. Kelm; AF)

Notes

1. Presiding Bishopric, "Financial, Statistical, and Historical Reports of Wards, Stakes, and Missions, 1884–1955," CR 4 12, 257.

2. Ingrid Freimann Juras, Irmgard Freimann Klindt, and Ruth Freimann Dietz, interview by the author in German, Salt Lake City, March 23, 2007; unless otherwise noted, summarized in English by Judith Sartowski.

3. Reinhard Freimann, interview by the author in German, Hanover, Germany, August 6, 2006.

4. Renate Klein and Sigrid Klein, interview by the author, St. George, Utah, October 9, 2006.

5. Inge Grünberg Seiffer, interview by Jennifer Heckmann in German, Backnang, Germany, August 17, 2006, summarized in English by the author.

6. The twelfth article of faith of The Church of Jesus Christ of Latter-day Saints reads thus: "We believe in being subject to kings, presidents, rulers and magistrates, in obeying, honoring, and sustaining the law."

7. Erika Jenschewski Koch, interview by Michael Corley, Bountiful, Utah, March 14, 2008.

8. Christel Freimann Schmidt, telephone interview with Judith Sartowski, February 25, 2008.

9. Karin Kremulat Bryner, interview by the author, Salt Lake City, February 2, 2007.

10. "Freimann Family History" (unpublished, 2001), 12; private collection.

11. Gudrun Hellwig Weber, interview by the author in German, Schwerin, Germany, August 17, 2006.

12. Maria Bresilge Berger, *Erinnerungen* (unpublished history, 1979), 12; private collection; trans. Renate Berger.

13. Helga Kremulat Freimann, interview by Michael Corley, West Valley City, Utah, March 21, 2008.

14. "Freimann Family History," 17.

15. Fritz E. Bollbach, *Fate Rules My Life* (Fritz E. Bolbach, 1993), 137–39.

16. Mission leaders had also recommended that the members in the eastern districts—at least the women and the children—move west to areas in the districts of Chemnitz and Zwickau.

17. Margarete Hack Hellwig, report (unpublished), recorded by Wilford Weber; private collection.

18. No official passenger records were kept for the fatal voyage but estimates run as high as 9,000 deaths. Retrieved October 30, 2008, from http://www.wilhelmgustloff.com.

19. Berger, *Erinnerungen*, 14–15.

20. Ibid., 15.

21. Bollbach, *Fate Rules My Life*, 142, 153.
22. Ibid., 161.
23. Ibid., 163–64.
24. Theodor Berger to Maria Bresilge Berger, private collection.
25. Bollbach, *Fate Rules My Life*, 169.
26. "Freimann Family History," 17.

MEMEL BRANCH

The eastward expansion of The Church of Jesus Christ of Latter-day Saints ended in Memel, Germany. Stretching north of East Prussia along the Baltic Sea, the Memel territory was annexed by Germany in 1939. It was one of the territories reclaimed by Hitler in what historians call a "bloodless conquest." The city of Memel was the capital of the region and was closer to Russia than it was to East Prussia and Germany.

Nothing is known about the status of the Memel Branch of the Church in Germany other than the membership numbers and the address of the meetinghouse ("Bommelsvitte 70 bei Herbst"). Bommelsvitte was a suburb on the north side of the city of Memel. The Herbst family was likely the core of the group of Latter-day Saints there.

Memel Branch[1]	1939
Elders	0
Priests	1
Teachers	0
Deacons	0
Other Adult Males	2
Adult Females	13
Male Children	0
Female Children	0
Total	16

Because there was no elder among the sixteen Saints in the Memel Branch, it is likely that an elder from another branch in the district was assigned to visit the group from time to time. There was a priest of the Aaronic Priesthood in the branch; therefore, the sacrament ordinance was available in their meetings.

The Soviet army invaded the Memel province in the fall of 1944. If the Saints there had not fled by that time, they would have been expelled by 1946 at the latest, and the branch was erased from the records of the East German Mission.

IN MEMORIAM

Only one known member of the Memel Branch did not survive World War II:

Theresa Henriette Rautenberg b. Mussaten Litauen 30 Sep 1863; dau. of Wilhelm Rautenberg and Wilhelmine Bartschat; bp. Mussaten 4 Aug 1912; m. August Gottlieb Bartschat; 2 children; d. Memel, Tilsit, Ostpreußen 23 Nov 1940 (*Sonntagsgruss*, no. 11, 16 Mar 1941, 43; FHL Microfilm 25718, 1930 Census)

NOTE

1. Presiding Bishopric, "Financial, Statistical, and Historical Reports of Wards, Stakes, and Missions, 1884–1955," CR 4 12, 257.

PILLAU BRANCH

The East Prussian town of Pillau was a very small port on the Baltic Sea. With a population of about ten thousand, it was a short ride on the train from Königsberg, eighteen miles to the east. The branch of Latter-day Saints in Pillau was quite small when World War II began.

The Pillau Branch held its meetings in the Prawitt home at Predigerstrasse 10. With two elders, the branch at least had sufficient priesthood leadership to perform the normal functions of a small Church unit. One of those elders was Branch President Arthur Prawitt.

By early 1943, the meetings of the Pillau Branch had moved to Schmiedestrasse 5. The location was likely a family residence, but the records do not give the name of a host family.[1]

Pillau Branch[2]	1939
Elders	2
Priests	0
Teachers	1
Deacons	1
Other Adult Males	2
Adult Females	11
Male Children	4
Female Children	5
Total	26

Due to a lack of eyewitness testimony nothing more is known about the Pillau Branch during the years 1939–45.

The members of the Pillau Branch most likely suffered the same fate as those in other branches in the Königsberg District—either they fled the advancing Red Army or were expelled from East Prussia when the territory was ceded to Russia after the war. In any case, the Pillau Branch would have ceased to exist by 1946. The name of the town was changed to Baltiysk.

In Memoriam

Only one member of the Pillau Branch did not survive World War II:

Otto Sawatzki b. Schackeln, Ostpreußen, Preußen 4 Jan 1912; son of Julius Sawatzki and Auguste Heinrich; bp. 11 May 1931; ord. teacher; m. Fischhausen, Ostpreußen, Preußen 1 Sep 1934, Gertrud Anna Charlotte Bagdon; 2 children; d. 10 Apr 1945 or MIA Breslau, Schlesien, Preußen 1 Apr 1945 (www.volksbund .de; FHL Microfilm 245257, 1935 Census; AF)

Notes

1. East German Mission, "Directory of Meeting Places" (unpublished manuscript, 1943); private collection.
2. Presiding Bishopric, "Financial, Statistical, and Historical Reports of Wards, Stakes, and Missions, 1884–1955," CR 4 12, 257.

Selbongen Branch

A unique branch in many ways, the Selbongen Branch was situated in a very isolated part of East Prussia from its inception in the 1920s until its demise in the 1970s. The branch was founded in great part thanks to the gospel dedication and missionary spirit of one member, Friedrich Fischer. He was converted in Berlin in 1918 and went home to Selbongen to share the gospel with his relatives and his friends. The branch grew so steadily that the Church decided that the Selbongen Branch needed its own meetinghouse. One was constructed there in just two months during the year 1929. As of the outbreak of World War II in 1939, this was the only meetinghouse owned by the Church in Germany or Austria.

Selbongen Branch[1]	1939
Elders	6
Priests	3
Teachers	8
Deacons	6
Other Adult Males	40
Adult Females	62
Male Children	17
Female Children	14
Total	156

The Selbongen Branch was, in many aspects of the word, a family. From its beginnings among the extended Fischer family, it came to include members of the Krisch, Kruska, Mordas, Pilchowski, Skrotzki, and Stank families. The branch had existed barely two decades when World War II ended, but by then many marriages had occurred among these families. The rate of activity among the members of the branch was also exceptionally high.

Emma Stank Krisch (born 1915) was one of the first members of the LDS Church in Selbongen. Later she described the meeting rooms inside their unique structure:

> Inside was just a chapel, and we had one room and one classroom. When you came in, on the left side was the classroom and straight [ahead] was the chapel. And there was a stage, a platform at the back. There was no electricity in the building.[2]

Regarding the decor in the meetinghouse, Günther Skrotzki (born 1930) recalled the following: "On the right wall was a picture of Heber J. Grant, and on the left wall one could see the quotation 'Who will go up to the mountain of the Lord? . . . He who hath clean hands and a pure heart,' embroidered on a large banner. On the right side there was a pump organ below the picture of the prophet [Heber J. Grant]."[3]

Emma's daughter, Renate Krisch (born 1941), added these details: "There was no running water in the building and no restrooms, so we had to go next door to the Kruska home."

Emma Stank Krisch recalled that many of the members of the Selbongen Branch did not live in the town of about six hundred inhabitants, but came from various small towns and farms in the vicinity. For this reason, the Sunday meetings were held consecutively in the morning.

For young Heinz Grühn (born 1934), "Christmas celebrations were always the most wonderful times." He provided this description:

> The Relief Society organized many get-togethers with food and a bazaar. We already started in July to practice for the Christmas program. Those programs lasted over two hours, and the entire village came to watch—the building was full of people, and there was no room left. These Christmas celebrations always happened on Christmas Eve. Sometimes, we had snow up to [four feet deep].[4]

Heinz Grühn lived just across the street from the church building in Selbongen. His father, Otto, was a policeman who was not fit for military service, having burned his arm severely as a youth. Due to this condition, Otto was at home for nearly the entire duration of the war.

Renate Krisch provided an excellent description of the family home and domestic functions during the war and for several years thereafter:

> It was a fairly new brick house, so it was nice. The only modern convenience it had was electricity . . . for lights. . . . There were no electrical appliances at all except for an electrical iron. There was no running water in the house. Drinking water and water for cooking, etc., was brought into the house from the well beside the house. . . . Water for washing clothes was "softer" from the lake. . . . Mother scrubbed all the clothes on a washboard with lye soap; there was no detergent. All the water had to be heated on the stove. . . . There was no bathroom in the house. . . . A steel tub that an adult could sit in was used for the weekly Saturday nights' baths. The outhouse was in the back of the stable. . . . All the cooking was done on a "two burner" stove that was fueled with wood or coals. The big room was heated with a tile stove. It also served for baking bread.[5]

Emma's husband, Wilhelm Krisch, was already in the Wehrmacht when World War II began. As a draftee, he was required to take his own motorcycle when he reported for duty. He participated in the campaign against Poland and then the campaign against France. By the time his first child, Renate, was born, it, he was serving in Russia.

Shortly after the German invasion of the Soviet Union, Wilhelm Krisch and his comrades came under fire from enemy artillery. As he was running to join a group of seven of them in what appeared to be a good defensive position,

> a soft, quiet voice called me by name, telling me that I should go back. When I heard the

voice I started to run back. I got thirty to forty steps when I threw myself on the ground. Only a few seconds elapsed before a direct hit struck the group. . . . They were dead or wounded. The only thing that happened to me was marks on the stock of my rifle. . . . Our Heavenly Father warned me with the soft voice. I don't know, perhaps I would have been dead also.[6]

At one point, Wilhelm was wounded in Russia and was sent to a hospital in Allenstein, about forty miles southwest of Selbongen. His wife was allowed to visit him there. Then it was back to war for Brother Krisch, who returned home on leave perhaps twice, but he was not home when his two daughters were born. His last furlough was Christmas 1943, after which he was separated from his family for many years. According to his wife, Emma, "The loneliest days were Christmas and Mother's Day. I felt sorry for my dear husband being gone for so long."[7]

Regarding her husband's experience in the army, Emma Stank Krisch later explained, "He did not get along well with the other soldiers. It was hard for him to live as a Latter-day Saint under those conditions. Once he had a Bible, but he really felt alone." By the early summer of 1944, Wilhelm Krisch was near the Atlantic Coast in France, and he was captured by the Americans shortly after the D-day invasion in June 1944. He was allowed to write a card to his family so that they knew he was still alive.

Emil Skrotzki (born 1904) was a husband and father of six. He was no die-hard Nazi wishing to fight wars for the Führer; he just wanted to be home with his family. His son, Walter (born 1939), remembered that on his last visit home, this young father told his children, "I might not be coming back again." Indeed, Emil was killed on the Eastern Front, and the *Sonntagsgruss*, the publication of the East German Mission in Berlin, announced his death on April 5, 1942.[8]

Fig. 1. *The East German Mission constructed this meetinghouse for the Selbongen Branch in 1929. This photograph was taken for the Deseret News in 1938. The building still stands.*

Günther Skrotzki, another one of Emil's six children, remembered the experience as one of the worst things that can happen to a boy:

We were six children at home that waited for him to come back. I will never forget the day that we found out about my father [dying]. The mayor and a teacher came to our apartment, and I already heard my mother crying when I walked inside the house. Later, we received a little package with my father's Bible and some other small things. One day, my mother and I visited a man who was in one room with my father. He told us that he would never forget the day when my father died. They had gotten a call to get ready because there was an alarm, and my father Emil was nowhere to be found. He went to look for my father, and he found him on his knees praying. He was the only one out of his group who died.

According to Günther, the branch conducted baptisms in three different small lakes near Selbongen. The water was not very cold when Günther was baptized in July 1939. Because the Church was well known and accepted in

Fig. 2. *Former branch president Emil Skrotzki, father of six, was killed in 1942. (R. Krisch George)*

Selbongen, there was no need for secrecy on those occasions.

Annie Butschek (born 1927) remembered that even in a small town such as Selbongen, National Socialism was important to some of the citizens. For example, all of the programs for the youth were in place. "I was a part of the BDM and I liked it there. Our leader was a kindergarten teacher, and she practiced songs with us. There were no politics included at all."[9]

In other instances, fanatics made sure that people toed the party line. Günther Skrotzki's mother supported the foreign laborers and gave them clothing that her family no longer needed. Günther explained, "A farmer reported her to the local party officials. She was required to meet with the local political leader, and he explained that she was lucky that her husband [had] died in the war or she would have been taken to a [concentration] camp."

Hitler Youth groups were known for their discipline and obedience, but there were exceptions. An odd incident happened in 1944 in the Jungvolk group to which Heinz Grühn belonged: "Some of the boys went to our leader's home one night because he did not treat us well that day, and they told him what they thought of him and even hurt him on his way home. After that, he started to treat us better again."

For the last year or so of the war, older men like branch president Alfred Kruska (who lived next to the church) and August Fischer were the only adult priesthood holders left to direct the activities of the branch. They were instrumental in looking after the many women and children who were trying to survive without their husbands or fathers.

Located far from any major city, Selbongen was spared the constant air raids and false alarms. Life was very calm there until the fall of 1944, when the Soviet Army set foot on German soil for the first time. Edith Mordas recalled living with her widowed mother and five siblings "in a beautiful house by a lake . . . a dream world" that included eight acres of land, a few chickens, and several pigs. Her grandmother also lived in the home and tried to calm their fears about the invading Russians: "The Russians are human beings, too," she said.[10]

The invaders arrived in Selbongen on January 25, 1945; there was no armed resistance. Edith soon learned that her grandmother had overestimated the goodness of the enemy soldiers. "They didn't treat us well. They executed lots of people, and we knew it, because we knew everybody in town." The fear was constant in Edith's mind:

> It was always frightening when a wagon stopped in front of our house. [The soldiers] would storm into our house with their guns pointed at us. My sister Eva (7) and I (6) hung on to Mother's dress. They took everything they liked, but they didn't harm us.

Living under military occupation was not comfortable, but the war was over in Selbongen nearly four months before it concluded in Berlin.

According to the recollections of Emma Stank Krisch, the Red Army soldiers were allowed to do anything they desired for three days after taking the town. For the first time in the war, Germans civilians were experiencing the anger and revenge that characterized the typical Soviet soldier when he set foot on German soil. No woman—young or old—was safe in Selbongen, but as if by a miracle, only a few of the members of the branch were assaulted. Nevertheless, at least two sisters later gave birth to children of enemy soldiers.

Soon after their arrival, the conquerors impressed many Selbongen men into involuntary labor service in the Soviet Union.[11] A short time later, they began to kidnap women for the same purpose. When the word went out that this was happening, Emma Stank Krisch left her girls with her good friend Maria Niehsit and went into hiding. As Emma later wrote:

> I stayed in the chicken coop all day, hoping that the Russians would not find me. The good Lord surely did protect me. So many mothers were taken to Russia, and had to leave their children behind. It was heartbreaking! Most of these mothers never came back.

At age fifty-eight, August Fischer had not served in the German army during the war, but for all practical purposes, he became a prisoner of war before the conflict ended. In early February, he and fourteen other Selbongen men were impressed into service. He had no opportunity to say good-bye to his wife and was not in great health to start with. One day while marching through deep snow, he could not go on and attempted to climb onto a wagon for a ride. As he wrote in 1948:

> A Russian soldier sitting on the wagon wanted to shoot me. I said I didn't care. He took aim at me and was about to shoot when a young sergeant came by and stopped him. Later I regretted the fact that he didn't kill me then, because he would have spared me from a great deal of suffering.[12]

By March 21, August Fischer had been transported deep into Russia near the Ural Mountains. Under the terrible conditions of the transport, hundreds of Germans had already died. It was soon clear to August that a life of hard labor under grueling conditions awaited him. Right from the start, he battled illness after illness and spent much of his time in camp hospitals. "I only survived all of those illnesses because of my great energy and will to live."

Eventually some degree of calm came back among the inhabitants of Selbongen as they sought an existence without a government to regulate matters (such as food distribution). Emma Krisch later recalled that they had always had enough to eat during the war because they lived in a rural area. However, all of that

changed when the Russians arrived and stole their animals and their stored grains. She explained that they often buried food supplies in the ground to keep them from being discovered and taken by the Soviets. In response, the invaders used long metal rods to search for hidden food and valuables.

Annie Butschek recalled somebody having the idea "that we should hide everything that was really valuable to us underneath the podium in the meetinghouse. We hid nice tableware and special clothing. Nothing happened to those things, and a few months later, we were able to get them back."

Walter Skrotzki was only five years old when the Russians invaded the town, but he recalled one item of family property that was lost: "We had a picture of Jesus Christ holding the lost lamb in his arms, and the frame for this picture looked like it was gold. So [the soldiers] wanted to find out [if it was gold] and burned it."[13]

Walter recalled the problem of involuntary forced labor under Soviet domination:

> Two of my siblings were taken by the Russians in 1945. My brother was hurt on the way to Russia and they had left him [behind]. A week later, he returned home. My sister was less fortunate and had to stay with them [in Russia] for five years. She returned in the 1950s.

Although the war was replete with senseless tragedies, a particularly sad example took place in Selbongen on Sunday, January 28, 1945. Adolf Ernst Kruska (born 1925), a young husband in the Selbongen Branch, had returned on convalescent leave shortly before the invasion. He (on crutches) and his wife, Frieda, were crossing the street toward his father's home next to the church that Sunday morning. Still wearing his uniform, he was challenged by enemy soldiers to give them cigarettes, which he told them he did not have. They shot and mortally wounded him at the gate in front of his father's home.

Eyewitnesses such as Renate Krisch never forgot the incident. The shots rang out while they were holding Sunday School in the church next door to the Kruska home. Adults and children alike first looked out the window and then rushed out to see what had happened. Renate described the event in these words:

There was Frieda Butschek [Kruska] leaning over her lifeless husband, and she was uncontrollably wailing—not just crying. The blood, of course, was very visible on the white snow and very disturbing to me. It was only minutes before his parents were there and the whole neighborhood. The Russians kept on talking to the adults and looked very mean and told them to go into the house.[14]

Adolf was laid to rest in a grave next to the church, about twenty feet to the right of the front stairway. Helmut Mordas (born 1933) later wrote that "the burial took place two or three days later and in the dark of night, because we were scared of the Russians. We were so sad. Adolf's father made the coffin."

Helmut Mordas recalled a Sunday when the Russian soldiers went through town in search of women and girls:

Several women gathered in church, hiding out with Brother Kruska, and I was there too. We sang the hymn "Come, O Come, Thou Day of Glory" on page twenty-six. After the hymn, we knelt down and two or three sisters and Brother Kruska prayed. We could feel the Spirit of God among us. Despite the fact that the singing could be heard out on the street, no Russian entered the church. That strengthened our faith that God had heard our prayers.

Erich Stank (born 1933) gained a testimony of the Savior Jesus Christ at the age of thirteen during a particularly harrowing event in February 1945. As he later wrote:

About fifteen of us (four families) found ourselves in a life-threatening situation. About

fifteen Russian soldiers pointed their rifles at us to shoot us. In this dangerous situation, my mother stood between their bullets and us children (five of us). She said, "Children, take each other by the hand." Then she sang the hymn, "Abide with Me, Fast Falls the Eventide." . . . I was only thirteen years old and I wanted to live. I prayed to my Father in Heaven, told him that I wanted to live, and made a pact with him: if he allowed me to live, I would live according to his commandments and laws.[15]

It should not be assumed, of course, that every Soviet or Polish soldier was capable of inhumane acts: "In all fairness, I have to say that where there were lots of children, [the conquerors] left the family one cow and a few chickens so that the children would have something to eat and some milk to drink." Otherwise, all animals were taken and sent eastward. Helmut was forced to herd animals in that direction for six weeks until he could escape and return to Selbongen.

In the spring of 1945, Emma Krisch was working in the garden when an enemy soldier approached her. She walked in the opposite direction, pretending not to see him:

I knew that he was following me. I kept on walking to the neighbors, the Kruska's, but I did not make it. He picked up a piece of wood, a board, and hit me on the head from behind. Brother Kruska came out of the house and scared him off. Otherwise, he could have killed me. Here,

Fig. 3. Heinrich Stank visits the grave of a friend in Russia. Heinrich was wounded in Latvia in 1944 and died in a field hospital. (R. Krisch George)

again, the Lord was with me and protected me because I was needed to take care of my two little girls.

All eyewitnesses agreed that by May 1945, when the war ended, Brother Kruska was still conducting church services in the Selbongen Branch. There had been brief interruptions when the Russians arrived, and the soldiers actually inhabited the hall for a week or two, but the Saints there did their best to restore order in the Church at a time when order was not possible in so many other aspects of life.

If the Saints in Selbongen thought that the Soviets were brutal rulers, they found out differently when the region was turned over to the Polish. Emma Krisch later wrote that any offenses committed by the Russians were surpassed by the Polish. "Nothing was safe; everything was fair game for the Poles. If they wanted something they just took it from the Germans."

At eighteen years of age, Annie Butschek was a prime target for abuse by the conquerors. She must have been quite scared when called to the local police office one day. She described the experience in these words:

> They brought us to the Polish GPU (police) and we had to answer questions about what we did during the war and if we were a member of the Party in any way or even a member of the BDM. After I answered all these questions, a secretary took a ruler and hit me in the face a few times, after which I was allowed to leave. They brought me to a cellar space below a living room, and I had to climb into it through a door in the floor. All the others who came with us were already in there. The people asked me if they had hit me, and I responded that it was nothing compared to all of this. A little later, they opened the door and we could climb out. We got a little to eat.

Annie's mother called her treatment "nothing compared to all that was being inflicted on women all over East Prussia."

Life in the Selbongen region was helter-skelter at best for several months after the war. For example, in the fall of 1945, Martha Krisch Pilchowski (born 1909) was ordered by Polish soldiers to vacate her home within thirty minutes. Along with her sons and her sister-in-law, Antonie, and some belongings (a maximum of thirty pounds per person), they began the trip to Germany by walking thirty miles to a railroad station. Under deplorable conditions, they were transported to eastern Germany. A trip that once took two days now lasted five weeks. The refugees were cold, starving, and sick, and Martha's health failed. According to her sister-in-law Emma Krisch, "She died en route to East Germany. When the train stopped, the relatives wrapped her body in a blanket and left it on the platform of a train station. They were not allowed, nor was there time to bury her."[16]

The youth of the area faced another particular challenge. Helmut Mordas wrote that "we young people didn't have any future in those days. There was no school and no occupational training. We stayed alive by working the farms and the gardens."

Thinking back about the challenges faced by his widowed mother, Emilie, during the horrific last days of the war, Walter Skrotzki offered this short statement: "My mother was very faithful. Nothing could take her away from the Church."

"We were among the first members who left Selbongen," recalled Heinz Grühn.

> We stayed in Selbongen until August 20, 1947, when we took a transport out of the town. Because my father worked for the police, he left for western Germany in 1945. For him, it was too dangerous to stay. The Russians were not the problem but rather the Polish. When we left Selbongen, we were assigned to a transport train in which we slept on straw for two weeks with thirty-one people.

All through the years of 1946 and 1947, August Fischer tried to maintain his health enough to do the work required of him in the POW camps of Russia. It seemed like his work was always outdoors, where he was subjected to numbing cold and wet conditions. Fighting lice and the illnesses of other prisoners in his immediate vicinity, he rarely had a warm meal or a warm place to sleep. On the few occasions when he was given a delousing or a shower in lukewarm water, he was grateful to enjoy any condition resembling cleanliness. However, his health was never good, and he narrowly escaped death on several occasions.

As a POW, Wilhelm Krisch was first taken to the United States and interned in Alabama. In 1946 he was sent to Scotland and was released there in 1947. Unfortunately, he dared not return to Selbongen. By that time, the town was under Polish administration. While Latter-day Saints in all other German towns

Fig. 4. The interior of the Selbongen church in 1958. Eyewitnesses say that the decor was essentially the same during the war years.

that became Polish after 1945 were compelled to leave and go west to Germany, this was not the case in Selbongen. The Polish county government there allowed (or forced) only some of the surviving Germans in the branch to emigrate. Under those circumstances, Wilhelm Krisch felt it safer to stay in West Germany and wait until his family could come to him. As the years went by, he decided to immigrate to the United States with his brother. He was not reunited with his wife and his children until they were allowed to leave Selbongen and travel to the United States in 1957.

The list of illnesses suffered by August Fischer for three years as a forced laborer in Russia is long, amazing, and discouraging. Twice he was told that a release was forthcoming and each time was disappointed. He was finally able to establish communications with his family in 1947, and this bolstered his spirits. Unfortunately, by the time he was released in 1948, his health was permanently weakened. He was not allowed to return to his wife and family in Selbongen but was sent to western Germany and ended up in Wolfshagen near Kassel, where he was put into a hospital. It was there that he concluded his memoirs of the years in Russia with these words: "I don't know how long I will stay in this hospital; my illnesses are fairly serious." He had contracted tuberculosis in Russia and died on September 9, 1951, in a Heidelberg hospital. His family was still in Selbongen, and he had not seen them since being kidnapped in February 1945.

The members of the Selbongen Branch who stayed there after World War II were allowed to continue to meet in the church but were required to conduct their services in the Polish language. They translated their songs and their talks into Polish, but their German heritage refused to be totally conquered. After 1947, theirs was the only branch of the Church for hundreds of miles; they were isolated except for periodic visits from leaders of the Church from East Germany.[17]

Beginning in the 1950s, the Latter-day Saints in Selbongen sought a way to immigrate to Germany one by one. For example, Helmut Mordas availed himself of illegal means to leave Poland and travel to West Berlin. By 1974, the branch ceased to exist. As of this writing, the LDS meetinghouse in Selbongen (now Zelwagi, Poland) is being used by the Catholic Church. The grave of Adoft Ernst Kruska is carefully maintained.

IN MEMORIAM

The following members of the Selbongen Branch did not survive World War II:

Auguste Bauik b. Rhein/Lötzew, Ostpreußen, Preußen 2 Jan 1863; dau. of Gottlieb Bauik and Amalie Walter; bp. 15 Aug 1924; conf. 15 Aug 1924; m. —— Hartwich; d. 8 Apr 1940 (CHL Microfilm 2448 pt. 27, no. 26)

Manfred Johannes Bojahra b. Selbongen, Sensburg, Ostpreußen, Preußen 24 Jun 1936; son of Alfred Fritz Bojahra and Hedwig Louise Kruska; d. diphtheria Selbongen 5 May 1940 (*Sonntagsstern*, no. 21, 23 Jun 1940, n.p.; CHL Microfilm 2448 pt. 27, no. 156; IGI; PRF)

Julius Czwiowski b. Liebenberg, Ostpreußen, Preußen 7 Jul 1870; son of Samuel Czwikowski and Eva Polkowski; bp. 6 Oct 1929; conf. 6 Oct 1929; m. Kumilsko, Ostpreußen, Preußen 3 May 1896, Wilhelmine Gutowski; 4 children; d. old age Selbongen, Ostpreußen, Preußen 5 May 1940. (*Sonntagsstern*, no. 21, 23 Jun 1940, n.p.; FHL Microfilm 245749; IGI)

Horst Fritz Fischer b. Turnowen, Ostpreußen, Preußen 12 Aug 1923; son of Michael Fischer and Wilhelmine Jedamzik; bp. Selbongen, Sensburg, Ostpreußen, Preußen 1 Jun 1932; conf. Selbongen 1 Jun 1932; ord. deacon Selbongen 1 May or Oct 1939; k. in battle 13 Mar or May 1943 (CHL Microfilm 2448 pt. 27, no. 23; IGI; PRF)

Walter August Fischer b. Selbongen, Ostpreußen, Preußen 5 Mar 1920; son of August Fischer and Amalie Bukowski; bp. Selbongen 28 Apr 1928; conf. Selbongen 28 Apr 1928; ord. deacon Selbongen 24 Jun 1934; ord. teacher Selbongen 6 May 1938; MIA Luga, Sabzje, Russia 1 Jan 1944 or d. 10 Mar 1944 (CHL Microfilm 2448 pt. 27, no. 5; IGI; PRF; www.volksbund.de)

Fig. 5. The grave of Heinrich Stank in distant Russia. (R. Krisch George)

Willy Fritz Fischer b. Selbongen, Ostpreußen, Preußen 11 Jul 1921; son of August Fischer and Amalie Bukowski; bp. 14 Jul 1929; conf. 14 Jul 1929; ord. deacon 13 Sept 1936; ord. teacher 1 Oct 1939; d. 20 Jul 1944 (CHL Microfilm 2448 pt. 27, no. 6; IGI; PRF)

Johann Fladda b. Neu Ukta, Sensburg, Ostpreußen, Preußen 22 Feb 1885; son of Michael Fladda and Friedrike Czesny; bp. Selbongen, Sensburg, Ostpreußen, Preußen 6 Jul 1930; conf. Selbongen 6 Jul 1930; ord. deacon Selbongen 25 Dec 1938; m. Nicolaiken, Ostpreußen, Preußen 11 or 19 Jul 1919, Marie Hoffmann; 1 child; d. Sensburg, Ostpreußen, Preußen 27 Jan 1945 (CHL Microfilm 2448 pt. 27, no. 11; IGI; PRF)

Paul Fladda b. Selbongen, Sensburg, Ostpreußen, Preußen 4 Dec 1901; son of Karl Fladde and Charlotte Gruenske; bp. Selbongen 6 Nov 1924; conf. 6 Nov 1924; ord. deacon Selbongen 1 Nov 1925; ord. teacher Selbongen 26 Oct 1930; m. 16 Nov 1928, Anna Brisewski; d. POW France 28 Sep 1945 (Krisch-George; CHL Microfilm 2448 pt. 27, no. 9; IGI; PRF)

Wilhelmine Giesewski b. Selbongen, Ostpreußen, Preußen 20 Jul 1878; dau. of Samuel Giesewski and

Karoline Eichel; bp. 3 Jul 1924; conf. 3 Jul 1924; m. 2 or 3 Oct 1903, Emil Piotrowski; 5 children; d. Selbongen 13 or 17 Feb 1940 (*Sonntagsstern*, no. 17, 26 May 1940, n.p.; CHL Microfilm 2448 pt. 27, no. 49; NG-IGI; AF; PRF)

Heinriette Grudda b. Neuwalde, Sensburg, Ostpreußen, Preußen 31 Mar or May 1868; dau. of Johann Grudda and Marie Marzenowski; bp. 15 Aug 1924; conf. 15 Aug 1924; m. 24 Nov 1889, Fritz Walter; d. 11 Jun 1943 (CHL Microfilm 2448 pt. 27, no. 92; IGI)

Auguste Huebner b. Plowczen, Ostpreußen, Preußen 17 Dec 1872; dau. of Samuel Huebner and Catharine Staschewski; bp. 4 Jun 1932; m. —— Sabotka; d. 19 Oct 1942 (IGI)

Johann Kelbch b. Klein Schwignainen, Ostpreußen, Preußen 28 May 1896; son of Leopold Kelbch and Wilhelmine Schliski; bp. 30 June 1917; conf. 30 Jun 1917; d. 1940 or 1942 (CHL Microfilm 2448 pt. 27, no. 131; IGI)

Martha Krisch b. Ododyen, Johannesburg, Ostpreußen, Preußen 19 Jan 1908; dau. of Gottlieb Krisch and Marie Penski; bp. 23 Oct 1922; conf. 23 Oct 1922; m. Ostpreußen, Preußen 6 or 9 June 1930, Rudolf Pilchowski; d. as refugee Feb 1945 (Krisch-George; CHL Microfilm 2448 pt. 27, no. 136; IGI)

Adolf Ernst Kruska b. Selbongen, Sensburg, Ostpreußen, Preußen 29 Oct 1916; son of Adolf Kruska and Amalie Fischer; bp. 20 Jun 1925; conf. 20 Jun 1925; ord. deacon 13 May 1932; ord. teacher 6 May 1938; ord. priest 26 Aug 1943; m. Nikolaiken, Sensburg, Ostpreußen, Preußen 6 Nov 1942, Frieda Buschek; k. by Russian soldiers 28 or 29 Jan 1945; bur. at Selbongen LDS Church (Krisch-George; CHL Microfilm 2448 pt. 27, no. 91; IGI)

Anna Kulinna b. Pietzarken, Angerburg, Ostpreußen, Preußen 10 Oct 1903; dau. of Friedrich Kulinna and Auguste Masannek; bp. 1 Aug 1923; conf. 1 Aug 1923; m. 14 Nov 1930, Richard Jestremski; k. by Russians 1945 (CHL Microfilm 2448 pt. 27, no. 30; IGI)

Auguste Massannek b. Siemanowen, Ostpreußen, Preußen 18 Jun 1864; dau of Daniel Massannek and Justine Schwüller; bp. 16 Aug 1923; conf. 16 Aug 1923; m. 15 Apr. 1892, Friedrich Kulinna Sr.; d. exposure 1945 (CHL Microfilm 2448 pt. 27, no. 37; IGI)

Margott Hildegard Mordas b. Selbongen, Sensburg, Ostpreußen, Preußen 27 Aug 1929; dau. of Gustav Mordas and Anna Stopka; bp. 29 Aug 1937; conf. 29 Aug 1937; d. typhoid 27 Aug 1945 (Mordas-Hohmann; CHL Microfilm 2448 pt. 27, no. 46; IGI; PRF)

Gustav Pieniak b. Selbongen, Sensburg, Ostpreußen, Preußen 24 Aug 1906; son of Gottlieb Pieniak and Auguste Benzka; bp. 19 Sep 1937; conf. 19 Sep 1937; ord. deacon 25 Dec 1938; ord. teacher 25 Apr 1943; ord. priest 1 Oct 1944; m. Nikolaiken, Ostpreußen, Preußen 29 Dec 1933, Anna Marie Heyduck; 2 children; d. Ural Tu, Russia 22 Mar 1945 (CHL Microfilm 2448 Pt. 27, no. 165; IGI)

Fritz Karl Piotrofski b. Selbongen, Sensburg, Ostpreußen, Preußen 10 Jan 1917; son of Emil Piotrofski and Wilhelmine Giesenki; bp. Selbongen 12 Sep 1925; conf. Selbongen 12 Sep 1925; lance corporal; d. 30 May 1944; bur. Cassino, Italy (CHL Microfilm 2448 pt. 27, no. 52; IGI; PRF; www.volksbund.de)

Martha Karoline A. Przygodda b. Bettmar, Braunschweig 17 Jul 1899; dau. of August Przigodda and Frieda E. Hentis; bp. 19 Sep 1924; conf. 19 Sep 1924; d. surgery 23 Aug 1942 (CHL Microfilm 2448 pt. 27, no. 82; IGI)

Heinrich Friedrich Schirrmann b. Gross Jauer, Ostpreußen, Preußen 20 or 27 Feb 1920; son of Wilhelm Schirrmann and Amalie Schwalgin; bp. 9 Sep 1928; conf. 9 Sep 1928; k. in battle 1944 or 1945 (CHL Microfilm 2448 pt. 27, no. 62; IGI)

Waldemar Ernst Schirrmann b. Gross Jauer, Ostpreußen, Preußen 30 Aug 1925; son of Wilhelm Schirrmann and Amalie Schwalgin; bp. 2 Aug 1936; conf. 2 Aug 1936; lance corporal; k. in battle St. Pol,

Fig. 6. The newspaper obituary for Otto Stank in 1943. (R. Krisch George)

Fig. 7. Otto Paul Stank (left) and Heinrich August Stank.

France 9 Nov 1944; bur. Bourdon, France (CHL Microfilm 2448 pt. 27, no. 65; IGI; www.volksbund.de)

Emil Skrotzki b. Salza, Lötzen, Ostpreußen, Preußen 4 Feb 1904; son of Gottlieb Stank and Heinriette Skrotzki; bp. 15 or 16 May 1924; conf. 16 May 1924; ord. deacon 2 Nov 1925; ord. teacher 20 Mar 1928; ord. priest 14 Jul 1929; ord. elder 13 Mar or 5 Sep 1932; former branch president; m. Salza, Ostpreußen, Preußen 14 Oct 1927, Emilie Grabowski; 6 children; policeman; k. in battle San. Kp. 1/181 Ortslaz. Welikije Luki, Russia 18 or 19 Jan 1942; bur. Welikije Luki, Russia (*Sonntagsgruss*, no. 7, 5 Apr 1942, pg. 28) (CHL Microfilm 2448 pt. 27, no. 69; www.volksbund.de; IGI; PRF)

Heinrich August Stank b. Gross Jauer, Lötzen, Ostpreußen, Preußen 1 Aug 1917; son of Gottlieb Stank and Heinriette Skrotzki; bp. 25 Sep 1927; conf. 25 Sep 1927; lance corporal; d. wounds Field Hospital 2/608 Riga, Latvia 4 Feb 1944 (Krisch-George; CHL Microfilm 2448 pt. 27, no. 80; www.volksbund.de; IGI; PRF)

Otto Paul Stank b. Gross Jauer, Ostpreußen, Preußen 20 Jul 1913; son of Gottlieb Stank and Heinriette Skrotzki; bp. 31 May 1926; conf. 31 May 1926; noncommissioned officer; k. in battle 4 km north of Kelkowo b. Mga, Russia 12 Aug 1943; bur. Sologubowka, St. Petersburg, Russia (Krisch-George; CHL Microfilm 2448 pt. 27, no. 77; www.volksbund.de; IGI)

Werner Stank b. Fasten, Sensburg, Ostpreußen, Preußen 15 Oct 1940; son of Fritz Stank and Frieda Hahn Stank; d. heart ailment Fasten 8 Apr 1942 (Krisch-George; CHL Microfilm 2448 pt. 27, no. 185; IGI; PRF)

Notes

1.   Presiding Bishopric, "Financial, Statistical, and Historical Reports of Wards, Stakes, and Missions, 1884–1955," CR 4 12, 257.

2.   Emma Stank Krisch and Renate Krisch George, interview by the author, Fruit Heights, Utah, May 25, 2006.

3.   Günther Skrotzki, interview by the author in German, Strausberg, Germany, June 8, 2007; unless otherwise noted, summarized in English by the Judith Sartowski.

4.   Heinz Grühn, telephone interview with Judith Sartowski, May 8, 2008.

5.   Renate Krisch George, autobiography (unpublished, 2002), 9–10; private collection.

6.   Wilhelm Krisch, autobiography, 122; private collection.

7.   Emma Stank Krisch, "How and Why We Came to America" (unpublished manuscript, 1994); private collection.

8.   *Sonntagsgruss*, no. 7 (April 5, 1942): 28.

9.   Annie Butschek Skrotzki, interview by the author in German, Strausberg, Germany, June 8, 2007.

10.   Edith Mordas Hohmann, autobiography (unpublished); private collection.

11.   Helmut Mordas claims to remember clearly that this "manhunt" occurred on April 10, 1945. Helmut Mordas, "Mein Bericht: Geschrieben aus meiner Erinnerung von 1939 bis 1957" (unpublished memoir); private collection.

12.   August Fischer, "Meine Erinnerungen 1945–1948" (unpublished memoir); private collection.

13.   Walter Skrotzki, interview by the author in German, Munich, Germany, August 9, 2006.

14.   George, autobiography, 18.

15.   Erich Stank, report (unpublished, 2005); private collection.

16.   Emma Stank Krisch, report (unpublished, 2006).

17.   Walter Krause and Henry Burkhardt each visited the Selbongen Branch on a number of occasions.

Tilsit Branch

Internationally famous for its distinctive cheese, the city of Tilsit was located in the northeast corner of East Prussia, approximately forty-two miles from the capital city of Königsberg. The population of the city in 1939 was fifty-nine thousand.

In early 1939, the Tilsit Branch was meeting in rented rooms at Schlageterstrasse 54, on the main floor. Waltraut Naujoks (born 1921) described the meeting rooms as follows:

We entered the house from the street side and went up some stairs, which led to a room before the actual room for our meetings. Then, there was a small room that was used as a cloakroom. There was also another small room for the Primary and the Young Women (called Beehives). The large meeting room was used for Sunday School and sacrament meeting.[1]

Eva Schulzke (born 1930) provided the following detail from her memories:

It was two rooms, one in the front and the other room was [for] little classes. And there was terrible cold in the wintertime; we didn't have any heat and the toilet was frozen. There were no pictures on the walls and we didn't have a pulpit—just a table. We didn't have a pump organ or anything—we just sang from our books.[2]

Helga Meiszus (born 1920) remembered a less attractive characteristic of the rooms at Schlageterstrasse:

It used to be a restaurant and a beer hall. The smell of beer doesn't go away overnight and then of course [there was] a lot of smoke in the walls and curtains and whatever. . . . Before we started our meetings, we had to open all the windows first because it was quite a smell.[3]

There were few decorations, but Helga also remembered having fresh flowers in the rooms on a regular basis.

Tilsit Branch[4]	1939
Elders	2
Priests	3
Teachers	2
Deacons	6
Other Adult Males	22
Adult Females	52
Male Children	1
Female Children	5
Total	93

The branch observed the typical meeting schedule, with Sunday School in the morning and sacrament meeting in the evening. For many families, it was very inconvenient to take little children back to church in the evening.

Waltraut Naujoks remembered walking for one hour each way from their home outside of town to church. "In the evenings, my mother and father rode bikes to Church so that they could attend sacrament meeting."

Arthur Naujoks had fond memories of the social life in the Tilsit Branch:

Without question, the social event of the year was a gala New Year's Eve party, held at the meetinghouse, complete with refreshments and a stunning array of cakes and sweets.[5]

The missionaries from America were evacuated from Germany on August 25, 1939. The move came so quickly that most of the local Saints did not have the opportunity to send them off. Arthur Naujoks was fortunate to be there as they departed:

When the news came calling the missionaries to Copenhagen [Denmark], I helped Elder Oscar Sither load his bags onto a handcart and then hauled them to the train station. . . . I was sad to see the elders go but was relieved that they would get out safely before any serious trouble began.[6]

Eva Schulzke was baptized in the Memel River when she was nine years old. When she turned ten, she and her classmates were inducted into the Hitler Youth. She missed a few meetings early on due to church attendance and was told that if she continued to be absent, the police would come for her. Fortunately, she found a way to avoid conflict, but the sports and the craft activities never particularly interested her.

"I was part of the Hitler Youth although I did not support their methods," recalled Bruno Stroganoff (born 1923). "In the Hitler Youth, I got the chance to participate in training for firefighters. I also learned how to ride a horse. This training took place outside of Königsberg."[7]

The Augat family lived in the small rural community of Rautengrund, about ten miles

Fig. 1. The Tilsit Branch Sunday School in about 1935. (H. Meiszus Birth Meyer)

from Tilsit. Because of the inconvenience of travel from Rautengrund to Tilsit, and because her husband was not a member of the Church, Berta Augat usually went to the meetings by herself. According to her daughter, Ursula (born 1935), and her son, Heinz (born 1936), their mother took the horse-drawn wagon to the town of Unter Eisseln on the Memel River. From there, she took the boat downriver to the city of Tilsit and then walked through town to church. Ursula and Heinz did not recall going to Tilsit to church with their mother, but they clearly remembered having Sunday School with her in their home, where she taught them the gospel and sang the hymns of Zion with them.

While at work in a pharmacy on Friday, September 1, 1939, Helga Meiszus heard the announcement that Germany had invaded Poland:

I was there in the store, and it was not even noontime and the people came and bought everything under the sun. They bought everything, whatever they could. Whatever they needed, and the store was empty. It was not even noontime. . . . It was not long then the news came that the first of the soldiers got killed. So it was a gloomy day. It seems like the streets were . . . empty. It was like a numbness. Everybody was shocked.

Helga's father, a sergeant in the Wehrmacht, was immediately activated and sent to Poland. The family at home had time to consider what they had heard the previous year from LDS Apostle Joseph Fielding Smith, when he spoke at a district conference in Königsberg. Helga recalled his message:

The year before [1938], we had a special meeting in Königsberg, the capital of East Prussia . . . with then Elder Joseph Fielding Smith. He was there, and I will never forget, he gave a talk—of course it was in English and then translated. He encouraged all the members to have a storage of coal to make fire. Wood and coal and special briquettes. He encouraged us to

Fig. 2. A New Year's celebration in the Tilsit Branch. (E. Schulzke Bode)

fill our basements with it and to have blankets. It seems like he really prepared us for this time.

Ursula Lessing (born 1927) also lived with her family far from the Tilsit Branch. Her parents, Willi and Emma Lessing, lived in a small house in Kallwehlen, a farming community on the north side of the Memel River in the Memelland. They were just a mile from the Russian border in what is now Lithuania, probably farther east than any other LDS family in Germany. The Lessings rarely made the fifty-mile trip to Tilsit to church; their only real connection came through the parents of Emma Lessing, Carl Otto and Ida Hübner.[8]

The Hübners operated a riverboat in the region. They cruised the Memel River and several other rivers and canals in the Memelland and East Prussia. It was an odd lifestyle, but the Hübners were happy members of the Church and attended meetings whenever possible.

Berta Augat's husband, Fritz, was not a member of the Church. He was drafted in the first year of the war. Leaving his wife and little children, he was destined to serve for the remainder of the war and was allowed to come home on leave only a few times. He was assigned to an engineering corps and spent his time building roads and bridges.[9]

In about 1942, some soldiers walked

Fig. 3. Ursula Lessing in the uniform of a BDM girl in about 1941. (U. Lessing Mudrow)

into the church rooms where Helga Meiszus was conducting a Primary meeting. They informed her that they needed to confiscate the rooms for army storage purposes. She insisted that the Church needed the rooms and was actually successful in defending some of the property. The soldiers eventually used only the larger room at the back, leaving the front rooms for regular meetings.

Helga Meiszus continued to work in Tilsit and lived with her grandparents. On February 11, 1942, she married Gerhard Birth of the Schneidemühl Branch. He was a fine young man, and the wedding was a joyous occasion, but their life together was brief. A few days after the wedding, Gerhard returned to the front and was killed on April 1—less than two months later. The report of Gerhard's death reached Helga on Hitler's birthday (celebrated all over Germany each year on April 20). That anniversary became one of very bad luck for Helga Meiszus Birth. On April 20, 1943, she was sitting in a bomb shelter when a bomb landed just a few feet away. She explained the circumstances:

> I was wounded by shrapnel in my neck. I had my fur coat on, and the fur coat had a big lining, a heavy lining, and one piece [of shrapnel], instead of going into my intestines, it didn't go in because of the lining of my fur coat. . . . In that moment I thought, *I'm going to die and I will see my husband.* I twisted around and then when you are in a situation like that it is hard to believe how fast your thoughts are going. I saw my whole life like a film rolling [by] and all my thoughts and I knew my family will be sad.

Fortunately, Helga was lucid enough to leave the air-raid shelter and walk to the hospital, where a physician pronounced, "[You are] very lucky. You could have been paralyzed."

The Lessing family moved to Szillen in East Prussia (about ten miles south of Tilsit) during the war. Willi Lessing had been inducted into the rural police and stationed there. About that time, the Hübners gave up their life on the riverboat and went to live on the farm in Kallwehlen. Both families were isolated from the Church.

Life in rural Rautengrund during the war was a pleasant experience for the Augat children, but they missed their father. In the last year of the war, the city of Tilsit came under attack by Soviet airplanes. The Augat children vividly recalled seeing the "Christmas trees" (illumination flares) over the city from their distant vantage point. They were only eight and nine years old at the time, but they were sufficiently aware of the events to be very frightened of the pending invasion. They saw the red lights on the horizon when Tilsit burned, observed the last German defenders digging defensive trenches and retreating, and watched as German and Soviet fighter planes dueled in the sky. Eventually, they heard the Red Army artillery in the distance. According to Ursula, "It was horrible, and I was very scared, and I didn't even understand the full extent of what was happening."

When Germany attacked the Soviet Union in June 1941, Arthur Naujoks was a witness to some of the first events of the campaign because the Russian border was barely twenty miles to the east of Tilsit. As he later wrote, "In a matter of hours, thousands of Soviet POWs were marching through Tilsit. I was headed to my Sunday School class, barely able to hear the artillery moving away into Belarus."[10]

Arthur was drafted a few months later and in 1942 took part in the offensive that was designed to take the German army into Moscow. By January 4, 1943, he was with his unit in what was possibly the worst place on earth for German soldiers at that time: just west of the city of Stalingrad. He had just been informed by his commanding officer that the Soviets had surrounded their position and that he hoped they could break out and head west to rejoin

Fig. 4. Tilsit Saints enjoyed a social occasion in the home of branch president Otto Schulzke in 1943.

German units. Then the commander took his men totally by surprise, as Arthur recollected:

> Mounting his horse, he stood in the saddle and called out to all the men in a firm, strong voice: "Every man for himself!" Drawing his pistol from his holster, he laid it against his temple and pulled the trigger. In stunned silence we watched his lifeless body slide from the saddle and land in a crumpled heap in the snow. After a few moments to collect ourselves, we quietly wrapped his body in a blanket and buried him where he fell. We were now on our own.[11]

Thus began a terrible trial of survival for Arthur and his comrades. With the odds against him, he resolved to survive:

> I knew that my faith in God would support me and that He would be with me no matter what happened. For the next three months, that knowledge was the only comfort and strength I would have.[12]

Over the next twelve weeks, Arthur trudged through the snow westward, away from Stalingrad, where an estimated 295,000 German soldiers had been killed or captured.[13] He suffered terrible cold and lack of food and shelter and saw his comrades fall and perish around him, but the worst danger was perhaps potential death or loss of body parts to frostbite. At one point, an officer had noticed his sad condition and found a spot on a sled to carry him along.

Arthur later described his condition toward the end of their retreat in the spring of 1943: "The pain in my feet and legs was so intense that I could no longer walk. The skin on my feet had fallen away, and there was horrible infection everywhere. The pain was terrible and excruciating, almost unbearable."[14] Fortunately, he was soon shipped back to Germany and taken to a hospital where he received excellent care.

After months in the hospital, Arthur was given leave to visit his family in Tilsit for a month. The image of the bold hero returning to an enthusiastic welcome by adoring admirers at home was clearly not applicable in his case, as he later observed:

> My arrival was a somber one, tears both of joy and of gratitude. . . . The effect Stalingrad had on me was evident in my limp and walking cane. My family also saw deep spiritual wounds, which would take time to heal. They saw the sadness in my eyes and steeliness in my composure that still held a lot inside. I was not the jovial soldier home on leave they had seen [the] last November.[15]

Because Arthur Naujoks's physical condition improved, he was not released from the army but was given a training assignment. By the summer of 1944, he had recovered

sufficiently to be sent again to the Eastern Front, which was creeping steadily toward Germany. There was little that he and his comrades could do to stop the advance of the seemingly innumerable soldiers of the Red Army.

Waltraut Naujoks married in 1944 in Tilsit. While visiting her parents-in-law in Elbing near Danzig, she learned that an air raid had occurred in Tilsit on April 20 and that her parents' apartment had been destroyed. The Naujoks were the first Saints in Tilsit to lose their home. Even for faithful members of the Church, this could be a spiritual test, as she later explained: "We asked ourselves if we were not faithful enough for the Lord to protect us. We prayed long and hard to know why it had happened to us." Later, the branch president's home was also destroyed, and they knew that it did not happen because they were not faithful

Fig. 5. The youth of the Tilsit Branch clown around on a wintry Sunday afternoon in 1941. Four of them did not survive the war. (H. Meiszus Birth Meyer)

Fig. 6. The letter every family feared most: "I have the sad duty to inform you that your son, Corporal Siegfried Meissus . . . has died in our army hospital." The letter detailed Siegfried's five major wounds; after eight days in the hospital, he died, despite the best efforts of the surgeons. (H. Meiszus Birth Meyer)

enough. "It just happened." Waltraut remained in Elbing.[16]

On July 24, 1944, the Tilsit Branch had a memorial service in the chapel for Helga Birth's brother, Siegfried Meiszus, and for Heinz Millbrecht. The loss of faithful priesthood holders was hurting this and most other branches in the East German Mission. Later that evening, Helga decided to stay the night with her aunt rather than with her grandparents, Eduard and Anna Wachsmuth, with whom she had stayed many times before. During the night, a terrifying air raid took place, and the next day Helga stood staring at the rubble of the Wachsmuth home. It would be two weeks before the bodies of her grandparents could be removed from the rubble. Regarding her escape from certain death, she later stated, "I cannot even explain anymore how I felt. I only knew that my Father in Heaven had a different plan for me."

In August 1944, Helga Meiszus Birth took the train to Berlin, where she began a term of missionary service that would last eighteen months. Paul Langheinrich, second counselor to the mission supervisor, had called her in April, but in accordance with the law, she was not allowed to leave her employment until she could find her own successor.[17]

Bruno Stroganoff's occupational training program was not yet finished when he was drafted into the Waffen-SS, the elite combat troops under the command of Heinrich Himmler. Bruno had no way of knowing that he would soon be exposed to some of the more sinister happenings of the war on the Eastern Front:

> When I saw what they did with the Jews, I could not believe my eyes. I did not see any sense in what I was ordered to do.[18] As soon as I realized what their [SS] methods were, a Hungarian and I fled but were soon caught in Czechoslovakia.[19] We then had to explain the situation to a judge in court. I was kept in prison in Krakau [Poland] in concentration camps.

Bruno Stroganoff could easily have lost his life. Desertion was punishable by death in every European country at the time. Being sent to a concentration camp was the closest thing to death and often did result in death. At one point in his incarceration, Bruno Stroganoff was sent to Dachau, one of the most infamous concentration camps. He explained: "In Dachau, I did not have to work in the concentration camp, but they treated me horribly." He was one of many political prisoners there, of whom thousands died from 1933 to 1945. After making the rounds of numerous camps, Bruno had serious health problems that put him into a hospital in Heidelberg. Tuberculosis was part of the diagnosis. He underwent surgery, and by the time he had recovered, the war

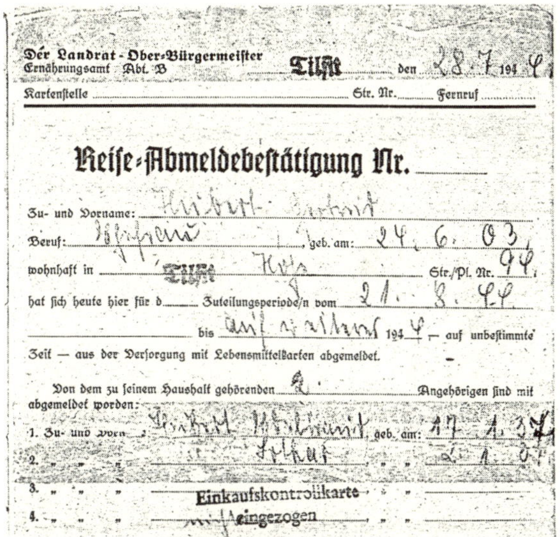

Fig. 7. Refugees who expected to receive food ration stamps in a new location needed official permission to leave their homes. This certificate was issued to Gertrud Hubert when she left Tilsit with her son Lothar in July 1944. (L. Hubert)

Fig. 8. The Schulzke family's apartment (upper balcony) was bombed and burned out in late 1944. (E. Schulzke Bode)

was over. The Americans took him prisoner, and he was not released until 1946.

"I did not always keep the commandments during the war, but I never forgot that I was a member of the Church," admitted Bruno Stroganoff. This is a reminder that the life of a soldier could be spiritually challenging. He continued, "During the war, I didn't have any contact with the Church after I left home. I wasn't allowed to carry the scriptures with me." Like so many Latter-day Saint soldiers in the service of the fatherland, Bruno was isolated from organized religion.

Sometime in the last year of the war, the Schulzke home was destroyed. Eva and her parents were in the habit of hiding in their basement when the air-raid alarms went off, except on that very night:

> My mother had a feeling; she said we have to leave tonight, we cannot stay here, and she had the feeling to go to the farm. We went to members of the Church, and the same night we got bombed out, totally destroyed. If we had stayed at home that night, we would have been killed.

On July 24, 1944, Anna Maria Moderegger heard bombs fall on Tilsit and saw the glare of fires at night. She lived in Heinrichswalde (about eight miles from Tilsit), but decided to walk to town the next day to see what had happened. She described the scene:

> I could hardly recognize the city. Entire streets were burning. People who had lost their homes and had escaped the basement shelters wandered about, crying out in desperation for their loved ones. Some were mourning their property, as they watched it go up in flames. They all seemed to have lost their minds.

She found that branch president Otto Schulzke had survived, but his home had been destroyed. The Wachsmuths and their daughter, Anna, had been killed in the basement of their home. Brother Schulzke asked the surviving Saints to come to Tilsit for one last meeting on Sunday. They were to meet in the home of the Naujoks family. Sister Moderegger later described that event:

> All of the survivors came. There were so few of us that we could all sit around two tables. We had a very modest meal, to which we had all contributed what we had. We had become a literal city of Enoch, because we literally shared everything. There was little left, but we did not speak of hunger. We also shared what clothing we had with those who had lost everything. Brother Schulzke gave the sermon. His vibrant testimony gave us all strength. We gained new courage. Nobody knew what the future would bring, but we relied on the Lord. All of us were discouraged and sad, but nobody was desperate or hopeless as were most people in those days. Toward the end, we had a moment of silence in honor of our fallen brethren who had once been the pride of their parents and the hope of our branch. Then we sang the hymn "God Be with You till We Meet Again." We shook hands for the last time. For some it was the last good-bye. Brother Schulzke [a warden at the local prison] was ordered to take his prisoners to Königsberg. The survivors were given permission to leave the city. They fled to the countryside with their last possessions. Mothers with children were allowed to head westward. We no longer had a branch president. The Tilsit Branch had ceased to exist.[20]

In the fall of 1944, Red Army soldiers set foot on German soil for the first time, and

Fig. 9. The house at the far left was the home of Sister Hedwig Hubert Bütow in Tilsit. It was bombed out in 1944. (L. Hubert)

stories of the brutal treatment of civilians at the hands of the Soviet invaders spread quickly. Despite the encouragement of neighbors to stay, Berta Augat felt strongly that they must flee. They loaded a good-sized wagon with their most treasured possessions and a good supply of food. As Heinz later recalled, the bed of the wagon bowed down under the weight, and one horse strained to pull the wagon:

> The wagon looked like a pioneer wagon. We had those woven rugs, kind of like you would put a tent over to shield us from the cold. On our way back there was a column of German tanks that approached, and they stopped, and we stopped, and we gave them some food, and one of the soldiers climbed over the fence onto a deserted farm and [found] another horse [to hitch to] our wagon.

The day before their departure, Sister Augat received a letter from her brother's family. They

had departed about six weeks earlier and had written to inform her that they had found temporary housing in Freiberg in Saxony. Ursula Augat recounted the following details about their exodus:

> Then we went several days on this wagon, and then my mom said, "I can't do this." And she felt so strong. . . . She was guided by the Spirit all the time. She knew just what to do. She went to this train station and said, "Look, I'm [a] woman alone with two small children. I need to get on this train." They said, "Absolutely not, unless you have a relative." And she said, "Yes, I do, I have my brother there." And she showed them the letter that she got the day before. [Without that] we would have not gotten onto the train.

The train they boarded was heading west, overcrowded with refugees attempting to flee for their lives yet bent on taking everything they could with them. According to Ursula:

I, myself, was very scared. I thought I was being crushed to death because people were standing so close together. And it was horrible. And I remember we were standing and always looking up to adults, and they were old men and women. And they looked at their watches and pocket watches, and they said, "Oh, boy, oh, boy, are we going to make it?" [The Soviets] were closing in, and our train went through, and nothing more. We just made it! Just made it!

After arriving in Freiberg in about January 1945, the Augats were given a room in the meetinghouse of the Freiberg Branch. For the first time, they experienced air-raid warnings and nights in the basement shelter. Also for the first time, they attended church meetings on a regular basis. Ursula was surprised to see the other members singing from hymnals, something she had never seen. "I knew all of the songs by heart. My mother had taught them to us at home."

In the fall of 1944, Lothar Hubert (born 1939) was taken by his mother north to the city of Memel for a short time. From afar, they listened and watched the air raid taking place over Tilsit. Lothar told this story:

The next day, we went back to Tilsit together with my foster brother and we heard that in the Grabenstrasse, where my grandmother lived, the houses were destroyed. We cried. When we looked at the house, we could see the inside of the apartment from the street. I remember the kitchen cabinet that was still standing.[21]

When Sister Hubert decided to leave Tilsit for good in the fall of 1944, they needed specific permission from the city government. With that paper in hand, they headed west and south and experienced the end of the war in the town of Oberneuschönstein near the Czech border in Saxony. Several months later, they moved to Bernburg, Saxony, and soon found themselves living in what had been the Buchenwald Concentration Camp. Sister Hubert was joined there by her husband, Arthur, after he

was released from an American POW camp. Their daughter, Klara, had been a prisoner of the British and likewise found her way to her parents at Buchenwald. Unfortunately, the sins of the concentration camp guards were visited upon the heads of these innocent civilians, in that they were required to help bury the bodies of Buchenwald inmates.

During the last few months of the war, the Lessing family was split up. Brother Lessing was away on police duty and daughter Ursula was employed by the German postal system and assigned to work at a railway station post office in Dirschau. Sister Lessing and the three youngest children moved west to Braunsberg, then on to Dirschau near Danzig to live with a relative. Sister Lessing's parents, the Hübners, left the Kallwehlen farm and moved westward. The Hübner property may have been the first German Latter-day Saint home to be conquered by the invaders.

In March 1945, Emma Lessing took her three youngest children and began the trek west to escape the invaders. They were able to board a train and made it all the way (nearly three hundred miles) to the main station at Swinemünde, a port on the Baltic Sea. However, their timing could not have been worse. Just as the train pulled into the main station, where thousands of refugees were competing for places on trains bound for cities to the west, the air-raid sirens began to wail. As daughter Inge recalled:

When the alarm went off, there was panic in the station. People were running around trying to find a place to hide from the attack. We were still on the train, so my mother told my brothers and me, "Quick, get under the seats!" Then the bombs began to fall and it was terrible. I was only six at the time and don't remember much of what happened. The next thing I knew was that a nurse or a Red Cross lady was holding my hand and leading me out of the railroad station.[22]

The attack on Swinemünde on March 12, 1945, left approximately twenty-three thousand civilians dead. Emma Hübner Lessing and her sons Kurt (born 1932) and Fritz (born 1936) perished when the railroad station was destroyed. Somehow, Inge survived the attack unharmed. The names of her mother and her brothers are included in the roster of the dead buried in mass graves in the suburb of Golm, but most of the people killed that day could not be identified. This was the first tragedy that struck the Lessing family.

Despite the tremendous confusion in German provinces east of Berlin in the spring of 1945, Ursula Lessing remembered that the German mail system was still functioning fairly well. By then, she had been sent to a postal sorting station near the Baltic Sea and was working long days there, sorting thousands of pieces of mail each day. "It was a kind of camp facility. We lived in barracks. I had to memorize all of the names of towns in the east. And we got to eat lots of fish from the Baltic," she explained.

When government services began to fail in April 1945, Ursula Lessing was released from her job in the postal system. She joined other refugees headed west, fleeing from the invading Red Army. On one occasion, she was riding a bicycle from Schönberg to Dassow. For all practical purposes, the war was over, but the following incident occurred and remained vivid in her memory:

> All of a sudden we were in [the] woods there and everyone said, "Get off the road!" And we all went off and just laid flat in the woods and when we came out of those woods the Russians had shot the refugees in their wagons, their horses and wagons, and they had shot them to pieces. It was horrible. . . . In the woods they didn't see anyone or anything so [we were] all right, but when we got out our horses were half dead and everyone was screaming.

Shaken but unharmed, Ursula continued her flight to the west.

In early 1945, Anna Maria Moderegger took her five-year-old son and found a train out of town. They were taken to Czechoslovakia and then used the only available transportation to take them west to southern Germany: their feet. They walked most of the way to Deggendorf, Bavaria. From there they found trains to Munich, Kaufbeuren, and Buchloe, where she met her husband and her daughter. She later wrote of the journey as the worst experience of her entire life, characterized by intense suffering.[23]

The Moderegger family members were reunited in Buchloe, Bavaria. In the summer of 1945, Brother Moderegger was given permission to establish a garden and landscaping business in Langen, just south of Frankfurt am Main. Anna Maria and her children joined him there a few months later. The first Saints in that town, they became the founding members of what was by 1946 a very large branch of the Church, consisting exclusively of refugees.[24]

On April 18, 1945, Arthur Naujoks narrowly missed being killed in a battle with the Soviets when he and his unit ran out of ammunition. His commanders told him that because they had nothing to fight with, their war was over, and they might as well leave. Arthur was armed with only a pistol when he headed west among a huge stream of refugees. His goals were to avoid capture by the Soviets and to survive.[25]

Near Neubrandenburg, he approached a checkpoint where SS soldiers were monitoring military traffic. Soldiers in good condition were being ordered to turn around and go back to fight the Soviets. Some had apparently refused and were hanged as deserters. Only wounded soldiers were allowed to pass and proceed westward. At that point, Arthur began to contemplate a terribly difficult option. After agonizing about the problem all night long, he decided to inflict a small wound upon himself in order to pass the guards and avoid execution. Later he would write about trying to listen to the still, small voice to know what to do, but "my head filled with so much noise that this small voice could not be heard."

He chose the fleshy part of his arm below the elbow and aimed his pistol carefully, in order to avoid serious damage. He pulled the trigger and nearly lost consciousness. Despite the simplicity of his wound, he was in shock. Fortunately, his calculations were good; he had missed the critical parts of the arm, but had bled enough to give the appearance of a serious wound. He thus faked his way past the guards and continued west to Schwerin and freedom. The Americans arrived in Schwerin while Arthur was there.

In western Germany, Ursula Lessing sought assistance from government agencies and the Red Cross to locate her parents and her siblings. She had last heard in 1945 that her father, Willi Lessing, was serving in the military police somewhere in Poland. Eventually she received a card from him; he was a POW in Soviet captivity. Unfortunately, he died in Leningrad, Russia, on September 20, 1948—still a prisoner of war. It is very likely that he had not learned that his wife and his two sons had been killed; only Ursula and Inge were still alive.

Ursula Lessing was finally able to locate her sister, Inge, in 1947. After the deaths of her mother and brothers, the little girl had been sent first to Denmark, then back to Germany after the war, and was living with an aunt. Until their reunion, Ursula had no idea what had become of Inge and the rest of the family. In the meantime, her grandparents, the Hübners, had made their way as far west as Danzig before the conquerors caught up with them. For some reason, they did not evacuate to the west. Carl Otto Hübner succumbed to malnutrition in Danzig on September 4, 1945.

When the war ended, the Augat family exodus had not yet concluded. According to Ursula and Heinz, they spent about nine months in Freiberg (where both of them were baptized on August 28, 1945), then in 1946 moved farther west to Wolfsgrün, where the East German Mission leaders had been granted the use of a castle (a large villa) to house Latter-day Saint refugees. Nine months later, in 1947, Sister Augat took her children on another trip, this time to Langen, where they joined the largest Latter-day Saint refugee colony in Germany. Things were looking up for the Augats, whose husband and father finally joined them in 1949 when he returned from his POW term in the Soviet Union.

All Germans who declined to become Polish citizens in Tilsit were expelled from the territory by the end of 1946. The expellees likely included the remaining members of the Tilsit Branch of the Latter-day Saints, leaving the city of Tilsit with no Church representation. Today the city is known as Sovetsk, Russia.

IN MEMORIAM

The following members of the Tilsit Branch did not survive World War II:

Therese —— bp. 4 Aug 1912; m. —— Bartschat; d. 23 Nov 1940, age 77, Memel, Tilsit (*Sonntagsgruss*, no. 11, 16 Mar 1941, 43)

Kurt Brahtz b. Tilsit, Ostpreußen, Preußen 24 May 1924; son of Fritz Karl Brahtz and Berta Emma Wachsmuth; bp. 29 Jun 1934; engineering corps; d. wounds army hospital Rela Aussig, Russia 14 Jan 1944; bur. Sovetzk, Russia (H. Meiszus Meyer; www.volksbund.de; IGI)

Emil Eduard Ernst Berthold Flach b. Tilsit, Ostpreußen, Preußen 24 Nov 1924; son of Emil Eduard Hermann Erich Flach and Ida Helene Martha Hoost; bp. 17 Jun 1937; rifleman; d. wounds Lublin, Poland 19 Jan 1944 (H. Meiszus Meyer; www.volksbund.de; IGI)

Berta Johanne Hoffmann b. Augustlauken, Ostpreußen, Preußen 4 Apr 1865; dau. of Karl Hoffmann and Henriette Dwillies; bp. 3 Dec 1916; m. Argelothen, Ostpreußen, Preußen, Eduard Wilhelm

Fig. 10. Emma Hübner Lessing and her two sons are some of the thousands of victims of the March 12, 1945, air raid on Swinemünde who were buried in this mass grave. (http://www.erwin-rosenthal.de/swinemuende/GolmfrontNa1.jpg)

Wachsmuth; 9 children; k. air raid Tilsit, Ostpreußen, Preußen 24 Jul 1944 (IGI; AF; H. Meiszus Meyer)

Karl Otto Hübner b. Trapönen, Ragnit, Ostpreußen, Preußen 17 Nov 1867; son of Otto Wilhelm Hübner and Karoline Wilhelmine Zielinsky; bp. Tilsit, Ostpreußen, Preußen 26 May 1912; m. 25 or 26 Dec 1894 Motzwethen, Niederung, Ostpreußen, Preußen, Ida Minna Schlenther; 6 children; d. malnutrition as refugee Danzig Free City 4 Sep 1945 (U. Lessing Mudrow; IGI; AF)

Emma Agnes Hübner b. Trapönen, Ragnit, Ostpreußen, Preußen 25 Oct 1899; dau. of Karl Otto Hübner and Minna Ida Schlenther; bp. 8 Jul 1924; m. Wischwill, Pogegen, Lithuania 27 Jun 1926, Willi Lessing; 4 children; k. air raid Swinemünde, Pommern 12 Mar 1945; bur. Golm, Swinemünde, Pommern Mar 1945 (U. Lessing Mudrow; IGI; AF)

Marie Jokuschies b. Tutteln, Ostpreußen, Preußen 12 Jun 1867; dau. of Jurgies or Georg Jokuszies and Ermuthe Emilie Swars; bp. 3 Sep 1908; missing refugee 1945 (FHL Microfilm 271372, 1930/35 Census; IGI)

Fritz Adolf Lessing b. 1 May 1936 Kallwehlen, Wischwill, Pogegen, Lithuania; son of Willi Lessing and Emma Agnes Hübner; k. air raid Swinemünde, Pommern 12 Mar 1945; bur. Golm, Swinemünde, Pommern (U. Lessing Mudrow; IGI; AF)

Kurt Erich Lessing b. Kallwehlen, Wischwill, Pogegen, Lithuania 29 Feb 1932; son of Willi Lessing and Emma Agnes Hübner; k. air raid Swinemünde, Pommern 12 Mar 1945; bur. Golm, Swinemünde, Pommern (U. Lessing Mudrow; IGI; AF)

Willi Lessing b. Lasdehnen, Tilsit, Ostpreußen, Preußen 17 Jul 1899; son of Hermann Gottfried Lessing and Maria Dilba; bp. 16 Jun 1926; m. Wischwill, Pogegen, Lithuania 27 Jun 1926, Emma Agnes Hübner;

4 children; d. POW Leningrad, Russia 20 Sep 1948; bur. Leningrad (U. Lessing Mudrow; IGI; AF)

Henry Martin Meiszus b. Tilsit, Ostpreußen, Preußen 17 Feb 1926; son of Martin Meiszus and Minna Berta Wachsmuth; MIA Normandy 1944 (H. Meiszus Meyer; IGI)

Siegfried Adalbert Meiszus b. Tilsit, Ostpreußen, Preußen 27 Jan 1923; son of Martin Meiszus and Minna Berta Wachsmuth; bp. 25 Jul 1931; d. wounds army hospital Romania 8 Jun 1944 (H. Meiszus Meyer; IGI)

Fritz Bruno Millbrecht b. Tilsit, Ostpreußen, Preußen 18 May 1922; son of Ludwig Millbrecht and Bertha Louise Pastowsky; k. in battle 2 Jun 1944 (H. Meiszus Meyer; FHL Microfilm 245233, 1930/35 Census; IGI)

Karl Heinrich Millbrecht b. Tilsit, Ostpreußen, Preußen 21 May 1919; son of Ludwig Millbrecht and Bertha Louise Pastowsky; k. in battle Russia 1 Apr 1944 (H. Meiszus Meyer, FHL Microfilm 245233, 1930/35 Census; IGI)

Fritz Negraszus b. ca. 1918; MIA (H. Meiszus Meyer)

Bertha Louise Pastowsky b. Meldienen, Tilsit, Ostpreußen, Preußen 5 Nov 1882; dau. of Hans Nuckmann and Wilhelmine Pastowsky; m. Laugallen, Tilsit, Ostpreußen, Preußen ca. 1905, August Friedrich Raeder; 2m. Ludwig Millbrecht; d. 11 Jun 1945 (H. Meiszus Meyer; IGI)

Erich Kurt Pechbrenner b. Wischwill, Pogegen, Lithuania 2 Oct 1925; son of Fritz Pechbrenner and Ells Frieda Minna Hübner; non-commissioned officer; MIA Pulawy bridge head, Glogow Jan 1945 (U. Lessing Mudrow; www.volksbund.de; IGI)

Olga Viktoria Romanowski b. 13 May 1881; dau. of J. Romanowski and F. Koresna; m. Königsberg, Ostpreußen, Preußen ca. 1922, Johann Kusmin Stroganoff; 1 child; disappeared (IGI)

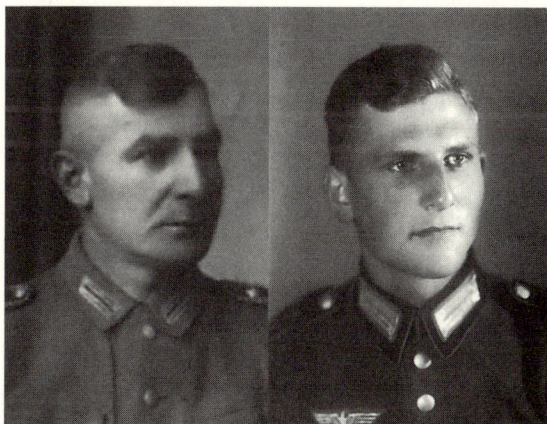

Fig. 11. Willi Lessing. (U. Lessing Mudrow) *Fig. 12. Siegfried Meiszus (H. M. Meyer)*

Fritz Stanull b. Tilsit, Ostpreußen, Preußen; m. Hedwig Anna ——; k. in battle Russia 1943 or 1944 (H. Meiszus Meyer)

Anna Wachsmuth b. Ragnit, Ostpreußen, Preußen 4 Jan 1901; dau. of Eduard Wilhelm Wachsmuth and Berta Johanne Hoffmann; m. Altona, Schleswig-Holstein, Preußen 9 Jul 1937, Otto Hermann Paul Schulze; k. air raid Tilsit, Ostpreußen, Preußen 24 Jul 1944 (IGI; H. Meiszus Meyer)

Eduard Wilhelm Wachsmuth b. Schaaken, Ostpreußen, Preußen 24 Aug 1859; son of Heinrich Wachsmuth and Friederike Wilhelmine Gassner; bp. 24 Aug 1920 Tilsit, Ostpreußen, Preußen; m. Heinrichswalde, Ostpreußen, Preußen 20 Oct 1889, Berta Johanne Hoffmann; 9 children; k. air raid Tilsit, Ostpreußen, Preußen 24 Jul 1944 (IGI; AF; H. Meiszus Meyer; www.volksbund.de)

Adelbert Zapick b. 1916; gef. (MIA) Russia 1941 (U. Lessing)

NOTES

1. Waltraut Naujoks Schibblack, telephone interview with Jennifer Heckmann in German, February 15, 2008; unless otherwise noted, summarized in English by Judith Sartowski, and transcript or audio version of the interview is in author's collection.

2. Eva Schulzke Bode, interview by the author, Salt Lake City, February 9, 2007.

3. Helga Meiszus Meyer, interview by Michael Corley, Salt Lake City, February 15, 2008.

4. Presiding Bishopric, "Financial, Statistical, and Historical Reports of Wawrds, Stakes, and Missions, 1884–1995," CR 4 12, 257

5. Arthur G. Naujoks Jr. and Michael S. Eldredge, *Shades of Gray: Memoirs of a Prussian Saint on the Eastern Front* (Salt Lake City: Mill Creek Press, 2004), 29.

6. Ibid., 51.

7. Bruno Stroganoff, interview by Jennifer Heckmann in German, Neckargemünd, Germany, August 20, 2006.

8. Ursula Lessing Mudrow, interview by the author, Ogden, Utah, March 9, 2007.

9. Ursula Augat Black and Heinz Augat, interview by the author, Salt Lake City, December 1, 2006.

10. Naujoks and Eldredge, *Shades of Gray*, 56.

11. Ibid., 115.

12. Ibid.

13. William L. Shirer, *The Rise and Fall of the Third Reich: A History of Nazi Germany* (New York: Simon & Schuster, 1990), 932.

14. Naujoks and Eldredge, *Shades of Gray*, 132–33.

15. Ibid., 139.

16. For a description of subsequent events in Waltraut's life, see the chapter on the Elbing Branch of the Danzig District.

17. For a report of her activities in the mission home in Berlin, see the East German Mission chapter.

18. The "Final Solution of the Jewish Problem" (a euphemism for the murder of European Jews) was well under way by that time.

19. Men from many European countries were recruited by the Waffen-SS. One of the organization's prime arguments was that the Waffen-SS was responsible for the eradication of communism in Europe, specifically in the Soviet Union. Bruno himself was not a German but the son of Latvian citizens.

20. Anna Maria Moderegger, "Mein Weg in die Freiheit" (unpublished history, 1977), 2–3; private collection; trans. the author. In the introduction of her autobiography, Sister Moderegger made this comment: "If my readers believe that I had included too much detail in the story of my flight from Saxony to Bavaria, they should remember that this was the most violent and disturbing experience of my entire life."

21. Lothar Hubert, interview by the author in German, Schwerin, Germany, August 17, 2006.

22. Inge Lessing, interview by the author, Ogden, Utah, May 30, 2006.

23. Moderegger, "Mein Weg in die Freiheit," 5–17.

24. Ibid., 23.

25. Naujoks and Eldredge, *Shades of Gray*, 189.

LEIPZIG
DISTRICT
East German Mission

At the west-central border of the East German Mission was the Leipzig District. The territory comprised the northwest portion of the province of old Royal Saxony, most of Prussian Saxony, and all of Saxony-Anhalt. The city of Leipzig was in the southwestern portion of the district.

In 1939, there were two branches of the LDS Church in Leipzig itself—the Center Branch and the West Branch. The other branches in the district were located in Magdeburg (sixty miles north), Aschersleben (fifty miles northwest), Halle (twenty miles northwest), Dessau (thirty-six miles north), and Naumburg (twenty-seven miles southwest). Mission records indicated that a group was holding meetings in Halberstadt (sixty-six miles northwest of Leipzig).

Church units bordering the Leipzig District were the Berlin District on the northeast, the Spreewald District on the east, the Chemnitz District on the southeast, and the Zwickau District on the south. Districts of the West German Mission were the neighbors to the west (Hanover) and the southwest (Weimar). The leader of the Leipzig District in 1939 was Erich Hein, and his first counselor was Erich Gützlaff.[1]

Leipzig District[2]	1939	1940	1941	1942
Elders	27	27		
Priests	18	18		
Teachers	17	16		
Deacons	29	35		
Other Adult Males	97	77		
Adult Females	370	346		
Male Children	24	20		
Female Children	24	23		
Total	606	562	564	562

Although the years just prior to the war were a time of growth and prosperity for the Church in general in Germany, there were challenges in certain areas. For example, the East German Mission history reported on September 30, 1938, that the full-time missionaries in the Leipzig District were forbidden to tract or to use other means of missionary work. One may presume that their activities were restricted to responding to inquiries, teaching interested persons in the homes of Church members, and giving public lectures. The mission history indicates that the restriction was in force "during the month of September" and thus may have been only short-lived.[3] In addition, baptisms were allowed only if the local police office gave permission, but there is no indication that anyone was denied the privilege of being baptized.

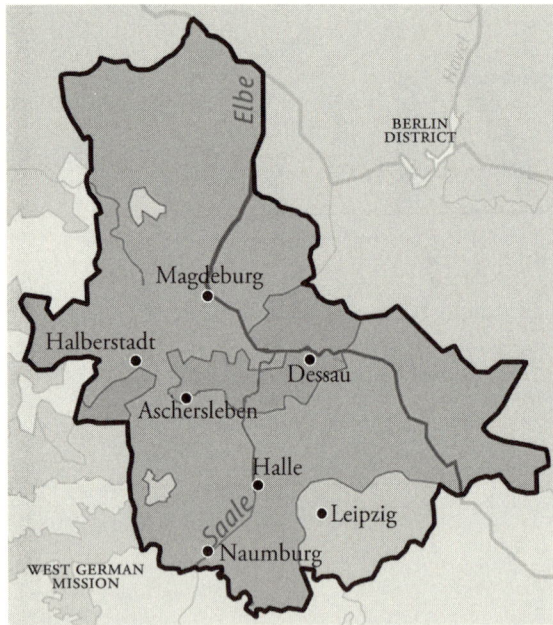

Fig. 1. The Leipzig District of the East German Mission in 1939.

Because the historical records of the East German Mission were not preserved after 1941, the last entry made regarding the Leipzig District was a report of a district conference held on March 25–26, 1939 (Saturday and Sunday), in Leipzig. The main meeting held on Sunday evening was attended by 205 members and thirty friends.[4]

The two branches in the city of Leipzig were combined in 1941, and all meetings were held in the Moritzstrasse until those rooms were destroyed in December 1943. Thereafter, meetings were held in the homes of members.[5]

NOTES

1. East German Mission Quarterly Reports, 1938, no. 13, East German Mission History; 1939, no. 58.
2. Presiding Bishopric, "Financial, Statistical, and Historical Reports of Wards, Stakes, and Missions, 1884–1955," CR 4 12, 257.
3. East German Mission Quarterly Reports, 1938, no. 40.
4. Ibid., 1939, no. 59.
5. The Church of Jesus Christ of Latter-day Saints, *Die Gemeinde in Leipzig* (Leipzig, Germany: The Church of Jesus Christ of Latter-day Saints, 1988), 10; trans. the author.

ASCHERSLEBEN BRANCH

The city of Aschersleben is located in the historical Prussian province of Saxony, some fifty miles northwest of Leipzig. Shortly before World War II began, there were only sixty-one members of the Church there. The city had a population of about thirty-five thousand people.

Aschersleben Branch[1]	1939
Elders	0
Priests	1
Teachers	0
Deacons	4
Other Adult Males	9
Adult Females	45
Male Children	2
Female Children	0
Total	61

East German Mission records indicate that the meetings of the Aschersleben Branch were held at Feldstrasse 21A by the end of 1938. Irene Hampel (born 1928) recalled that the rooms were part of a shoemaker's business. "The branch was permitted to use one main room and two smaller rooms." As in most other branches, Sunday School was held in the morning and sacrament meeting in the evenings. Irene and her mother walked home between meetings and back again in the evening. They lived about thirty minutes (walking time) from the meetinghouse.[2]

Rolf Richter (born 1930) remembered that branch meeting location all through the war. They began with one or two rooms and eventually expanded to five rooms.[3]

Just days before the war began, Irene came home from school. Her father was at home, and

Fig. 1. The Aschersleben Branch at the end of the war. (R. Richter)

she asked him why he was not at work. He explained that he had been called into the army. His first tour of duty lasted only three months, after which he stayed home until February 1945.

It was common to see large proportions of German branches in those days consisting of women. The Aschersleben Branch may be an anomaly, however, in that 74 percent of the branch members were in this category. There were very few men. According to Rolf Richter, Melchizedek Priesthood holders from neighboring branches or members of the district presidency attended meetings in Aschersleben on a regular basis. He specifically recalled H. Friedler of Magdeburg coming to Aschersleben to take charge of meetings. On March 30, 1940, Paul Wanke became branch president. He had moved from Breslau in Silesia to nearby Stassfurt.

"Until I was fourteen years old I was a member of the Jungvolk," recalled Rolf Richter:

I was a drummer in the brass band. I was in that group with body and soul. I liked it so much, and music was my life. When the transition [to Hitler Youth at age fourteen] was supposed to take place, my group leader said to the Hitler Youth leaders that I needed to stay in his group. I was lucky that I did not have to [advance].[4]

Irene's brother, Heinz Hampel, was hoping to serve in the merchant marine. His plan worked shortly before the war started. However, after Germany attacked Poland on September 1, 1939, Heinz was inducted into the navy and became a signal specialist. On one occasion, he was on shore leave when his ship was attacked and sunk. Several of the crew were lost.

When Irene Hampel became fourteen years of age, she was to be inducted into the League of German Girls. She refused and was threatened by the local police. Her mother came to her defense with the excuse, "She works from dawn to dusk, so there's no time." Irene was allowed to miss the meetings if her father wrote a letter requesting her release. He was not a member of the Church, but wrote the letter.

As the war dragged on, attendance at the meetings of the Aschersleben Branch declined. Irene recalled having as few as six persons in attendance. Sometimes, the only man present was an old man of very poor health. Nevertheless, the meetings continued.

There were eight air raids of mention over the city of Aschersleben during World War II.[5] At least 352 apartments were damaged or destroyed in the city and 244 residents were killed. In addition, several hundred foreign workers lost their lives. Irene Hampel recalled that the sirens began to blare one Sunday during a worship service. "We had a prayer then we went on with our meeting. We didn't have anywhere to go. . . . There were no public shelters anywhere close. Then we heard the bombs falling on another city a few miles away."

The Hampel apartment was one of those damaged in the attack of March 31, 1945. Irene was not at home, but her mother was in the cellar. A piece of concrete crashed through the roof and landed in one of their beds, but the damage was soon repaired.

Rolf Richter was trained in civil defense procedures. He later described those functions:

> When there was an alarm, I had to be where my group leader was to make sure he knew when something happened and to see that the lights were all turned off. I also had to go to factories that were attacked and that was the first time that I saw dead people. I did not have to retrieve the bodies.

On April 18, 1945, the American army conquered Aschersleben. There was enough resistance offered by the defenders that several persons were killed in the process. The Americans stayed in the city until May 23, 1945, when the British forces moved in. They in turn were replaced by the Soviet army.[6]

Rolf Richter recalled watching the American army moving into town. "They marched past our home with their tanks on both sides of the street. Being little boys, we stood in our doorway watching them. We weren't scared and they smiled at us. I saw many black people." When the Soviets came, conditions deteriorated. Rolf described the situation in a single phrase: "I never experienced anything like that!"

"We had enough food under Hitler's government, but when the Russians came, that all changed," recalled Irene Hampel.

Irene Hampel's father was taken prisoner by the French and remained in their custody until February 1946. He had been in poor health but was in even worse shape when he came home. Heinz Hampel also returned home safely, arriving in late 1946.

Fig. 2. The young women of Aschersleben with their leader, Sister Liebing. (R. Richter)

By the end of the war, the auxiliary organizations were no longer holding meetings during the week, but the two Sunday meetings continued to take place, as Rolf Richter later wrote in his branch history. Relief Society, Primary, and MIA began anew in the summer of 1945.

In Memoriam

The following members of the Aschersleben Branch did not survive World War II:

Rudolf Karl Hintz b. 23 Apr 1925; d. wounds 1945 (I. Hampel Kupitz)

Minna Karchner k. air raid Aschersleben, Sachsen 1944 or 1945 (I. Hampel Kupitz)

Notes

1. Presiding Bishopric, "Financial, Statistical, and Historical Reports of Wards, Stakes, and Missions, 1884–1955," CR 4 12, 257.
2. Irene Hampel Kupitz, interview by the author, Taylorsville, Utah, March 3, 2006.
3. Rolf Richter, "Geschichte der Gemeinde Aschersleben" (unpublished history); private collection; trans. the author.
4. Rolf Richter, interview by the author in German, Aschersleben, Germany, May 31, 2007; summarized in English by Judith Sartowski.
5. Angelika Adam, "Seit Zehn Jahren Ehrenbürger," *Ascherslebener Zeitung*, April 16, 2005.
6. Ibid.

Dessau Branch

Famous as the birthplace of the Bauhaus school of architecture, the city of Dessau is located in the old province of Saxony-Anhalt and was the capital city. In 1939, there were approximately seventy thousand people living in Dessau, about thirty-six miles north of Leipzig.

The East German Mission history contains a single entry regarding the small branch in Dessau, dated May 15, 1938: Walter Gerstner was appointed president of the Dessau Branch, with Franz Ackermann as first counselor.[1]

The directory of meetinghouse addresses for the mission indicated in late 1938 that the Dessau Branch held meetings at Georgenstrasse 11A.

Dessau Branch[2]	1939
Elders	2
Priests	1
Teachers	2
Deacons	5
Other Adult Males	8
Adult Females	25
Male Children	2
Female Children	4
Total	49

A native of Plauen and a member of the Latter-day Saint branch there, Irmgard Fassmann came to Dessau in 1941 as a new office employee at the Junkers Aircraft Company factory. She looked for the branch and only found it when she hummed a Church hymn melody while riding the bus and thereby came to the attention of Brother Gerstner.[3]

Irmgard was surprised to see only about a dozen members at the meetings. She later wrote this description of the members in Dessau:

> The church was just three rooms, and they were located at the back of an older building. The members were mostly older people, but at least we had three priesthood holders, Bro. Gerstner, Bro. Ackermann, and Bro. Quente. Gerstners was [sic] a very nice family with three little children. Bro. Quente was here as a visiting soldier, and Bro. Ackermann was a native. Soon after I came there all three men were sent to war.

Franz Ackermann was ordained a teacher in the Aaronic Priesthood in 1938. He entered the service of the Reich and was in uniform for the duration of the war. His service was outstanding, and he was promoted to first lieutenant by January 1945.

Fig. 1. Franz Ackermann's military service record. (G. Ackermann)

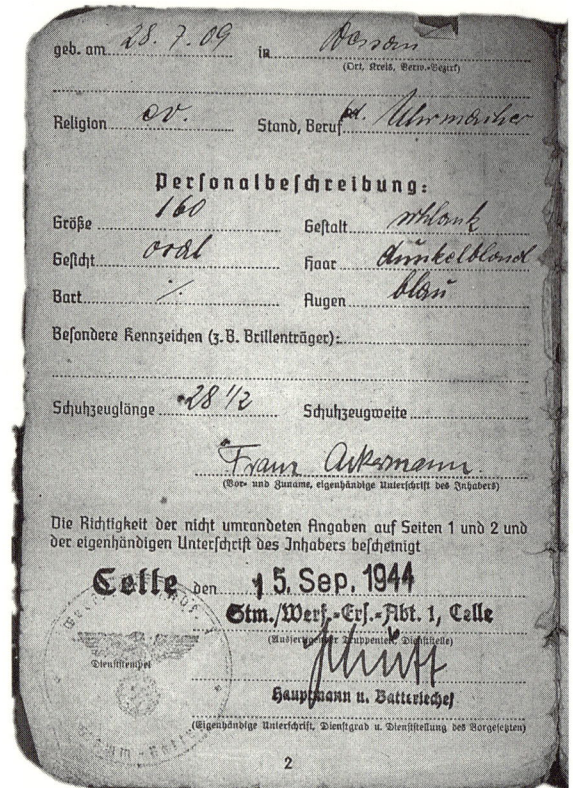

Fig. 2. Franz Ackermann's physical description from his military record. (G. Ackermann)

Irmgard Fassmann was likely a welcome addition to the Dessau Branch. While Franz Ackermann was still at home, the two went to the meetinghouse on Saturdays and cleaned the rooms, brought in firewood, and generally kept things in good shape for Sundays. Irmgard had many assignments, including Sunday School superintendent, chorister, Sunday School teacher, and speaker in sacrament meeting.

At the Junkers Aircraft Company, Irmgard became acquainted with a nice young man named Heiner Pakendorf. He wanted to marry her, but she made it clear that membership in the Church was a requirement for marriage. He began to study the gospel, and they became engaged and planned to marry during his next furlough. Tragically, Heiner was killed in Ukraine before the couple had that chance.

Irmgard also met Gaby Feurich at the office, and the two became inseparable friends. Eventually, Gaby learned about Irmgard's faith and was converted to the Church. Irmgard had waited for several months to invite Gaby to church "because there were just a few of us. I wanted to take Gaby one day with me to a [district] conference in Leipzig." Apparently, Gaby was not concerned about the small number of Saints in the Dessau Branch.

The Junkers factory attracted the attention of the Allied air forces and local residents began to spend significant amounts of time in air-raid shelters as of about 1943. Irmgard found her lifestyle drastically changed and learned to dread the sirens. One evening, she and Gaby were at the Gerstner home for MIA when the sirens sounded. Before they even reached the basement shelter, they heard the airplanes and the bombs. They prayed, waited, and heard the all-clear siren two hours later. She later described the night:

What [Gaby and I] saw was so awful. The whole city was burning. . . . We couldn't go home [through] the streets, we had to go far around the city. . . . It was just burning everywhere, it looked so sad. It took us three hours to get to the house I lived in. There the neighbors' house was burning and flames leapt toward the house where I had my room. We both ran upstairs to my room on the third floor, the house was full of smoke, so we put scarves on our faces, . . . grabbed some clothes and a few items, and ran out again. . . . Gaby's apartment was still all right.

The Junkers factory was severely damaged, but operations were moved into temporary facilities in a nearby forest and production continued through the remainder of the war.

In order to replace the clothing and other household items she had lost, Irmgard took the train home to Plauen. She arrived just in time to experience a terrifying air raid there as well. Along with her parents, she was trapped in a bomb shelter for several hours, because the door was covered with rubble.

According to Max Gerstner Jr., the meeting rooms of the Dessau Branch at Georgenstrasse 11A were destroyed in the spring of 1945—either in air raids or by the American artillery.[4]

> When we came out, we saw many dead people on the streets—many houses were burned and exploded. What a terrible sight. When we came to my parents' house only half of the house was still standing, the other half was gone. I looked up to the second floor where we lived, and there was the coat rack with my father's Sunday suit hanging, and his golden pocket watch on a golden chain was hanging down. I [could] still see it there in the hallway.

Back in Dessau, Irmgard experienced the entry of the American army. Just after the war ended, she took a bicycle and started for home. Hoping to avoid having her bicycle stolen, she let the air out of the tires and pushed it all the way to Zwickau, nearly 130 miles due south. She left Monday morning and arrived there safely on Friday. She was next escorted home to Plauen by her uncle, district president Walter Fassmann of Zwickau, along with President Sellner of the Plauen Branch.

Apparently the French authorities felt it very important to determine the political leanings of their POWs. This is evident from the case of Franz Ackermann, as reflected in

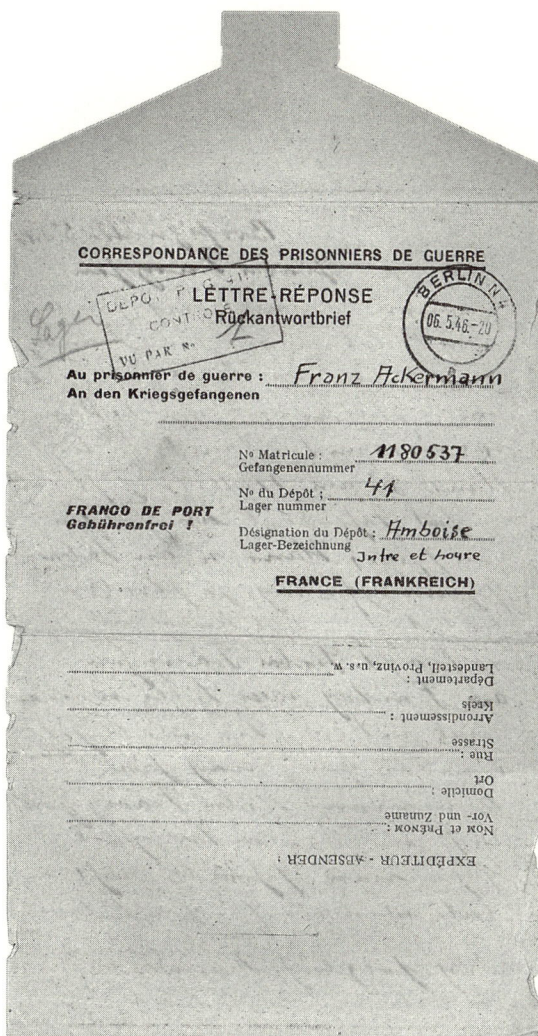

Fig. 3. Franz Ackermann wrote this letter to his wife from a French POW camp. (G. Ackermann)

the letters written to him in captivity by his brother, Walter, back in Dessau. For example, on April 22, 1946, Walter wrote the following:

> In the third letter you will receive the proof that you were an anti-fascist, i.e., an opponent of the Hitler [Nazi] Party. After all, you constantly gave money to the support of the underground. I visited the SED [Socialist Unity] party offices again today in order to get the papers. Those papers must first be examined by the SED. Then I will send them to you and you must have the camp commandant look at them.[5]

It is not known whether the papers were sent or whether they were used by Franz

Ackermann to secure an early release from the French POW camp.

In Memoriam

Only one member of the Dessau Branch did not survive World War II:

Marie Charlotte Weise b. 28 Oct 1868; dau. of Karl Weise and Louise Berger; m. —— Fleischer; d. 12 Jun 1942 (CHL CR 375 8 #2459, 1388–89)

Notes

1. East German Mission Quarterly Reports, 1938, no. 20, East German Mission History.

2. Presiding Bishopric, "Financial, Statistical, and Historical Reports of Wards, Stakes, and Missions, 1884–1955," CR 4 12, 257.

3. Irmgard Fassmann Messina Schwarz, autobiography (unpublished), 9; private collection.

4. Max Gerstner, telephone interview with the author, June 3, 2006.

5. Walter Ackermann to Franz Ackermann, April 22, 1946; private collection; trans. the author.

HALBERSTADT GROUP

A fledgling group of Latter-day Saints existed in Halberstadt at the beginning of World War II. There is no way to know how many Church members were living there at the time. The only details we have regarding the Latter-day Saints and their friends in Halberstadt come from the diary of Anton Larisch.

About sixty-six miles northwest of Leipzig, Halberstadt was the home of a critical military industry—the Junkers Aircraft Company factory. Brother Larisch was drafted to work in the factory for six months and left his family in Görlitz (Dresden District), where he had served as branch president. Within weeks of arriving for what was to be a six-month term of duty, he was called by Herbert Klopfer, the mission supervisor, to serve as a missionary in Halberstadt

Fig. 1. Anton Larisch at work in the Junkers aircraft factory in Halberstadt. (F. Larisch)

and nearby Aschersleben (twenty-miles to the southeast). Brother Larisch did not question this call, although he was required to work sixty-three hours in seven days each week.[1]

The mission records show that the group in Halberstadt met at Gutenbergstrasse 6 when the war began. A description of the rooms is not available. The first few meetings held by Brother Larisch were a disappointment to him, in that only four to eight persons attended.[2] Nevertheless, he prayed for guidance in his missionary work and purchased copies of the Book of Mormon.

Anton's missionary efforts and his clean lifestyle led to trouble at the aircraft factory. He explained it in his diary on June 27, 1940:

After [my co-workers'] repeated challenges against me to justify . . . to them [my] strange take on life, they finally learned a few things about my religion. Since they are all opposed to religion, they tried to take out their hatred on me. After I assured them that my church is permitted (legal), they tried to entangle me in politics. They fronted [sent as spies] their own people, who would "in passing" ask me questions that indicated that they were interested in (my) religion. My answers were immediately brought to the "windmill," who would [mis]interpret it so completely that they could formulate an accusation against me, and that [went] immediately to the police! So, consequently, on June 19, 1940, at 9:00 o'clock in the morning, I was picked up in the factory by the criminal police.[3]

After a day of questioning, Anton was formally charged with making five specific treasonous statements (such as "I shall never take a gun in my hands to defend my country!") and translating foreign letters. He then took four hours to write a response of eight pages in length. The judge then dismissed the charges and set him free. He had spent eleven days in jail, five of them in solitary confinement. He

Fig. 2. In 1939, there were few young members of the Halberstadt group. (F. Larisch)

thanked the Lord for his release with these words: "Well, . . . my ancient God still lives. He has helped me miraculously, and my accusers crumbled in their lies and deceit."[4]

His comments about friends of the Church are interesting, such as these made on December 8, 1940: "By now Miss Ahrens has become a faithful attendee of our meetings. She even went to the Fall [District] Conference in Leipzig. . . . She enjoyed it very much."[5]

Anton was not the only member of the Halberstadt group who was in trouble with the authorities. He recounted the following situation in his entry of March 29, 1941:

> Last Saturday two criminal police officers came to Sister Fischer and searched her home. They suspected secret (outlawed) Jehovah's Witnesses' activity and confiscated our Church books. . . . At the hearing last Monday she was told, that for the time being we can still meet in her home, as long as we [the Church as an organization] are not forbidden. . . . Sister Fischer willingly gave up the Jehovah's Witness literature, since she had withdrawn from them already in 1926.[6]

Fig. 3. Members of the Halberstadt Group celebrate Christmas together in 1941. (F. Larisch)

In March 1942, the group attempted to acquire a piano and collected 300 marks for the purpose. However, the mission leaders recommended that they first buy a pump organ. None could be found in Halberstadt, so the money was returned to the donors.[7]

The entry dated June 15, 1942, exudes happiness through its good news:

> We received the harmonium [pump organ] from the Magdeburger Branch, which has completely ceased to be. On June 7 we celebrated our dedication service in our new meeting quarters at the home of Sister Kuhne. It was wonderful. We had many visitors from Aschersleben. Eight persons. So altogether we were 15 in attendance. It was like in a small meeting room.[8]

More good news followed on Sunday, August 2, 1942: "I have performed the first baptism here. I baptized Christa Kuhne, 16 years old, in the Goldbach Waterfall in Langenstein [three miles southwest of town]. It was wonderful."[9]

Brother Larisch made the best of his free time away from his family. He read about world religions and philosophy, took night classes in English, French, and Russian ("because we have to take the gospel to that nation"), and prepared several hundred names for temple work. In his diary he commented about Germany's chances of winning the war ("We are fighting on too many fronts"). He also had some distracting physical ailments. Every six months, Anton was granted one or two weeks off to visit his family. As the end of each six-month employment period approached, he was promised a release, but time after time it did not happen. He left Halberstadt in January 1945, but certainly not in the way he had expected. On January 4, he was arrested again and spent the next six weeks in confinement in Halberstadt and Berlin.[10] He survived the experience and returned twenty pounds lighter to Görlitz, found his family in Löbau, and

Fig. 4. Sister Kuhne and her daughter Christa of the Halberstadt group. (F. Larisch)

brought them to Halberstadt, where they arrived on April 8, 1945.

Anton Larisch was made branch president in Halberstadt in July 1945. "So now, after decades, Halberstadt is again a branch."[11] For the past five years, the Halberstadt group had been his surrogate family, and his missionary service in that town was likely the reason for the expanded branch. In February 1946, he and his family returned to their home in Görlitz.

No members of the Halberstadt Branch are known to have died during World War II.

Notes

1. Anton Larisch, diary, November 26, 1939, 2; private collection; trans. Ruth Larisch Hinkel. See Görlitz, Dresden District, for the beginning and ending of the Larisch family story.

Fig. 5. Anton Larisch (with bicycle) and his family left Halberstadt with their few possessions in February 1946. Two missionaries, Elders Draegger (left) and Blietschau (rear), assisted the family. The little boy is Fred Larisch. The typical Leiterwagen was a very sturdy vehicle. (F. Larisch)

2. Ibid., December 16, 1939, 5.
3. Ibid., June 27, 1940, 13.
4. Ibid., July 18, 1940, 14–15.
5. Ibid., December 8, 1940, 18.
6. Ibid., March 29, 1941, 22.
7. Ibid., April 22, 1942, 28.
8. Ibid., June 15, 1942, 30.
9. Ibid., August 2, 1942, 31.
10. Ibid., January 4, 1945, 46.
11. Ibid., August 25, 1945, 48. The diary does not mention any other male members in the Halberstadt group.

HALLE BRANCH

According to the records of the East German Mission, the Halle Branch of The Church of Jesus Christ of Latter-day Saints held its meetings in rented rooms at Rathausstrasse 14 in the Hinterhaus. Whereas the city had nearly two hundred thousand inhabitants when World War II began, only thirty-three were members of the Church.

Halle Branch[1]	1939
Elders	2
Priests	0
Teachers	2
Deacons	3
Other Adult Males	8
Adult Females	18
Male Children	0
Female Children	0
Total	33

The Halle Branch had only a few youth and no children (under twelve) at the end of the year 1939. Nevertheless, there is evidence suggesting that the branch was vibrant and perhaps even growing. For example, the history of the East German Mission shows that when the branch moved into the rooms on Rathausstrasse 14 on July 3, 1938, there was a formal dedication ceremony, on which occasion Alfred C. Rees, the president of the mission, delivered the dedicatory address. More than seventy persons attended.[2]

The new rooms must have been of ample size for the branch membership because a conference of the Leipzig District was held there later that year. Once again, President Rees presided over the meeting and this time 203 members and friends attended. The conference sessions were held on Saturday and Sunday, December 3–4, 1938, and most of the attendees would have come by train from as far as fifty miles away (Halberstadt and Magdeburg).[3]

As of this writing, no eyewitnesses or writings of members of the Halle Branch during the war have been located.

IN MEMORIAM

Only one member of the Halle Branch did not survive World War II:
Ida Therese Knorre bp. 7 Sep 1935; d. 1 Apr 1941, age 81 (*Sonntagsgruss*, no. 24, 15 Jun 1941, 96)

NOTES

1. Presiding Bishopric, "Financial, Statistical, and Historical Reports of Wards, Stakes, and Missions, 1884–1955," CR 4 12, 257.

2. East German Mission Quarterly Reports, 1938, no. 29–31, East German Mission History.

3. Ibid., 1938, no. 49.

LEIPZIG CENTER BRANCH

When World War II began, Leipzig had been the capital of the German book market for several centuries. The international book fair took place there every year, and the world looked to Leipzig for new books. In this metropolis of about six hundred thousand people, The Church of Jesus Christ of Latter-day Saints had two branches: Center and West.

Leipzig Center Branch[1]	1939
Elders	16
Priests	11
Teachers	7
Deacons	14
Other Adult Males	52
Adult Females	206
Male Children	13
Female Children	9
Total	328

The Leipzig Center Branch met in rented rooms at Moritzstrasse 10 in the second Hinterhaus—just two blocks from the New City Hall and thus near the commercial center of this bustling city. According to the branch history, the rooms there were on the second floor and included a large meeting hall, a cloakroom, and a kitchen where the members who lived farther away could enjoy their noon meal between Sunday meetings. There was also a Relief Society room where the sisters met on Monday evenings for discussions and craft circles.[2]

Elfriede Waldammer Werner (born 1918) later indicated that the branch had both a piano and a pump organ. "Sometimes there were more than eighty people in the meetings. There were many children and teenagers."[3] With 328 members at the end of the year 1939, this was the fifth-largest branch in the mission and the sixth-largest in all of Germany.

All of the programs of the Church were functioning in the Leipzig Center Branch when the war began in 1939. According to Elfriede Werner:

> Sometimes, we were at church nearly every day. We were always there Sundays, Mondays, and Wednesdays. On Sunday mornings, we went to church for Sunday School, went home again for lunch, and then came back to the church for sacrament meeting.

According to Sister Werner, politics had no place in the branch. "When we had our meetings, we didn't talk about anything but the gospel. We also didn't pray for Adolf Hitler."

The history of The Church of Jesus Christ of Latter-day Saints in Leipzig includes the following about the war years:

> When the Second World War broke out, most of the brethren were drafted into the army. The lack of leadership led to the combining of the two Leipzig branches in 1941. Brother Johannes Hurst was the branch president at that time. The members gathered for meetings in rented rooms at Moritzstrasse 10. In the early hours of 4 December 1943, the rooms were hit by bombs during an air raid over Leipzig and burned out. The branch was "bombed out" as they used to say in those days. Thereafter, the meetings took place in the home of Sister Herz on Schletterstrasse, then in the rooms of another church on Josephstrasse.[4]

Just before the rooms at Moritzstrasse were destroyed, Elfriede Schiele, longtime secretary of the Relief Society, considered taking the

Fig. 1. A celebration in the Moritzstrasse. (Leipzig Branch History)

records home with her for safekeeping. Then she wondered what the other sisters would say about that and did nothing. After the destruction of the church, she regretted not heeding those promptings.[5]

Herbert Werner was thirty-one, married, and the father of two when he was drafted in 1942. That same year he was wounded in action in the Soviet Union and taken to Charkov for treatment. From there he was put on a train heading home, with a cast on his leg. Unbeknownst to the doctor, there was still a piece of shrapnel in his leg. Herbert's son, Eberhard, later described what happened:

> He was in great pain during the train ride and even passed out a few times. He asked for help, but the doctor told him to not exaggerate his pain. A friend who knew that Herbert was not exaggerating went over to check him out and smelled something very bad inside the cast. At the next train station, the doctor took Herbert off the train and into a restroom where he amputated the leg. The conditions of the operation were poor, and the doctor predicted that his patient would not live another hour, but he

survived and never had trouble with the stump of his leg again.

When Herbert Werner returned to Leipzig, city officials assigned his family an apartment at Eisenbahnstrasse 157. There he learned to walk with an artificial leg but could no longer participate in the dancing and water sports he and his wife, Elfriede, had enjoyed before. He told her that he was grateful to be alive and that he could live with the condition. He convinced her that she would have to do the same or they would both be unhappy. She spent many hours in the corridor of their apartment building teaching him how to walk.

Elfriede's reaction was natural. Herbert's leg may not have caused him much pain, but he had other physical ailments when he came home:

> He came home with lots of illnesses he contracted while he was in the army hospital. It was a drastic change for all of us when he came home. He suffered a lot. . . . He was very brave and he expected us to be brave. . . . He

was home and he was alive and that was all that really mattered. It never affected his testimony.

Elfriede Werner had three children by the time the air raids over Leipzig became frequent. She described the trials of a young mother at such times:

> Whenever we had an attack, we went into our basement. Sometimes it took very long and it was hard to be patient. I had three little children to take care of and a husband. I prepared everything and put out clothing before we went to bed so that my children would not have to go into the basement in their night gowns. . . . Sometimes, the children got their clothes mixed up because everything was so hectic. The children knew very well what was going on outside.

As the war went on and attacks on Leipzig increased in frequency, Sister Werner was encouraged to take her family out of town. She first went north to Heiligendamm on the Baltic Sea, then to Ahlbeck to the former home of a wealthy family after the home was converted for use by mothers with little children. Finally, she took her children and her husband and found a place to live in Warmbad Wolkenstein. Those locations were physically safer, but had one distinct disadvantage:

> When I was gone from Leipzig, we did not have much contact with the Church. I always had a Bible and Book of Mormon with me whenever I could. Often, I would not take them because I was afraid that somebody would take them away from me or I would lose them—they were so precious to me.

Siegfried Schmidt's father had been the president of the Düsseldorf Branch in the West German Mission before he moved with his family to Leipzig. He was employed by the Rheinmetall Company (a critical war industry) and was thus exempt from military service. Because there was no housing available in Leipzig, the Schmidts found a home in nearby Zehmen. Siegfried (born 1939) recalled the

very long walk from Zehmen to the outskirts of Leipzig, then the ride on the streetcar for twenty minutes. Because the way home was equally long, the family usually could not stay for sacrament meeting in the evening.[6]

When the Schmidt family was bombed out, Siegfried recalled that they escaped their burning apartment building by crawling through a hole broken into the basement of the adjacent building. This was a common practice all over Germany and saved the lives of the Schmidt family members.

The American army entered Zehmen toward the end of April 1945. According to Siegfried, "I did not have a reason not to like them. They gave me a bar of chocolate and a pat on the back." Even when the Soviets replaced the Americans a few weeks later, there were few incidents.

According to the branch history, "six brethren of the Leipzig Branch lost their lives in the war, but in 1945 every family was suffering and in need."[7]

The Leipzig Branch conducted an extensive welfare drive and collected hundreds of items to be shared with members throughout the district who had lost their homes and property. A list dated 1944 shows shoes, clothing, household items, and infant supplies. Branch president Johannes Hurst reported the success of the campaign to district president Arthur Böhme and indicated that persons receiving supplies were also given forty marks in cash.[8]

Walter Schiele (born 1927) was not quite seventeen when he was drafted into the Reichsarbeitsdienst in 1944. By that time, Germany had a greater need for soldiers than for laborers, so Walter was sent to East Prussia to be trained as an antiaircraft gunner. He was then transferred to Belgium, but when the Allied troops landed at Normandy, he was sent home for six days. The call to the German army awaited him there.[9]

Fig. 2. The old city hall in Leipzig. (R. P. Minert, 1992)

After six weeks of training in Böhmisch-Leipa in Czechoslovakia, Walter was sent to Norway for additional training. At the age of seventeen, he then participated in the Battle of the Bulge in Belgium, where he was taken prisoner by the Americans on January 14, 1945. By the end of April, he was in the United States. Over the next year, he lived and worked in POW camps in Missouri, Nebraska, Colorado, and New York. He wrote home many times but never received an answer.

In 1946, Walter Schiele was sent to England. He and his comrades had been promised a release but were simply transferred to the British POW system. He had read in an American newspaper that a German prisoner did the work of 3.77 Italian prisoners, which explained why the Italians were sent home sooner. "They were smarter than we were; they didn't work as hard," Walter explained.

Walter's sister wrote to the office of European mission president Ezra Taft Benson in 1947 and the letter found its way to Walter. He told his friends, "See, it's good to be a Mormon. This church helps its members." He was given an early release due to the fact that

his father was dying of tuberculosis. During his days in uniform, Walter had met only one other member of the Church—an American guard in a POW camp in Missouri who claimed to be a descendant of Brigham Young. Walter asked him to find a Book of Mormon in German, but the two lost contact soon thereafter.

Looking back on the wartime experience, Elfriede Werner had the following observations:

> I never gave in to the thought that we could die. . . . I never doubted Heavenly Father. Not me. I have to say that there were members who doubted Him, but I always replied that it was we who did all of these horrible things and not Heavenly Father. . . . There were some members who did not attend the meetings any more because they did not have a strong testimony and were influenced by the war. It was not simple at all to keep a testimony during a time like that. Even very faithful people found themselves doubting.

In Memoriam

The following members of the Leipzig Center Branch did not survive World War II:

Fritz Wilhelm Bernau b. Kriescht, Brandenburg, Preußen 13 Jan 1912; son of Otto Karl Bernau and Bertha Auguste Kirsten; bp. 6 Nov 1920; m. Dresden, Dresden, Sachsen 24 Dec 1934, Margarete Marie Paeschel; 4 children; corporal; d. dysentery POW Russia Apr 1945; bur. Charkow, Ukraine (CHL CR 375 8 #2458, 1458–59; www.volksbund.de; IGI)

Bruno Rudolf Gotty b. Oberneuschönberg, Dresden, Sachsen 2 Feb 1913; son of Bruno Joseph Gotty and Martha Elisabeth Fritzsche; bp. 4 Nov 1923; lance corporal; k. in battle Schukowo, Uljanowo, Russia 7 Sep 1942 (*Sonntagsgruss*, no. 1, 3 Jan 1943, 4; E. Werner; www.volksbund.de; AF)

Hedwig Heweick b. Greiz, Reuss j.L. 6 May 1866; dau. of Wilhelm Heweick and Minna Lippold; m. —— Windisch; d. senility 18 Nov 1939 (CHL CR 375 8 #2458, 1939 data)

Emma Elisabeth Koetz b. Borna, Leipzig, Sachsen 28 Jun 1863; dau.of Karl Gottlob Koetz and Christiane Friedericke Schumann; bp. 6 Aug 1935; m. Groitzsch, Leipzig, Sachsen 15 Dec 1887, Friedrich Edmund Oskar Graf; 4 children; d. Groitzsch, Leipzig, Sachsen

3 Mar 1940 (*Sonntagsstern*, no. 17, 26 May 1940 n.p.; FHL Microfilm 25776, 1935 Census; IGI)

Friedrich Richter b. Grimma, Sachsen 25 Mar 1875; bp. 13 Apr 1921; m. Marie Anna Friedericke Backhaus; d. heart attack Leipzig 25 Mar 1941 (*Sonntagsgruss*, no. 22, 1 Jun 1941, 88; FHL Microfilm 271402, 1930/35 Census; IGI)

Gertrud Berta Schroedter b. Gohlis, Leipzig, Sachsen 18 Sep 1908; dau. of Franz Heinrich Gustav Franz Heinrich Schrodter and Martha Jakob; d. stroke Leipzig, Sachsen 15 Mar 1940 (*Sonntagsstern*, no. 17, 26 May 1940, n.p.; IGI; AF)

Karl Alfred Schulz b. Leipzig, Leipzig, Sachsen 9 Apr 1914; son of Johann Karl Schulze and Anna Martha Zimmer; bp. 17 Jul 1924; k. in battle Eastern Front 1942 (*Sonntagsgruss*, no. 1, 3 Jan 1943, 4; E. Werner; IGI)

August Schwob b. Walddorf, Reinerz, Schlesien, Preußen 7 Apr 1862; son of Franz Schwob and Beate Rieger; bp. 9 Aug 1930; ord. deacon; d. old age Leipzig, Sachsen 24 Sep 1939 (*Stern*, no. 23, 1 Dec. 1939, 372; FHL Microfilm 245260, 1935 Census; IGI)

Karoline Franziska Swaboda b. Przlautsch, Böhmen, Austria 4 or 6 May 1875; bp. 17 Sep 1921; m. 14 May 1901, Albert Franz Lippold; 1 child; d. Leipzig, Sachsen 7 Mar 1941 (*Sonntagsgruss*, no. 17, 27 Apr 1941, 68; FHL Microfilm 271388, 1935 Census; AF; IGI)

Emma Lina Troll b. Beutha, Zwickau, Sachsen 25 Jun or 26 Jul 1858; dau. of Christian F. Troll and Friedricke Schmidt; bp. 22 Apr 1914; m. Beutha 31 Oct 1886, Ernst Otto Sonntag; 8 children; d. Leipzig, Sachsen 24 Apr 1941 (*Sonntagsgruss*, no. 24, 15 Jun 1941, 96; FHL Microfilm 245270, 1935 Census; IGI)

NOTES

1. Presiding Bishopric, "Financial, Statistical, and Historical Reports of Wards, Stakes, and Missions, 1884–1955," CR 4 12, 257.

2. "Auf Spurensuche, Wo Seit 1920 in Leipzig Die Kirche Jesu Christi der Heiligen der Letzten Tage Ihr Domizil Hatte" (unpublished history); private collection.

3. Elfriede Waldammer Werner, interview by the author in German, Leipzig, Germany, June 1, 2007; unless otherwise noted, summarized in English by Judith Sartowski.

4. The Church of Jesus Christ of Latter-day Saints, *Die Gemeinde in Leipzig* (Leipzig, Germany: The Church of Jesus Christ of Latter-day Saints, 1988), 10; trans. the author.

5. *History of the Leipzig Branch* (unpublished), 179; private collection; trans. the author.

6. Siegfried Schmidt, telephone interview with Judith Sartowski in German, February 25, 2008.

7. *Die Gemeinde in Leipzig*, 10.

8. *History of the Leipzig Branch*, 179b.

9. Walter Gerd Schiele, interview by Matthew K. Heiss in German, Leipzig, Germany, October 11, 1991, OH 1144; The Church of Jesus Christ of Latter-day Saints, Church History Library, Salt Lake City; trans. the author.

LEIPZIG WEST BRANCH

The Leipzig West Branch was a relatively young unit of The Church of Jesus Christ of Latter-day Saints in 1939. The population was far smaller than that of the Leipzig Center Branch. The West Branch met in rented rooms at Angerstrasse 18 in the first Hinterhaus.

Leipzig West Branch[1]	1939
Elders	3
Priests	6
Teachers	0
Deacons	4
Other Adult Males	7
Adult Females	40
Male Children	2
Female Children	2
Total	64

The history of the East German Mission contains two entries regarding this branch, both from October 1938, one year before the war began. On October 19, Johannes Hurst was appointed branch president with Fritz Berndt as his first counselor.[2] Ten days later, a branch conference was held, including a social on Saturday night. The attendance was twenty-four members and forty-five friends.[3]

Very little is known about the members and activities of the Leipzig West Branch. A history of the Leipzig Branch written four decades after the war indicates that the West and Center Branches were merged in 1941. Johannes Hurst was the branch president thereafter, and the meetings were held at Moritzstrasse 10 for the next two years.

Kurt Nägler and his family were members of the Leipzig West Branch when he was drafted into the army. His wife, Martha, was faced with the same challenges experienced by several hundred Latter-day Saint women in Germany—rearing their children alone. Whereas many of those women had to be employed to do so, Martha was blessed to be able to stay at home and make do with her husband's army pay.[4]

In 1944, Sister Nägler was informed that her husband was missing in action somewhere in Romania. According to their daughter, Gerda, "My mother never gave up hope that he would return until long after the war. She never doubted her testimony." However, Kurt was officially declared dead several years after the war. His two daughters became some of the many Latter-day Saint children who grew to adulthood with only one parent. The army pay Sister Nägler received from the government ended in May 1945, and she became the sole support of her daughters.

In Memoriam

The following members of the Leipzig West Branch did not survive World War II:

Fig. 1. The family of Kurt Nägler in 1944, just before he was reported missing in action. (G. Nägler Fischer)

Gerolf Johannes Hurst b. Leipzig, Leipzig, Sachsen 16 Nov 1923; son of Johannes Georg Hurst and Klara Martha Koch; bp. 24 Nov 1931; k. in battle Saporohsja, Russia Sep 1943 (Werner Nägler; FHL Microfilm 162794, 1930/35 Census; AF)

Kurt Nägler b. Leipzig, Leipzig, Sachsen, Germany 4 Oct 1907; m. Martha Beyer; 2 children; MIA Romania 1944 (G. Nägler Fischer)

Amalie Selma Ulbricht b. Mittweida, Leipzig, Sachsen 22 or 23 Jul 1856; dau. of Karl Wilhelm Ulbricht and Christiane Rosine Eichhorn; bp. 6 Jun 1912; m. Chemnitz, Sachsen 3 Aug 1885, Gottlieb David Gustav Groeschke; 7 children; d. Leipzig, Sachsen 4 or 5 May 1940 (*Sonntagsstern*, no. 23, 7 Jul 1940, n.p.; FHL Microfilm 25778, 1930/35 Census; IGI)

Notes

1. Presiding Bishopric, "Financial, Statistical, and Historical Reports of Wards, Stakes, and Missions, 1884–1955," CR 4 12, 257.

2. East German Mission Quarterly Reports, 1938, no. 41, East German Mission History.

3. Ibid., no. 43.

4. Gerda Nägler Fischer, telephone interview with the author, June 2, 2007.

Magdeburg Branch

One of the most important venues in the Thirty Years' War (1618–48), the city of Magdeburg is located on the west bank of the Elbe River. The city survived the ravages of that terrible war and eventually became the capital of the Prussian province of Saxony. With a population of nearly three hundred thousand, it was the largest city for many miles in any direction.

The LDS Church had only a small branch in this large city. According to the official records of the East German Mission, there were only forty-three members in this branch at the end of the year 1939. It is interesting to note that there were fourteen adult males (age twelve and up) who did not have the priesthood; this constitutes thirty-three percent of the branch population.

Magdeburg Branch[1]	1939
Elders	2
Priests	2
Teachers	0
Deacons	1
Other Adult Males	14
Adult Females	22
Male Children	0
Female Children	2
Total	43

According to East German Mission records, the members of the Magdeburg Branch held their meetings in rooms rented at Blumenthalstrasse 11, about a half mile southeast of the city's main railroad station. It is not known just how many rooms were used by the branch or what they looked like.

Anton Larisch was working in Halberstadt (thirty miles to the southwest) and serving as the group leader there (the membership was not sufficient for branch status). In his diary entry of June 15, 1942, he mentioned that the group had acquired the pump organ "of the Magdeburger Branch, which has completely ceased to be."[2] There is no explanation regarding how the Magdeburg Branch population of forty-three in 1939 had decreased to zero four years later.

As of this writing, no eyewitnesses from the Magdeburg Branch could be located, nor could any biographical or autobiographical writings by members of that branch be found.

In Memoriam

The following members of the Magdeburg Branch did not survive World War II:

Minna Pauline Amalie —— b. Sangerhausen, Sachsen, Preußen 3 Jul 1868; bp. 15 Sep 1936; m. Erdmann Adolf Hermann Koebel; d. Magdeburg or Aschersleben, Sachsen, Preußen 7 Jun 1940 (*Sonntagsstern*, no. 23, 7 Jul 1940, n.p.).

Erdmann Adolf Hermann Koebel b. Benstedt, Halle, Sachsen, Preußen 1 Apr 1868; bp. 19 Dec 1932; m. Minna Pauline Amalie ——; d. Aschersleben, Sachsen, Preußen 18 Sep 1942 (IGI)

Notes

1. Presiding Bishopric, "Financial, Statistical, and Historical Reports of Wards, Stakes, and Missions, 1884–1955," CR 4 12, 257.
2. Anton Larisch, diary, June 15, 1942, 30; private collection; trans. Ruth Larisch Hinkel.

Naumburg Branch

Old, small, and historic, the city of Naumburg was the home to a very small branch of Latter-day Saints as World War II approached in 1939. With only twenty-seven members, the branch nevertheless had a place of its own at Grosse Marienstrasse 5–6. The rented rooms were located in the second Hinterhaus.

Naumburg Branch[1]	1939
Elders	0
Priests	0
Teachers	3
Deacons	1
Other Adult Males	3
Adult Females	17
Male Children	1
Female Children	2
Total	27

Gustav Mudrow was born in Kreuz in Pomerania. He was drafted and chose to serve in the German air force. Assigned to the central Luftwaffe headquarters on Wilhelmstrasse in Berlin, he became a member of the Schöneberg Branch. While in Berlin, he met and married Else Focker, a native of the capital city, in 1941.[2]

During the next few years, Gustav served in the Soviet Union, North Africa, and France—seeing more of the landscapes of the war than most men. By 1944, conditions in Berlin had become so insecure that he had his wife leave the city and move into the home of her grandparents in the town of Gebstedt in Thuringia (about twenty miles east of Erfurt). By doing so, she became a member of the branch in Naumburg, about twelve miles distant.

The war was for all practical purposes over in Thuringia in April 1945. Nevertheless, the locals were still cautious, wondering how the conflict would end in their vicinity. The American army was just a few miles from Gebstedt when an incident occurred that could easily have ended the life of an infant. Gustav Mudrow's daughter, Renate, was just eleven months old when Else put her in the stroller for a few moments in the sun.

The stroller stood in the small courtyard between the family home and Sister Mudrow's father's workshop. Else was working in the kitchen when she heard the sound of an airplane. Because most Germans had sufficient experience to associate specific sounds with specific aircraft, she knew that a fighter plane—an enemy aircraft—was approaching very low. There were no military targets in the small town, but enemy pilots were looking for ways to disrupt the lives of civilians.

Else Mudrow ran out the door to bring her daughter into the house at precisely the moment the fighter plane began to fire. Fifty-caliber bullets tore across the courtyard and struck the stroller, tearing it in half. Little Renate tumbled out onto the cobblestones—totally unscathed. More bullets buried themselves in the ground and pierced the wall of the grandfather's workshop.

A few days after this near miss, the American army arrived. Soldiers moved into the home of Else's grandparents and stayed there for two

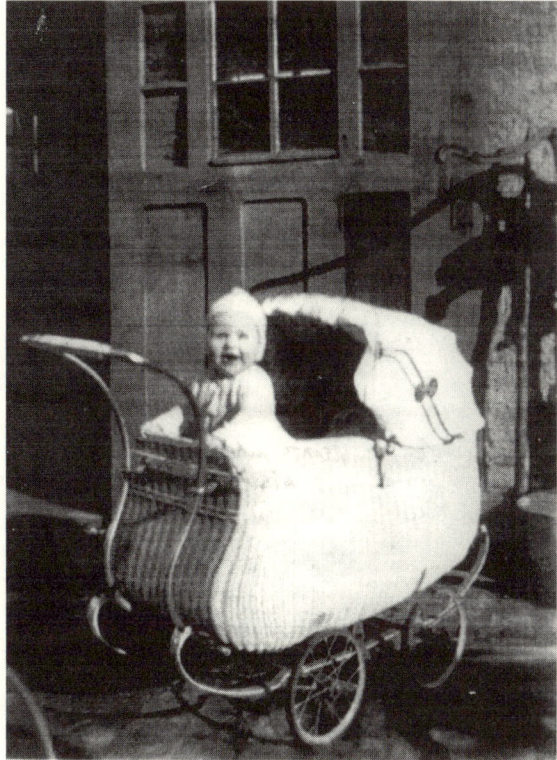

Fig. 1. Little Renate Mudrow in her stroller just days before it was torn in half by bullets from a fighter plane. (R. Mudrow Buttars)

months. On July 1 they moved out and were replaced by Soviet occupation forces.

Before the year 1945 ended, Gustav Mudrow was released as a prisoner of war and joined his family in Gebstedt. He had nearly lost his leg to a frightful wound but convinced the surgeons that he could be healed—as he was. From Gebstedt, the Mudrows enjoyed making the trip to church, walking about two miles to the railroad station in Tromsdorf and riding the train about twenty miles to Naumburg.

As of this writing, no other eyewitnesses in the Naumburg Branch have been located.

No members of the Naumburg Branch are known to have died during World War II.

NOTES

1. Presiding Bishopric, "Financial, Statistical, and Historical Reports of Wards, Stakes, and Missions, 1884–1955," CR 4 12, 257.
2. Renate Mudrow Buttars, interview by the author, Ogden, Utah, May 30, 2006.

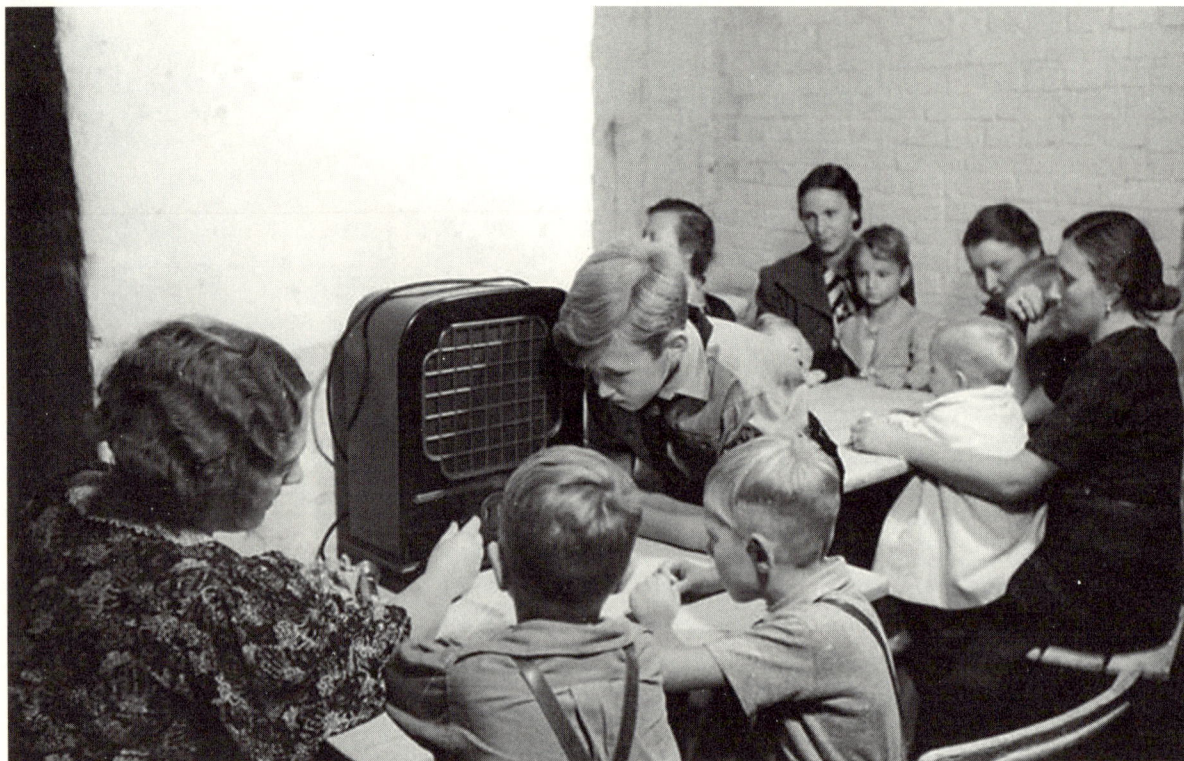

Fig. 2. Hitler Youth boys were often assigned to monitor radio broadcasts while local residents sat in air-raid shelters hoping that the enemy bombers were headed elsewhere. (Deutsches Bundesarchiv, Bild 146-1981-076-29A)

ROSTOCK
DISTRICT
East German Mission

With only 248 members of The Church of Jesus Christ of Latter-day Saints within its boundaries at the end of the momentous year 1939, the Rostock District, with its four branches and two groups, was the second smallest in the East German Mission. On the other hand, the territory covered by the district was significant. The historic provinces of Mecklenburg-Schwerin and Mecklenburg-Strelitz were the core of the district, which also included a small portion of western Pomerania.

The landscape along the Baltic Sea is relatively flat, sandy countryside with very few cities, many of which are close to the sea. The principal city in the district was Rostock, a stronghold of the old Hanseatic League. The Barth Branch was twenty-five miles to the northeast, also a coastal town. Demmin, in Pomerania, was thirty-five miles to the east. In 1939, there were groups of Saints meeting in Stralsund (thirty-five miles northeast) and Wolgast (sixty miles to the east).

The president of the Rostock District in 1939 was Walter Czerny.[1] He was succeeded on January 14, 1940, by Rudolf A. Noss of Rostock.[2] Arno Dzierzon is listed as district president as of April 23, 1941.[3] Little is known about the service of these three men in this important calling.

The Rostock District was annexed to the Stettin District (to the east) on February 15, 1942. The announcement made in the sacrament meeting in Rostock on that date did not include details for the change. Perhaps the lack of priesthood leadership within the three branches of the district required more direct involvement of district presidents Erich Berndt and Ernst Winter of Stettin.

Rostock District[4]	1939	1940	1941	1942
Elders	17	16		
Priests	3	4		
Teachers	6	8		
Deacons	17	14		
Other Adult Males	35	39		
Adult Females	145	146		
Male Children	13	11		
Female Children	12	13		
Total	248	251	249	242

It appears that at least three branches of the Rostock District were holding some meetings (usually in private homes) at the end of the war. From the accounts of eyewitnesses, few members fled the invading Red Army. As difficult as life under the conquerors was, the

Fig. 1. The Rostock District was one of the most sparsely populated in the mission.

Latter-day Saints in the district were usually able to maintain their homes.

The group meeting in Stralsund had declined into historical obscurity, but at least one family is known to have belonged to the group in Wolgast (see that chapter).

Notes

1. The Church of Jesus Christ of Latter-day Saints, *Geschichte der Gemeinde Rostock, 1893–1944* (Rostock, Germany), October 30, 1939; trans. the author.
2. Ibid., September 15, 1940.
3. Ibid., March 23, 1941.
4. Presiding Bishopric, "Financial, Statistical, and Historical Reports of Wards, Stakes, and Missions, 1884–1955," CR 4 12, 257.

BARTH-STRALSUND BRANCH

Located not far from the Baltic Sea in the province of Pomerania, Barth was a town of about ten thousand inhabitants in 1939. Of those, only thirty-eight were Latter-day Saints at the onset of World War II. As part of the Rostock District, the members in Barth rode the train west twenty-five miles (forty minutes) to attend district conferences in Rostock.

The closest branch was in Demmin, thirty-five miles to the southeast.

In September 1938, the members of the Barth Branch met in rented rooms at Baustrasse 36 on the main floor. The same rooms were used for the next few years.

Before the war, the branch was home to two American missionaries, but the city government was not enthusiastic about their presence. The mission history includes the following statement in November 1938: "Elders Burke M. Snow and Everett L. Cooley were not allowed to register with the police, either in Barth or Stralsund. Therefore, they were transferred to Rostock, where the permission still was pending at this time."[1] The practice of having all residents register with city hall allowed the city to deny a person the privilege of living there.

Barth Branch[2]	1939
Elders	1
Priests	1
Teachers	1
Deacons	3
Other Adult Males	6
Adult Females	19
Male Children	5
Female Children	2
Total	38

Konrad Friedrich Langer was the president of the Barth Branch from 1933 to 1941. After he was killed in the Soviet Union that year, he was replaced by Günther Zühlsdorf, who served simultaneously as the president of the Rostock District and the president of the Barth Branch. The branch likely relied heavily on priesthood visitors from other branches or on the district leaders for important functions and events in the Church.

Brother Langer's son, Karl Werner, later wrote, "Unfortunately, we four children did not enjoy a long and happy family time with

Fig. 1. The Barth-Stralsund Branch in the 1930s at perhaps the height of its prosperity. (F. Harris)

our parents because Father was taken from us in 1941 and Mother in 1946. . . . Mine was certainly no easy childhood . . . , but through the faith of my parents I had a basis for recognizing the truth of the gospel."[3]

The branch in Straslund to the east was struggling in those years. The mission history indicates the following in an entry dated March 31, 1939: "A family of five members moved away from Stralsund, Rostock District. Consequently the small branch was closed, and the remaining few members attended meetings in the Barth Branch henceforth." It is not known which members came to Barth from Stralsund or how often they made the trip.

During the war, members of the Barth Branch occasionally visited the Rostock Branch. The Rostock Branch history mentions the surnames Zühlsdorf, Neumann, and Ihns as one-time or occasional visitors from 1939 to 1942. The Zühlsdorf family moved from Barth to Rostock in January 1942.[4] The loss of an active family was unfortunate for such a small branch.

Nothing is known of the fate of the Barth and Stralsund Latter-day Saints. Because the war ended the week the Soviet forces entered those cities, it is probable that the members of the branch remained in their homes.

In Memoriam

The following members of the Barth Branch did not survive World War II:

Anna Rosa Minna Bandelow b. Anklam/Pomm. 2 May 1864; dau. of Wilhelm Bandelow and Marie Beusel [?]; bp. 11 Aug 1934; conf. 11 Aug 1934; d. 4 Aug 1940 (CHL LR 537 21, no. 78; NG-IGI, AF, PRF)

Konrad Friedrich Heinrich Langer b. Lüdershapen, Stralsund, Pommern, Preußen 7 Mar 1908; son of August Langer and Johanna Henriette Wilhelmine Ehlert; bp. 5 May 1929; conf. 5 May 1929; ord. deacon 16 Nov 1930; ord. teacher 29 May 1932; ord. priest 3 Dec 1933; ord. elder 12 Mar 1939; m. Barth, Pommern, Preußen 15 Apr 1933, Martha Frieda Else Ihns; 4 children; soldier; k. in battle Petersburg, Luga, USSR 9 or 19 Aug 1941 (FHL Microfilm 271383, 1935 Census; CHL LR 537 21, nos. 7 and 57; IGI)

Fritz Gustav Theodor Matthies b. Ramitz, Rügen, Pommern 31 Dec 1875; son of Fritz Matthies and Friederike Pahl; bp. 8 Oct 1933; conf. 8 Oct 1933;

m. 22 Jul 1923, Marta Zillmann; d. asthma 13 Dec 1942 (CHL LR 537 21, no. 69)

Hertha Martha Thesenvitz b. Stralsund, Pommern 20 Dec 1918; dau. of Paul Wichmann and Hertha Thesenvitz; bp. 11 Jul 1933; conf. 11 Jul 1933; m. —— Wunna; d. tuberculosis 5 Sep 1939 (CHL LR 537 21, no. 28; NG-IGI, AF, PRF)

Anna Marie Johanna Ziems b. Barth, Franzburg, Pommern, Preußen 1 Nov 1871; dau. of Johann Heinrich August Ziems and Johanna Karoline Wilhelmina Freese; bp. 5 May 1929; conf. 5 May 1929; m. 9 Jul 1909, Otto Zajek; m. Friedrich Carl Linck; 2 children; d. lung ailment 23 Nov 1941 (CHL LR 537 21, no. 20 and 65; IGI)

NOTES

1. Presiding Bishopric, "Financial, Statistical, and Historical Reports of Wards, Stakes, and Missions, 1884–1955," CR 4 12, 257.

2. East German Mission Quarterly Reports, 1938, no. 48, East German Mission History.

3. Karl Werner Langer, "Ostdeutsche Mission" (unpublished history), 96; private collection.

4. The Church of Jesus Christ of Latter-day Saints, *Geschichte der Gemeinde Rostock, 1893–1944* (Rostock, Germany), January 26, 1942; trans. the author.

DEMMIN
BRANCH

Demmin is located thirty-five miles west of the city of Rostock and had about fifteen thousand inhabitants when war broke out in 1939. This small Pomeranian town was located along the main railway line from Neubrandenburg to Stralsund on the Baltic Sea. The branch meetings were held in rented rooms in Reuterstrasse 13 in the first Hinterhaus. Annaliese Ahlwardt Dieckmann (born 1915) recalled the meeting rooms:

> We went through a corridor and outside, and then we entered the Hinterhaus. We had a large room and a smaller one. Outside was a toilet we could use. These rooms had been a candy factory before, and we then separated the large rooms by a portable wall so that we could have

two smaller classrooms. There was a picture of Joseph Smith and a picture of Jesus Christ and his disciples at the Last Supper. There was an organ. I played the organ for a very long time in our branch.[1]

Demmin Branch[2]	1939
Elders	2
Priests	2
Teachers	0
Deacons	7
Other Adult Males	7
Adult Females	27
Male Children	3
Female Children	3
Total	51

Jutta Ruetter recalled that there were some benches in the church rooms and some very old chairs that had come to Demmin from the Neubrandenburg Branch. "Somebody always crashed to the floor each Sunday, since the chairs were old. . . . We did not have many pictures on the wall, but I remember a banner reading 'The Glory of God Is Intelligence.'"[3]

Annaliese married Franz Dieckmann in 1937. The official ceremony took place in the civil registry office in city hall, as was required by law. Then there was a second marriage ceremony in the church. Her friend, Helmut Plath of the Stettin Branch, conducted the ceremony. "All of the branch members celebrated with us," she recalled.

The Demmin Latter-day Saints were few in number, but the missionary spirit was strong in that branch. Jutta Ruetter recalled how Elisabeth Ahlwardt (Annaliese's mother) encouraged her to bring other children her age to church. Sister Ahlwardt was both Relief Society president and Beehive leader.

Regarding the Church meetings in the years just prior to the war, Annaliese later explained:

> We had a very large Sunday School. Even children who were not members attended because

we knew each other well. Sunday School was in the morning. Sacrament meetings depended on the season; in the summer it was in the evening hours, during the winter we held it in the afternoon. We had three Sunday School classes based on age. For Sunday School, we had about thirty-five people attending.

Annaliese's father, Max Ahlwardt, served as branch president for several years. The walk to the church from their home on Luisenstrasse took about ten minutes.

In 1940, Anneliese Dieckmann's lifestyle began to be somewhat nomadic. She followed her husband, Franz, with his military employment, visited her parents, and hardly stayed anywhere for more than a few months at a time. Her two sons were born in 1937 and 1941. She had her hands full with them all during the war.

Franz Dieckmann was a civilian employed by the Luftwaffe. His first move with the family was to Stargard, a town twenty-five miles east of Stettin and fifty-five miles southeast of Demmin. Annaliese was just ninety miles from her parents' home and was able to visit them relatively often. Thus she did not often attend Church meetings in Stargard and did not get to know the members of that small branch very well. "We lived on Zarziegerstrasse, which was about twenty minutes from the meeting rooms at Radestrasse 31 in the first Hinterhaus."

Soon after moving his family to Stargard, Franz was required to travel to France, where he was responsible for aircraft security.

The burdens on a young mother are difficult under any circumstance, but Annaliese was alone by 1941 when her second son arrived. Years later, she described this crisis:

My youngest son was sick with diphtheria. I had to take him to the hospital, and the doctor gave him the serum right away, but I was not allowed to stay with my son. I paced in front of the door all night. . . . I then remembered a regulation or law that allowed having someone with diphtheria

stay at home when the neighborhood was without children or the nearest child was very far away. The person at the health office had to give me the paper. Now I was alone with both children, and I had all the responsibility. How often did I find myself on my knees praying for help!

A neighbor lady felt compelled to leave her own little girl in the hospital, and the child died just days later. Annaliese learned an important lesson from the experience: "This is something that has made me strong—this has made my testimony stronger. This feeling that you have to do something different than what other people tell you to do has helped me."

From Stargard, Annaliese could take the train home to Demmin without buying a ticket because the distance was less than one hundred kilometers [sixty miles].[4] This allowed her to see her family with some regularity. Her mother also went to Stargard to visit her.

During the fall of 1944, Franz Dieckmann was stationed just south of Berlin and was able to visit his family on weekends. In early February 1945, he was sent to Breslau in Silesia. Annaliese was given permission to take winter clothing to him there; she left her children with her mother. However, the Red Army invaders were advancing on Breslau, and Franz insisted that his wife turn right around and go back to her children. "We even heard [the army] shooting at night," she explained. She was able to find a place aboard a hospital train headed west.

The war had left Stargard in relative peace for years, but things were changing fast. As Annaliese recalled, "When I got back to Stargard, my apartment was already filled with German soldiers and refugees. In my children's room there lived a mother with two little children; she must have been from somewhere in the East."

Annaliese found railroad travel to be increasingly difficult in the late winter of 1945.

She had left practically everything in Stargard, hoping to return, but soon realized that this was not possible. Because Demmin had a large airfield, the town was subjected to air raids in the last few months of the war. She described her next move in these words:

In April 1945, I took my mother and my children and followed my husband's letters that came from the west [near Hanover]. He, at the same time, looked for a way to come back to Demmin and managed to arrive there. All he could see was that the whole city was destroyed and burning for three days. I was so happy that I had made the decision to [go west], although my father stayed in Demmin.

When the war ended on May 8, 1945, Annaliese, her children, and her mother were safely at Timmendorfer Strand in what became the British Occupation Zone. Franz Dieckmann left Demmin in search of his family and located them with the help of Annaliese's cousin in Hamburg. He took them back to Demmin in the fall of 1945.

Jutta Ruetter and her mother did not leave Demmin when the invaders came. According to her recollection:

The women had to hide very often, but [the Russians] were always very friendly to us children and strangers. They never did anything to us. One cousin of mine was allowed to sit on a tank once, and my aunt was afraid that something would happen to her. As children, we did not worry much about [the events of the war].

The Ahlwardt home in Demmin had been destroyed, but Max Ahlwardt was able to procure building materials and start over again. To his new little home, he added a small room for the Dieckmann family. They had survived the war in good health and were pleased to be together again. Their story of being separated and having to live in different places is not at all a rarity among Latter-day Saints in Germany at the time.

No members of the Demmin Branch are known to have died during World War II.

NOTES

1. Anneliese Ahlwardt Dieckmann, interview by the author in German, Kassel, Germany, June 17, 2007; unless otherwise noted, summarized in English by Judith Sartowski.
2. Presiding Bishopric, "Financial, Statistical, and Historical Reports of Wards, Stakes, and Missions, 1884–1955," CR 4 12, 257.
3. Jutta Ruetter Meyer, telephone interview with Judith Sartowski, April 14, 2008.
4. To purchase a ticket for a longer journey, the passenger had to justify the trip. This requirement allowed officials to regulate long-distance traffic.

NEUBRANDENBURG BRANCH

Just a few hundred feet south of the famous "Baker's Wife" monument on the main street of the city of Neubrandenburg, the small but vibrant Neubrandenburg Branch met in rented rooms next to the post office. The address at the time was Adolf Hitler Strasse 12, and the rooms were on the main floor at this very central location in town.

Neubrandenberg Branch[1]	1939
Elders	4
Priests	5
Teachers	4
Deacons	4
Other Adult Males	21
Adult Females	49
Male Children	4
Female Children	4
Total	95

The city of Neubrandenburg in the historic province of Brandenburg, Prussia, is located fifty miles west of Stettin. It was decided in December 1938 that the Neubrandenburg Branch of the Stettin District should be shifted

Fig. 1. Members of the Neubrandenburg Branch in 1938. (E. Klappert Bergmann)

to the Rostock District (to the northwest).[2] The official justification for the change was that better railroad connections existed between Neubrandenburg and Rostock (even though the distance to Rostock was twelve miles greater). However, the very low population of the Rostock District may also have influenced the decision to move the branch with its ninety-five members to the Rostock District.

Frida Bauer (born 1922) later described the rooms in which the branch held its meetings:

> It was a nice meeting room. It had a little po-dium with a pump organ. It was nice, in very good shape. It was almost too large for our branch. . . . We had three classrooms. A rest-room was not right there. We had to go over to another building, the Hinterhaus. It was not very convenient, but we children were pretty disciplined. We went to the bathroom at home before going to church.[3]

Church activities in the East German Mission in the days leading up to World War II

included cultural programs. For example, in the Neubrandenburg Branch, Erich Berndt gave a presentation on the Word of Wisdom on November 13, 1938, and one week later, an illustrated lecture entitled "The Life of Christ" was given by Adolf Klappert and Georg Dauss. Attendance was sixty-four and fifty-seven per-sons, respectively.[4]

On Saturday and Sunday, March 11–12, 1939, the Rostock District spring confer-ence was held in Neubrandenburg, with dis-trict president Günther Zühlsdorf presiding. Mission president Alfred C. Rees and Stettin District president Erich Berndt also attended. As reported in the mission history, "The [large] attendance of Saints and friends was very gratifying."[5]

In early 1939, the branch president in Neubrandenburg was Karl E. Toebe, and his counselors were Ludwig Renter and Philipp Bauer.[6] Bruno Rohloff was the branch

Fig. 2. Members of the Neubrandenburg Branch on an outing in 1941. (A. Bauer Schulz)

president in January 1941, when he visited the meetings of the Rostock Branch.[7] His son, Walter (born 1922), was the Sunday School president until he was drafted by the Wehrmacht in February 1942.

Sunday School began at 10:00 A.M., and sacrament meeting was held in the evening ("Children usually did not attend sacrament meeting," recalled Frida Bauer). Priesthood and Relief Society groups met on Monday evenings, and MIA was held on Wednesdays. Primary meetings were held on Wednesdays after school.

Frida managed to avoid involvement in the Hitler Youth. Because her mother was already deceased, Frida's official excuse was that she had to take care of the household. While other girls participated in the Jungvolk activities on Saturdays, Frida had to remain in school.[8] In one sense, attending school on Saturdays became a punishment for nonparticipation in the party program.

Frida Bauer's sister, Anni (born 1925), was encouraged by her father to avoid associating with the Hitler Youth. This caused her serious

problems at school, but she found a way out by assisting in the association known as the Society for Germans in Foreign Nations. She invested substantial efforts on behalf of the thousands of Germans who were moved out of nations in Eastern Europe back to Germany, where they would be safe from persecution. Upon finishing her schooling, Anni was awarded a beautiful memorial book by the school's principal. She later explained, "To me, this job was one of the greatest accomplishments in my life for a good cause, without being in the Hitler Youth."[9]

The family of Paul and Ilse Meyer lived in Cammin, eleven miles south of the city. Daughter Waltraud (born 1920) recalled seeing only seven children in the Primary meetings. Attendance at church for her family was a bit complicated, as she explained:

My family could not attend church regularly because the train schedule did not work out for us. We lived sixteen kilometers away from the branch. Today, it does not sound like much, but back then we had to take the horses to go to church, and we could not let them stand outside for that long while we were in the meeting.[10]

Waltraud Meyer's brother, Kurt, was drafted soon after Germany invaded Poland in September 1939. Waltraud recalled her reaction to hearing that war had begun:

When the war started back then, I remember being kind of excited since we all thought that Germany would conquer the entire world. I could not understand why my father had to be careful about his political views or why he did not express them more often. I was nineteen years old when the war started and had no political knowledge about the war whatsoever.

Waltraud was inducted into the German Red Cross in 1940 and spent much of the war away from Cammin and the branch in Neubrandenburg. After a short stint in a local hospital, she was sent to Forst in Silesia, then to France.

Tragedy struck the family of Ernst and Ida Schulz just weeks after the war began. Vera Schulz Bamberger (born 1917) later described the incident:

My father, Ernst Schulz, was a worker and also spent much time helping out at the airport in Trollenhagen near Neubrandenburg, where he died on October 6, 1939. . . . On that day, my father saw an airplane that was on the runway and was stopped by a large branch of a tree. He jumped over a ditch and wanted to remove that branch and although his colleagues warned him and shouted at him, they later said that he seemed to be drawn to do it. When he attempted to remove the branch, the pilot started the engines and the propeller started and hit my father.[11]

After the death of her father, Vera Schulz and her mother, Ida, worked at a munitions factory where the brother of branch president Bruno Rohloff was the head of personnel. Vera soon married and was the mother of three children by 1943.

Günter Streuling's father was a member of the Church and also of the Nazi Party. According to Günter, "We had a picture of Hitler hanging on the wall, and a copy of *Mein Kampf* was tucked away in the closet.[12] The Hitler picture was a profile in black, and it hung over the door from my parents' bedroom to the living room."[13] Günter's father was often at odds with the neighbors in their apartment building because most of them were communists. Fortunately, debates conducted in the stairway never became violent.

Young Günter Streuling (born 1935) could hardly wait to join the Jungvolk because the older boys seemed to be having such a great time. As he later explained:

I envied them, so I pushed my mother to let me join. I don't know why she opposed that plan. Finally, she said yes, so I joined. I was accepted. My mom got me a shirt and sewed me some pants. After school on Wednesdays, we went to march and had weekend activities. They taught us not to smoke and to help old ladies across the street. I wore a knife on my belt but was never taught to use it.

During the first few years of the war, the Nazi Party confiscated the main branch meeting room at Adolf Hitler Strasse 12 for the use of the local Hitler Youth group. According to Walter Rohloff, "they left us only the three classrooms."[14] The directory of the East German Mission shows the next meeting address as Pasewalkerstrasse 11 (the home of the Rohloff family) in January 1943—with the notation that meetings were not being held at that time. "We still met for Relief Society," recalled Frida Bauer. "I know, because I was the secretary. But very few sisters came."

While other Latter-day Saint women were required to take jobs in offices or industry during the war, Waltraud Meyer served in the Red Cross for nearly five years. "I did not have any problems working for the Red Cross," she recalled,

[But] it was hard for me to see the wounded people because it always made me think about people I knew whom I could lose during the war or who could get hurt. . . . When I was in France, we worked in different shifts in the Red Cross. We started at eight in the morning, and sometimes things would not go as well, and we would have to work until eight the next morning. The normal shift ended late in the afternoon.

Waltraud found herself in hospitals in various larger cities during her work with the Red Cross. She attended Church meetings in Stettin and Berlin, for example, whenever she had the chance.

On several occasions in 1941, Walter Rohloff was approached by recruiting officers of the Waffen-SS. Each time, he lied to avoid their offers, telling them that he planned to join the air force. At the time, he enjoyed immunity from the draft, because he was employed in a critical war industry. However, by January 1942, Walter decided to volunteer for military service. He later explained this decision:

> I wanted to go because none of my friends were home anymore. All had been drafted and had joined the armed forces. Some had died already in war action, and when I met the parents they asked me why I was still home. I was embarrassed and hated it. They probably thought I was a draft dodger. I was not afraid of going to war, even though I did not really understand what it meant.[15]

For Walter Rohloff, the question of religion had a genuine impact on his military career. Wehrmacht officials wanted to register him simply as Catholic or Protestant, but he indicated that he was a member of The Church of Jesus Christ of Latter-day Saints, whereupon the entry "Jes.Chr." was made. One officer asked him "What is that?" but there was no time for a discussion. Later, Walter pondered long and hard over the question, "What is that?" A few months later, a soldier asked him if he was a "Latter-day Saint" by conviction or simply because his parents were. These two events caused Walter a great deal of

soul-searching, and he studied the scriptures intently to find an answer to those questions.[16]

Vera Bamberger was not able to attend church often during the war, but was involved in several activities in the branch. For example, she remembered a wintry baptismal ceremony:

> I can remember that we also had baptisms during the war, but I cannot tell who was baptized. I only know that there was one day when we baptized three people—it was a cold winter day, and they chopped a hole in the ice on the Tollensesee [Lake] and it was cold. We did not have to do baptisms in secret.

Vera remembered that while there were no air raids over Neubrandenburg, the alarms sounded as often as three times a week, and she had to take her children to the shelter in the basement. "We also packed a little suitcase for each of the girls, and although they could not carry them on their own, the suitcases stood in the corner prepared."

Life for Vera and her mother in Neubrandenburg was tolerable through most of the war. Her husband was away in the Wehrmacht, but Vera's existence was relatively free of privations. As she later explained, "We still had some heat, electricity, and water, and although we could only use a certain amount, we had enough. All in all, we did not have many wants when it came to food, water, or the standard of living in general."

Shortly after completing her schooling, Anni Bauer moved to Stettin to serve her Pflichtjahr in the home of the wealthy family of Dr. Xaver Meyer. It was an "attractive and sophisticated home," and she enjoyed the experience, but was soon quite overworked and became ill. Nevertheless, she was very much at home in the Stettin Branch. Having attended district conferences there in the 1930s, she knew most of the members. It was there that she became acquainted with young Juergen

Schulz: "I certainly had a crush on him, ever since I met him."

In 1942, Anni Bauer's employment required that she move east to Schneidemühl. For nine months, she worked in a stressful environment that included harassment from the local Hitler Youth officials. She was so miserable that she became seriously ill and was bedridden for six weeks. She felt quite fortunate to find a physician to sign papers attesting to her maladies and allowing her to return to Stettin.[17]

While in the Wehrmacht during the second half of 1942, Walter Rohloff suffered from various illnesses, including nerve paralysis. In January 1943, he was released from a hospital and was given leave to spend two weeks at home. He later wrote of the condition of the Neubrandenburg Branch at the time: "Our little branch of the Church was almost nonexistent. After discussing this with my parents, I visited the remaining members, and we had Sunday meetings at our home."[18]

In 1943, Walter was stationed in Gnesen in Poland. From there, he found a way to travel sixty-five miles to Schneidemühl to attend church, where he met the Birth family with their ten children. He felt so much at home there that he found many occasions to visit them again before February 1945. With time, he also fell in love with Edith Birth, one of several very attractive daughters in the family.[19] Later that year, Walter was enrolled in Officer Candidate School and learned early on that if he were unwilling to embrace National Socialist ideology (and deny his faith), he had little chance of successfully completing the program. By March 1944, this became a reality. He was returned to his unit without promotion and later learned what had been written about him in the Officer Candidate School (where his performance was better than most other participants): "Religious fanatic. Belonging to the Mormon sect. Politically not trustworthy."

He was proud to have defended his faith and did not regret not being promoted.[20]

On the Eastern Front in June 1944, Walter Rohloff was hit in the face by shrapnel. In the confusion caused by an enemy attack, he was nearly left behind in a hospital that was eventually surrounded by Soviet soldiers. At the last moment, he was rescued and taken west, then sent to a hospital in Kirchhain, Silesia. While there, he found a way to sneak out of the hospital to attend church in Cottbus, a few hours away by train; he was able to sneak back into the hospital in the evening before his absence was discovered. After surgery to remove the shrapnel from his forehead, he was assigned to a new unit and sent to the Western Front.[21]

During the fall of 1944, Walter was constantly under fire from the Americans who were approaching Germany's western border. Decorated for valor with the Iron Cross, Second Class, he came very close to being killed when American tanks advanced toward his foxhole. As he later explained, "There was no help in sight. This was the end. I prayed. I always said my prayers, but this time it was different. It was a cry for help. I didn't want to be run over by tanks." As if by a miracle, a German howitzer was moved into position and quickly put two tanks out of action. The rest retreated, and Walter was saved. "A thanks went up to my Heavenly Father. That was a close call."[22]

Due to his fine record of bravery under fire on the Western Front, Walter was given leave from December 12 to January 3. While he was in Schneidemühl visiting Edith Birth, the German army launched its Ardennes Offensive, and the Battle of the Bulge was under way. By the time he returned to the front, nearly all of the soldiers serving with him had been killed or wounded. Just before he left Neubrandenburg, Walter had been admonished by his father to "stay close to the Lord" and to contact the mission office in Berlin, in order to find the family after the war.[23]

In early 1945, while attempting to cross the Rhine River to the east side and temporary safety, Walter was rowing a small boat under fire from the west bank. Just yards from the east bank, he was hit by a bullet that penetrated his abdomen. Fortunately, he was transported to a nearby hospital and given the necessary medical treatment. Over the next few weeks, he was moved town by town east and north to Lüdenscheid, where he was taken prisoner by the advancing American army on April 13, 1945. His wound had not yet fully healed, but his condition was improving.[24]

By December 1944, it was clear that the Red Army's advance toward the city of Neubrandenburg could not be halted. Frida Bauer recalled thinking to herself, "This is it! Where is God? We could not believe the government any longer. Hitler continued to speak [over the radio] until January 30. He said we were going to win and we were going to have those new ['miracle'] weapons. But we didn't believe him."[25]

In January 1945, Anni Bauer left Stettin to visit her fiancé, Juergen Schulz, in Thorn in West Prussia—close to the advancing Soviets. Her father had warned her against making the trip, but she went nevertheless. Arriving in Thorn just hours after Juergen was moved closer to the front, she had no option but to turn around and head for home. Unfortunately, the chaos of the refugee territory resulted in a three-week journey filled with terror and suffering. Anni had already endured several serious illnesses and surgeries during the previous three years and was no longer physically capable of making a trip of two hundred miles, some of it on foot. In temperatures near zero, with shoes falling apart and with little or nothing to eat, she found that the physical suffering led to emotional suffering: "I reached the point, where I really didn't care, one way or another, whether I would be able to get out or not. I prayed to Heavenly Father to let me die without much suffering. I was very discouraged." At one point in the exodus, she was shoved onto an open railroad car and watched infants die in the bitter cold as the train crept slowly westward. The train was attacked several times by enemy fighter planes and Anni could feel the discouragement growing:

> A change in attitude overcame me—I turned very bitter. For the first time in my life I couldn't pray. I couldn't understand why Heavenly Father could let little, innocent babies and children suffer so much. . . . The exhaustion seemed to have killed everything in us. . . . Maybe my thoughts were so distorted because of cold, lack of sleep, hunger, and pain.[26]

Despite being so weak during the three-week trip that she fell unconscious more than once, Anni also had to endure several attempts by Polish men to assault her. She was successful in fending them off each time. She finally reached Stettin, found another train to Neubrandenburg, and dragged herself from the railroad station to the apartment of her sister, Wanda, who took her in and nursed her back to health. Anni was only nineteen years old at the time.[27]

As the danger of invasion seemed to intensify, the women of the Bauer family made preparations to flee Neubrandenburg. Frida recalled saving the fat from bacon for three months to spread on bread. She also began listening to the news broadcasts of the BBC "because German radio news came a day late and was not reliable. . . . This was really dangerous, and I had the sound really low and put a blanket over my head and the radio so nobody [else] could hear."[28]

Frida's father, Phillip Bauer, managed to return to Neubrandenburg from West Prussia just before Christmas 1944. Over the next three months, the situation became increasingly critical, especially since he not only had two young adult daughters at home but was responsible also for the twelve children of his three married daughters, Emmi, Wanda, and Marthel (all of the grandchildren being under the age of nine). Frida recalled that he went to the forest one day to pray about what to do and came home to announce: "We are getting out of here—quickly!"

On about April 27, 1945, the Bauer family (seventeen persons in all) loaded a small Bollerwagen and headed westward out of town amid throngs of refugees. Everyone was looking to catch a ride on a truck, and the roads were filled with all kinds of vehicles—both civilian and military. By some miracle, a truck offered to take the whole family, with the exception of Frida and her sister, Anni, because they had bicycles. Unfortunately, the girls were strangers to bicycles and found them very difficult to ride. Thus they basically pushed the vehicles down the road, using them at least to transport their meager supplies of food and clothing. They eventually reached Güstrow—about forty-five miles to the west. Luckily for them, the invaders, at the same time, were more interested in moving south toward Berlin.

At the age of ten, Günter Streuling could probably not understand why Nazi Germany was making war on the Jews. However, after one experience at the Neubrandenburg railroad station, he understood that some people were not treated well by the government:

> In early 1945, we were asked to go to the train station to hand out food to refugees. One day I was on the platform, and a cattle train pulled in. I noticed that there was barbed wire over the airhole at the upper right. That looked strange. We heard movement inside, then suddenly faces appeared in the opening. . . . I thought that these people had done something really bad to be in that situation. They held out tin cans and said, "*Wasser, Wasser!*" We could easily reach

the airhole, and we took the tin cans, filled them with water, and carried them back. [The prisoners] spilled most of it in the process. We kept doing that until the SS troops came running and pointed their rifles at us and yelled, "Get out of here!" The last thing I saw was the soldiers pounding their rifles against the sides of the cars, telling [the prisoners] to get away. The train came from the east and was headed west.[29]

Günter Streuling's father was in the Luftwaffe, assigned to a hospital on the island of Sylt (off the west coast of the North Sea, in Schleswig-Holstein near the Danish border). He sent his wife a forged document authorizing her and their son to join him on Sylt. After an adventure-filled week of travel by train, by bicycle, and on foot, Günter and his mother arrived on the island. Although the island was very isolated, they were not free from the sights and sounds of the war. American and British airplanes were constantly flying overhead on their way to targets in Germany and back home. Günter recalled gruesome scenes: "On the way back [to England], the crippled [Allied] aircraft were shot at by our antiaircraft batteries. Several times, we found dead British airmen washing up onto the shore. That was really traumatic for a young [ten-year-old] boy."

By the time Red Army soldiers were approaching Neubrandenburg, Waltraud Meyer was twenty-four years old, unmarried, and back at home in Cammin. The town of one hundred fifty inhabitants had swollen to twice its size as the local residents took in refugees from the east—family, friends, even strangers. When the enemy approached the town, Waltraud went into hiding ("because I expected something terrible to happen") and was for a short time separated from her parents. When she returned, she was greeted with the news that her parents had taken their own lives in their home. This was a horrible experience, as she later explained:

At first, I wanted to go into our house [to see the bodies of my parents], but the neighbors told me not to. I walked back into the village and other people offered to let me stay in their home for the night because they did not want me to be alone. My parents were buried the same night. Following that experience, many others committed suicide also—even families with up to six children. It was a horrible time.

According to Waltraud Meyer, "I have to confess that I did not really have a testimony of the gospel when I was young. I followed my parents, and if they had been Protestant, I would have been the same also. My testimony grew during and after the war." Waltraud escaped harm at the hands of the Soviet occupiers in Cammin and assisted her neighbors where she could. Her brother, Kurt, returned to Cammin in July 1945. He had been told when he arrived in a nearby town that his parents and Waltraud were dead, but fortunately he did not believe the reports and was happy to see his sister still alive. They eventually made their way west to Elmshorn (north of Hamburg) where they were again associated with the Church.

Vera Bamberger and her children were still in Neubrandenburg, along with her mother and her sister, when the Soviets entered the city at the end of April. Overnight, the citizens were ordered to evacuate the town. This was a severe challenge to the women who had no men to support them. Vera recalled the move:

I had a bike with a basket in the front, and my youngest daughter was in her stroller. My mother pushed the stroller, and we loaded as much as we could into the bags that we had on it. We walked to Podewall, near Trollenhagen [three miles north of town] and slept near a forest for one night. My mother was concerned that we would lose all the things that we left behind in our home in Neubrandenburg, so she asked me to go back and get some of the important things, like a coat for my brother. One morning, I went back and got a bed cover for my children so they would not be cold anymore

and a coat for my brother. I stood outside and tried to fasten all the things onto my bike when the shooting began. The house next to us was hit and also the house I was standing in front of. Our windows burst and some splinters hit me. I could not ride my bike out of the city, so I just pushed it. When I was going back to where my family was, I met some [German] soldiers in civilian clothing who gave me a new bike and helped me.

Although hundreds of Latter-day Saint women later told of miraculous escapes from the conquerors, not all were spared the suffering associated with physical assault. Such was the case with Ida Schulz when the hiding place of the Schulz family was discovered by Red Army soldiers. As Vera recalled, "[The soldiers] took my mother away, and she kept her hands tightly around her handbag because she did not want to lose it. It was horrible to see what they did to her. When she came back, she did not talk to anyone for days."

After a few days in the forest by Podewall, Vera and her family returned to their apartment in Neubrandenburg but found enemy soldiers living there. After a few weeks in an army barrack, they were allowed into their apartment again. They were sad to see what had happened in the interim, as Vera explained:

Lots of things were missing. Two things that I was very sad about having lost were the Book of Mormon and the Bible that Elder Kronemann, the missionary who baptized me, had given me for my baptism. The Russians did not even know how to read them, but they must have seen how nice they looked with the gold writing on it, so they took them away.

At one point on their flight westward, Frida and Anni Bauer slept overnight in an inn but learned the next morning that their bicycles had been stolen. After "a good cry," they sat by the road again to hitchhike and were fortunate to have a troop of soldiers take them along. They eventually followed an older soldier toward

Denmark, but they were turned away at the Kaiser Wilhelm Canal and headed south toward Hamburg when they heard that the war was over. They then headed for Saxony to a friend's home but gave up the plan when it became evident that to live in the Soviet Occupation Zone in eastern Germany would not be a good thing. Shortly after the war ended on May 8, 1945, Frida and Anni joined other members of their family in the city of Celle near Hanover. All of her family had survived the war, with the exception of her soldier brother, Otto Bauer, who had been killed in Russia in 1941.

With his "thousand-year Reich" (only twelve years old at the time) crumbling all around, Germany's Führer, Adolf Hitler, committed suicide in his underground bunker in Berlin on April 30, 1945. Günter Streuling recalled that day:

One day the announcement came that the Führer was dead, that he had died when hit by artillery while directing the defense of Berlin. We went to school and sang the national anthem and also "Ich hatt' einen Kameraden" (a favorite song when a soldier died). I remember crying and going home. After the war was over, we found out that it was a lie [and that he had actually killed himself].

Otto Krakow (born 1910) returned from the war in search of his mother in Neubrandenburg. Years later, he told of coming home on crutches, hoping to get his family to safety, and described conditions there: "Just as everything else was in a state of destruction and disorder, so was the Church in Neubrandenburg. The branch no longer existed; no responsible brethren were left."[30]

By late 1945, Walter Rohloff had been moved through several POW camps and finally arrived in Belgium. By early 1946, he applied to work in a coal mine. As an officer, he was not required to do heavy labor but hoped to improve his condition with better food

rations and the minimal wage paid for POW labor. He also learned that year that his mother had survived the war and that his father was a prisoner of the victors. While working in the coal mines at nearly two thousand feet below the surface, Walter was buried alive on two occasions but managed to escape. After several months, he and other German POWs went on strike due to the dangerous work conditions. His reward for the successful strike effort was the transfer to a farm.[31]

During his incarceration in Belgium, Walter was able to spend significant amounts of time studying the Doctrine and Covenants in preparation for serving as a missionary when he returned to Germany. He also found opportunities to discuss religion with military chaplains and other soldiers. His conduct among common Belgians was so correct that some of the locals tried to convince him to remain there and to marry. However, his thoughts were on his mother in Neubrandenburg and his father somewhere in the Soviet Union. Of course, his desire to go home increased over time, and he actually attempted an escape. While crossing a bridge into Germany, he was caught and returned to the POW camp. Following a term of light punishment, he went back to work on the farm.[32]

Looking back on her wartime experiences, Waltraud Meyer came to the following conclusions:

I was protected so well so many times. The Lord had his hand in my life and guided me. . . . There were so many moments when I thought that I could not make it. Other people around me had horrible things happen to them, but I often felt that a protecting hand was over me. I often felt like I should go a different way or another direction. There was no other way than to develop a stronger testimony. . . . I did not have only one angel who protected me, but at least a hundred.

Anni Bauer wrote the following comments regarding her wartime experiences:

> After an inner struggle with myself, I regained my strong testimony of the love of our Heavenly Father. . . . The years of 1944–45 were the most difficult times of my life. But the knowledge of the gospel and the plan of eternal life and salvation truly gave me the strength to keep on going through those trying years.[33]

Juergen Schulz spent a year in Denmark after the war, recovering from serious wounds. Then he traveled to Celle to be reunited with Anni Bauer. They were married there in 1947.

In November 1947, Walter Rohloff was released as a POW in Belgium and made his way home. When he crossed the border into the Soviet Occupation Zone, he found conditions to be dismal and wondered if he should have remained in the American or British Zones. Nevertheless, he was needed by his mother and the Neubrandenburg Branch and made it home in a few days. He surprised his mother with his arrival, as he later wrote: "She looked tired and a little worn out, but when she recognized me, her eyes lit up and she fell into my arms crying. I was a little clumsy. I was not used to taking my mother into my arms. I let her feel I love her and was glad to be home after all." He also surprised her with a substantial supply of things she badly needed, such as shoes, yarn, and sweets.[34]

Seriously weakened by the departure and death of many of its members, the Neubrandenburg Branch barely survived the war. It would be several years before a strong branch would emerge there again.

In Memoriam

The following members of the Neubrandenburg Branch did not survive World War II:

Otto Bauer b. Biskopitz, Thorn, Westpreußen, Preußen 12 May 1918; son of Philipp Bauer and Luise Wilhelmine Kuhn; bp. 16 May 1931; m. Berlin,

Fig. 3. Otto Bauer and Vera Giehr were married in 1941. (A. Bauer Schulz)

Preußen 10 Mar 1941, Vera Gier; d. at WWII action Klin, Kalinin, Russia 15 Dec 1941 (IGI; AF)

Georg Albert Johannes F. Dauss b. Burg Stargard, Mecklenburg-Strelitz 15 Feb 1907; son of Gustav Friedrich Emil T. Dauss and Anna Auguste Luise Utech; bp. 16 May 1928; lance corporal; d. France 4 Sep 1944; bur. Bourdon, France (CHL CR 375 8 #2459, 1405–06; IGI; www.volksbund.de)

Gerhard R. O. Ebert b. Neubrandenburg, Mecklenburg-Strelitz 6 Sep 1910; son of Ernst Emil Reinhold Ebert and Alwine Karoline Wilhelmine Lahde; m.; corporal; k. in battle Karlovy Vary, Czechoslovakia 6 May 1945; bur. Karlovy Vary (CHL CR 375 8 #2460, 514–515; FHL Microfilm 25759, 1925/30/35 Census; www.volksbund.de)

Gustav Adolf Ebert b. Hohenkirch, Briesen, Westpreußen, Preußen 19 Oct 1882; son of Johann Ebert and Auguste Pauline Templin; bp. 8 Feb 1913; conf. 8 Feb 1913; ord. elder; m. 19 Oct 1908, Emma Furth Aksmann; d. 18 May 1941 or 2 Feb 1942 (FHL Microfilm 25759, 1935 Census; CHL LR 6008 21, no. 5; Geschichte der Gemeinde Rostock)

Otto F. W. Ebert b. Neubrandenburg, Mecklenburg-Strelitz 20 May 1912; son of Ernst Emil Reinhold Ebert

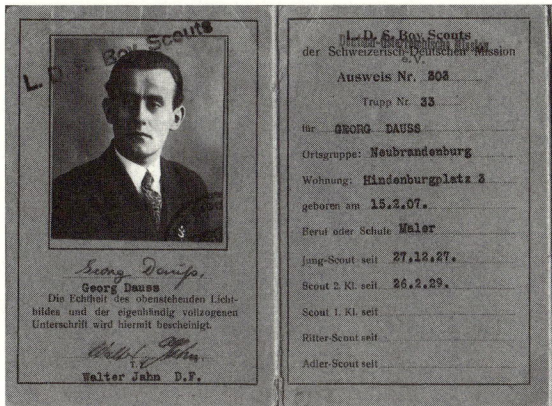

Fig. 4. Georg Dauss was killed in France in 1944. He is shown here as a registered Boy Scout. (W. Leonhardt)

and Alwine Karoline Wilhelmine Lahde; m.; k. in battle Aug 1944 (CHL CR 375 8 #2460, 514–515; FHL Microfilm 25759, 1925/30/35 Census)

Karl Ernst d. 1945 (CHL LR 6008 11)

Heline Luzinde Friederike Bernhardine Farnow b. Neubrandenburg, Mecklenburg-Strelitz 26 Aug 1875; dau. of Fritz Farnow and Auguste Boll; bp. 8 Oct 1919; conf. 8 Oct 1919; d. old age 20 Dec 1941 (CHL LR 6008 21, no. 11)

Gustav Adolf Klappert b. Ferndorf, Westfalen, Preußen 24 Aug 1902; son of August Heinrich Gustav Klappert and Auguste Dickel; bp. 27 Jul 1929; m. Neubrandenburg, Mecklenburg 18 May 1934, Emma Bauer; 6 or 7 children; d. POW Stalinsk, Russia 12 Apr 1946 (W. Rohloff, www.volksbund.de; IGI; AF)

Richard Klappert b. Ferndorf, Westfalen, Preußen 17 Sep 1912; son of August Heinrich Gustav Klappert and Auguste Dickel; k. in battle about 1943 (AF; IGI)

Willi Klappert b. Ferndorf, Westfalen, Preußen 25 Jul 1914; son of August Heinrich Gustav Klappert and Auguste Dickel; bp. 1 Sep 1929; conf. 1 Sep 1929; corporal; k. in battle Jegiorcive, Poland 2 Sep 1939; bur. Mlawka, Poland (CHL LR 6008 21, no. 80; www.volksbund.de; IGI)

Paul Karl Wilhelm Meyer b. Köpenick, Berlin, Brandenburg 12 Dec 1889; son of Karl Wilhelm Meyer and Klara Agnes Krause; bp. 9 Jul 1932; m. Köpenick 5 Dec 1914, Else Albertine Rosalie Utech; 2 children; d. suicide 30 Apr 1945, Cammin, Mecklenburg-Schwerin (IGI; Meyer-Dierking)

Alexander Friedrich Rosenow d. 9 Mar 1943 (CHL LR 6008 11)

Liddi Gertraud Charlotte Schell b. Nordhausen, Sachsen, Preußen 17 Jun 1926; dau. of Karl Franz Schell and Frieda Paulmann; bp. 18 Sep 1937; conf. 18 Sep 1937; k. air raid 4 Apr 1945 (CHL CR 375 8, no. 5; IGI)

Ernst Otto Gottfried Schulz b. Nörnberg, Pommern, Preußen 7 May 1885; son of August Friedrich Hermann Schulz and Auguste Wilhelmine Karoline Bloedow; bp. 27 Jun 1922; conf. 27 Jun 1922; m. Riudorf, Brandenburg, Preußen 23 Nov 1910 or 1911, Ida Wilhelmine Sophie Schmidt; 3 children; d. Accident, Trollenhagen, Neubrandenburg, Mecklenburg 6 Oct 1939 (CHL LR 6008 21, no. 30; Schulze-Bamberger; IGI)

Hans Steudt b. Pasewalk, Brandenburg, Preußen 20 Nov 1913; son of Rudolf Karl Steudt and Anna Wilhelmine Elfriede Johanne Leesch; k. in battle 8 Mar 1945 (CHL CR 375 8 2458, 1474; CHL 2458, Form 42 FP, Pt. 37, 1474–75; IGI)

Rudi K. A. Steudt b. Neubrandenburg, Mecklenburg 16 Mar 1927; son of Rudolf Karl Steudt and Anna Wilhelmine Elfriede Johanne Leesch; bp. 30 Aug 1930; conf. 30 Aug 1930; k. in battle 17 Apr 1942 (CHL LR 6008 21, no. 54; IGI)

Karl Ernst Eduard Toebe b. Lieteldam (?) 17 Feb 1893; ord. priest; ord. elder; m. Else Johanna Bertha Rosenow; 1 child; d. typhus before 1946 (FHL Microfilm 245286, 1925/30/35 Census)

Else Albertine Rosalie Utech b. Grabow, Pommern, Preußen 14 Dec 1891; dau. of Wilhelm Karl Heinrich Utech and Christine Albertine Friedericke Kuehl; bp. 19 Aug 1922; conf. 19 Aug 1922; m. Köpenick, Berlin, Preußen 5 Dec 1914, Paul Karl Wilhelm Meyer; 2 children; d. suicide, 30 Apr 1945, Cammin, Mecklenburg-Schwerin (CHL LR 6008 21, no. 34; Meyer-Dierking; IGI; AF)

Joseph Weigand b. München, Oberbayern, Bayern 15 Feb 1875; son of Karl Weigand and Marie Reiser; bp. 14 Feb 1931; conf. 14 Feb 1931; m. 30 Jan 1906, Anna Lange; d. 3 Jun 1941 (CHL, LR 6008, no. 85)

Notes

1. Presiding Bishopric, "Financial, Statistical, and Historical Reports of Wards, Stakes, and Missions, 1884–1955," CR 4 12, 257.

2. East German Mission Quarterly Reports, 1938, no. 50, East German Mission History.

3. Frida Bauer Kindt, interview by the author, Greendale, Wisconsin, August 19, 2007.

4. East German Mission Quarterly Reports, 1938, no. 46.

5. Ibid., 1939, no. 59.

6. Ibid., no. 52.

7. Rostock Branch, history (unpublished), January 12, 1941; private collection.

8. German public schools were in session every Saturday until noon in those days.

9. Anni Bauer Schulz, autobiography (unpublished), 45; private collection.

10. Waltraud Meyer Dierking, telephone interview with Jennifer Heckmann in German, April 12, 2008; unless otherwise noted, summarized in English by Judith Sartowski.

11. Vera Schulz Bamberger, interview by the author, Neubrandenburg, Germany, June 9, 2007.

12. *Mein Kampf* (*My Struggle*) was written by Adolf Hitler in 1925 and outlined his plans for Germany and Europe. Its length and boring presentation prevented most Germans from reading it. In many ways, however, it proved to be prophetic.

13. Günther Fred Streuling, interview by the author, Provo, Utah, March 26, 2006.

14. Walter Rohloff, autobiography (unpublished), 48; private collection.

15. Ibid., 51.

16. Ibid., 52.

17. Schulz, autobiography, 66.

18. Rohloff, autobiography, 56.

19. Ibid., 57.

20. Ibid., 70.

21. Ibid., 79–81.

22. Ibid., 83–84.

23. Ibid., 92.

24. Ibid., 97–99.

25. The promised weapons were the so-called *Vergeltungswaffen* (weapons of vengeance) such as the V2 missile and jet-engine aircraft. Both types existed at the time, but production never fulfilled Hitler's expectations.

26. Schulz, autobiography, 86–87.

27. Ibid., 87–88.

28. Listening to enemy radio broadcasts was illegal in Germany during the war. Several British broadcasts in German could be picked up on radios all over Germany.

29. During the final months of the war, concentration camp guards were ordered to transport camp inmates away from the advancing Allied armies. The train Günter saw apparently came from a camp in Poland and was headed west.

30. Otto Krakow, "Twenty-Five Years a Branch President in Neubrandenburg," in *Behind the Iron Curtain: Recollections of Latter-day Saints in Germany*, ed. Garold N. Davis and Norma S. Davis (Provo, UT: Brigham Young University, 2000), 101.

31. Rohloff autobiography, 109.

32. Ibid., 110–11.

33. Schulz, autobiography, 88.

34. Rohloff, autobiography, 118.

ROSTOCK BRANCH

The port city of Rostock is situated near the mouth of the Warnow River, just five miles south of the Baltic Sea. The Lower Warnow River links Rostock to the town of Warnemünde on the coast. Just prior to World War II, Rostock had about seventy-five thousand inhabitants and was home to a small LDS branch of sixty-eight members.

Rostock Branch[1]	1939
Elders	4
Priests	2
Teachers	2
Deacons	3
Other Adult Males	10
Adult Females	44
Male Children	1
Female Children	2
Total	68

At the end of 1938, the branch was holding meetings in rented rooms at August Brackmann Strasse 23 on the second floor. From available mission records, it appears the meetings continued there through much of the war, but there were significant interruptions. For example, Hans-Jurgen Schlüter later recalled attending meetings in the home of the Stöckigt family in the last months of the war.[2]

A detailed history of the Rostock Branch has survived and provides insight into the lives of the Latter-day Saints living there during the years 1939–45.[3] The following entries are representative of activities and events in the branch:

> June 5, 1939: Branch president [Walter] Ruthenberg was activated by the Wehrmacht for special training.

September 3, 1939: Our meeting rooms were occupied as public air-raid shelters.

October 30, 1939: District president Walter Czerny visited us.

January 14, 1940: Brother Rudolf A. Noss [of Rostock] was called to be the district president.

March 17, 1940: Our meeting rooms were made available to us again.

May 22, 1940: We acquired a new pump organ.

September 15, 1940: Relief Society meets from 9:30 to 10:15 and sacrament meeting from 10:15 to 11:00. Rudolf A. Noss was released as district president.

November 10, 1940: Relief Society begins at 3 P.M. and sacrament meeting follows directly.

March 23, 1941: The work of the Relief Society has been suspended temporarily by district president Arno Dzierzon.

April 13, 1941: Beginning today, sacrament meeting will be held biweekly.

May 15, 1941: Brother Gustav A. Ebert of Neubrandenburg, Dümperstrasse 12, is called to be the president of the Rostock District.

May 17, 1941: Sister Elisabeth Keil died and was taken to Plauen/Voigtland [Saxony] for burial.

May 25, 1941: Beginning today, Sunday School will begin at 10 A.M. and sacrament meeting at 3 P.M.

July 6, 1941: Beginning today, sacrament meeting will begin at 5 P.M.

August 17, 1941: Ten people attended Sunday School today. Only the branch leaders attended sacrament meeting.

November 2, 1941: Brother [Richard] Ranglack, counselor to the mission leader, visited us today. Brother Walter Ruthenberg was released as branch president due to his call to the army. Brother Richard Stöckigt is called as the temporary branch president.

January 18, 1942: The Relief Society begins holding meetings again today; the time will be 4–5 P.M.

15 February 1942: It was announced in sacrament meeting that the Rostock District has been annexed to the Stettin District.

February 22, 1942: In order to help district president [Erich] Berndt of Stettin, Brother [Bruno] Rohloff of Neubrandenburg has been assigned as a traveling elder to visit our branch.

March 15, 1942: Mission leader H[erbert] Klopfer visited us. Beginning today, sacrament meeting will begin at 3 P.M. and will be followed by Relief Society.

March 29, 1942: Brother Paul Langheinrich, [second] counselor to the mission leader, visited us.

May 3, 1942: Our meeting rooms were confiscated to be made available to people who have been bombed out or burned out of their homes.

June 30, 1942: Our meeting rooms were restored to us again.

October 25, 1942: Brother Joseph Kaiser, a deacon from the Schneidemühl Branch, visited us. He is in the army.

March 2, 1944: Brother Albert Zajek died in Fingerao (N.A.).[4]

District conferences were a favorite experience of Latter-day Saints in Germany during the war and most were held on a regular basis through 1944. Rostock Branch members attended district conferences in Neubrandenburg (May 1940), Demmin (October 1940 and September 1941), at home (March 1941), and in Stettin (September 1942).

It is clear from the history that a branch as small as Rostock appreciated visits from members of other branches. The names of many visiting members—not just district and mission leaders—appear throughout the pages dated 1939–43.

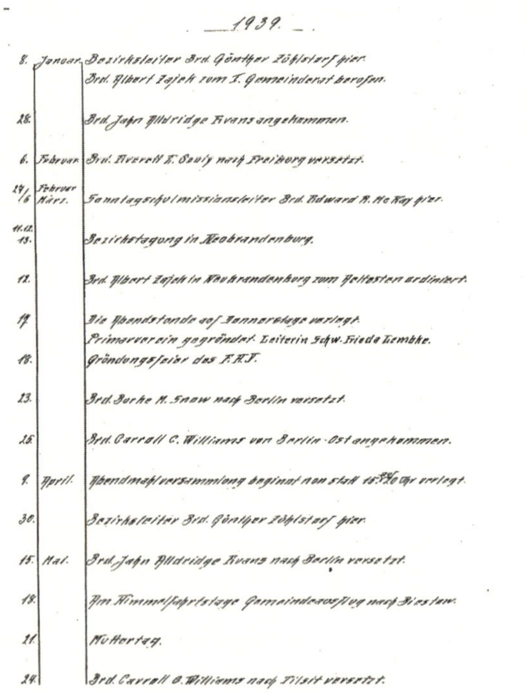

1939.

8.	Januar	Bezirksleiter Brd. Günther Zöllsdorf hier.
		Brd. Albert Zajeh zum I. Gemeinderat berufen.
28.		Brd. John Alldridge Evans angekommen.
6.	Februar	Brd. Everett E. Sauly nach Freiberg versetzt.
27/6	Februar März.	Sonntagschulmissionsleiter Brd. Edward R. McKay hier.
11.u. 13.		Bezirkstagung in Neubrandenburg.
12.		Brd. Albert Zajeh in Neubrandenburg zum Ältesten ordiniert.
17		Die Abendstunde auf Donnerstage verlegt.
		Primarverein gegründet. Leiterin Schw. Frieda Lembke.
18.		Gründungsfeier des F.H.V.
23.		Brd. Burke H. Snow nach Berlin versetzt.
26.		Brd. Carroll C. Williams von Berlin-Ost angekommen.
9.	April.	Abendmahlversammlung beginnt nun statt 15 [illegible] Uhr verlegt.
30.		Bezirksleiter Brd. Günther Zöllsdorf hier.
15.	Mai.	Brd. John Alldridge Evans nach Berlin versetzt.
18.		Am Himmelfahrtstage Gemeindeausflug nach Biestow.
21.		Muttertag.
24.		Brd. Carroll C. Williams nach Tilsit versetzt.

Fig. 1. A page from the detailed history of the Rostock Branch. (B. Ruthenberg)

After losing and regaining their meeting rooms several times, the Saints of the Rostock Branch lost the rooms at August Brackmann Strasse 23 for good on April 21, 1943, when Allied bombers reduced the building to rubble. The final entry of the Rostock Branch history is dated March 2, 1944. The author of this fine record is not identified.

Bodo Ruthenberg (born 1939) recalled that his father, Walter Ruthenberg, was a saddler in the army, and was determined not to have to shoot at the enemy. After serving in France, he was transferred to Norway. He learned to ski there and became very fond of that country.[5]

Bodo's mother, Erika Ruthenberg, had three little children to worry about when the bombs began to fall on Rostock. In April 1945, the area around her home at Kossfelderstrasse 6 was attacked by the Royal Air Force. According to Bodo's recollections:

> My mother tried to take furniture out of the apartment. She left some downstairs because she wanted to get more, but when she came back, everything had been taken by other people. We all just got out of the apartment and the basement when the house collapsed behind us—still burning. My mother carried me out holding me in her arms. We lost everything we had.

Erika Ruthenberg took her children and left Rostock, hoping to escape the immediate dangers of war. In the recollection of her son, Bodo, she was fairly successful in finding better living conditions:

> Later, we were evacuated to Steinhagen near Rostock in the countryside. It was a very refreshing experience. We lived in an empty farm house because the owner had fled. It was very idyllic, and we forgot that there was a war going on—no sounds of planes or bombs. But then the Russians came and jumped over the fence and broke it. I, as a little boy, went to them and told them that [their behavior] was absolutely not acceptable and that I didn't like what they just did.

Bodo's scolding of the enemy soldiers did not make him unpopular. They took him for rides in their vehicles, gave him some small food items, and in general treated him very kindly.

Walter Ruthenberg was captured toward the end of the war but was fortunate to be released in 1946. When he returned to Rostock, he found a new apartment for his family on Margarithenstrasse. According to Bodo, "We lived [there] many years . . . the bathroom was in the basement and only the third floor of the building was warmer." Nevertheless, the family was together again and in good health.

In Memoriam

The following members of the Rostock Branch did not survive World War II:

Clara Anna Wilhelmine Boeck b. Rostock, Mecklenburg-Schwerin 18 Oct 1893; dau. of Emma Boeck; bp. 15 Aug 1925; conf. 16 Aug 1925; m. 22 Dec 1922, Willi Fritz Karl Heinrich Hermann Moll; d. of effects of incarceration Neubrandenburg Prison 25 Apr 1946 (CHL, LR 7647 21, no. 57; IGI)

Anna Dorathea Sophia Boek b. Rostock; Mecklenburg-Schwerin 12 Apr 1875; dau. of Wilhelm Boek and Marie Meyer; bp. 24 Apr 1926; conf. 24 Apr 1926; m. 11 Oct 1931, Wilhelm Brandt; d. 4 Dec 1941 (CHL, LR 7647 21, no. 50; IGI)

Anna Elisabeth Feustel b. Ostritz, Bautzen, Sachsen 5 May 1892; dau. of Heinrich Wilhelm Feustel and Ida Conradi; bp. 8 May 1926; conf. 8 May 1926; m. Triebes, Reuss j.L. 8 Jul 1911, Max Friedrich Hugo Keil; 1 child; d. cancer, Rostock, Mecklenburg 17 May 1941 (Geschichte der Gemeinde Rostock; FHL Microfilm 271377, 1935 Census; CHL, LR 7647 21, no. 88; IGI; AF)

Hildegard Magdalene Johanna Guethner b. Rostock, Mecklenburg-Schwerin 23 Aug 1884; dau. of Hermann Guethner and Ida Friebe or Triepe; bp. 23 Aug 1923; conf. 23 Aug 1923; m. 16 May 1908, Robert Sievert; d. heart attack 17 May 1944 (CHL, LR 7647 21, no. 24)

Herta Ida Just b. Schneidemühl, Posen, Preußen 13 Jul 1922; dau. of Heinrich Christoph Just and Bertha Freek; bp. 13 Jul 1936; conf. 13 Jul 1936; d. heart ailment 18 Aug 1944 (CHL, LR 7647 21, no. 147)

Ferdinand Friedrich Max Louis Lembke b. Gross-Klein, Warnemünde, Mecklenburg-Schwerin 6 Aug 1886; son of Carl Christian Friedrich Lembke and Elise Sophie Johanna Friederike Randow; bp. 11 Jul 1919; conf. 11 Jul 1919; ord. deacon 7 Oct 1919; ord. teacher 16 Sep 1920; ord. priest 16 May 1921; ord. elder 25 Jul 1926; m. 14 Jul 1913, Frieda F. E. Kreuzmann; d. illness 28 May 1944 (CHL, LR 7647 21, no. 5; IGI)

Frieda Rudolphine Sophie Pagel b. Malchow, Mecklenburg-Schwerin 17 Feb 1898; dau. of Ludwig Pagel and Caroline Priegnitz; bp. 23 Apr 1920; conf. 23 Apr 1920; missing (CHL, LR 7647 21, no. 58)

Hans Otto Hubert Eugen Sauer b. Chemnitz, Chemnitz, Sachsen 23 Mar 1913; son of Hubert Robert Gustav Sauer and Margarete Wilhelmine Marie Bornhagen; bp. 16 Jul 1921; conf. 16 Jul 1921; m.; engineer; k. in battle, Italy, 2 Sep 1943; bur. Futa-Pass, Italy (CHL, LR 7647 21, no. 93; www.volksbund.de; IGI)

Albert Otto Anton Zajek b. London, London, England 13 May 1911 or 1913; son of Otto Zajek and Anna Maria Johanna Ziems; bp. 17 May 1931; conf. 17 May 1931; ord. deacon 13 Oct 1932; ord. teacher 14 Aug 1933; ord. priest 19 Apr 1936; ord. elder 12 Apr 1939; m. Rostock, Mecklenburg, Preußen 12 Jun 1936, Amalie Margarate Sophie Petersen; d. asthma, 2 Mar 1944 (CHL, LR 7647 21, no. 71; IGI)

NOTES

1. Presiding Bishopric, "Financial, Statistical, and Historical Reports of Wards, Stakes, and Missions, 1884–1955," CR 4 12, 257.
2. Hans-Jürgen Schlüter, and Ursula Höhle Schlüter, "The Way Things Were," in *Behind the Iron Curtain: Recollections of Latter-day Saints in Germany*, ed. Garold N. Davis and Norma S. Davis (Provo, UT: Brigham Young University Press, 2000), 247.
3. The Church of Jesus Christ of Latter-day Saints, *Geschichte der Gemeinde Rostock,* [1893–1944] (Rostock, Germany); trans. the author.
4. The meaning of "N.A." is unclear but is apparently a reference to a province or a country.
5. Bodo Ruthenberg, interview by the author in German, Rostock, Germany, June 10, 2007; summarized into English by Judith Sartowski.

WOLGAST GROUP

Too few in number to be accorded the status of a branch, the Latter-day Saints living in the town of Wolgast on the Baltic Sea in 1939 were far from any city with a branch. Sixty miles east of Rostock, Wolgast was a fishing village. Church meetings there were held at Langestrasse 17 on the main floor.

One eyewitness of the Wolgast group has left a detailed autobiography that offers very candid observations. Gerd Skibbe (born 1930) was just the right age to be exploited for political purposes by the National Socialists. In school and in the Jungvolk, he was harangued by leaders who exalted Germany over every other country and war over peace. As he later confessed in his book *Schritte durch zwei Diktaturen* (Traversing Two Dictatorships):

> I was too young to be a Nazi, but I was headed in that direction. My schoolbooks made it seem that a good German boy loved the swastika flag. That was clear to me by then anyway. My parents noticed all too late that I was being swept along by the spirit of the times. . . . I developed a National Socialist consciousness

and grew to be a gullible Hitler Youth who was thrilled by every new special announcement in the radio: Germany has won another battle! . . . *Deutschland, Deutschland über alles!*[1]

Gerd's parents, Wilhelm and Julianne Skibbe, were devoted members of the Church who were not attracted by Hitler's programs. Brother Skibbe tried to help Gerd understand what was most important in life, but the nationalistic allure of the times was very strong. As Gerd later wrote, "It made me angry when [my father] said that Germany would lose the war because its aims were evil."[2]

At some point, apparently close to the time (September 1938) that the group was known to have been meeting at Langestrasse 17, the Skibbe family moved to that street. According to Gerd, only one meeting on an evening during the week was being held from 1943 to the end of the war. Gerd recalled seeing missionaries for the last time in 1941, namely Arno Dzierzon and Rudolph Wächtler.[3]

Wolgast was not a target for Allied aircraft until the last few months of the war. When the first air raid came and bombs fell, Gerd's attitude about war changed a bit. "They were attacking me!" he realized. However, he did not understand what war was really about until the day when he and other Hitler Youth were ordered to report to the railroad station to help the Red Cross sisters with the occupants of a hospital train. Suddenly, war was no longer glamorous but bitterly serious. When the door opened, "the first thing that hit me was the terrible stench." Dead bodies and suffering soldiers crying for help robbed young Gerd of a bit of his nationalistic spirit. "Their sufferings seemed to be very much my own."[4]

On April 22, 1945, Gerd (barely fifteen years old) was drafted into the Volkssturm. With the Soviet invaders only a few miles to the east and approaching fast, this call could have been a death sentence, but his mother

intervened. Wilhelm Skibbe had been in uniform for several years already and was still far away, so Julianne Skibbe was in no mood to let her son be killed. She made it very clear to the local military authorities with one word that her son was not available for service: "Nein!"[5]

All through the war, Gerd had shown much more interest in the military and other worldly matters than in the Church. Even his father's serious Bible study and family prayers failed to impress and attract the young German patriot. However, the message of the gospel must have been sinking in to a small degree, as he learned during the last month of the conflict. He caught his mother listening to the forbidden BBC radio broadcast and instinctively began to yell at her. A crisis of conscience was tearing him apart, as he later wrote:

> I was incensed and wanted to do my duty as a loyal German boy, to turn her in. There was so much conflict within me. There had to be a punishment for this deed. Thank heavens my better side prevailed at the moment. The words "Don't do it!" rang in my mind. I was shocked at my own reaction and could do nothing more than slam the door and run away.[6]

On the last day of April 1945, the Wolgast police fled the town. With the Red Army still a few miles away, the town became a moral and military no man's land. Recent bombings had shattered shop windows, and suddenly civilians emerged and began looting on a grand scale. Gerd was in the main business street at the time and readily joined in the free-for-all. Again, he heard the voice saying, "Don't do it!" but this time he disregarded the advice. He stole some candy and took it home. Returning to the main street for another run at looting, he suddenly realized how wrong it was when he saw his little brother, Helmut, rolling a large cheese wheel toward him. "That's theft!" he yelled. When he considered the matter of his double standard, he decided, "I knew exactly what I was going to do from then on."[7]

Another important lesson was learned when Gerd confronted a Soviet soldier for the first time. Nothing the man did confirmed the terrible rumors spread by German radio about the beastly enemies. Of course, in the days after the Soviet takeover of the town, crimes were committed against the citizenry, but Gerd learned that it was not the uniform that made the man. Some enemy soldiers did indeed enter the Skibbe home and steal things, but others came to play their piano, behaved themselves quite correctly, and left without harming persons or property.

A few days after the war ended, Gerd and his friends swam to a deserted island where they found a huge supply of rifles and ammunition. As foolish teenage boys are wont to do, they fired several rounds into the sky, only to determine that the ammunition consisted of warning flares in various colors. One such flare flew close to a Soviet observation plane, and within minutes, the boys were surrounded by very angry and heavily armed soldiers. Wearing only swimming suits, the boys seemed rather harmless after all and were fortunate to talk their way out of trouble.

By the late summer of 1945, Sister Skibbe was hosting Church meetings in her home on evenings during the week. Refugees from eastern German provinces were some of the attendees. Whereas Gerd remembered only one or two attendees as the war drew to a close, the Church appeared to be on its way now to a healthier condition in the town of Wolgast.

IN MEMORIAM

Only one member of the Wolgast group did not survive World War II:

Gerhard Alfred Weigand b. Stettin, Stettin, Pommern 19 Jul 1913; son of Philipp Weigand and Meta Katilius; bp. 31 Jul 1923; conf. 31 Jul 1923; ord. deacon 2 Feb 1930; missing as of 20 Oct 1948 (CHL, LR 10261 22, no. 15)

NOTES

1. The German national anthem, the title of which means "Germany, Germany over/above all." Gerd Skibbe, *Schritte durch zwei Diktaturen* (Friedrichsdorf, Germany: LDS Service, 2004), 11, 13, 14.
2. Ibid., 15.
3. Ibid., 12, 15.
4. Ibid., 18.
5. Ibid., 18.
6. Ibid., 19.
7. Ibid., 22–23.

Fig. 1. These B-17F bombers used radar to attack targets in Germany in 1943. (U.S. Air Force Photograph 060517-F-1234S-004)

SCHNEIDEMÜHL
DISTRICT
East German Mission

The six branches of the Schneidemühl District formed essentially a line along the Berlin-Danzig railroad. The distance from Landsberg on the Warthe River in the southwest to Flatow in the northeast is only about sixty miles.

Between those two towns were four other towns with branches of The Church of Jesus Christ of Latter-day Saints: Driesen, Kreuz, Schönlanke, and Schneidemühl.

Schneidemühl District[1]	1939	1940	1941	1942
Elders	21	21		
Priests	8	11		
Teachers	13	15		
Deacons	18	18		
Other Adult Males	53	52		
Adult Females	134	138		
Male Children	19	17		
Female Children	11	10		
Total	277	282	272	269

In June 1937, Johannes Kindt (born 1897) of Schneidemühl was set apart as district president by mission president Roy A. Welker and in the presence of Elder Joseph Fielding Smith. President Kindt faithfully carried out the duties of this office until the end of the war. A photograph printed in *Der Stern* just prior to the war shows Brother Kindt with the six branch

Fig. 1. *The Schneidemühl District in 1939.*

presidents (one of whom was an American missionary at the time).[2]

When the war began, there were just enough elders in the district to direct the programs of the Church. In fact, Johannes Kindt selected his counselors from among the serving branch presidents, asking them to continue as the leaders of the branches. His first presidency consisted of Fritz Birth of Schneidemühl (a brother-in-law) as first counselor, Arnold Schmidt, branch president in Kreuz, as second counselor, and Wilhelm Jonischuss, branch president in Schneidemühl, as secretary.

Mission records indicate that a conference was held in the Schneidemühl District every six months until at least the fall of 1944. Because the Red Army had already conquered the region by April 1945, no spring conference was held that year.

Johannes Kindt and Frieda Fritz Kindt were the parents of four when she died from complications of surgery on August 7, 1939—just three weeks before World War II began. In order to sustain his family and maintain his high level of Church service, he married again on January 15, 1940. His second wife was Maria Bernau, only twenty-six years of age but mature in the gospel and dedicated to service in the family and in the Church.[3]

Fig. 2. Johannes Kindt (third from right) with the presidents of the branches of the Schneidemühl District (Der Stern, 1938)

President Kindt was employed at an army post in Schneidemühl and was therefore fortunate to live at home. According to

Fig. 3. Johannes Kindt married Maria Bernau on January 15, 1940. (W. Kindt)

Fig. 4. Survivors of the branches of the Schneidemühl District gathered for this photograph during a district conference in Dresden in July 1946. (W. Kindt)

his autobiography, he advanced to a "position of trust" and was thus a favorite of his commander, who then prevented any active duty call for him. In fact, when another officer tried to have Johannes assigned to active duty, the commander blocked the order twice. Eventually, however, the fact that he was not a member of the Nazi Party put an end to Johannes's favored status. On September 23, 1943, a third draft order came which could not be avoided.[4] Brother Kindt retained his Church calling for the duration of the war.

By the spring of 1944, Johannes had made two military journeys of four weeks' duration each. The first took him through Poland, Austria, and Yugoslavia to Serbia. "Following many losses and adventures," he later wrote, he was transferred back to Schneidemühl.

In March 1944, he was pleased to have both soldier sons at home for three full weeks—Hans from the Eastern Front and Walter from France. He was also back at work with all possible energy, visiting the branches in the district. "Little by little, I was dedicating more time and effort to my Church calling than to my personal affairs," he wrote.[5]

In August 1944, President Kindt was sent to the town of Schönau near Neustettin in Pomerania, where he was assigned as a guard at a POW camp. During the autumn, he was given leave for a month and was visited by his wife on two weekends. By January, his guard duty assignment was moved to Deutsch Krone, just fifteen miles from home.

During the war, the Flatow Branch was discontinued. President Kindt did not explain this development in his autobiography, but the lack of priesthood leadership was likely the cause. By the end of the war, the following men were serving the five remaining branches as presidents: Wilhelm Jonischuss (Schneidemühl), Karl Beyer (Schönlanke), Arnold Schmidt (Kreuz), Walter Jeske (Driesen), and Fritz Fleischhauer (Landsberg).[6]

As guards, Johannes Kindt and his comrades moved their prisoners ever westward, trying to avoid the advancing Red Army. By the end of April 1945, the American army (advancing from the west) found them and disarmed the German soldiers, who a few days later were turned over to the Soviets. Then as prisoners they began their journey eastward, nearly to East Prussia. Because he was seriously ill most of the way, Brother Kindt was put in the worst physical condition category and was released early. In his recollection, there was a routine in the life of the POWs: "On even days we pealed [sic] potatoes, on odd days we were deloused."[7]

On September 9, 1945, Brother Kindt and other prisoners who were unfit for hard labor were set free. "They gave us food for about ten days, lectured us one last time, then threatened to lock us back up again if they could still see us fifteen minutes later." The 380 men hurried westward. Ten days later, Johannes Kindt located his wife and their children in an apartment in Tremsbüttel near Hamburg. As it turned out, the other family members had already reached the west in safety. Within days, the children from his first wife visited him in Tremsbüttel.[8]

Because the entire territory of the Schneidemühl District was ceded to Poland following World War II, no German members of the Church living in that region were allowed to stay. The branches of the Schneidemühl District ceased to exist by the fall of 1946.

NOTES

1. Presiding Bishopric, "Financial, Statistical, and Historical Reports of Wards, Stakes, and Missions, 1884–1955," CR 4 12, 257.
2. Johannes Kindt, *My Book of Remembrance: My Life, Works, and Mission in the Family and the Church* (unpublished autobiography, 1948); private collection.
3. Ibid., 23.
4. Ibid., 28.
5. Ibid., 30.
6. Ibid., 35.
7. Ibid., 37.
8. Ibid., 38.

DRIESEN BRANCH

The town of Driesen is located about fifty miles southwest of Schneidemühl on the main railroad route from the latter to Berlin. During the generation between the world wars, the town was just a few miles from the Polish border. In 1939, Driesen (now Dresanus, Poland) had about seven thousand inhabitants.

Driesen Branch[1]	1939
Elders	5
Priests	2
Teachers	2
Deacons	4
Other Adult Males	9
Adult Females	27
Male Children	11
Female Children	3
Total	63

Before and throughout the war, the president of the Driesen Branch was Walter Jeske. The meetings were held in rented rooms on the main floor of the building at Kietzerstrasse 30. His daughter, Ilse (born 1921), later wrote about the meetings held there: "The branch observed the usual meeting schedule, with Sunday School in the morning and sacrament meeting

Fig. 1. Members of the Driesen Branch gathered for this photograph in 1942. (R. Sward)

in the evening. Priesthood meeting took place on Monday evening, MIA on Tuesday evening, Primary on Thursday afternoon, and Relief Society on Thursday evening."[2]

Walter Jeske's son, Siegfried (born 1924), was inducted into the Wehrmacht just after finishing his apprenticeship as a machinist. He had already fallen in love with a pretty girl from the Schneidemühl Branch. The distance between the two towns did not allow frequent meetings, as he later wrote:

> We had our district conference two times a year, and we had to travel to the town [Schneidemühl] where my [future] wife lived. It was there that we got to know each other. Our courting was somewhat different because we lived 75 [kilometers] from each other, and the only transportation we had was either a bicycle or the train. . . . We had to resort to letter writing only because telephones were only for rich people.[3]

President Jeske was called into military service soon after the war began. Due to the small number of priesthood holders in the branch, he authorized his daughter, Ilse, to write the reports and to send the tithing donations to the mission home in Berlin. Even after he returned in late 1940, Ilse continued to write the reports. She was later called to be the second counselor in the Relief Society while retaining all current callings.

As a soldier in the German army in September 1942, Siegfried Jeske went through basic training in nearby Poznan, Poland (previously Posen in Prussia). For the following six months, he had additional training in the Netherlands, Belgium, and France (near Bordeaux). Then he was shipped to Belgrade, Yugoslavia, where, he said, "We were actively involved in tracking down Tito, the leader of the guerilla movement." Such warfare usually involved women and even children, and Siegfried was soon put in a position that contradicted the standards taught to him in his family and in church. He described the potential crisis in these words:

> One of the men in our company claimed to have seen the women wave to their men on top of another mountain; and as a result of that, I was asked by my commanding officer, to whom I was an aid [sic], to shoot all of the women and children. Having been a member of the Church and taught all my life not to kill, I had to ask if it was an order or merely a suggestion that I do that. He in turn asked me if I did not want to, and I answered him, "No, I [have] no desire to do so." Well, all of the women and children did get killed by other men of the company. I realized that I could have been court-martialed for what I had done; but as a result of that, the commanding officer and I became very close friends. He found out that I was a member of the L.D.S. Church, which was not known too well in Germany. He treated me like a king after this incident.

As an infantry soldier, Siegfried did a lot of marching. After the war, he marked the routes he had walked and calculated more than three thousand miles on foot. In the spring of 1944, he was transferred to the northern sector of the Eastern Front. Soon after arriving there, he was surprised to be granted leave to go home. During his absence, his unit was involved in fierce combat that cost the lives of most of the men. He concluded, "Here again the Lord had known of this battle and the easy way to protect me from getting killed was to send me home."

Ilse Jeske married Gerhard Pagel, a Luftwaffe airman, on December 15, 1943. After a short leave, he returned to his station in the Soviet Union. They did not see each other again for nearly six years.

Siegfried Jeske's younger brother, Gerhard (born 1927), served in the German army for only the last few months of the war. On November 22, 1943, the Jeske family was temporarily in Berlin, where they experienced the same air raid that destroyed the mission home. It is interesting to note Gerhard's com-

ments about the property they lost when fire destroyed their apartment:

> I had done some genealogical research on my mother's line. . . . I went to some of the parishes about 100 miles east of Berlin, where my ancestors had lived, and I found many names of my people for whom I wanted to have the temple work done. This valuable information was also lost in the fire, which I regret to this day. . . . If I could have only saved those records. They were more important than anything else I possessed.[4]

In late 1944, Gerhard was drafted into the army and served seven months before being taken prisoner. Later, he wrote about ten specific occasions when he could have lost his life. Most of those were situations in which disaster struck the place he had been just hours before or involved soldiers who replaced him.

As a soldier on the Eastern Front, Gerhard took the opportunity to tell a close army buddy about the Church. Reinhard Schibblack was a typical German soldier who enjoyed cigarettes and alcohol, but he listened to Gerhard's description of the Word of Wisdom. The two also prayed together—a common practice among soldiers facing death. According to Reinhard, Gerhard "never officially instructed me, but we

Figs. 2 & 3. The wedding picture of Ilse Jeske and Gerhard Pagel. Gerhard's Russian captors destroyed his image in the copy he carried with him but allowed him to keep his bride's picture. She kept the original (left). (R. Sward)

often talked about God and the plans God has for us." Just before the war ended, the two were separated, and each became a POW.[5]

In June 1944, Siegfried Jeske was wounded, and in October he was sent to a hospital in Schneidemühl for treatment. Finally, he had a chance to spend a lot of time with his fiancée (they had become engaged in May). He later wrote, "I now had the opportunity to get to know her better and found out that I really loved her." In December, he was sent to a camp south of Munich in Bavaria.

In February 1945, Siegfried Jeske was sent to Königsberg, East Prussia, where the Red Army was advancing into Germany. "We had very little chance to get back to Germany without being captured by the Russians." His fear was justified, because as he was traveling a few weeks later, he heard the voices of Soviet soldiers. Under heavy artillery fire, he had not noticed them approaching from behind. The first thing he saw was their bayonets pointing at him. He was captured and imprisoned.

Conditions in the Soviet POW camps were terrible, according to Siegfried:

> Many of the prisoners died there. We got little or no food. Every day early in the morning a detail of prisoners was assigned to haul out a handcart full of dead prisoners, sometimes twice a day, and we all wondered when our time would come to die. We were glad when we were split up and sent off to other camps. . . . Many times we were kept at work for 24 hours, but we did not mind because many of the prisoners were sent to Siberia to work in the Russian salt mines in which many more prisoners died.

When the invaders approached Driesen in March 1945, Walter Jeske instructed his daughter, Ilse, to claim that her younger brother, Hartmut (born 1937), was her son so that the Soviets would not molest her. They walked for ten miles with a handcart over ice-covered roads to a larger town and managed to board a train. Walter did not go with the family

but returned to Driesen. With her mother and siblings, Ilse arrived in Holstein (northeastern Germany) after a week on the train. They managed to find a place to live with a kind family of farmers and were there when the war ended. They were far from home and miserable. As she later recalled,

> By that time, no one of us cared whether we were dead or alive. No family, no home. The big boys, Sig [Siegfried] and Rudy, still in Russia— Jerry [husband Gerhard Pagel] in Russia and my father was not with us either. Nothing to eat and we could not buy anything either.

Young Hartmut Jeske later recalled the evacuation of his family from Driesen:

> We were told the Russians were moving into Germany, and those who didn't want to be under Russian occupation [must leave]; there was one train going west, and we needed to be on it. So mother and my older sister Ilse and my brother Manfred, we got on that train. [We took] just a little wicker basket full of clothes is all. [But] most of the time, it was a horse-drawn carriage from town to town, and the women and small children were on the wagon, and the rest of them walked. Being young enough, I ended up on the wagon. I didn't have to walk.[6]

Hartmut recalled these impressions of Itzehoe, Schleswig-Holstein, his family's new home:

> One unfortunate thing was that, in Itzehoe, we lived across the street from a high school, which they had turned into a hospital for those German soldiers, and every once in a while, they would bring one in on a flatbed truck, haul him in, and fix him up. I saw some of those soldiers pretty banged up. But that's as close as I got to the [horrors of] war.

From Itzehoe it was only ten miles to Glückstadt, where the Jeske family established connections with a branch of Latter-day Saints.

For the first two years as a POW, Siegfried Jeske was allowed to write a card home with a maximum of twenty-five words. He said, "We had to be very selective with our words." Not

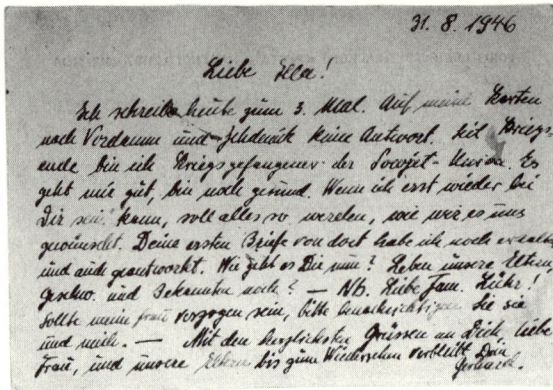

Fig. 4. This letter was written by Gerhard Pagel to his wife Ilse from a Russian POW camp in 1946. "Are our parents still alive? Our siblings? Our friends?" (R. Sward)

knowing where his parents were, he wrote to the mission home in Berlin, and his letters were forwarded to his parents and his fiancée.

Gerhard Jeske was also miserable as a POW in the Soviet Union, where he spent three and one-half years—"six times as long as my life in the army. . . . It seemed like an eternity to me." Regarding his state of mind during the incarceration, he later stated, "My faith in the gospel of Jesus Christ gave me great strength during the years in the Russian prison camps, and this was what sustained me, as well as the observance of the Word of Wisdom."

Gerhard Pagel wrote the following to his wife, Ilse, from a POW camp in the Soviet Union on February 26, 1947:

> Dear Wife,
> The monthly writing day has again arrived. I haven't received a message from you since October [19]46. My memories about you awake thoughts of the surroundings. That these have changed completely. In the case of my return, I hope to see you again healthy, and wish that our new secure home will meet our needs in every respect. How do you find your new surroundings? Many of my comrades here are from there. Things are bearable here. But there is a lot to wish for, especially a return home and freedom. Then it is my mission to pursue and make up for our happiness in Glückstadt. Please greet the parents and the boys. With heartfelt greeting to you, I am your Gerhard.[7]

On March 1, 1949, Siegfried was surprised to be released and sent home. For two days, he rode a freight train to Germany and was set free just inside West Germany, because his parents had settled there after fleeing Driesen. His fiancée was still in East Germany but was soon allowed to join him in the West. They were married on August 20, 1949.

Reinhard Schibblack returned to Berlin in June 1949 and was fortunate to find his friend, Gerhard Jeske, who immediately took him to church. Reinhard was readily accepted by the members of the Church in East Berlin and was baptized soon thereafter.[8]

Gerhard Pagel was released in the Soviet Union in October 1949 and joined his wife, Ilse, in Schleswig-Holstein.

Branch president Walter Jeske finally left Driesen in early 1947. He may have been the last member of the Church in the town. All members of the branch were expelled from the area by the new Polish government, and the branch ceased to exist.

No members of the Driesen Branch are known to have died during World War II.

Notes

1. Presiding Bishopric, "Financial, Statistical, and Historical Reports of Wards, Stakes, and Missions, 1884–1955," CR 4 12, 257.

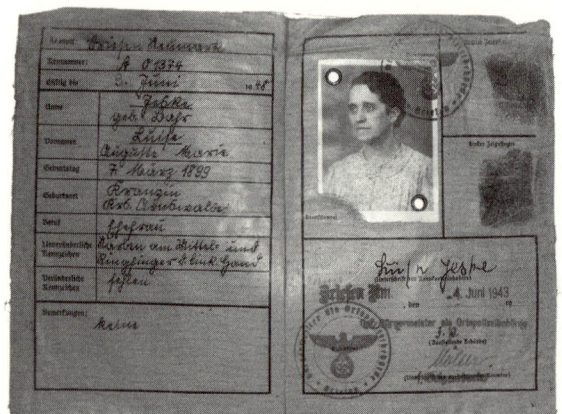

Fig. 5. This is the standard personal identification document issued to German citizens. Luise Jeske was a member of the Driesen Branch. (H. Jeske)

2.   Ilse Jeske Pagel, fireside address (unpublished); private collection.

3.   Siegfried L. Jeske, fireside address (unpublished); private collection.

4.   Gerhard Jeske, autobiography, 1979, MS 17127; Church History Library.

5.   *Church News*, August 1, 1970, 14.

6.   Hartmut Jeske, interview by Michael Corley, Ogden, Utah, March 7, 2008.

7.   Gerhard Pagel to Ilse Pagel, February 26, 1947; private collection.

8.   Reinhard Schibblack, autobiography (unpublished); private collection.

FLATOW
BRANCH

At the far northeast corner of the district, Flatow was a town of about five thousand when World War II approached. Just eighteen miles from Schneidemühl in the former Prussian province of West Prussia, it was also just eight miles from the Polish border. The modern name is Złotow, Poland.

Flatow Branch[1]	1939
Elders	1
Priests	0
Teachers	1
Deacons	0
Other Adult Males	3
Adult Females	4
Male Children	0
Female Children	1
Total	10

As of this writing, no eyewitnesses or writings of eyewitnesses have been located. There is no mention of the Flatow Branch in the history of the East German Mission for the years 1938 and 1939. With only ten members, this was the smallest official branch of The Church of Jesus Christ of Latter-day Saints in all of Germany in 1939.

Given the small number of priesthood holders in Flatow, it is very likely that District President Johannes Kindt visited the branch on numerous occasions (his home being only twenty minutes distant by train) or that he sent his counselors to assist on Sundays and other occasions. His records showed that the Flatow Branch became defunct during the war.

No members of the Flatow Branch are known to have lost their lives in World War II.

NOTE

1.   Presiding Bishopric, "Financial, Statistical, and Historical Reports of Wards, Stakes, and Missions, 1884–1955," CR 4 12, 257.

KREUZ
BRANCH

Often referred to as "Kreuz an der Ostbahn," the town of Kreuz in Pomerania was located on the north bank of the Netze River (the border of Germany and Poland) between the world wars. The Ostbahn was the main railway line running from Berlin east through Schneidemühl and the so-called Polish Corridor to the Free City of Danzig.

Kreuz Branch[1]	1939
Elders	2
Priests	0
Teachers	2
Deacons	2
Other Adult Males	4
Adult Females	19
Male Children	3
Female Children	0
Total	32

The Kreuz Branch had only thirty-two members when war began on September 1, 1939. The branch president at the time was

Arnold Schmidt, who served in that calling throughout the war.

The East German Mission history shows this entry for Monday, November 21, 1938:

> From this day until December 15th, all meetings were forbidden in the Schönlanke and Kreuz Branches, Schneidemühl District. This measure was taken on account of a foot and mouth epidemic which prevailed in this section of Germany.[2]

The largest family in the Kreuz Branch was that of Gustav and Emilie Mudrow. With ten children, the family constituted fully one-third of the branch. Sister Mudrow was awarded the Mutterkreuz (Mother's Cross) of the Nazi Party for having so many children.[3]

Son Helmut Mudrow (born 1925) described in detail the rooms rented by the branch at Hindenburgstrasse 2:

> It was a former apartment. There were two rooms in the apartment where a wall was taken out, and the big room was used for sacrament meetings and other meetings. And we had four classrooms. We had a primary class, a kindergarten class, and an art class. The art class was for teenagers. The kindergarten class was for children until about six. And then the primary class was from six until twelve. Those over twelve were in the youth class. There was only one main floor. We had a little show window on the street with a sign. The sign was about two by one foot with the name *Kirche Jesu Christi der Heiligen der Letzten Tage*.[4]

On Sunday mornings, priesthood meeting took place at 9:00 A.M. and was followed by a prayer meeting and Sunday School. Sacrament meeting was held in the evening.

To Helmut Mudrow, being a Latter-day Saint had its advantages:

> When we had the religion classes [in school], the woman [who] was teaching it knew that I knew more about the Bible than any of the other students, because I went to church and we learned that. I didn't have any problems whatsoever. Everybody knew that I was a Mormon.

Fig. 1. *The Mudrow Family in 1931. Eight of the ten children had war-related occupations or assignments. The entire family survived the war. (H. Mudrow)*

At age ten, Helmut was inducted into the Jungvolk with his classmates and at age fourteen made the transition to the Hitler Youth in 1939—the year World War II started. The activities took place on Wednesdays and Saturdays and did not interfere with church attendance. Helmut was large for his age and became a Hitler Youth leader. Some of the activities included schooling in political subjects.

Because they were living right on the German-Polish border, the members of the Kreuz Branch were aware of some of the conflicts that preceded the outbreak of the war. They knew of troubles between Polish citizens and ethnic Germans just across the river in Poland. There was apparently a very intense anti-German atmosphere in Poland.[5]

Helmut also recalled an incident that occurred in 1937 involving American missionaries: "Starting in 1935, the Germans were building some fortifications, some bunkers, and some fox holes along the border, about a half mile away from the border on a little hill there." A missionary named Walton disregarded the sign that read, "Sicherheitszone: Photographieren verboten!" ("Secure Area: No Photography!") and took pictures. When Elder Walton's pictures were developed in the local drugstore, the owner reported him to the Gestapo and he was arrested. While he was

Fig. 2. Members of the Kreuz Branch in 1938. (H. Mudrow)

interrogated in Schneidemühl for three days, his companion, George Larkin, stayed in the apartment in Kreuz. Elder Walton was released without harm, but the missionaries were required to leave Kreuz.

In the week before the invasion of Poland, large numbers of German troops moved into and around Kreuz in anticipation of the attack. By September 21, 1939, the Polish campaign was over and the Wehrmacht was victorious. For several years after the campaign, Kreuz was far from any action connected with the war.

Branch resident Arnoldt Schmidt had married Gertrud Blechschmidt of the Meerane Branch (Zwickau District) in 1934. She became a devoted member of the Kreuz Branch and had served already as the Relief Society president of the Schneidemühl District. In 1941, she was a Red Cross nurse and became seriously ill. As she later wrote:

I really fought for my very life. One time I clearly remember kneeling in my bed and praying to my Heavenly Father to spare my life, because I wanted to be with the Saints during the

gathering of Israel. I received the blessings of the priesthood, and I began to improve. For the doctor it was a great miracle since he thought that I would never live through an illness of this nature.[6]

In April 1942, Helmut Mudrow was completing his apprenticeship with the national railroad system. As a large young man, he was often asked why he had not yet joined the army. Finally, he decided to do so and got his father's permission. As a volunteer, he had a choice of assignments and requested flight training. The recruitment officer responded, "Everyone wants to be a pilot. What about the paratroops?" "That's fine! Sign me up!" Half of the volunteers were rejected, but Helmut was accepted. His jump training took place near Berlin, where representatives of the Axis nations watched with interest.

Helmut's first jump was done from 3,300 feet. He later recalled the experience:

That was really enjoyable except getting out, jumping out of the airplane there. But then once we get out there, hanging there, and you can see all the landscape there and coming down. The

Fig. 3. Kreuz Branch members digging for potatoes in 1940. (H. Mudrow)

sun was shining. I remember coming down and just went to my knees. . . . Hooked it on, and nothing happened at the end.

The paratroops were some of Hitler's favorites, and were thus constantly being observed, paraded, and filmed. Nevertheless, life for those who jumped from planes was not always romantic. For example, during one training jump (Helmut made nineteen jumps in all), the wind kicked up when he landed, and his parachute dragged him a half-mile across the ground before he could get to his feet.

Helmut's tour of duty took him to Africa, Italy, and Malta. When the German army retreated at El Alamein, Egypt, Helmut and thirty comrades wandered in the desert for ten days. At one point, they drank water from the radiators of abandoned vehicles in order to stay alive. By the time they were rescued, only five of them had survived.

In the desert climate, Helmut became seriously ill and lost one-third of his weight. This earned him sick leave, and he was sent to southern Germany to recuperate. In 1943, he went home on furlough. By then, most of his siblings were in the service of the Reich and were away from home. While at home, he was ordained a priest by branch president Arnold Schmidt with the approval of district president Johannes Kindt.

Back in action, Helmut was in Italy while the Americans were advancing northward up the peninsula toward Rome. Without jumping from an airplane, he fought at Monte Casino and Anzio. He was wounded by shrapnel five times, but never critically. In 1944, he was sent to France and stationed where German military leaders expected the Allied invasion to take place. When their calculations proved wrong, the paratroops were moved to Caen on the Normandy coast. However, it was too late for Helmut and his comrades to stop the American advance into France, and they were moved away from the combat zone again.

Helmut Mudrow may have seen action at more locations of the war than any other German LDS soldier. From the Normandy region, he was moved north and fought the Allied invaders in the Netherlands as part of the Allied Market-Garden operation of September 1944. He also participated in the Battle of the Bulge in December 1944 and January 1945.

Helmut's parents fled Kreuz on January 26, 1945, as the Soviet invaders approached. It is very likely that the remainder of the Saints in Kreuz left at the same time. Over the next three years, the Mudrow family members established contact with each other through various communications media. All twelve of them survived the war.

Gertrud and Arnold Schmidt also departed Kreuz in January 1945 as the Saints continued to abandon that city. The last branch activity

Fig. 4. Paratrooper Helmut Mudrow (second from left) received another medal in 1944. (H. Mudrow)

was a large party held in the Schmidt home. Gertrud's account reads thus:

> In honor of our 10th wedding anniversary we invited the entire branch membership and announced it as our "Adventsfeier" which means the "advent of Christmas." At the time nobody was thinking that this might be our last home gathering.[7]

The Schmidts then prepared to join the exodus from Kreuz. Gertrud later wrote,

> The rolling thunder of the battle front in the east was coming closer to our small town. . . . We visited the members of the branch for one last time to see if any help was needed. Many of the families had already left their homes. Early in the morning of that day, Arnold had said to me, "Gertrud, an inner voice tells me we should go now." . . . We loaded a small hand cart with some suitcases filled with clothing and church records of the Schneidemühl District, and before we left our so dearly beloved home we kneeled in prayer and thanked the Lord for so many blessings and for the comfortable home we had had, and asked Him for His protection and guidance.[8]

No trains were available to take the Schmidts west. Arnold Schmidt had a weak heart, and the journey on foot was very difficult for him. Fortunately, a ride on a wagon was possible at times. They arrived in Landsberg on the Warthe River that Saturday and were taken in by the branch Relief Society president. The next day, they attended a testimony meeting there. Gertrud Schmidt recalled, "The meeting was so inspiring and heart-warming, there among friends during such a difficult time; many tears were shed by all." The next morning, the word went out that the Soviets were very close to Landsberg. When the Schmidts left the city in the opposite direction, they took nothing along but the church records.[9]

The Schmidts were in a hurry to get to the home of Gertrud's parents in Meerane, but they made a detour and delivered the church records to the mission leaders in Berlin. Then they headed south without further delay. By February 1, they reached their destination, having been on the road for eight days and covering about 275 miles.[10]

By April 1945, Helmut Mudrow's unit had moved farther east into the Reich. One day he told his men that the war was essentially over and that they might want to consider discarding their uniforms in order to get home without being taken prisoner. He and several comrades then dressed as civilians and traveled through Germany, bypassing American army checkpoints as they went. They were stopped once but talked their way through and kept walking. Along the way, Helmut found work with a farmer and stayed on the farm for three years, waiting for the confusion of postwar Germany to subside.

In 1948, Helmut Mudrow left the farm to begin a new life. As a paratrooper, he had experienced the war on three different fronts, had earned the Iron Cross First Class, and was wounded five times. For a time, he had carried the Book of Mormon but never served with another Latter-day Saint soldier and never attended church except when on leave in Kreuz.

By 1946, at the latest, there were no Latter-day Saints left in Kreuz, and the branch ceased to exist. The name of the town was soon changed to Krzyż Wielkopolski, Poland.

IN MEMORIAM:

Only one member of the Kreuz Branch did not survive World War II:

Kurt Herbert Erwin Vielstich b. Kreuz, Pommern, Preußen 1 Oct 1915; son of Karl Friedrich Vielstich and Frieda Margarete Hildegard Quolke; bp. 5 Apr 1927; lance corporal; d. Braye, Chemin-des-Dames, France 5 Jun 1940; bur. Fort-de-Malmaison, France (H. Mudrow; www.volksbund.de; IGI ; PRF)

NOTES

1. Presiding Bishopric, "Financial, Statistical, and Historical Reports of Wards, Stakes, and Missions, 1884–1955," CR 4 12, 257.

2. East German Mission Quarterly Reports, 1938, no. 47, East German Mission History.

3. The Mutterkreuz was awarded in three degrees: for five, seven, and nine or more children.

4. Helmut Mudrow, interview by the author, Ogden, Utah, May 25, 2006.

5. See the story told by Rudi Seehagen in the chapter on the Spandau Branch, Berlin District.

6. Gertrud Schmidt, autobiography (unpublished), 14.

7. Ibid., 14.

8. Ibid., 14–15.

9. Ibid., 16.

10. Ibid., 16.

LANDSBERG BRANCH

Landsberg was a small branch at the western end of the elongated territory of the Schneidemühl District. The city was located on the Warthe River in the province of Brandenburg and had about forty-five thousand residents when World War II began. The modern name is Gorzów Wielkopolski, Poland.

Landsberg Branch[1]	1939
Elders	3
Priests	2
Teachers	3
Deacons	3
Other Adult Males	25
Adult Females	36
Male Children	1
Female Children	2
Total	75

In 1939, the Landsberg Branch held its meetings in rented rooms at Schiessgraben 1. Elsa Klein (born 1932) offered this description of the facility:

I always thought that the building in which we met was absolutely ugly and dark. On the first floor was an animal breeder. He was the only other person who used that building. The rooms were simple. . . . I know that we had a separate room for the Primary.[2]

Elsa's brother, Werner (born 1929), also recalled the setting:

It was a big warehouse building or a factory. We had a large room on the second floor. Attendance was twenty or thirty people on Sunday. Our branch president was Friedrich Fleischhauer and the Relief Society president was Sister Hintze.[3]

The family of Emil and Emma Klein was very attached to the Church and the branch. Werner recalled his mother singing Church hymns while cleaning the house. She also wrote little plays for the branch members to perform. Werner's brother, Horst, learned how to play the pump organ.[4]

At the onset of the war, Emil Klein was inducted into the city police force. He was a veteran of the Great War and was pressed into service to replace a policeman sent to Poland in the German invasion. Later, Brother Klein was drafted into the German army and was gone from home for the duration of the war. Initially, he was assigned to guard duty at a POW camp in northern Germany, and then the family lost contact with him.

Emil Klein was not at home when his daughter, Elsa, was baptized. The ceremony took place in the Warthe River in late March. As she explained, "We were a very active and busy branch in Landsberg. When somebody was baptized, we made a big event of it." On Elsa's baptismal day, "the entire branch was there," but no talks were given at the site. "I had only one thought: 'Heavenly Father, please help me so that my shirt is not above the water.' I knew that all of me had to be under the water."

In Elsa's school (as in all German schools), the day began with the singing of the national anthem.[5] She found it difficult to hold her right arm in the air in the Hitler salute for the duration of the song, so she switched to her left arm. This mistake earned her punishment from her music teacher. She recalled, "I was often punished for things that I did not do, because I was too shy to defend myself."

By 1943, the Landsberg Branch had moved to a new location at Schlageterstrasse 17. The space was smaller, as Werner later recollected:

> It was close to the marketplace. It was in a Hinterhaus. There we had a little room where we had to go up a very steep staircase. . . . We had a room where all of us met together. . . . It was like a business building but it was empty. . . . There was a little sign on the building by the street with the name of the Church on it.[6]

Elsa Klein was barely ten years old when she learned how a humanitarian act could be dangerous in Nazi Germany. Forced laborers from France used to pass her garden on their way to work in a local factory. Once she picked a handful of berries and reached through the fence to give them to the French laborers. A neighbor saw her and reported the family to the police, who sent Sister Klein an official warning. Elsa said, "I remember my mother telling me angrily that I was not to do that again or we would be dead. I could not understand why I was not allowed to do that since it was a nice thing to do."

Christmas 1944 should have been a time of rejoicing, but the spirit of the season was sobered by the news brought to Emma Klein by a neighbor who was a member of the Nazi Party. Emma's son, Horst, had been killed in the Soviet Union. Werner recalled being told that Horst "was shot in the abdomen and probably bled to death."[7]

Elsa remembered hearing the news of her brother's death. "I screamed, and my parents hid me. . . . My grandmother passed out when she heard the news. My mother did not say anything at all; she was very brave."

The war had no substantial effect on the town of Landsberg until the last. In early 1945, Werner (then fifteen) volunteered for service in the Red Cross and received some training. He was immediately put to work and learned about the results of war in a dramatic fashion:

> My job then was to meet the trains bringing wounded German soldiers from the Russian front and then transport the wounded to our army hospitals. These men were in horrible condition. The air was filled with the odor of blood, pus, dead flesh, and gangrene. There were young men with both legs amputated who screamed in pain when we moved them onto stretchers. It was difficult for a young boy such as I not to vomit or pass out from smelling the odors and seeing the condition of these men.[8]

As the Red Army approached Landsberg in the early spring of 1945, air raids began to leave their mark on the city. Several homes in the Klein family's neighborhood were destroyed. The Soviets (actually Mongolians) did in Landsberg what they had done elsewhere—they stole, vandalized, and molested women young and old. Werner was only sixteen years old but seemed to understand the terrible experience feared by women all over town—including his mother and his twelve-year-old sister. His fears were nearly realized on one occasion when an enemy soldier entered their apartment:

> He walked into the bedroom and motioned for Elsa to come in. . . . He put his rifle down. . . . My mother and I watched in horror, not knowing what to do. I could see and hear my mother praying with terror in her eyes. I concluded that I would grab the soldier's gun and shoot him. No matter what, I would not stay there and let him rape my little sister. Some kind of miracle took place. The man picked up his gun and left the house without saying a word. We felt that, once again, we had been protected by a higher power.[9]

Branch president Fleischhauer's shoe shop was burned down by the conquerors, and there was an explosion (probably of chemicals) while the shop burned. The family's house went up in flames as well, while Werner watched from his home down the street. "We never knew what happened to him and his family," Werner wrote years later.[10]

Sister Klein kept a constant vigil against marauding soldiers. She made her own hair white, and she had her daughter carry a doll so she would appear very young. They were always cautious and agreed upon specific hiding places. One night, a Russian soldier came into the room where Elsa was hiding. She recalled the situation later with great clarity: "He used a lighter to look all over the room to see if anybody was there. I was pressed against the wall, and I could see my own shadow, but he never saw me. He looked through the room three times while I was praying."

In the spring of 1945, peace was just weeks away; Werner Klein may have believed that, as a teenager, he was safe in Landsberg. However, one day everything changed, and he found himself being held prisoner along with other boys and girls his age. The Soviets rounded them up and imprisoned them under horrible conditions for several days while interrogations and beatings took place. (Werner was spared.) Next, they were sent home—not as free people, but in order to get clothing to take along, as they would soon be forced to leave their homes. Saying good-bye to his mother was very painful for Werner.[11]

Werner and the other youths were then transported by truck to various working sites. At one point, all personal property was taken from the prisoners and burned, but somehow Werner was allowed to keep a few items—his belt and his photographs being the most valuable. In the days to come, he was subjected to terrible food, his head was shaved, and he was deloused. This was a most difficult state of affairs for the young man. As he later explained,

> There was never a moment when I was alone; always I was surrounded by other prisoners and the guards. For prayer, I could only lie in bed and say to the Lord what was in my heart. Even when going about following orders, there was in my heart a prayer for protection and wisdom.[12]

For the next few days, the young people worked in a stone quarry and helped dismantle railroad tracks to be shipped to the Soviet Union.[13] A few days later, Werner and a friend named Günther were out in a field planting potatoes and decided to escape. Soon they were able to carry out the escape plan, running away while guards wildly shot at them. They were then on their own and determined to make their way home to Landsberg. The prison camp was in Schwiebus, about forty miles southeast of their hometown. The two boys traveled by night to avoid enemy soldiers. They passed abandoned, destroyed towns and the bodies of soldiers long since dead. At one point they were captured and put to work on a farm. Nevertheless, Werner was not satisfied being a prisoner, and the boys engineered another escape.[14]

Werner's accomplice was eighteen but a boy of little imagination and motivation. He allowed Werner to make essentially all decisions. The final decision led to their separation. Because the Warthe River was too wide to swim across, the boys had to cross a bridge guarded by enemy soldiers. Early in the morning, the soldiers were asleep, and Werner knew it was time to sneak across the bridge. Günther

Fig. 1. Werner Klein was only fifteen when he joined the Red Cross. (W. Klein)

wished only to sleep and refused to go along. With time being of the essence, Werner was compelled to go on alone, but he was too late. The bridge was guarded again. Fortunately, he found a rickety old boat and managed to paddle across the river. He never saw Günther again and was sad that their separation had come that way. Nevertheless, for the young adventurer, this was a moment of jubilation:

> Now I was exultant. I was on the right side of the river to reach Landsberg. After all I had been through, I thought that nothing could stop me from reaching my goal. My thoughts were of my mother and sister. . . . I was daydreaming like this when I was brought back to reality by the sound of a gunshot.[15]

Red Army soldiers had seen him, and they brought him back to the east bank of the Warthe, but they decided that he was harmless and let him go. As his odyssey continued, Werner again attempted to cross a bridge but was captured by Polish militia. "We Germans feared the Polish more than the Russians," he wrote. In an odd twist of fate, they released him when they learned that he had escaped from the Soviet prison camp in Schwiebus.

At this time, shortly before the war ended, Emma Klein must have thought that things could not get worse. One son was dead, and her husband and her two other sons were missing. Only her daughter, Elsa, was still with her. Werner recalled:

> What my mother went through, losing her sons and losing me when I was taken away, then receiving the note that my father was killed and me getting sick [later] with tuberculosis in a hospital. I never heard her mourn or complain or doubt—never![16]

Werner continued toward Landsberg and managed to reach home just days before the war ended on May 8. The reunion with his mother and his sister was glorious, and they immediately knelt in prayer to thank the Lord for bringing him home. For several days, his mother treated his feet that had been damaged by long walks without shoes and in new but ill-fitting tennis shoes.[17]

Werner was home again, but in his words, "The peace that followed was worse than the war." Landsberg was in territory given to Poland by the victorious Allies. During the summer of 1945, the Kleins were evicted. As Werner wrote:

> Polish soldiers came into our house and ordered us to leave. We had fifteen minutes to pack a few things into three suitcases, which we put in a small hand wagon. All poor people like us were forced to get out of the Mark Brandenburg country. We left behind what we could not carry. . . . It was summer; the sun beat down on us and water was scarce. It was a heart-breaking thing to see the human tragedy—homeless people moving along with what strength they had, tired and weak from the heat and starvation.[18]

The Kleins accompanied other refugees westward toward Berlin and found a place to stay and work on a farm near the town of Gransee. This lasted all summer, until their Soviet employers released them for lack of work. They walked to the nearby town of Königstett, where they again found employment and a place to live. The two jobs Werner had there were bizarre: he worked first as the local grave-digger, then with some other boys destroying ammunition at a defunct munitions factory in the forest. He later explained the danger: "There were a lot of unexploded mines lying around everywhere—in the grass, in the sand, and between the trees. We had to watch every step we took. One wrong step meant a serious injury or even death."[19]

The most terrifying experience Elsa Klein had in the year after the war was one that no girl could forget. The terror came not from an enemy soldier, but from a German farmer as Elsa was on a country road one evening, looking for her mother. The farmer pulled up beside her with his team. She recounted the event in these words:

> There was snow on the ground, and it was cold. He told me to get on his wagon, and being young, I got on. He stopped at the side of the road and [we got off.] He attempted to rape me and told me that if I screamed, he would kill me right away. He then said that he would kill me anyway. I didn't even have an elastic band on my pants but only leather which he could not untie. He got angrier and angrier. When I started screaming for help, he started to choke me. I begged him to stop and told him that even the Russians hadn't gotten that far with me. The moment I said a prayer in my heart, I heard the horses starting to pull the wagon away. He let go of me and ran after the horses. He told me that he would get me.

Fortunately, Elsa ran to a cemetery to hide and was discovered there by her mother and Werner. Because of the terror she had experienced, she could not speak for some time.

By the time spring 1947 had arrived, the Kleins had been without contact with the Church for two years. Sister Klein longed for that association and wrote a letter to the LDS branch in Cottbus, Germany, near the Polish border. She was then invited to go to Cottbus. With this development, the story had a relatively happy ending. Emma Klein took Elsa and Werner south to Cottbus. They made their way to the home of Fritz Lehnig, where a veritable Latter-day Saint refugee colony had been established. There Emma found her husband, Emil, who had been taken prisoner on the Western Front and released in 1945 by his American captors. With a heavy beard, he was hardly recognizable but alive and well.[20]

Their son Siegfried Klein was never found. Werner explained years later that his brother was drafted in late 1944 and was involved in the final, hopeless effort to stop the Soviet advance on Berlin. Siegfried was probably killed in or near the city of Küstrin, between Landsberg and the Reich capital. No official word was ever received.

The Kleins were probably the last Latter-day Saints to leave Landsberg. With their departure, the branch ceased to exist.

In Memoriam

The following members of the Landsberg Branch did not survive World War II:

Heinz Siegfried Klein b. Memel, Ostpreußen, Preußen 1936 OR 4 Sep 1927; son of Emil Max Klein and Emma Helene Teichert; bp. 21 Sep 1935; MIA or d. Sep 1949 (Klein; AF; IGI)

Horst Helmut Klein b. Memel, Ostpreußen, Preußen 1924 OR 27 Jul 1923; son of Emil Max Klein and Emma Helene Teichert; bp. 25 Jun 1932; corporal; k. in battle, Ljubimowka, southwest of Tschunaki, Ukraine 24 Dec 1943; bur. Dmitrijewka, Nikopol, Ukraine (Klein, 13; www.volksbund.de; AF; IGI)

Emma Emilie Piska b. Krumthis, Deutsch Krone, Westpreußen, Preußen 3 or 5 Nov 1880; bp. 22 Jul 1924; m. Leo Julius Krueger; 4 children; d. Landsberg, Pommern 29 Mar 1940 (*Sonntagsstern*, no. 17, 26 May 1940 n. p.; FHL Microfilm 271381, 1935 Census)

Kurt Ludwig Stubbe b. Kreuz, Posen, Preußen 5 Nov 1909; son of Ludwig Carl Stubbe and Emma Louise Auguste Kemnitz; bp. 2 Apr 1926; ord. deacon; corporal; d. wounds in Res. Field Hospital IV Lemberg Bergsanatorium, Ukraine 21 Sep 1942 (*Sonntagsgruss*, no. 1, 3 Jan 1943, 4; www.volksbund.de; FHL Microfilm 245277, 1935 Census)

Notes

1. Presiding Bishopric, "Financial, Statistical, and Historical Reports of Wards, Stakes, and Missions, 1884–1955," CR 4 12, 257.
2. Elsa Klein Tietjen, interview by the author in German, Amtsberg, Germany, May 30, 2007; summarized in English by Judith Sartowski.
3. Werner Klein, interview by the author, Salt Lake City, March 23, 2007.
4. Werner Klein and Joy Robinson, *Under the Eye of the Shepherd* (Springville, UT: Cedar Fort, 2006), 6.
5. In some schools, the national anthem ("Deutschland über Alles") was followed by the Horst Wessel song—the anthem of the Nazi Party.
6. Klein, interview.
7. Klein and Robinson, *Under the Eye*, 13.
8. Ibid., 14.
9. Ibid., 20.
10. Ibid., 18.

11. Ibid., 30.
12. Ibid., 33.
13. For several years following the war, the Soviets also dismantled machinery in their military occupation zone and shipped it to Russia to replace what they had lost at the hands of the Germans.
14. Klein and Robinson, 45.
15. Ibid., 47.
16. Klein, interview.
17. Klein and Robinson, 52.
18. Ibid., 56.
19. Ibid., 64.
20. Ibid., 69.

SCHNEIDEMÜHL BRANCH

The city of Schneidemühl was not located in the center of the district of the same name, but at the end of 1939 there were substantially more priesthood holders in that branch than in any other. Perhaps that was the reason for the selection of Schneidemühl as the home of the district. During the war, the branch president was Wilhelm Jonischuss, and his counselors were Richard Rieve and Friedrich Wolff.[1]

This branch was a fine example of the role played by larger families in smaller branches. Fritz Birth had eleven children and Johannes Kindt had seven (from two wives—his first wife had died). Together the two families made up almost one-quarter of the branch population.

Schneidemühl Branch[2]	1939
Elders	7
Priests	3
Teachers	4
Deacons	3
Other Adult Males	12
Adult Females	44
Male Children	3
Female Children	6
Total	82

For the duration of World War II, the Schneidemühl Branch met in rented rooms on Gartenstrasse. The address was house 31, in the main floor of the first Hinterhaus.

Hans Kindt (born 1922), the eldest child of district president Johannes Kindt, recalled that the branch rooms in the Hinterhaus included a main meeting hall, three or four small classrooms, a cloakroom, and restrooms. He remembered that the phrase "The Glory of God is Intelligence" was painted on the wall at the front of the chapel. There was a pump organ, and the rooms were heated by a stove.[3]

Ruth Gärtner (born 1923) recalled that a picture of the prophet Joseph Smith hung on one of the walls. Her family's Church attendance was stellar, thanks to the character of her mother, a "very dedicated member of the Church":

> We had to be [in church] rain, snow, or ice. We walked an hour to church for Sunday School and went back home. Then at 7:00 was the sacrament meeting, and then we walked another hour, and by 9:00 we were back home. So we walked four hours on Sundays.[4]

President Johannes Kindt was not a follower of Adolf Hitler and encouraged his sons to avoid involvement with the Hitler Youth.[5] According to Hans, "He told me to say that we didn't have the money to pay for the uniforms. So [the leaders] gave me the uniform and then I didn't have an excuse. I liked it at first because I liked the competition of sports."

Hans's younger brother, Walter (born 1923), planned to be a surveyor and needed to be in the organization or he risked losing his apprenticeship. Walter was a talented young man and eventually became the leader of a group of 350 boys. On one occasion, a friend wondered why Walter did not attend Hitler Youth activities on Sundays, so on the next Sunday, all 350 boys came to the Kindt home to pick Walter

Fig. 1. Mission supervisor Herbert Klopfer came from Berlin in about 1940 to visit the Saints in Schneidemühl. (W. Kindt)

up. He went with them, but he was still able to attend Sunday School promptly at 10:00 that morning. "Already, in my early life, I worked with the principle of faith."[6]

The first meeting on Sundays was for the teachers and began at 9:00 A.M., followed by Sunday School. Sacrament meeting was held in the late afternoon. The Kindt family lived at Bölkestrasse 6, about fifteen minutes from church, and had plenty of time to go home between meetings for Sunday dinner. Most parents did not bring their little children to sacrament meetings in those days due to the lateness of the hour, but the children had already partaken of the sacrament during Sunday School.[7]

Walter was the Sunday School secretary in 1939. He recalled recording an average attendance of 110 persons. Although this number exceeded the total population of the branch at the time, it is quite credible. All over Germany,

it was the practice of the Saints to invite friends to Sunday School, especially children.

Hans Kindt was inducted into the Reichsarbeitsdienst while doing an apprenticeship in tailoring. For the next nine months he practiced his craft while attached to a quartermaster unit behind the lines in Lithuania and Russia. Upon returning home, he worked only one month in a tailor shop before his draft notice arrived in December 1941. While in basic training in Thorn, West Prussia, he was one of twenty men tested as possible radio men. He was musically inclined and thus quickly learned Morse code, winning the job.

Ruth Gärtner was doing an apprenticeship as a seamstress when she was called into the Reichsarbeitsdienst in 1940. She spent the first six months working on a farm with other girls as replacements for the young men who had been drafted. The next six months saw her in Berlin, where she helped run the

Fig. 2. The city of Schneidemühl in about 1940. (W. Kindt)

S-bahn commuter trains through town. Air raids were already plaguing the city, and riding the S-bahn at night was a bit risky. She later recalled a humorous incident that took place while the air-raid sirens were blaring:

> One night I was still in the shower [when the alarm sounded], and a girl [air raid warden] had to go around and see if everyone was out of the rooms, and she said, "Is somebody still in the shower?" I said, "Yes, I am!" and she said, "Come out!" and she grabbed me by my hand, and she didn't allow me to go back and get my clothes. I was just wrapped in a towel, and the bombs were falling. And we ran and had to go over a big yard into the bunker; I was sitting all night in that towel wrapped around me, that's all I had on.

Friedrich "Fritz" Birth and his wife, Emma, already had eleven children when World War II began. The family had two sources of income—Fritz's glass shop in town and Emma's small grocery store in a side room of the family home in a suburb of Schneidemühl. The children were instrumental in the operations of both businesses.

When the American missionaries were evacuated from Germany in August 1939, a vacuum was created that could only be filled by German Latter-day Saints. In 1941, the Births' daughter, Edith Gerda (born 1921), was called to serve as a full-time missionary in the mission office in Berlin. "My heart stood still. Why me? . . . I was nervous. . . . And I needed greater faith." She served honorably until November 3, 1943—just three weeks before the mission office was destroyed.[8]

At age seventeen, Walter Kindt began serving his country. He first spent three months in the Reichsarbeitsdienst, helping to build a dam near Pogegen, East Prussia. From there, he was fortunate to attend church in both Tilsit and Königsberg. At one point during this term of service, Walter Kindt and his elder

Fig. 3. Walter Kindt (front right) with his Hitler Youth group. (W. Kindt)

brother Hans were both home on leave and went to church on Sunday, June 22, 1941. That morning, the German army attacked the Soviet Union. Upset by this violation of the Ten Commandments, Walter predicted to his brother that Germany could not win the war because the invasion had begun on the Sabbath Day.

While still in the Reichsarbeitsdienst, Walter volunteered for military service and by doing so secured a much better wage. He spent seven months in basic training in Pasewalk near Stettin. While he was home on leave toward the end of his basic training, his unit was transferred to the Soviet Union, but Walter was not sent with them. At first, Walter was disappointed to be separated from his friends, but he later learned that all twenty-four of his comrades were killed on the Eastern Front. Years later, he wrote, "This woke me up, and I offered a special prayer of thanks to my Heavenly Father for being alive."

Not following his comrades to the Soviet Union, Walter was instead sent to the Western Front. In France, he resolved to keep the Lord's commandments though he was out of contact with the Church. He consistently said his prayers and faithfully mailed his tithing back to Germany to his branch president.

The district conference was always a grand event that took place on a Saturday and Sunday. It was an especially exciting time for the youth, who were generally in small numbers in each branch. Ruth Gärtner recalled how all of the local youth escorted the youth from other branches to the Schneidemühl railroad station on Sunday night to send them home to other towns. On one such occasion in 1942, Siegfried Jeske of the Driesen Branch asked Ruth if she would write to him. She did so, but he was soon in the army, and their relationship was one of correspondence over long distances.

By April 1942, Hans Kindt was in a combat zone on the Eastern Front. As a radio man, he was right up at the front line. He earned his combat infantry badge (awarded after three combat engagements) right away. By October 1942, the German army had advanced far into enemy territory, but Soviet resistance was stiffening. At one point, Hans's unit was surrounded and cut in half. Fortunately, they were able to fight their way out of the predicament.

Like so many other Latter-day Saint soldiers, Hans had no desire to kill enemy combatants. However, as a radio man at the front, he also carried a rifle and was expected to fight. He later explained how he resolved the conflict in his mind and in practice:

> Very soon in [battle] I discovered that when I was aiming after fleeing Russian soldiers with the tracer bullets, I discovered how closely I [came to hitting] [one], and then I said, "I could have killed him. Maybe he had a wife and children." And so from there on I would always aim a little higher. I never told anyone for years and years because they would think I was a coward. But that was my decision, and that's what I did. So I was lucky; I got through it, I didn't have to kill anyone.

Fig. 4. Members of the Schneidemühl Branch pose for a picture in the courtyard next to the meetinghouse. (S. Dunbar)

In the fall of 1942, Hans contracted diphtheria and dysentery. He was sent home on leave, then was assigned to a post in France, where he served from October 1942 to February 1943. After another furlough at home, he returned to the Soviet Union in April 1943.

Hans Kindt came within inches of being killed in July 1943. During a Soviet offensive, he was given the order to radio for tank support then to destroy his equipment and join the retreat. However, he decided that he could simply disconnect the antenna and take his radio with him. While doing so, he saw a Red Army soldier shoot at him from more than one hundred yards away. He felt the bullet pierce his arm, and he fell down in shock. He lay there all night while the Soviets infiltrated the German lines. He unbuttoned his shirt and, using a flashlight, learned that the bullet had cut across his chest from left to right and then passed through his right arm. The flesh on his chest was wide open. The next morning, a buddy ran by and Hans called for help:

[My comrade] didn't want to [take me along,] but then he came, and I was hanging on to him and completely exhausted. That was a time in my life where I said to him, "Leave me. There's no hope anyway," and so he gave me the courage to go because he could see there was a hill going down, and we would find cover there. He saved my life. I was still walking, hanging on.

Initially, because he was nowhere near a bona fide medical facility, Hans's gaping flesh wound was simply taped together. By the time a surgeon was found, the wound could no longer be repaired cosmetically, and he had a ghastly scar that would serve as a reminder of the experience for the rest of his life. He convalesced in a hospital in Czechoslovakia near the German border. His arm was taped up to his shoulder "in a primitive fashion," and the wound refused to heal for months due to recurring infections. After nine months, he was released and eventually gained full use of and strength in his arm. By then it was the spring of 1944.

At age ten, Werner Birth (born 1932) was inducted into the Jungvolk program with his

Fig. 5. Members of the Schneidemühl Branch during a picnic in a nearby forest. (W. Kindt)

classmates. With the war at a high pitch, the youngsters were given some training with rifles "perhaps twice a year." When it came time to learn how to box, Werner protested. He was not interested in hitting his friends.[9]

The first Church assignment given Werner Birth was that of usher. He later clearly recalled the instructions he was given: "'Stay by the door, and when we have the sacrament, don't let anyone in.' So I put my shoulder under the [door] handle so nobody could get it open. I must have been pretty small at the time."

During the first years of the war, there were few disturbances to life in Schneidemühl. Esther Rieve (born 1926) was similar to teenagers all over Germany in that she was less interested in the war than she was in her apprenticeship program, which was to last for three years. She was trained in the fine points of salesmanship in a small store. "In the evenings we came home, and it was so dark [due

to blackout regulations] that we could hardly see our own hands."[10]

In 1943, Esther was assigned to work on a farm as part of the government's Pflichtjahr program. That assignment lasted six months, after which she was required to work in an underground aircraft factory near Berlin.

As air raids brought destruction to Schneidemühl, there were ample reasons to wonder who or what would be spared and who or what would be lost. Ruth Gärtner recalled the case of Sister Bauer of the Schneidemühl Branch:

She was young and married, and she had a beautiful apartment just all decorated beautifully, and she came home [after church], and a bomb had destroyed her house. . . . I could not believe it because my mother had always said, "If you keep the commandments, nothing will happen to you." And I said, "Why did this happen to her?" . . . We had a lot of *why*s.

Fig. 6. Four young men and a young lady contribute to the spirit of the branch meetings through their musical talents. (W. Kindt)

Edith Birth had met Helmut Kinder of Chemnitz while on her mission. In early 1944, he visited her in Schneidemühl, and soon the two were engaged to be married. When he was transferred from France to the Eastern front, she became seriously concerned for his welfare; her eldest brother, Gerhard, had been killed there in 1942 and another brother, Nephi, had been reported missing in action there in July 1944. On September 8, 1944, Edith wrote Helmut a letter and placed it on a crystal bowl in her bedroom for mailing the next day. In the morning, a noise woke her up. As she later recalled:

> It was like someone threw a rock through my window. I jumped up and saw my crystal bowl I had placed the letter on, was broken. The crystal fragments had formed a heart and a cross. When my father saw the fragments, he said to me: "I am sorry, my child, but I have to tell you, your fiancé was killed this morning. He did this to let you know he was dying."

As the Births had feared, Helmut Kinder was reported missing in action in Latvia on September 9, 1944.[11] A "missing in action" notice represented a particular hardship for a soldier's family, as Edith explained in her autobiography:

> It was very hard to hear that one of your loved ones [was] killed in action, but it [was] almost

Fig. 7. In March 1944, Johannes Kindt was pleased to have sons Walter (left) and Hans home on furlough at the same time. (W. Kindt)

even harder to read that he [was] missing in action. . . . You never knew how they died. Nephi was such a special fine young man. How did he die? Was he shot? Was he taken prisoner? Did he die of starvation as so many did in the Russian prisoner of war camps? Just missing in action, that was hard to take.[12]

Brigitte Birth (born 1935) recalled the heartbreak her mother suffered when Nephi was reported missing. "The first prayer I ever said beside the Lord's Prayer was that my mother would finally stop crying." As it happened, comfort came in a most unexpected way. According to Brigitte, her mother woke up one morning and told her elder daughters that Nephi had visited her during the night to say that he was, in fact, dead. Then she knew that all was right and that he would not be coming home.

A few weeks before the Allied landing in Normandy on June 6, 1944, Walter Kindt had a significant spiritual experience in France, a reminder that even (or especially) in wartime, there is time for reflection about one's spiritual condition:

> One Sunday morning, I prayed in the woods, asking my Heavenly Father to help me find a way to increase my faith and testimony and to always have His Holy Spirit. I was then told by a great impression of the Spirit, "Read the Book of Mormon." Immediately I sent a letter to my parents asking them to send me a copy of the book, and they, of course, sent it to me at once.

After the Normandy invasion, Walter Kindt's unit retreated steadily into the interior of France. As a member of the signal corps, he always had access to automobile transportation and quickly learned survival tactics which he used when attacked by Allied fighter planes: he tried to hide the car underneath a tree to stay out of sight and then used smoke bombs to trick the pilots into assuming that his car had been hit and damaged.

In his new assignment in Berlin, Hans Kindt was dangerously close to participation in a plot to assassinate Adolf Hitler on July 20, 1944. Hans's commanding officer had conspired to have his troops capture and hold in house arrest certain high-ranking officers in Berlin while other conspirators took over the national army headquarters and the radio stations. Hans and his comrades were told that SS troops were planning a rebellion against Hitler and that Hans and his unit would be instrumental in saving Germany's Führer.

The truth was quite the opposite. The plan was to have Hans's unit assist in killing troops loyal to Hitler. By some quirk of fate, the bomb left in a conference room in Rastenburg, East Prussia, only superficially injured Hitler; the conspiring generals (including Hans's commander) were rounded up and executed. Hans

Fig. 8. Walter Kindt (right) with his comrades in France. (W. Kindt)

and his comrades were never ordered to carry out the plan for which they were trained. Had it come to that, he too might have been executed for treason.

Back home in Schneidemühl, Hans's sister, Sigrid Kindt (born 1928), turned sixteen and was called to serve in the Pflichtjahr program. Her first assignment was on a farm. "They fed us as if we were in the army," she wrote of the experience. Up at 4:00 A.M., they were marched every day to work, "singing as we marched." It was not long before the work became military in nature—digging defensive positions for the German army. Due to the famous sandy soil of Prussia, the digging was relatively easy. However, life in the camp was not pleasant because, like soldiers, the young women were plagued by lice.[13]

In the fall of 1944, Fritz Birth was drafted. A veteran of the Great War, he was deaf in one ear and had hoped to be spared another tour of duty at his age (fifty-one) in order to stay at home with his wife and his nine surviving children.

"I remember watching my mother keep very careful records every night of the food ration stamps she collected during the day [in her grocery store]," recalled Brigitte. "She sent the records to city hall, and the distribution of food was organized very well." Sister Birth was so concerned about the ration stamp audit that she even took some of the stamps with her when she fled Schneidemühl in 1945.[14] Initially she did not wish to flee, but her daughters were finally able to convince her of this necessity. Sister Birth left in January 1945 with her five youngest children and was able to reach Dresden safely by train. They were taken in by a family in the southwest suburb named Dölzschen.[15]

In their parents' and brothers' absence, Irmgard took over the operation of the glass shop, and Christel and Edith took over the grocery store. Edith recalled, "We thought we would be safe for a while. We never were so wrong." Packing some belongings onto two children's sleds, the girls joined the throngs of refugees leaving the city on January 26 while the enemy artillery thundered close by. Edith later wrote of the painful separation:

> We [had grown] up here, and it was a terrible feeling to leave everything behind. Everything in this home had a meaning to us. We loved this place, where we used to sing, play music and games, and had our harmonious family life. We loved our neighbors, our friends, and we loved our LDS branch in town. . . . We left with the hope someday to return.[16]

As many as three thousand Latter-day Saints shared Edith's emotions as they left eastern Germany.

What had usually been a trip of three hours to Berlin became one of eight days and nights. The Birth girls and Wilford Kindt (younger brother of Hans and Walter) rode in a freight car devoid of supplies or amenities. From Berlin, the Births found another train headed south to Dresden, where they located their mother. Just a few days later, they watched from the Dölzschen suburb as downtown Dresden was reduced to rubble in the firebombing of February 13–14, 1945.[17]

Sigrid Kindt, then 16, was released from government service in November 1944 when the winter frost and ice set in, and she returned home to Schneidemühl. Very soon thereafter, she began to suffer from odd physical maladies that may have been related to overproductive glands. "I had horrible dreams, was skeptical of everything, and had spasms in my left arm. They gave me iodine and some kind of nerve medication." At one point, a physician conducted a lumbar puncture "with a bent needle." No particular results were reported.

From the summer of 1944, Hans Kindt lived near the Olympic Village in Berlin's Charlottenburg district. He worked there as a tailor until January 1945, when he experienced the confusion of the fall of the Third Reich. Sent to fight the Soviets near Meseritz (just thirty miles east of the Oder River), he found chaos at an Eastern Front that was fast disintegrating. Under threat of death if he appeared to any fanatical military police to be retreating

Fig. 9. The Birth home on the outskirts of Schneidemühl. Sister Birth operated a grocery store in a room on the side of the house. (S. Dunbar)

or deserting, Hans managed to keep out of harm's way by pretending to deliver messages toward the rear. Eventually, he was sent back to Berlin, then to the west to oppose the oncoming American army.

When it came time to flee Schneidemühl in January 1945, Wilford Kindt went to the hospital to pick up his sister, Sigrid, who was still suffering from her unexplained illness. He took her to Fritz Birth, who gave her a priesthood blessing that healed her immediately. The two young people then went to the railroad station, where a Nazi Party leader stopped Wilford (who was then fifteen but looked much older) and ordered him to stay in the city to defend it from the Soviet invaders. Fortunately Wilford was able to find his Birth cousins, and they walked to nearby Lebehnke, where they boarded a train for Dresden.

Maria Kindt and her children made their way by train across northern Germany with several friends, and by early February they arrived in Tremsbüttel near Hamburg. They were quartered one by one in various farm homes and looked forward to the day when they could live together again.

Ruth Gärtner and her mother had visited Ruth's sister near the Baltic Sea and returned home to Schneidemühl on the very day the last civilians left the town by train. In the confusion of a city in preinvasion panic, the last train departed before the Gärtners learned that they needed to leave with it; they were trapped in the city with no way out. They went to church that next Sunday and were disappointed to find that they were the only ones there. According to Ruth, German defenders fought valiantly for several weeks to save the city. During the fighting, her family stayed in a formidable air-raid bunker. One day, a Soviet soldier opened the door, and all occupants of the bunker were ordered out.

The invaders burned down most of the houses in the city center while searching for German defenders. However, civilians were also endangered during and after the conquest of the city. At one point, Ruth was lined up with seven other women:

> There were eight of us ladies. And I was standing here in the middle and two [soldiers] were standing there, pointing their rifles at us. I just prayed and said, "Dear Lord, please let me be the first one to die," and the minute I said that, I was looking to see if anyone had fallen yet. That same minute I finished my prayer, the bayonets went down, [the soldiers] turned around and walked off. . . . I didn't want to see anyone else die. I wanted to be the first one, but [Heavenly Father] let me live.

The war in Schneidemühl ended in late February when the Red Army arrived, but a new phase of challenges and suffering began. The Gärtner women were impressed into clean-up crews, clearing rubble from streets and helping the conquerors systematically take valuables from private homes. By an odd stroke of fate, they found themselves one day in the rooms at Gartenstrasse 31, where the Schneidemühl Branch had held meetings for several years. According to Ruth:

> I think [the Russians] kept all the chairs. There were loose chairs that we sat on. There was an organ there, too. They goofed around on the organ; they didn't know how to play it anyway. They told us to pile the songbooks and other books in the street and burn them. They told us to take the big picture of the prophet Joseph Smith off the wall and put it in the fire. . . . I couldn't throw that picture in; it was precious to me. . . . So I broke the glass, and I took the picture out and put the frame in the fire. I rolled the picture up and set it behind the door. I don't know if anybody later on threw it in the fire or not. When the Russians began to get drunk on their vodka, we left the scene.

Soon after the destruction of the city of Dresden, Sister Emma Birth decided to seek

Fig. 10. Friedrich Birth with his wife and eleven children. The two sons in the back row, Gerhard and Nephi, were both killed in Russia. (W. Kindt)

refuge in a smaller, safer location. Her daughter, Edith, contacted her former mission companion, Gretel Dzierzon, who lived in Geyersdorf in the Annaberg-Buchholz Branch near the Czechoslovakian border. In response to Gretel's invitation, the Births headed south, arriving by train two days later. There they were taken in by gracious hosts and quickly fell in love with the people and the region. Nevertheless, even in such an isolated region, fighter planes menaced the civilians, and Edith recalled being in danger every day of the week:

> When we walked to church . . . on Sundays, we had to watch out and take shelter, when airplanes attacked. Seeking shelter meant falling to the ground in our Sunday clothing and not moving. [It was] a miracle no one of us was hurt.[18]

Brigitte Birth was only nine years old at the time, but she was personally offended when dive-bombers attacked civilians:

> I remember hearing those [planes,] and I knew that the best idea was totally falling down on the ground and hiding in the flowers as much as I could. I almost had tears in my eyes because I said, "I didn't do anything to that fellow up there." I just didn't.

By early 1945, Walter Kindt's unit had retreated from France to Germany, and he drove his car across the Rhine River bridge at Cologne just before the bridge collapsed. Days later, the members of the unit were nearly surrounded by the advancing Americans. At the last minute, Walter managed to send a letter to his father in Yugoslavia and another to his brother, Hans, on the Eastern Front. He informed them that his mother had arrived in Tremsbüttel, northeast of Hamburg.

On April 15, 1945, Walter's commander disbanded the unit, and Walter joined eleven comrades for a long trek to the north, his goal being a reunion with his family in Tremsbüttel. They traveled by night, using the North Star as their guide, then slept in hiding by day. The war had not yet ended. As they moved north, they traded their uniforms for civilian clothing at the homes of farmers. Although they went without food for several days, they were usually fortunate to receive food from sympathetic countrymen as they traveled. On May 1, they entered the large city of Hanover and witnessed the traditional celebration then observed by the victors. Walter was disturbed by his status: "Just the day before, we, the men in the army, were the heroes of the Fatherland—today we felt like criminals in hiding."

While stationed in and near Berlin, Hans Kindt was occasionally able to attend Church events. This was still the case as the end of the war approached. Regarding one conference, he wrote the following:

> I will never forget the last mission conference I attended as a soldier in Berlin. The people would come with a great outpouring of love for the gospel. They had lost their homes, some of them their loved ones, their possessions—but not their testimonies. We all knew that this would be the last time we would meet, and soon the war will come to an end, and deliverance was on its way. In defeat, and in all our suffering, we as LDS rejoiced, for it meant for us that our church [would] survive.[19]

By April 1945, Hans Kindt was in action south of the city of Berlin. At one point, a young soldier without a rifle was accused of desertion, and the officer in charge ordered that he be shot. Hans was the only soldier present who could carry out the execution order. While the young man cowered by a tree and the officer paced back and forth, "I had to make a decision," recalled Hans years later:

> I would not do it. I could not do it. My life, my upbringing, my testimony had prepared me for this moment, and I was ready to suffer the consequences. I firmly believe that in coming to this decision, standing firm in my conviction, that the Lord blessed me when the officer had a change of heart and let him go.

In early May, Hans was told to round up as much food as he could in anticipation of being taken prisoner. He was fortunate to surrender to the Americans on May 8, 1945—the day the war in Europe ended. POW Hans Kindt worked for his captors as a tailor and gained the favor of several officers. Hans was soon transferred to a British POW camp. At one point, he was suspected of having been a soldier in the SS and was intensely interrogated. He even spent a few days in a regular prison but eventually fended off the accusations and was returned to the POW camp. He managed to secure a release as early as July 1945 and rode a bicycle nearly 150 miles to Tremsbüttel to join his family.

During the six weeks of his trek northward, Walter Kindt saw his companions go their various ways one by one. Along the way, they were twice stopped by American military police but not detained. Fortunately, it did not rain once during that time. Only one friend, Hans Gaedt, was still with Walter when he reached Hamburg, 250 miles from the starting point of their trek. The two found a man who took them across the Elbe River into town, and they continued northeast to Tremsbüttel, arriving two weeks after the end of the war.

Walter was thrilled to be able to attend church again—the first time was in a private home in the Hamburg suburb of Wandsbek. His account reflects the feelings of the occasion:

> I will never forget this day. There I stood. . . . I had lost my home, all my belongings, my beautiful bank account, my friend, my job, and my hometown. I had even lost the war. . . . So at this sacrament meeting at the cottage, my first church gathering for long years, I felt the spirit of the Lord as I had never ever felt it before. I was facing a seemingly impossible situation, starting over with my life. Yet, I rejoiced in God. I prayed and promised my Heavenly father that I would do whatever was necessary to have this power of the Holy Ghost—this wonderful peace I felt at this moment on this day—all the days of my life.

Of the surviving Births, only father Fritz was not in Annaberg-Buchholz when the war ended on May 8, 1945. Wilford Kindt received a letter from a friend indicating that Fritz Birth had been killed in the fighting near Schneidemühl. He informed the Birth girls, who dared not tell their mother. However, Sister Birth sensed from her daughters that something was amiss and learned the secret by reading Edith's diary. Sister Birth refused to give up hope and took to fasting every Friday that her husband might still be alive.[20]

In July 1945, Emma Birth and several of her children accepted an invitation to join the large colony of LDS refugees on the Fritz Lehnig property in Cottbus. A month later, Margaretha Birth was ill with what some people thought was typhoid fever. From her sick bed, she told her brother, Werner, "Go downstairs and open the gate. Father is there." They could not see the gate from her bed, so Werner did not go. She told him again, and once more he did not carry out her request. After the third time, Werner went downstairs and found his father standing by the gate.

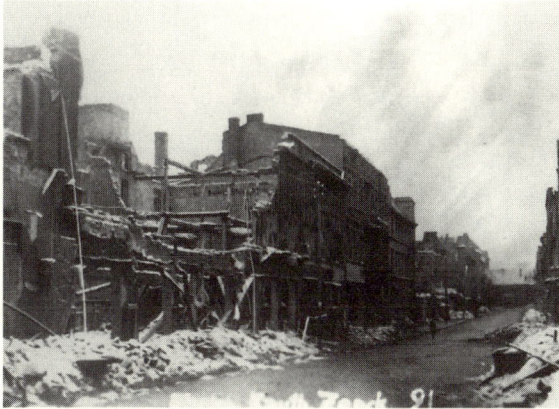

Fig. 11. The Wolff family once lived in this building on the Kleine Kirchenstrasse in Schneidemühl. (W. Kindt)

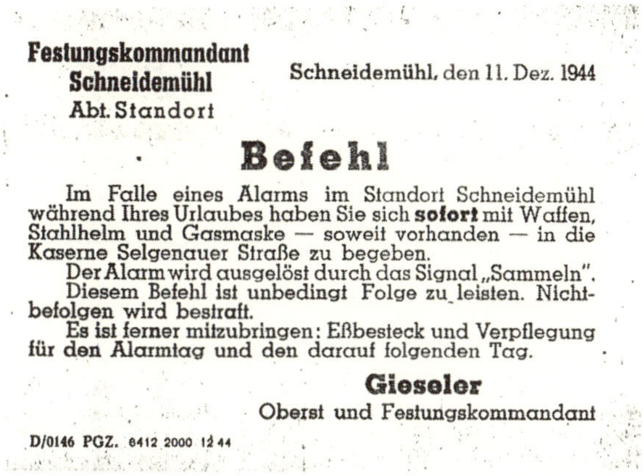

Festungskommandant
Schneidemühl
Abt. Standort

Schneidemühl, den 11. Dez. 1944

Befehl

Im Falle eines Alarms im Standort Schneidemühl während Ihres Urlaubes haben Sie sich **sofort** mit Waffen, Stahlhelm und Gasmaske — soweit vorhanden — in die Kaserne Selgenauer Straße zu begeben.

Der Alarm wird ausgelöst durch das Signal „Sammeln".

Diesem Befehl ist unbedingt Folge zu leisten. Nichtbefolgen wird bestraft.

Es ist ferner mitzubringen: Eßbesteck und Verpflegung für den Alarmtag und den darauf folgenden Tag.

Gieseler
Oberst und Festungskommandant

D/0146 PGZ. 6412 2000 12 44

*Fig. 12. These instructions for emergency mobilization were issued to soldiers on leave in Schneidemühl in December 1944: "Should an alarm be sounded in Schneidemühl during your furlough, you are to report **immediately** at the Selgenauer Street army post with weapons, helmet and gas mask—if those are readily available." (W. Kindt)*

Fritz Birth had been released from a Soviet POW camp and located the family with the help of the LDS mission office in Berlin. Edith recalled the unexpected, astonishing reunion:

> My mother and the children that were with my mother were excited to see our father home. My mother's feelings had not betrayed her! She knew all the time her husband, our father, was alive! It was a great reunion. . . . He had lost his right arm and was thin and old looking but full of enthusiasm and full of plans to start over again.[21]

On January 27, 1945, Anna Rieve and her five children were evacuated from Schneidemühl and transported to the town of Stralsund near the Baltic Sea. When the Red Army entered the city of Stralsund in the first week of May 1945, Anna and her children were hiding in a small apartment. While enemy soldiers scoured the city for women and girls, Sister Rieve found a secret door into an attic space, where she could hide her eldest two daughters. "During the night, the screaming of the women and the girls was terrible; we could hear it from our attic room," recalled Esther years later.

Toward the end of May, Sister Rieve was told that if she expected to receive food ration stamps, she would have to leave Stralsund and return east to her home in Schneidemühl. When she arrived, she found that her apartment had been taken over by a Polish family. Her father had lost his large farm and his many horses and cows. The town had suffered extensive damage. "We didn't like what we saw," recalled daughter Esther. "The Russians and Poles were competing for the spoils."

The Rieve family spent the summer months of 1945 in temporary housing, while Anna and her elder daughters were assigned to labor crews under Soviet supervision. Every night they were escorted under guard back to their homes, where they hid from potential molestation and brutality. It was a tense existence in a town that was no longer their home.

In August, Anna Rieve was allowed to leave Schneidemühl with her children. A military train transported them to the town of Burg, west of Berlin near Magdeburg. Always on the lookout for members of the Church, Sister Rieve eventually located other Latter-day Saints, and they began to hold meetings in Magdeburg. Her husband, Richard, was fortunate to be united with his family in Burg before the year was out.

Looking back on the end of the war, Esther Rieve recalled being in grave danger at least once. While traveling by train one day, she was pursued by a drunken enemy soldier who apparently had a venereal disease, which possibly meant both momentary and lasting torture for Esther. He chased her through the station, and for a few moments she escaped him by hiding under a pile of refugee belongings at a railroad station. As the train began to leave the station, she emerged from her hiding place and ran for the train, looking for a place to jump on. "My mother thought that I was going to throw myself in front of the train, but I didn't have that in mind." She was very blessed to avoid being assaulted.

The Gärtners were able to leave Schneidemühl in October 1945. The new Polish government had informed them that they would have to become Polish citizens if they wished to stay. They corresponded with the LDS mission office in Berlin and were instructed to travel to Barth (on the Baltic Sea north of Berlin), where three surviving Latter-day Saints would welcome them. Initially, the Gärtners had no money to purchase railroad tickets, but one day they found some paper money lying in the streets, discarded by other Germans who found that their money could not be used in local stores. With that money, they bought the tickets. They arrived at the home of the in-laws of Ruth's sister, bringing with them only the clothes they were wearing and a 1941 Church hymnal.

Regarding her experience as a Latter-day Saint during the horrific last days of the war and the Soviet invasion, Ruth Gärtner offered this explanation:

> It was like being in a dream world. You really didn't know if you were alive or if you were dead. You felt kind of nauseous, kind of numb; you didn't know what was going to happen the next minute. For what we went through after the Russians came in, it was unbelievable. And I gained my testimony there. But still you sometimes ask yourself, "Why did this happen?"

Ruth had been engaged to Siegfried Jeske of the Driesen Branch since 1944. She lost track of him for two years before learning that he had survived the war. He was released from a Soviet POW camp in 1949, and they were married shortly thereafter.

Looking back on his years in the Wehrmacht, Hans Kindt recalled attending church only when on leave—there were no LDS meetings at the front. His father had given him a small New Testament that he took with him everywhere he went. He also tried to have religious conversations with other soldiers, but such occasions were not common. Speaking for himself and Walter, he said that despite their isolation from other Latter-day Saints, "I think we had a good upbringing that stayed with us. We would never even doubt anything [about the Church]."

By the fall of 1946, all surviving members of the Schneidemühl Branch had left the area and resettled in what remained of Germany. The once strong and vibrant branch disappeared into history.

In Memoriam

The following members of the Schneidemühl Branch did not survive World War II:

Gerhard Fritz Birth b. Zechendorf, Deutsch Krone, Westpreußen, Preußen 5 May 1918; son of Friedrich Martin Birth and Emma Pauline Hedwig Fritz; bp.

Fig. 13. Walter Kindt standing at the entry to the wartime church meeting rooms at Gartenstrasse 31 in 1999. (W. Kindt)

27 Feb 1927; ord. teacher; ord. priest, 15 May 193—; m. Tilsit, Ostpreußen, Preußen 11 Feb 1942, Rita Helga Meiszus; artilleryman; k. in battle Ssytschewo, Staraja, Russia 1 Apr 1942 (H. Meiszus Birth Meyer; LDS Ordination Certificate; www.volksbund.de; IGI; AF)

Nephi Albert Ferdinand Birth b. Schneidemühl, Posen, Preußen 6 Apr 1925; son of Friedrich Martin Birth and Emma Hedwig Pauline Fritz; bp. 9 May 1934; d. Russia 16 Jul 1944 (H. Meiszus Birth Meyer)

Friedrich Julius Preuss b. Norkitten, Insterburg, Ostpreußen, Preußen 28 Jul 1851; son of Gottlieb Preuss and Charlotte Laubichler; bp. 14 Aug 1920; ord. elder 1930; m. 7 Oct 1880, Ottilie Julianne Augusta Vogel; d. Schneidemühl, Pommern, Preußen 18 Apr 1940 (*Sonntagsstern*, no. 17, 26 May 1940 n.p.; IGI)

Alfred Heinrich Wilhelm Ross b. Schneidemühl, Posen, Preußen 15 Feb 1913; son of Adolf Wilhelm Ross and Anna Marie Wilhelmine Klingenhage; bp. 27 Mar 1922; m. Stargard, Pommern, Preußen 8 Apr 1938, Ilse Herta Marta Moeser; infantryman; d. near Obergänserndorf, Austria 28 Feb 1945 or Apr 1945; bur. Oberwoelbling, Austria (Anni Bauer Schulz; www.volksbund.de; AF; IGI; PRF)

Ottilie Julianne Auguste Vogel b. Bovenwinkel, Danzig, Westpreußen, Preußen 22 Jan 1852; dau. of Alexander Vogel and Julianne Plaeger; m. 7 Oct 1880, Friedrich Julius Preuss; d. old age Schneidemühl, Pommern, Preußen 3 Dec 1939 (*Sonntagsstern*, no. 17, 26 May 1940 n.p.; IGI)

Notes

1. East German Mission Quarterly Reports, 1938, no. 8, East German Mission History.
2. Presiding Bishopric, "Financial, Statistical, and Historical Reports of Wards, Stakes, and Missions, 1884–1955," CR 4 12, 257.
3. Hans Kindt, interview by the author, Greendale, Wisconsin, August 19, 2007.
4. Ruth Gärtner Jeske Hadley, interview by the author, Ogden, Utah, March 9, 2007.
5. See the Schneidemühl District chapter for extensive information on Johannes Kindt.
6. Walter Kindt, autobiography (unpublished); private collection.
7. Walter Kindt, interview by the author, Greendale, Wisconsin, August 19, 2007.
8. Edith Gerda Birth Rohloff, *Life Is a Gift from God* (unpublished history, about 2003), 19; private collection. See the chapter on the East German Mission for details about her missionary service and the destruction of the mission office.
9. Werner Birth, interview by the author, Salt Lake City, July 19, 2007.
10. Esther Rieve Vergin, interview by Rachel Gale, Salt Lake City, June 6, 2007.
11. Rohloff, *Life*, 26–27.
12. Ibid., 22.
13. Sigrid Kindt, autobiography (unpublished, about 1952); private collection.
14. Brigitte Birth Foster, interview by the author, Salt Lake City, January 10, 2008.
15. Rohloff, *Life*, 27–28.
16. Ibid., 28–29.
17. Ibid., 33.
18. Ibid., 35.
19. Hans Kindt, *Story* (unpublished personal history); private collection.
20. Rohloff, *Life*, 36.
21. Ibid., 40.

SCHÖNLANKE BRANCH

The town of Schönlanke belonged to West Prussia until 1918, when the region was added to the province of Pomerania through the Treaty of Versailles. The Polish border was only six miles away along the Netze River; this was truly the German frontier in the days just prior to World War II.

Waltraud Schimming (born 1926) had a wonderful childhood in Schönlanke. Her mother, Martha Kennert Schimming, provided a very happy household in their apartment at Gartenstrasse 31 at the edge of town. Her father, Hermann, worked in a furniture factory and was an enthusiastic member of the firemen's brass band. Waltraud later wrote about the "dreamy" town of Schönlanke, but admitted that not everything was beautiful there:

One morning in November [9,] 1938, there was tumult in town. The relatively quiet synagogue had been put to the torch. The flames were threatening the very foundation. The target of the attack [were] the Jewish citizens. The men were herded together to the livestock market place and from there driven to the old gymnasium and finally to the railroad station. The catastrophe went through the town like wildfire. Nobody knew just what to think.[1]

Conditions in the Schimming home may have been idyllic, but this was not the case for everybody in Germany. There was nothing they could do about the persecution of the Jews, and Waltraud learned that people simply preferred not to discuss the matter.

Schönlanke Branch[2]	1939
Elders	1
Priests	2
Teachers	2
Deacons	4
Other Adult Males	4
Adult Females	9
Male Children	2
Female Children	0
Total	24

Though there was no persecution of the Church by the German government in the Schneidemühl District in the late 1930s, other forces seemed determined to interrupt the functions of the Church. In the mission history, we read the following under the date November 21, 1938:

From this day until December 15th, all meetings were forbidden in the Schönlanke and Kreuz Branches, Schneidemühl District. This measure was taken on account of a foot and mouth epidemic, which prevailed in this section of Germany.[3]

The disease continued to disrupt daily activities for several months. On January 31, 1939, the following entry was made in the mission history:

The continuation of the flu and grippe epidemic in the Schönlanke Branch, Schneidemühl District, made it necessary to discontinue all public Church meetings. However, several cottage meetings were held in the homes of members.[4]

The branch president for the duration of the war was Karl Bayer. When World War II began, the Schönlanke Branch was meeting in rented rooms at Friedrichstrasse 40. Hyrum Hardel (born 1924) recalled the appearance of the rooms:

The branch met in a former carpenter's workshop on the first floor. We had a large room with an oven in it to heat the room, and then there were also smaller classrooms in the back for the smaller meetings. The rooms were in a Hinterhaus. There were about sixty members who were in attendance, and we held our Sunday School in the morning, went home, and then went back to church for sacrament meeting in the evening.[5]

Hyrum recalled other meetings that took place during the week, such as MIA. According to him, there was a pump organ in the room, and music was a part of each get-together. He also remembered that a sign was displayed forbidding Jews to enter the rooms ("Juden verboten"). He offered this explanation: "The sign did not state that this idea came from the Church. It was a general sign that one could find anywhere."

Regarding politics, he said, "We had members of the branch who were members of the Nazi Party. One brother had the Party emblem on his jacket but he did not talk about the Party when he was at church—not in his talks nor with anybody else." In what was definitely a rare occurrence in the East German Mission during the war, Hyrum recalled, "We also had to hang up a picture of Adolf Hitler on the side wall of the room." On the other hand, "we did not talk about Hitler in our meetings or generally at church."

Being named after the brother of the Prophet Joseph Smith, Hyrum found that people had trouble pronouncing his name. His religion teacher in school simply called him Heinrich. However, his religion did not cause him any problems in school or in the neighborhood.

Martha Schimming had enjoyed contacts with Latter-day Saints since 1923 but had not been baptized. In May 1942, she heeded promptings to join the Church. Her daughter, Waltraud (then sixteen), went along to witness the baptism in a local lake but later admitted that she did not comprehend the act of immersion.[6] However, thanks to a young man in the branch, Hans Boelter, Waltraud eventually became interested in the Church and was baptized later that year. She described the event in these words:

> On November 1, 1942, I was baptized by Brother [Karl] Bayer in a lake in the woods. It was raining and a slight mist arose from the water. After the prayer, I didn't feel any cold at all. Brother Johannes Kindt gave me the gift of the Holy Ghost.[7]

Waltraud later noticed that Jews were allowed to attend meetings in the Schönlanke Branch (despite the "Juden verboten" sign); nobody ever tried to stop them. In her recollection,

> There was always somebody standing near the front door to give a signal if the Gestapo came. They were not allowed to interrupt our meetings and were always gone by the time we finished because our meetings lasted so long.[8]

Under the government's Pflichtjahr programs, Hyrum Hardel worked on a farm for a year then began an apprenticeship as an automobile mechanic. In 1942, he was serving in the Reichsarbeitsdienst and from there was drafted directly into the army. His basic training took place in Stettin. While there, he learned an important lesson regarding Latter-day Saints as fallible human beings:

> I was able to attend the Stettin branch when I was stationed close to there as a soldier. One experience I had, I will never forget. I was waiting

at the bus stop after the meeting was over, and I saw an elderly man approaching me; he had blessed the sacrament just earlier and I recognized him. As he came closer, he got out his pipe and started smoking. He did not recognize me.

Following basic training, Hyrum was invited to enter the Officer Candidate School. This was an attractive option because it would allow him to delay his departure to the Eastern Front. At one point, he was sent to Berlin for weapons training for seven months. While there, he had an interesting and disturbing experience: "We were allowed to listen to a case in court. One man was on trial because, while drunk, he had called Hitler a 'litterbug.' He was sentenced to death that very day."

Due to army politics, Hyrum never made it past the rank of noncommissioned officer, although he showed excellent military skills. Eventually, he was sent to Russia and experienced combat on the Eastern Front. On one occasion, a bullet narrowly missed him when he ducked at the last instant. Another time, he was hit in the thigh. Fortunately, he recovered from that wound.

By 1944, Hyrum was an instructor for army training courses in the Baltic States. When the Soviets invaded the area, he was able to board a ship to Danzig then found a train to southern Germany. Along the way, he was wounded again and ended up in a convent hospital in Reiningen near Nördlingen, Bavaria. It was there that he experienced the end of the war. Once he recovered and could walk again, he was imprisoned by the Americans and spent two years working in their POW system. For most of that time, he was on a farm near Neu Ulm on the Danube River.

Ruth Schimming (born 1933) recalled that life in Schönlanke was peaceful: "We did not feel much of the war because we were so far away [from large cities]. The first refugees came before Christmas 1944, and then came the trucks." Martha Schimming worked in a military hospital at the time and wanted very much to stay in Schönlanke. In January 1945, she suffered from a severe kidney ailment, and her daughter, Waltraud, recalled that Karl Bayer from Schneidemühl came to give Sister Schimming a blessing. She was not yet fully recovered when retreating German soldiers convinced her to take her daughters and flee. It was January 28, and the invaders were at the gates of the town. According to Ruth, "My mother did not think twice; she took her linen bag where she kept her bible and her tithing, and we left with a blanket wrapped around us."[9]

Years later, Waltraud described the desperate setting:

> The only possessions we had were the clothes on our backs. Everywhere we looked we saw hopelessness. Young and old passed us, pulling little carts and strollers. People were screaming for their lives, and babies were crying. Destruction was everywhere. Entire villages were on fire. The roar of artillery was heard over the trees. . . . All around us, the attitude was "Every man for himself!"[10]

Ruth recalled that they walked nearly twenty miles to Arnsfelde. On the way, German soldiers passed them on the road; later, Soviet tanks were going by. The women first took them for German tanks but then saw the Soviet markings. As Ruth explained, "The people [tank crew] must have been blind, because they didn't see us."

In Arnsfelde, they found a hospital train at the station, and Waltraud begged long enough to get her mother a place on the train. Ruth was allowed to go with her, but Waltraud was left behind. Fortunately, she joined up with them later in Deutsch Krone, about seven miles to the north. From there they found rail transportation to the province of Mecklenburg, north of Berlin. However, as Ruth recollected, "The people there were not very nice to us at all. We

stayed for a few weeks, but then we decided to go to Sondershausen, where the family of my mother's brother still lived." They arrived in Sondershausen just in time to witness the last air raid. Days later, the war was over.

In Sondershausen, Martha Schimming found work in the city hall. The family located a branch of the Church in nearby Erfurt. Eventually, Hermann Schimming found his wife and children there, and they began a new life together.

All ethnic Germans in the Schönlanke community were expelled by the new Polish government by the fall of 1946. It is likely that no members of the Schönlanke Branch were still living there by that time. The town soon became known as Trzcianka, Poland.

In 1947, Hyrum Hardel was released as a POW and made his way to Hamburg, where he had located his parents through correspondence. Driven from their home in Schönlanke at the end of the war, they never returned. Although they had lost their home and most of their possessions, the family considered themselves immensely blessed; the parents and all seven children had survived World War II.

In Memoriam

The following members of the Schönlanke Branch did not survive World War II:

Johannes Werner Boelter b. Schönlanke, Posen, Preußen 14 Apr 1925; son of Friedrich Wilhelm Boelter and Bertha Auguste Kersten; bp. 3 Oct 1933; k. in battle Russia 13 or 14 Apr 1944 (Froelke; Waltraud Hansen book, 45–46; IGI; AF; PRF)

Rosalie Elisabeth Jaster b. Altnippnow, Posen, Preußen 13 or 23 Jan 1861; dau. of Johann Jaster and Cecilie Stelter; bp. 24 or 29 Nov 1919; m. Wilhelm Kaiser; 5 children; d. Schönlanke, Pommern, Preußen 1940 (IGI, AF, PRF)

Notes

1. Waltraud Schimming Hansen, *Die Erde liegt unter den Füßen der Mütter* (Berlin: Frieling, 2001), 35; trans. the author.

2. Presiding Bishopric, "Financial, Statistical, and Historical Reports of Wards, Stakes, and Missions, 1884–1955," CR 4 12, 257.

3. East German Mission Quarterly Reports, 1938, no. 47, East German Mission History.

4. Ibid., 1939, no. 53.

5. Hyrum Hardel, interview by the author in German, Hamburg, Germany, August 13, 2006; unless otherwise noted, summarized in English by Judith Sartowski.

6. Hansen, *Die Erde liegt unter den Füßen der Mütter*, 43.

7. Ibid., 47.

8. Ibid.

9. Ruth Schimming Froelke, interview by Marion Wolfert in German, Salt Lake City, February 2006.

10. Hansen, *Die Erde liegt unter den Füßen der Mütter*, 50–51.

Fig. 1. Millions of Germans were evicted from provinces ceded to Poland by 1947. Most were allowed to take with them only what they could carry. Many traveled more than 500 miles. (Deutsches Bundesarchiv, Bild 146-1985-021-09)

Fig. 2. Children of the Schneidemühl Branch. (W. Kindt)

SPREEWALD
DISTRICT
East German Mission

The only district in the East German Mission not named for a city was the Spreewald District. The Spreewald ("the forest through which the Spree River flows") is located roughly between the city of Berlin and the province of Silesia to the southeast. Only four cities comprised the district throughout World War II: Frankfurt/Oder (about sixty-five miles east of Berlin), Cottbus (ninety miles southeast of Berlin), Forst (fifteen miles east of Cottbus), and Guben (thirty-eight miles south of Frankfurt/Oder).

Spreewald District[1]	1939	1940	1941	1942
Elders	24	24		
Priests	8	10		
Teachers	7	7		
Deacons	30	31		
Other Adult Males	45	40		
Adult Females	188	184		
Male Children	28	29		
Female Children	21	21		
Total	351	346	347	344

The district included the southeast section of the historic province of Brandenburg. To the northwest was the Berlin District, to the northeast the Schneidemühl District, to the east Poland, to the southeast the Breslau District, and to the southwest the Dresden District.

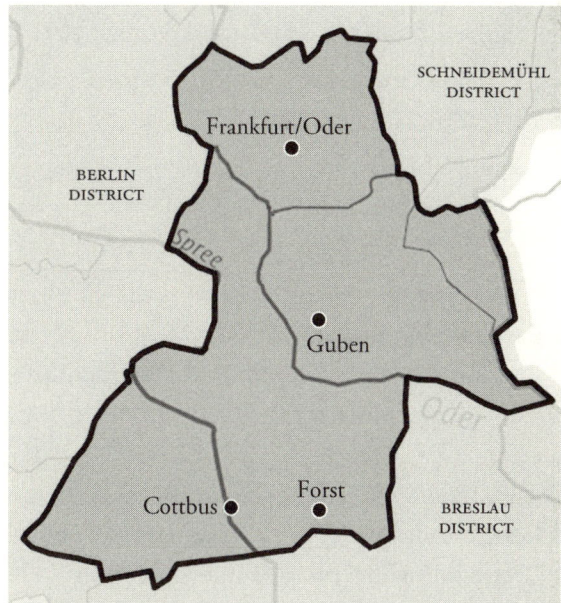

Fig. 1. The Spreewald District had only four branches.

The president of the Spreewald District throughout the war was Fritz Lehnig (born 1893) of Cottbus. According to eyewitness accounts, Brother Lehnig also functioned for at least part of the war era as the president of the Cottbus Branch.

Little is written about this district in the history of the East German Mission. The following entry is found under the date May 18, 1938:

On this, the previous, and the following day, special meetings were held in Frankfurt/Oder, Cottbus and Forst Branches, Spreewald

Fig. 2. The property owned by Fritz Lehnig in Cottbus as it appeared in the 1990s. The upper floor was the residence of more than one hundred Saints in 1945–46. (E. Grünewald Schulz)

District, by Elder Edward R. McKay, to discuss the new genealogy plan, which was presented at that time.[2]

As was the case all over the East German Mission, genealogical research was in full swing when the war started, and members were active in sending family data to the mission office in Berlin to be checked for completeness and accuracy. Approved data were forwarded to the LDS Genealogy Department in Salt Lake City.

The following entry is dated February 16, 1939:

> Members and friends of the Spreewald District met in Cottbus to attend a special entertainment. A spirit of better cooperation and service was obtained. More than eighty percent of the district membership was present.[3]

The reason for a need of better cooperation is not mentioned, but the percentage of the membership in attendance on that occasion is impressive.

Doris Schäler (born 1933) recalled attending district conferences during the war:

Our branch loved to go to the regularly-scheduled *Bezirkskonferenz*, which was usually held in Cottbus. We met other members from different branches, such as Guben, were taught, and heard all the latest news, which usually included the most recent casualties of war.[4]

During the last year of the war, many Latter-day Saint refugees arrived in Cottbus at the home of Fritz Lehnig. At Lausitzerstrasse 53 he owned a small factorylike building, one floor of which had been used as a restaurant. The structure became a haven for Saints driven from their homes in districts to the east by the advancing Red Army. Brother Lehnig was a hero in the minds of many surviving eyewitnesses in that he was able to harbor many Saints on his property and find food for all of them and jobs for some. This was the case for more than a year after the war as well, until many of the refugees were forced by the city government to move out; they traveled farther west in search of new homes.

Brother Lehnig was a great proponent of priesthood power and insisted that a blessing on the sick was superior to the powers of physicians and surgeons.[5] Under his direction, each day in the refugee camp began with a hymn and a prayer, after which work assignments for the day were determined. Several eyewitnesses recalled that despite the privations of 1945 and 1946, they enjoyed the feeling of living in a "united order" where everybody shared what they had.

Nevertheless, the cramped conditions caused predictable stress. Jutta Obst (born 1939) later recalled the conditions in the months after the war ended in May 1945: "The number of Saints now exceeded two hundred. For nine months we were packed like sardines in a can." One evening, two young women decided that they could not tolerate the conditions and returned to their apartment. They were molested repeatedly that night by Red Army soldiers; in despair the following morning, they turned on the gas and ended their lives.[6]

In September 1945, Brother Lehnig was apparently required to submit to the city a list of persons residing under his roof. That list shows precisely 118 persons, some of whom had come from as far away as Königsberg, East Prussia, and Breslau, Silesia. The mayor's office required a response within twenty-four hours regarding the official registration status of each person on the list. It is very possible that other Latter-day Saint refugees were living on the property at the time but had not yet been registered with the city.[7]

Due to the lack of bread in the Lehnig refugee camp, the ordinance of the sacrament included other types of food, principally potato peelings. According to Jutta Obst, "I'm sure the Lord was pleased to accept our offering, no matter what emblems were used, so long as they were blessed and partaken for the renewing of the sacred covenants."[8]

In the summer of 1946, many members of the Church left the Lehnig property to seek new surroundings farther west (in the American or British Occupation Zones, if possible). Eventually, activity at the Lehnig property declined.

The parts of Brandenburg that lay east of the Neisse River were ceded to Poland following the war. That territory included suburbs of the cities of Guben and Forst. By the end of 1946, members of the Church living on the east side of the river in those towns were evicted from their homes and never returned.

By the end of World War II, all four branches were still officially in existence, but the Guben Branch had been decimated and ultimately did not survive.

NOTES

1. Presiding Bishopric, "Financial, Statistical, and Historical Reports of Wards, Stakes, and Missions, 1884–1955," CR 4 12, 257.
2. East German Mission Quarterly Reports, 1938, no. 22, East German Mission History.
3. Ibid., 1939, no. 56.
4. Doris Charlotte Schäler Shapardanis, "World War II Experiences of the Schaeler Family and Members of the Forst Branch" (unpublished), 3; private collection.
5. Jutta Obst Burch, "Portrait of My Family" (unpublished family history, 2003), 9; private collection.
6. Ibid.
7. Mayor of the City of Cottbus to Fritz Lehnig, September 28, 1945; private collection.
8. Burch, "Portrait of My Family," 11.

COTTBUS BRANCH

The branch in Cottbus, Brandenburg, played a very significant role in the history of The Church of Jesus Christ of Latter-day Saints toward the end of World War II and in the following months. Located ninety miles southeast of Berlin, Cottbus had about fifty-five thousand inhabitants when the war began. Industrially insignificant, the city was largely spared the ravages of war until January 1945.

By the end of the war, it had become the gathering place for Saints from many branches in eastern Germany.[1]

Cottbus Branch[2]	1939
Elders	7
Priests	4
Teachers	3
Deacons	6
Other Adult Males	9
Adult Females	42
Male Children	11
Female Children	5
Total	87

The history of the East German Mission shows that Wilhelm Eckert was appointed president of the Cottbus Branch on May 1, 1938. His counselors were Adolf Duschl and Guido Schröder.[3] Eyewitnesses later identified the branch president as Fritz Lehnig, but this may have been a temporary and additional responsibility toward the end of the war because Brother Lehnig was officially the president of the Spreewald District throughout the war. The branch met in rented rooms at Lausitzerstrasse 53, a two-story structure owned by the Lehnig family. The upper story had been used as a restaurant but was converted into a chapel and a few classrooms. The cloakroom and the restrooms were located in an anteroom.

Joachim Lehnig (born 1935) recalled the following about the location of the building:

> The restaurant in the building used to be called Zum Grauen Affen ("At the Sign of the Grey Ape"), but it was then used as a place where potentially recyclable materials such as paper or bones were collected. This property was very close to the train station, only a five-minute walk away, five minutes into the city and with the streetcar station close by.[4]

The branch observed the typical meeting schedule, with Sunday School held at 10:00 A.M. and sacrament meeting in the evening. Priesthood and Relief Society meetings were held on Monday evening with MIA meeting on Wednesday evenings. Jutta Obst (born 1939) later recalled that her parents always attended the meetings on Monday and Wednesday evenings, leaving their children at home under the care of their eldest son, Lothar.[5]

Although full-time missionaries were a rarity in Germany during the war, individual members continued to tell others about their church and their faith. So it happened that Heinrich Grünewald of Cottbus, a railroad employee, was introduced to the Church by an unidentified member riding the train one day. Heinrich was interested in the message and began to attend Church meetings in Cottbus. His wife, Anne Marie, was busy with their four little children but eventually attended with him. They were baptized together on July 18, 1943, in the Spree River. Heinrich and Anne Marie Grünewald had a very happy home. They taught their children the truths of the gospel and loved the gospel dearly. Like so many other Latter-day Saint fathers, Heinrich did not want to go away to war, but in 1944 the call came. With a premonition about not returning, Brother Grünewald asked the branch president to watch over his family, and he requested of his wife that she marry again if he died, for the children's sake. Shortly before the end of the war, Heinrich Grünewald disappeared in the Soviet Union.[6]

The family of Otto and Marie Hagen lived at Neustädterstrasse 3 during the war. Brother Hagen was gone for most of the war as a test pilot for new airplanes. Sister Hagen took care of their three little boys. Their home was spared destruction during the air raids and the artillery bombardments. Sometime after the Allied invasion of France on June 6, 1944, Otto Hagen was taken prisoner by the Americans.

Church events continued to be observed as well as possible during the war, as Joachim Lehnig attested:

I was baptized in January 1944 in the Spree River. Brother Schröder baptized me—a faithful member with five sons. The place where we usually baptized people was where the river was a little faster than normal so there was also no ice. The baptism took place in the evening hours when it was already dark. My father did not like to give in and accept restrictions for the Church.[7]

Max Obst (born 1903) was a supervisor at the Cottbus railway station. As such, he was classified as exempt from military service. This allowed him to spend the entire war era at home with his wife, Elfriede (born 1907), and their family; however, work days of twelve or more hours were not uncommon for him. In 1944, the Obst family moved to Moltkestrasse, just ten walking minutes from the main rail station.

During the last year of the war, Cottbus became a target of the approaching Red Army. Air-raid sirens wailed on a regular basis, but attacks were fortunately not common occurrences. At times, Brother and Sister Obst were in church when the sirens went off, and young Lothar (now twelve) would carry his three younger sisters, one by one, down into the basement shelter of their home.

The invading Red Army arrived in the vicinity of Cottbus in early 1945. Jutta Obst later recalled one terrifying afternoon in February when Allied airplanes brutally pounded the city. She huddled with her mother and her siblings in the basement for two hours in "earth-shattering terror." When the attack was over, the house still stood but was substantially damaged:

The power of the explosions broke loose all the doors, including their frames. The wall plaster had fallen off, and all the wall hangings and pictures were broken up; all over the floors. It was a bad scene, a terrible and depressing scene. But we were grateful that we were alive and physically

Fig. 1. Elfriede Grünewald on her first day in school in September 1944. The traditional Schultüte was filled with goodies. (E. Gruenewald Schulz)

unharmed. Poorly and scanty, we repaired everything and covered the windows with paper.[8]

Volker Hagen (born 1940) recalled what may have been the same air raid. The house next to his was destroyed by the bombs. He later told how the rescue squad "had to come into our fallout shelter and knock a hole in the wall to get to the people in the other bomb shelter next door. [That way they] got them into our bomb shelter to save them because their house was destroyed."[9] The system used throughout Germany had worked again successfully.

As the war intensified in Cottbus, it was not even safe to walk the streets. Fighter planes swooped down and shot at civilians. On one occasion, Elfriede Grünewald (born 1938) and her brother, Gerhard, were playing outside. Gerhard was tied to a little wagon like a horse by a long rope. Suddenly, an airplane attacked, and Elfriede fled to the house while her brother crawled under the wagon. "We were terrified, but Heavenly Father protected us," she explained. After that, when Elfriede's mother sent her to the bakery, the little girl went from one house entrance to the next to make her way down the street safely.[10]

During one harrowing afternoon when as many as eight thousand people were killed in air raids on Cottbus, Anne Marie Grünewald had wanted to work in her garden but could not find the gate key anywhere.[11] When three successive alarms sounded, she prayed with her children and took them to the basement shelter. One bomb landed so close to the house that significant damage was done. When they returned to the kitchen, Sister Grünewald found the garden key on the kitchen table. She realized that if she had found the key earlier, she would likely have been in the garden when the bomb that damaged the home hit the ground. There were six bomb craters between their apartment and their garden plot.[12]

Early in 1945, the city government confiscated part of the Lehnig building. According to young Joachim:

> [They took] the large meeting rooms because they used them as a station for the refugees from Silesia and East Prussia. They put wooden beds covered with straw and equipped with blankets in the rooms. They also installed bathrooms and a small kitchen.

Young Gisela Vogt (born 1939) had vivid memories of the dangers experienced in the last months of the war. As she recalled, "We went to bed with our clothes on [to be ready for an alarm]. Once, we were trapped in the basement, and it took about an hour to dig our way out. I once saw a little black body underneath a burned-out automobile. It apparently was the driver who had tried to hide there. You don't forget those sights and smells."[13]

By March, the Soviets were approaching the city of Cottbus, and the government encouraged women and children to leave, while the men were required to stay and defend the city. Along with about eighty other members of the Cottbus Branch, Max and Elfriede Obst took their four children and headed west. They were privileged to ride in a delivery van owned by a Brother Sasse. They stayed for several days in a barn near the town of Stradow, about ten miles west of Cottbus. In the meantime, the Red Army conquered Cottbus and just days later streamed past Stradow on their way to Berlin. The LDS refugees decided to return to Cottbus. As they did so, they were surrounded by confusion and destruction, as Jutta Obst recalled:

> Everything around us was burning and on fire. Along the way we passed corpses of dead soldiers and dead horses everywhere. The stench of death filled the air. This gruesome sight of death, heaps of twisted steel and concrete, naked blasted walls, was so enormously frightening. . . . I remember being so anxious, nervous, scared, and trembling. The other side of the highway was crowded with Russians and their tanks with trucks, cannon, armored cars, soldiers, etc.[14]

Several eyewitnesses recalled that one of the wagons used on the return trek to Cottbus was pulled by two strong horses. Soviet soldiers confiscated those horses and replaced them with two very old and decrepit animals. On the way, Elfriede Grünewald was instructed to hold tightly to a beautiful young woman named Gerda Eckert (who was only twenty-one) and to call her "Mama" in case the invaders tried to molest Gerda.[15]

Marie Hagen also took her three sons and fled before the Soviets. When they returned from Stradow, their apartment was still intact but inhabited by another LDS family.

After a short stay at the Lehnig home, the Hagens moved back into their apartment. According to young Volker, the Soviets soon went through the apartment looking for items to confiscate—principally radios and bicycles. The conquerors ordered that those and other specific items be surrendered at city hall by the citizenry.

Back in Cottbus, the Obst family joined the LDS refugee colony at the Lehnig property. In an attempt to protect the women from enemy soldiers (some of whom lived in a building next door), American flags were displayed on the property and were worn by the members of the group. However, as much as Fritz Lehnig and the other priesthood leaders of the group tried to protect the women from molestation, it simply was not possible on an everyday basis. Jutta Obst recalled that "in spite of Lothar's tender age of thirteen–fourteen, he was made to witness one of the many rapes that even happened in Lehnig's home."[16]

Church meetings were held regularly at the Lehnig property, but the members had to gather in secret. The Soviet military occupation authority did not allow such meetings. On at least one occasion, enemy soldiers barged into the chapel during the sacrament service and menaced the congregation. Fortunately, they left without further incident.

The family of Fritz Lehnig suffered from the loss of two sons killed in the war: Alfred and Reinhold. In the recollections of young Joachim:

> After 1945, we received notice from the Red Cross that Alfred and Reinhold could not be found. I was the only one who saw my father sitting at his desk crying with his face in his hands. He stopped after a while and went back to work. He explained to us later that the gospel needs to be taught to every person and that Reinhold and Fredi would now also be teachers [in heaven]. Reinhold had served in the East

German Mission in 1938 and 1939 and was drafted right after he came home.

Similar sentiments were not the reaction of the Lehnig family when they heard of the death of Adolf Hitler: "We burned his picture," explained Joachim.

Volker Hagen recalled visiting his father in a POW camp in the American Occupation Zone in 1946. Otto Hagen was freed in 1947 and joined his wife and sons in Cottbus. Marie Hagen had been working in a savings and loan company while he had been gone for nearly five years. He was in relatively good health but was tall and—according to Volker—"very skinny; he was just like a straight line." Shortly after his return, Otto Hagen baptized his son, Volker, in the Spree River.

Sister Grünewald waited for years for Heinrich to return and did not remarry. When she died in 1987, there was still no information regarding his fate. In 1998, her children learned that he had died in a Soviet POW camp two days before Christmas in 1944.[17]

The Obst family left Cottbus in April 1946 and took up residence in another Latter-day Saint refugee colony—Langen, south of Frankfurt am Main in the West German Mission. Many other Cottbus refugee camp veterans joined them there. By the time most refugees had fled, the Cottbus Branch was smaller than it had been in 1939.

In Memoriam

The following members of the Cottbus Branch did not survive World War II:

Ernst August Wilhelm Heinz Grabke b. Cottbus, Brandenburg, Preußen 27 Aug 1919; son of Ernst Fritz Wilhelm Grabke and Anna Hedwig Martha Feiertag; bp. 27 Oct 1927; ord. deacon; k. in battle eastern Germany 1943 or 1945 (E. Gäbler; FHL Microfilm 25776, 1930 Census)

Ernst Fritz Wilhelm Grabke b. Cottbus, Brandenburg, Preußen 6 Jan 1881; son of Wilhelm Grabke and Marie Noack; bp. 3 Dec 1925; m. Berlin,

Brandenburg, Preußen 8 Oct 1908, Anna Hedwig Martha Feiertag; 3 children; m. Cottbus, Brandenburg, Preußen 30 Mar 1930, Pauline Helene Marks or Voigt; d. Cottbus 6 Feb 1944 (IGI)

Heinrich Grünewald b. Neu-Beideck, Samara, Russia 3 May 1911; son of Balthasar Grünewald and Katharina Elisabeth Hill; bp. 18 Jun 1943; m. Cottbus, Brandenburg, Preußen 5 Mar 1938, Anna Maria Melcher; 4 children; corporal; d. POW Woroschilograd, Russia 20 Dec 1944 (E. Grünewald Schulz; IGI; AF; PRF; www.volksbund.de)

Reinhold Fritz Lehnig b. Crimmitschau, Sachsen 20 Mar 1919; son of Fritz Alfred Lehnig and Anna Hildegard Salzbrenner; bp. 20 Mar 1927; missionary East German Mission, 1938–39; m. 22 May 1940, Elsa Elisabeth Erna Niepraschk; 2 children; d. Stalingrad, Russia 9 Jan 1943 (www.volksbund.de; IGI)

Wilhelm Alfred Lehnig b. Forst, Brandenburg, Preußen 26 Feb 1927; son of Fritz Alfred Lehnig and Anna Hildegard Salzbrenner; bp. 11 Mar 1935; d. 26 Mar 1945 (IGI)

Fig. 3. Heinrich Grünewald shortly after he joined the Church in 1943. (E. Gruenewald Schulz)

Fig. 4. Reinhold Lehnig. (J. Lehnig)

Die Schulferien dauern vom 9. Juli bis 6. August 1944.

Verwaltung der Textilingenieur-Schule Cottbus

Oberinspektor

Fig. 2. Alfred Lehnig is shown here on his official school card. He died in March of 1945. (J. Lehnig)

NOTES

1. Elfriede Grünewald Schulz, autobiography (unpublished), 2; private collection.
2. Presiding Bishopric, "Financial, Statistical, and Historical Reports of Wards, Stakes, and Missions, 1884–1955," CR 4 12, 257.
3. East German Mission Quarterly Reports, 1938, nos. 20–22, East German Mission History.
4. Joachim Lehnig, interview by the author in German, Salt Lake City, June 16, 2007; summarized in English by Judith Sartowski.
5. Jutta Obst Burch, "Portrait of My Family" (unpublished family history, 2003), 4; private collection.
6. Schulz, autobiography, 13–14.
7. There is no official record of restrictions having been placed on the Church in Cottbus.
8. Burch, "Portrait of My Family," 7.
9. Volker Hagen, interview by the author, Midvale, Utah, December 8, 2006. For details on this civil defense practice, see the introduction.
10. Schulz, autobiography, 15.
11. It was the custom in most of Europe to fence in the family garden plot (which was often not close to the home), and the gate was usually locked.
12. Schultz, autobiography, 16.
13. Gisela Vogt Berndt, interview by the author in German in Berlin, Germany, August 20, 2006; summarized in English by the author.
14. Burch, "Portrait of My Family," 8.
15. Schulz, autobiography, 17–18.
16. Burch, "Portrait of My Family," 11. For additional details regarding life in the refugee colony, see the chapters on the Spreewald District and the Guben and Forst Branches.
17. Schulz, autobiography, 14.

FORST BRANCH

Numbering 142 members, the branch in Forst was by far the largest of the four in the Spreewald District. The city is situated on the west bank of the Neisse River but in 1939 included homes on the east side of the river in what is now Poland. As World War II approached, there were about forty-five thousand inhabitants in Forst.

Forst Branch[1]	1939
Elders	7
Priests	2
Teachers	2
Deacons	11
Other Adult Males	21
Adult Females	85
Male Children	7
Female Children	7
Total	142

The meetings of The Church of Jesus Christ of Latter-day Saints were held in rented rooms at Frankfurterstrasse 17 in the Hinterhaus. Helga Schäler (born 1930) recalled that the building looked like a factory.[2]

We were on the second floor, and we had it fixed up as a meeting place. There was a little stage and some classrooms. When you came in, there was a cloakroom with a tiny little iron stove that would keep it warm.

Eberhard Gäbler (born 1927) added these details about this meeting place:

There was a sign out front, at the right of the portal where we drove through to the Hinterhaus. We were in the third floor [classrooms]. We could play ping-pong up there too. We had a cloakroom that was used as a classroom. The main room had a stage, and another classroom

was behind that. Attendance may have been sixty or seventy. That location was used by the branch during the entire war.[3]

Sunday School was held at 10:00 A.M. and sacrament meeting in the evening. As was the case in many wartime branches, Helga recalled, "A lot of times the young kids stayed home, and the older people went to sacrament meeting in the evenings."

The history of the East German Mission shows the following entry for Wednesday, May 18, 1938:

On this, the previous and the following day, special meetings were held in Frankfurt/ Oder, Cottbus and Forst Branches, Spreewald District, by Elder Edward R. McKay, to discuss the new genealogy plan, which was presented at that time.[4]

Apparently, all Church programs of that era were operating successfully in the Forst Branch.

Another entry in 1938 leaves room for speculation—Saturday, November 26 and Sunday, November 27: President and Sister Rees attended special meetings in the Forst and Guben Branches, spoke, and "brought new enthusiasm and cheer into the hearts of the attending members and friends."[5] One wonders what may have dampened the spirits of the members in those days.

Morale among the citizenry in Germany in 1939 was predominately positive but not for those Jews who had not yet left the country. Helga Schäler recalled experiences with a Jewish family who lived down the street from her Forst home. Three boys from that family attended LDS Church meetings, and Helga's mother, Rosa, was their teacher. Later, while Sister Schäler worked as a cleaning lady at city hall, she met the mother of that Jewish family, who was being incarcerated temporarily in the basement. The woman was despondent and asked, "Sister Schäler, why does this happen to us? We

Fig. 1. The building in which the Forst Branch met during the war as it now appears. (H. Schäler Price)

have never done any harm to anyone." Helga recalled her mother quietly weeping as she told her husband, Georg Schäler, of the situation.

Günther Gäbler (born 1923) had a positive experience in the Hitler Youth organization. He enjoyed the road trips, the camping, and the singing. "There was no heavy-duty political training," he later explained. At sixteen, he began an apprenticeship as a carpenter and was able to complete it, despite interruptions caused by the war.

Eberhard Gäbler was in a cavalry unit of the Hitler Youth and enjoyed his training with horses. His brother, Horst (born 1932), did not have time for the organization because he was busy delivering newspapers during the last years of the war.

Irmgard Gäbler (born 1935) turned eight in 1943 and was baptized in the Neisse River. "I remember being swept away by the current, but my father [Bruno Gäbler] grabbed me and saved me." A year later, she wanted to join the Jungvolk, but her mother objected.[6]

Shortly after the war began, Helga Schäler turned ten and was inducted with her classmates into the Jungvolk. She explained her reluctance to participate and described a strategy she developed to avoid attending the meetings:

> I hated it. They threatened that the police would come for us if we didn't go. Once a leader found me at the store, took me home, and then escorted me to the meeting. If you lived on the fourth floor, you could watch the street from the window and see [other girls] coming [and] hide in the attic.

Despite the shortages of war, Christmas celebrations were still observed at church, according to the recollections of Helga Schäler. Traditionally, a Christmas program was held which involved all of the children. The story of Christmas was told, songs were sung, and poems were recited. Santa Claus came with his sled or on a white horse and handed out sacks with presents. "If we didn't know a poem to recite, we didn't get any presents."

Doris Schäler (born 1933) was seen by her school teacher while walking to church on several Sundays. Once, she stopped Doris and asked where she was headed. After the teacher found out that Doris attended church, the little girl was subjected to an inquiry in school. Doris later described the experience in these words:

> In front of the entire class, she asked me if my father was in the [Nazi] Party. I answered honestly and said no. Then she asked if my mother was in the Nazi Party women's auxiliary. I again said no. Then she asked if anybody in my family would support the country by being in the army or in other organizations. I answered that my brother was in the Wehrmacht. After that, she seemed satisfied and left me alone.[7]

As in nearly all branches of the East German Mission, most of the young men in Forst were drafted into the Wehrmacht but enough older men were still in town to guide the branch and exercise the powers of the priesthood. For most

Fig. 2. The family of Georg and Rosa Schäler in 1939. Brother Schäler was unfit for military service, because it was said that without his glasses "he could not distinguish between friend or foe." (D. Schäler Shepardanis)

of the war years, Paul Schulze was the branch president. At the conclusion of the war, Georg Schäler (who was exempt from military duty due to poor health and eyesight) led the branch.

The Schäler family lived in several different apartments during the war years. At first, they were in the main part of town close to church then they moved across the river to a suburb called Berge. The walk from there to church was substantially longer, "about forty-five minutes, through the whole city," as Helga recalled. She also said, "Basically, all I remember about being young was the war. It lasted from about the time I was eight until I was nearly fifteen." However, she also indicated that she and her friends had plenty of opportunities to play and live a somewhat normal life:

> We didn't have television or even a radio at first, so we went outside. We went to the river and the woods; we loved the outdoors. We used to get coins and put them on the railroad tracks and wait until the train ran over them. When you picked them up, they would be about twice the size of normal. Once we were playing in the woods and it rained and we got all wet. We took off our clothes and hung them in the trees to dry, and when they were dry we put them back on.

During his six months in the Reichsarbeitsdienst, Günther Gäbler served aboard three ships, two of them being the battleships *Scharnhorst* and *Gneisenau.* Just a week after his release, a draft notice arrived, and he was inducted into the Wehrmacht. His basic training took place in Zülichau, Brandenburg, and from there he was transferred to a unit bound for Africa.[8] He was next trained in the use of light and heavy machine guns and arrived in Africa on July 30, 1942, to serve under Field Marshall Erwin Rommel.

In Africa, Günther and his comrades actually used captured British weapons to fire upon British tanks. Nevertheless, the German campaign in North Africa was a failure, and Günther was captured on October 25, 1942. After six months in a POW camp in Egypt, he was shipped to the United States. The voyage took him east to Bombay, then west and south along the east coast of Africa, past Capetown, across the Atlantic, around Cape Horn, along the coast of Chile, through the Panama Canal, and up the east coast of the United States to New York City. The extensive voyage lasted nearly two months.

Aboard the *Cape Horn Castle,* the German POWs had managed to make and hang out swastika flags without their captors finding out. This embarrassed the British crew when they docked in New York City. As Günther later recalled, "The British then [turned us over] to the Americans, [telling us] that we should make life as hard for them as we had made it for the British. The British were always nice to us; that I have to admit."

After a long train ride ("very comfortable—leather seats!"), Günther found himself in Alberta, Canada, where he worked from 1943 to 1944. Then he volunteered for a logging detail and remained at that job through 1945. His pay was fifty cents per day or thirty marks per month. He was allowed to write as many as two letters and four cards per month, so his family knew of his whereabouts in

Fig. 3. The Forst Branch met in the upstairs rooms of this building behind the main building at Frankfurterstrasse 17. (R. P. Minert, 2008)

North America before a notice arrived in Forst reporting him missing in action in Africa.

For most of the war, the city of Forst was spared air raids. Helga Schäler recalled the first time a bomb—apparently a dud—was dropped on the city:

> They showed it in the city hall, and we went to look at it. We were basically very lucky that we did not have any bombing (hardly at all) until the very end when the Russians came in, and then everything went kaput.

As in many cities with large factories, Forst was a city where Dutch and Polish laborers were brought to work. Horst Schäler (born 1937) recalled that his mother invited a few foreign laborers to join the family for Sunday dinner each week, although food supplies were short. One Sunday after dinner, a man in a long leather coat knocked on the door and identified himself as an agent of the Gestapo. He had heard that foreign laborers had been in the apartment and wanted to know what was going on there. Rosa Schäler told him, "Mister, we invite them for Sunday dinner. We are Christians, and we

believe that one should be kind to prisoners of war." He replied, "Is that all?" then searched the apartment for radios and similar items. Finding only the standard Volksempfänger radio, he was satisfied and left.[9]

As the war drew to its conclusion, Eberhard Gäbler and his Hitler Youth group were pressed into service to dig trenches on the east side of the river for German defensive troops. However, Eberhard was no longer at home when the invaders arrived. The country needed soldiers, so he was not drafted into the Reichsarbeitsdienst but directly into the Wehrmacht at age seventeen. His military career was quite short and fairly uneventful, as he recalled:

> It was the end of 1944, and I was assigned to an antiaircraft battery. I had quick basic training in Schleswig-Holstein, then went to an airfield up by Eckeberg by the Danish border, then was assigned to an airfield near Schleswig [in Germany] at Easter 1945. I was there when the war ended. We were attacked by both bombers and dive-bombers. When the Allied planes headed for cities in the interior, the fighter planes stayed around our area and tried to find our planes on the ground to destroy them. I was in the air force [ground troops]. We didn't see the enemy until the war was over. My life was never really at risk, but twice while I was at the gun, our barracks were destroyed (a few hundred yards from our gun position).

Johannes (Hans) Georg Schäler was eighteen when he was drafted into the Waffen-SS. His younger brother, Horst, recalled the instruction their mother gave to Hans before he left home as a soldier:

> She said that if he had to take a life in order to defend his own, that would be all right. But if he did not need to defend his own life, he was not to take the life of another person. My brother promised my mother that he would not kill anybody who was innocent, but that he would defend himself.

Hans Schäler was wounded in the Battle of the Bulge, spent some time in a hospital,

Fig. 4. Members of the Forst Branch celebrated the centennial of the Relief Society in 1942. (H. Gäbler)

then went home to Forst on leave in early 1945. When it came time for him to return to his unit in western Germany in the spring of 1945, railroad service was interrupted by air raids, and his departure was apparently delayed. According to his sister, Doris, Hans was jailed by the military police:

> My parents tried desperately to convince the police that he was not a deserter. My father met one of Hans's former teachers and explained the problem. . . . The teacher, also a soldier at the time, wrote a letter to the Wehrmacht. . . . My father then asked me to take the letter to the commander. I was eleven years old. I asked if I had to go, and he said that I had to go. I delivered the letter. The commander looked at me, took the letter, and told me that I could leave. They released my brother that same day.

The last general meeting of the Forst Branch in wartime was a conference of the Primary that was attended by seventy-five people on February 11, 1945. According to Eberhard

Gäbler, "It was a spiritual event in peaceful harmony." Days later, the German army retreated to the west bank of the Neisse, and the Soviets moved to the outskirts of Forst (to the suburb of Berge). In their apartments between the armies, the four Latter-day Saint families living east of the river were starving and prayed specifically that they might find food. Soon after the prayer was offered, Red Army artillery shells hit a supply depot, and German soldiers crossed the river to the Schäler apartment with substantial supplies of food that otherwise would have been wasted.

With this direct answer to prayer in mind, the children of those families gathered to pray for something they had not seen for a long time: chocolate. They had faith that their prayer would also be answered. It was, the answer coming with the unwitting help of Hans Schäler, then a soldier defending his own hometown. According to his younger brother, Horst, Hans

429

found a large supply of chocolate in a bombed-out and abandoned store downtown and gathered up some to take home. The prayer of the children was answered as expected. As Horst considered the event years later, he commented that "the Lord always used other people to help us; those other people might have thought that those events were only coincidences, but those things were a little too obvious."

As little boys will do, Horst Schäler played soldier in his neighborhood in the days prior to the Soviet invasion. On one occasion, he found a grenade and tucked it into his belt, not realizing that the pin had been removed. A passing German soldier grabbed Horst by the collar, took the grenade from him, and threw it as far as he could. Fortunately, it did not explode. "He then put me across his knee and gave me a really good spanking," recalled Horst.

When the Red Army approached Forst, the Schäler family thought that the German defenders would stop the invaders. As Helga recalled, "We thought we wouldn't be like the other refugees and have to leave, but we had to do that, too." They left their home on the east side of the Neisse River and moved in with an LDS family (the Voigts) on the west side. Two of the Schäler girls—Ruth and Helga—later decided to go back across the river to their apartment to retrieve the family accordion. Doris later called this a "foolish" plan and described what happened in these words:

> Off they went to the river to cross the bridge, which was ready to be blown up. The soldiers did not want Ruthie to cross the bridge because it was much too dangerous. She begged for 15–20 minutes, which was granted reluctantly. She literally flew across the bridge, while Helga cowered in a trench praying with all her heart for the safety of her sister. Ruthie ran up the four flights, grabbed the instrument, which was heavy, ran down toward the bridge again, almost passing out from this effort. The German soldiers were truly relieved when she returned.[10]

The German defenders of Forst put up stiff resistance for several weeks, holding on to the bridgeheads on both sides of the river. However, their resources were simply not sufficient to hold off the invaders, and they retreated across the river to the main part of town in February 1945. The enemy arrived in the Berge suburb with such speed that young Horst Gäbler was surprised to see them. He had delivered his newspapers one evening and asked his aunt Dora to go home with him. As they crossed the bridge to the east bank, they were suddenly confronted by an enemy soldier, who first fired a warning shot, then (fortunately) allowed them to pass without hindrance. Aunt Dora was not a practicing Christian but learned the importance of prayer while hiding in the Gäbler's basement shelter for the next few days.

The effort to recover the accordion was rewarded shortly after the invaders arrived in Forst. When a soldier bent on evil deeds entered the basement room where the Schäler women were hiding, they convinced him to leave them undisturbed and take the accordion as his great prize instead.

During the war, the population of Latter-day Saints living in Berge on the east bank of the Neisse River consisted almost totally of the families of Paul Schulze, Max Riedel, Georg Schäler, and Bruno Gäbler. In February 1945, Brother Gäbler gathered his family for prayer to ask the Lord's guidance about whether to go or stay. The answer received by all seemed to be unanimous: "We're staying here!" they decided. The Schulzes also stayed, while the Schälers and Riedels evacuated the neighborhood. Irmgard Gäbler was not quite ten at the time but vividly recalled what happened when the Soviet soldiers arrived in the neighborhood:

> The day came when we were to be forced out of our homes. The Russians acted as if they were going to kill all of us. Then they marched us out of town into the forest. My father had a

briefcase with all kinds of genealogical papers, and he brought them with us. He kept it all the way—[thirty] miles out [east] and [thirty] miles back. He was mocked for bringing such a thing along, but those were all of the genealogical papers about my ancestors.

The residents were marched thirty miles eastward by the conquerors and lived in the country for about the next two months. Horst Gäbler described what transpired next: "We came back home in April 1945. Much of the housing was burned down, including our home. The town was destroyed 85 percent. We then lived in a neighbor's house because they had fled."

It was a Sunday in April when Red Army soldiers reached the place where the Schäler family was staying. They could hear sporadic firing and hid in the basement. At one point, Georg Schäler took his wife and his children upstairs to the living room and held a sacrament service with them around a little table. Then he told his family that Heavenly Father would bless them so that they would not need to be afraid. They sang and prayed together, after which Rose Schäler said that if they were righteous and did everything the Lord wanted them to do, they would someday go to America. A few minutes later, the soldiers searched the house and stole some of the Schäler's property, but did not harm them.

"In about mid-February, the first Russians came into our house," wrote Charlotte Schulze. "They were clean and spoke broken German."[11] The next enemy soldiers were not as nice, and Charlotte went into hiding. Her father was in the Volkssturm and her sister was working in a communications office. A few weeks later, Charlotte, her mother, and her siblings headed east toward the town of Pförten, passing horrible scenes of dead soldiers and decaying animals along the way. After a walk of nearly twenty miles, they stopped and searched for a place to stay while enemy soldiers watched. "Never have I prayed so fervently," she later wrote.

A few days later, Charlotte and her mother were thrown into a cellar and incarcerated there with other women. One by one, the women were taken away and assaulted. The two Saints held fast to each other and prayed to the Lord for help. "Peace overcame our hearts, and we felt that nothing would happen to us; and so it was." This was not the last time when the danger of molestation was imminent, but Charlotte was spared every time.[12]

The Schulze women eventually went fifteen miles north to Bobersberg, then south back to Sommerfeld, then finally west back to Forst. The town was policed by both the Soviets and the Polish, but the women were able to cross the river and find a place to stay with the Voigt family in Nossdorf. "We had lost literally everything, but nobody could take from us our faith and our testimonies," Charlotte later wrote.[13] Her father was missing, and the family later heard that he too had been sent east of Forst at the end of the war; he had died of starvation as a prisoner of the conquerors.

Eberhard Gäbler later functioned as the unofficial historian of the Forst Branch and, in 1995, compiled stories under the title *Gemeinde Forst Vor 50 Jahren—1945* (The Forst Branch Fifty Years Ago—1945). The following are extracts from that history:[14]

> Sunday, February 18: We met in the Voigt family home. . . . We are in God's hands.
>
> Friday, February 23: People are confused and hopeless. . . . The Schulze family are missing. . . . We are praying for them.
>
> Sunday, February 25: Flames seen in Nossdorf. . . . We are worried about the members living there.
>
> Monday, February 26: The Lord blessed us in a wonderful way today: we received food for the first time in a long time. . . .

Wednesday, February 28: [Several members] moved from the city to Nossdorf today. [Several more] left for Niederbarnim by Berlin.

Friday, March 2: Today we were told "Women and children are to leave the city." . . . We all felt like we need to stay and trust in God.

Saturday, March 3: We met for a fast meeting at 6:00 P.M. We prayed for all of the members. . . . There were sixteen in attendance.

Sunday, March 4: Fast meeting. Elder Paul Schulze spoke to us: "[So far] the destroying angel has passed over us."

Thursday, March 15: Life in the homes of the Saints goes on. Many members have taken non-members [refugees] into their homes.

Sunday, March 18: Sunday School at 10:00 A.M.; at 3:30 we held a memorial service for Brother Wolfgang Dommaschk who died on January 23 1945 for *Führer, Volk, und Vaterland.*

Sunday, March 25: We held Sunday School and sacrament meeting. Reinhold and Betha Schwier were again with us after being absent for a while. All were pleased at the reunion. Twenty-two persons were in attendance.

Saturday, March 31: We left Forst . . . with heavy hearts.

According to Eberhard Gäbler, the first postwar meeting of the Forst Branch took place on May 20, 1945, in the home of Sister Kolo:

In addition to the hostess, the following were in attendance: the Schwier and Gäbler families, Anni Kleemann, Laasner, Brother Riedel, and Sister Domke. On this occasion, the members reported on their experiences in fleeing Forst and bore testimony to the way the Lord had led them through this difficult time and how each had to take "his own path." When they returned to Forst, the city was totally destroyed, including the meeting house. Most of the families had lost their homes.

The surviving Latter-day Saints of the Forst Branch headed west to Cottbus (ten miles) to join other LDS refugees at the Fritz Lehnig home.

By May 1945, Sister Schäler and her children had joined the LDS refugee colony in Cottbus. Georg Schäler had been compelled to stay and defend Forst. After the Soviets arrived, they destroyed his glasses, without which he

Fig. 5. The Gäbler family lived in Berge in the closest house to the left. (E. Gäbler)

432

was nearly blind. Fortunately, he was not detained and joined his family in Forst just days after the war ended. The family did not return to their Forst neighborhood again for another year, and when they did, there was nothing left of their apartment building.

When Bruno Gäbler took his family back to Forst, they found that the Polish (to whom the area east of the Neisse River now belonged) had burned their house down. With no place to stay, they were forced to leave. They crossed the river to the German side and began life anew in the southwest Forst suburb of Nossdorf.

In the summer of 1945, Charlotte Schulze prayed for a way to get back to Berge to rescue her Church books from the family apartment. She managed to find a work detail for the Polish across the river and was able to carefully sneak into her home. She found some scriptures and hymnals "amid a terrible mess" but not what she sought most—"the history of the Forst Branch that I had so carefully and lovingly compiled. I was in the house again on three occasions and was very saddened by this loss."[15]

At war's end, Eberhard Gäbler's unit was officially taken prisoner by British troops in northern Germany. They were classified as POWs but lived in a barn and were allowed to move about in the area. Later, when the English were looking for an aide for a military judge, Eberhard volunteered to do that job.

In September 1945, Eberhard was released as a British POW. After working on a nearby farm until November, he sneaked across the border into the Soviet Occupation Zone and headed home to Forst. The trip took five days. When he got off the train in Forst, he was delighted to run into his sister who had come to pick up a friend.

In early 1946, Günther Gäbler was shipped to the British Isles, where he worked first in Scotland and then in southern England. In 1947, he was released as a POW and returned to Germany and his hometown of Forst. As a priest in the Aaronic Priesthood, Günther had been isolated from the Church and other Latter-day Saints for five years. However, he lost no time in rejoining the Saints:

> When I went home, I attended the meetings again right away. There were most of the people I knew because the branch slowly started to come together again. I also received a calling very soon after my return because every person was needed.

Looking back on the branch and its members during the war, Doris Schäler offered the following comments:

> We boosted each other's faith and expectations although things looked horrible all around us. But knowing that there are others who also suffer and on whom you can rely for support and who believe in the same source of comfort really helped us through hard times—particularly in 1944 and 1945. Without having other Saints and the meetings and the prayers and sharing everything we had, . . . we would not have been so strong.

Relatively few members of the Forst Branch died during the war, and enough of them returned to the city to begin Church meetings and activities anew in the summer of 1945.

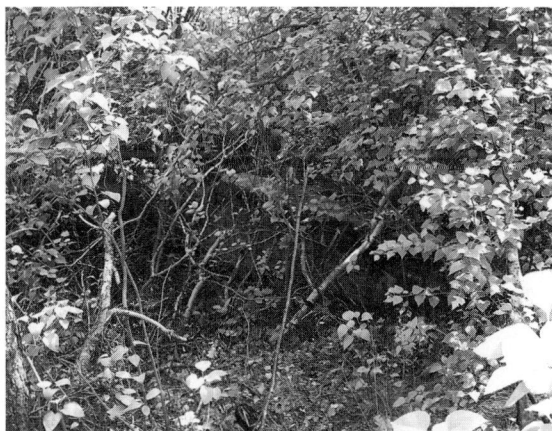

Fig. 6. All that remains of the Gäbler home in Berge today is the foundation. All usable building materials in Berge after the war were taken for the reconstruction of Warsaw. (R. P. Minert, 2008)

In Memoriam

The following members of the Forst Branch did not survive World War II:

Ida Klara Bredsch b. Hennersdorf, Sorau, Brandenburg, Preußen 29 Aug 1861; dau. of Eduard Bredsch and Amalia Lipscher; bp. 23 Aug 1924; m. —— Paul; d. stroke 9 Mar 1945 (CHL CR 375 8 #2458, 1410–11; IGI)

Günter Wolfgang Dommaschk b. Forst, Brandenburg, Preußen 24 Dec 1925; son of Willy Mensel and Dora Gertrud Erna Dommaschk; blessed Forst 21 Mar 1926; bp. 26 Jul 1941; k. in battle Stuhlweißenburg, Hungary 23 or 25 Jan 1945 (E. Gäbler; www.volksbund.de; IGI)

Karl Falkner b. Bostenhofen, Nuremberg, Mittelfranken, Bayern 14 Jun 1885; son of Paul Heinrich Falkner and Anna Katharina Lauterbach; bp. 14 Nov 1925; m. Chemnitz, Chemnitz, Sachsen 1 Dec 1907, Ida Klara Taubert; 5 children; 2m. Chemnitz 11 Sep 1926, Lina Ella Tierlich; 3 children; 3m. Helene Mehnert; d. Chemnitz 22 Dec 1942 or 1944 (FHL Microfilm 25764, 1930 Census; IGI; AF)

Auguste Pauline Lerche b. Reichersdorf, Brandenburg, Preußen 14 May 1864; dau. of —— Lerche and Maria Elisabeth Lorisch; bp. 25 Jul 1921; m. Forst, Brandenburg, Preußen 1 Dec 1888, Johann Karl August Schimmack; 1 child; d. Forst 19 Mar 1941 (*Sonntagsgruss*, No. 15, 13 Apr 1941, 60; FHL Microfilm 245259, 1935 Census; IGI)

Max Paul Schulze b. Forst, Brandenburg, Preußen 4 Nov 1895; son of Johann Schulze and Marie Johanna Koinzer; bp. Forst 27 Sep 1923; conf. Forst 27 Sep 1923; m. Forst 18 Sep 1920, Frieda Anna Marie Stahn; 3 children; Volkssturm; MIA 1945; declared dead 31 Jul 1949 (E. Gäbler; www.volksbund.de; IGI; AF)

Lina Ella Tierlich b. Gablenz, Chemnitz, Sachsen 11 Feb 1900; dau. of Heinrich Franz Tierlich and Lina Anna Taubert; bp. 17 Mar 1926; m. Chemnitz, Chemnitz, Sachsen 11 Sep 1926, Karl Falkner; 3 children; d. Chemnitz 7 Jan 1944 (FHL Microfilm 25764, 1930 Census; IGI; AF)

Paul Friedrich Helmut Wirth b. Forst, Brandenburg, Preußen 18 Oct 1916; son of August Bruno Wirth and Therese Berta Hulda Wandtke; bp. Forst 21 or 31 Jul 1926; conf. Forst 21 Jul 1926; m. 24 Nov 1939, Gerda Weise; corporal; k. in battle Western Front 18 Jun 1940; bur. Andilly, France (E. Gäbler; www.volksbund.de; IGI)

Notes

1. Presiding Bishopric, "Financial, Statistical, and Historical Reports of Wards, Stakes, and Missions, 1884–1955," CR 4 12, 257.

2. Helga Schäler Price, interview by the author, Highland, Utah, February 17, 2006.

3. Eberhard Gäbler, interview by the author in German, Forst, Germany, June 7, 2007; unless otherwise noted, summarized in English by Judith Sartowski.

4. East German Mission Quarterly Reports, 1938, no. 22, East German Mission History.

5. Ibid., no. 47.

6. Irmgard Helga Gäbler Henkel, interview by Jennifer Heckmann in German, Bretzfeld, Germany, August 17, 2006; unless otherwise noted, transcript or audio version of interview in author's collection.

7. Doris Charlotte Schäler Shapardanis, telephone interview with Jennifer Heckmann, March 5, 2008.

8. "Before we went to Africa, they looked for three people who wanted to go. We [three friends] did not want to be separated because we were used to each other as companions and got along well. So we volunteered and went to Africa. Everybody else in our group went to Stalingrad [Russia]. That was a blessing. Heavenly Father had his hand in things." Günther Gäbler, interview by the author in German, Forst, Germany, June 7, 2007.

9. Horst Schäler, telephone interview with Jennifer Heckmann in German, May 8, 2008.

10. Doris Charlotte Schäler Shapardanis, "World War II Experiences of the Schaeler Family and Members of the Forst Branch" (unpublished), 7; private collection.

11. Charlotte Schulze Riedel, report (unpublished), 1; private collection; trans. the author.

12. Ibid., 5–6.

13. Ibid., 8.

14. Eberhard Gäbler, *Gemeinde Forst Vor 50 Jahren—1945*, in *Der junge Zweig* (unpublished history, 1995); private collection.

15. Riedel, report, B2.

Frankfurt/Oder Branch

About sixty-five miles east of Berlin, the city of Frankfurt lies on the west bank of the Oder River. An industrial city, it was the home of about seventy-five thousand people when World War II began.

The Latter-day Saints of the Frankfurt/Oder Branch were led in 1939 by Walter Krause, who had arrived in the city in 1931, married there, and fathered three children. As an independent carpenter, he led a modest life and was a devoted branch president. Just prior to the war, the branch held its meetings in rented rooms at Park 11–12, on the main floor of the Hinterhaus.

Frankfurt/Oder Branch[1]	1939
Elders	7
Priests	0
Teachers	1
Deacons	3
Other Adult Males	9
Adult Females	38
Male Children	6
Female Children	4
Total	68

"The rooms were in an old factory building," said Ilona Gertrud Henkel (born 1940). "Some of the members lived in the same building."[2]

An interesting entry is found in the history of the East German Mission under May 18, 1938:

> On this, the previous and the following day, special meetings were held in Frankfurt/Oder, Cottbus and Forst Branches, Spreewald District, by [missionary] Elder Edward R. McKay, to discuss the new genealogy plan, which was presented at that time.[3]

As it was elsewhere in Germany, the work of genealogical research in support of temple ordinances for the deceased was being carried out with enthusiasm in the Spreewald District.

At the onset of the year 1939, the Frankfurt/Oder Branch had strong adult priesthood leadership, but younger priesthood holders were rare. More than one half of the branch membership consisted of women.

In 1938, Walter Krause was classified as "conditionally fit" for military service. When the war began, he was thirty years old and relatively confident that at his age he would not be needed for the war effort. This hope was

dashed in January 1940 when he was drafted into a police unit. He later wrote of his feelings at the time: "Nobody mentioned how my family would survive or what would happen to my shop or all the work I was doing for the branch. I was disappointed but what good did that do?"[4]

Walter was posted to occupied Poland and soon found himself assigned as a cook (something he had never done before). For the next three years, he served under safe conditions well away from the front. He informed his comrades of his avoidance of alcohol and tobacco and sought opportunities to speak with them about religion. He even prayed with other Christians and delivered funeral sermons for fallen friends.[5]

Young Manfred Henkel (born 1933) grew up with the Third Reich, but his parents were not comfortable under Hitler's government. Manfred recalled problems using the required salutation "Heil Hitler!" and wrote this description:

> We were very careful about what we said during the Hitler years. . . . We didn't really like saying "Heil Hitler" all the time. When my mother sent me [to the store]—I might have been nine at the time—I said "Guten Tag," and they sent me out and said that I could come back in when I was ready to say "Heil Hitler!"[6]

As if there were not sufficient ways for a family to suffer in wartime, an accident took the life of ten-year-old Winfried Henkel in 1943; he drowned while swimming in the Oder River by Frankfurt. According to his younger sister, Ilona, "My father had been drafted into the Wehrmacht, and he was not allowed to come home for the funeral."

As a soldier, Walter Krause was probably not the best example of obedience. He found too often that the actions of soldiers were not in harmony with the teachings of the gospel. On one occasion, for example, he watched as

Fig. 1. Members of the Frankfurt/Oder Branch in the late 1930s. (Der Stern, May 1993)

his commanding officer knocked a piece of bread from the hand of a Russian child and crushed it in the dust with his heel. Walter could not contain himself and yelled, "You jerk! Our children and grandchildren will pay for such deeds!" Walter was led away in handcuffs, but a higher-ranking officer prevented punishment. On another occasion, he was ordered to shoot an old man and some children who were suspected partisans. He refused to do so, insisting that they were not partisans. The officer responded, "If you refuse to carry out my order, you will be shot along with them." But the officer did not dare follow through with his threat.[7]

Brothers Karl and Hermann Henkel were stationed in Norway for a time and were actually able to attend the meetings of a branch of Saints there. Hermann became well acquainted with the Jacobsen family in Oslo.[8]

Walter Krause became a successful and popular cook and was rewarded at times with additional leave to visit his family. However, by 1943, he lost his comfortable assignment.

That year he was wounded twice as his unit retreated before the advancing Red Army. All in all, he was blessed with the fulfillment of a sincere wish, namely never having to shoot at the enemy.[9]

In the absence of Brother Krause, Karl Baukus directed the affairs of the branch until he, too, was drafted. During the war, several involuntary laborers from the Netherlands attended meetings with the members in Frankfurt/Oder. Due to the lack of priesthood leadership, district leaders from Cottbus and Forst also visited on several Sundays.[10]

As a young girl, Ilona Henkel did not understand the complexities of war, but she understood, to a degree, the plight of a Jewish family who lived in the same building: "My mother always told me that we were not allowed to give them anything to eat though they were hungry. [But] she gave them food because she felt that we were so blessed that she had to share with others."

Life during wartime in Frankfurt/Oder was fairly comfortable until the last year when air raids plagued the city and the invaders approached. Manfred Henkel recalled, "We lost our home in 1944. . . . The windows in our apartment were blown out, and we moved out to live with my grandparents until the place could be repaired." Things then went from bad to worse for Maria Henkel, whose husband, Hermann Heinrich, was away at the front. Manfred recounted:

> Frankfurt/Oder was declared a fortress during the last months of the war and most of the members left town. Some of us took the last train out of town and went to Annaberg-Buchholz. It was an adventuresome trip. Members there took us in. Then the place we were staying was hit and burned out with the last of our property.

Margarete Krause later wrote of a particular tragedy among the members in Frankfurt/Oder:

> When the Russians came, Sister Jenny Reinemann chose to take her life along with her son['s], Georg, and her daughter['s], Regina, by taking poison. Regina survived the event, having developed immunity to the drug; she had taken it previously for a nervous condition.

In early 1945, Walter Krause was assigned to guard an ammunition train moving toward Germany. When Walter's unit was attacked by Polish partisans, the wagon on which Walter was riding collapsed, and he was crushed underneath large boxes. Taken for dead, he was nearly buried by his comrades but saved by an alert medic. Walter's injuries were extensive, and he was removed from the front lines for treatment.[11]

Following his recovery, Walter was ordered to accompany a railroad car full of documents and equipment back to Germany. He and a friend made it as far as Dresden, where they arrived in the Neustadt district at precisely the wrong time—a few hours before the terrible firebombing of February 13–14, 1945. When a railroad train loaded with ammunition exploded nearby, Walter lost the hearing in his left ear. He and his comrade survived and traveled on to the south and west in the Erzgebirge Mountains. He hoped that he would find his wife and his children there.

Margarete Krause had indeed left Frankfurt/Oder when the Red Army approached. With several other Saints, she found her way to the town of Annaberg-Buchholz near the Czechoslovakian border. In the late spring, she left that town and traveled east to Cottbus where she joined the LDS refugee colony at the Fritz Lehnig home.

Walter and his friend decided in April 1945 that the best way to survive was to change into civilian clothing and hide out in the forest. They easily could have been shot by fanatic police for not actively contributing to the hopeless defense of the fatherland. During this time of uncertainty, Walter wrote the following in his diary:

> Heavenly Father, what is to become of all these people [refugees]? Wilt thou ever again grant them peace? Will they ever have the opportunity to hear of Thy gospel? . . . Today I truly cannot comprehend thee. Why do so many innocent people, old and young, have to suffer because a few madmen lived a riotous life and started a murderous war? . . . Only thou, oh, Lord, canst remedy this situation and I beg thee to do so.[12]

Eventually, Walter and his friend surrendered to American soldiers. During his initial interrogation, he found himself talking with an officer who demanded to know if Walter was a fascist. His response was to show the officer a certificate proving his membership in the Church. The American knew quite a bit about the LDS Church in Utah (his brother was a member of the Church) and asked for information regarding LDS beliefs as proof. Walter's answers were satisfactory.

The Henkel family had to leave their home on the east side of the Oder River. That territory had been ceded to Poland, and they were not allowed to stay. The exodus to the west and south must have been a real adventure to little Ilona, who described part of their journey in these words:

> I remember taking the train for a short distance and sitting on top of the train. . . . Often we stopped in the middle of nowhere. When we were forced to walk, we were glad to meet people with handcarts who let us put our backpacks on them so we did not have to carry them for so long. . . . It seemed chaotic and none of the [transportation] systems seemed to work anymore.

According to Ilona, her mother changed residence at least five times in the next few years, including short stays in the Latter-day Saint

Fig. 2. Hermann Henkel became a master saddlemaker in 1943. This document recognizes his status in the guild. (M. Henkel)

refugee colonies of Cottbus and Wolfsgrün. An uncle eventually found an apartment for them in Freiberg, Saxony, where they joined the strong Latter-day Saint branch.

Manfred Henkel explained the fate of his soldier father, Hermann Heinrich Henkel, in these words:

> My father died in the war, on April 30, 1945, in Lenggries, Bavaria, Germany. I have the death certificate. It says that he was Catholic, but that is not correct. His papers were in his pocket, and he apparently was wounded near that pocket and the blood got on his papers and they could not tell what he was. He was buried in the Catholic cemetery in Lenggries.

Brother Henkel's death is extensively documented. The mayor of Lenggries wrote to Marie Henkel in November 1945 to inform her of the burial of her husband there. One month later, an army comrade wrote to her and indicated that her husband had died quickly. Nearly seven years later, she received word that her husband's remains had been removed to a military cemetery in Traunstein near Munich in Bavaria.

In June 1945, Walter Krause was anxious to find his family but found himself assigned as a military policeman in the tiny town of Brünlos in Saxony. He was charged with keeping order among the populace and preventing violence on the part of fanatics. When the Red Army assumed authority in the region a few weeks later, his assignment was confirmed (he was even offered the job of mayor of the town but declined). By July, he was fortunate to be released and was miraculously accompanied by Soviet officers by train to Cottbus, where he knew his family was staying. The reunion with his wife and his children took place under the Lehnig roof in early July 1945. Walter had avoided becoming a prisoner of war and was pleased to join the LDS refugee colony in Cottbus.

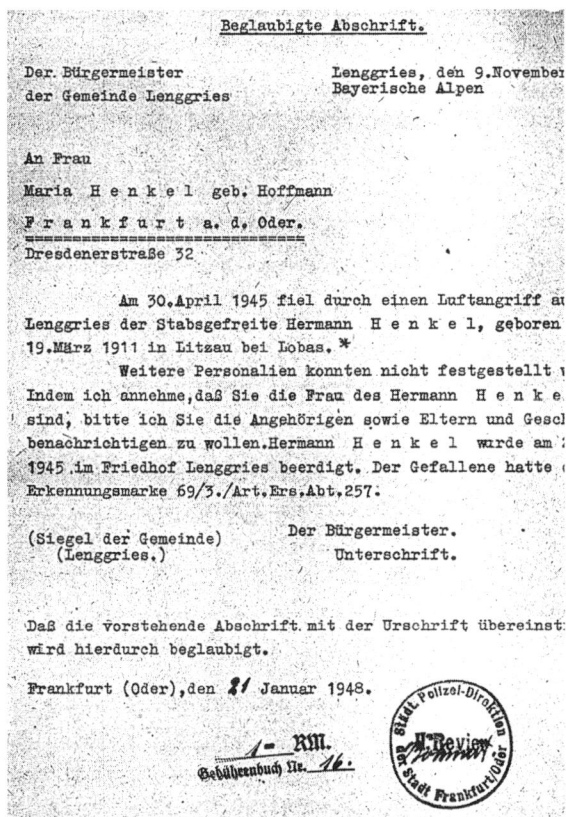

Fig. 3. *This letter dated November 9, 1945, was the first official notice of the death of Hermann Heinrich Henkel just days before the war ended. (M. Henkel)*

Very few of the wartime members of the Frankfurt/Oder Branch were able to return to their homes. For the next few years, the branch struggled to survive.

In Memoriam

The following members of the Frankfurt/Oder Branch did not survive World War II:

Karl Ferdinand Baukus b. Magotten, Ostpreußen, Preußen 24 Jan 1888; son of Johann Ferdinand Baukus and Maria Plaehn; bp. 7 Jun 1934; m. Hafstrom, Kalgen, Ostpreußen, Preußen 13 Jan 1916, Theresia Luise Murningkeit; 3 children; d. field hospital Wandern, Halbe, Brandenburg, Preußen 31 Dec 1945 (M. Henkel; IGI; www.volksbund.de)

Hermann Heinrich Henkel b. Lietzen, Brandenburg, Preußen 19 Mar 1911; son of Friedrich Wilhelm Henkel and Auguste Marie Ruttke; bp. 29 Mar 1932; m. Frankfurt/Oder, Brandenburg, Preußen 15 Dec 1932, Frieda Marie Hofmann; 4 children; staff corporal; k. in battle Lenggries, Bayern 30 Apr 1945;

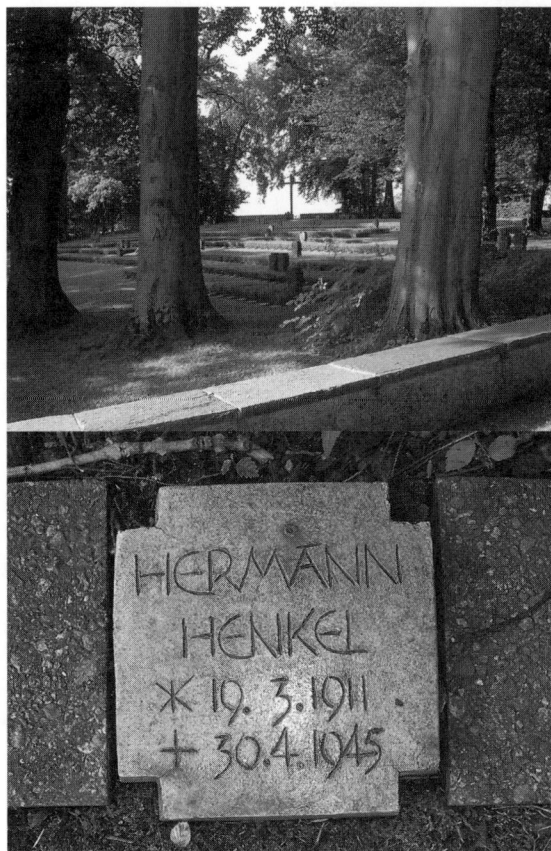

Figs. 4 & 5. *Hermann Henkel's remains were moved to this military cemetery in Traunstein, Germany, in 1952. He may be the only LDS soldier of the East German Mission buried in what is now Germany. (R. P. Minert, 2008)*

bur. Traunstein, Oberbayern, Bayern (M. Henkel; www.volksbund.de; IGI)

Winfried Karl Henkel b. Frankfurt/Oder, Brandenburg, Preußen 19 Nov 1933; son of Karl Friedrich Henkel and Gertrud Elsa Hofmann; bp. Frankfurt/Oder 1941; drowned in the Oder River, Frankfurt/Oder 3 Aug 1943; bur. Frankfurt/Oder (I. Henkel-Hartz; FHL Microfilm 162781, 1935 LDS Census)

Wolfgang Karl Georg Reinemann b. Frankfurt/Oder, Brandenburg, Preußen 25 Jan 1928; son of Karl Reinemann and Jenny Sophie Wilke; k. in battle Berlin, Preußen 30 Apr 1945; bur. Berlin-Wilmersdorf, Schmargendorf Cemetery (M. Krause; www.volksbund.de)

Jenny Sophie Wilke b. Berlin-Weis, Brandenburg, Preußen 5 Aug 1903; m. Karl Reinemann; 3 children; d. suicide Frankfurt/Oder, Brandenburg, Preußen Jan-Feb 1945 (M. Krause; FHL Microfilm 271401, 1930/35 Census)

NOTES

1. Presiding Bishopric, "Financial, Statistical, and Historical Reports of Wards, Stakes, and Missions, 1884–1955," CR 4 12, 257.

2. Ilona Gertrud Henkel Hartz, telephone interview with Jennifer Heckmann in German, February 22, 2008; unless otherwise noted, summarized in English by Judith Sartowski.

3. East German Mission Quarterly Reports, 1938, no. 22, East German Mission History.

4. Edith Krause, *Walter Krause in seiner Zeit* (Hamburg: Mein Buch, 2005), 59.

5. Ibid.

6. Manfred Henkel, interview by Jennifer Heckmann in German, Bretzfeld, Germany, August 17, 2006.

7. Edith Krause, *Walter Krause*, 63.

8. Manfred Henkel to the author, August 17, 2006.

9. Edith Krause, *Walter Krause*, 59, 73.

10. Margarete Krause, *Gemeinde Frankfurt/Oder* (unpublished history); private collection; trans. the author.

11. Edith Krause, *Walter Krause*, 69–70.

12. Ibid., 72–73.

GUBEN BRANCH

The city of Guben is situated on the Neisse River in the southwest region of the historic province of Brandenburg. During the decades before World War II, the city had expanded to the east across the river. Approximately forty thousand people lived in Guben in 1939.[1]

Guben Branch[2]	1939
Elders	4
Priests	1
Teachers	1
Deacons	7
Other Adult Males	7
Adult Females	22
Male Children	4
Female Children	3
Total	49

An interesting notice is found in the history of the East German Mission on February 28, 1938: "In Dresden and Guben the elders, without any specific reasons, were asked to leave these cities within a specified time. At the intervention of [mission president] Alfred C. Rees, the elders were not banished, and they were told to remain until further notice."[3] It is not known why the missionaries were asked to leave or in what office the mission president petitioned to have the order rescinded.

For reasons unknown, the morale of the Guben Branch must have been a bit low in late 1938. However, the following entry in the mission history lent hope to the situation:

> Sunday, November 27: President and Sister Rees attended a special meeting in the Guben Branch, where they spoke and brought "new enthusiasm and cheer into the hearts of the attending members and friends."[4]

In September 1938, the acting branch president in Guben was Otto Sasse, with Walter Czerny and Helmut Kleeman serving as acting counselors.[5] Eyewitnesses identified Willi König as the branch president several years later. The branch met in rented rooms at Lindengraben 13. Helmut Schulz (born 1932) recalled that the street was on the east side of the river, very near the bridge over the Neisse. He described the meeting rooms as follows:

> First you came into a corridor, a small room, a cloakroom. We even had a class in there too after the Sunday School split. You came into a bigger room like a big living room, and there was even a little stage in there too; there was a curtain there, and it was in the regular [apartment] house where people lived. There was not an extra building around it, nothing like that.[6]

Sunday School was held at 10:00 A.M. and sacrament meeting in the afternoon. Other meetings were held on evenings during the week, according to Walter Luskin (born 1922).[7]

Fig. 1. Members of the Guben Sunday School posed for this picture in 1934. (P. Czerny)

Helmut Schulz's father was drafted right away when the war started. He saw action in the Polish and French campaigns and then was transferred to Russia. It was there that he was severely wounded in the right shoulder by an artillery round. It took him a full year to heal, but fortunately he was sent to a hospital in Guben where he could be visited by his family. By 1943, he was back in France but no longer able to carry a rifle.

Because his father was away from home for long periods of time, Helmut was not baptized in 1940 but had to wait until he was nine. Walter Czerny, home on leave, conducted the ceremony. After he left, the only priesthood holder in Church meetings was young Walter Luskin, a teacher in the Aaronic Priesthood. A priest or elder from another branch in the district came each week to conduct the meetings and to administer the sacrament to the members in Guben. As Walter recalled, "I was asked by Brother Ranglack (first counselor in

the mission leadership) to lead the meetings until the branch president came back."[8]

Walter Luskin's father was born to Jewish parents but married a Lutheran girl. During the Third Reich, his ancestry provided reason for local persecution and could have led to his incarceration. However, the Luskin family's neighbors were Latter-day Saints, and they prayed for a peaceful resolution to the problem. Soon afterward, Herr Luskin passed away. Walter, one-half Jewish by blood, was thus spared military service. He was baptized into the Church with his mother on June 13, 1942. Walter's status in the eyes of the government changed dramatically after the death of his father, as he explained:

> From this time on we were a little bit more free. For me being half-Jewish was the greatest blessing that could happen because they did not take me into the German army. They asked me if I would go as a volunteer and I didn't do this. They didn't draft me into the army. They drafted me to work for the army. I was a tailor.

441

I worked in the army tailor shop [in Guben] until the end of the war.

Young Helmut Schulz was forced to make a personal sacrifice for the war effort in early 1943. The sled he had received for Christmas was confiscated just a few weeks later by the German army for military use. Helmut cried and ran after the soldiers, but they did not return his sled.[9] Nearly eleven years old, Helmut was already a member of the Jungvolk but was not prepared to sacrifice everything for his country.

Helmut's father was captured by the Allies after the invasion in Normandy, France, in 1944. Via Africa, he was shipped to the United States where he spent his time in a POW camp until the summer of 1945. A postcard from the Red Cross informed Sister Schulz of her husband's status.

Records of the East German Mission indicate that the meeting place of the Guben Branch had moved by 1943 to Crossenermauer 13a. Walter Luskin indicated that the street was in the older section of Guben on the west side of the river. "When we left home [in 1945] I did see the meetinghouse in flames, burning."

Young Peter Czerny (born 1941) recalled participating in the ordinance of the sacrament in the last days before evacuating Guben:

The [meeting] rooms were all intact because the war hadn't arrived yet. There was one row of smaller chairs up front for little children. This was one of the first times I was allowed to sit up there. As they passed the sacrament, I noticed that there was one piece of bread that was extra large, so I thought, "Oh, wow, I'll get this before anyone else." I reached way over trying to get it and knocked the tray out of the young man's hand. It was very embarrassing. But [because of that experience] I know that we had at least the Aaronic Priesthood in the branch.[10]

The city of Guben was not a crucial industrial town so it was not the target of numerous air raids. Helmut Schulz could remember only one (as well as constant blackouts), but he recalled that the town was extensively damaged when the invaders arrived in early 1945. German defenders held the Soviets at bay for a while but ultimately gave way. Walter Luskin reported that the Red Army shelled the city for six weeks and tried several times to conquer it. At one point, Sister König, the wife of the (absent) branch president, asked Walter and his mother to come to her apartment on the east side of the river. They complied, and that night the bombardment became so fierce that they could not return home. For the next eleven days, they lived in the basement of the König family's apartment house. Then the German defenders instructed them to leave because a counterattack was expected at any time.

As the threat of a Soviet invasion intensified, a young mother in the branch, Sister Iseke, came to Walter. She appealed to him for advice, in that he was the only priesthood holder of the branch who was still at home. Should she take the train and flee Guben with her three little boys? He said that she should, but if there were no room on that train, she was not to take the next train twenty minutes later, but to stay in Guben. She did indeed miss the first train and stayed home. Later they learned that the second train had been destroyed in the Cottbus railroad station during an air raid.

Walter Luskin and his mother fled Guben with several other branch members, stopping first in Sedlitz, then in Vetschau—both small towns a few miles to the west. From there they were able to visit the branch in Cottbus on several Sundays. Eventually, the Soviets arrived and forced them to leave. They headed back toward Guben but were fortunate that their path took them to Cottbus. There they decided to stay in the building that Fritz Lehnig had acquired and converted into a refugee home.[11]

Fig. 2. *The Guben Branch Christmas party of 1936 featured a visit by Sankt Nikolaus. (P. Czerny)*

Helmut Schulz, his mother, and his baby brother fled Guben with other members of the branch. They first tried to reach Berlin, but Red Army soldiers prevented that and instructed them to return to Guben. At first, Polish soldiers did not allow them to cross the Neisse River to their neighborhood on the east side, but the three wanted very much to see their home and to learn the fate of other members of the branch. They constructed a makeshift American flag and used it to talk their way across the pontoon bridge that the invaders had erected. The Schulz home had been totally destroyed, but the homes of other members were still standing. The Polish soldiers did not allow them to stay, so they made their way to Cottbus, about fifteen miles to the southwest.

On the train headed for Cottbus, the Schulzes were subjected to an unexplained delay. The train halted in the country for two hours, and nobody understood why they weren't moving. When they finally proceeded and arrived in Cottbus, they learned that a major air raid had struck the city while the train waited in the country. Many people were killed when the railroad station was bombed. Helmut was convinced that his Heavenly Father had saved them by delaying the train's arrival in Cottbus.

Peter Czerny later quoted the handbill posted around Guben that announced the departure of women and children from the town: "The way the Germans wrote was interesting; they said it would be a well-disciplined evacuation (*Wir wollen die Evakuierung in Ruhe und Besonnenheit vollziehen*), but we were all running for our lives."

Helene Czerny (whose husband was on the Eastern Front at the time) took her two young boys and moved westward. They were first assigned to live with farm families in the little community of Stradow, west of Cottbus. From there, they hoped to make it west far enough to see the Americans as conquerors. The conquerors had different ideas and prevented any westward migration. They actually tried to stop refugees from moving eastward as well, which meant that Sister Czerny could not take her family to Cottbus to join the Saints there. Fortunately, when she and other women and children approached the guard station on the road to Cottbus, the guard was distracted by a cow that had not been milked in days. While he chased after the distraught animal, the women and children hurried past the checkpoint.

It was still February 1945 when the small group of Saints approached Cottbus. Fritz Lehnig met them on the road with several wagons, but they dared not travel at night, fearing attack by soldiers. One night they sought refuge in a small cemetery chapel. Peter Czerny recalled the tense overnight vigil:

> We ran to a nearby cemetery and took refuge in the chapel there. . . . It was freezing outside, so they had just stacked up [dead] bodies and put some blankets over them. The adults kept it secret from us children so we wouldn't be scared. I think if we had known, we would have gone nuts. There was no toilet inside the building, so we used empty flowerpots. . . . The majority of us were children. There were a few teenage boys and girls, and the rest were women.

The tension inside the cemetery chapel was almost unbearable for a child, but Fritz Lehnig instructed the children to be totally silent. In the vivid recollection of little Peter:

> I wanted to cry. But in that same instant, a spirit came into my heart that made me feel so wonderful. It said to me, "Peter, everything is going to be all right. This is one time you don't have to cry, even though you want to. Just go to sleep and it'll be okay." I immediately recognized it as my Father in Heaven, helping me not to cry. I know that same spirit was touching all the little babies and children in the group, but I

was the only one old enough to remember what happened. None of us could cry.

Most of the LDS women made it to the cemetery chapel, but a few were raped because they arrived too late from the previous hiding place. One teenage LDS girl was assaulted by at least eight men. Several other women suffered the same tribulation before they could reach the Lehnig home in Cottbus.

Sister Schulz and her two sons were also members of the large refugee colony at the Fritz Lehnig property in Cottbus in the summer of 1945. They had survived the war but would never return to their home in Guben. Helmut later stated: "I missed my hometown, yes, [but] in the [Lehnig] refugee camp, I had no time to think about it. I went back later and visited my aunt; she was still there. No friends, they were all gone. They were all killed."

Life at the Lehnig property was remarkable in the recollection of Walter Lehnig. He later explained that as many as one hundred fifty persons lived there shortly after the war ended. Feeding them was such a challenge that the adults fasted twice each week in order to leave enough food for the children. Care was taken to hide the women every time a Soviet soldier approached the property, and the Saints were nearly always successful in this

Fig. 3. The cemetery chapel where the LDS refugees sought safety one cold night in February 1945. (E. Gruenewald Schulz)

effort. Eventually, city officials came by and ordered that all persons not originally residing in Cottbus leave. From there, most of the refugees headed west to find a new place to live.[12]

When the adults went out into the countryside to forage for food, they often took children along and instructed them to sing and make merry when soldiers came by, to distract them from a possible search for contraband food in the wagons, according to Peter Czerny.

Apparently, no Latter-day Saints returned to live in Guben after the destruction of the city. The few who had not yet evacuated the city soon left. With their departure, the branch ceased to exist.

In Memoriam

The following members of the Guben Branch did not survive World War II:

Helmut Erhard Ewald Kleemann b. Hildesheim, Hanover, Preußen 2 Feb 1922; son of Karl Friedrich Richard Kleemann and Frieda Auguste Schmidt; ord. priest; m. Forst, Brandenburg, Preußen 3 Sep 1943, Martha Erna Anni Gäbler; 1 child; engineer; k. in battle Göppingen, Württemberg 16 Apr 1945; bur. Göppingen (E. Gäbler; www.volksbund.de; IGI)

Karl Heinz Peter Rechenberg b. Guben, Brandenburg, Preußen 6 Oct 1924; son of Eitel Waldemar Ferdinand Julius Rechenberg and Leokadia Julia Scheibner; bp. 15 May 1936; ord.; k. in battle Tschitomir, Russia 11 or 18 Nov 1943 (W. Luskin; IGI)

Wolf-Dieter Eitel Rechenberg b. Guben, Brandenburg, Preußen 2 May 1923; son of Eitel Waldemar Ferdinand Julius Rechenberg and Leokadia Julia Scheibner; bp. 15 May 1936; ord.; corporal Waffen-SS; k. in battle Crespina, Pisa, Italy 10 Jul 1944; bur. Futa Pass, Italy (W. Luskin; www.volksbund.de; IGI)

Notes

1. The name of the city in the local Wendisch dialect is Gubin, the same spelling used in modern Poland.
2. Presiding Bishopric, "Financial, Statistical, and Historical Reports of Wards, Stakes, and Missions, 1884–1955," CR 4 12, 257.
3. East German Mission Quarterly Reports, 1938, no. 12, East German Mission History.
4. Ibid., no. 47.
5. Ibid., no. 39.
6. Helmut Schulz, interview by the author, Sandy, Utah, July 26, 2007.
7. Walter Luskin, interview by Rachel Gale, Salt Lake City, July 6, 2007; transcript or audio version of interview in author's collection.
8. Walter Luskin, "Lebensgeschichte von Walter Luskin" (unpublished personal history), 5; private collection.
9. Helmut Schulz, "Helmut's Life" (unpublished personal history), 72; private collection.
10. Peter Czerny, interview by the author, Pleasant Grove, Utah, February 24, 2006.
11. Luskin, "Lebensgeschichte," 7.
12. Ibid., 10.

Fig. 4. Mothers hurrying to the air-raid shelter had to leave their Kinderwagen *near the entrance. (Deutsches Bundesarchiv Bild 146-1976-032-22)*

STETTIN
DISTRICT
East German Mission

Situated near the mouth of the Oder River by the Baltic Sea, the city of Stettin was a major port and industrial center in northeastern Germany. The Church of Jesus Christ of Latter-day Saints had a substantial population of members in the region beginning in the early twentieth century. In addition to the large branch of Saints in the city of Stettin, there were branches in Prenzlau (thirty-three miles to the west), Stargard (nineteen miles to the east), and Kolberg (sixty-five miles to the northeast).

Stettin District[1]	1939	1940	1941	1942
Elders	17	21		
Priests	16	9		
Teachers	21	23		
Deacons	22	22		
Other Adult Males	93	92		
Adult Females	265	268		
Male Children	27	26		
Female Children	18	16		
Total	479	477	478	469

The history of the East German Mission shows the following entry for Sunday, May 8, 1938:

> On this, the previous and the following day, the spring conference of the Stettin District was

held in Stettin. Miss. Pres. and Sister Alfred C. Rees attended, as well as the elders of the Stettin and Rostock Districts, and the two lady missionaries, Martha Kruger and Erna Boehme. The public meeting held on Sunday night was attended by one-hundred seventy members and friends. At this meeting, district president Hellmuth Plath was honorably released and Bro. Erich Berndt sustained as president of the Stettin District. Bro. Plath was then appointed first counselor to the chairman of the Mission Genealogy Association.[2]

Erich Berndt lived with his family in a suburb of Stettin. In the fall of 1938, he had his first opportunity to represent the Church to the police in Stettin; they wanted information regarding the district conference held in that

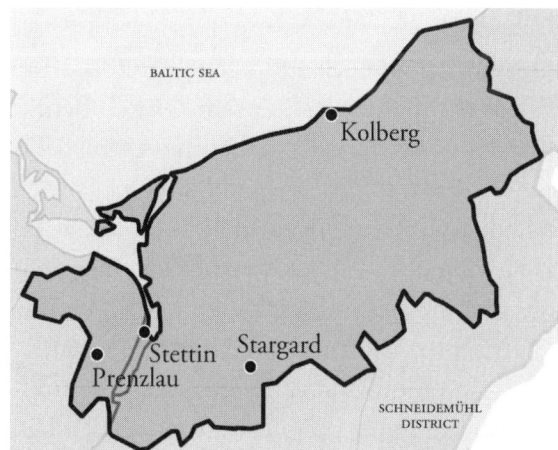

Fig. 1. The branches of the Stettin District during World War II.

Fig. 2. District president Erich Berndt (third from left) with colleagues at the factory where he was killed in an air raid in 1944. (D. Berndt)

Fig. 3. Elder Joseph Fielding Smith and his wife, Jessie Evans Smith, attended a Berlin conference in the summer of 1939. They are shown here with members of the Stettin District. (Boehme)

city on October 1–2. Brother Berndt provided that information and also helped the foreign missionaries, who had just returned from the evacuation to Denmark,[3] to register to live and work in Stettin.

East German Mission records show a second district president serving during the years 1940–42, namely, Ernst Winter. This condition may have been a result of the fact that Brother Berndt was traveling a great deal to visit not only the branches of the Stettin District, but also those of the Rostock District to the west. The history of the Rostock Branch lists Erich Berndt as a visitor in the meetings there on several occasions. Indeed, the history of the Rostock Branch included the announcement on February 15, 1942, that the Rostock District had been annexed to the Stettin District.[4]

Erich Berndt was a supervisor in a factory producing motors for airplanes and was probably doing a great deal of overtime work when

he was released as district president in 1942. Brother Winter continued as district president and served for the next few years, at least until November 1943.[5] At that time, Willi Dretke signed an announcement as district president.[6]

Erich Berndt was one of the few members of the Church in the Stettin District to be educated beyond public school and an apprenticeship. In the field of precision mechanics, he supervised industrial apprentices in an aircraft factory on the outskirts of Stettin.[7] On April 11, 1944, enemy aircraft unloaded their bombs onto the factory. The story was told that Brother Berndt had gone back at the last minute to close the door of an aboveground bunker—one not sufficiently sturdy to withstand the bombs—and was killed by a sudden blast. The news of the tragedy was conveyed to Erich Berndt's wife, Erika, by her father; she was staying at that time with her two children in a small town in the countryside east of Stettin. Erich Berndt had been a popular figure in the Church and was decidedly opposed to Hitler's government and the Nazi Party.

From statements made by the leaders of the East German Mission, it is clear that district and branch conferences continued to be held in the Stettin District through at the least the end of the year 1944. Christel and Edith Wilms, then

448

Fig. 4. Members of the Stettin District Choir (I. Boehme)

young women in the Stargard Branch, recalled
fondly those district conferences:

> We always liked the activities and conferences we
> held in Stargard and in the district. One time,
> there was an opera singer; her voice was abso-
> lutely beautiful. Those conferences sometimes
> lasted for several days. On those Saturdays, they
> performed a play, and we usually stayed at the
> home of some members because we did not have
> enough money to go back home [to Stargard]
> and then come back the next morning.[8]

Because the branches in Stettin, Kolberg,
and Stargard were in territory ceded to Poland
in 1945, the German members of those three
branches were evicted and the survivors moved
across the Oder River to the west. Only the
branch in Prenzlau was still in existence by the
fall of 1946.

NOTES

1. Presiding Bishopric, "Financial, Statistical, and Historical Reports of Wards, Stakes, and Missions, 1884–1955," CR 4 12, 257.

2. East German Mission Quarterly Reports, 1938, no. 20–22, East German Mission History.

3. East German Mission Quarterly Reports, 1938, no. 44. See the chapter on the East German Mission for details regarding the evacuation of foreign missionaries in September and October 1938.

4. Rostock Branch, "Manuscript History and Historical Reports, 1917–1962," February 15, 1942, LR 7647 2, Church History Library. The Rostock District had been organized from the Stettin District on January 21, 1938.

5. Ibid., July 26, 1924.

6. Stettin Branch, meeting minutes: announcement, November 1943, LR 12728 11, Church History Library.

7. Dieter Berndt, interview by the author in German, Berlin, Germany, August 20, 2006.

8. Christel Wilms Radukoswki and Edith Wilms, interview by the author in German, Dortmund, Germany, August 7, 2006; summarized in English by Judith Sartowski.

Kolberg Branch

In 1939, the historic Prussian province of Pomerania extended for more than three hundred miles along Germany's Baltic Sea coast. The coast features gigantic sand dunes and has relatively few port cities. One of the larger cities very near the coast was Kolberg (now Kolobrzeg, Poland), located sixty-five miles northeast of Stettin.

Kolberg Branch[1]	1939
Elders	3
Priests	0
Teachers	1
Deacons	4
Other Adult Males	5
Adult Females	26
Male Children	0
Female Children	0
Total	39

With only about thirty thousand inhabitants, the city of Kolberg was home to a very small branch of The Church of Jesus Christ of Latter-day Saints. Prior to January 21, 1938, the branch was part of the Stolp (later Danzig) District of the mission.[2] This small branch officially included no children but was apparently quite active, as reflected in the following entries from the East German Mission history:

Thursday, March 17, 1938: Programs, celebrating the organization of the Relief Society in the branches of Stettin and Kolberg, were held, in the latter city an attendance of sixty-one, in the former an attendance of seventy-five persons was reported.[3]

Sunday, April 10, 1938: Franz Schroder was appointed first and Paul Reimer second counselors in the Kolberg Branch Presidency.[4]

Friday, April 29, 1938: A spring festival for the Kolberg Branch Primary Association was held in Kolberg with an attendance of fifty-seven persons. All children, belonging to the Primary there, were those of friends.[5]

Sunday, October 30, 1938: The fall conference of the branch was held, with forty-three members and friends in attendance.[6]

Monday, 14 November 1938: A special meeting was held with Pres. Rees; attendance was twenty-five members and thirty-five friends.[7]

Saturday, 11 February 1939: Elder Edward R. McKay, mission supervisor of Sunday Schools and chairman of the Mission Correlation Committee, visited with the different auxiliary organizations of the Kolberg Branch, Stettin District, discussed their problems, and suggested to them ways and means for improvement.[8]

It is interesting to note the large numbers of children (apparently none of whom had parents who were Church members) who took part in meetings and festivities. The adult leaders of the branch likely had personalities that attracted children. At the same time, few families in Germany attended their own church services in those days.

Wynn S. Andersen, a missionary from Brigham City, Utah, served in Kolberg just before the war. He described the modest group of Saints who met in a Hinterhaus at Lindenstrasse 34: "We met in a single room with only about twelve members. I recall the family names Schröder and Reimers."[9]

Being a missionary in Kolberg was not without excitement, according to Elder Andersen: "When Elder Hilbert and I were tracting, he only wrote in our tracting book in hiding because he was afraid that the Gestapo would see him doing it."[10] While in Kolberg, the missionaries witnessed some of the terrible acts of the Nazi Party hooligans on November 9, 1938—Reichskristallnacht (the "Night of Broken Glass"):

Fig. 1. Members of the Kolberg Sunday School posed for this picture in 1937. (I. Reimer Ebert)

We heard a lot of noise and went downtown cautiously to see what was going on. There were a lot of people in front of a Jewish store. We saw party members in uniform smashing the windows. I saw them pushing a man around. They took a piano out of the store (possibly a music store) and smashed it up.

One of the principal ways in which the German Latter-day Saints differed in lifestyle from their friends and neighbors was in their strict health code. Ilse Reimer (born 1914) learned as a young woman that the health standards she was taught in Church, based on the Word of Wisdom, could earn her the respect of others. While attending a Nazi Party Christmas program for young women, she declined to drink the coffee that was served. She later wrote about what happened next:

> Because my girl friend knew that I didn't drink [coffee], she spoke with the other girls. When I came to their table, they were all sitting around it. I noticed to my astonishment that there was

a cup full of cream at my place. All of the girls (I didn't even know them all) had agreed to put their cream into my cup so that I would have something to drink. I was deeply touched by their love and understanding because they were not members of the Church.[11]

In January 1940, Ilse received a letter from President Thomas E. McKay of the East German Mission. He called her to serve as a full-time missionary in the office in Berlin. Although a young man in the nearby Stettin Branch, Fritz Ebert, was poised to ask for her hand in marriage, Ilse accepted the call and was on her way to Berlin in March. She served honorably for the next twenty-five months, visiting many districts of the Church in the East German Mission.[12]

Ilse Reimer was released as a missionary in April 1942. Mission supervisor Herbert Klopfer wrote her a gracious letter in recognition of her service. The following lines are included in that letter dated April 6, 1942:

The Lord looks with satisfaction upon you and the work that you always fulfilled with such loyalty and dedication. Nobody appreciates your industry and constant readiness to help in the promotion and orderly administration of the East German Mission in the war years 1940–42 more than your brethren in the mission leadership. . . . When you return to your loved ones, the spirit of missionary work will radiate among them, and they will have ample opportunities to hear of your experiences and to remember the hours you spent in the service of the Lord.[13]

Ilse Reimer and Fritz Ebert married in Kolberg that June and moved to Stettin. They survived the war and were parents when peace returned to Germany.

It is highly probable that all members of the Kolberg Branch were evicted from their homes in the year that followed the war, during which time the territory was ceded to Poland. With the members gone, the Kolberg Branch slipped into obscurity by the summer of 1946. No members of the Kolberg Branch are known to have died during World War II.

Fig. 2. Former missionary Ilse Reimer married Fritz Ebert in Kolberg on 20 June 1942. (I. Reimer Ebert)

NOTES

1. Presiding Bishopric, "Financial, Statistical, and Historical Reports of Wards, Stakes, and Missions, 1884–1955," CR 4 12, 257.

2. East German Mission Quarterly Reports, 1938, no. 10, East German Mission History.

3. Ibid., no. 14.

4. Ibid., no. 17.

5. Ibid., no. 19.

6. Ibid., no. 43.

7. Ibid., no. 47.

8. Ibid., 1939, no. 56.

9. Wynn S. Andersen, interview by the author, Brigham City, Utah, October 19, 2006.

10. The term "tracting" describes the process of taking their message from door to door.

11. Ilse Reimer Ebert, autobiography (unpublished), 16; private collection.

12. Ibid., 16–17. For stories from her mission experience, see the East German Mission chapter.

13. Herbert Klopfer to Ilse Reimer, April 6, 1942; private collection; trans. the author.

PRENZLAU BRANCH

Situated at the northern tip of the Unteruckersee Lake, the city of Prenzlau is located about thirty-three miles southwest of Stettin and one hour by rail northeast of Berlin. When World War II approached, the city was home to about twenty-three thousand residents and a small branch of Latter-day Saints.

The Prenzlau Branch held its meetings in rented rooms at Steinstrasse 415 on the main floor of the first Hinterhaus. As of this writing, there were no eyewitnesses available to describe the setting. A list of meetinghouse addresses for the East German Mission compiled on January 31,

1943, shows that the address had changed to Vincentstrasse 267. Again, there is no available description of the rooms.

Prenzlau Branch[1]	1939
Elders	2
Priests	0
Teachers	1
Deacons	0
Other Adult Males	7
Adult Females	20
Male Children	3
Female Children	6
Total	39

The history of the East German Mission includes the following three entries regarding the branch in Prenzlau:

Saturday, 19 March 1938: Fifty-one persons attended a program in Prenzlau, commemorating the organization of the Relief Society.[2]

Wednesday, 16 November 1938: A meeting was held with Pres. Rees and the German and American missionaries of the Stargard and Prenzlau Branches; 146 members and friends were in attendance.[3]

Sunday, 11 December 1938: A branch conference was held, including a genealogy lecture by district president Erich Berndt; attendance was five adults and sixty-two children.[4]

Smaller branches in the East German Mission were usually visited by members of the district presidency and by traveling elders. There is every reason to believe that Prenzlau was not neglected. It is also very probable that some of the members regularly took the short train ride to Stettin to attend semiannual district conferences during the war.

The Prenzlau Branch survived World War II. No members are known to have lost their lives during the war.

NOTES

1. Presiding Bishopric, "Financial, Statistical, and Historical Reports of Wards, Stakes, and Missions, 1884–1955," CR 4 12, 257.
2. East German Mission Quarterly Reports, 1938, no. 14, East German Mission History.
3. Ibid., no. 47.
4. Ibid., no. 49.

STARGARD BRANCH

The city of Stargard was located nineteen miles east of Stettin in the province of Pomerania and had a population of about twenty-five thousand in 1939. The railroad line from Kreuz to Stettin made travel between Stargard and Stettin very convenient, so members from the small branch could attend district conferences in Stettin.

Stargard Branch[1]	1939
Elders	1
Priests	1
Teachers	1
Deacons	1
Other Adult Males	8
Adult Females	21
Male Children	2
Female Children	1
Total	36

The history of the East German Mission includes several notes on the Stargard Branch. The following are of interest:

Sunday, October 16, 1938: Wilhelm Pobanz was appointed first counselor to the branch president and Philipp Bauer Jr. second counselor.[2]

Tuesday, November 15, 1938: A special meeting was held with Pres. Alfred C. Rees. The Stettin Branch choir of eighteen members attended and furnished music.[3]

Wednesday, November 16, 1938: A meeting was held with Pres. Rees and the German and American missionaries of the Stargard and Prenzlau Branches; 146 members and friends were in attendance.[4]

Tuesday, November 29, 1938: A special meeting was held in Stargard, with district president Erich Berndt in attendance. The renovation of the branch hall was discussed with the branch presidency.[5]

December 19–24, 1938: Renovation work was done in the Stargard Branch hall.[6]

At the onset of the war, sisters Christel (born 1923) and Edith Wilms (born 1925) each served a Pflichtjahr for the government. Christel worked in the office of an attorney, then for a book editor. Edith was assigned to work in a children's home because a woman she knew was the owner. She later had this to say about the owner:

> She only took tall girls with blond hair—all others would not be Aryan enough. She fired everybody else, and I was there to take care of everything—cleaning, cooking, doing laundry, and taking care of the children.[7]

Sister Wilms was not politically involved and did not encourage Christel and Edith to participate in Hitler Youth activities. The girls recalled their mother's attitude toward the Nazi Party as follows:

> Our mother did not like to salute the flag whenever it passed us. Every Sunday, on our way to church, [Party members] would pass us with the flag, but our mother would go into the nearest building and tell us that her nylons were torn or she had to fix something really quick. During the last years, we realized that she just did not want to salute.

Elders Lloyd Gunther of Pleasant Grove, Utah, and Burton Watson of Idaho were the last American missionaries in Stargard before World War II. Lloyd later recalled that Otto Bork came from Stettin to lead the Stargard Branch and that perhaps ten to fifteen persons attended the meetings on Sundays. Lloyd recalled: "I remember baptizing a child of the Zühlsdorf family. We did it in a pond after dark, in order to keep the ceremony secret from the public."[8] The missionaries boarded with a Jewish family and enjoyed a very pleasant relationship with them. "We even left our bicycles with them when we left town, fully expecting to return." The elders were instructed to leave for Denmark on August 24 and never saw Stargard again.

When World War II began, the members of the Stargard Branch were holding their meetings in the first Hinterhaus at Radestrasse 31. The Wilms sisters later described the setting in these words:

> In the front, there was an apartment building. . . . We walked through the gate to the back yard and then into the Hinterhaus and up the stairs. Brother Willhelm Pobanz lived on the side of the building; he was the branch president. There was one large room that we also divided with curtains so that we could hold more than one class at the same time. In the Radestrasse, we did not have a sign for the Church. For Sunday School, we had our Deseret hymnbook, but for our sacrament meetings, we used only the black hymnbook.

As was the tradition in most branches, Sunday School was held at 10:00 A.M. and sacrament meeting in the evening. The average attendance in those days may have been twenty people, including for the most part the women and children of the Möser, Drews, Günzel, Hänsel, Wilms, and Würfel families. As is evident from the table above, the largest category of members in the Stargard Branch was that of adult females—nearly 60 percent.

As a widow, Sister Wilms was permitted to stay at home while she sewed military clothing. She also sewed small items for neighbors and traded services for additional food rations to support herself and her two daughters.

Fig. 1. A celebration of the Stargard Branch in 1939. (M. Wilms Deppe)

Philipp Bauer (born 1915) was drafted into the Wehrmacht early in 1938. Fortunately, he was assigned to a unit stationed in Stargard and did not have to leave town until September, when the Germany army marched into Czechoslovakia. This was the second of Hitler's so-called bloodless conquests (after Austria in March 1938). Philipp later wrote of the reception the German troops received upon crossing the border near Breslau:

> We slept on German soil that night and drove into [Czechoslovakia] the next morning. In our unit not one single shot was fired. As we drove through the northern part, the people were German and were real friendly toward our soldiers. In Slovakia it was different. People didn't like us, but they didn't have any choice and tolerated us. Occasionally there was shooting.[9]

One year after the conquest of the German-language region of Czechoslovakia (the Sudetenland), Philipp Bauer's unit crossed the Polish border on the first day of the

war—September 1, 1939. For the first time, he saw death and destruction. That night, his unit came under fire, and the terror of combat lasted for hours. He would later recall:

> I didn't think anybody would come out alive. I was scared, scared to death. I thought this would be my end. I prayed to the Lord like I prayed never before. I promised Him if I would come out alive of this terrible shooting, I would serve Him and do whatever He asked me all my life. I never forgot this incident.[10]

Philipp had met and fallen in love with Elfriede Ross of the Schneidemühl Branch just before the war began. This relationship flourished, and he applied for permission to marry her while still in uniform. Permission was granted while he was stationed in Heckholzhausen in the Rhineland, far from home. His leave was for only three days, so he hurried to Schneidemühl for the ceremony on November 29, 1939. They then parted, not knowing when they would be together again (with a war against France looming).[11]

Due to an injury to his foot sustained in a soccer game, Philipp Bauer was in an army hospital when Germany attacked France on May 10, 1940. His division suffered heavy casualties. By the time he was released, the short campaign against France was over.[12] Elfriede had been able to visit him for several weeks during his hospitalization. He believed that the Lord had provided for the injury that kept him out of combat in France.[13]

For the next year, Philipp had noncombat duties but then was shipped to the Soviet Union. After a short tour of duty at the front, he was transferred to the city of Orel behind the lines, away from the fighting. His father had requested this, based on the law that the only son in the family did not have to serve in a combat zone. Philipp's elder brother, Otto (born 1918), had been killed in the Soviet Union in December 1941. In Orel, Philipp lived a much more comfortable and safe life than at the front. He also had time to study the Book of Mormon and the New Testament.[14]

By June 1942, Philipp and Elfriede Bauer had two children—a son, Eckhard, and a daughter, Renate. Except for 1944, Brother Bauer was always able to go home for Christmas. While at the front, his assignment was usually that of a messenger on a motorcycle. "It was dangerous, especially in Russia. But I liked challenging jobs," he explained.[15]

The family of Johann and Frieda Zunkowski had moved from Driesen to Stettin in late 1940. Soon thereafter, Brother Zunkowski—an employee at a large aircraft factory in Stettin—was asked to serve as the branch president in Stargard. His son, Bernard, recalled that "every Sunday he traveled by train [to Stargard], early in the morning; he came home late at night, while our family went to the branch in Stettin."[16]

The city of Stargard was essentially untouched by the war until nearly the end. However, the town was close to Stettin, and the possibility of an attack by enemy airplanes was real. The Wilms sisters recalled their preparations for such events:

> The Church also counseled us that we should store food and have blankets ready. We heeded that counsel—everybody in our family had a blanket to stay warm. Our documents and identification papers were ready, and whenever we went into the basement [for shelter], we took all those things with us and covered ourselves with our blankets. We stored the documents in a suitcase that we always took with us. Nothing else fit in that suitcase (it was only twenty inches by ten inches)—no clothing or food.
>
> The documents consisted of family history papers. Other papers (like our baptism certificate and birth certificate) were in separate bags that we carried individually. When we left the apartment, we were always fully dressed, had a blanket and our individual bags. We did not go to sleep fully dressed—we had enough time to get dressed. . . . Alarms sounded about three to four times a week, and we stayed longer than an hour in our shelter each time.

Christel Wilms recalled how women in Stargard were employed in the summer of 1944 in digging trenches for the defense of the city. It was about that time that she was inducted into the Reichsarbeitsdienst, but her service was interrupted, as she explained:

> They only seemed to find fault with me, so I did not have to go. Once, they put me to work in a munitions factory, but then they told me that I did not work in a team very well and did not have to stay. And then I was assigned to work for the railroad in the summer of 1944. I think that Heavenly Father had a plan for me because all these happenings made it so that [our family was] able to leave Stargard together.

The Stargard Branch continued to meet until the Red Army approached the town in January 1945. As the Wilms sisters explained:

The last Church meetings we had were in the apartment of Brother Pobanz. We could also still partake of the sacrament. We did not baptize people anymore but everything else still went on normally. The branch was still like it used to be before—people had not left yet.

By January 1945, Philipp Bauer's unit had retreated as far as Gotenhafen and Danzig on the Baltic Sea in Germany. They were trapped there against the sea as the Soviets moved past in their rush toward Berlin. Philipp was still there when the war ended.

The invaders were only a few miles from Stargard in January 1945, when the order was given that women and children were to be evacuated. The Wilms sisters took their mother and boarded a train headed west. Their brother was required to stay and defend the city, but his children left with their aunts and their grandmother. The train ride took the Wilms party only about 130 miles to the northwest, but the journey lasted nearly a full week. At one point, they stood on a siding near Berlin and Christel left the train to forage for food. When she returned, the train had moved on. Although she wore out the soles of her shoes, she managed to catch up with the train, which was moving at an agonizingly slow pace. A few miles west of Rostock, the train deposited its passengers in the small coastal town of Kühlungsborn on February 8, 1945.

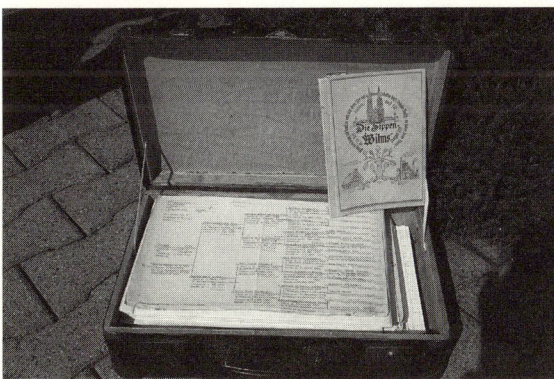

Fig. 2. The small suitcase used to safeguard the Wilms family history documents survives to this day. (M. Wilms Deppe)

In April, Kühlungsborn was invaded by the Red Army, and the women of the Wilms family were in grave danger. They tolerated well the loss of their watches and other property, but the threat of physical abuse provided lasting tension. On one occasion, Christel was out looking for salt. She was told by an enemy soldier that he would give her salt if she would sleep with him. She responded that she did not need the salt after all. On another occasion, she took a job as a cook (for which she was not at all qualified) because she knew that she would be cooking in the town square—out in the open where nobody could harm her.

Philipp Bauer later wrote about the day he and his comrades surrendered their weapons to their Soviet captors:

> How can I describe our feelings? Sure we were happy the war was over, but when we thought what is going to happen to us, loneliness and emptiness filled our hearts. It was all over. Without our rifle, our companion for years, we felt we had given a part of ourselves away. . . . Now we knew the enemy could do whatever they wanted with us.[17]

Fortunately, Philipp was a POW for only a few days. Fearing nothing but disaster in the Soviet Union as POWs, he and two comrades decided to escape. When they were herded into a church cemetery one night, they climbed over the wall and ran away. They were able to throw away their uniforms and change into civilian clothing, then pass themselves off as railroad and shipyard laborers. For the next few weeks, they worked their way west, avoiding cities and main roads. On several occasions, they were confronted by conquering soldiers or police but managed to maintain their cover. Their route took them to Dübzow, Philipp's hometown, and he went to the cemetery to visit the grave of his mother. He later described the visit: "Even [as] a hard soldier who has seen many deaths, tears came to my eyes. How I wished I could have talked to her. I was thirteen years old when she passed away, and I was thirty years now and still missed her."[18]

By June, Philipp arrived in Berlin, where he was taken in by Vera, the widow of his brother, Otto. He stayed there for a few weeks then decided to head west to Celle, where he believed his wife and his children to be. Taking sixty letters to people in the British Occupation Zone, he made his way to the Elbe River, where he gained permission to cross the bridge by conversing with the guard in Russian. Upon arriving in Celle (near Hanover), he located the branch president and was told that his family lived at Bultstrasse 23. Philipp later wrote: "It was a joyous welcome with Elfriede, with our children and her mother. Nobody can really describe the feeling, the happiness and the joy we experienced on July 15, 1945."[19]

In the summer of 1945, the Stargard refugees were told that they must return to their hometown. At the time, Sister Wilms was seriously ill and was not allowed to travel, but she encouraged her daughters to go to Stargard. Christel declined, explaining that in a dream she had seen their apartment burning; she would stay in Kühlungsborn. Her married siblings, one brother and one sister, went back. As the sisters recalled, "They were in Stargard for about two weeks when the Polish went through the streets and wanted all the Germans to leave. They had ten minutes to pack their things and leave the city by foot." They were likely the last of the Stargard Branch members to leave the city that was by then in territory annexed by Poland.

Christel Wilms summed up their survival in these words: "Our Father in Heaven always had his hand in our lives—in whatever happened. I don't think that we were ever in serious danger in those years. Even when it was very dark around us, literally, a light always came at some point."

By the end of the year 1945, all members of the Latter-day Saint branch in Stargard had been evicted from their homes and made the trek west to one of the Allied occupation zones in what remained of Germany. The branch ceased to exist, and the name of the town was changed to Szczeciński.

In Memoriam

The following members of the Stargard Branch did not survive World War II:

Ernestine Luise Daehn b. Dobberphul, Pommern, Preußen 19 Dec 1877; dau. of Herrmann Daehn and Regine Wichmann; m. 16 May 1898, Friedrich Sack; 11 children; d. Beelitz, Rostock, Mecklenburg 7 Feb 1945 (LDS Census)

Else Anna Drews b. 2 Dec 1925; dau. of Johann Friedrich Drews and Emma Emilie Kleiner; d. appendicitis Stargard, Pommern, Preußen ca. 1943 (Wilms-Radukowski; FHL Microfilm 25757 Census 1935; IGI; AF)

Notes

1. Presiding Bishopric, "Financial, Statistical, and Historical Reports of Wards, Stakes, and Missions, 1884–1955," CR 4 12, 257.
2. East German Mission Quarterly Reports, 1938, no. 41, East German Mission History.
3. Ibid., no. 47.
4. Ibid.
5. Ibid.
6. Ibid., no. 50.
7. Christel Wilms Radukoswki and Edith Wilms, interview by the author in German, Dortmund, Germany, August 7, 2006; summarized in English by Judith Sartowski.
8. Lloyd Gunther, interview by the author, Brigham City, Utah, October 29, 2006.
9. Philipp Bauer, "This Is My Life" (unpublished history), 15; private collection.
10. Ibid., 16.
11. Ibid., 17–18.
12. The French army was defeated in June 1940, but the exile government in England continued the struggle.
13. Bauer, "This Is My Life," 18–19.
14. Ibid., 21.
15. Ibid., 22.
16. Bernard Zunkowski, interview by Michael Corley, Salt Lake City, April 24, 2008.
17. Bauer, "This Is My Life," 24–25.
18. Ibid., 28–30.
19. Ibid., 34.

STETTIN BRANCH

One of the largest and strongest branches in the East German Mission, the Stettin Branch, was about forty years old when World War II began in 1939. With a substantial number of priesthood holders, it was the logical administrative center of the Stettin District. The city of Stettin was home to approximately 260,000 people at the time.

Stettin Branch[1]	1939
Elders	12
Priests	14
Teachers	17
Deacons	18
Other Adult Males	75
Adult Females	194
Male Children	17
Female Children	12
Total	359

The Stettin Branch held its meetings in rented rooms at Hohenzollernstrasse 32. Elli Zechert Polzin (born 1913) later described the setting in these words:

> Before the Church rented these rooms and made them pretty for us, it was a cow shed. This place was the second Hinterhaus. It was a very long building, and . . . there was a sign attached to the first building on the street; it was black with white lettering. Inside, the building was divided into smaller rooms. The first rooms one could see were the cloak room and a small classroom. On the right side was the chapel with a podium and a curtain, which one could move. I remember a picture of Christ hanging on the wall.[2]

Margarethe Dretke (born 1912) remembered that the branch had both a piano and a pump organ in those days. "We heated the large room in the building with wood and coal that members contributed," she recalled.[3]

Heinz Winter (born 1920) explained that the chapel was usually filled and a classroom was used as an overflow area. Because there was no microphone in the room, the speakers had to speak very loudly.[4] Heinz also recalled that after the meetings, groups of Latter-day Saints walked toward home, often stopping at street corners, where "more meetings were held before we went our separate ways. People took each other home, and that was really nice."

Regarding the schedule of meetings, Elli Polzin recalled that Sunday School began at 10:00 A.M., preceded by a leadership meeting. Sacrament meeting took place in the evening at seven o'clock. The Relief Society met on Tuesday evenings and MIA on Thursday evenings. She recalls an average attendance on Sunday of about one hundred persons.

Elli also recalled the departure of the American missionaries in August 1939: "We all cried when we said our good-byes in the branch. We hoped that it would not take long until they were allowed to come back." Elli Zechert had married Hans Alfred Polzin in 1936. A daughter was born to them in 1937 and a son in 1940. Hans was drafted in May of that year and was gone for nearly ten years, except for a few furloughs during the war. The hairdressing business they had operated had to be closed down, and his wages as a soldier were substantially less than their business income, but she made ends meet for herself and the children in his absence.

Young Dieter Berndt (born 1938) recalled the branch as a "big family." He also remembered that when the children filed out of the main meeting room to their classes, they did so very reverently and orderly, namely, with their hands behind their backs "with a bit of a military air."[5]

Fig. 1. The interior of the Stettin Branch rooms at Hohenzollernstrasse 32. (I. Boehme)

Only six years old when the war began, Ruth Krakow (born 1933) later recalled being scared to be alone after her father left for military service and her mother was assigned to work in the post office:

> As a child in the war, I was very tense. My mother . . . had to leave very early for work. I had to take the train to school every morning, and I went alone. After school I went to my grandmother's home, where I stayed until my mother picked me up late in the evening. I was scared being alone so much.[6]

Waltraut Kuehne (born 1929) was inducted into the Jungvolk with the rest of her classmates when she turned ten. She later recalled being only minimally active in the organization: "I didn't have any uniform. I attended meetings but mostly sports meetings and that. I never went to any other meetings because my parents didn't believe in it."[7]

Margarethe Dretke's husband, Willi, had been the branch president and a member of the district presidency in Stettin. He was a lathe operator and worked in a factory that produced items critical to the war effort. This allowed him to be exempt from military service for the entire war, though the army attempted to draft him at least once.

A barber by trade, Alfred Bork (born 1920) was a teacher in the Aaronic Priesthood when he was drafted by the Wehrmacht very early in the war. A devout Latter-day Saint, he was planning to serve a mission some day and was soon to be engaged to a pretty young lady in the Königsberg Branch. These plans were put on hold when he donned the uniform of the German army. An avid writer, Alfred kept two journals—one for matters of daily life and military service and one for religious experiences and thoughts. The entry dated July 30, 1939, in his religious journal is indicative of the spirit of this young man:

> Today was a beautiful Sunday for us. Three-quarters of the Stettin Saints traveled to Berlin to hear Apostle Joseph Fielding Smith and his wife speak. . . . The high point of the meeting came when this apostle stood to give us his message. . . . We were all shocked to hear that this will be the last time we hear Pres. Alfred C. Rees speak, because he is being released from his mission. . . . Pres. Rees shook my hand and said these words to me: "Brother, you will be called on a mission soon." . . . When I shook the hand of Apostle Joseph Fielding Smith, I felt the Holy Ghost flow over me, as if he were confirming the words spoken to me by President Rees.[8]

Further entries in Alfred's religious diary recount visits to many branches around Germany and Austria. He sought out the local Saints every time he could. In several entries, he pled with the Lord that he might never take another human life. He was fortunate to have several assignments away from combat zones and to not carry a rifle for much of his time in the service of his country.[9]

Heinz Winter had been in the Stettin Branch's Boy Scout troop in 1934, when the German government banned all such groups in favor of the new Hitler Youth program. At first, Heinz resisted joining the organization but then found out that there was a navy arm of the Hitler Youth. This he joined and was enthusiastic about the water sports. This interest guided his path into and within the German military.

When Germany attacked Poland on September 1, 1939, Heinz Winter was

Fig. 2. Heinz Winter in the uniform of the German navy. (H. Winter)

aboard a merchant vessel at the eastern end of the Baltic Sea. He was finishing a tour of duty that lasted two years and hoped to become a merchant marine engineer. On Hitler's birthday that year, April 20, 1939, Heinz had survived an accident that sank his ship. According to his recollection, "we were passing a reef, and it ripped open the whole side of the ship, and I was in the engine room. I could see the water coming in like a waterfall." The crew of thirty men managed to get off safely before the ship went down.

The fact that Latter-day Saint meetinghouses did not look like the traditional Christian churches in Germany is evident in the recollections of Gerda Stenz (born 1921), who was introduced to the Church by her future husband, Heinz Winter. He was back home for eighteen months of additional navy training. When he took her to see the main building on Hohenzollernstrasse 32, in the second Hinterhaus, she wondered: "It didn't look like a church to me. So I was really anxious what it would be [like] inside."[10] As she became acquainted with the Church and the branch, the physical setting no longer bothered her, and she was baptized in 1941.

The general minutes of the Stettin Branch survived the war. The branch secretary was meticulous in his record-keeping, including the names of all persons who presided at meetings, prayed, gave talks, or otherwise contributed to the worship services. The attendance figures for the years 1940 through early 1943 show an average of sixty to sixty-five persons in sacrament meeting.[11]

The German army invaded the Soviet Union on Sunday, June 22, 1941. Alfred Bork had the dubious privilege of participating in the invasion and made note of it in his diary:

> June 22, 1941, Sunday: At 3:15 A.M. we were the first troops to cross the border into Russia. The enemy artillery fire was quite intense. Six

men of our company were killed, including our company commander. When our artillery responded at 3:15 A.M., I ran with my horse from our hiding place behind a house through the forest to the Bug River in order to cross the river with the first boat. The Russian artillery immediately opened fire. As I was running through the forest holding on to my horse, I tripped and fell. At that moment, a shell landed just seven feet from me, and a piece of shrapnel hit the horse in the chest—right at the point where I had been running alongside of him. I then jumped up again and ran to the Bug River. Just as I got there the first boat pushed off, so I had to go with the second boat. When the first boat reached midstream, it received a direct hit and went down. I thank the Lord for saving me in this amazing way.[12]

One month later, Alfred Bork was shot through the lung and was taken to the rear. During his recovery, he spent time in Stettin and in Vienna, where he visited the branch meetings. He was back in Russia with his unit in December 1941.[13]

One Sunday, Alfred Bork was on his way to Stettin, and his train was held over in Küstrin for five hours. He went looking for a branch of the Church (not knowing that there was none there) and while doing so asked directions of an older lady (seventy-six years old). She knew nothing about the Church, but they conversed for a few minutes about religion while standing at an intersection. Minutes after they parted, Alfred felt inspired to return to that intersection and found her coming back to that place as well. She then invited him to her home, and he wrote the following in his diary:

We talked about God and His word, then I got out my Bible that I always have with me. We had a fine conversation. She was a very sincere woman who wished to obey God and serve Him. She had suffered through many trials with her husband, who was a drunkard. She had given birth to retarded children because of her husband's alcoholism. . . . But she was a happy person. . . . She told me, "You are a nice and sweet young man, and you have brought

the sun into my home." And I thank God that I was allowed to do this.[14]

Hans Polzin happened to be home on leave one night in 1942 when a bomb hit the pharmacy down the street. His family had chosen to stay in their apartment that evening rather than to seek shelter in the basement. The force of the explosion in the pharmacy sent them all flying off of the couch. As his wife, Elli, later explained, "We really thought that we would not make it. We prayed and held each other close." At the time, they were living in the town of Finkenwalde, about eight miles from downtown Stettin.

Heinz Winter and Gerda Stenz were married on her birthday, August 5, 1942. Gerda had overcome many obstacles to find a wedding dress, shoes, roses, food, and a suit for Heinz. Years later, she described her wedding day:

After hunting for many items for several months, the big day finally came. [Heinz] and his father came with the horse-drawn buggy to pick my father and me up to go to the *Standesamt* (civil registrar) to be married. The official was so serious that I could not stop laughing during the whole ceremony. We [were given] the book *Mein Kampf*. . . . When we got home, I got dressed in my bridal gown. I can hardly remember it because it was like a dream to me. I was beautiful, weighing only 95 lbs.; my dress was made out of silk and lace. We both were good looking, [Heinz] was only 156 lbs., thin and handsome. . . . At 4 P.M. in the afternoon our church wedding was. . . . Willi Dretke, the branch president, married us.[15]

Following five days spent with his bride, Heinz Winter was shipped off to Nantes, France, where he was assigned to a tanker. While the ship was being repaired, it was attacked and sunk. Heinz never went to sea on that ship, and the same fate claimed the next ship to which he was assigned. During his travels to and from various ports, Heinz once found himself in Amsterdam, where he set out to find the local branch. He was successful in doing so and walked into an apartment where fifteen to twenty men were holding a meeting. He later described the precarious event:

> I was wearing my regular blue navy uniform and had a pistol on my belt. That was important. I came there as a German soldier. First, there was a little quiet, and I looked at them quietly. Now, I couldn't really say much because I couldn't speak their language a lot. But finally they all sat down, and I took my belt off and hung it up on the clothes rack, and they all gasped. . . . The meeting was pretty nice. After a while we shook hands and said good-bye, and then I never saw them again.[16]

His visit in the Amsterdam Branch was a rare treat for Heinz Winter. Otherwise, he was able to attend church only when home on leave, which happened about once a year. He had no scriptures with him and never had contact away from home with any German sailors or soldiers who were Latter-day Saints.

The first contact for Anna Kopischke (born 1924) with the Church came through an elderly member. As she recalled: "Sister Kuehne was about eighty years old. She came to pick up her grandson to go to Sunday School, and they invited my brother to go along. He came back very enthusiastic and wanted me to go with them the next time." The year was 1942, and Anna's entire family eventually became acquainted with the gospel. She and her parents, Erich and Meta Kopischke, were baptized on September 26, 1942. The ceremony was conducted at a Stettin lake called Glambecksee under the direction of Ernst Winter. Anna later recalled, "I remember being wet even before we went into the water, because the weather was so bad that day. . . . Even though it was wet that day, the moment I went into the water, it was warm and it did not matter."[17]

Ruth Krakow once traveled with her grandmother by train from Stettin to Breslau to visit an uncle. On the way, her grandmother suddenly left the first passenger car where there were empty seats and took Ruth to the last car, where there were no available seats and they had to stand. As Ruth recounted, "We had not been in the back for very long when we were thrown around the train and the luggage fell on us. We later saw that two trains had collided. Had we stayed in the first car, we would all have died. . . . This experience helped us build a strong testimony."

Sieglinde Dammaschke (born 1937) and her younger siblings were not safe in Stettin when the bombs began to fall. Her father was in the army, so her mother took the family to Hamburg (180 miles to the west). Unfortunately, it was no safer there because the city was attacked on many occasions. Sieglinde recalled that her mother had difficulty waking her children up to take them to the basement. Apparently, the local block warden chastised her for considering leaving her children in bed when the sirens went off. The next time, she got them out and downstairs, later learning that a bomb had come through the roof and landed in their apartment.

On another occasion, the Dammaschkes' apartment house was hit, and they could not escape because the basement door was blocked by debris. They utilized the holes cut through the walls into adjacent basements to move through the block.[18] At the end of the row of apartment houses, they learned that the fires outside were too severe to allow them to exit, so they retraced their path through the basements to another exit. "I don't know how we ever got out of there," explained Sieglinde. After another raid, she and her siblings were sent to an open area near the Elbe River to wait until it was safe to move through the streets. The Dammaschke family was bombed out three times in Hamburg before returning to Stettin, a city they considered safer.[19]

Fig. 3. Members of the Stettin Branch on an outing for Ascension Day in about 1939.

Waltraut Kuehne's parents, Georg and Margarete, lost all of their property on April 20, 1942, in an air raid that nearly took their lives as well. Waltraut described the terrifying incident in these words:

> We lived on the top floor, and a phosphorus bomb hit the bedroom of our apartment, and it was in flames right away. We didn't get out [of the basement] until the all-clear siren went on. Where we lived there were only seven houses on the street, big apartment houses. Because bombers [probably knew] the whole street was military buildings, maybe they wanted to hit them, . . . but nothing military got hit there, but all seven of [the apartment houses] were heavily damaged. There were no stairs left to go up and rescue anything out of the apartment. . . . My sister Renate had only a doll when she went into the basement, and when the air raid was over and we got out, she only had a leg from the doll left in her hand.

When her school was destroyed in an air raid, Waltraut Kuehne was sent to the city of Kolberg (fifty-five miles to the northeast) to complete the school year. Back in Stettin, she was then pressed into service digging antitank ditches around the city. A year later, she was called to do her Pflichtjahr for the government and found herself assigned to a hotel in Heringsdorf where school children were housed.[20] There she served for seven months as a cook and cleaning lady. When the Red Army approached the area, she was released from her service and sent back to Stettin.

Heinz and Gerda Winter's first son, Eberhard, was born in 1943. Heinz came home on leave from France with a suitcase full of food. Just after he left again, Eberhard contracted a serious illness and was in a hospital in Finkenwalde for six weeks. Gerda made the trip to the hospital every day to see him (a return trip that took all day). She recalled her fears for her son: "I surely prayed hard for his recovery." Fortunately, no operation was needed.[21] Soon thereafter, Gerda was evacuated to the town of Christinenberg, about fifteen miles to the northeast. She stayed there for more than a year and had no contact with the Stettin Branch, with the exception of a woman who visited her once. There was no other branch in the vicinity.

For most of the year 1943, Heinz Winter was stationed in the French harbors of Nantes, Brest, and Calais. In Brest, the Germans had constructed enormous submarine pens, where Heinz and his fellow sailors took refuge during the constant Allied air raids. Toward the end of the year, Heinz was assigned to a minesweeper patrolling the French coast of the English Channel. For ten months, his ship with its crew of seventy-five was under fire from sea and air. As he later explained, "We had [shrapnel] holes all over the ship. Every night we would weld plates of steel over them as repairs then paint them. The next morning, off we went again!"

During that ten-month tour of duty, nearly three hundred men who served aboard Heinz's vessel were killed or wounded, but Heinz never suffered a scratch. He later stated, "If I had a scratch, I would have gotten a medal." He worked a twelve-hour shift each day—the first six hours in the engine room and the next six on deck on fire patrol or doing repairs. From their position along the French coast, Heinz could see across the Channel to England. Every ship was visible. By the time he left that ship, his rank was equivalent to that of an ensign in the United States Navy.

Anni Bauer (born 1925) had moved to Stettin from Neubrandenburg to work and soon became an enthusiastic member of the Stettin Branch. By 1943, due to the absence of so many men in the Wehrmacht and so many

Fig. 4. Heinz Winter served aboard a minesweeper of this class in the English Channel. (H. Winter)

women and elderly members of the branch (who had moved away from the city to escape the air raids), Anni took on several Church responsibilities: "I was doing just about every secretarial job in our [branch], except for Primary. Most of my free time was spent with the branch president, helping him to balance his financial records and reports. . . . Relief Society I also taught once a month."[22]

Thea Bork (born 1931) recalled that government agents attended Church meetings on occasion, but apparently they did not disturb the proceedings. She also explained that they were not allowed to sing certain hymns (those featuring such "Jewish" words as *Zion* and *Israel*). "We circled the [hymn] numbers and knew that we should choose others."[23]

The branch meeting minutes include a sad entry for 1943: "During the night of April 20–21, Stettin was attacked from the air. In this attack our meeting rooms were damaged." The last meeting held at that location took place on April 25, after which the police declared the building unsafe and off limits.[24] The record then states that future meetings would be held in the homes of member families. During the same air raid, the following members lost their homes: Gertrud Schmidt, Julius Schmidt, Gerda Wittkopp, the Heinz Winter family, and the Georg Kühne family.

Elli Polzin and her children were evacuated to the town of Gielow (about ninety miles west

Fig. 5. The women and girls of the Stettin Branch gathered together for a Mother's Day photograph in 1939.

of Stettin) in 1943. There she lost touch with the branch but had periodic meetings with the Gabrecht family, who had also gone there from Stettin.

Otto Bork (born 1896) was activated from his reserve status and assigned to supervise a camp of Soviet POWs near Grimmen, north of Demmin (about seventy miles northwest of Stettin). He was allowed to move his family to Demmin. From that time until the end of the war, Brother Bork spent most of his time at the POW camp. In Demmin, his wife and the three youngest children (son Hellmut and daughters Thea and Ruth) attended Church meetings with the tiny branch. "We met in the branch president's home, and I don't think that there were more than ten people most Sundays," recalled Ruth.[25]

Just as all other German cities, Stettin was under strict blackout regulations at night for most of the war. In order to be seen on the streets in the pitch dark, pedestrians wore

fluorescent badges on their outer clothing. According to Gerda Stenz Winter:

We could see when somebody was coming. We always walked because we had no other transportation. We were never afraid that we would be molested. It never occurred to anybody that maybe you were afraid that somebody would do something to you—including women walking alone.

When the meetinghouse was no longer available to the branch, members met in the villa owned by a Sister Schroeder. In her large living room, they held only a sacrament meeting. There were still enough older men in the city to preside and to administer the sacrament. "Many younger people talked to me about what they had always done together with the branch before the war started," Anna Kopischke recalled. Many branch activities and programs went by the wayside due to the restrictions imposed by wartime conditions.

"The air raids were horrible for me," recalled Ruth Krakow. "We lived on the fifth floor of our building, and the shelter was in the basement. We were very scared because we thought that the house might fall on us if a bomb hit it." There were a few public shelters in downtown Stettin for use by people away from home, and signs directed people to those shelters. "In every apartment house there was a man who was responsible to ensure that everybody in the building was safe in the basement and not upstairs in their apartments," according to Ruth.[26] The Krakow home was destroyed in the night of April 30, 1943. "That night, it seemed to me that we would never leave the shelter." Fortunately, there was time to escape from the basement while the fire engulfed the upper floors of their apartment house. Following the destruction of their home, the Krakows moved to Neubrandenburg, where Ruth's other grandmother lived.

The branch meeting minutes include a "joyous announcement" dated November 22, 1943: Branch meetings were to begin again at 4:00 P.M. on November 28 in the rooms of the Evangelical Free Church at Deutschstrasse 30. For the next few months, attendance again approached sixty persons, whereas only about forty had been attending services held in the homes of member families.[27]

Later in the war, Margarethe Dretke and her son Ulrich ("Ulli," born 1938) were evacuated to a farm in Kannenberg. From there, she was required to leave her son for a month to dig antitank ditches near Driesen. As she explained, "The ditches were supposed to be four meters [thirteen feet] deep so that the tanks would fall into them. It happened differently than we expected; [the invaders] just drove past them." Sister Dretke protested being absent from her son and was allowed to return to Kannenberg.

Ulli's recollection of the time on the farm was that of a little boy. "I was so homesick. I never wanted to go to bed." He loved the animals and even sneaked into their pens to sleep with them at night. He recalled spending one night with a huge bull that was fed on a fermented sugar beet substance ("it kept the animals drunk, and they slept better"). Ulli ate some of the same feed and later recalled that "when they got me out [of the pen] I felt pretty good."[28] This incident apparently added to his father's insistence that his wife and his son return to Stettin without delay.

When Sister Dretke returned to Stettin, she was again assigned to dig fortifications around the city. She tried hard to avoid the work, insisting that she had already done enough. "Brother Oppmann of the branch recommended that I do as I was told so [the government] would not take my child away. It was a great blessing, and I am still grateful today for his advice."

In August 1944, Elli Polzin had the following distinct dream:

> I dreamed of a large hall. . . . At the end of the hall, I saw my husband standing. He wore a white coat like he always did as a hairdresser. He was cutting somebody's hair, and I was so excited to see him. I went over to him, but we were not allowed to show anybody that we knew each other. I offered him a glass of water, and our hands touched. We looked each other in the eyes, and that was a wonderful moment. The [other] people then told me that I had to leave again. It was so hard for me to leave him.

The next morning, the local Lutheran pastor came to inform Elli that her husband had been reported missing in action in Romania. The pastor was sorry and explained that Hans might be dead. Her response was as follows: "I looked him in the eye and said that [Hans] was alive and that I knew it. I told him about the dream, and he said that it was not coincidental." For the next three years, Elli did not know anything about her husband's whereabouts.

A massive air raid hit Stettin on April 11, 1944. Former district president Dieter Berndt was killed at his workplace—an aircraft factory just outside of town.[29]

Johannes Zunkowski (serving at the time as the president of the Stargard Branch) worked at the same factory and was buried under the rubble of his building. For approximately sixteen hours, he waited to be rescued. According to his son Bernard, "The building just collapsed, and there was a pocket underneath, and he was able to breathe in there, but nobody knew he was under there. For some reason, one of the bombs didn't go off [on impact], but exploded hours later and uncovered my father. So he came home. His hair turned white overnight."[30]

Bernard recalled the prologue to that devastating attack, when he and his friends were playing cowboys and Indians:

> There was an open field where we used to build teepees. . . . All of a sudden I heard this rumbling, and I looked up in the sky, and the sky was just covered with airplanes. It was just covered. And you could see all the bomb doors were open and the fighter planes. And there was a big fight because we had an air base in Stettin, a big air base. So there was a big fight above us, and shrapnel was flying everywhere. That day, my dad was buried alive.

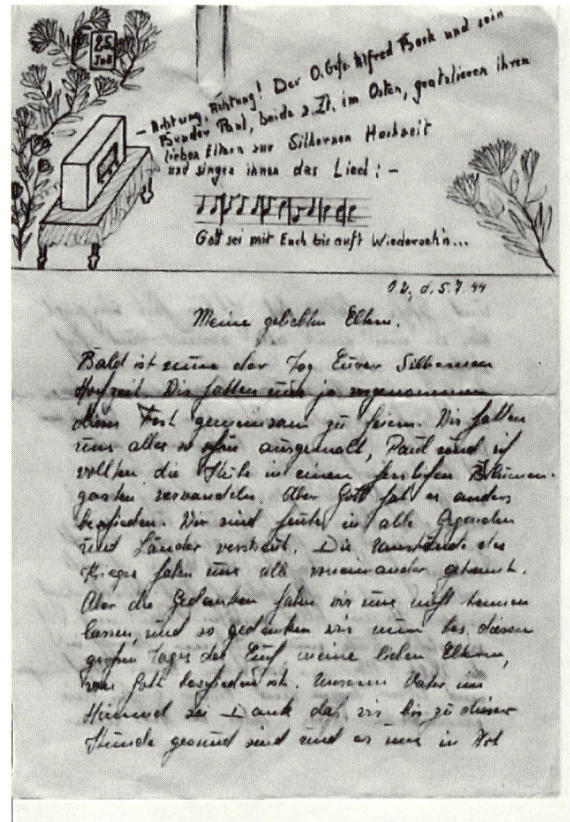

Fig. 7. Alfred Bork wrote this letter to his parents in July 1944 on the occasion of their silver wedding anniversary. The illustration at the top is a reference to the bombastic national radio broadcasts of German victories. The music notes represent the hymn "God Be with You till We Meet Again." (H. Bork)

On August 30, 1944, Stettin was visited with the full fury of the war, as enemy airplanes reduced large sections of the city to rubble. Anni Bauer had joined her neighbors in the basement of a large apartment house that suffered a direct hit. The terror she experienced is evident from the story she wrote:

> The walls were cracking and caving in, but the worst was still to come. . . . For a moment I thought my life was over because I had difficulty breathing with the pressure that was on my lungs. . . . One thing I shall never forget: seeing all the people crowding together in the shape of a great "ball" . . . all of them crying to God for help. . . . I had only one thought in mind, to get out of the terrible fire . . . Another bomb shook our ruins, and I cried to the Lord to take my life now and not let me be smothered by rubble or be burned alive.[31]

Fig. 6. The family of Otto and Margaretha Bork in 1943. Soldiers Alfred (left) and Paul were "missing in action" when the war ended—and still are. The parents never gave up hope that their sons would return someday. (H. Bork)

Anni drenched herself with water from the barrel in the basement, then raced through the flames upstairs into the street. Then she ran to the park at Blücher Square, assuming that the park would be free of fire and smoke. She was wrong because phosphorus bombs had spread fire everywhere. "The trees were burning, bushes and benches were in flames. The heat was so tremendous and the smoke would have killed us if it hadn't been for the underground shelter." Anni saw several people burning alive in the streets. "It was the greatest horror," she would recall in her memoirs.[32]

The apartment building in which the family of Otto and Margarethe Bork lived in Stettin was also destroyed in 1944 in their absence, and the family was instructed to come back long enough to see if they could salvage anything important from the ruins. Young Hellmut (born 1933) recalled hearing from a neighbor that his older brother, Paul, had been reported killed in the building during the bombing. There was even an announcement in the newspaper to that effect, but the family had since received letters from Paul in the Soviet Union; they knew that he was still alive.[33] This was, however, not the case for long. In September 1944, the Borks received a letter from Paul's company commander indicating that their son's unit had been surrounded

Fig. 9. Anni Bauer was nearly buried alive in the basement of this building. (A. Bauer Schulz)

during a recent battle. He had not been seen since and was believed to be a POW.

In the fall of 1944, the Red Army was approaching Christenenberg, so Gerda Stenz Winter took her son back to Stettin. Her husband was temporarily in Stralsund for more navy training and encouraged her to join him there. Unfortunately, the trip was very difficult because refugees were overloading all trains headed west. Gerda's father went with her to the railroad station and successfully used cigarettes to bribe the conductor to take his daughter and his grandson onto the train—along with their baby stroller. At one point on the journey, she left the stroller in a place where it easily could have been stolen but came back to find it still standing there. In Stralsund, she found her husband, and they were successful in

Fig. 8. Helmut Plath conducted the funeral of former district president Erich Berndt in 1944. (D. Berndt)

renting a room to stay in. It was cold, so Heinz went out to a local park to gather enough wood to keep a small fire going. A few days later, they parted as Heinz returned to duty. They agreed to meet after the war in Varel in the western province of Oldenburg because they believed that it would not be safe to be in any region where the Red Army was likely to be the occupation force. It was February 1945.

When Heinz Winter left Stralsund, he was no longer bound for the sea. He had responded to a call for more ground troops and had transferred voluntarily to the army, as he explained:

They said that if I volunteered for the infantry, I could choose my unit and area of service. I wanted to help defend Stettin, but they sent me to Czechoslovakia instead. . . . I was trained as a forward observer [for artillery], sitting out there in front of the infantry. [Forward observers] were all lieutenants, and losses among them were very high.

Back in Stettin in 1944, the Dammaschke family moved into some barracks outside of town. From there, Sieglinde's mother went to church now and then by herself. She dressed the children, prayed with them, and then made the long trek into town to join with other branch members for meetings. Neighbors were unhappy with this young mother for leaving her children alone in the camp, but she did nevertheless, explaining, "They'll say their prayers, and they'll be safe."

During the fall of 1944, Germans from the eastern provinces of the Reich began to evacuate their homes as Soviet soldiers moved toward the Reich. Johann Zunkowski's family lived on the outskirts of Stettin, and young Bernard observed the stream of refugees moving westward:

Our little home was maybe a couple of blocks away from the autobahn, and you could see the people. Day and night they were walking down the road trying to get away from Russian

troops. At night, a lot of times, they used to come in our backyard and settle down for the night. Sometimes we used to help them out as much as we could. We'd supply the food, and we'd find shelters for the horses.

The Zunkowski family eventually joined the throngs of refugees in January 1945. The beginning of their flight was not encouraging, as explained by young Bernard:

We left at one o'clock in the morning, and there was about a foot of snow on the ground, and most of the neighbors had already left. We put my grandma on top of the wagon and just a couple of suitcases. My dad and I were pulling. My mom was pushing. My brother [Wilford] was drafted [and gone]. So that's how we left. Then after we were going along the side of the road, they came down with the fighter planes and just strafed the roads. Somehow, all of a sudden, a truck came by and stopped, and two soldiers got out. They lifted our little wagon inside and us, and they drove all night long.

In January 1945, the Red Army moved through Gielow, and Elli Polzin decided to return to Finkenwalde. The war was not yet over, and the Soviets occupied the entire area, so she was instructed to leave again. This time she went to the island of Rügen in the Baltic Sea, where conditions were relatively calm and safe. She lived there in a hotel with her children. There was no branch of the Church on the island, thus by the end of 1945, the mission leaders recommended that she move west to Schwerin, where refugees from the east had established a branch. It was there that her husband found them.

In early 1945, Anna Kopischke and her family left Stettin on a train heading west for Strasburg. Moving ahead of the advancing Red Army, they went through Neubrandenburg, where they were joined by Anna's fiancé, Horst Röhl. He had been recuperating in a military hospital and accompanied them through Malchin and Wismar to a castle near Plüschow.

From there, they crossed the border into the British Occupation Zone and then settled in the town of Elmshorn. Writing to an address she found in an old issue of *Der Stern*, Anna established contact with the Altona Branch in Hamburg, and they began to attend Church meetings again.

The apartment house in which the Dretke family lived survived the war undamaged, but a dud once landed in the henhouse just ten feet behind the building. As the invaders approached the city, Waffen-SS troops set up defensive positions in the apartment house. Thanks to them, the family had enough food to eat when things got very scarce. The soldiers also promised to help them escape the city when the Soviets got too close. During those last months, Brother Dretke was often required to stay overnight in the factory where he was employed.

When the time came to leave Stettin, Margarethe Dretke took her son, Ulli, and a few important items, as she recalled: "a pan with oatmeal, my papers, and a bottle of water." The train was already full, and refugees from eastern Germany were trying to board with grains, animals, and other items for which there simply was no room. "People dragged my son and me into the train through the windows. In that train, some of the wounded soldiers were dying, while others sang." Margarethe and Ulli rode the train west as far as the port city of Lübeck and found a place to stay in a chicken coop.

Branch president Kurt E. Lehmann made his last entry in the Stettin Branch minutes on March 25:

> Six members gathered today. They walked from the meetinghouse to the home of Brother and Sister Pautsch at Mackensenstrasse 22. There they had a short discussion under the leadership of Brother Johannes Zundkowski. This was the last meeting. Everybody was to evacuate Stettin because the city was under artillery barrage. The members have been scattered in all directions. Some have been evacuated to [the province of] Mecklenburg. This is the end of the Stettin Branch.
> [signed] Branch President Kurt E. Lehmann.[34]

In April 1945, Otto Bork instructed his wife, Margarethe, to take the three children and work her way toward the advancing American Army (away from the Soviets). The four of them headed north and west and soon found themselves in the company of German soldiers whose task was to destroy every bridge they crossed on the way west. This would prevent or at least delay the advance of the Soviet Army. Each time the Borks crossed a river, the soldiers dynamited the bridge behind them. One night, the soldiers left while the Borks were asleep, and they were awakened by a tremendous explosion. The soldiers had blown up the next bridge, leaving the Borks stranded on the east side. That day, they were overtaken by the advancing Soviets, who ordered them to return to Demmin.

As they retraced their route to Demmin, Hellmut Bork found a nice bicycle, but the chain was gone, so he pushed it along as a luggage carrier. A Russian solder went by and demanded that Hellmut trade for the older bicycle the Russian had. Hellmut tried to make the man understand that his newer bicycle was not functional, whereas the older one the soldier had was in good condition. The trade took place anyway. Hellmut's gain was short-lived, however. When they arrived in Demmin, he had to surrender his bicycle to the conquerors, as did everybody else in town.

After hearing of her husband's death in the air raid the day after Easter of 1944, Erika Berndt took her two children back to Stettin, where their home still stood. In the spring of 1945, her father joined them in the trek west, their Bollerwagen loaded with their most valued possessions. By the time they arrived in Neubrandenburg, the advancing Soviet Army had caught up with them. They saw enemy soldiers for the first time while hiding in the basement of an aunt. The conquerors ordered them to return to Stettin.

Following the destruction of their home, Margarete Kuehne moved with her daughters and Waltraut's grandparents to Anklam (fifty miles to the northwest). They were there when the Soviets arrived in April 1945. The first night, the local residents were ordered into the hospital across the street, while the invaders searched for German soldiers. Then they were sent back to their homes and were terrorized by the enemy soldiers soon thereafter. According to Waltraut:

> [The Russians] came every night and in every house to steal . . . They came in, and [one of them] took my [little] sister from my mother's arms. And they all stood there with machine guns, we thought that was the end. But my mom ran to him and grabbed my sister from him. We were so scared, and they were so drunk. They were laughing when they left the house. That's the first bad experience that I had.

The American army entered Czechoslovakia in April 1945, and Heinz Winter's unit confronted the invaders west of the city of Plzen. Heinz later described the successful German attack, planned for a hilly location where the road was quite narrow: "We just had bazookas [*Panzerfaust*], but we shot the first tank, and the whole [column] stopped. Then they were practically at our mercy." Later, the Germans fought the invaders near an orphanage where the Americans had established their headquarters, again winning the day. "We took forty [Americans] prisoner, some badly wounded. Since we didn't have any facilities, we couldn't help them. We put them on one of their jeeps, put a Red Cross flag up, and drove to the next little town."

In an odd situation, Heinz and his comrades negotiated with the Americans and won a very important concession: the German soldiers were to be given release papers to go home, meaning that they would not become POWs. Within two weeks after the war ended on May 8, Heinz was on his way to Germany. He knew that his father was working in a salt mine near Nordhausen, so he went there, walking the 180-mile route.

Gerda Winter was to go to Varel in western Germany, but decided instead to join her parents-in-law in Nordhausen in central Germany. She sought the security of family and moved in with a Schneider family in the town of Kleinberndten, where her mother-in-law was staying. It was in Kleinberndten that Gerda experienced the end of the war—the arrival of the American army. Under the command of a Jewish officer, the Americans moved into the Schneider home and evicted the residents. Gerda later wrote what they found when the Americans left: "The whole house was in chaos, they trampled on the baby's feather bed, ripped open every glass of fruit in the house, took all the cooking pots and urinated in them. My two beautiful rings were gone, which I [had] left on the counter."[35]

Just before Stettin was conquered by the Red Army, Willi Dretke and his colleagues loaded their factory's machinery onto flatbed railroad cars and transported it west to Lübeck. Willi was required to ride on the open freight car with his machine and contracted a lung ailment along the way. He was eventually able to join his family in Lübeck but did not recover from the malady. Without proper medication, he died there on August 25, 1945.

The Dretke family had left almost everything they owned in Stettin. As Margarethe explained:

Fig. 10. Willi Dretke at work at his lathe. (H. Dretke)

When we left Stettin, we . . . thought that we would just go back when the war was over. We left our apartment clean so we would find it proper and nice when we returned. We could have gone back to Poland, but we didn't want to be in a country that wasn't ours anymore. [The Polish] also didn't want us to go back anymore.

After living in her grandmother's home in Neubrandenburg for a short time, Ruth Krakow's family moved in with the Huppel family across town on Demminer Strasse, where they lived in cramped quarters. Ruth later described the conditions in these words:

It was an apartment in which the owner had one room; another family from Tilsit lived in the other with their four children, and my mother and I lived in the last room. We all had to share the kitchen, and we often had arguments about it. Because we still had to heat with coal, we had to have schedules of who would cook when. We did not have much, and if somebody had a piece of meat still on the stove, that person had to be careful.

When the conquerors entered Neubrandenburg in 1945, Ruth Krakow and her mother were fortunate to escape harm. "My father had taken a couch and built a hiding place for us so nobody could see us. . . . The Russians were not nice to adults, but they never did anything to children. They gave [us] bread."

Sieglinde Dammaschke left Stettin with her mother and siblings, bound for Hamburg with their possessions loaded in a baby buggy and a small wagon. Along the way they were persuaded to travel to Erfurt instead (225 miles to the southwest). Living there in a small attic space, they experienced the arrival of the American army in April. Two months later, the Americans moved out, and the Soviets came into Erfurt, which upset many of the locals. Sieglinde's mother decided to leave while she had the chance and traveled north to Hamburg. Her husband joined the family there after being released from a POW camp.

By the spring of 1945, Alfred Bork had not seen his parents for nearly a year, but a sister of the branch later told of seeing him in Stettin in early May. She was watching as hundreds of German POWs were being marched through the city by their Soviet captors. She thought she recognized Alfred among them and called out to him. Just at the moment when he turned to look at her, she was knocked down by a guard. By the time she got back to her feet, he was too far down the street to see him again.

When the Red Army approached the prison camp where Otto Bork was in command, his two comrades took to the hills. Brother Bork stayed and handed over the camp to a Soviet officer in a jeep. Just when it looked like Otto would be killed, inmates came forward to testify that he had treated them very correctly under the circumstances. Because of this, he was given a written statement to allow him safe passage back to Demmin. He set out, carrying a small briefcase full of invaluable family documents, such as his genealogical papers, family photographs, and Alfred's diaries (he had kept this suitcase with him since the war began). Along the way, he was confronted by a squad of Red Army soldiers who proceeded to rough him up. They opened the suitcase and threw his papers all over the road. Despite his agony about losing those treasures, he remembered the certificate in his pocket and quickly produced it in his defense. The squad leader was shocked to read it and immediately apologized for the mistake. The soldiers gathered up the papers and returned them to Brother Bork, asking him to not report their misconduct. He was relieved to be able to continue his walk to Demmin, where he joined his family about two weeks after they had returned from their abortive flight west.

Shortly after the war ended, Georg Kuehne took his family back toward Stettin. With a small Bollerwagen, they walked the entire distance (fifty miles) from Anklam. Because there was no place for them to stay in Stettin, they continued on to the home of Waltraut's grandparents in a nearby village. The home had already been confiscated by a Polish family, so the Kuehne party moved on to a refugee camp about one half hour away.

In late May 1945, Heinz Winter showed up in Kleinbernten to be with his family. Gerda (who had not heard from him since February) later wrote of their reunion: "Nobody can believe how I felt when I saw my husband standing in front of me alive after the most horrible war." Then Gerda and her son both contracted what was called the *Russische Krätze*—a frightening and painful skin condition. Fortunately, they were treated in a local hospital. Grandpa Winter also gave them a blessing, and they were healed in two weeks; the doctors called them "miracle people." The Winters moved onto a farm, where both parents worked for room and board. The work was extremely hard for Gerda, but she realized how blessed they were that they had employment and food while others were dying of hunger. For the next two years, Heinz had to be on the lookout for Russian soldiers who were often hunting for former German soldiers, especially those with technical skills. Many were sent to the Soviet Union as involuntary laborers. Heinz escaped that fate.[36]

The Zunkowskis were fortunate to get to Güstrow, north of Berlin, where there was some degree of safety. However, in the summer of 1945, they were ordered to return to Stettin, but those orders were countermanded and they were stopped at the Oder River. Turning back westward, they made their way to Berlin and were taken in at the mission home on Rathenowerstrasse. In September, Wilford (only fifteen and a Soviet POW at the time) was able to escape and join his family in Berlin. They eventually moved to the suburb of Charlottenburg, where Brother Zunkowski became the president of a new branch.

Looking back on the war years, Sister Dretke summarized her feelings:

> I had a very strong testimony of the gospel during the war. There was no doubt about anything even though the war situation was difficult. There was nothing that could weaken my testimony. Difficult things only made it stronger. My husband's testimony stayed strong in the same way.

The nightmare that began for the Kuehne family in Anklam continued in Poland. On December 2, 1945, Polish soldiers broke into the home and subjected the family to heinous abuse. The next day, Waltraut found her girlfriend dead. She had been shot in the stomach by the soldiers and had then jumped out of a window. Waltraut's grandmother Schoening had been quite ill and passed away that same night. The next morning, a wagon came by, and several bodies were loaded on and taken away. By this time, it was clear that there was no reason for the Kuehne family to remain in the territory that had been ceded to Poland, so they applied for permission to head west into Germany. By April 1946, they found a new home in Schleswig-Holstein in the British Occupation Zone.

When asked how she maintained a testimony of the gospel during those hard times, Waltraut Kuehne made these comments:

[My testimony] wasn't there once in a while. It was gone once in a while. It was gone that time in Anklam. It was gone that time near Stettin. That night I said there couldn't be a God. Little did I know. But that's the way I felt. But the thing that kept me going was my dad. It didn't matter how bad things got, my dad never doubted.

Erika Berndt survived the first postwar months in her home on the outskirts of Stettin. In February of 1946, she was evicted from her home and headed west with her children. She arrived a few weeks later in northwest Germany near the town of Bad Segeberg. According to her son, Dieter, "My mother immediately prayed that we could find a branch of the Church nearby." After sleeping on straw in a barn for six weeks, the Berndts finally found a place to live, and life began again.

One day in December 1949, the Schwerin radio station named Hans Polzin as one of the POWs scheduled to arrive from the Soviet Union that day. Elli and her children waited at the railroad station for an hour in anticipation of his arrival. As she later recalled:

That hour for us seemed longer than any other hour we ever went through. When the train came, I saw him getting off of the last car. I recognized him, but he looked different. At first, I asked myself if it was really him. We went home together but we could really not believe it for the longest time. We had to get used to each other again. The children stared at their father often, not believing that he was home. . . . The first few weeks he was home, it was not very easy. . . . He had changed; he had gone through so much.

By the summer of 1946, the many surviving members of the Stettin Branch had left the city voluntarily or when compelled by the conquerors. The branch disappeared into history.[37]

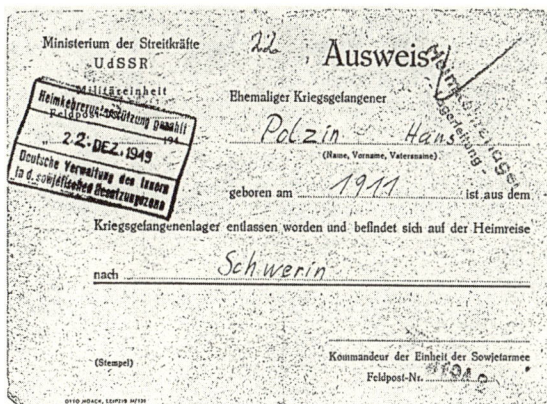

Fig. 11. The certificate of release of Hans Polzin as a POW in Russia.

In Memoriam

The following members of the Stettin Branch did not survive World War II:

Erich Hermann Wilhelm Berndt b. Stettin, Stettin, Pommern, Preußen 25 Jul 1907; son of Hermann Gustav Berndt and Marie Magdalene Koch; bp. 8 Sep 1923; m. Stettin 9 Jan 1937, Erika Edith Gerda Boldt; 2 children; k. air raid Arnimswalde, Pommern, Preußen 11 Apr 1944 (D. Berndt; AF; IGI)

Fritz Otto Karl Berndt b. Stettin, Stettin, Pommern, Preußen 15 Feb 1910; son of Hermann Gustav Berndt and Marie Magdalene Koch; bp. 8 Sep 1923; m. Stettin 12 Apr 1937, Dora Gertrud Luise Geschke; noncommissioned officer; k. in battle Bol.-Orahewo, Belarus 5 Jul 1944 (D. Berndt; www.volksbund.de; AF; IGI)

Johanne Elfriede Boenke b. Stettin, Stettin, Pommern, Preußen 7 Oct 1904; dau. of Wilhelm Boenke and Klara Mueller; k. air raid Stettin Feb 1945 (CHL CR 375 8 2458, 1378)

Otto Rudolf Böhnke b. Stettin, Stettin, Pommern, Preußen 6 May 1912; son of Wilhelm Adolf Böhnke and Anna Therese Pauline Schugk; bp. 5 Jun 1920; ord. priest; d. Stettin 11 or 12 Feb 1941 (*Sonntagsgruss*, no. 20, 18 May 1941, p. 80; *Sonntagsgruss*, no. 11, 16 Mar 1941, 43)

Guenter Karl Hermann Boldt b. Stettin, Stettin, Pommern, Preußen 9 Nov 1920; son of Karl August Friedrich Boldt and Anna Ida Marie Schuenke; k. in battle 19 Jun 1943 (D. Berndt; AF; IGI)

Alfred Karl Otto Bork b. Lötzen, Ostpreußen, Preußen 18 Jan 1920; son of Otto Franz Paul Bork and Margarethe Emilie Kuehn; bp. 14 Apr 1928; conf. 14 Apr 1928; ord. deacon 5 Jul 1936; ord. teacher 2 Apr 1939; MIA Russia 2 Apr 1945 (H. Bork; IGI)

Paul Walter Artur Bork b. Stettin, Stettin, Pommern, Preußen 7 Jan 1924; son of Otto Franz Paul

Fig. 12. Fritz Berndt.   *Fig. 13. Günter Boldt.*

Bork and Margarethe Emilie Kuehn; bp. 4 Jun 1932; conf. 5 June 1932; ord. deacon 2 Apr 1939; ord. teacher 25 Oct 1942; corporal; MIA Brody, Galicia, Russia 22 Jul or Sep 1944 (H. Bork; www.volksbund.de; IGI)

Hulda Marie Mathilde Schmalofski b. Breitenwerder, Friedeberg, Neumark Brandenburg, Preußen 10 Mar 1879; dau. of Friedrich Wilhelm Schmalofski and Wilhelmine Karoline Viedt; bp. 4 Aug 1924; m. 1 Sep 1906, Johann Gustav Franz Borrmann; d. malnutrition as refugee Güstrow-Schliefenberg, Mecklenburg Sep 1945 (Zdunkowski, IGI)

Franz Johannes Albert Brüsch b. Pommerensdorf, Pommern, Preußen 10 Mar 1876; son of Johann Christian Michael Brüsch and Friederike Juliana Neumann; bp. 30 May 1924; m. Stettin, Stettin, Pommern, Preußen 28 May 1902, Minna Marie Amalie Kirchoff; 4 children; d. heart disease Stettin 1 Nov 1939 (*Stern*, 1 Jan 1940, no. 1, 15; IGI)

Gustav Buyny b. Schwente, Westpreußen, Preußen 13 Aug 1872; son of August Buyny and Christine Holzer; bp. Schwendain, Stettin, Pommern, Preußen 2 Jul 1901; m. Auguste Boldt; d. Stettin 8 Jun 1942 (CHL LR 12728 11, 57; IGI)

Heinz Dieckmann b. Stettin, Stettin, Pommern, Preußen 2 Oct 1919; son of Albert Emil Dieckmann and Johanna Ebert; bp.; ord. deacon; MIA Russia Sep 1944 (I. Dieckmann Whitlock)

Heinrich Wilhelm Karl Diekmann b. Welstorf, Lippe 28 Apr 1864; son of Christian Heinrich Diekmann and Dorothea Catharina Johanna Haak; d. 14 Apr 1944 (IGI)

Max Dretke b. Schmiedeberg, Posen, Preußen 27 Dec 1918; son of Wilhelm Dretke and Emilie Riehm; bp. 2 Dec 1937; m. 1 Feb 1941; MIA Orel, Russia 17 Mar 1943 (court ruling; H. Dretke)

Willi Artur Herman Dretke b. Wongrowitz, Posen, Preußen 17 Jul 1912; son of Wilhelm Dretke and Emilie

Riehm; bp. 14 Apr 1928; m. Stettin, Stettin, Pommern, Preußen 30 Mar 1935; d. pneumonia Lübeck 25 Aug 1945 (H. Dretke; IGI)

August Friedrich Ferdinand Ebert b. Schillersdorf, Randow, Pommern, Preußen 25 Nov 1865; son of Carl Friedrich Ferdinand Ebert and Henriette Karoline Friederike Winkelmann; bp. 24 Mar 1901; ord. elder; m. Stettin, Stettin, Pommern, Preußen 27 Dec 1892, Hedwig Johanne Karoline Suhr; 9 children; d. old age Stettin 25 Dec 1944 (I. Dieckmann Whitlock; FHL Microfilm 25759, 1935 Census; IGI)

Herbert Karl Arthur Habedank Memel, Ostpreußen, Preußen 23 Mar 1923; son of Friedrich Carl Habedank and Anna Martha Berscheit; k. in battle Eastern Front 22 Oct 1943 (CHL LR 12728 11, 86; IGI)

Auguste Matilda Harwald b. Klein Zappeln, Schwetz, Westpreußen, Preußen 8 Feb 1870 or 1871; dau. of Gustav Harwald and Henriette Schmeichel; bp. 26 Dec 1908; m. Taschau, Jeschowa Westpreußen, Preußen 31 Mar 1904, Gustav Adolph Kuhn; 3 children; m. Gustav Krebs; d. Stettin, Pommern, Preußen 15 Aug 1943 (FHL Microfilm 271381, 1925/30/35 Census; AF; IGI)

Elisabeth Matilde Hennig b. Stettin, Pommern, Preußen 21 or 22 Oct 1883; dau. of Friedrich Wilhelm Hennig and Bertha Anna Ernestine Korth; k. air raid 30 Aug 1944 (CHL LR 12728 11, 78; FHL Microfilm 162781, 1925/30/35 Census)

Erwin Karl Otto Hönig b. Stettin, Pommern, Preußen 17 May 1923; son of August Hermann Hönig and Agnes Helene Emilie Burtelt; bp. 1932; rifleman; k. in battle by Tureni, Romania 21 or 29 Sep 1944; bur. Cluj, Romania (CHL LR 12728 11, 78; www.volksbund.de; IGI)

Hermann Gustav Jahn b. Landsberg/Warthe, Brandenburg, Preußen 5 Dec 1916; son of Gustav Jahn and Anna Nowakowsky; bp. 13 Dec 1931; ord. deacon; noncomissioned officer; d. 24 Nov 1940; bur. Norderney, Hanover (www.volksbund.de; FHL Microfilm 271365, 1035 Census)

Ernst Robert Otto Lehmann b. Pommerensdorf, Pommern, Preußen 12 Sep 1872; son of Albert Julius Alexander Lehmann and Marie Luise Koeckeritz; bp. 30 Mar 1907; m. Pommerensdorf 3 Aug 1895, Mathilde Pauline Alwine Loehn; d. heart failure Stettin, Stettin, Pommern, Preußen 2 Sep 1939 (*Stern*, no. 21, 1 Nov. 1939, 340)

Karl Willi Rudi Lehmann b. Stettin, Stettin, Pommern, Preußen 16 Oct 1920; son of Karl Ernst Otto Lehmann and Hertha Bertha Elfriede Appelgruen; bp. 26 Jun 1929; soldier; k. in battle 28 Jul 1941 (*Sonntagsgruss*, no. 28, 21 Sep 1941, 112)

Anna Maria Elisabeth Oehlke b. Schwenz, Cammin, Pommern, Preußen 20 Oct 1873; dau. of Johann Friedrich Oehlke and Johanna Friedricke Henriette Manthey; bp. 31 May or 1 Jun 1924; m.— Lange; d. Stettin, Pommern, Preußen 14 Feb 1944 (CHL LR 12728 11, 91; IGI)

Julius Karl August Schmidt b. Seeligsfelde, Pommern, Preußen 15 Feb 1871; son of Friedrich Wilhelm Schmidt and Karoline Friederike Wilhelmine Dummer; bp. 14 May 1910; m. Seeligsfelde 16 May 1905, Bertha Anna Augusta Reeck; 3 children; d. old age Stettin, Pommern, Preußen 11 Dec 1943; bur. Stettin 13 Dec 1943 (CHL LR 12728 11, 88; IGI)

Hedwig Johanne Karoline Suhr b. Stettin, Stettin, Pommern, Preußen 12 Jul 1874; bp. 24 Mar 1901; dau. of Friedrich August Johann Suhr and Luise Wilhelmine Sophie Suhr; m. Stettin 27 Dec 1892, August Friedrich Ferdinand Ebert; 9 children; d. heart attack Wismar, Mecklenburg-Schwerin 4 Apr 1945 (I. Dieckmann Whitlock; FHL Microfilm 25759, 1935 Census; IGI; AF; PRF)

Gerhard Alfred Weigand b. Stettin, Stettin, Pommern. Preußen 19 Jul 1913; son of Philipp Weigand and Meta Katilius; missing as of 1948 (CHL CR 375 8 2458, 824; CHL 2458, form 42 FP, pt. 37, 824–25)

Franz Rudolf Wichmann b. Deutsch Wilten, Ostpreußen, Preußen 31 Jan 1862; son of Gottlieb Wichmann and Julianne Charlotte Schulz; bp. 29 Nov 1896; ord. elder; m. Stettin, Stettin, Pommern, Preußen 14 Aug 1890, Marie Regine Helene Garbrecht; 8 children; d. Stettin 4 or 8 Feb 1941 (*Sonntagsgruss*, no. 11, 16 Mar 1941, 43; IGI)

Wilhelmine Johanna Sophie Günther b. Anklam, Pommern, Preußen 30 Mar 1866; dau. of Friedrich Günther and Wilhelmine Masch; bp. 14 May 1927; k. air raid 30 Aug 1944 (CHL LR 12728 11, 78; IGI)

Notes

1. Presiding Bishopric, "Financial, Statistical, and Historical Reports of Wards, Stakes, and Missions, 1884–1955," CR 4 12, 257.
2. Elli Martha Marie Zechert Polzin, interview by the author in German, Schwerin, Germany, August 17, 2006; unless otherwise noted, summarized in English by Judith Sartowski.
3. Margarethe Boehme Dretke Schmidt, interview by the author in German, Salt Lake City, July 12, 2007.
4. Heinz Winter, interview by the author, Salt Lake City, April 13, 2006.
5. Dieter Berndt, interview by the author in German, Berlin, Germany, August 20, 2006.
6. Ruth Krakow Meyer, interview by Anne Regina Leonhardt in German, Neubrandenburg, Germany, October 16, 2007; unless otherwise noted, transcript or audio version of the interview is in author's collection.
7. Waltraut Kuehne Dretke, interview by the author, Salt Lake City, February 2, 2007.
8. Alfred Bork, diary, July 30, 1939; private collection; trans. the author.
9. Ibid., October 19, 1941 and April 5, 1942.
10. Gerda Stenz Winter, interview by the author, Salt Lake City, April 13, 2006.
11. Stettin Branch, meeting minutes, 1940–1943, LR 12728 11, Church History Library; trans. the author.
12. Alfred Bork, diary, June 22, 1941.
13. Ibid., July 24, 1941–December 3, 1941.
14. Ibid., June 21, 1942.
15. Gerda H. Winter, "My Life Story" (unpublished history), 4; private collection.
16. This was most probably a priesthood meeting because only men were in attendance and no sacrament service took place. Heinz was a teacher in the Aaronic Priesthood throughout the war.
17. Anna Kopischke Roehl, telephone interview with Jennifer Heckmann in German, March 28, 2008.
18. For a description of the preparations made by civil defense authorities in large cities, see the introduction.
19. Sieglinde Dammaschke Zwick, interview by Rachel Gale, Salt Lake City, June 29, 2007.
20. Under a program called Kinderlandverschickung, entire classes of schoolchildren (usually ages ten to fourteen) were evacuated from large cities and sent with their teachers or Jungvolk leaders to vacation areas where hotels stood empty. This is most likely the situation where Waltraut worked.
21. Winter, "My Life Story," 5.
22. Anni Bauer Schulz, autobiography (unpublished), 73; private collection.
23. Thea Bork Gierschke, interview by Jennifer Heckmann in German, Stuttgart, Germany, August 18, 2006.
24. Stettin Branch, meeting minutes, April 20–21, 1943, 78.
25. Ruth Bork Rügner, interview by Jennifer Heckmann in German, Stuttgart, Germany, August 18, 2006.
26. Very common are stories regarding people in German cities who were too tired to go downstairs during alarms or who simply assumed that the bombs would not strike their neighborhood.
27. Stettin Branch, meeting minutes, 87.
28. Hans Ulrich Dretke, interview by the author, Salt Lake City, February 2, 2007.
29. See the details of the tragedy in the Stettin District chapter.
30. Bernard Zunkowski, interview by Michael Corley, Salt Lake City, April 24, 2008.
31. Schulz, autobiography, 78.
32. Ibid., 79.
33. Hellmut Bork, interview by the author, Kearns, Utah, January 20, 2006.
34. Stettin Branch, general minutes, 118; meeting minutes, 1940–1943, 118.
35. Winter, "My Life Story," 7.
36. Ibid, 7–8.
37. The modern Polish name for the city is Szczecin.

Stettin district president Erich Berndt presides over yet another wartime funeral.

ZWICKAU
DISTRICT
East German Mission

In the former kingdom of Saxony, where The Church of Jesus Christ of Latter-day Saints had its highest concentration of members in Germany before World War II, the Zwickau District had the highest number of branches in the smallest territory. The district measured approximately forty-two miles north–south and twenty-five miles east–west. Within that small area were eight branches and one group of the Church with a total membership of 690 at the end of 1939.

Zwickau District[1]	1939	1940	1941	1942
Elders	38	36		
Priests	9	10		
Teachers	18	23		
Deacons	32	29		
Other Adult Males	111	109		
Adult Females	438	433		
Male Children	24	24		
Female Children	20	22		
Total	690	686	675	666

Traveling distances to district conferences in Zwickau were relatively short. Meerane is ten miles to the north, Wilkau-Hasslau two miles to the southeast, Beutha twelve miles to the east, Schwarzenberg eighteen miles to the southeast, Auerbach seventeen miles to

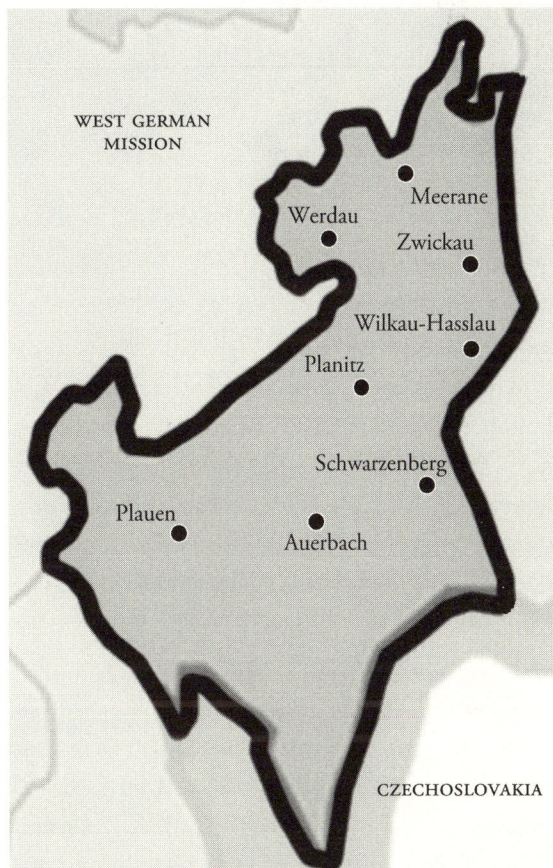

Fig. 1. *The Zwickau District of the East German Mission shared borders with the nation of Czechoslovakia, the West German Mission, and the districts of Chemnitz and Leipzig.*

the south, Planitz two miles to the southwest, Plauen twenty-four miles to the southwest, and Werdau five miles due west. One could take the train from Zwickau to every branch city

Fig. 2. Members of the Zwickau District gathered for a conference in 1940. (M. Gangien Mannek)

in the district except Planitz (in the Zwickau metropolitan area) and Beutha (where a small group of Saints met).

Adult women constituted the major demographic group in the Zwickau District—more than 63 percent. There was also a very large number of adult males who did not hold the priesthood—111. Relatively few children (barely 6 percent) lived in the nine units of the district when World War II approached.

The district president was Bernhard Unger until November 6, 1938, when Walter Fassmann, Sr. of the Zwickau Branch was named to that office.[2] Brother Fassmann served throughout World War II and for several years thereafter. As of March 19, 1939, Carl Neumärker was the first counselor in the district presidency and Alfred Klopfer the second counselor.[3] Sister Lina Ebisch of the Zwickau Branch was appointed district Relief Society president on August 7, 1938.[4]

The history of the East German Mission provides interesting details regarding the Zwickau District until March 1939, beyond which the mission records have been lost. For example, from November 5 to 23, 1938, Elder Roger A. Brown of the East German Mission Auxiliary Committee visited the branches of the Zwickau District "and discussed with the branch presidents and leaders of auxiliary organizations their various problems and gave suggestions and advice for improvement."[5]

On Saturday and Sunday, November 5–6, 1938, the fall conference of the district was held in Zwickau. President Alfred C. Rees of the East German Mission presided. The attendance at the general session on Sunday included 250 members and eighty-two friends.[6] It seems that the members in the district were quite willing to invite friends to join with them on these occasions. As in other districts in the East German Mission, the district conferences in Zwickau included cultural events such as concerts, dances, and theatrical performances in the years leading up to the war. Unfortunately, many such events were no longer possible when the privations of the war increased. Nevertheless, district conferences in Zwickau were held twice annually, at least through the year 1944.

The last pre-war conference for which a report exists in the record of the mission office in Berlin was held in Zwickau on Saturday and Sunday, March 18–19, 1939. Herbert Klopfer of the mission office staff represented President Rees on that occasion. The main session on Sunday evening was attended by 280 members and friends.[7]

NOTES

1. Presiding Bishopric, "Financial, Statistical, and Historical Reports of Wards, Stakes, and Missions, 1884–1955," CR 4 12, 257.
2. East German Mission Quarterly Reports, 1938, no. 46, East German Mission History.
3. Ibid., 1939, no. 58.
4. Ibid., 1938, no. 35.
5. Ibid., 1938, no. 46.
6. Ibid., 1938, no. 46.
7. Ibid., 1939, no. 59.

AUERBACH BRANCH

Nine miles from the border of Czechoslovakia, the town of Auerbach was home to a tiny branch of Latter-day Saints in 1939. Amidst the beautiful Erzgebirge Mountains of Saxony, the town is just seventeen miles south-southeast of the city of Zwickau. When the war began, there were about fifteen thousand inhabitants in Auerbach. Only sixteen were members of The Church of Jesus Christ of Latter-day Saints.

At the end of the year 1938, the Auerbach Branch was holding meetings at Kreuzstrasse 8B, apparently the home of a family named Seifert. That location is not in Auerbach itself, but rather in the neighboring community of Rodewisch, one mile to the north.

Auerbach Branch[1]	1939
Elders	1
Priests	0
Teachers	0
Deacons	1
Other Adult Males	1
Adult Females	12
Male Children	0
Female Children	1
Total	16

The adult female members constituted three-quarters of the branch population. The one elder may have been Brother Seifert.

By 1943, the location of the meetings was listed as Ottostrasse 17. This address in Auerbach was likely the home of some of the members of the branch.

As of this writing, there were no eyewitnesses to describe life in the Auerbach Branch during the war or the fate of the Latter-day Saints there.

No members of the Auerbach Branch are known to have lost their lives in World War II.

NOTE

1. Presiding Bishopric, "Financial, Statistical, and Historical Reports of Wards, Stakes, and Missions, 1884–1955," CR 4 12, 257.

Beutha Group

The group of Latter-day Saints holding meetings during World War II in the small community of Beutha in Saxony comprised principally two families: Schettler and Weinholdt. In this predominately Lutheran territory, the few members of The Church of Jesus Christ of Latter-day Saints were generally known and accepted. The meetings were held in the Schettler home on Hauptstrasse. Baptisms were conducted in a small pond just a few hundred yards from the home.

The history of the East German Mission contains but one entry regarding the Saints in Beutha, dated Friday, February 25, 1938: "The Beutha Branch gave an illustrated lecture, attended by fifteen persons."[1] Some of those persons would have been friends, because there were not fifteen members of the Church in the village. The history does not identify the topic of the lecture, but the Book of Mormon and genealogy were the most popular themes for such events in the mission in those days.

The only eyewitness for the Beutha group available for an interview as of this writing is Gertrude Schettler Sehm (born 1926). She made the following statements about life in Beutha and about the members of the group there just prior to and during World War II.[2]

> We held Church once a month. The only meeting was sacrament meeting. Because my father was deceased and Mr. Weinholdt was not a member of the Church, a priesthood holder came from Zwickau to administer the sacrament to us. Sometimes a second brother came along, and we had a rare Sunday School meeting as well. My mother taught us the gospel in the home. She could sing well (we had the Church hymnal), and she told us stories from the Book of Mormon.

Fig. 1. May 9, 1943, was a significant day for the Beutha Group: Sonja Weinholdt and Margarete Schettler were baptized by Bernhard Unger of the Zwickau Branch. (G. Schettler Sehm)

> Sometimes we traveled to Zwickau to attend meetings, including Relief Society and MIA (we did not have those in Beutha). About ten to fifteen of us made the trip together. We walked about one hour, then took the streetcar to the Zwickau Branch meetinghouse. We always left very early in the morning and came back late at night, since they held meetings twice a day in Zwickau. We usually stayed with other members between meetings because we couldn't go home yet.
>
> My father was very much against the [National Socialist] system, so I didn't participate in the Hitler Youth, nor did my brothers. He even locked my brothers in the house when it came time for the meetings so that they couldn't go. Nobody reported us because the people in the villages outside of the big cities didn't take these things very seriously.
>
> Although we lived in a village, the war raged all around us. The airplanes didn't drop bombs on us, but they did in nearby towns, and the air pressure broke windows in Beutha. There was a crater behind our house caused by an artillery shell. We hid in various places during the air raids, but our basement was the best place. One [neighbor] girl was killed when shrapnel flew through her window and hit her.
>
> The Americans came through Beutha first, but they didn't stop and didn't bother us. The Russians came next, and they did go through our houses. German soldiers were in our home once, and that was dangerous. They brought lice with them.
>
> There were food shortages during the war. I didn't see any foreign foods like bananas. The local stores went out of business. To heat our home, we used what little coal was distributed

and we gathered wood from the forest. When the Russians came, we didn't dare collect wood in the forest because they were camped there.

Two of my brothers were killed on the Russian Front. For one of them [Emil Ernst], we received an official notice on July 24, 1944. We never found out what happened to my other brother, Hans Gustav. He was declared dead by a court order on December 31, 1949.

My mother never doubted the gospel—even when she found out that her two sons were dead. She always said that she was looking forward to seeing them again.

Regarding life as a teenager during World War II, Gertrude made the following statement: "I was nineteen years old [when the war ended]. It should have been the most wonderful age for me, but under those circumstances, it was a disappointment."

In Memoriam:

The following members of the Beutha group did not survive World War II:

Emil Ernst Schettler b. 28 Feb 1921 in Beutha, Zwickau, Sachsen; son of Gustav Emil Schettler and Melitta Freida Löffler; bp. 11 Oct 1931; non-commissioned officer; k. in battle Lemieszow, Russia 24 July 1944 (Schettler-Sehm; CHL CR 275 8 2458, 1522; IGI; AF; www.volksbund.de)

Johannes Schettler b. 23 Nov 1919 Beutha, Zwickau, Sachsen; son of Gustav Emil Schettler and Melitta Freida Löffler; bp. 4 Aug 1929; corporal; d. Romania aft 25 Jul 1944; officially declared dead 31 Dec 1949 (Schettler-Sehm; IGI; AF)

Fig. 3. Emil and Johannes Schettler were both casualties of the war. They are shown here in their sister's photo album. (G. Schettler Sehm)

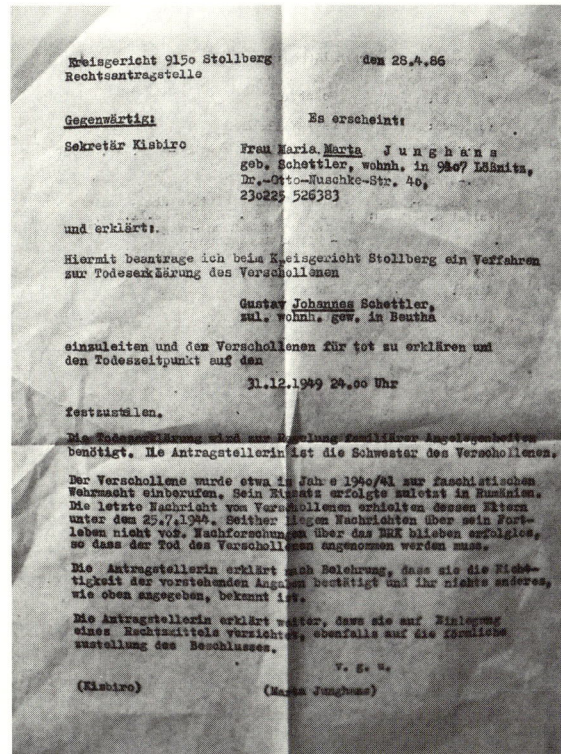

Fig. 2. Johannes (Hans) Schettler was reported missing in action in 1944. This 1986 letter officially established his death effective December 31, 1949—the date used for many missing soldiers in Germany. (G. Schettler Sehm)

Notes

1. East German Mission History Quarterly Reports, 1938, no. 12, East German Mission History.

2. Gertrude Schettler Sehm, interview by the author in German, Beutha, Germany, May 30, 2007; summarized in English by Judith Sartowski.

Meerane Branch

Very little is known about the small branch of Latter-day Saints living in Meerane in 1939. The town is located ten miles north of Zwickau. As of July 3, 1938, the following men led the branch: Erwin Auerbach, president; Hermann Blechschmidt, first counselor; Max Paul Frenzel, second counselor; Kurt Auerbach, secretary.

Meerane Branch[1]	1939
Elders	3
Priests	1
Teachers	3
Deacons	3
Other Adult Males	5
Adult Females	34
Male Children	3
Female Children	2
Total	54

The Meerane Branch is mentioned on several occasions in the history of the East German Mission before the spring of 1939. The following entries are of interest:

Sunday, August 14, 1938: A branch conference was held and sixty-two members and friends attended.[2]

Wednesday, November 30, 1938: In the Meerane Branch, the members of the priesthood were the guests of the Relief Society at a program and social; the attendance was very good.[3]

Friday, January 13, 1939: A special meeting was held under the direction of the full-time missionaries of the Chemnitz and Zwickau Districts; twenty members and seventeen friends attended.[4]

Friday, March 3, 1939: A social was held in the Meerane Branch, Zwickau District. It was attended by members and friends of the Zwickau, Werdau, and Planitz Branches. The sum of RM 10.00 was collected for the Meerane Branch Welfare Association.[5]

Based on such reports, it appears that the basic meetings were being held in Meerane and that some of the auxiliaries of the Church were also functioning as World War II approached.

At the conclusion of the year 1939, the Meerane Branch was holding its meetings at Marienstrasse 42 on the main floor. The location had changed to Augustusstrasse 99 in the home of the Blechschmidt family by January 1943. However, a note in the mission directory on that date indicates that meetings were sporadic

at best. It may then be that the Meerane Branch was substantially weakened by 1945.

In Memoriam

The following members of the Meerane Branch did not survive World War II:

Selma Emma Ahnert b. Niederschindmaas, Chemnitz, Sachsen 3 Dec 1863; dau. of Johann Christian Gottlieb Ahnert and Christiana Johanna Hochmuth; bp. 9 May 1929; conf. 9 May 1929; m. Niederschindmaas 2 or 29 Nov 1887, Hermann Theodor Trummer; 4 children; 2m. Niederschindmaas 23 Sep 1901 or 18 Feb 1904, Ernst Strangfeld; 1 child; d. old age 29 Mar 1945 (CHL CR 375 8 2444, no. 11; IGI)

Egon Auerbach b. Glauchau, Zwickau, Sachsen 19 Nov 1938; son of Karl Erwin Auerbach and Anna Elsa Neubert; d. lung ailment 21 or 22 Mar 1940 (CHL CR 375 8 2444, no. 63; IGI; AF)

Erich Willi Bauer b. Zschornewitz, Sachsen, Preußen 24 Jun 1919; son of Robert Alfred Bauer and Marie Sophie Wassmus; bp. 30 Jun 1927; m. 21 Aug 1943, Ruth Adina Blechschmidt; lance corporal; d. field hospital Brest-Litowsk, Russia 23 or 28 Oct 1943 (Sonja K. Nesbitt; IGI; www.volksbund.de)

Karl Hermann Blechschmidt b. Stangendorf, Chemnitz, Sachsen 18 Jul 1873 or 1875; son of Hermann Alexander Nienhold or Carl Louis Meinhardt and Augusta Amalia Blechschmidt; bp. 29 Mar 1929; conf. 29 Mar 1929; ord. deacon 3 May 1931; ord. priest 2 Apr 1933; ord. elder 28 Nov 1937; m. Marienthal, Zwickau, Sachsen 5 Nov 1898, Klara Hulda Daemmler; 13 or 14 children; d. weak heart Meerane, Zwickau, Sachsen 2 Feb 1940 (CHL CR 375 8 2444, no. 4; IGI; AF)

Auguste Louise Grundmann b. Meerane, Zwickau, Sachsen 31 Oct or Nov 1862; dau. of Johann Wilhelm and Christiana Johanna Peterman; bp. 29 Mar 1929; conf. 29 Mar 1929; m. Meerane 4 Dec 1897, Max Paul Frenzel; d. old age 25 Jun 1943 (CHL CR 375 8 2444, no. 9; IGI; AF)

Elsa Marie Koehler b. Meerane, Zwickau, Sachsen 18 Jan 1881; dau. of Alfred Theodor Koehler and Bertha Emilie Schwalbe; bp. 3 Apr 1931; conf. 3 Apr 1931; m. Meerane 21 Apr 1900, Paul August Bartko; 2 children; d. liver cancer Meerane 10 Oct 1940 (CHL CR 375 8 2444, no. 28; IGI; AF)

Anna Therese Scheithauer b. Ölsnitz, Chemnitz, Sachsen 4 Nov 1859; dau. of Johann Gottlieb Scheithauer and Christiane Johanne Hartel; bp. 3 Apr 1931; conf. 3 Apr 1931; m. 28 Aug 1884, Paul Heinrich Haertel; d. old age 17 Dec 1941 (CHL CR 375 8 2444, no. 31; IGI)

Erich Gerhard Schirner b. Bad Kösen, Sachsen, Preußen 8 or 18 Apr 1921; son of Rudolph August Schirner and Elsa Klara Belchschmidt; bp. 21 Apr 1930; conf. 21 Apr 1930; ord. deacon 3 Mar 1935; ord. teacher 5 Dec 1937; ord. priest 23 Jun 1940; d. tuberculosis 22 or 24 Mar 1943 (CHL CR 375 8 2444, no. 37; IGI)

Notes

1. Presiding Bishopric, "Financial, Statistical, and Historical Reports of Wards, Stakes, and Missions, 1884–1955," CR 4 12, 257.

2. East German Mission History Quarterly Reports, 1938, no. 35, East German Mission History.

3. Ibid., no. 47.

4. Ibid., 1939, no. 53.

5. Ibid., no. 59.

Planitz Branch

The town of Planitz lies not quite three miles south of the city center of Zwickau, yet the concentration of Latter-day Saints in the neighborhood warranted the establishment of a branch in Planitz.

Planitz Branch[1]	1939
Elders	6
Priests	1
Teachers	4
Deacons	5
Other Adult Males	7
Adult Females	38
Male Children	4
Female Children	6
Total	71

The meetings were held at Moritzstrasse 13. Manfred Röhlig (born 1921) described the setting in that building:

It was a large room that had previously been a shoe factory, and there were still iron pillars in the room. One time, I ran into one, and I still have a scar on the left side of my forehead. We also had a coal stove inside so the rooms would stay warm, but when we came on Sunday mornings, we could not breathe. Some of our members worked in a mine, and they made sure that we never ran out of coal. Next to the large room, there were two smaller ones—one for Sunday School and the Primary and the other for Priesthood meeting and Relief Society. . . . There was a picture of Jesus Christ in front of the room. . . . I think that we had a sign on the side of the building saying that [the Church] met there.[2]

The history of the East German Mission has two entries featuring the Planitz Branch just prior to World War II:

Sunday, July 17, 1938: The Planitz Branch, Zwickau District, held a conference. Attendance was sixty-three members and sixteen friends.[3]

Friday, March 3, 1939: A social was held in the Meerane Branch, Zwickau District. It was attended by members and friends of the Zwickau, Werdau, and Planitz Branches. The sum of RM 10.00 was collected for the Meerane Branch Welfare Association.[4]

According to Manfred Röhlig, the branch observed the typical meeting schedule, with Sunday School in the morning and sacrament meeting in the evening. Relief Society and priesthood meetings were held on Monday evening and MIA on Wednesday. When the weather was favorable, they often met outside in a field about two miles away. The locals called it "Mormon Field." Manfred recalled an average attendance at Sunday School of about seventy persons. With nearly 10 percent of the branch being elders, this was a strong group of Latter-day Saints.

When World War II began, Manfred Röhlig was serving in the Reichsarbeitsdienst in the Palatinate (the territory of the state of Bavaria west of the Rhine River). He was inducted directly into the Wehrmacht, receiving his new uniform as soon as he returned to the city of Kaiserslautern following three days of leave. One of his first assignments after the victorious campaign against France in the summer of 1940 was a leadership position in an office. "I did not think about it much but went along with it, although I could not understand why they chose me. That was the proof for me that Heavenly Father had his hands in these happenings." He was stationed in Calais, France, on the English Channel until 1944.

At home on leave in 1940, Manfred was ordained a teacher in the Aaronic Priesthood by branch president Albrecht Hochmut. Manfred felt that the gospel knowledge he took with him to the military was what he had received from Sunday School. He was never able to attend church away from home, but he observed the standards of conduct taught to him in his early years, and his comrades respected that. He also found it advantageous to trade his cigarette rations for better food. ("The others smoked and I lived," he claimed.)

It was on July 7, 1944, that Manfred married Gertraut Pfrötzschner of nearby Rottmannsdorf. After the obligatory ceremony in the office of the civil registrar in Zwickau, they went to the Marienkirche for the Church ceremony (she was still a Lutheran at the time).[5] The bride was driven to the church in a carriage. Because her aunt had connections to local stores, there was plenty of food available for the wedding dinner that followed. The army had granted Manfred eight days for the occasion, but that included travel time from and back to Calais, France.

A year later, Manfred was transferred to the Netherlands, then to Denmark, and finally to Hungary. On his way to Hungary, he was fortunate to go through Planitz, where he spent a few minutes with his wife; she was employed in an armaments factory there. From Hungary, Manfred's unit retreated gradually toward Germany. They met up with the advancing American Army in Czechoslovakia in April 1945, and Manfred became a POW. The war was over for him, but the challenges became more difficult. As he recalled his wartime service, he came to the following conclusions:

> I never used a weapon nor heard somebody shoot at anything or anybody. I had been issued a weapon, but I never knew where it was, so I could not carry it with me. (To be honest, I was never a good shot, either.) I did not have to walk or march—I was always lucky to have a vehicle to take me places.

By some quirk of fate, Hermann Hans had been wounded slightly and shipped from one army hospital to another, as medical personnel attempted to keep the wounded out of the hands of the invading Red Army. On the morning of May 8, Hermann was evacuated from a field hospital in Aue, just ten miles from his home. By that evening, he was thrilled to watch his transport roll into Planitz. American soldiers monitored traffic at key intersections, but Hermann had the driver stop at an intersection where no guards were present. Hopping off of the truck, he made his way around the corner on crutches and was home in minutes. A few days later, it was announced that anybody harboring German soldiers did so at the risk of punishment, so Hermann went to surrender himself to the Americans. He was interned in town, but with the help of local connections, he managed to be released officially on June 1, 1945.[6]

Manfred Röhlig's comfortable life ended for a time in May 1945, because the Americans turned him and his comrades over to the Soviets. As POWs, they were marched through Austria to Romania and from there to the Soviet Union. For the next two years, his wife did not know of his whereabouts. Like any common soldier, Manfred was required to perform hard labor during his time in the Soviet Union. While he spent some of the time in a kitchen, he also worked for three years in a mine and in a quarry. At one point in time, he was so ill from dysentery that he nearly died. In fact, he awoke one day and found that those around him in the hospital had died.

Part of the program of Manfred's Soviet captors was a detailed education in socialism. Manfred used the writing materials provided to write copious notes about that philosophy because he did not wish to simply sit around and waste his time. When he was released, a guard took his papers from him and threw them away. He was told that if he did not yet have the knowledge in his head, the notes would do him little good.

Herta Hans (born 1911) had to survive wartime Germany without the assistance of her husband, Hermann, who had been in the army since 1933. He was gone all during the war, with the exception of a few furloughs. They had married in 1938, and their son, Peter, was born in 1940. Sister Hans moved to Dresden for a time during the war, then back to Planitz. A small miracle occurred in her life when her husband arrived at home on May 8, 1945—the day the war ended.

When Manfred Röhlig was released from the Soviet POW camp in June 1949, he reentered Germany at Frankfurt/Oder. There he was given 50 marks, which he used to buy some white bread "and ate it fast!" as he recalled. He then took the train to Zwickau, arriving after the last bus left for Planitz. However, it was still light, and he simply walked the last two miles to his home. He had served for ten years in a German uniform. Unlike most German POWs in the Soviet Union, he had been fed fairly well; his wife was surprised by his good condition.

Looking back on his life as a Latter-day Saint in the German army, Manfred said that "without prayer, nothing worked for me. . . . The connection to my Heavenly Father never broke down. I could not have survived without that connection. . . . After the ten years I was

gone, I went back to activity in the Church as if I had never even been gone. I was only absent physically."

In Memoriam:

The following members of the Planitz Branch did not survive World War II:

Heinz Albert Hochmuth b. Planitz, Sachsen, Zwickau, Sachsen 19 Dec 1924; son of Albrecht Max Hochmuth and Martha Camilla Hertel; bp. 31 Aug 1932 or 1933; d. 20 or 22 Apr 1945 (CHL CR 375 8 2458, 1522; IGI)

Margarete Alma Hoffmann b. Halsbach, Freiberg, Sachsen 21 Feb 1888; dau. of Karl Emil Hofmann and Alma Hulda Froebe; bp. 20 Jul 1926; conf. 20 Jul 1926; m. 6 Jan or Jun 1908, Ernst Krügel; d. esophageal tumor 28 Oct 1944 (CHL, LR 6986 21, no. 25; IGI)

Willy Rainer b. Planitz, Zwickau, Sachsen 16 Aug 1944; son of Erich Alfred Mueller and Elfriede Lina Dietel; d. tongue inflamation 1 Nov 1944 (CHL, LR 6986 21, no. 96; IGI)

Heinz Georg Stribrsky b. Buchholz, Chemnitz, Sachsen 7 or 15 Mar 1915; son of Johann Georg Stribrsky and Hedwig Johanne Mueller; bp. 12 Apr 1923; conf. 12 Apr 1923; ord. teacher; m. 21 Dec 1940, Johanna Elfriede Kehrer; soldier; k. in battle 31 Aug 1942 (*Sonntagsgruss*, no. 20, Oct 1942, 80; M. Roehlig; CHL LR 6986 21, no. 63; FHL Microfilm 245277, 1930/35 Census; IGI)

Notes

1. Presiding Bishopric, "Financial, Statistical, and Historical Reports of Wards, Stakes, and Missions, 1884–1955," CR 4 12, 257.

2. Manfred Röhlig, interview by the author in German, Planitz, Germany, June 3, 2007; summarized in English by Judith Sartowski.

3. East German Mission History Quarterly Reports, 1938, no. 31, East German Mission History.

4. Ibid., 1939, no. 59.

5. For some reason, the civil registrar did not present the newly-weds a copy of *Mein Kampf* by Adolf Hitler, nor did he give them a family book to record major events in their lives.

6. Hermann Hans, autobiography (unpublished); private collection.

Plauen
Branch

The city of Plauen in Saxony was located in the extreme southwest corner of the East German Mission territory. The city is twenty-four miles southwest of Zwickau and had a population of about one hundred thirty thousand people when the war began.

Plauen Branch[1]	1939
Elders	8
Priests	1
Teachers	0
Deacons	8
Other Adult Males	31
Adult Females	114
Male Children	6
Female Children	2
Total	170

Plauen was the home of a very strong branch of The Church of Jesus Christ of Latter-day Saints in 1939. The history of the East German Mission has several entries regarding the rooms in which the Plauen Branch met:

Thursday, September 1, 1938: The Plauen Branch, Zwickau District, moved temporarily into a new hall at Rahnitzer Strasse 103.[2]

November 1938: During the month of November, various improvements took place in the Plauen Branch. Among other things the stage was re-built, a wall replaced, a banister remodeled.[3] During the month of January [1939], the meeting hall in the Plauen Branch, Zwickau District, was completely renovated.[4]

The mission history also gives evidence that the Plauen Saints enjoyed interacting with the members of other nearby branches. We read this entry under Sunday, October 16, 1938:

Fig. 1. To reach the branch meeting rooms in Plauen, members walked through this portal to the Hinterhaus. (F. Fassmann)

Members of the Zwickau, Werdau, and Wilkau[-Hasslau] Branches made a trip by bus to Aschberg. A special meeting was held in Schwarzenberg in the morning and one in Plauen in the evening. Fifty percent of the members participated.[5]

As is true throughout the Zwickau District, the Plauen Branch also had a prominent group of adult women (67 percent of the branch population).

Perhaps the best source of information on the Plauen Branch is the journal kept by branch member Louis Christian Fassmann (born 1889). Along with stories of events in the branch and records of branch members, priesthood ordinations, mission and district leaders, family tithing payments and statistics, he kept a record of all of the full-time missionaries who served there. For example, he recorded the departure of elders Ralph H. Kmetzsch and Parry H. Harryson on August 26, 1939, due to "danger of war." They were replaced that day by one German missionary, Ernst Landschulz, who stayed in Planitz until November 24, 1940.[6]

In January 1943, the mission directory showed a different address for the Plauen Branch, namely Beethovenstrasse 14. Fritz Fassmann (born 1927) recalled moving into the rooms at Beethovenstrasse near the onset of the war and meeting there into the postwar era. He also recalled going to church early to heat the rooms so that there would be a comfortable temperature by the time most of the members arrived.[7]

Ruth Pfund (born 1931) provided the following description of the rooms at Beethovenstrasse: "The meeting rooms were located in a Hinterhaus. The branch was not very large, but we had a comfortable and large meeting room. There were one large room and two or three smaller rooms. It was decorated very simply."[8]

Fritz Fassmann also recalled attending Church meetings on occasion in his Hitler Youth uniform. "Sometimes when we had [Jungvolk] meetings on Sunday mornings, we went over to church in our uniforms. . . . I know

of one brother who was in the Sturmabteilung [SA] because of his occupation. Sometimes he came to Sunday School in his uniform."[9]

Fritz's elder sister, Irmgard (born 1924), served her Pflichtjahr at the age of fifteen (from April 1939 to April 1940). She was sent

Fig. 2. A modern view of the Hinterhaus at Beethovenstrasse 14, which served the branch from 1942 through the end of the war. (F. Fassmann)

Fig. 3. The chapel of the Plauen Branch during World War II. At left is Louis Christian Fassmann, the author of the branch records. The banner reads, "The Glory of God Is Intelligence." (F. Fassmann)

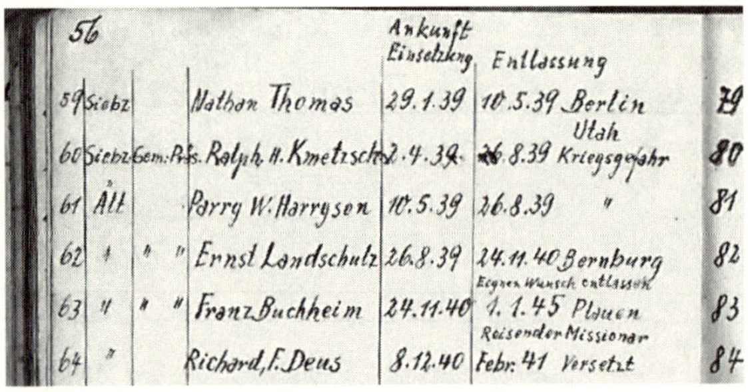

56				Ankunft Einsetzung	Entlassung	
59	Siebz		Nathan Thomas	29.1.39	10.5.39 Berlin Utah	79
60	Siebz.	Gem. Präs.	Ralph H. Kmetzsch	2.4.39	26.8.39 Kriegsgefahr	80
61	Ält		Parry W. Harrysen	10.5.39	26.8.39 "	81
62	"	" "	Ernst Landschulz	26.8.39	24.11.40 Bernburg Eigenen Wunsch entlassen	82
63	"	" "	Franz Buchheim	24.11.40	1.1.45 Plauen Reisender Missionar	83
64	"		Richard F. Deus	8.12.40	Febr. 41 Versetzt	84

Fig. 4. A page of Louis Christian Fassmann's journal showing the comings and goings of full-time missionaries in Plauen. (F. Fassmann)

with twenty-four other girls her age to work on a farm in eastern Silesia. Her day began at five o'clock, and she spent the morning feeding and milking cows, cleaning stalls, feeding chickens, collecting eggs, turning hay, planting potatoes, and doing other farm chores. The conclusion of the day was apparently the most entertaining:

> We worked till six at night, ate again, and at 8:00 we girls could go back to our camp. The camp was fun, too. We girls had a lot to giggle [about] and tell about our experiences and then fell dead tired into bed. . . . During this time I could not go to my church so I sent my tithing home. We got about 20 marks a month. When I started . . . I was a skinny little thing, but after this year on the farm, I grew strong and big. I was able to carry a 100 lb. bag of wheat to the miller some houses away.[10]

World War II began while Irmgard was working on the farm. At age sixteen, she finished school and signed up for a secretarial course sponsored by the Junkers Aircraft Company of Dessau. After three months of office training, she was hired and moved to Dessau. Her wage at Junkers was 120 marks a month. In Dessau, she could not find the branch of Latter-day Saints, so she hummed Church melodies on the bus and thereby met Brother Gerstner. She recalled, "The next Sunday I went to church. I was surprised at how small the branch was, only about twelve people present." She remained in Dessau until the last year of the war.

According to Fritz Fassmann, life in Plauen did not change much during the first years of the war. "Our daily lives were normal for us. The adults worked or did something at home, while the children were at school or participated in extracurricular activities." Air raids and invading armies were experiences of the last year of the war in Plauen.

Toward the end of the war, Fritz Fassmann was inducted into the Reichsarbeitsdienst and sent to Czechoslovakia to work. While he was there, his time elapsed and, as was common practice at the time, he was automatically drafted into the army. While still in Czechoslovakia for training, he and his unit were captured by the invading Red Army in April 1945.

The diary of Louis Christian Fassmann contains a list of all members of the Plauen Branch, as well as a record of current events. No fewer than fifteen members died during the war, including several who were killed in air raids over Plauen. The last few days of the war in Plauen were perilous times in that large city while the residents were being bombed into submission by the Allies:

> Air raids day and night.
>
> February 23, March 5, 1945: Little damage.
>
> March 19, 1945: day time air raid; windows damaged.
>
> March 21, 1945: terrible attack; everything bombed out; our house is totally destroyed.
>
> March 25, 1945: had regular [Sunday] meetings.
>
> March 26: huge raid with incendiary bombs; both of us were hiding in a bomb crater outside and were showered by debris and suffered bruises; I suffered a broken rib; we moved to the home of Sister Wunderlich at Bahnhofstrasse 84 until April 10, 1945.

Fig. 5. Members of the Plauen Branch posed for the photographer between the main building at Beethovenstrasse 14 (right) and the Hinterhaus where they met (to the left). (F. Fassmann)

April 1, 1945: held regular meetings, with branch president Erich Sellner of Werdau in attendance.

April 3, 1945: night attack.

April 8, 1945: Sunday night air raid; alarms prevented us from holding meetings.

April 9, 1945: night air raid; city center on fire.

April 10, 1945: huge air raid; worst attack yet; city center and Haselbrunn [neighborhood] all burned out; incendiaries; only 55,000 people left in Plauen; it is a ghost town; almost all of the members have been bombed out or burned out. Most of the members are living out of town.

Spent a night in the Schönfeld home at Rossviertelstrasse 10.

April 12, 1945: stayed in the home of a farmer named Wenk in Trieb.

April 15, 1945: no meetings. Our rooms are slightly damaged. Plaster has fallen from the ceiling and window panes are broken.

April 22, 1945, Sunday: we were at church; windows are all right; no meeting because of bad weather; we have to clean up first; things are not in order; Sister Ellie Kurzendörfer cleaned up the rooms.

Many members have left town. Nobody can get into or out of the city. We plan to meet on Sunday, April 29, 1945 at 3 o'clock.

I have to report to work every day.

April 29, 1945: Six persons were in attendance; the meetings were cancelled because of bad weather.

May 6, 1945: first meeting, fast meeting. District president Walter Fassmann and branch president Erich Sellner [of Werdau] were in attendance.

Brother Fassmann's daughter, Irmgard, arrived home from Dessau on Pentecost Sunday, six weeks after Easter in 1945. She and two friends went to church and on the way saw two elderly people walking, the woman helping the man climb the hill. "Coming closer I saw that they were my parents going to church, true and faithful. I cried to see them alive even though not too strong. We got to church and . . . had a very good reunion. . . . We [were] like a real family, the whole branch."

The Fassmanns continued to live in the apartment that was half destroyed by the bombs. "It was difficult to climb up the broken stairway, but we made it," Irmgard recalled. Soon she went to work helping to clear the rubble from the streets.

Fritz Fassmann had heard rumors that his Soviet captors might ship German POWs to Siberia to work and decided that "I did not want that to happen to me." As a young man, he had confidence in his ability to survive and soon escaped from the Soviet POW camp. Making his way west, he surrendered to the Americans in Czechoslovakia. Conditions in the new camp were primitive, as he later explained:

> The camp was just one wide field, without any fences, no buildings, and not even tents. We just lay in the field out in the open. I knew that Plauen was not very far away. I made plans to flee from there also. The Americans were pretty sure that nobody would escape, because the Czechs had the reputation of killing the Germans [they caught].

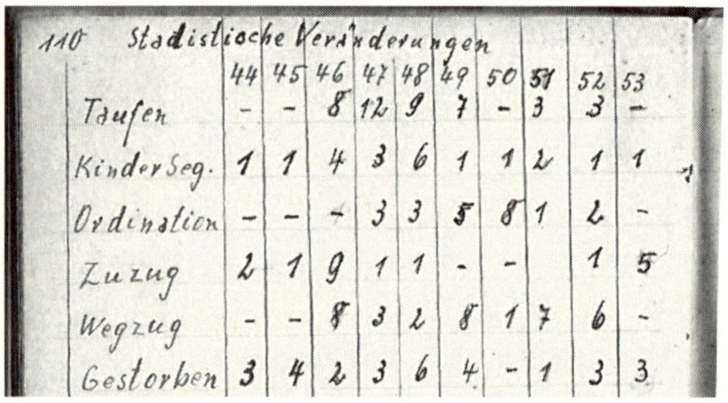

110 Stadistische Veränderungen	44	45	46	47	48	49	50	51	52	53
Taufen	-	-	8	12	9	7	-	3	3	-
Kinder Seg.	1	1	4	3	6	1	1	2	1	1
Ordination	-	-	-	3	3	5	8	1	2	-
Zuzug	2	1	9	1	1	-	-		1	5
Wegzug	-	-	8	3	2	8	1	7	6	-
Gestorben	3	4	2	3	6	4	-	1	3	3

Fig. 6. This page from Louis Christian Fassmann's journal shows "statistical changes" in the Plauen Branch beginning in 1944. The categories are baptisms, blessings of children, ordinations, arrivals, departures, and deaths. (F. Fassmann)

Nevertheless, Fritz escaped and made it safely home to Plauen. There he found a bombed-out city. "Although our [apartment] house was destroyed, the families living in the building had posted notes [in the ruins] telling people where they had moved to. That is how I found my family again." It was about June 1945. Fritz assisted the surviving branch members in reconstructing the branch. Latter-day Saints who had fled the city began to come home.

In Memoriam:

The following members of the Plauen Branch did not survive World War II:

Emilie —— b. 9 Jan 1869; bp. 18 Sep 1909; m. 14 Sep 1901, —— Menicke; d. 21 Feb 1944 (L.C. Fassmann journal)

Emilie Maximiliane —— b. 11 Feb 1885; bp. 31 Jul 1926; m. 2 Aug 1913, —— Rothe; 2 children; d. heart attack 7 Mar 1942 (L. C. Fassmann journal; FHL Microfilm 271407, 1930/35 Census; IGI)

August Karl Adler b. Rittersgrün, Zwickau, Sachsen 9 May 1852; son of Karl Ludwig Adler and Christiane Friederike Taubner; bp. 5 Apr 1909; m. Werdau, Zwickau, Sachsen 3 Jul 1871, Ernestine Pauline Adam; 8 children; 2m. Auerbach, Zwickau, Sachsen 6 Mar 1930, Emma Clara Krause; d. old age Plauen, Zwickau, Sachsen 24 Sep 1943 (L. C. Fassmann journal; IGI)

Martin Hermann b. 30 Apr 1897; bp. 2 Sep 1911; m. 9 Nov 1919; k. in air raid 20 Apr 1945 (L. C. Fassmann journal)

Elsa Klara Hoyer b. Plauen, Zwickau, Sachsen 2 May 1880; dau. of Bernhardt Albin Hoyer and Emilie Louise Schwinger; bp. 13 Sep 1907 or 22 Aug 1922; m. Plauen 4 Jan 1900, Franz Otto Buchheim; 5 children; d. stroke Plauen 5 Nov 1944 (L.C. Fassmann journal; IGI)

Paul Hermann Koch b. Adorf, Zwickau, Sachsen 25 Jan 1904; son of Gottfried Franz Koch and Lina Augusta Ebner; bp. 20 Mar 1926; soldier; d. Austria 16 Apr or 8 May 1945; bur. Nuremberg South Cemetery,

Nuremberg, Bayern (FHL Microfilm 271380, 1935; AF; IGI; www.volksbund.de)

Gustav Emil Koenig b. Schöneck, Zwickau, Sachsen 1 Aug 1872; son of Friedrich August Koenig and Marie Louise Meyer; bp. 17 Jun 1910; ord. deacon 3 Sep 1914; m. Plauen, Zwickau, Sachsen 18 Jul 1896, Elisabeth Hirschmann; d. intestinal illness 21 or 27 Mar 1943 (L. C. Fassmann journal; IGI)

Reinhard Johannes Roeder b. Plauen, Zwickau, Sachsen 15 May 1919; son of Hans Fritz Roeder and Olga Selma Schmidt; bp. 25 Oct 1929; m. 22 Jan 1944; non-commissioned officer; k. in battle Monor, Romania 11 Nov 1944 (L. C. Fassmann journal; IGI; www.volks-bund.de)

Gerhardt Paul Schieck b. Plauen, Zwickau, Sachsen 27 or 28 Oct 1910; son of Isidor Valentin Schieck and Johanna Georgine Spindler; bp. 19 Jan 1924; m. 27 Apr 1940, Elly Fischer; k. in battle 27 Jan 1945 (L. C. Fassmann journal; IGI)

Rosa Gertrud Schleicher b. Plauen, Zwickau, Sachsen 1 Dec 1900; dau. of Gotthardt Heinrich Schleicher and Anna Augusta Weiss; bp. 2 Sep 1911; m. 24 Dec 1924, —— Gerstner; d. 6 Feb 1944 (L. C. Fassmann journal; IGI; FHL Microfilm 25773, 1930/35 Census)

Johanne Schleizer b. Plauen, Zwickau, Sachsen 23 Jan 1898; dau. of August Wartmann and Wilhelmine Schleizer; bp. 11 May 1911; m. 24 Feb 1923, —— Wagner; k. in air raid 10 Apr 1945 (L. C. Fassmann journal; IGI; FHL Microfilm 245291, 1930/35 Census)

Wilhelmine Schleizer b. Pöhl, Zwickau, Sachsen 6 Feb 1870; dau. of August Schleizer and Wilhelmine; bp. 11 Mar 1911; m. 5 Apr 1895, —— Wartmann; k. in air raid 10 Apr 1945 (L. C. Fassmann journal; FHL Microfilm 245294, 1930/35 Census; IGI)

Paul Werner Sorger b. Reichenbach, Zwickau, Sachsen 23 Dec 1911; son of Emil Otto Sorger and Martha Lina Keller; bp. 9 Jul 1930; k. in battle Eastern Front 1 Nov 1942 (L. C. Fassmann journal; IGI)

Anna Rosa Wolf b. Plauen, Zwickau, Sachsen 12 Aug 1909; dau. of Bruno Wolf and Martha Rosa Baumgaertel; bp. 31 Jul 1926; m. 25 Nov 1933, —— Hölzel; k. air raid 6 Feb 1945 (L. C. Fassmann journal; FHL Microfilm 163788, 1935 Census)

NOTES

1. Presiding Bishopric, "Financial, Statistical, and Historical Reports of Wards, Stakes, and Missions, 1884–1955," CR 4 12, 257.
2. East German Mission History Quarterly Reports, 1938, no. 40, East German Mission History.
3. Ibid., no. 47.
4. Ibid., 1939, no. 53.
5. Ibid., 1938, no. 43.
6. Louis Christian Fassmann, diary, 56; private collection.
7. Fritz Louis Fassmann, telephone interview with Jennifer Heckmann in German, May 2, 2008; unless otherwise noted, summarized in English by Judith Sartowski.
8. Ruth Pfund Adler, telephone interview with Judith Sartowski, March 5, 2008.
9. The SA (Sturmabteilung) was the arm of the Nazi Party for adult males.
10. Irmgard Fassmann Messina Schwarz, autobiography (unpublished); private collection.

SCHWARZENBERG BRANCH

The town of Schwarzenberg in Saxony is located eighteen miles southeast of Zwickau, seven miles north of the Czech border. In 1939, approximately seven thousand people lived in Schwarzenberg; fifty-one were members of The Church of Jesus Christ of Latter-day Saints.

Schwarzenberg Branch[1]	1939
Elders	2
Priests	1
Teachers	2
Deacons	1
Other Adult Males	11
Adult Females	33
Male Children	1
Female Children	0
Total	51

As of this writing, no eyewitnesses could be found, and thus no description of the branch, its meeting place, or its membership is available. The mission directory for September 1938 shows an address of Grünhainerstrasse 8, on the main floor of the first Hinterhaus of "Hecker's factory."

In the final months of the war, the rooms in which the Schwarzenberg Branch met were confiscated; throngs of refugees pouring into the region needed housing, and the city government appropriated space wherever possible.[2]

No members of the Schwarzenberg Branch are known to have lost their lives in World War II.

Notes

1. Presiding Bishopric, "Financial, Statistical, and Historical Reports of Wards, Stakes, and Missions, 1884–1955," CR 4 12, 257.
2. "Die Geschichte der Gemeinde Zwickau in Kurzfassung" (unpublished history); private collection.

WERDAU BRANCH

The city of Werdau, with its twenty-three thousand inhabitants, was home to a branch of the Latter-day Saints in 1939. The city is just six miles west of Zwickau.

Werdau Branch[1]	1939
Elders	4
Priests	3
Teachers	5
Deacons	5
Other Adult Males	10
Adult Females	52
Male Children	6
Female Children	5
Total	90

The Werdau Branch met throughout the war in rented rooms at Reichenbacherstrasse 22, rooms that were officially opened for Church use on March 5, 1939. On that occasion, seventy-six members of this and other branches in the district met for the celebration under the leadership of district president Walter Fassmann.[2]

Hannelore Ehrler (born 1930) recalled that the church location was right next to the railroad station and that the building had previously been used as a house of ill repute. As she explained years later, "We cleaned it up nicely, and to us it was our meetinghouse." Regarding the number of persons who attended, she said "When there were thirty, we thought we had a wonderful meeting."[3]

Marianne Suhrmann (born 1926) later described the Church facility as follows:

The rooms were on the ground floor in the main building. We had a really nice and large main room, and one or two classrooms. We had about 100 to 120 persons in attendance on a typical Sunday. Sunday School was at 10:00 A.M. and sacrament meeting at 4:00 P.M. [My family] walked about [two miles] one way to church. During the week, we had Beehives (Sister Sellner was our leader); all young women were Beehive Girls; the older ones were Golden Gleaners.[4]

The history of the East German Mission sheds significant light on the condition of the Werdau Branch when World War II approached:

Sunday, August 28, 1938: A very successful branch conference was held.[5]

Sunday, September 11, 1938: Recreation committees were formed in thirteen branches throughout the mission, including Werdau.[6]

Sunday, October 16, 1938: Members of the Zwickau, Werdau, and Wilkau[-Hasslau] branches made a trip by bus to Aschberg. A special meeting was held in Schwarzenberg in the morning and one in Plauen in the evening. Fifty percent of the members participated.[7]

Friday, March 3, 1939: A social was held in the Meerane Branch, Zwickau District. It was attended by members and friends of the Zwickau, Werdau, and Planitz branches. The sum of RM 10.00 was collected for the Meerane Branch Welfare Association.[8]

Marianne's mother, Johanna Suhrmann, was the local Relief Society president. The branch president was Alfred Klopfer (father of mission supervisor Herbert Klopfer), and his counselors were Brother Fritzsching and Erich Sellner.

Marianne Suhrmann's experience in the Hitler Youth was not exemplary, as she explained:

> I was inducted into the Jungvolk, then at fourteen into the BDM. I was a real troublemaker. Whenever they did something religious, I was not allowed to stay there with them. I was considered a troublemaker, so they punished me by taking away my neckerchief knot. And sometimes I had to stay away from the meetings for a month as a penalty, but they never kicked me out totally. They wanted to maintain a hold on all of us.

Her reputation was known in school as well. "They knew that I was a Mormon, and they sent me out when they had the religion class."

In early 1943, Herbert Klopfer, the supervisor of the East German Mission, and a soldier in active duty since 1940, moved his wife and his two sons from the mission home in Berlin back to Werdau, his hometown. There they lived with his parents. Sister Erna Klopfer and her sons were safe in this small town, far from the terror of air raids over Berlin. Her parents (Brother and Sister Hein) joined them by the end of the war, as did Herbert's sister, Maria. Brother Klopfer was able to visit the family here several times before the year 1943 came to a close.

Hannelore Ehrler was not interested in the Hitler Youth program. "They did a lot of marching with music. I wanted to sing to music, not march to it." As in many German cities in those days, public school ended at 1:00 P.M. on Wednesdays and the Jungvolk met that afternoon as well as on Saturdays. Fortunately for

Fig. 1. A modern view of the building in which the Werdau Branch held its meetings throughout World War II: Reichenbacherstrasse (now August Bebel Strasse) 22. (G. Brokatzky)

Hannelore, a piano teacher suggested that she take lessons from him on Wednesdays. She accepted his offer and had a fine excuse for missing Jungvolk meetings. "But on Saturdays, I had to go," she recalled. At the age of fourteen, she was sworn in as a member of the League of German Girls, but just a few weeks after that, the war ended.

Marianne Suhrmann's half-brother, Rolf Armin Fugmann, was a sailor in the German navy in 1943 when he was on leave at Plöner See (a lake in northern Germany). He drowned in a boating accident, and his body was taken by four other sailors to Werdau for burial. Johanna Suhrmann received a telegram with the tragic news, but Marianne had sensed her brother's death the night after the accident. She described the experience in these words:

> On the Sunday when he died, I was in bed that night, and I felt like there was somebody in our house. I heard steps and breathing—three times somebody came close to me. I told my mother, and she searched all over the house and found nobody. Later, when we had learned of Rolf's death, I knew that he had come to say good-bye to me. We were very close.

After two years of training as a telephone operator, Marianne went to work for the railroad office in Werdau. As a young woman, she was interested in normal social activities such as dancing. On one occasion, she and a friend were on their way to a dance when they met two French workers, who introduced themselves. Marianne soon found herself romantically involved with one of the men and her mother liked him as well. Unfortunately, this led to trouble. Sister Suhrmann gave the Frenchman the key to their garden cottage and invited him to spend the night there. However, a local policeman saw him on the property one night and charged him with espionage. When the investigation revealed his relationship with Marianne, she was fired from her job (based on her "un-German activities") and was sent to faraway Kühlungsborn on the Baltic Sea. There she became a member of an antiaircraft battery. Luckily for her, an officer came by the next day in search of a telephone operator, and she was spared the hard labor of the antiaircraft battery crew. In February 1945, she was sent home on convalescent leave. Weeks later, she was baptized a member of the Church in an outdoor swimming pool. She was home when the American army arrived in late April 1945.

Marianne welcomed the invaders with a large white flag, but the neighbors worried that fanatic defenders might shoot her for treason in the last hours of a war already lost. Fortunately nothing came of it, and soon Americans were in Sister Suhrmann's store, asking for drinks and food ("and behaving themselves very well," according to Marianne). The war had done little damage to Werdau, and both the Suhrmann home and the Werdau Branch meeting rooms were undamaged.

As the war drew to a close, the residents of Werdau found their city approached from the east by the Soviets and from the west by the Americans. Hannelore Ehrler recalled hearing the roar of artillery from each side. The Americans entered the city first, and Hannelore went out to greet them, holding

the photographs of two missionaries from her mother's collection.[9] She was able to communicate to one soldier that she was "a Mormon" and he helped her find his buddy, who was actually related to one of the missionaries in her photographs.

In the first week of July 1945, Marianne and a girlfriend headed for the border of the Soviet and American Occupation Zones. There they were caught by Soviet guards but released the next day without harm and crossed into southern Germany. Marianne returned to Werdau in 1946, very grateful to have escaped ill treatment at the hands of the victors.

On July 1, 1945, the American army moved out of Werdau and the Soviets moved in. Hannelore was one of many young girls who feared being assaulted by the soldiers. She explained the frightening situation:

> I had just graduated from public school in April, and 63 percent of my classmates had to go to the hospital with venereal diseases because they had been raped. At that time, I prayed, "Heavenly Father, I cannot be raped!" I had it in my mind that if I got old enough, I wanted to go to Salt Lake City and be married in the temple. We had been told that if you [go to] get married in the temple and you're not morally clean, the temple door won't open. So I needed to be morally clean.

Both Hannelore Ehrler and her mother exercised great caution to protect themselves from assault at the hands of conquerors, and they were blessed with success—though there were several close calls. Looking back on her association with the Werdau Branch during World War II, Hannelore had these comments:

> It wasn't a big branch, but we had some pretty good people. We all knew that the Lord was with us, otherwise we wouldn't have made it through. The priesthood holders were very [solid] and did everything they needed to do. If somebody needed a blessing for the sick, they were there, even if they had to ride a bicycle or walk for an hour or two to get there.

In Memoriam

The following members of the Werdau Branch did not survive World War II:

Heinz Erich Fritzsching b. Werdau, Zwickau, Sachsen 9 May 1922; son of Arthur Paul Fritzsching and Anna Frieda Günnel; bp. 2 Jul 1930; conf. 2 Jul 1930; ord. deacon 3 Jul 1928; ord. teacher 8 Dec 1940; corporal; k. in battle Gragau, Memel, Ostpreußen 2 or 22 Feb 1945 (FHL Microfilm 68808, no. 14; Kosak; www.volksbund.de; AF; IGI; PRF)

Walter Franz Fritzsching b. Werdau, Zwickau, Sachsen 30 Mar 1919; son of Arthur Paul Fritzsching and Anna Frieda Günnel; bp. 22 Oct 1927; conf. 22 Oct 1927; ord. deacon 11 Aug 1935; ord. teacher Jul 1938; lance corporal; k. in battle Smolensk, Russland 29 Nov 1942 (FHL Microfilm 68808, no. 13; Kosak; www.volksbund.de; IGI; AF; PRF)

Rolf Armin Fugmann b. Werdau, Zwickau, Sachsen 9 Mar 1925; son of Max Fugmann and Johanna Gerstner; bp.; sailor; d. Plöner See, Schleswig-Holstein 22 Aug 1942; bur. Werdau Aug 1942 (Marianne Suhrmann Young)

Franz Heinzl b. Platten, Böhmen, Austria 18 or 19 Jun 1862; son of Franz Eusebius Heinzl and Elisabeth Schippel; bp. 11 Sep 1920; conf. 11 Sep 1920; m. Werdau, Zwickau, Sachsen 28 Dec 1886, Johanna Franziska Petzold; 8 children; d. old age Werdau 20 Jan 1945 (FHL Microfilm 68808, no. 35; IGI; AF)

Minna Auguste Schmutzler b. Stenn, Zwickau, Sachsen 31 Mar 1864; dau. of Johann Gottlieb Schmutzler and Christiane Friederike Grimm; bp. 11 or 17 Apr 1909; m. Zwickau, Zwickau, Sachsen 12 Apr 1887, Bernhardt Albin Edmund Ritter; d. old age Werdau, Zwickau, Sachsen 16 Jan 1941 (*Sonntagsgruss*, no. 6, 9 Feb 1941, 24; FHL Microfilm 271403, 1930/35 Census; FHL Microfilm 68808, no. 64; IGI; AF)

Anna Franziska Sterer b. Werdau, Zwickau, Sachsen 1 Jun 1849; dau. of Georg Franz Sterer and Christiane Wilhelmine Hochmuth; bp. 8 Mar 1911; conf. 8 Mar 1911; m. 20 Jan 1874, Franz Oskar Reiz; d. old age 29 Apr 1942 (FHL Microfilm 68808, no. 61; IGI)

Notes

1. Presiding Bishopric, "Financial, Statistical, and Historical Reports of Wards, Stakes, and Missions, 1884–1955," CR 4 12, 257.

2. East German Mission History Quarterly Reports, 1939, no. 60, East German Mission History.

3. Hannelore Ehrler Mueller, interview by Michael Corley, North Salt Lake City, Utah, March 21, 2008; transcript or audio version of the interview in the author's collection.

4. Marianne Suhrmann Young, interview by the author, Draper, Utah, June 16, 2008; summarized in English by the author.

5. East German Mission History Quarterly Reports, 1938, no. 35.

6. Ibid., no. 37.

7. Ibid., no. 43.

8. Ibid., 1939, no. 59.

9. Prior to World War II, Latter-day Saint missionaries from the United States usually had photographs of themselves printed on the reverse of post cards. These they handed out freely to German Saints and friends.

Wilkau-Hasslau Branch

Situated on a steep hill above the Zwickauer Mulde River, the town of Wilkau-Hasslau is slightly more than one mile east of Planitz. In this small town, The Church of Jesus Christ of Latter-day Saints consisted for all practical purposes of the Damm family at Eichleite 4 and several older ladies. Friedrich Damm was the branch president during the war.

Wilkau-Hasslau Branch[1]	1939
Elders	1
Priests	0
Teachers	1
Deacons	1
Other Adult Males	6
Adult Females	25
Male Children	1
Female Children	1
Total	35

With nine children, the family of Friedrich and Rose Damm was the core of the small branch, and the meetings were held in their home for several years. With adult women constituting 72 percent of the branch membership, this branch would have benefited from more priesthood holders. As of this writing, three of the nine Damm children were the only persons available as eyewitnesses to the life of the branch in Wilkau-Hasslau and the experiences of its members.

Jutta Damm (born 1933) was the youngest child. According to her memory, the branch meetings held in her home took place in various rooms. Sacrament meeting was held in the main room upstairs. A bedroom was used for an additional Sunday School class, and the children met in the kitchen downstairs for their instruction. Sunday School took place in the morning and sacrament meeting in the evening. On the first Sunday of the month, only a morning meeting was held. According to Jutta, there might have been fifteen persons in attendance on a typical Sunday.[2]

Because there were so few men in this branch, district leaders and other visitors from nearby Zwickau often attended church in the Damm home, including district president Walter Fassmann and his predecessor Bernhard Unger. Music was provided by a small pump organ. "We had some old hymnbooks and the scriptures," explained Jutta Damm.

Friedrich (Fred) Damm (born 1929), the seventh of the nine children, described the family home during the war years:

> It was three stories in all (basement, main floor, and upstairs). We had running water and electricity as well as an indoor WC [toilet]. There was no telephone. We had only one heater—in the kitchen on the main floor; we heated with coal and wood.[3]

The neighbors all knew about the Damms' membership in the Church. Those neighbors were Lutherans and did not bother attending their own church services except on religious holidays. Nobody seemed to care much about the religious services held in the Damm home, but Jutta recalled that her baptism in 1942 was conducted quietly. After the public indoor swimming pool had closed for the night, the members of the branch were allowed to enter and to use the facility for a baptismal service.

Fig. 2. Jutta Damm Sedlacek stands in what was the main meeting room for the Wilkau-Hasslau Branch during the war. She is now the homeowner and uses the room as a bedroom. (J. Larsen 2007)

Manfred Damm (born 1931) recalled that an official government visitor would come by now and then during the war to listen to the meetings and the lessons. No interruptions ensued.

When Manfred turned ten, he and his classmates were inducted into the Jungvolk. He later described some of the activities:

> We had meetings after school with songs and stuff. Hitler was trying to promise so much for the young people. . . . We had the same organization as the military. . . . On a Saturday, we walked through the streets. We had learned special songs, and every group had a different flag with their number.[4]

As of January 1943, the mission directory showed a different address for the Church meetings: Friedhofstrasse 4. Jutta described this facility in these words:

Fig. 1. The Damm home at Eichleite 4 as it appeared in 2007. (J. Larsen)

It was an impossible building to meet in, [but] we tried to make it look better on the inside. Because the rooms were located inside a large rock, there were steep stairs that all of the children had to climb up to hold Sunday School (there was no Primary meeting at the time).

Fred Damm later explained that in order to attend district conferences in Zwickau, the family first had to walk about twenty minutes to the nearest streetcar station, then ride to downtown Zwickau, then finally walk about ten minutes again. The entire trip might have taken an hour.

Two of the Damm sons served in the Wehrmacht. Paul came home, but Johannes did not. In November 1941, the letter every family dreaded arrived at the Damm home. The text is exemplary of the spirit of the time, when Germany was still generally victorious on all fronts:

Dear Mr. Damm,

Due to constant combat conditions, I have only now found an opportunity to send you the sad tidings that your son, Corporal Johannes Damm, lost his life on the field of honor on the morning of November 15, 1941. During a cavalry attack against an established position, he was assigned to retrieve the wounded and while doing so, was hit in the head and the shoulder by shrapnel. He died in accordance with the motto "Be faithful unto death."

In the name of the entire squadron, I would like to extend to you and your family my most sincere condolences at your loss. May you be assured that your son did not die a hero's death in vain, but rather gave his life so that we might live. He gave his life for our leader, our people, and our country and for the future of the German Reich. May this be a comfort to you. Your son shall remain a shining example to all of us, and our memories of him will inspire us to new triumphs.

When the shrapnel struck your son, he died instantly. Thus I can at least assure you that he passed out of this life without suffering. We laid

Fig. 3. Members of the Wilkau-Hasslau Branch and friends gathered for this photograph in front of the Damm home in 1939. (J. Damm Sedlacek)

499

him to his eternal rest by the church in the town of Gorbowo (twelve miles east of Rusa) among his fallen comrades. His grave is the humble grave of a soldier.

If all soldiers were as fine in their conduct as your son, for whom it was a natural thing to give his life for his comrades and his country (and of whom I can claim that his motto was "I know a word of iron—the word is loyalty"), then we will win this campaign in a short time. God will give you comfort and strength to bear this great loss. It is in God's hands to make such decisions over our lives, and we must bow to His will and bear whatever burden He places upon us.

With my repeated and sincere condolences, I remain,
Count Lehndorff
First Lieutenant and Squadron Leader

For most of the war, life did not change much for the residents of Wilkau-Hasslau. Jutta Damm was only a child and explained, "I didn't think about the war very much. On the other hand, we were surprised when the

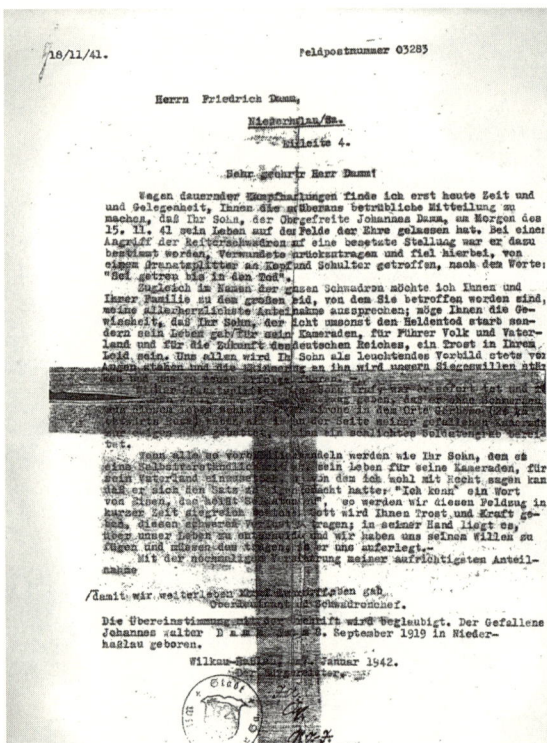

Fig. 4. *The commander of Johannes Damm's unit wrote this sad letter announcing the death of the young soldier in November 1941. This is the first of two pages. (M. Damm)*

war came home to us, because we lived in a rural setting." The war "came home" when larger cities nearby were bombed, such as Zwickau. Sometimes the Damms watched out the window as other cities were bombed, and on several occasions, they hurried down to the basement for shelter.

The rationing of food was a part of daily life there as well, but Jutta did not recall much deprivation until the war was over. With such a large family, Rose Damm had a challenge to keep food on the table. Once in a while, she came up short with the ration coupons and had to depend on such people as the local baker to extend her credit.

A very rare incident occurred in the Damm home in the last year of the war. This version of the story was offered by Fred Damm:

One time, an American POW went by our house and asked my mother for some water. She took him into the kitchen, and while she was getting water for him, he saw our *Buch Mormon* on the kitchen table and said, "I'm a Mormon!" He couldn't speak German, but he got the message across. The family did not see him again.

As air raids over Zwickau became more severe, Manfred had a grisly assignment. Bombs had missed their probable target and hit the Zwickau Cemetery. Manfred and his Hitler Youth comrades were required to help clean up the mess. They dug around amid the rubble. "When we found a dead person, we had to raise our hand. Then the old people (too old for the military) came around and took the dead people out. We were not supposed to touch the bodies. We did that in Wilkau too."

Toward the end of the war, the National Socialist propaganda machine promised the German people *Wunderwaffen* (miracle weapons) that would destroy the enemy and preserve the victory for Germany. Manfred recalled hearing about those Wunderwaffen and claimed, "Nobody believed it anymore." While

Fig. 5. The Damm family of Wilkau-Hasslau in about 1942. Johannes (back row in uniform) had already died in battle, but his picture was inserted into this photograph to complete the family group. (M. Damm)

German troops were retreating on nearly all fronts, conditions worsened on the home front. Interruptions in utility services made life more challenging. For example, Manfred told of using candles on the sacrament table during evening meetings: "In the wintertime, it was dark during sacrament meetings. We had to use candles to read the sacrament prayers."[5]

The American army entered Wilkau-Hasslau in April 1945. The soldiers stayed in the area until July and then withdrew in accordance with the borders established by the victorious powers. Manfred later explained the reactions of the locals:

> When the Russians came in, the difference [from the Americans] was like night and day. They didn't look at us. They had nothing to eat. They started raping the women. . . . When we had Mutual, we didn't let the girls go [home] alone. There always had to be a couple of boys with them.

Regarding his experience as a young Latter-day Saint in Germany during World War II, Manfred said simply, "You had to be very strong [in the faith] in Germany."

In Memoriam

Only one member of the Wilkau-Hasslau Branch did not survive World War II:

Johannes Walter Damm b. Niederhasslau, Zwickau, Sachsen 8 Sep 1919; son of Friedrich Albin Damm and Rosa Alma Morgenroth; bp. 3 Dec 1927; lance corporal; k. in battle Weljkino, Russia 15 Nov 1941 (F. Damm; *Sonntagsgruss*, no. 2, 18 Jan 1942, 8; www.volksbund.de; IGI; PRF)

Notes

1. Presiding Bishopric, "Financial, Statistical, and Historical Reports of Wards, Stakes, and Missions, 1884–1955," CR 4 12, 257.
2. Jutta Damm Sedlacek, interview by the author in German, Wilkau-Hasslau, Germany, June 4, 2007; summarized in English by Judith Sartowski.
3. Fred Damm, interview by the author, Bountiful, Utah, April 18, 2006; unless otherwise noted, audio version or transcript of the interview in the author's collection.
4. Manfred Damm, interview by Michael Corley, Spanish Fork, Utah, February 15, 2008.
5. After arriving in the United States, Manfred heard Church members telling about the Saints in Germany using candles on the sacrament tables as if it were a deviation from proper procedure, even comparing the German Saints to Catholics in that regard. "This had nothing to do with Catholic practices!" Manfred insisted.

Zwickau Branch

Zwickau is one of the largest cities in the former kingdom of Saxony, located just nineteen miles southwest of Chemnitz. As World War II approached, the city was home to eighty thousand people and a thriving branch of Latter-day Saints.

The rented rooms in which the Zwickau Branch met throughout the war years were located in the Hinterhaus at Bahnhofstrasse 37. Maria Gangien (born 1926) described the setting:

> The main meeting room was just a few steps up from the ground level. We had to go upstairs to the classrooms; there may have been three of them. Sunday School was in the morning and sacrament meeting in the afternoon.[1]

The Gangien family lived on Crimmitz-schauerstrasse 5 and walked about twenty minutes to church. "There was no streetcar in our neighborhood," Maria explained. Her family went home for dinner after Sunday School then returned for sacrament meeting. Relief Society and MIA meetings took place on Wednesday evening, as did choir practice. Regarding the attendance at meetings, Maria recalled about fifty people as an average. Other eyewitnesses estimated the attendance at closer to one hundred.

Zwickau Branch[2]	1939
Elders	12
Priests	2
Teachers	4
Deacons	6
Other Adult Males	44
Adult Females	137
Male Children	3
Female Children	3
Total	211

An excellent history of the branch (and subsequent ward) in Zwickau was produced in 2007 in connection with the centennial celebration. As is typical of Latter-day Saint branch histories, few details about life under Hitler's government are provided. It is interesting to note that Elder Joseph Fielding Smith presided over a conference in Chemnitz in the summer of 1939, and 170 members of the Zwickau Branch went there to take part in the meeting.[3]

The following events in the branch took place shortly before World War II:

Sunday, February 13, 1938: A conference of the Zwickau Branch Primary Association was held. It was attended by one hundred and five persons.[4]

Tuesday, February 22, 1938: The Zwickau Branch Mutual Improvement Association presented a musical program, followed by an illustrated lecture. One hundred and thirty-two persons were in attendance.[5]

Sunday, March 13, 1938: A program commemorating the organization of the Relief Society was given in the Zwickau Branch. It was attended by one hundred and twenty-six persons.[6]

Friday, March 3, 1939: A social was held in the Meerane Branch, Zwickau District. It was attended by members and friends of the Zwickau, Werdau, and Planitz branches, The sum of RM 10.00 was collected for the Meerane Branch Welfare Association.[7]

Unfortunately, not all news reported to the mission office in Berlin was positive. Under the date Thursday, March 31, 1938, it was reported that the police had forbidden the branch Mutual Improvement Association to hold an Easter celebration. There was no justification provided.[8]

"I was in the Reichsarbeitsdienst when the war started," recalled Erika Fassmann (born 1920). To Erika, being a teenager in Hitler's Germany was not all bad. She loved associating with other girls in the League of German Girls. "But my father knew that [Hitler] was not a righteous man, and he always told me that."[9] However, district president Walter Fassmann and his wife seldom expressed their critical opinions about National Socialism, Hitler, or the war. Daughter Helga Fassmann (born 1930) recalled that her sister, Erika, and her brother, Walter (born 1922), were enthusiastic members of the Hitler Youth at the time; it was feared that they would unwittingly relay to leaders negative political comments made at home, which could have had serious consequences.[10]

The Zwickau Branch made a substantial contribution to the German war effort from the very beginning. By September 21, 1939 (the successful end of the German campaign against Poland), no fewer than nineteen brethren had been drafted. Evening meetings were set for earlier times in response to regulations regarding blackouts.[11]

One of those young men drafted in the first month of the war was Heinz Gangien (born 1915), Maria's brother. By then, he had actually received a letter from mission president Alfred C. Rees and was preparing to leave on a mission. With Germany at war, the mission call could not be honored. Heinz was drafted by the Wehrmacht right away and served for more than five years.

Just after the war started, Maria Gangien finished public school and applied for admission to a business college. Because her father had not allowed her to participate in the Hitler Youth organization, her entry into the college was almost blocked by the party. Fortunately, her scholastic record was so strong that she could not be denied admission.

Daily life for teenagers in Zwickau was not all work and suffering during the war. According to Maria Gangien, the youth of the Zwickau Branch continued to enjoy get-togethers on Saturdays when they went to the woods and played ball. "We had a very good youth group in our Church. We always tried to stick together and do fun things. On New Year's Eve we celebrated in the [branch]. We had nice programs." Helga Fassmann later recalled

Fig. 1. The first Hinterhaus at Bahnhofstrasse 37 was the home of the Zwickau Branch. The entrance is at the far right. (Zwickau Branch History)

that there were no disturbances in the normal church routine. Until 1945, "Everything was fine."

Air-raid warnings were commonplace in Germany as early as 1940. In Zwickau (where peace prevailed for the first few years of the war), the branch leadership organized pairs of members to watch out for the meeting rooms. They were to go there as soon as possible after an attack, in case there was a fire to put out. Young Walter Fassmann recalled going to Bahnhofstrasse 37 in the middle of the night. Even young women were assigned to this service and were safe in doing so, despite the blackout conditions.[12]

In 1940, Erika Fassmann was called to be a full-time missionary and to serve in the office of the East German Mission in Berlin. For the next five years, she traveled all over the mission to participate in district conferences and conduct training sessions for the auxiliary programs of the Church.

The official Zwickau Branch history recounts a very sad story that unfolded in 1941:

Brother Ewald Beckert was arrested in 1941 because he had smuggled bread to Russian POWs. He was taken into custody and placed in the Zwickau jail. From his cell, he wrote to his family, told them that he was fine and that he hoped to be released the next day. However, his family received notification the next day that he had taken his own life. [When they saw the body] . . . they found that his wrists had been slit, but also that there was an injury to his neck.[13]

As a teenager in a prosperous Germany, Walter Fassmann had "shared in the pride of the German people" as Hitler achieved bloodless conquests in the Rhineland, Austria, Czechoslovakia, and other territories bordering Germany. "As I grew older, my enthusiasm for National Socialism waned." Nevertheless, he had a good experience serving for seven months in the Reichsarbeitsdienst in Czechoslovakia.

Fig. 2. A priesthood gathering in Zwickau. Apostle John A. Widtsoe was the special guest on this 1937 occasion. He is seen in the front row, third from left. The banner reads, "The glory of God is intelligence." (M. Gangien Mannek)

Walter returned from his service in the Reichsarbeitsdienst and in less than one week was drafted into the military. Assigned to the German navy, he began a long journey that took him first to Stralsund, Rügen Island, then to Sweden and Norway. He ended up at a coastal artillery battery near Haugesund, Norway, and received additional training there. Next, he was assigned to a battery on the island of Kvitso, where he lived under very isolated conditions for six months. While there, he became enthralled with the sea and with nature in general. He saw no military action during that time.

Some of the events of the year 1941 were described in a second (unpublished) history of the Zwickau Branch:

On September 5, two converts were baptized, along with six children (of member families) who had reached the age of eight years. Fourteen sisters married nonmembers during the year and most of them became inactive. Some also married soldiers at the front. Some elderly members passed away, having been faithful to the end. The population of the branch continued to decrease.

Inge Beckert (born 1927) finished school at the age of fourteen and was immediately called upon to do her Pflichtjahr on a farm in Marienthal (about ninety minutes walking time from Zwickau). She later described the situation: "I had to work hard. We got up at 5:00 A.M. and worked all day long. They were good people on that farm, but I hated the farm work. I only got one Sunday a month free."[14]

Fig. 3. The youth of the Zwickau Branch took a trip to Meerane in April 1939. (W. Fassmann)

On March 17, 1942, Heinz Gangien married Maria Graf, a recent convert to the Church. The ceremony took place in the office of the civil registrar, after which another ceremony was held at church. The ensuing celebration was of necessity quite simple; as Heinz's sister, Maria Gangien, recalled, "We just had a simple meal at home with close family members."

Despite the privations of wartime, branches in Germany tried to observe special events as they believed was done among Saints around the world. One such event was the centennial of the founding of the Relief Society that was celebrated throughout Germany in 1942. In Zwickau, the program was attended by 190 persons.[15]

Unfortunately, as the war continued, the rich variety of branch activities began to wane.

As of 1943, only two meetings were still being held in Zwickau: Sunday School at 10:00 A.M. and sacrament meeting at 7:00 P.M.[16] Eight persons were baptized on September 2 that year. Later that month, a musical talent night was held, and voluntary donations collected on that occasion were used to purchase a new organ.[17]

For a land-based seaman like Walter Fassmann, life on an island was idyllic for a time, but eventually he longed for something more exciting. In June 1942, he volunteered for training as an artillery mechanic and was transferred to the town of Wesel on the Rhine River. In October, he was sent to Kiel, a Baltic seaport. On the way, he found the opportunity to visit his sister, Erika, in the mission office in

Berlin. While in Kiel, Walter hoped to attend church, but was unsuccessful, as he described:

> After finding out the address of an LDS branch in Kiel, I started out one Sunday to go to church. I had to walk a long time before I reached the place, only to find a sign on the door that read "Closed for remodeling." That was the only time I had a chance to go to church as a soldier.

From Kiel, Walter moved on to Swinemünde, Germany, and finally to Russia, just west of Leningrad. He was never in combat during that assignment and very much enjoyed being there, where he interacted with Russian civilians. During his travels in August 1943, Walter had a dream that he described years later:

> Alone in a train compartment, I had fallen asleep in the middle of the day. I can no longer recall the details, but I was aware that [my brother] Heinz had lost his life. I could trace back the day and the hour of that dream and found that it coincided with the day and hour of his death.

Heinz Fassmann had been killed in battle in the Soviet Union, and Walter's dream was confirmed when he spoke with Erika again in the mission office in Berlin. She had received the news from their family in Zwickau.

Following a second training course in Wesel on the Rhine, Walter was sent through northeast Germany to Greece, traveling through his hometown and Austria on the way. After seeing Athens, he moved on to the harbor in Piraus, where he was assigned to service large weapons aboard

Fig. 4. Young Walter Fassmann in the uniform of the Reichsarbeitsdienst. (W. Fassmann)

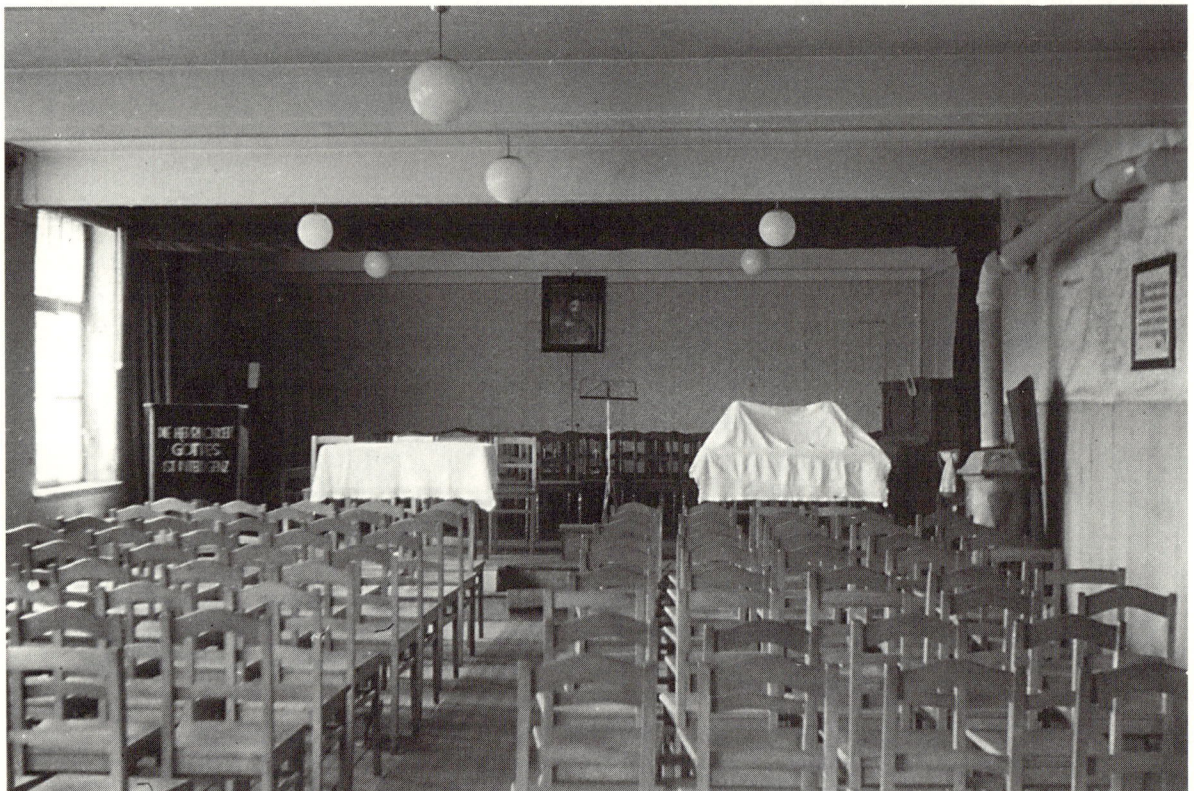

Fig. 5. The interior of the branch meeting rooms at Bahnhofstrasse 37. (M. Gangien Mannek)

transport vessels. He never left the mainland. In September 1944, the German forces in Greece began to retreat. On the way, Walter had time to pray and to reflect upon his good fortune: "My whole career in the navy passed before my eyes and it became clear to me that my Heavenly Father had always protected and guarded me so that I never had been directly involved in the battles of the war." However, as he continued to pray a different feeling came over him:

> While I was pouring out my heart in a prayer of gratitude and thanksgiving, I suddenly saw gruesome, grotesque faces approaching me. They looked as if they were made of thick strands of wool. After coming directly in front of me they vanished into thin air. But more and more multitudes of them appeared from no-where, rushing toward me. I was wide awake. Opening or closing my eyes did not change anything in the gruesome apparition. These ugly, terrifying faces were grinning and looking at me as if to say that from now on the wind would blow from a different direction.

The move north from Greece took Walter to Yugoslavia, where progress was slow due to the gradual breakdown of the German military system. Transportation was seriously hampered by the actions of local partisans, and supplies and food were difficult to come by. By Christmas, Walter's physical condition was pitiful, as he later wrote:

> I really must have been a sight! Just imagine: My disheveled beard was crusted with ice. Over my head I had pulled a lady's stocking to keep my ears warm. On the top of my head I wore a filthy field service cap. For a shawl worn over my gray leather jacket, I had another lady's stocking. . . . For gloves I had two socks. On one foot I wore a boot and on the other a shoe. All my possessions, consisting of a few toilet articles and a few pieces of underwear, were in a haversack. I carried my rifle upside down, like a stick over my shoulder.

In distant Berlin in 1944, Walter's sister, Erika Fassmann, was in her fifth year as a missionary. That year, she married Rudi Müller, a member of the Danzig Branch, whom she had known for more than two years. She explained her formal deportment in relation to Rudi in these words: "I was a missionary and was not supposed to have anything to do with men. He called me 'Sister Fassmann' and asked me in a letter to marry him. I said 'yes' in a letter." Later, she traveled with her mother to Danzig to meet the Müller family. The marriage took place in the civil registry in Zwickau on the morning of October 26, 1944, followed by a ceremony in the church that afternoon. Erika's story continued:

> Brother [Ernst] Ebisch prayed and promised that we would someday marry in the temple. We thought this would be impossible in our lifetime. Such a wonderful promise. My cousin carried the train of my dress and we had flower girls, too. We had a wedding dinner in our apartment. . . . My mother had connections with a farmer and got enough food to feed the relatives and a few people from the branch. It was a great meal.[18]

Fig. 6. Maria Gangien and Inge Beckert at the entry to the meeting rooms at Bahnhofstrasse 37 in 1942. The word Luftschutz-raum *above the door means "public air-raid shelter." (M. Gangien Mannek)*

Newlyweds Erika and Rudi Müller spent three days in her parents' apartment, and then he took the train back to his post with the German navy and she returned to the mission office in Berlin, where she served until March 1945. She did not see him again for more than four years. She returned to missionary service in early 1948 and was released when Rudi returned later that year from his term as a prisoner of war in Yugoslavia.

When the year 1945 arrived, few people in the Zwickau Branch believed that Germany could still win the war. Under this cloud of discouragement, the priesthood holders in the branch met on New Year's Day for a testimony meeting. They were able to strengthen each other and to gain renewed dedication to carry out their duties.

Walter Fassmann's situation had improved somewhat after Christmas 1944, when he found himself on duty in the port city of Trieste, Italy. The previous three months had represented what he later called "the greatest hardships of my entire life." Cleaned up and fed, he was actually allowed a furlough and went home to Zwickau for two weeks in January 1945. By the time he returned to Trieste, he was a naval mechanic petty officer with duty in a very safe area.

Maria Gangien graduated from business college in 1943 at the age of seventeen and was called right away to serve her Pflichtjahr on a farm. She returned home in time to experience the Allied air attacks on Zwickau. When the bombs began to fall, the Gangien family sought shelter in their own basement; there was no public air-raid shelter close by. "Our basement would not have been sufficient protection if a bomb hit our house, but it was the only shelter we had. Our house was not destroyed in the war," Maria explained.

Inge Beckert recalled two specific occasions when Zwickau was attacked from the

Fig. 7. Maria Gangien spent six months in government service on a farm after graduating from business college. (M. Gangien Mannek)

sky—September 11, 1944, and March 19, 1945. On the first occasion, her sister Marianne was giving birth in the local hospital, and the second time, all of the windows were broken in the neighborhood where her sister Hanne lived. Fortunately, the Church rooms were not damaged in either attack.

Elenore Gangien (born 1938) was just a little girl when Allied bombers dropped their loads on Zwickau. She was not old enough to understand why nations were at war, but she recalled being scared:

The only fear I would say we had was when we heard the sirens, and it was usually in the middle of the night, and everything had to be closed off, and as a child you got carried out. . . . Your mother dressed you and took you down to the cellar where all the neighbors met. You're half

508

asleep and you sit there and hope the bombs don't fall on your house.[19]

After one air raid, Grandpa Gangien came by with a bus and offered to take the family on a little ride. What they saw impressed little Elenore and she clearly recalled it years later: "He showed us the newly bombed houses [in a suburb]. It was shocking to me because there was still smoke coming [out] and these were all the single homes out there. It was just a village of single homes, nice homes. That gave me as a child a strange feeling."

In March 1945, Paul Langheinrich, second counselor in the leadership of the East German Mission, granted Erika Fassmann Müller permission to go home to Zwickau. She planned to attend the festivities associated with the silver wedding anniversary of her parents, then return directly to Berlin. She experienced an adventuresome railroad journey south to Zwickau, lasting several days rather than the usual several hours. Along the way, she found herself on a train loaded with soldiers. When airplanes attacked the train, everybody scrambled out and sought hiding places near the tracks. Always the missionary, Erika saw a fine opportunity:

> I preached the gospel to those soldiers, but they didn't want to listen. One was a lieutenant who was trembling with fear. I asked if I could pray. They said yes, so I prayed loudly enough to be heard. Not one bomb hit the train. Then we got back into the train, and I continued to preach the gospel, and this time nobody protested.

Sister Müller arrived in Zwickau in time to help celebrate the silver wedding anniversary of her parents on March 20. By the time she was ready to return to Berlin a few days later, the Soviets had nearly surrounded the capital, and travel to that city was impossible.

On one occasion, Maria Gangien was at work in an office downtown when the air-raid sirens went off. Her boss instructed her to go home, so she left. Arriving at home with her sister, Elinore, they stopped in front of the house to take a few pictures. The sirens were wailing, and the roar of the approaching bombers could be heard already, but the girls took a moment to take photographs. "We were crazy and did it just for fun. It was an adventure," she explained. Fortunately for the Gangiens and the other residents of Zwickau, the great majority of air-raid alarms were false alarms as the airplanes passed by the city on their way to other targets.

Maria Gangien's brother, Heinz, was reported missing in action while fighting the invading Soviets in March 1945. Maria recalled her parents' reaction to the news of Heinz's disappearance:

Fig. 8. Maria Gangien remembered taking this photograph of her sister, Elinore, just as American bombers entered the air space over Zwickau. (M. Gangien Mannek)

My father kept saying "My only son! My only son!" [Heinz] was there [in the Wehrmacht] from 1939 to 1945, [nearly] six years. It was very sad. . . . We don't know how he died. We don't know where. . . . The last letter we got from him said that he was close to St. Petersburg [Russia]. Three [of our] letters were returned with the comment "killed in battle."

Young Elenore Gangien remembered the sorrow in her home when they received the news. She also recalled her grandmother saying, "Well, they can't find him, so he's still alive." She was not prepared to relinquish her hope. The custom in Germany at the time was still to wear black clothing for a year of mourning. According to Maria Gangien, they did not observe that custom for the entire year because the war had ended and conditions had changed.

On April 17, 1945, American artillery fired upon the city of Zwickau for several hours. Airplanes overhead threatened more destruction when (according to several eyewitnesses) a few brave citizens climbed the tower of the Marienkirche downtown and hoisted a white flag. An act that could have resulted in execution for treason apparently spared the city additional destruction and suffering.

During the American artillery barrage, members of the Zwickau Branch were gathered in the home of the Ficke family, where district president Walter Fassmann led a prayer circle. According to his daughter, Erika Müller, "he prayed that the Lord might protect us and our city. . . . We heard the planes approaching the city, but not one bomb fell." Later, she wrote in her diary, "Zwickau surrendered. Our city has survived. We should build an altar to the Lord."[20]

The American army entered the city of Zwickau just days before Germany surrendered and the war came to an end. According to Maria Gangien, "We were so happy to see

[the Americans]. We came out of church and saw white flags flying. It was very quiet."

"We lived on the second floor of the [apartment house]," recalled Elenore Gangien. "As a child, you would look out the window and wave and they were happy people—those Americans. They'd toss their candy and . . . it was really fun. Those were two glorious weeks."

In accordance with an agreement among the Allied nations, the Americans vacated Zwickau and all of Saxony on July 1, and the Soviets moved in. Undisciplined Russian soldiers immediately set out in search of women to assault, as Maria Gangien recalled:

My father was a husky man. When he opened the door, [the Russian soldiers] asked, "Frau hier? Frau hier?" There were four of us girls, and my father said "No!" We were hiding under the beds. Then they left. . . . For some reason we were protected. We had extra help. . . . It was a very dangerous situation.

Helga Fassmann recalled how the conquerors moved into her family's apartment:

We couldn't lock the door and so they could get in anytime they wanted. But when they lived in our house, the only thing we actually lost were my mother's nice drinking glasses. Sometimes they would drink their vodka and throw the glasses out of the window. One day they asked me to drink with them, and I said to them, "I don't drink that." One day I was angry enough that I threw their vodka out the window, and boy, I thought they were going to kill me. . . . But they were usually friendly with me and gave me lots of food.

On May 1, 1945, Walter Fassmann's position in Italy was attacked by Yugoslav partisans. The German forces retreated into the city of Trieste, and it was there that Walter Fassmann was taken prisoner just days before the war ended. He was soon to understand the meaning of the grotesque faces in the dream he had years before. Life as a POW in Yugoslavia was torture at best. For nearly four years, he would suffer, work, and survive in that country, while thousands of his comrades perished.

Soon after his capture, Walter ran into Rudi Müller of the Danzig Branch, who had married Walter's sister, Erika. The two POWs were able to stay together for several months. While marching through the Yugoslavian countryside for weeks, Walter discovered that he was holding up better than most of his comrades. He attributed his ability to "run and not be weary and walk and not faint" to his adherence to the Word of Wisdom.

During his years of incarceration, Walter contracted several life-threatening illnesses, including typhus, and was incoherent for days at a time. With no proper medical facilities or personnel at hand, he came very close to death more than once. When healthy enough to work, he spent his time building houses, doing farm work, and repairing army vehicles. "None of these chores was too hard for me," he wrote.

On Easter Sunday 1947, Walter had a moving experience. While he languished inside the POW camp, a girl of perhaps thirteen came and gave him a colored Easter egg, reaching her hand through the fence to him. Then she quickly ran away.

> It was quite risky for her to come so close to the fence. I cannot remember into how many pieces we [prisoners] divided the egg. Nobody got much. But a gift under these circumstances was something special. . . . The effect of this gift was profound. From that moment on, I was no longer hungry all the time.

Living conditions for German POWs such as Walter Fassmann and Rudi Müller improved markedly in 1947 and 1948. They were allowed to send and receive mail, to wander about town after their working day, and to purchase goods in local stores with their meager wages. They were fed well, and their physical and emotional health improved substantially.

Fig. 9. Surviving priesthood holders of the Zwickau Branch. (W. Kindt)

In January 1949, Walter was released to return to Germany (Rudi Müller had left a few months earlier). Looking back on the end of his POW term and his experiences in uniform in general, Walter wrote:

Thus, the most difficult period of my life had come to an end. I had been away from home almost exactly eight years. Several months in the Reichsarbeitsdienst, three years and eight months in the Germany navy, and three years and nine months as a prisoner of war in Yugoslavia. Many people would consider time spent under these conditions as time wasted. I do not share this feeling. I value this span of my life because during this time I had experiences I could have had no other way. These experiences have enriched my life, strengthened my character, strengthened my testimony of The Church of Jesus Christ of Latter-day Saints, and brought me closer to God. I have never had feelings of hate toward the so-called enemy, even when I was mistreated by them, and I never needed to point a gun toward another human being.[21]

Looking back on her experiences in Zwickau during the war years, Maria Gangien made this comment: "I am grateful for the members in Zwickau because we really helped each other in faith."

In Memoriam

The following members of the Zwickau Branch did not survive World War II:

Ernst Hermann Ackermann b. Zwickau, Zwickau, Sachsen 7 Jun 1871; son of Karl Gottlieb and Wilhelmine Liewald; bp. 15 Jul 1909; m. Verronica Kohlert; d. old age 12 Dec 1944 (FHL Microfilm 25708, 1930 Census)

Max Ewald Beckert b. Weissbach, Zwickau, Sachsen 7 Apr 1889; son of Friedrich Wilhelm Beckert and Lina Ida Kunz; bp. 18 Mar 1908; ord. deacon; m. Zwickau, Zwickau, Sachsen 4 Jul 1914, Marie Elisabeth Schmitzler; 4 or 5 children; d. questionable circumstances Zwickau Jail Zwickau 22 Oct 1941 (Zwickau Branch History; FHL Microfilm 25721, 1930 Census; IGI; AF)

Ernst Louis Ebisch b. Stein, Hartenstein, Zwickau, Sachsen 29 Jul 1865; son of Louis Friedrich Ebisch and Ernestine Wilhelmine Bochmann; bp. 4 Apr 1922;

m. Zwickau, Zwickau, Sachsen 23 Jun 1891, Aurora Lina Reich; 7 children; k. in air raid Zwickau 19 Mar 1945 (E. Fassmann Mueller; Zwickau Branch History; IGI)

Heinz Fassmann b. Zwickau, Zwickau, Sachsen 20 Nov 1924; son of Walther Fassmann and Anna Clara Förster; bp. 4 or 7 Oct 1934; d. wounds Sokolowo, Russia 22 Aug 1943 (E. Fassmann Mueller; IGI; AF; PRF)

Lina Fassmann b. Zwickau, Zwickau, Sachsen 19 Dec 1890 or 1891; dau. of Louis Franz Fassmann and Margarethe Raithel; bp. 4 Dec 1909; m. Hamburg 28 Oct 1919, Wilhelm Ernst Louis Mauber; 2 children; k. air raid Hamburg 1 Jul 1943 (H. Fassmann; IGI; AF)

Louis Franz Fassmann b. Strassberg, Zwickau, Sachsen 6 May 1861 or 1863; son of Johann Christian Fassmann and Antonie Mathilde Lautenschlaeger; bp. 3 May 1909; m. Plauen, Zwickau, Sachsen 20 Apr 1889, Margarethe Raithel; 10 children; d. pneumonia Zwickau, Zwickau, Sachsen 13 Sep 1941 (CHL Microfilm LR 10378 11, Zwickau Branch General Minutes; IGI; AF)

Hedwig Carola Fischer b. Oberlochmühle, Chemnitz, Sachsen 18 Jun 1889; dau. of Otto Heinrich Fischer and Albine Sidonie Schmerler; m. 20 Oct 1912, Paul Georg Rost; 6 children; d. by abdominal cancer 20 Jun 1942 (FHL Microfilm 271407, 1930/35 Census; IGI; AF; CHL Microfilm LR 10378 11, Zwickau Branch General Minutes)

Rolf Wolfgang Guenther b. Zwickau, Zwickau, Sachsen 16 Sep 1919; son of Ernst Erich Guenther and Edith Lea Waldbrunn; d. in WWII (CHL CR 375 8 #2460, 562–63)

Heinz Kurt Günter Walter Gangien b. Kötitz, Dresden, Sachsen 11 Oct 1914; son Kurt Julius Walter Gangin and Ella Franziska Tierlich; bp. 9 Aug 1924; ord. teacher; ord. elder Zwickau, Zwickau, Sachsen 1939; m. Zwickau 17 Mar 1942, Maria Graf; 1 child; k. in battle Eastern Front Feb or Mar 1945 (Gangien-Mannig; AF; IGI; FHL Microfilm 25771, 1935 Census)

Paul Rudolf Hermann d. suicide Crossen 17 Aug 1941 (CHL Microfilm LR 10378 11, Zwickau Branch General Minutes)

Konrad Meixner b. Vorra, Mittelfranken, Bayern 17 Dec 1864; son of Johann Georg Meixner and Christine Sperber; bp. 8 May 1925; m. Hohenleuben, Reuss-jüngere Linie 4 Jul 1886, Rosa Antonie Gerstner; 5 children; d. Zwickau, Zwickau, Sachsen 8 Sep 1940 (*Sonntagsgruss*, no. 3, 19 Jan 1941, 12; IGI)

Frieda Helene Mothes b. Pölbitz, Zwickau, Sachsen 26 May 1878; dau. of Otto Mothes and Helene Marie Wagner; bp. 18 May 1920; m. —— Weichelt (div.); 1 child; d. cerebral embolism 31 Oct 1939 (CHL

Microfilm LR 10378 11, Zwickau Branch General Minutes; IGI; FHL Microfilm 245296, 1930/35 Census)

Antonie Rosa Notzold b. Oberhohoudry [?], Germany 1 Apr 1904; m. —— Markert; k. in air raid 1945 (FHL Microfilm 245226, 1935 Census; Zwickau Branch History)

Margarethe Raithel b. Streitau, Oberfranken, Bayern 15 Apr 1866; dau. of Franz Julius Jahnsmueller and Barbara Raithel; bp. 3 May 1909; m. Plauen, Zwickau, Sachsen 20 Apr 1889, Louis Franz Fassmann; d. Zwickau, Zwickau, Zwickau, Sachsen 2 Apr 1943 (IGI; AF; CHL Microfilm LR 10378 11, Zwickau Branch General Minutes)

Horst Erhard Schaller b. Zwickau, Zwickau, Sachsen 22 Mar 1927; son of Edmund Alfred Schaller and Helene Gertrud Böttcher; bp. 13 Jun 1935; k. in battle Eastern front 19 Apr 1945; bur. Schwedt/Oder, Brandenburg, Preußen (A. Langheinrich; CHL Microfilm LR 10378 11, Zwickau Branch General Minutes; IGI; AF)

Auguste Jenny Waechtler b. Chemnitz, Chemnitz, Sachsen 5 Aug 1888; dau. of Max Friedrich Waechtler and Emilie Auguste Wunderlich; bp. 29 Nov 1907; m. Kurt Bendel; d. 28 Nov 1943 (CHL Microfilm LR 10378 11, Zwickau Branch General Minutes; IGI)

Selinna Werdauen d. heart attack, 24 Nov 1944 (CHL Microfilm LR 10378 11, Zwickau Branch General Minutes)

NOTES

1. Maria Gangien Mannek, interview by the author, Salt Lake City, July 6, 2007.
2. Presiding Bishopric, "Financial, Statistical, and Historical Reports of Wards, Stakes, and Missions, 1884–1955," CR 4 12, 257.
3. The Church of Jesus Christ of Latter-day Saints, *Geschichte der Gemeinde Zwickau,* 1907–2007, 25; private collection.
4. East German Mission Quarterly Reports, 1938, no. 11, East German Mission History.
5. Ibid., no. 12.
6. Ibid., no. 14.
7. Ibid.
8. Ibid.
9. Erika Fassmann Mueller, interview by the author in German, Salt Lake City, February 3, 2006; summarized in English by Judith Sartowski.
10. Helga Fassmann Kupitz, interview by Michael Corley, West Jordan, Utah, March 7, 2008.
11. "Die Geschichte der Gemeinde Zwickau in Kurzfassung" (unpublished history); private collection.
12. Walter K. Fassmann, autobiography, 41.
13. *Geschichte,* 25.
14. Ingeborg Beckert Fassmann, interview by Michael Corley, Salt Lake City, February 1, 2008; unless otherwise noted, transcript or audio version of the interview in the author's collection.
15. *Geschichte,* 26.
16. Ibid.
17. Ibid.
18. In April 1945, Ernst Ebisch was killed in an air raid in Zwickau.
19. Elenore Gangien Vielstich, interview by the author, Salt Lake City, July 12, 2007.
20. Sister Müller lost her first three diaries when the office of the East German Mission in Berlin was destroyed in 1943.
21. Seven months after Walter arrived at home in Zwickau, he was called upon to baptize an eight-year-old boy named Dieter Friedrich Uchtdorf. Dieter grew up to become an apostle of the Church and a member of its first presidency. He recounted the story of Aurora Reich Ebisch, the widow of Ernst Ebisch (see note 18 above), who introduced Dieter's mother to the church. See Dieter F. Uchtdorf, *Sister Eternal* (Salt Lake City: Deseret Book, 2005).

Fig. 10. The ruins of the apartment building in which Anni Bauer Schulz was nearly killed (see Stettin Branch). Note the messages written in chalk to help friends and relatives locate the former residents of the building. (A. Bauer Schulz)

CONCLUSION

To say that the East German members of The Church of Jesus Christ of Latter-day Saints experienced difficult times during World War II would be an understatement. I have presented the first-person stories of more than three hundred eyewitnesses. The episodes included represent what I consider to be the most significant among the thousands of incidents recounted by these eyewitnesses. Many survivors had experiences that could be presented sufficiently only in book-length format. I leave that daunting task to other authors.

The collective experiences of these Saints are unique in the history of the Church since the era of Joseph Smith. To be sure, other groups of Saints have suffered harrowing trials, including those who lived in the countries attacked, conquered, and occupied by the German Wehrmacht during World War II. Their story, too, remains to be told and will likely mirror in many respects the accounts on the foregoing pages.

Without any attempt to present the Latter-day Saints in the East German Mission exclusively as martyrs or victims of the war, I offer below some observations about their experiences in general.

THE GERMAN LATTER-DAY SAINTS AS OUTSIDERS

The German citizenry during World War II belonged principally to the Catholic and Protestant churches. Latter-day Saints represented one of the tiniest religious groups in the nation. Several eyewitnesses admitted being somewhat ashamed to tell friends and relatives that the local branch met not in a large and beautiful church but in a Hinterhaus, often a former restaurant or office building or a back-street factory. Unlike their neighbors of other faiths, the Saints attended church services twice on Sunday and met for activities as often as four times during the week.

Latter-day Saint youth were often left out of religious instruction in school because they did not fit either the Catholic or the Protestant mold. To serve a mission (usually within the confines of the East German Mission), they separated themselves from their non-LDS friends and appeared to be fanatics. When it came time to marry, LDS young adults looked to distant branches for partners or chose non-LDS spouses, hoping for a subsequent conversion. Many longed for the day when they could enter the temple in Salt Lake City (the closest one to Germany at the time). Only four

Saints in this mission are known to have been endowed in the temple, and only one couple was sealed there before the war.

Just as the Saints could not point to ostentatious meetinghouses, neither could they identify members of the Church in the higher socioeconomic strata. This investigation has not yielded evidence of Latter-day Saints as doctors, lawyers, or teachers; university graduates were extremely rare. The men of the Church in the East German Mission were primarily laborers and craftsmen. A few owned their own shops as carpenters or glazers. Several were supervisors in local factories, but there is no evidence of Church members who sat on boards of directors or owned industries and department stores. As the war escalated, many of the men in the Church who were not drafted were required to increase their work weeks to sixty hours or more and many were compelled to work on Sundays (see the story of Anton Larisch of the Görlitz and Halberstadt Branches).

LATTER-DAY SAINTS AND THE GERMAN EXPERIENCE IN WORLD WAR II

As mentioned above, the population of Germany in 1939 was approximately eighty million. Just over thirteen thousand of the inhabitants of the Reich were members of The Church of Jesus Christ of Latter-day Saints. It appears that they shared nearly all of the wartime experiences of their neighbors—the average citizens and families in Germany. Just as their non-Mormon countrymen, Latter-day Saints attended schools, worked in factories, lived in huge apartment complexes in large cities, bought their food in small specialty shops, participated in local harvest festivals, and swam in city lakes. They dreamed of owning their own home or an automobile or of enjoying the convenience of a telephone in the home.

Most Latter-day Saints attended parades and watched Hitler and his troops pass in review. Some raised their arms in the Nazi salute and greeted others with the obligatory "Heil Hitler!" They sang the national anthem in movie theaters with their neighbors and in schools with their classmates. Some believed that Hitler's plans to regain German territory from neighboring countries (especially from Poland and Czechoslovakia) were justified and his methods appropriate.

A few members of the Church belonged to the Nazi Party but most avoided political involvement and seldom spoke of Hitler at home. Most Latter-day Saint boys and girls wore the uniforms of various branches of the Hitler Youth for a year or longer. Young men and young women answered the call to serve in government labor programs such as Pflichtjahr and Reichsarbeitsdienst. Most recalled enjoying their term of service and believed it an important contribution to their nation, though it usually meant a delay in their occupational progress. Declining to serve in Hitler's Germany was not an option.

Under the universal conscription laws passed in Germany in 1935, Latter-day Saint men served in the German army, navy, and air force, as well as in elite combat forces such as Heinrich Himmler's Waffen-SS and as paratroopers. They were there when Germany mounted offensives against Poland, France, and the Soviet Union and were still there when the Allies struck back and invaded the fatherland. Just as their Catholic and Protestant comrades, Latter-day Saint German soldiers were buried where they fell. Some lost limbs and returned home as invalids, while others suffered for years from wounds unseen. They died as prisoners of war thousands of miles from home. The final resting places of many LDS German soldiers remain unknown.

Latter-day Saint men too old to be drafted were pressed into service as local auxiliary police or in the Volkssturm (home guard). For most of them, this was something to be avoided and some were able to do so (thanks to the confusion that reigned in the final months of the war). Women, too, were compelled to serve in soup kitchens, hospitals, refugee shelters, and in other critical war capacities. Many had to leave the home and replace men as full-time employees in factories and offices. Some were pressed into temporary service in hospitals or in constructing fortifications around the cities. However, most women were thinking more of their families and how they might later survive the Soviet invasion or escape to the West.

Some female Church members were honored by the government with the Mutterkreuz for giving birth to five or more children. (Eyewitness accounts support the assumption that no LDS women gave birth to children specifically for their country.) They bore children without the attendance of their husbands and raised those children for years in the absence of the fathers. Latter-day Saint women contributed to relief programs with donations of money, goods, or labor. To provide for their children, they stood in long lines to purchase food on ration coupons and made do with less and less as the war drew to a close.

When Germany came under attack from the air, Latter-day Saint civilians huddled in air-raid shelters, praying for heavenly protection. They died there in significant numbers—some as family groups (such as the Fischers of the Chemnitz Center Branch). Some members of the Church died in their basement shelters or in their apartments, were killed in artillery barrages or by invading soldiers as they ran through the streets for cover. Many witnessed and some died in the horrific firebombing of Dresden in February 1945. Church members died of disease or starvation during the long trek to the west after being forced from their homes by the invaders or subsequent occupation forces. Several young women or members of the Relief Society suffered physical abuse at the hands of their conquerors, the mental scars of which, in some cases, never disappeared. Latter-day Saints assisted in fighting fires and rescuing neighbors after air raids and from other life-threatening calamities.

Approximately 60 percent of the members of the Church in the East German Mission lost their homes. Many more lost some or all of their personal property—in some cases their most cherished possessions. They lost pets, farm animals, photographs, heirlooms, genealogical documents, personal scriptures, the money in their savings accounts, silverware—everything but the clothes on their backs. Many of the buildings in which they held their meetings were destroyed. Membership records, hymnals, chairs, and pulpits vanished and usually could not be replaced for years.

German citizens who were not of "Aryan" (Caucasian) ancestry or who criticized Hitler's government were subject to incarceration in jails and concentration camps. Such was the fate of several Latter-day Saints (such as Elisabeth Jung Süss of the Chemnitz Center Branch). Thousands of mentally or physically infirm persons became victims of government sterilization and euthanasia programs; at least two members of the Church in the West German Mission were among the mentally impaired persons who were put to death in secret. Annalies Höhle of the Dresden Altstadt Branch (Dresden District) considered her son a potential victim but was able to protect him from such a fate.

Nearly everything experienced by the general populace in Hitler's Third Reich was experienced by one or more members of The Church of Jesus Christ of Latter-day Saints in the East German Mission.

Lest the impression be made that the war years meant nothing but death and suffering for the Saints of the East German Mission, it should be clearly stated that they enjoyed good times as well. Eyewitnesses often told of joyous occasions in the home or with other Church members—visits by soldier fathers and brothers on leave, Christmas holidays, wedding celebrations, the births of sons and daughters, and baptismal ceremonies for member children and converts. One of the most frequently mentioned Church events was the district conference that usually lasted two or three days and to which members often traveled substantial distances. Those from out of town were usually housed in the homes of local members, and friendships were born and cultivated. Such events were especially meaningful for young adults. Life for the Saints in many locations in Germany did not involve personal suffering until the final stages of the war.

FINAL COMMENTS

One of the goals of this research was to ascertain how members of The Church of Jesus Christ of Latter-day Saints in the East German Mission fared during the years of 1939 to 1945. It would be interesting to know how they interacted with the Nazi Party. Another goal was to determine the losses they suffered as individuals, families, and branches. In this regard, I offer the following conclusions based on the testimonies of eyewitnesses:

THE NATIONAL SOCIALIST PARTY AND THE LATTER-DAY SAINTS OF THE EAST GERMAN MISSION

A few adult Latter-day Saints joined the National Socialist Party. Others were asked to do so but found ways to decline the invitation or avoid the issue altogether. Some were pressured to join but declined and suffered penalties

for their opposition. Of those who joined, some did so only because it was required of them as employees of the government, such as Max Hegewald (district president in Dresden and a bailiff in the Freiberg City Court). Based on the stories told and written by eyewitnesses, it appears that fewer than three percent of the Latter-day Saints in the East German Mission joined the Nazi Party. Douglas F. Tobler, a professor of German history, estimated that "only about five percent of Mormon adults either joined the party or its various organizations. . . . The overwhelming majority of German Mormons remained apolitical and quiescent."[1] There is no indication that any Latter-day Saint had a significant leadership position within the party. Reports of party members making overt political statements in branch meeting facilities are rare. Even rarer were Saints who belonged to other political parties.[2]

Eyewitnesses are in agreement that some of those Saints who were known to be members of the Nazi Party were enthusiastic about Adolf Hitler's leadership in the early years and convinced that the Führer had the answers to Germany's problems, but those individuals did not promote their political views or agenda in Church meetings.[3] Only in rare instances was a portrait of Adolf Hitler seen in a Church facility and never on a lasting basis (see Breslau South Branch chapter).

Photographs of Latter-day Saint homes (interior and exterior) rarely show pictures of Adolf Hitler or the German swastika flag (see Berlin East Branch chapter). However, to avoid flying the flag on specific occasions meant to risk incurring the wrath of a fanatical neighbor (and there was often one living close by). Eyewitnesses told of parents who did their best to simply keep out of sight rather than to openly oppose the government. Survivors also recalled hearing infrequent criticism of Hitler or the party from their parents, who understood that they dare not voice such criticism outside of the home.

While it could be suggested that Latter-day Saints should have opposed the rise of Hitler in the 1930s through political activism, historians generally agree that such opposition could only have led to personal and collective suffering for the dissidents and their families (and possibly for the Church).[4] Any overt or violent resistance after 1933 could have merited capital punishment, as is evident from the deaths of thousands of alleged revolutionaries in Germany, especially after the abortive plot to assassinate Hitler on July 20, 1944. If there is any question of guilt on the part of Latter-day Saints for tolerating an evil government (and in my mind there is not), they certainly paid a terrible price for their lack of action.

Several eyewitnesses have admitted that one or more of their parents listened to broadcasts of BBC London or Moscow. Such actions were, of course, illegal, but there is no record of any Latter-day Saint being charged with that crime. In all cases, it was believed that information received through this medium was never transmitted to persons outside of the immediate family—even to trusted friends at church.

In many ways, it appears that the leaders of the mission, the districts, the branches, and the families increased their efforts to safeguard the Saints and support the branches during the war years. They could neither stop nor (as they learned later) win the war, but they could care for the members, maintain Church worship services and programs, and in general keep the Church alive until the war ended. In this regard, they were immensely successful.

In general, German Latter-day Saints found it possible to live their lives as good German citizens who had no valid reason to rebel against the government, even if it meant leaving their homes and Church callings to fight and die in far-off lands. According to eyewitnesses, most

adult Saints did not like Adolf Hitler in 1939 because they saw in his overt militarism the prospect of another devastating war. Regarding military service, they often quoted the twelfth article of faith ("We believe in being subject to kings, presidents, and rulers") to justify serving Hitler's government. Latter-day Saint soldiers often expressed a hope for two things: that they would not be compelled to hurt their fellow man and that they might return to their families in good health. For many, the first wish was fulfilled; for most, the second was as well.

THE LATTER-DAY SAINT FAMILY UNDER FIRE

As Hitler and his cronies gained power in the nation, the family came under increasing pressure. National Socialist philosophy emphasized the importance of the Party over that of the family and the Church. Organizations such as the Hitler Youth served in part to take young Germans from their homes and place them in an atmosphere where they could be schooled carefully in the Nazi concept of patriotism and the philosophies of the party. Children were raised to serve *Führer, Volk, und Vaterland* rather than God, church, and country. Fortunately, it seems that in many cases, the goal was not achieved among Latter-day Saint youth.

It is evident that many parents in the Church understood that while some aspects of the Hitler Youth program were positive, others were sinister. In some cases, the parents of eyewitnesses forbade their children to join the Hitlerjugend or the Bund Deutscher Mädel at age fourteen, insisting that the programs of the Church would provide the necessary education, training, and entertainment. Although such non-compliance was not tolerated under the law, most Latter-day Saint parents got away with it. According to eyewitnesses, punishments for non-cooperation were rare and seldom had any lasting effect.

Another method used by the party to weaken the influence of parents in the lives of their children was the program under which schoolchildren were moved as school classes to rural settings. Under the auspices of protecting the children from harm through air raids by Allied forces, teachers (required by law to be members of the party) and party leaders often used the setting to indoctrinate the children. The program was called *Kinderlandverschickung*, and in the case of nearly every eyewitness interviewed, this absence from home prevented any contact with the Church. When Latter-day Saint mothers independently took their children away from the big cities, they rarely had the opportunity to attend Church services. The absence from formal worship was perceived as a very negative aspect of life during the war. The corresponding decline in member populations also had a negative effect on the programs of the local branch.

The national labor service required of teenage boys and girls (under programs called Reichsarbeitsdienst and Pflichtjahr or Landjahr) also separated family members. For as much as a year at a time, Latter-day Saint youth lived too far from home to visit their families and were totally subject to the leadership of Party officials. Again, none of the eyewitnesses reported ever having had the opportunity to attend church during this period of their lives and few were able to take or study the holy scriptures.

Any time a country goes to war, fathers are removed from their homes. When a lengthy war is fought and lost, many fathers do not return to their families. When German Saints were away at the front, their wives and children survived without the presence of patriarchal and priesthood leadership in the home—in some instances for as long as eight to ten years. The eyewitnesses expressed universal sadness regarding this aspect of their lives. Furloughs granted German Latter-day Saint soldiers were rare and brief—sometimes just long enough to produce another child who was then brought into the world to be raised by a mother without a father. Several children of Latter-day Saint soldiers never knew their fathers.

THE EAST GERMAN MISSION IN ISOLATION

After the United States and Germany declared war upon each other in December 1941, communications between the office of the East German Mission in Berlin and the headquarters of the Church in Salt Lake City were interrupted. This state of isolation persisted until the summer of 1945 (forty-two months), when attempts were made to re-establish the connection. President Max Zimmer of the Swiss Mission traveled into Germany to inquire regarding the status of both German missions and their leaders. Several American soldiers who had served in the German missions before the war were allowed to travel to Berlin and Frankfurt to ascertain the fate of the members.[5] Elder Ezra Taft Benson of the Quorum of the Twelve Apostles arrived in the fall of 1945 to establish a system through which welfare supplies from Salt Lake City could be distributed to the surviving Latter-day Saints.[6]

It was learned in 1945 that the German Saints had maintained meeting schedules and branch activities as consistently as possible since 1939—at times under challenging conditions. There is no evidence that Church procedures or practices were altered or allowed to deviate from the established norms. Tithing funds were paid, collected, and transferred to the mission office carefully throughout the war and after, as is evident from the accounts of eyewitnesses like Marie Jenschewski of the

Königsberg Branch. Church literature was produced and distributed faithfully until paper shortages or government regulations hindered the effort.

The work of the priesthood was carried on faithfully and correctly throughout the war. Babies were blessed, children and converts were baptized, blessings of healing and comfort were given, miracles were performed. The priesthood was conferred upon worthy brethren all over the mission. Priesthood leaders who were absent or killed were replaced via the established means. Meetings were conducted and presided over by the proper authorities. In cases where no priesthood holders were present to preside over the ordinance of the sacrament, there simply was no such ordinance. In the absence of priesthood leadership, women did not usurp authority or stewardship but simply held study groups, Primary classes, and choir rehearsals in an attempt to maintain the community of the Saints.

Eyewitnesses attested to the dedication of the Saints to the branches and programs of the Church. In cases where the branch organization broke down totally, individual members prayed, read the scriptures, fasted, and taught their families the gospel. Many eyewitnesses told of their attempts to find a branch of the Church whenever they found themselves away from home. For them, life was not complete without regular interaction with the Saints.

A short explanation regarding priesthood ordinations in those days is warranted. Ordinations were not done primarily on the basis of age but rather on the basis of need in the branch. Whereas some young men were ordained deacons soon after turning twelve, advancement within the Aaronic Priesthood followed no regular pattern thereafter. Almost exactly one-half of the male members over twelve years of age in 1939 were not holders of

the priesthood, though some were quite active in the branch.

Ordination to the Melchizedek Priesthood took place when the man was needed as a branch leader. Many men became elders after the age of thirty or forty. Because there was no stake of Zion in Germany until 1961, there were no high priests in that country during the war.[7]

The German Government and the East German Mission

From the testimony of eyewitnesses and the surviving records of the East German Mission, it is evident that the government of Germany made no attempt during the Hitler era to shut down The Church of Jesus Christ of Latter-day Saints in that nation. The only substantiated intervention by the government came when the Berlin police instructed leaders of the mission to have the members avoid singing hymns featuring words associated with the Jewish culture, such as *Zion* and *Israel* (see the East German Mission chapter). In fact, with the exception of rare and short-lived episodes of police inquiries and the occasional private harassment of individual Saints by local Nazi Party leaders, members of the Church and the branches to which they belonged in the East German Mission were never at risk of extinction. The government either had no intention at the time of eradicating the Church, or did not consider the 13,000 members of the Church in Germany worthy of special attention.

Several eyewitnesses told of seeing official observers in church meetings. Such observers always entered without fanfare, were recognized as "strangers," inevitably sat on the back row, and avoided any kind of participation. Not one account of an interruption of meetings by such officials was proffered.[8]

Changes in the Mission, the Districts, and the Branches during World War II

As can be seen in previous chapters, the East German Mission leadership continued to function with dedication and efficiency throughout the war. Despite the total destruction of the mission office at Händelallee 6 in Berlin in November 1943 and the disappearance of mission supervisor Herbert Klopfer in 1944, mission leaders were true to their stewardship. Following the departure of foreign (principally American) missionaries in August 1939, only German Saints served as full-time missionaries. By 1941, all male missionaries had been released and there were only a few women left in these callings; according to eyewitnesses and available documents, those young women performed admirably.

Of the thirteen districts in the mission, only one (faraway Hindenburg with a total of seventy-two members) appears to have discontinued district conferences before 1944. All others were under the direction of faithful district presidents, of whom three lost their lives in the war or in the immediate aftermath: Martin Werner Hoppe (Breslau), Karl Göckeritz (Chemnitz), and Max Freimann (Königsberg). Many eyewitnesses reported seeing members of district presidencies visiting the weaker branches to offer priesthood support. Conditions during the war often required district leaders to travel to outlying branches via bicycle.

Nearly every branch in the East German Mission (seventy-two in number when war broke out in 1939) was still holding meetings in 1943. By that time, several had lost their meeting facilities (through destruction or confiscation) but had found other rooms. By the end of the war, nearly half of the branches had lost their meeting places and could hold sacrament services only in the homes of members and on an irregular basis.

Branches without priesthood leadership often held only Sunday School meetings. With few exceptions, meetings were still held across the mission as late as April 1945, and in a few cases, there were no interruptions at all.

The Effects of the War on the Programs of the Church

As mentioned above, sacrament and Sunday School meetings survived the war in most branches, but this is not true with other meetings. The Primary organization was weakened or even discontinued in branches in cities where the Jungvolk units were very active. However, the resourcefulness of the members came into play when the Primary meetings no longer took place: the adults invested their energies in the education of the children in Sunday School classes. It should be noted, of course, that in several branches there were only very small numbers of children (see membership tables of individual branches).

The Mutual Improvement Association (*Gemeinschaftliche Fortbildungsvereinigung*) in German branches involved essentially every unmarried member from the age of twelve up. Many married members also participated in the activities of the MIA. As might be expected, the absence of young men who were serving in the military and young women performing their duties under the Pflichtjahr program weakened the branches' MIA groups considerably. As the privations of war increased, there were also fewer resources available to support the cultural activities of the MIA, (typically, musical and theatrical performances, outings, dances, and dinners). Only in the largest branches of the mission were these meetings still taking place regularly in 1945.

Fig. 1. "Who knows our parents and our origins?" This 1971 Red Cross poster was designed to help young adults locate persons who could identify them. Each was found in the last few months of the war in the ruins of bombed-out cities or on the roads among dead refugees. Most had no option but to adopt new names and birth data.

The Relief Society groups survived the war in nearly all branches. The sisters intensified their compassionate service during the first years of the war, but as they left the big cities with their children, lost their homes, became widows, or were otherwise distracted by the task of daily survival, their service to others did in many cases decline. In the last year of the war, even those sisters still carrying out their society duties had little to offer others in the way of welfare items and food. Eyewitness reports make it clear that most of those who still had the means to survive were willing to share whatever they had (see Leipzig Center Branch chapter).

MILITARY LOSSES AMONG LATTER-DAY SAINTS

Prophets and Apostles of The Church of Jesus Christ of Latter-day Saints have never taught that members of the Church would be spared trials and suffering in this life. Indeed, Church doctrine holds that negative experiences are an integral part of life. It can come as no surprise that hundreds of Saints of the East German Mission lost their lives during the war. In addition to the mission supervisor and the district presidents named above, several branch presidents or their counselors also perished under various circumstances.

It is probable that one thousand members of the Church in the East German Mission served in the various branches of the German armed forces (Wehrmacht). Fewer than fifty were in the navy, approximately 150 in the Luftwaffe (mostly ground personnel), and the rest in the army. Several dozen served in various police assignments or as POW camp guards, such as did Otto Bork of the Stettin Branch. An additional one hundred to two hundred older male members of the Church were inducted into the Volkssturm after October 1944.

Of those Saints of the East German Mission in German military service, 181 died in wartime (by May 8, 1945) and 55 more died by the end of 1950. Available data suggest that more than 50 percent of those men had been ordained to the priesthood, the majority holding offices in the Aaronic Priesthood. For purposes of this discussion, all soldiers reported missing in action are assumed to have died by 1955, when the last German prisoners of war were officially released from incarceration in the Soviet Union.

Except for those whose wounds were debilitating, no Latter-day Saint men in uniform in 1943 were released before the end of the war. Many who were drafted as early as 1940 served for the duration, and several served from 1938 until at least 1946 (such as Erhard Wagner of the Annaberg-Buchholz Branch and Wilhelm Werner of the Berlin Moabit Branch). From eyewitness testimony it is clear that only a few Latter-day Saint German soldiers escaped being taken prisoners by war's end. Rare are the stories of soldiers who in May 1945 simply went home and became civilians again, as did Walter Kindt of the Schneidemühl Branch. If all needed data were available to investigate this matter, we might see that at least 90 percent of the regular Wehrmacht soldiers in the Church spent time behind barbed wire. Several died while incarcerated. The majority of the Latter-day Saint POWs were held in camps in the Soviet Union, but significant numbers spent time in the United States, Canada, Great Britain, France, and Belgium. Very few returned home as early as 1945, several in 1946, most in 1947, and many in 1948. The last Latter-day Saint POW is believed to have returned to Germany in 1950.

German Latter-day Saints Who Died in Military Service in World War II	
Killed in battle or died of wounds	181
Missing in action*	39
Died as prisoners of war	16
Total deaths	236

*It is assumed that all soldiers missing in action were in fact killed or died later.

Due to the confusion existing in German military units toward the end of the war and the lack of records in POW camps, it is very probable that several more LDS men died during their military service. Essentially all were buried where they died and only one is known to be buried in modern Germany (Hermann Henkel of the Frankfurt/Oder Branch).

CIVILIAN LOSSES AMONG LATTER-DAY SAINTS

The primary cause of death among Latter-day Saint civilians cannot be directly attributed to the war. However, as explained earlier in the Memorial Book, some non-violent deaths among members of the Church would certainly not have happened in peace time. Many Saints died due to what in German is called Kriegseinwirkung (enemy action). Among those whose deaths came through enemy action, the most common cause was Allied air raids over their cities. The second most common cause of death through enemy action occurred when the Red Army invaded Germany from the east. The third category of civilian losses includes those members who died while fleeing the invaders or after being forced from their homes by Polish authorities during the years 1945 to 1947. In many cases, the trek to Germany (the Soviet Occupation Zone or what became East Germany—the German Democratic Republic) was as far as three hundred miles. Those refugees who made it to the British or American Occupation zones traveled at least one hundred fifty miles farther. Many Latter-day Saint refugees made part or all of the journey on foot and in seasons of extreme cold. Some used the standard little Bollerwagen or Leiterwagen—reminiscent of the wagons and handcarts pulled by the American Mormon pioneers who were driven from their homes a century earlier (see photographs in the Chemnitz South and Halberstadt Branch chapters).

International negotiations between the Allied victor nations in 1945 resulted in the annexation of a great deal of east German territory. The northern half of East Prussia was ceded to Russia. The southern half of East Prussia, most of Pomerania and Silesia, and about one-fourth of Brandenburg, were ceded to Poland. Essentially all of the members of the

Church living in those provinces of Germany in 1939 fled the area before the arrival of the Soviets or were forcibly evicted from their homes by 1947. This included the East German Mission districts of Breslau, Danzig, Hindenburg, Königsberg, Schneidemühl, and Stettin. Those members of the Forst and Guben Branches (Spreewald District) who lived on the east side of the Neisse River also lost their homes. The total number of Latter-day Saints who left those areas was 3,161 (42 percent of the population of the East German Mission).[9]

According to one modern study, 9,476,900 Germans fled or were driven out of what was then eastern Germany (now Poland and Russia), and more than one million died in the process.[10] It has been established that some of the Latter-day Saints who made that trip also perished on the way or as a result of the experience. Several members simply disappeared and may be presumed dead.

The only Church branch in the former eastern German territories that did not become defunct by 1947 was Selbongen (Königsberg District). The members who survived the war and did not flee Selbongen were forced to become Polish citizens and to conduct their church services in the Polish language. This they did for nearly thirty years, after which they immigrated to Germany.

German Latter-day Saint Civilians Who Died during or as a Result of World War II	
Killed in air raids	48
Killed during the invasion of Germany	18
Died from diseases or starvation	99
Died from other causes	177
Died in concentration camps or euthanasia facilities	6
Missing	21
Total deaths	369

As was the case among the soldiers, it is very possible that dozens more civilian deaths actually occurred among the members of the Church.

Though it is evident that the members of The Church of Jesus Christ of Latter-day Saints in the East German Mission were not always spared suffering and death, there are hundreds of stories told by survivors who believe that they were shielded from harm on specific occasions—some of the Saints more than once. Soldiers and civilians alike told of occasions when they "should have been killed" or at least when their survival or rescue defied human explanation as told for example by Willi Dzierzon (Freiberg Branch, Dresden District).

German Latter-day Saints and the Crimes of Nazi Germany

Several eyewitnesses stated that they were aware before the war that Jewish neighbors and business acquaintances were being mistreated. The events of Reichkristallnacht (the Night of Broken Glass) on November 9–10, 1938, shocked Latter-day Saints as much as they did millions of Germans across the Reich. Saints saw some of the destruction of Jewish businesses as it happened. Others noticed that Jews they knew disappeared soon after that fateful night. The account of Heinz Koschnike (Breslau South Branch, Breslau District) is especially impressive. Siegfried Dietze's father came under pressure because he had business dealings with Jews (Dresden Neustadt Branch, Dresden District). As it turned out, his (Christian) German customers did not support the Party boycott instituted against Brother Dietze. The fact that young people were being poisoned against Jews is evident from the confession of Gerd Skibbe (Wolgast Branch, Rostock District): one day he thought himself bold enough to shout insults at a local Jewish businessman but was then sternly chastised by his father who understood that such social misbehavior could lead the German people down the road to destruction.

At the end of the war, Richard Müller (Danzig Branch, Danzig District) saw evidence of the mistreatment of Jews near the Bergen-Belsen concentration camp. However, only one LDS eyewitness indicated knowing of the terrible treatment to which Jews were subjected in concentration camps in Germany or of the genocide that was being practiced in the extermination camps located east of Germany in occupied territories (Bruno Stroganoff of the Tilsit Branch, Königsberg District). As with most Germans, Latter-day Saint survivors were shocked to learn the details of the atrocities after the war.

The story of Franz Nolte (Breslau South Branch, Breslau District) is the only account among Latter-day Saints in the East German Mission of a Church member formally punished for his interactions with Jews. Fortunately, his imprisonment lasted only one year. Other Saints rendered support to Jews during the war and risked serious consequences, as was the case with the Berlin Schöneberg Branch in their care of Sister Heber. The fact that Walter Luskin (Guben Branch, Spreewald District) was half-Jewish turned out to be an advantage rather than a disadvantage; he was exempt from military duty and spent the war years tailoring uniforms at the local army post.

The East German Mission at the End of World War II

With six of the thirteen districts of the East German Mission practically defunct by the end of the war, the mission territory was reduced by more than one half. Thousands of members were left homeless and hundreds of families left without fathers (at least temporarily). Nearly one-half of the surviving branches had no meeting rooms large enough to accommodate the active branch population. Most branches were led by aging priesthood holders, while a few branches held only Sunday School meetings (essentially study groups) organized by the surviving women while they hoped and waited for their men to return (see Bischofswerda Branch, Dresden District).

In many surviving or newly acquired meeting rooms, there were no glass windows left; the materials used to cover the openings were opaque and the rooms were dark. At many such locations, there was also no functional electricity or water supply. Meetings taking place in the late afternoon or evening often required the use of candlelight. These conditions may have given rise to the commonly held Latter-day Saint misconception that members of the Church in wartime or postwar Germany using candles on the sacrament table had adopted deviant practices and rituals during the time when the German missions were out of contact with Church leaders in Salt Lake City.[11]

Most Latter-day Saint refugees from East Germany sought new lodgings in the Soviet Occupation Zone. In the southern portion of that zone (Chemnitz, Dresden, and Zwickau Districts), they were often able to establish connections with existing branches (that being the area in which the highest density in Latter-day Saint populations was found). In the northern areas of the Soviet Occupation Zone (Rostock District), the branches of the Saints were few and far between. In several locations, those branches attracted refugees, and in other places new branches were established by and for the new arrivals.

Following the destruction of the mission office in Berlin in 1943, the office operations and surviving equipment were moved to the apartment building in which Paul Langheinrich (second counselor to Herbert Klopfer since early 1940) lived on Rathenowerstrasse (see East German Mission chapter). Even before the war ended, the mission leaders and office staff (young women missionaries) began to compile lists of Latter-day Saints who had left their homes. Many eyewitnesses tell of family members who agreed that they would contact the mission office if they were separated during the war. A veritable "missing persons" registry was established and maintained for several years.

Mission leaders were concerned about the refugees finding housing and maintaining contact with the Church. During the summer of 1945, Richard Ranglack (interim mission supervisor) and Paul Langheinrich set out to ascertain the status of the surviving branches and to see to the welfare of refugees. They were fortunate to be granted the use of a fine modern villa south of Zwickau at Wolfsgrün, where a substantial colony of Saints evolved, eventually numbering nearly two hundred persons. Another refugee colony was established in Langen, nine miles south of Frankfurt am Main in the American Occupation Zone (the first Saints there being the Moderegger family of the Tilsit Branch). These Saints erected their own church building there, and the population swelled to more than three hundred by 1950.

It seems that wherever they found themselves, the Saints of the East German Mission began in May 1945 to pick up the pieces of

Fig. 2. Refugee Saints established a colony in the Wolfsgrün Castle in the summer of 1945 (L. Eichler Love)

their branches or to join and strengthen whichever branch was close at hand. By the fall of 1945, several young men (most of them veteran soldiers) had been called as full-time missionaries, charged first and foremost with the task of helping Church members recover from the war. The Church was in capable hands and conditions steadily improved.

According to the statements of eyewitnesses, the general state of mind of Church members in the East German mission in the summer of 1945 represented a combination of sadness and relief. Hundreds of members were dead or still missing, men were in short supply, homes and meetinghouses were destroyed or damaged, food was scarce, utilities were interrupted, and transportation was unreliable. Nevertheless, the Saints were alive and had maintained their testimonies of the gospel of Jesus Christ—or in the words of many survivors, their testimonies had maintained the Saints. World War II had weakened the Church as an organization in significant respects, but the faith was alive and well.

A fitting example of the mission membership after the war is Fritz Birth of the Schneidemühl Branch in Pomerania. Brother Birth was an elder, a father of eleven (two of whom had died as German soldiers in the Soviet Union), the former owner of a house and two businesses, and later a refugee in Cottbus (Soviet occupation zone). Brother Birth had been inducted into the home guard in late 1944 and ended up losing his right arm. After rejoining his family in Cottbus (Spreewald District) in the summer of 1945, he found a new apartment for them and assisted in caring for the refugees in the growing colony of Saints in that city. By the fall of 1945, Fritz Birth had established a new shop as a glazer and was installing window panes with his one remaining arm. Despite serious personal losses, he was determined to make the best of his new circumstances in postwar Germany.

All over Germany, the surviving Saints of the East German Mission were busy in the summer of 1945 rebuilding their lives, their homes, and their branches. Years would pass before some of the bad memories faded, but the work of the kingdom of God on the earth was carried forth with dedication by Saints who praised God for preserving their lives.

NOTES

1. Douglas F. Tobler, "German Mormons as 'Righteous Gentiles': Trying to Save a Few Jewish Friends," 1995, 7 (unpublished MS). Private collection.

2. After the Reichstag (parliament building) fire of 1933, Hitler had used the German government to legally outlaw the Communist Party and to at least severely repress other political parties. Activity in any but the Nazi Party was thus grounds for suspicion on the part of the state.

3. See the story told by Heinz Koschnike in the Breslau South Branch chapter.

4. See the chapter on the Chemnitz Center Branch for an example of punishment for low-intensity opposition to the government. The chapter on the Hamburg St. Georg Branch in the West German Mission provides the only known example of serious resistance to Hitler's regime by Latter-day Saints—the case of teenagers Helmut Hübener, Karl-Heinz Schnibbe, and Rudi Wobbe.

5. J. Richard Barnes, a veteran of the West German Mission, was an officer with the U.S. Army forces that entered Germany in 1945. Several of his reports on the status of the Church in Germany were published in the *Deseret News* in the summer of 1945.

6. See Frederick W. Babbel, *On Wings of Faith* (Salt Lake City: Bookcraft, 1972).

7. Church records show that only one man in the East German Mission at the end of 1938 was a Seventy and that was mission president Alfred C. Rees of Salt Lake City, Utah. The numbers of priesthood holders are shown in a table in the East German Mission chapter.

8. Indeed, the only interruptions described by eyewitnesses to the author occurred after the war, principally under the occupation of the Soviet army.

9. The total of 3,161 refugees would of course have to be reduced by the number of Saints who had been killed or had died prior to that time and the very few who remained in the region (See Selbongen Branch chapter).

10. K. Erik Franzen, *Die Vertriebenen: Hitlers letzte Opfer*, 280; see also Martin K. Sorge, *The Other Price of Hitler's War* (New York: Greenwood, 1986), 126–28.

11. Eyewitness Ruth Schumann Hinton of the Chemnitz Schloss Branch offered this explanation years later: "How were the brethren to read the sacrament prayers in those dark rooms without light? With the power out, we had to use candles."

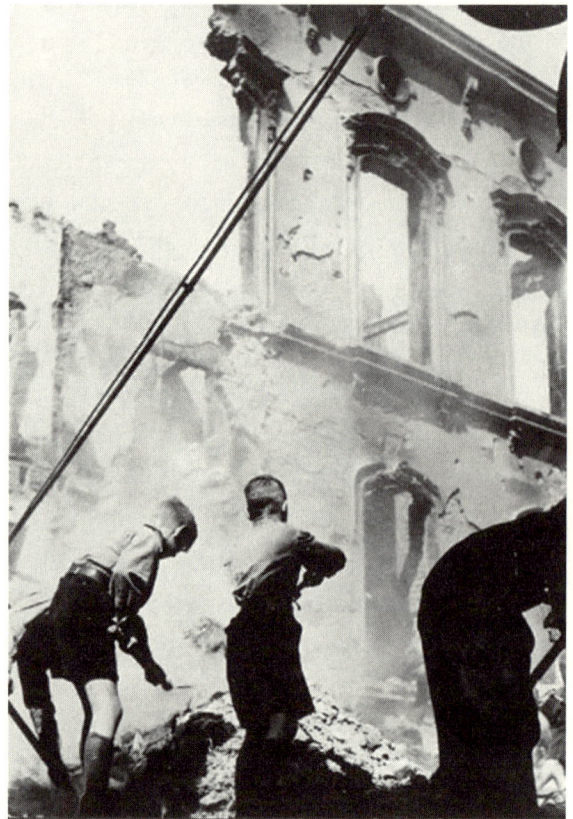

Members of the Hitler Youth participating in a more sobering aspect of their service—searching for survivors after an air raid. [Bundesarchiv 146-1974-120]

GLOSSARY

CIVILIAN PROGRAMS OF THE THIRD REICH

Bund Deutscher Mädel (League of German Girls): Beginning at age fourteen, all German girls were to join the Bund Deutscher Mädel (BDM) for two or three years. Like the boys of the same age, many girls were already employed or in occupational training and thus not free to attend the meetings. BDM girls were trained extensively in domestic skills such as baking and sewing, but were also carefully schooled in patriotic virtues and taught to prepare to be model German mothers who would bear children for the state. Their uniforms reflected conservative standards of virtue and discipline. Meetings were often held on Sundays.

Jungvolk (Young People): All German boys and girls were to be inducted into the Jungvolk at the age of ten. The program was organized through the public schools, and participation was required. There were official penalties for noncompliance, but some Latter-day Saint parents were able to invent excuses for the absence of their children from Jungvolk activities. Jungvolk groups wore uniforms, marched in parades, memorized nationalistic songs and details of Hitler's life, and engaged in wholesome activities, often out of town.

Meetings were held weekly, but usually not on Sundays.

Hitler Jugend (Hitler Youth): All German boys were expected to enroll in the Hitler Jugend (HJ) when they turned fourteen years of age. Since some boys had already finished public school and were busy in apprenticeships, it was not as easy for local officials to determine whether a certain boy was attending his HJ meetings. Again, penalties were promised those who did not comply. Activities included sports, war games, political lectures, political rallies, and camping. HJ members wore a distinctive uniform, were taught to observe strict health standards, to deport themselves as gentlemen, and to act in every way as loyal citizens of the National Socialist state. Quite a few HJ units conducted meetings and activities on Sundays. Training with actual weapons was not common among HJ units.

National Sozialistische Deutsche Arbeiter Partei (National Socialist German Workers Party, or Nazi Party): Founded in Munich in 1920, the party attracted far-right reactionaries who were antirepublican, anticommunist, and rabidly anti-Semitic. Adolf Hitler joined the party early and soon became its leader. By 1929, the Nazi Party was one of the largest political parties in Germany. It steadily gained power until in 1932 it earned the greatest number of seats in the parliament. As the leader of the Nazi Party, Hitler was appointed chancellor of Germany in January 1933.

Pflichtjahr (duty/service year): Because so many young men were taken from the local economy to serve in the military, the program known as Pflichtjahr was introduced to provide substitutes. Each teenage girl in Nazi Germany could expect to be inducted into the Pflichtjahr program, which would usually require her to render service in one or two capacities: as a farm laborer or as a domestic helper in a home without a father. The call to begin Pflichtjahr service came in the form of a draft notice, and the term of service lasted from six months to one year. During the Pflichtjahr, many girls had Sundays free, but Latter-day Saint girls were usually too far from a branch of the Church to attend meetings. Service on a farm within this program was often called Landjahr.

Reichsarbeitsdienst (Reich labor force): Preparing for and waging war required all the manpower Germany could muster. Thus the Reichsarbeitsdienst (RAD) was formed early on to provide that labor and simultaneously to prepare young men for military service. The call to the RAD came to seventeen-year-olds in the form of a draft notice. They wore uniforms very similar to those of the army, marched with shovels rather than with rifles, and lived in camps that closely resembled boot camps. The most common activity for RAD units was the construction of roads, airfields, harbor facilities, and fortifications—often in foreign countries. A full term with the RAD was one year, and a young man could expect to be drafted into the military very soon after he returned home.

MILITARY ORGANIZATIONS OF THE THIRD REICH:

Geheime Staatspolizei or Gestapo (secret state police): Under the command of one of Hitler's closest cronies, Heinrich Himmler, the Gestapo was reponsible for the identification and arrest of enemies of the Nazi Party and the state in general. Known for their long leather coats, Gestapo agents instilled terror in the hearts of German citizens by their mere presence. They were occasionally seen in LDS branch meetings but came and went in silence, never causing any interruptions or cancellations of meetings.

Marine: The German navy.

Luftwaffe: The German air force.

Polizei: Police; the term was also used to designate military police and police officials stationed in occupied territories, where they assisted the military.

Volkssturm: home guard; these were civilians inducted toward the end of the war to defend the fatherland; they were often more than sixty years old and in some cases younger than seventeen.

Waffen-SS: The elite combat forces under the command of Heinrich Himmler, whose personal titles included "Reichsführer-SS and Chief of the German Police." Waffen-SS troops wore black uniforms (with the SS lightning bolt insignia), fought on various fronts, and enjoyed better living conditions (see the story of Lothar [John] Flade in Chemnitz Center Branch, Chemnitz District). The term *Waffen-SS* is often confused with the regular SS—police units whose infamous duties included the command of concentration camps and death camps.

Wehrmacht: Technically referring to all armed forces together, the word *Wehrmacht* was also used to describe the regular army, i.e., the land forces (officially *Heer*).

OTHER ITEMS OF INTEREST:

Adolf Hitler: Born in Braunau, Austria, on April 20, 1889, Hitler was a decorated veteran of World War I and became a member and leader of the Nazi Party in the early 1920s. His rise to power in German politics culminated in the combination in his person of the office of Reichskanzler (chancellor) and Präsident (President) in 1934. He was the so-called Führer (leader) of the German nation until he committed suicide in Berlin on April 30, 1945.

Hinterhaus: In German cities, Hinterhäuser were buildings constructed in the space behind the main buildings on the block. The tradition of building Hinterhäuser dates back to the Middle Ages. Access to such a building was usually gained through a portal in the main building at that address. In some cases, one went through the entry hall of the main building, out the back door, and then across a courtyard (Hinterhof) to the Hinterhaus. In the largest cities, there were often several Hinterhäuser within a given block; they were usually designated Hof I, Hof II, and so forth (see Forst Branch Chapter, Spreewald District).

Kinderlandverschickung: As early as 1941, German city leaders found it advisable to send children to rural areas where their lives would not be threatened by enemy air raids. The program had two aspects: the transfer of entire classes of schoolchildren (from eight to fourteen years of age) with their respective homeroom teachers to hotels in tourist regions, and the evacuation of mothers with small children to the homes of relatives in rural regions. Under this program, school children were often away from their parents for a year or more. Many families disapproved of the program but did not wish to see their children in danger at home.

***Mein Kampf* (My Struggle):** This autobiography of Adolf Hitler was written while he was incarcerated in Landsberg following a failed coup against the government of Bavaria in Munich. The book was published after he left prison in 1925. Although some statements made in the book proved prophetic, the work was not popularly read. It was often given by the civil registrar to newlyweds.

Reich (Empire): This term was exalted to prominence during the Hitler regime (*das Dritte Reich* or "the Third Reich") of 1933–1945. The word was frequently used in connection with other nouns describing government programs, such as Reichsarbeitsdienst (described above).

Reichskristallnacht (Night of Broken Glass): Ostensibly as a spontaneous reaction to the assassination of the German ambassador to France, Nazi Party strongmen (SA members) attacked hundreds of Jewish synagogues and thousands of Jewish-owned businesses all over Germany during the night of November 9–10, 1938. Nearly one hundred Jews were killed. Most Germans were shocked by the open violence, but it was finally clear that there was no longer a place for Jews in Hitler's Germany.

Die Kirche Jesu Christi der Heiligen der Letzten Tage

Tauf und Konfirmation **Schein**

Dies bestätigt *die Taufe und Konfirmation*

des Mitgliedes *Edith Luise*

Johanna Wilms

von *Otto Bork und Wilhelm Pobanz* vollführt

der *Stargarder* Gemeinde.

Stargard; den *2. Aug.* 19*33*

Otto Bork

Gemeinde-Präsident

Baptisimal certificates like this one were used in both German missions throughout World War II. This one was issued to Edith Louise Johanna Wilms of the Stargard Branch, Stettin District. (E. Wilms)

INDEX
of Personal Names

A woman who was married before the war began in 1939 is listed under her married name.

A woman who married after the war began is listed under her maiden name as well as her married name, as shown in this example of Edith Rehbein, who married Hans Marquardt in 1940:

Rehbein Marquardt, Edith, 144, 166, 188
Marquardt, Edith Rehbein. *See* Rehbein Marquardt, Edith

Names containing the German umlaut characters *ä*, *ö*, or *ü* are alphabetized as if those characters were spelled *ae*, *oe*, or *ue*, respectively.

Adult LDS Church members for whom no given name is known are listed as *(Brother)* or *(Sister)* after the surname. American missionaries whose given names are unknown are listed as *(Elder)*.

For those listed in the *In Memoriam* sections, only the principal is included in the index—not his or her parents or spouse(s).

Page numbers in italics refer to images.